SIXTH EDITION

CONCEPTS OF STRATEGIC MANAGEMENT

FRED R. DAVID

Francis Marion University

Prentice Hall
Upper Saddle River, New Jersey 07458

Dedicated to:
Joy, Forest, Byron, and Meredith—my wife and children—
for their encouragement and love.

Acquisitions Editor: David Shafer
Associate Editor: Lisamarie Brassini
Editorial Assistant: Brett Moreland
Editor-in-Chief: James Boyd
Marketing Manager: Sandra Steiner
Production Editor: Cynthia Regan
Production Coordinator: Renee Pelletier
Managing Editor: Carol Burgett
Manufacturing Supervisor: Arnold Vila
Senior Designer: Ann France
Design Director: Patricia Woszczyk
Interior Design: Rosemarie Votta and Lorraine Castellano
Cover Design: Maureen Eide
Illustrator (Interior): Carlisle Communications, Ltd.
Composition/Project Management: Carlisle Publishers Services
Cover Art/Photo: © 1996 Picture Crew/Picture Perfect™

Library of Congress Cataloging-in-Publication Data
David, Fred R.
  Concepts of strategic management / Fred R. David. — 6th ed.
      p.   cm.
    Includes bibliographical references and index.
    ISBN 0-13-565466-1
    1. Strategic planning.   2. Strategic planning—Case studies.
  I. Title.
  HD30.28.D3785   1997   96-46648
  658.4'012—dc21   CIP

Printed in the United States of America

10 9 8 7 6 5 4 3 2 1

ISBN 13-565466-1

Prentice-Hall International (UK) Limited, London
Prentice-Hall of Australia Pty. Limited, Sydney
Prentice-Hall Canada Inc., Toronto
Prentice-Hall Hispanoamericana, S.A., Mexico
Prentice-Hall of India Private Limited, New Delhi
Prentice-Hall of Japan, Inc., Tokyo
Simon & Schuster Asia Pte. Ltd., Singapore
Editora Prentice-Hall do Brasil, Ltda., Rio de Janeiro

Brief Contents

Contents

Preface

The business world today is much different than it was just two years ago when the previous edition of this text was introduced. Today, voice mail, e-mail, the World Wide Web, the Internet, globalization, and concern for the natural environment have radically changed the way managers think and operate. Downsizing, rightsizing, and reengineering, coupled with thousands of mergers and acquisitions, have permanently altered the corporate landscape. Hundreds of recent strategic management articles in journals, magazines, and newspapers have impacted strategic thinking. Great opportunities for export and investment have surfaced worldwide, especially in the developing countries of Southeast Asia and South America. Changes made in this edition are aimed squarely at illustrating the effect that our rapidly changing world has on strategic management theory and practice.

Our mission in preparing this sixth edition of *Strategic Management* was, "to create the most current, well written business policy textbook on the market; a book that is exciting and valuable to both students and professors." To achieve this mission, significant improvements have been made to every item in the teaching package. The time basis for all cases included in this edition is through 1995, resulting in the most up-to-date compilation of cases ever assembled in a business policy text. Strategic management research and practice from the 1994–1996 era are incorporated throughout the chapters. Nearly all examples used in the text are 1994–1995 based. The Cohesion Case on Hershey Foods and the 53 Experiential Exercises are fully updated. There are 40 new Internet exercises.

TIME-TESTED FEATURES

This edition continues many of the special time-tested features and content that have made this text so successful over the last decade. Trademarks of this text are as follows:

◆ The text meets AACSB guidelines which support a more practitioner orientation rather than a theory/research approach. This text aims to support that effort by taking a skills oriented approach to developing a mission statement, performing an external audit, conducting an internal assessment, and formulating, implementing, and evaluating strategies.

◆ The author's writing style is concise, conversational, interesting, and supported by numerous current examples throughout.

◆ Global Strategy coverage has doubled in a thoroughly revised Chapter 10: Global Strategic Management Issues, and updated Global Perspective boxes are found throughout the text.

◆ The Natural Environment theme is unique to Strategic Management texts. In this edition the Natural Environment boxes found in each chapter have been updated to stress the need for firms to conduct operations in an environmentally sound manner or face increasingly stiff penalties and criticism.

◆ A simple, integrative management model is introduced early and appears in all subsequent chapters.

◆ Excellent coverage of strategy implementation issues such as *corporate culture, organizational structure, marketing concepts,* and *financial tools and techniques.*

◆ Experiential Exercises—53 end-of-chapter exercises effectively apply concepts and techniques in a challenging, meaningful, yet enjoyable manner.

  ◆ 18 exercises apply text material to the Cohesion Case

  ◆ 10 exercises apply textual material to a college or university

  ◆ 4 exercises use the software that accompanies the text

  ◆ 10 especially popular exercises send students into the business world to explore important strategy topics

◆ Hershey Foods Cohesion Case—fully updated, appears after Chapter 1 and is revisited at the end of each chapter. This case allows students to apply strategic management concepts and techniques to a real organization as chapter material is covered. This integrative (cohesive) approach readies students for case analysis. Hershey encourages professors and students to call 1–800–468–1714 for additional information, or visit Hershey's homepage on the Internet at **http://www.hersheys.com**

◆ Split paperback versions of the text chapters or cases continue to be available.

◆ Introductory material in the text gives (1) guidelines for using the *Case Analyst and Strategy Formulator* software and (2) Guidelines for Analyzing a Business Policy Case.

NEW TO THIS EDITION

In addition to the special time-tested trademarks described above, this edition includes some exciting new features designed to position this text as the clear leader and the best choice for teaching business policy and strategic management. Changes to this edition include the following:

◆ The *Information Technology Theme* is completely new to this edition and has been included in response to accelerated strategic use of computer technology to gather, analyze, send, and receive information. Many important U.S. Government documents such as *U.S. Industrial Outlook,* are now online and monthly updated services such as the National Trade Data Bank (NTDB), can be accessed on the Internet at **Gopher.stat.usgov** or **FTP.stat.usagov**

◆ Information Technology Boxes now appear in each chapter with topics ranging from home shopping to online capabilities of developing countries.

◆ "Take It to the Net" end-of-chapter exercises. By visiting **http://www.prenhall.com/davidsm** students can practice searching for, and analyzing information on the Internet in the context of Strategic Management.

◆ The chapter material is now published in four color; increasing the clarity and amount of information conveyed in the illustration program.

◆ Chapter 6 now takes a more systematic and analytical approach, including matrices such as TOWS, BCG, IE, GRAND, SPACE, and QSPM.

◆ New topics covered in the chapters include reengineering, downsizing, rightsizing, restructuring and use of the World Wide Web, the Internet, CompuServe, AOL, and Prodigy for strategic purposes.

ANCILLARY MATERIALS

To meet the different needs of the many professors who teach business policy or strategic management at the undergraduate or graduate level, this text is accompanied by what we feel is the best ancillary package available.

◆ Instructor's Resource Manual with Test Item File—Includes Chapter outlines, Answers to discussion / review questions, Experiential Exercise Notes, Glossary and Test Question Answers. Test Items include a per chapter average of 70 T/F, 45 Multiple Choice, and 20 Essay questions.

◆ Case Solutions Manual—Provides comprehensive notes for all thirty-eight cases. Each case discussion is organized into thirteen sections, including summary, major issues, discussion questions, various analytical ratios and matrices, and an epilogue.

◆ Transparencies—Fifty four-color transparencies on high quality Mylar featuring illustrations from the textbook.

◆ Software—

Strategy Formulator—A DOS based software package that helps students organize case information and data. A master is included in the Instructor's Resource Manual and may be copied.

Case Analyst—Includes year-end 1995 financial data for most of the cases. A master is included in the Instructor's Resource Manual and may be copied.

PowerPoint—100, four-color electronic transparencies available on 3.5" disk with illustrations and tables from text.

Computerized Test Item File—PH Custom Test Software with technical support. Instructors can modify existing questions, or add additional questions of their own.

Instructor's Resource Manual on disk—IRM on 3.5" disk allows instructors to add their own lecture notes, examples, and information.

◆ Videos—Five new color videos to accompany the existing collection of fourteen corporate video case studies. These include Circus Circus, Greyhound, Biomet, Avon, and Boeing.

◆ Web Site Support—40 new End-of-Chapter Internet exercises allow students to practice searching for information and using it for strategic decision making. Visit us at **http://www.prenhall.com/davidsm**

A SPECIAL NOTE TO STUDENTS

Welcome to business policy. This is a challenging and exciting course that will allow you to function as the owner or chief executive officer of different organizations. Your major task in this course will be to make strategic decisions and to justify those decisions through oral and written communication. Strategic decisions determine the future direction and competitive position of an enterprise for a long time. Decisions to expand geographically or to diversify are examples of strategic decisions.

Strategic decision making occurs in all types and sizes of organizations from General Motors to a small hardware store. Many people's lives and jobs are affected by strategic decisions, so the stakes are very high. An organization's very survival is often at stake. The overall importance of strategic decisions makes this course especially exciting and challenging. You will be called upon in business policy to demonstrate how your strategic decisions could be successfully implemented.

In this course you can look forward to making strategic decisions both as an individual and as a member of a team. No matter how hard employees work, an organization is in real trouble if strategic decisions are not made effectively. Doing the right things (effectiveness) is more important than doing things right (efficiency). For example, Digital Equipment Corporation was prosperous in the 1980s, but ineffective strategies led to annual billion dollar losses in the 1990s.

You will have the opportunity in this course to make actual strategic decisions, perhaps for the first time in your academic career. Do not hesitate to take a stand and defend specific strategies that you determine to be the best. The rationale for your strategic decisions will be more important than the actual decision, because no one knows for sure what the best strategy is for a particular organization at a given point in time. This fact accents the subjective, contingency nature of the strategic-management process. Use the concepts and tools presented in this text, coupled with your own intuition, to recommend strategies that you can defend as being most appropriate for the organizations that you study. You will also need to integrate knowledge acquired in previous business courses. For this reason, business policy is often called a capstone course; you may want to keep this book for your personal library.

This text is practitioner-oriented and applications-oriented. It presents strategic-management concepts that will enable you to formulate, implement, and evaluate strategies in all kinds of for-profit and nonprofit organizations. The end-of-chapter Experiential Exercises allow you to apply what you've read in each chapter to the Hershey Foods Cohesion Case and to your own university.

Be sure to use *Case Analyst* and *Strategy Formulator* because this software will save you time in performing analyses and will make your work look professional. Read and follow the guidelines provided after this preface for using the software and for making oral presentations. Work hard in policy this term and have fun. Good luck!

ACKNOWLEDGMENTS

Many people have contributed time, energy, ideas, and suggestions for improving this text over six editions. The strength of this text is largely attributed to the collective wisdom, work, and experiences of business policy professors, strategic-management researchers, students, and practitioners. Names of particular individuals whose published research is referenced in this text are listed alphabetically in the Name Index. To all individuals involved in making this text so popular and successful, I am indebted and thankful.

Many special people and reviewers contributed valuable material and suggestions for this edition. I would like to thank my colleagues and friends at Auburn University, Mississippi State University, East Carolina University, Pembroke State University and Francis Marion University. These are universities where I have served on the management faculty. Professors at these schools who shaped development of this text are Bill Holley, Achilles Armenakis, and Bob Neibuhr at Auburn University; Johnny Giglioni, Dennis Ray, and Dan Cochran at Mississippi State University; Louis Eckstein, Tilton Wilcox, and Buc Keush at East Carolina University; and Don Kelley, Bob Pugh, Jack Goebel and Bob Barrett at Francis Marion University.

Individuals who develop cases for the North American Case Research Association Meeting, the Midwest Society for Case Research Meeting, the Eastern Casewriters Association Meeting, the European Case Research Association meeting, and Harvard Case Services are vitally important for continued progress in the field of strategic management. From a research perspective, there is no question that writing business policy cases represents a valuable scholarly activity among faculty. Extensive research is required to structure business policy cases in a way that exposes strategic issues, decisions, and behavior. Pedagogically, business policy cases are essential for students in learning how to apply concepts, evaluate situations, formulate strategies, and resolve implementation problems. Without a continuous stream of up-to-date business policy cases, the strategic-management course and discipline would lose much of its energy and excitement.

The following individuals wrote cases that were selected for inclusion in this text and helped develop the most current compilation of cases ever assembled in a business policy text:

David Adams, Marywood College
Claire Anderson, Old Dominion University
Robert Anderson, College of Charleston
Jill Austin, Middle Tennessee State University
Stephen Barndt, Pacific Lutheran University
Henry Beam, Western Michigan University
David Bradbard, Winthrop College
James Camerius, Northern Michigan University
Thomas Carey, Western Michigan University
Dr. John Champion, University of Florida
James Clinton, University of Northern Colorado
Carol Cumber, South Dakota State University
Charles Doryland, Francis Marion University
Bahman Ebrahimi, North Texas State University
Caroline Fisher, Loyola University
Giovanni Giglioni, Mississippi State University
Jack Goebel, Francis Marion University
Doug Gray, Business owner

Jean Hanebury, Texas A & M University at Corpus Christi
James Harbin, East Texas State University
Paula Haynes, University of Tennessee at Chattanooga
Marilyn Helms, University of Tennessee at Chattanooga
Charles Hofer, University of Georgia
Sharon Johnson, Baylor University
Mike Keeffe, Southwest Texas State University
Gerald Kohers, Sam Houston State University
Charles Kuehl, University of Missouri, St. Louis
Joseph Lampel, New York University
Kay Lawrimore, Francis Marion University
Ted Legatski, Texas A & M University
Dean Lewis, Sam Houston State University
Robert Losik, New Hampshire College
Charles Manz, Arizona State University
John Marcis, Francis Marion University
James McFayden, Francis Marion University
Bill Middlebrook, Southwest Texas State University
Francine Newth, Providence College
Shelby Nickell, Business owner
Joni Norby, Sam Houston State University
Sharon Oswald, Auburn University
Dr. Dennis Patzig, James Madison University
Rich Priesmeyer, St. Mary's University
Valerie J. Porciello, Bentley College
Paul Reed, Sam Houston State University
Lawrence Rhyne, San Diego State University
John Ross, Southwest Texas State University
George Rubenson, Salisbury State University
Pete Schoderbek, University of Iowa
Amit Shah, Frostburg State University
Jamal Shanusie, New York University
Frank Shipper, Arizona State University
Charles Shrader, Iowa State University
Christy Sloan, University of Tennessee at Chattanooga
Matthew Sonfield, Hofstra University
Timothy Stearns, Marquette University

Carolyn Stokes, Francis Marion University
John Stanbury, Indiana University
Craig Tunwall, Ithaca College
Joan Twenter, Iowa State University
Andrew Varanelli, Pace University
Richard Wagner, Indiana University
Charles Watson, Miami University, Ohio
Steve Williams, Baker College
Lucretia Zienert, Auburn University

Prentice Hall employees and salespeople have worked diligently behind the scenes to make this text a leader in the business-policy market. David Shafer, Natalie Anderson, Lisamarie Brassini, Tom Nixon, Bill Oldsey, Cynthia Regan, and Brett Moreland, for example, have supported this text immensely. I appreciate the continued hard work of all Prentice Hall employees and salespeople.

I also want to thank you, the reader, for investing time and effort reading and studying this text. As we approach the twenty-first century together, this book will help you formulate, implement, and evaluate strategies for organizations with which you become associated. I hope you come to share my enthusiasm for the rich subject area of strategic management and for the systematic learning approach taken in this text.

Finally, I want to welcome and invite your suggestions, ideas, thoughts, and comments and questions regarding any part of this text or the ancillary materials. Please call me at 803-661-1419, or write to me at the School of Business, Francis Marion University, Florence, South Carolina 29501. My e-mail address is FDavid @ F Marion. edu and my fax number is 803-661-1432. I appreciate and need your input to continually improve this text in future editions. Drawing my attention to specific errors or deficiencies in coverage or exposition will especially be appreciated. Thank you for using this text.

F.R.D.

Case Description Matrix

COMPANY-CASE/INFO CODE	Manufacturing or Service	Profit or Nonprofit	Publicly-Traded Stock (Yes or No)	Small, Medium, or Large	International or Domestic
1. Splatterball	S	P	N	S	D
2. Norwood Funiture Company	S	P	N	S	D
3. Woodlands Cleaning Service	S	P	N	S	D
4. Citicorp	S	P	Y	L	I
5. Banc One	S	P	Y	L	D
6. The Limited	S	P	Y	L	I
7. Nordstrom	S	P	Y	L	D
8. Wal-Mart Stores	S	P	Y	L	I
9. Promus Corporation	S	P	Y	L	D
10. Circus Circus Enterprises	S	P	Y	L	I
11. Carnival Corporation	S	P	Y	L	I
12. DMN&E Railroad	S	P	N	M	D
13. Greyhound Corporation	S	P	Y	M	D
14. Cineplex Odeon	S	P	Y	L	I
15. Audubon Zoo	S	N	N	S	D
16. Classic Car Club	S	N	N	S	I
17. Elkins Lake Baptist Church	S	N	N	S	D
18. Walnut Creek Baptist Church	S	N	N	S	D
19. Metropolitan Museum of Art	S	N	N	S	I
20. E.L. Nickell	M	P	N	S	D
21. NSP Corporate Graphics	M	P	N	S	D
22. Material Handling Engineering	M	P	N	S	I
23. Harley-Davidson Inc.	M	P	Y	L	I
24. Winnebago Industries	M	P	Y	L	I
25. McDonnell Douglas	M	P	Y	L	I
26. Boeing Company	M	P	Y	L	I
27. Weyerhaeuser	M	P	Y	L	I
28. Georgia-Pacific	M	P	Y	L	I
29. W.L.Gore	M	P	N	L	I
30. Nike	M	P	Y	L	I
31. Playboy	M	P	Y	L	I
32. Biomet	M	P	Y	M	I
33. Stryker	M	P	Y	M	I
34. Avon Products	M	P	Y	L	I
35. UST	M	P	Y	M	I
36. Campbell	M	P	Y	L	I
37. Pilgrim's Pride	M	P	Y	L	I
38. Perdue Farms	M	P	Y	L	I

Headquarted in which state	Revenues: Falling or Rising	Profit: Falling or Rising	Complexity (High, Medium or Low)	Financial Statements Included (Yes or No)	Mission Statements Included (Yes or No)	Org. Chart Info Included (Yes or No)	Industry Note Precedes (Yes or No)	First Appearance Ever in this Text (Yes or No)
TN	R	R	L	Y	Y	N	N	N
NY	R	R	L	Y	Y	Y	N	N
TX	R	R	L	Y	Y	N	N	Y
NY	R	R	H	Y	Y	N	Y	N
OH	R	F	H	Y	Y	N	Y	N
OH	R	R	H	Y	Y	N	Y	N
WA	R	R	M	Y	Y	Y	Y	N
AR	R	R	M	Y	N	N	Y	N
TN	R	F	H	Y	Y	N	Y	N
NV	R	R	M	Y	N	Y	Y	N
FL	R	R	M	Y	Y	N	Y	Y
SD	R	R	M	Y	Y	Y	Y	N
TX	F	F	M	Y	N	N	Y	Y
CN	F	F	M	Y	N	N	Y	Y
LA	F	F	L	Y	Y	Y	N	N
IL	R	R	L	Y	N	Y	N	N
TX	R	R	L	Y	N	N	N	Y
TX	R	F	L	Y	N	N	N	N
NY	R	R	M	Y	Y	N	N	N
MI	R	R	M	Y	N	Y	N	Y
AL	R	R	L	Y	N	Y	N	N
SI	R	F	H	Y	N	Y	N	N
WI	R	R	M	Y	Y	N	N	N
IA	R	R	M	Y	N	N	N	N
MO	F	R	H	Y	N	N	Y	N
WA	F	F	H	Y	N	Y	Y	N
WA	R	R	H	Y	N	Y	Y	N
GA	R	R	H	Y	N	N	Y	N
DR	R	R	M	N	N	Y	Y	N
OR	R	R	M	Y	Y	Y	Y	N
IL	R	R	H	Y	Y	Y	Y	N
ID	R	R	M	Y	N	Y	Y	Y
MI	R	R	M	Y	N	Y	Y	Y
NY	R	R	H	Y	Y	Y	Y	Y
CT	R	R	H	Y	N	N	Y	Y
NJ	R	R	H	Y	Y	Y	Y	N
TX	R	R	M	Y	Y	Y	Y	N
MD	R	R	M	N	Y	N	Y	Y

How to Analyze a Business Policy Case

OUTLINE

- **WHAT IS A BUSINESS POLICY CASE?**
- **GUIDELINES FOR PREPARING CASE ANALYSES**
- **PREPARING A CASE FOR CLASS DISCUSSION**

- **PREPARING A WRITTEN CASE ANALYSIS**
- **MAKING AN ORAL PRESENTATION**
- **FIFTY TIPS FOR SUCCESS IN CASE ANALYSIS**

OBJECTIVES

After studying this chapter, you should be able to do the following:

1. Describe the case method for learning strategic-management concepts.

2. Identify the steps in preparing a comprehensive written case analysis.

3. Describe how to give an effective oral case analysis presentation.

4. Discuss fifty tips for doing case analysis.

NOTABLE QUOTES

The essential fact that makes the case method an educational experience of the greatest power is that it makes the student an active rather than a passive participant. —Wallace B. Donham

The great aim of education is not knowledge, but action. —Herbert Spencer

Two heads are better than one. —Unknown Author

Good writers do not turn in their first draft. Ask someone else to read your written case analysis, and read it out loud to yourself. That way, you can find rough areas to clean up. —Lawrence Jauch

One reaction frequently heard is, "I don't have enough information." In reality, strategists never have enough information because some information is not available and some is too costly. —William Glueck

I keep six honest serving men. They taught me all I know. Their names are What, Why, When, How, Where, and Who. —Rudyard Kipling

Don't recommend anything you would not be prepared to do yourself if you were in the decision maker's shoes. —A.J. Strickland III

A picture is worth a thousand words. —Unknown Author

*T*he purpose of this section is to help you analyze business policy cases. Guidelines for preparing written and oral case analyses are given, and suggestions for preparing cases for class discussion are presented. Steps to follow in preparing case analyses are provided. Guidelines for making an oral presentation are described.

WHAT IS A BUSINESS-POLICY CASE?

A *business-policy case* describes an organization's external and internal condition and raises issues concerning the firm's mission, strategies, objectives, and policies. Most of the information in a business-policy case is established fact, but some information may be opinions, judgments, and beliefs. Business-policy cases are more comprehensive than those you may have studied in other courses. They generally include a description of related management, marketing, finance/accounting, production/operations, R&D, computer information systems, and natural environment issues. A business-policy case puts the reader on the scene of the action by describing a firm's situation at some point in time. Business-policy cases are written to give you practice applying strategic-management concepts. The case method for studying strategic management is often called *learning by doing.*

GUIDELINES FOR PREPARING CASE ANALYSES

THE NEED FOR PRACTICALITY   There is no such thing as a complete case, and no case ever gives you all the information you need to conduct analyses and make recommendations. Likewise, in the business world, strategists never have all the information they need to make decisions: information may be unavailable, too costly to obtain, or may take too much time to obtain. So, in preparing business policy cases, do what strategists do every day—make reasonable assumptions about unknowns, state assumptions clearly, perform appropriate analyses, and make decisions. *Be practical.* For example, in performing a pro forma financial analysis, make reasonable assumptions, state them appropriately, and proceed to show what impact your recommendations are expected to have on the organization's financial position. Avoid saying, "I don't have enough information." You can always supplement the information provided in a case with research in your college library. Library research is required in case analyses.

THE NEED FOR JUSTIFICATION   The most important part of analyzing cases is not what strategies you recommend, but rather how you support your decisions and how you propose that they be implemented. There is no single best solution or one right answer to a case, so give ample justification for your recommendations. This is important. In the business world, strategists usually do not know if their decisions are right until resources have been allocated and consumed. Then it is often too late to reverse the decisions. This cold fact accents the need for careful integration of intuition and analysis in preparing business policy case analyses.

THE NEED FOR REALISM   Avoid recommending a course of action beyond an organization's means. *Be realistic.* No organization can possibly pursue all the strategies that could potentially benefit the firm. Estimate how much capital will be required to implement what you recommended. Determine whether debt, stock, or a combination of debt and stock could be used to obtain the capital. Make sure your recommendations are feasible. Do not prepare a case analysis that omits all arguments and information not supportive of your recommendations. Rather, present the major advantages and disadvantages of several feasible alternatives. Try not to exaggerate, stereotype, prejudge, or overdramatize. Strive to demonstrate that your interpretation of the evidence is reasonable and objective.

THE NEED FOR SPECIFICITY   Do not make broad generalizations such as "The company should pursue a market penetration strategy." *Be specific* by telling what, why, when, how, where, and who. Failure to use specifics is the single major shortcoming of most oral and written case analyses. For example, in an internal audit say, "The firm's current ratio fell from 2.2 in 1993 to 1.3 in 1994, and this is considered to be a major weakness," instead of, "The firm's financial condition is bad." Rather than concluding from a SPACE Matrix that a firm should be defensive, be more specific, saying, "The firm should consider closing three plants, laying off 280 employees, and divesting itself of its chemical division, for a net savings of $20.2 million in 1995." Use ratios, percentages, numbers, and dollar estimates. Businesspeople dislike generalities and vagueness.

THE NEED FOR ORIGINALITY   Do not necessarily recommend the course of action that the firm plans to take or actually undertook, even if those actions resulted in improved revenues and earnings. The aim of case analysis is for you to consider all the facts and information relevant to the organization at the time, generate feasible alternative strategies, choose among those alternatives, and defend your recommendations. Put yourself back in time to the point when strategic decisions were being made by the firm's strategists. Based on information available then, what would you have done? Support your position with charts, graphs, ratios, analyses, and the like—not a revelation from the library. You can become a good strategist by thinking through situations, making management assessments, and proposing plans yourself. *Be original.* Compare and contrast what you recommend versus what the company plans to do or did.

THE NEED TO CONTRIBUTE   Strategy formulation, implementation, and evaluation decisions are commonly made by a group of individuals rather than by a single person. Therefore, your professor may divide the class into three- or four-person teams to prepare written or oral case analyses. Members of a strategic-management team, in class or in the business world, differ on their aversion to risk, their concern for short-run versus long-run benefits, their attitudes toward social responsibility, and their views concerning globalization. There are no perfect people, so there are no perfect strategists. Be open-minded to others' views. *Be a good listener and a good contributor.*

PREPARING A CASE FOR CLASS DISCUSSION

Your professor may ask you to prepare a case for class discussion. Preparing a case for class discussion means that you need to read the case before class, make notes regarding the organization's external opportunities/threats and internal strengths/weaknesses, perform appropriate analyses, and come to class prepared to offer and defend some specific recommendations.

THE CASE METHOD VERSUS LECTURE APPROACH   The case method of teaching is radically different from the traditional lecture approach, in which little or no preparation is needed by students before class. The *case method* involves a classroom situation in which students do most of the talking; your professor facilitates discussion by asking questions and encouraging student interaction regarding ideas, analyses, and recommendations. Be prepared for a discussion along the lines of, "What would you do, why would you do it, when would you do it, and how would you do it?" Prepare answers to the following types of questions:

- What are the firm's most important external opportunities and threats?
- What are the organization's major strengths and weaknesses?
- How would you describe the organization's financial condition?
- What are the firm's existing strategies and objectives?
- Who are the firm's competitors and what are their strategies?
- What objectives and strategies do you recommend for this organization? Explain your reasoning. How does what you recommend compare to what the company plans?
- How could the organization best implement what you recommend? What implementation problems do you envision? How could the firm avoid or solve those problems?

THE CROSS-EXAMINATION Do not hesitate to take a stand on the issues and to support your position with objective analyses and outside research. Strive to apply strategic-management concepts and tools in preparing your case for class discussion. Seek defensible arguments and positions. Support opinions and judgments with facts, reasons, and evidence. Crunch the numbers before class! Be willing to describe your recommendations to the class without fear of disapproval. Respect the ideas of others, but be willing to go against the majority opinion when you can justify a better position.

Business-policy case analysis gives you the opportunity to learn more about yourself, your colleagues, strategic management, and the decision-making process in organizations. The rewards of this experience will depend upon the effort you put forth, so do a good job. Discussing business policy cases in class is exciting and challenging. Expect views counter to those you present. Different students will place emphasis on different aspects of an organization's situation and submit different recommendations for scrutiny and rebuttal. Cross-examination discussions commonly arise, just as they occur in a real business organization. Avoid being a silent observer.

PREPARING A WRITTEN CASE ANALYSIS

In addition to asking you to prepare a case for class discussion, your professor may ask you to prepare a written case analysis. Preparing a written case analysis is similar to preparing a case for class discussion, except written reports are generally more structured and more detailed. There is no ironclad procedure for preparing a written case analysis because cases differ in focus; the type, size, and complexity of the organizations being analyzed also vary.

When writing a strategic-management report or case analysis, avoid using jargon, vague or redundant words, acronyms, abbreviations, sexist language, and ethnic or racial slurs, and watch your spelling. Use short sentences and paragraphs and simple words and phrases. Use quite a few subheadings. Arrange issues and ideas from the most important to the least important. Arrange recommendations from the least controversial to the most controversial. Use the active voice rather than the passive voice for all verbs; for example, say, "Our team recommends that the company diversify," rather than, "It is recommended by our team to diversify." Use many examples to add specificity and clarity. Tables, figures, pie charts, bar charts, time lines, and other kinds of exhibits help communicate important points and ideas. Sometimes a picture *is* worth a thousand words.

THE EXECUTIVE SUMMARY Your professor may ask you to focus the written case analysis on a particular aspect of the strategic-management process, such as (1) to identify and evaluate the organization's existing mission, objectives, and strategies; or

(2) to propose and defend specific recommendations for the company; or (3) to develop an industry analysis by describing the competitors, products, selling techniques, and market conditions in a given industry. These types of written reports are sometimes called *executive summaries.* An executive summary usually ranges from three to five pages of text in length, plus exhibits.

THE COMPREHENSIVE WRITTEN ANALYSIS Your professor may ask you to prepare a *comprehensive written analysis.* This assignment requires you to apply the entire strategic-management process to the particular organization. When preparing a comprehensive written analysis, picture yourself as a consultant who has been asked by a company to conduct a study of its external and internal environment and make specific recommendations for its future. Prepare exhibits to support your recommendations. Highlight exhibits with some discussion in the paper. Comprehensive written analyses are usually about ten pages in length, plus exhibits.

STEPS IN PREPARING A COMPREHENSIVE WRITTEN ANALYSIS In preparing a comprehensive written analysis, you could follow the steps outlined here, which correlate to the stages in the strategic-management process and the chapters in this text.

Step 1 Identify the firm's existing mission, objectives, and strategies.

Step 2 Develop a mission statement for the organization.

Step 3 Identify the organization's external opportunities and threats.

Step 4 Construct a Competitive Profile Matrix.

Step 5 Construct an EFE Matrix.

Step 6 Identify the organization's internal strengths and weaknesses.

Step 7 Construct an IFE Matrix.

Step 8 Prepare a TOWS Matrix, SPACE Matrix, BCG Matrix, IE Matrix, Grand Strategy Matrix, and QSPM as appropriate. Give advantages and disadvantages of alternative strategies.

Step 9 Recommend specific strategies and long-term objectives. Show how much your recommendations will cost. Itemize these costs clearly for each projected year. Compare your recommendations to actual strategies planned by the company.

Step 10 Specify how your recommendations can be implemented and what results you can expect. Prepare forecasted ratios and pro forma financial statements. Present a timetable or agenda for action.

Step 11 Recommend specific annual objectives and policies.

Step 12 Recommend procedures for strategy review and evaluation.

MAKING AN ORAL PRESENTATION

Your professor may ask you to prepare a business policy case analysis, individually or as a group, and present your analysis to the class. Oral presentations are usually graded on two parts: content and delivery. *Content* refers to the quality, quantity, correctness, and appropriateness of analyses presented, including such dimensions as logical flow through the presentation, coverage of major issues, use of specifics, avoidance of generalities, absence of mistakes, and feasibility of recommendations. *Delivery* includes such dimensions as audience attentiveness, clarity of visual aids, appropriate dress, persuasiveness of arguments, tone of voice, eye contact, and posture. Great ideas are of no value unless others can be convinced of their merit through clear communication. The guidelines presented here can help you make an effective oral presentation.

ORGANIZING THE PRESENTATION Begin your presentation by introducing yourself and giving a clear outline of topics to be covered. If a team is presenting, specify the sequence of speakers and the areas each person will address. At the beginning of an oral presentation, try to capture your audience's interest and attention. You could do this by displaying some products made by the company, telling an interesting short story about the company, or sharing an experience that you had related to the company, its products, or its services. You could develop or obtain a video to show at the beginning of class; you could visit a local distributor of the firm's products and tape a personal interview with the business owner or manager. A light or humorous introduction can be effective at the beginning of a presentation.

Be sure the setting of your presentation is well organized, with chairs, flip charts, a transparency projector, and whatever else you plan to use. Arrive at least 15 minutes early at the classroom to organize the setting, and be sure your materials are ready to go. Make sure everyone can see your visual aids well.

CONTROLLING YOUR VOICE An effective rate of speaking ranges from 100 to 125 words per minute. Practice your presentation out loud to determine if you are going too fast. Individuals commonly speak too fast when nervous. Breathe deeply before and during the presentation to help yourself slow down. Have a cup of water available; pausing to take a drink will wet your throat, give you time to collect your thoughts, control your nervousness, slow you down, and signal to the audience a change in topic.

Avoid a monotone by placing emphasis on different words or sentences. Speak loudly and clearly, but don't shout. Silence can be used effectively to break a monotone voice. Stop at the end of each sentence, rather than running sentences together with *and* or *uh*.

MANAGING BODY LANGUAGE Be sure not to fold your arms, lean on the podium, put your hands in your pockets, or put your hands behind you. Keep a straight posture, with one foot slightly in front of the other. Do not turn your back to the audience, which is not only rude but which also prevents your voice from projecting well. Avoid using too many hand gestures. On occasion leave the podium or table and walk toward your audience, but do not walk around too much. Never block the audience's view of your visual aids.

Maintain good eye contact throughout the presentation. This is the best way to persuade your audience. There is nothing more reassuring to a speaker than to see members of the audience nod in agreement or smile. Try to look everyone in the eye at least once during your presentation, but focus more on individuals who look interested than on persons who seem bored. Use humor and smiles as appropriate throughout your presentation to stay in touch with your audience. A presentation should never be dull!

SPEAKING FROM NOTES Be sure not to read to your audience, because reading puts people to sleep. Perhaps worse than reading is memorizing. Do not try to memorize anything. Rather, practice using notes unobtrusively. Make sure your notes are written clearly so you will not flounder trying to read your own writing. Include only main ideas on your note cards. Keep note cards on a podium or table if possible so that you won't drop them or get them out of order; walking with note cards tends to be distracting.

CONSTRUCTING VISUAL AIDS Make sure your visual aids are legible to individuals in the back of the room. Use color to highlight special items. Avoid putting complete sentences on visual aids; rather, use short phrases and then elaborate on issues orally as you make your presentation. Generally, there should be no more than four to six lines of text on each visual aid. Use clear headings and subheadings. Be careful about spelling and grammar; use a consistent style of lettering. Use masking tape or an easel for posters—do not hold posters in your hand. Transparencies and handouts are excellent aids; however, be careful not to use too many handouts or your audience may concentrate on them instead of you during the presentation.

ANSWERING QUESTIONS   It is best to field questions at the end of your presentation, rather than during the presentation itself. Encourage questions and take your time to respond to each one. Answering questions can be persuasive because it involves you with the audience. If a team is giving the presentation, the audience should direct questions to a specific person. During the question and answer period, be polite, confident, and courteous. Avoid verbose responses. Do not get defensive with your answers, even if a hostile or confrontational question is asked. Staying calm during potentially disruptive situations such as a cross-examination reflects self-confidence, maturity, poise, and command of the particular company and its industry. Stand up throughout the question and answer period.

FIFTY TIPS FOR SUCCESS IN CASE ANALYSIS

Business policy students who have used this text over two editions offer you the following fifty tips for success in doing case analysis:

1. View your case analysis and presentation as a product that must have some competitive factor to differentiate it favorably from the case analyses of other students.
2. Prepare your case analysis far enough in advance of the due date to allow time for reflection and practice. Do not procrastinate.
3. Develop a mind-set of "why," continually questioning your own and others' assumptions and assertions.
4. The best ideas are lost if not communicated to the reader, so as ideas develop, think of their most appropriate presentation.
5. Maintain a positive attitude about the class, working *with* problems rather than against them.
6. Keep in tune with your professor and understand his or her values and expectations.
7. Since business policy is a capstone course, seek the help of professors in other specialty areas as needed.
8. Other students will have strengths in functional areas that will complement your weaknesses, so develop a cooperative spirit that moderates competitiveness in group work.
9. Read your case frequently as work progresses so you don't overlook details.
10. When preparing a case analysis as a group, divide into separate teams to work on the external analysis and internal analysis. Each team should write its section as if it were to go into the paper; then give each group member a copy.
11. At the end of each group session, assign each member of the group a task to be completed for the next meeting.
12. Have a good sense of humor.
13. Capitalize on the strengths of each member of the group; volunteer your services in your areas of strength.
14. Set goals for yourself and your team; budget your time to attain them.
15. Become friends with the library.
16. Foster attitudes that encourage group participation and interaction. Do not be hasty to judge group members.

17. Be creative and innovative throughout the case analysis process.
18. Be prepared to work. There will be times when you will have to do more than your share. Accept it, and do what you have to do to move the team forward.
19. Think of your case analysis as if it were really happening; do not reduce case analysis to a mechanical process.
20. To uncover flaws in your analysis and to prepare the group for questions during an oral presentation, assign one person in the group to actively play the devil's advocate.
21. Do not schedule excessively long group meetings; two-hour sessions are about right.
22. A goal of case analysis is to improve your ability to think clearly in ambiguous and confusing situations; do not get frustrated that there is no single best answer.
23. Push your ideas hard enough to get them listened to, but then let up; listen to others and try to follow their lines of thinking; follow the flow of group discussion, recognizing when you need to get back on track; do not repeat yourself or others unless clarity or progress demands repetition.
24. Do not confuse symptoms with causes; do not develop conclusions and solutions prematurely; recognize that information may be misleading, conflicting, or wrong.
25. Work hard to develop the ability to formulate reasonable, consistent, and creative plans; put yourself in the strategist's position.
26. Develop confidence in using quantitative tools for analysis. They are not inherently difficult; it is just practice and familiarity you need.
27. Develop a case-writing style that is direct, assertive, and convincing; be concise, precise, fluent, and correct.
28. Have fun when at all possible. It is frustrating at times, but enjoy it while you can; it may be several years before you are playing CEO again.
29. Acquire a professional typist and proofreader. Do not perform either task alone.
30. Strive for excellence in writing and technical preparation of your case. Prepare nice charts, tables, diagrams, and graphs. Use color and unique pictures. No messy exhibits!
31. In group cases do not allow personality differences to interfere. When they occur, they must be understood for what they are and put aside.
32. Do not forget that the objective is to learn; explore areas with which you are not familiar.
33. Pay attention to detail.
34. Think through alternative implications fully and realistically. The consequences of decisions are not always apparent. They often affect many different aspects of a firm's operations.
35. Get things written down (drafts) as soon as possible.
36. Read everything that other group members write, and comment on it in writing. This allows group input into all aspects of case preparation.
37. Provide answers to such fundamental questions as what, when, where, why, and how.
38. Adaptation and flexibility are keys to success; be creative and innovative.
39. Do not merely recite ratios or present figures. Rather, develop ideas and conclusions concerning the possible trends. Show the importance of these figures to the corporation.
40. Support reasoning and judgment with factual data whenever possible.
41. Neatness is a real plus; your case analysis should look professional.
42. Your analysis should be as detailed and specific as possible.
43. A picture speaks a thousand words, and a creative picture gets you an *A* in many classes.

44. Let someone else read and critique your paper several days before you turn it in.
45. Emphasize the Strategy Selection and Strategy Implementation sections. A common mistake is to spend too much time on the external or internal analysis parts of your paper. Always remember that the meat of the paper or presentation is the strategy selection and implementation sections.
46. Make special efforts to get to know your group members. This leads to more openness in the group and allows for more interchange of ideas. Put in the time and effort necessary to develop these relationships.
47. Be constructively critical of your group members' work. Do not dominate group discussions. Be a good listener and contributor.
48. Learn from past mistakes and deficiencies. Improve upon weak aspects of other case presentations.
49. Learn from the positive approaches and accomplishments of classmates.
50. Be considerate, dependable, reliable, and trustworthy.

READINGS

Fielen, John. "Clear Writing Is Not Enough."*Management Review* (April 1989): 49–53.

Holcombe, M., and J. Stein. *Presentations for Decision Makers* (Belmont, Calif.: Lifetime Learning Publications, 1983).

———. *Writing for Decision Makers* (Belmont, Calif.: Lifetime Learning Publications, 1981).

Jeffries, J., and J. Bates. *The Executive's Guide to Meetings, Conferences, and Audiovisual Presentations* (New York: McGraw-Hill, 1983).

Shurter, R., J. P. Williamson, and W. Broehl. *Business Research and Report Writing* (New York: McGraw-Hill, 1965).

Strunk, W., and E. B. White. *The Elements of Style* (New York: Macmillan, 1978).

Zall, P., and L. Franc. *Practical Writing in Business and Industry* (North Scituate, Mass.: Duxbury Press, 1978).

Instructions for Using the *Strategy Formulator* and *Case Analyst* Software

*T*he *Strategy Formulator* and *Case Analyst* software that accompanies this text are user-friendly programs that run on any IBM or IBM-compatible machine with at least one floppy disk drive and 512K (or greater) memory. Step-by-step instructions for using this software are provided in this section. *Strategy Formulator* and *Case Analyst* will greatly reduce the time it takes you to prepare quantitative, professional exhibits to support your oral case presentations and written case assignments.

The *Strategy Formulator* program generates strategy-formulation matrices that are widely used among organizations. The matrices are described in Chapters 4, 5, and 6 of the text. You will want to use *Strategy Formulator* in analyzing all business policy cases. No prior experience with computers is needed to use this software, which is DOS-based.

The *Case Analyst* program consists of a set of 37 data files that contain the income statements and balance sheets for nearly all the cases in the text. These data files are presented in Lotus 1-2-3 format and can be loaded into any spreadsheet program. *Case Analyst* enables you to generate pro forma financial statements and projected financial ratios. Pro forma analysis is described in Chapter 7 of the text. Generating pro forma financial statements is an important part of analyzing a case because you need to show what impact your recommendations will have on the firm's future.

MAKING A BACKUP COPY OF THE DISKETTES   It is a good idea to make a working copy of both the *Strategy Formulator* and *Case Analyst* diskettes. Keep the original copies in a safe place as a backup. The operating system manual that came with your computer contains instructions on how to make backup copies. Follow instructions in your computer manual for creating a subdirectory, (or folder) and copy the original diskette to that subdirectory (or folder).

THE *STRATEGY FORMULATOR* SOFTWARE

Strategy Formulator is an innovative program that enables managers and students to formulate strategies for organizations. This personal computer software program incorporates the most modern strategic planning techniques in a simple way. The simplicity of *Strategy Formulator* enables this software to facilitate the process of strategic planning by promoting communication, understanding, creativity, and forward thinking among users.

Strategy Formulator is not a spreadsheet or database program; it is a structured brainstorming tool that enhances participation in strategy formulation. The software begins with development of an organizational mission statement as described in Chapter 3. Then, the software guides you through an internal strategic planning audit of the company, followed by an external audit of the firm as described in Chapters 4 and 5. Next, the software generates alternative strategies for the firm, using analytical tools discussed in Chapter 6.

Strategy Formulator enables students or managers to create an organizational mission statement, identify key internal strengths and weaknesses as well as key external opportunities and threats, and then generate, evaluate, and prioritize alternative strategies that the firm could pursue. Individuals can work through the software independently and then meet to discuss particular strategies.

Strategy Formulator runs on any IBM-compatible personal computer system that has a high density (HD) disk drive. It includes numerous help screens and examples and offers clear printouts. No documentation manual is needed with *Strategy Formulator.* Simply boot DOS, type SF, and follow directions.

Strategy Formulator gives you hands-on experience using actual strategic planning software and facilitates business policy case analysis. This new software is similar to the

CheckMATE strategic planning software that is widely used among organizations world-wide. (For additional information about CheckMATE, contact the author of Strategic Planning Systems, P.O. Box 13065, Florence, SC 29504; Phone 803-669-6960; Fax 803-673-9460, e-mail FDavidaFMarion.edu) CheckMATE is windows-based and costs $95.

THE STRUCTURE AND FUNCTION OF *STRATEGY FORMULATOR*   The first and second screens that appear in the *Strategy Formulator* software are given in Figures 1 and 2. Note from the first screen that the F1, F2, and F3 keys are the Save key, Load key, and Print key, respectively. Note that the second screen gives an outline or flow-chart of the *Strategy Formulator* program. This second screen is a main menu that returns throughout the program; you simply highlight the particular area you wish to work on and hit Enter to begin that part of the program.

FIGURE 1

THE FIRST SCREEN
Strategy Formulator Software

The *Strategy Formulator* program provides a systematic approach for managers to devise strategies their organizations could pursue. *Strategy Formulator* incorporates the most modern strategic planning techniques in a simple way.

The recommended approach for using *Strategy Formulator* is for managers to work through the software independently and then meet together to discuss the results and develop a single set of joint recommendations. This approach to strategic planning facilitates communication, forward thinking, understanding, commitment, and performance. The help key (F1) is available at all times throughout the *Formulator* program to give you more information. Press the F1 key now to obtain information about the Save key (F2), Load key (F3), Print key (F4), and Escape key.

Press the Return key on the highlighted topic on the menu to activate the various parts of the program.

FIGURE 2

THE SECOND SCREEN

The Structure and Function of *Strategy Formulator*
  I. Create a Mission Statement
 II. Identify Key Internal Strengths and Weaknesses
III. Identify Key External Opportunities and Threats
 IV. Generate Alternative Strategies Using:
      IE Analysis
      TOWS Analysis
      SPACE Analysis
      GRAND Analysis
  V. Refine Alternative Strategies
 VI. Select Strategies to Pursue
    Other functions:
      Load Data from Disk
      Save Data to Disk
      Print
      Quit Program

GETTING STARTED   Run the *Strategy Formulator* software by typing SF at the DOS prompt or double click on the SF.EXE program from Windows Explorer.

Read the first screen. Hit the F1 key just to get familiar with the Help routine. Hit the Escape key to return to the main menu. Hit Enter to go to the second screen. Note from the second screen that you may simply highlight the Create a Mission Statement line and hit Enter to begin work on developing a mission statement—which is the first activity in formulating strategies. Hit Enter again when you are ready to return to the main menu. You may hit the F1 key anytime in the program for help. The Program Mechanics Help, as shown in Figure 3, will appear on the screen if you hit the F1 key twice.

After completing the mission statement, highlight the next line, Identify Key Internal Strengths and Weaknesses. Hit Enter and begin development of a list of the company's key strengths and weaknesses. When you have completed this work, return to the main menu. Continue working sequentially in this manner through the program.

THE SAVE AND LOAD ROUTINES   It is easy to save and load your work in the *Strategy Formulator* program. The Help Screens (F1 key) associated with the Save and Load routines are given in Figures 4 and 5.

THE PRINT ROUTINE   The *Strategy Formulator* software generates nine planning reports that can be printed separately or together, (as indicated on a print screen as shown in Figure 6) that appears near the end of the program.

Simply highlight the reports you desire to be printed, and hit Enter to begin printing your work. You could highlight Print All Reports to print all of your work. If you press the F1 key, the screen shown in Figure 7 appears.

FIGURE 3

THE PROGRAM MECHANICS HELP SCREEN

- Movement between screens within a module is accomplished by pressing the UP and DOWN arrows. This is true both within the Help facility and within the main program.
- If you wish to delete to the left of the cursor, you should press the BACKSPACE key. If you wish to delete to the right of the cursor, you should press the DELETE key.
- If you wish to insert text, place the cursor where you wish to begin the insertion and press the INSERT key. When the insert mode is in operation, the cursor changes its size and the word "Insert" appears in the bottom right corner of the screen. Insert is turned off again either by pressing the INSERT key or by moving to another answer.
- You can access the HELP facility at any time by pressing the F1 key. From the Help facility, you can return to the screen you were working on by pressing the ESCAPE key.
- You can SAVE all of your work at any time by pressing the F2 key.
- You can LOAD all of your work at any time by pressing the F3 key.
- You can PRINT all or part of your work at any time by pressing the F4 key.
- You can return to the menu at any time by pressing the ESCAPE key.

FIGURE 4

THE SAVE ROUTINE HELP SCREEN

The Save routine is where the information that has been entered into the system is saved for later use.

The Drive is the disk drive where the data is saved.

The Path is the logical place on the drive where the information is saved. You should either read up on this in the DOS manual or go with the default. The default is the drive and path where the program is located.

The File Name is the name that is given to the information that is saved. This name is used later to retrieve the information. It is eight characters long.

The Directory List will give you a list of files that already exist. If you save over a file (use the same name), the contents of that file are lost. It is a good idea to save your files in two places so that there will be a backup if the primary file is lost. To do this, put a floppy disk in the drive and change the disk drive letter to the letter corresponding to the drive you are using. Usually the letter is A; sometimes it is B.

FIGURE 5

THE LOAD ROUTINE HELP SCREEN

The Load routine is where the information that has been saved on the disk is brought back into the system.

The Drive is the disk drive where the data is saved.

The Path is the logical place on the drive where the information is saved. For more information on this, you should read the DOS manual.

The File Name is the name that is given to the information that is saved. This name is used to retrieve the information. It is eight characters long.

The Directory List will give you a list of files that exist on the disk and path that are listed on the screen. The name must show up on the directory in order for the information to be read.

FIGURE 6

STRATEGY FORMULATOR PRINT REPORTS

Print ALL Reports	TOWS Analysis Report
Mission Statement Report	SPACE Analysis Report
Internal Analysis Report	GRAND Analysis Report
External Analysis Report	Alternative Strategies Report
IE Analysis Report	Selected Strategies Report

FIGURE 7

THE PRINT ROUTINE HELP SCREEN

The Print routine is accessed by hitting the F4 key or the print option on the main menu.

Within the print menu, select the report you wish by pressing the up and down arrow keys. You can print all reports or individual ones.

If there is a "printer off line" error, you should locate the on-line button on your printer and press it. This should put your printer on-line.

If there is a "printer paper out" error, you should load paper into your printer. This should correct this problem.

If you wish to bypass the program's printer error detection features for any reason, press the "D" (for disable) key. This is usually not needed, but if the user has nonstandard software or hardware, it may be necessary.

THE *CASE ANALYST* SOFTWARE

CONTENTS OF THE DISKETTE   Income statements and balance sheets for 36 cases are provided in Lotus 1-2-3 format on the *Case Analyst* diskette. The only cases in the text that do not include financial statements are W. L. Gore, E. L. Nickell, and Perdue Farms. All modern spreadsheet programs can read these files. Ample space is provided on the diskette for projected income statement and balance sheet information to be entered.

The *Case Analyst* data files are listed below in alphabetical order. Note that in June 1995, the Promus Company split into two publicly-traded companies. Financials for each are included under the file names Promus1 and Promus2.

File Name	Corresponding Organization
AUDUBON.WK1	The Audubon Zoo
AVON.WK1	Avon
BANCONE.WK1	Banc One
BIOMET.WK1	Biomet
BOEING.WK1	Boeing
CAMPBELL.WK1	Campbell Soup
CARNIVAL.WK1	Carnival Cruise
CCCA.WK1	Classic Car Club of America
CIRCUS.WK1	Circus Circus Enterprises
CITICORP.WK1	Citicorp
CPO.WK1	Cineplex-Odeon
DMERR.WK1	Dakota, Minnesota, & Eastern Railroad
ELKIN.WK1	Elkins Lake Baptist Church
GEORGPAC.WK1	Georgia-Pacific
GREYHOUN.WK1	Greyhound Bus
HARLEY.WK1	Harley-Davidson
HERSHEY.WK1	Hershey Foods
LIMITED.WK1	The Limited
MCDONNEL.WK1	McDonnell Douglas
MET.WK1	The Metropolitan Museum of Art
MHE.WK1	Material Handling Engineering
NIKE.WK1	Nike
NORDSTRO.WK1	Nordstrom
NORWOOD.WK1	Norwood Funiture
NSP.WK1	NSP Corporate Graphics
PILGRIM.WK1	Pilgrim's Pride
PLAYBOY.WK1	Playboy Enterprises
PROMUS1.WK1	Promus Hotels
PROMUS2.WK1	Harrah's Entertainment
SPLATTER.WK1	Splatterball Adventure Games
STRYKER.WK1	Stryker
UST.WK1	US Tobacco
WALMART.WK1	Wal-Mart Stores
WALNUT.WK1	Walnut Creek Baptist Church
WEYERHAE.WK1	Weyerhaeuser
WINNEBAG.WK1	Winnebago Industries
WOODLAND.WK1	Woodlands Cleaning Service

Most of the data in these spreadsheets was gathered from the Securities and Exchange Commission's Internet site (HTTP://WWW.SEC.GOV/). A search of the EDGAR database will provide you with a great deal of information. Companies that file with the SEC have their 10K as well as other forms online for download. Some of these files are rather large (greater than 1 megabyte). Also, you may want to refine your search. Some companies must file many statements with the SEC. Try searching for the company name and 10K.

After you have downloaded a file, you may wish to place the financials contained in it into a spreadsheet form. First, isolate the section of the form you wish to put into a spreadsheet. You must use a word processor that does not add its own formatting codes to the text. I used Microsoft's Write program. Find the section of the form you wish to place in the spreadsheet and copy it. In Write or another text editor, paste the text into a new, blank sheet. Save this sheet as a *text* file.

Open the new text file with your spreadsheet program. If you are using the new Excel, you will see a set of screens that may aid you in parsing the data. You may have a problem here if you have more than one financial statement in your file. If you have more than one statement in your file, do not use the wizard that starts up automatically when you open the text (press Cancel). The columns in a balance sheet will not line up with the columns in an income statement. This makes parsing the whole sheet at one time impossible. You either must move each statement into a separate file or manually parse each section. Parsing each section is easier.

To parse a section of text into columns, first select (with the mouse or by holding the shift key and moving the arrows) the text you want to separate into columns.

In Excel, choose:

Data

Text to Columns...

And inside the Convert Text to Columns Wizard

On step one choose:

Original Data Type—Fixed Width

On step two, move the break lines between the columns of data so that all, or as much as possible, of the data is separated by the lines. Use the scroll bar on the right to view your data to make sure you have not split a number with a break line. If you want to delete a break line (this does not affect your data) double click on the line. Click on an empty spot on the sheet to create a new break line.

Step three allows you to format your data. The default setting of "General" works fine.

Press finish and your data should be parsed. Quickly scan your data for errors. If you see more errors than you want to correct by hand, choose:

Edit

Undo

and start the parse process over.

Almost all spreadsheet programs have this capability although some are easier to use than others. You should look in your spreadsheet's manual under the word "Parse" or "Parsing data."

Part 1

OVERVIEW OF STRATEGIC MANAGEMENT

The Nature of Strategic Management

CHAPTER OBJECTIVES

After studying this chapter, you should be able to do the following:

1. Describe the strategic-management process.
2. Explain the need for integrating analysis and intuition in strategic management.
3. Define and give examples of key terms in strategic management.
4. Discuss the nature of strategy formulation, implementation, and evaluation activities.
5. Describe the benefits of good strategic management.
6. Explain why good ethics is good business in strategic management.

NOTABLE QUOTES

If we know where we are and something about how we got there, we might see where we are trending— and if the outcomes which lie naturally in our course are unacceptable, to make timely change. —ABRAHAM LINCOLN

Without a strategy, an organization is like a ship without a rudder, going around in circles. It's like a tramp; it has no place to go. —JOEL ROSS AND MICHAEL KAMI

Plans are less important than planning. —DALE McCONKEY

The formulation of strategy can develop competitive advantage only to the extent that the process can give meaning to workers in the trenches. —DAVID HURST

Most of us fear change. Even when our minds say change is normal, our stomachs quiver at the prospect. But for strategists and managers today, there is no choice but to change. —ROBERT WATERMAN, JR.

If business is not based on ethical grounds, it is of no benefit to society, and will, like all other unethical combinations, pass into oblivion. —C. MAX KILLAN

If a man take no thought about what is distant, he will find sorrow near at hand. He who will not worry about what is far off will soon find something worse than worry. —CONFUCIUS

It is human nature to make decisions based on emotion, rather than fact. But nothing could be more illogical. —TOSHIBA CORPORATION

No business can do everything. Even if it has the money, it will never have enough good people. It has to set priorities. The worst thing to do is a little bit of everything. This makes sure that nothing is being accomplished. It is better to pick the wrong priority than none at all. —PETER DRUCKER

*T*his chapter provides an overview of strategic management. It introduces a practical, integrative model of the strategic-management process and defines basic activities and terms in strategic management and discusses the importance of business ethics.

This chapter initiates several themes that permeate all chapters of this text. First, *global considerations impact virtually all strategic decisions!* The boundaries of countries can no longer define the limits of our imaginations. To see and appreciate the world from the perspective of others has become a matter of survival for businesses. The underpinnings of strategic management hinge upon managers' gaining an understanding of competitors, markets, prices, suppliers, distributors, governments, creditors, shareholders, and customers worldwide. The price and quality of a firm's products and services must be competitive on a worldwide basis, not just a local basis. A Global Perspective is provided in all chapters of this text to emphasize the importance of global factors in strategic management.

A second theme is that *information technology has become a vital strategic-management tool.* An increasing number of companies are gaining competitive advantage by using local area networks (LANs) for internal communication and online services—such as the *Internet, World Wide Web, Prodigy, America Online,* and *CompuServe*—for external communication. Internally, for managers and employees who may be dispersed across continents, LANs provide capabilities ranging from *e-mail* to *video conferencing.* Externally, for suppliers, customers, creditors, partners, shareholders, clients, and competitors who also may be dispersed globally, online services allow firms to sell products, advertise, purchase supplies, bypass middlemen, track inventory, eliminate paperwork, and share information. In total, *electronic commerce* is minimizing the cumbersomeness of time, distance, and space in doing business, which yields better customer service, greater efficiency, improved products, and higher profitability. Using up-to-date, rather than out-of-date, information as a basis for decisions is perhaps the benefit offered a firm operating online. An Information Technology Perspective is included in each chapter to illustrate how electronic commerce impacts the strategic-management process.

A third theme in this text is that *the natural environment has become an important strategic issue.* With the demise of communism and the end of the Cold War, perhaps no greater threat exists to business and society than the continuous exploitation and decimation of our natural environment. Mark Starik at George Washington University says, "The 1990s decade is critical in halting and reversing worldwide ecological destruction and deterioration; this is a strategic issue that needs immediate and substantive attention by all businesses and managers." A Natural Environment Perspective is provided in all chapters to illustrate how firms are addressing environmental concerns.

WHAT IS STRATEGIC MANAGEMENT?

Once there were two company presidents who competed in the same industry. These two presidents decided to go on a camping trip to discuss a possible merger. They hiked deep into the woods. Suddenly, they came upon a grizzly bear that rose up on its hind legs and snarled. Instantly, the first president took off his knapsack and got out a pair of jogging shoes. The second president said, "Hey, you can't outrun that bear." The first president responded, "Maybe I can't outrun that bear, but I can surely outrun you!" This story captures the notion of strategic management.

DEFINING STRATEGIC MANAGEMENT   *Strategic management* can be defined as the art and science of formulating, implementing, and evaluating cross-functional decisions that enable an organization to achieve its objectives. As this definition implies, strategic management focuses on integrating management, marketing, finance/accounting, production/operations, research and development, and computer information systems to achieve organizational success. The term *strategic management* is used at many colleges and universities as the title for the capstone course in business administration, Business Policy, which integrates material from all business courses.

STAGES OF STRATEGIC MANAGEMENT   The *strategic-management process* consists of three stages: strategy formulation, strategy implementation, and strategy evaluation. *Strategy formulation* includes developing a business mission, identifying an organization's external opportunities and threats, determining internal strengths and weaknesses, establishing long-term objectives, generating alternative strategies, and choosing particular strategies to pursue. Strategy-formulation issues include deciding what new businesses to enter, what businesses to abandon, how to allocate resources, whether to expand operations or diversify, whether to enter international markets, whether to merge or form a joint venture, and how to avoid a hostile takeover.

Since no organization has unlimited resources, strategists must decide which alternative strategies will benefit the firm most. Strategy-formulation decisions commit an organization to specific products, markets, resources, and technologies over an extended period of time. Strategies determine long-term competitive advantages. For better or worse, strategic decisions have enduring effects on an organization and major multifunctional consequences. Top managers have the best perspective to fully understand the ramifications of formulation decisions; they have the authority to commit the resources necessary for implementation.

Strategy implementation requires a firm to establish annual objectives, devise policies, motivate employees, and allocate resources so that formulated strategies can be executed; strategy implementation includes developing a strategy-supportive culture, creating an effective organizational structure, redirecting marketing efforts, preparing budgets, developing and utilizing information systems, and linking employee compensation to organizational performance.

Strategy implementation is often called the action stage of strategic management. *Implementing* means mobilizing employees and managers to put formulated strategies into action. Often considered to be the most difficult stage in strategic management, strategy implementation requires personal discipline, commitment, and sacrifice. Successful strategy implementation hinges upon managers' ability to motivate employees, which is more an art than a science. Strategies formulated but not implemented serve no useful purpose.

Interpersonal skills are especially critical for successful strategy implementation. Strategy-implementation activities affect all employees and managers in an organization. Every division and department must decide on answers to questions such as, "What must we do to implement our part of the organization's strategy?" and "How best can we get the job done?" The challenge of implementation is to stimulate managers and employees throughout an organization to work with pride and enthusiasm toward achieving stated objectives.

Strategy evaluation is the final stage in strategic management. Managers desperately need to know when particular strategies are not working well; strategy evaluation is the primary means for obtaining this information. All strategies are subject to future modification because external and internal factors are constantly changing. Three fundamental strategy-evaluation activities are (1) reviewing external and internal factors that are the bases for current strategies, (2) measuring performance, and (3) taking corrective actions. Strategy evaluation is needed because success today is no guarantee of success tomorrow! Success always creates new and different problems; complacent organizations experience demise.

Strategy formulation, implementation, and evaluation activities occur at three hierarchical levels in a large organization: corporate, divisional or strategic business unit, and functional. By fostering communication and interaction among managers and employees across hierarchical levels, strategic management helps a firm function as a competitive team. Most small businesses and some large businesses do not have divisions or strategic business units;

they have only the corporate and functional levels. Nevertheless, managers and employees at these two levels should be actively involved in strategic-management activities.

Peter Drucker says the prime task of strategic management is thinking through the overall mission of a business:

> . . . that is, of asking the question, "What is our Business?" This leads to the setting of objectives, the development of strategies, and the making of today's decisions for tomorrow's results. This clearly must be done by a part of the organization that can see the entire business; that can balance objectives and the needs of today against the needs of tomorrow; and that can allocate resources of men and money to key results.[1]

INTEGRATING INTUITION AND ANALYSIS   The strategic-management process can be described as an objective, logical, systematic approach for making major decisions in an organization. It attempts to organize qualitative and quantitative information in a way that allows effective decisions to be made under conditions of uncertainty. Yet, strategic management is not a pure science that lends itself to a nice, neat, one-two-three approach.

Based on past experiences, judgment, and feelings, *intuition* is essential to making good strategic decisions. Intuition is particularly useful for making decisions in situations of great uncertainty or little precedent. It is also helpful when highly interrelated variables exist, when there is immense pressure to be right, or when it is necessary to choose from several plausible alternatives.[2] These situations describe the very nature and heart of strategic management.

Some managers and owners of businesses profess to have extraordinary abilities for using intuition alone in devising brilliant strategies. For example, Will Durant, who organized General Motors Corporation, was described by Alfred Sloan as "a man who would proceed on a course of action guided solely, as far as I could tell, by some intuitive flash of brilliance. He never felt obliged to make an engineering hunt for the facts. Yet at times he was astoundingly correct in his judgment."[3] Albert Einstein acknowledged the importance of intuition when he said, "I believe in intuition and inspiration. At times I feel certain that I am right while not knowing the reason. Imagination is more important than knowledge, because knowledge is limited, whereas imagination embraces the entire world."[4]

Although some organizations today may survive and prosper because they have intuitive geniuses managing them, most are not so fortunate. Most organizations can benefit from strategic management, which is based upon integrating intuition and analysis in decision making. Choosing an intuitive or analytic approach to decision making is not an either-or proposition. Managers at all levels in an organization should inject their intuition and judgment into strategic-management analyses. Analytical thinking and intuitive thinking complement each other.

Operating from the "I've already made up my mind, don't bother me with the facts" mode is not management by intuition; it is management by ignorance.[5] Drucker says, "I believe in intuition only if you discipline it. 'Hunch' artists, who make a diagnosis but don't check it out with the facts, are the ones in medicine who kill people, and in management kill businesses."[6] In a sense, the strategic-management process is an attempt to duplicate what goes on in the mind of a brilliant intuitive person who knows the business. Successful strategic management hinges upon effective integration of intuition and analysis, as Henderson notes:

> The accelerating rate of change today is producing a business world in which customary managerial habits in organizations are increasingly inadequate. Experience alone was an adequate guide when changes could be made in small increments. But intuitive and experience-based management philosophies are grossly inadequate when decisions are strategic and have major, irreversible consequences.[7]

ADAPTING TO CHANGE   The strategic-management process is based on the belief that organizations should continually monitor internal and external events and trends so that timely changes can be made as needed. The rate and magnitude of changes that affect organizations are increasing dramatically. Consider, for example, palmtop computers, color fax machines, voice mail, monoclonal antibodies, completion of the English Channel tunnel, the aging population, the Hong Kong annexation, and normalization of relations between the United States and Vietnam. To survive, all organizations must be capable of astutely identifying and adapting to change. The strategic-management process is aimed at allowing organizations to effectively adapt to change over the long run.

> In today's business environment, more than any preceding era, the only constant is change. Successful organizations effectively manage change, continuously adapting their bureaucracies, strategies, systems, products, and cultures to survive the shocks and prosper from the forces that decimate the competition.[8]

Information technology and globalization are external changes that are transforming business and society today. On a political map, the boundaries between countries are as clear as ever, but on a competitive map showing the real flow of financial and industrial activity, the boundaries have largely disappeared.[9] Speedy flow of information has eaten away at national boundaries so that people worldwide readily see for themselves how other people live. People are traveling abroad more; ten million Japanese travel abroad annually. People are emigrating more; Germans to England and Mexicans to the United States are examples. As the Global Perspective indicates, U.S. firms have become second-tier competitors in many industries. We are becoming a borderless world with global citizens, global competitors, global customers, global suppliers, and global distributors!

The need to adapt to change leads organizations to key strategic-management questions, such as What kind of business should we become? Are we in the right fields? Should we reshape our business? What new competitors are entering our industry? What strategies should we pursue? How are our customers changing? Are new technologies being developed that could put us out of business?

GLOBAL PERSPECTIVE
The World's Largest Companies

Fortune's annual ranking of the world's largest companies reveals that only three U.S. firms make the top ten. Based on total revenues the ten largest firms in the world in rank order are Mitsubishi, Mitsui, Itochu, Sumitomo, General Motors, Marubeni, Ford Motor, Exxon, Nissho Iwai, and the Royal Dutch/Shell Group. As indicated below in *Fortune's* global ranking of firms in several industries, U.S. companies no longer dominate competitors.

BANKS	ELECTRONICS	INSURANCE
Deutsche Bank, Germany	Hitachi, Japan	Nippon Life, Japan
Citicorp, U.S.	Matsushita, Japan	Dai-ichi Mutual, Japan
Industrial Bank of Japan	General Electric, U.S.	Sumitomo Life, Japan
Fuji Bank, Japan	Siemens, Germany	State Farm Group, U.S.
Mitsubishi Bank, Japan	Toshiba, Japan	Prudential, U.S.
Sumitomo Bank, Japan	Sony, Japan	Meir Mutual Life, Japan
Sanwa Bank, Japan	NEC, Japan	Asahi Mutual Life, Japan
Credit Agricole, France	Daewoo, South Korea	Yasuda Mutual Life, Japan
Dai-ichi Kangyo, Japan	Philips, Netherlands	Metropolitan Life, U.S.
Credit Lyonnais, France	Mitsubishi, Japan	Mitsui Mutual Life, Japan

Source: Adapted from *Fortune,* August 7, 1995: 130–50.

KEY TERMS IN STRATEGIC MANAGEMENT

Before we go any further in discussing strategic management, we should define eight key terms: strategies, mission statements, external opportunities and threats, internal strengths and weaknesses, long-term objectives, strategies, annual objectives, and policies.

STRATEGISTS   *Strategists* are individuals who are most responsible for the success or failure of an organization. Strategists have various job titles, such as chief executive officer, president, owner, chairman of the board, executive director, chancellor, dean, or entrepreneur. Jonas, Fry, and Srivastva recently reported that strategists' three principal responsibilities in organizations are creating a context for change, building commitment and ownership, and balancing stability and innovation.[10]

Strategists in the 1990s are expected to change in ways outlined in Table 1–1. For example, strategists in the year 2000 will provide more visionary leadership, will better link compensation to performance, will communicate more frequently with employees, and will emphasize business ethics more. Coverage of these topics is expanded in this edition of this text.

Strategists differ as much as organizations themselves, and these differences must be considered in the formulation, implementation, and evaluation of strategies. Strategists differ in their attitudes, values, ethics, willingness to take risks, concern for social responsibility, concern for profitability, concern for short-run versus long-run aims, and management style. Some strategists will not consider some types of strategies due to their personal philosophy. For example, David Wickins, who replaced Colin Chapman as chairman of the board of Lotus, the car manufacturer, says, "Lotus has never been run with the objective of being a profitable company. Colin Chapman was quite simply interested in making cars go fast. I have a different viewpoint."[11]

Some strategists agree with Ralph Nader, who proclaims that organizations have tremendous social obligations. Others agree with Milton Friedman, an economist, who maintains that organizations have no obligation to do any more for society than is legally required. Most strategists agree that the first social responsibility of any business must be to make enough profit to cover the costs of the future, because if this is not achieved, no other social responsibility can be met. Strategists should examine social problems in terms of potential costs and benefits to the firm, and address social issues that could benefit the firm most.

TABLE 1–1

What Traits CEOs Have—and Will Need: Percent Describing Traits or Talents Dominant Now in the CEO and Important for the CEO of 2000

PERSONAL BEHAVIOR	NOW	YEAR 2000	KNOWLEDGE AND SKILLS	NOW	YEAR 2000
Conveys Strong Sense of Vision	75%	98%	Strategy Formulation	68%	78%
Links Compensation to Performance	66%	91%	Human Resource Management	41%	53%
Communicate Frequently with Employees	59%	89%	International Economics and Politics	10%	19%
Emphasizes Ethics	74%	85%	Science and Technology	11%	15%
Plans for Management Succession	56%	85%	Computer Literacy	3%	7%
Communicates Frequently with Customers	41%	78%	Marketing and Sales	50%	48%
Reassigns or Terminates Unsatisfactory Employees	34%	71%	Negotiation	34%	24%
Rewards Loyalty	48%	44%	Accounting and Finance	33%	24%
Makes All Major Decisions	39%	21%	Handling Media and Public Speaking	16%	13%
Behaves Conservatively	32%	13%	Production	21%	9%

Source: Lester Korn, "How the Next CEO Will Be Different," *Fortune* (May 22, 1989): 157.
Note: This information is based on a Columbia University survey of 1,500 senior executives, 870 of them CEOs, in 20 countries.

MISSION STATEMENTS   *Mission statements* are "enduring statements of purpose that distinguish one business from other similar firms. A mission statement identifies the scope of a firm's operations in product and market terms."[12] It addresses the basic question that faces all strategists: "What is our business?" A clear mission statement describes the values and priorities of an organization. Developing a business mission compels strategists to think about the nature and scope of present operations and to assess the potential attractiveness of future markets and activities. A mission statement broadly charts the future direction of an organization.

Research suggests that 60 percent of all organizations have developed a formal mission statement and that high-performing firms have more well-developed mission statements than low-performing firms.[13] Note that the mission statement of Adolph Coors Company below should, but does not, reveal that Coors is in the brewery business:

> We are a highly successful, innovative company of stand alone and self-sustaining businesses. We are leaders in technology, quality products and services that provide recognizably superior customer satisfaction. We are growth and profit oriented, developing new businesses from internally generated technology and synergistic acquisitions. Our business is known for quality relationships which are honest, ethical, and caring. Our employees grow personally as the company grows. Our work life is exciting, challenging and rewarding in a friendly atmosphere of teamwork and mutual respect. We are socially responsible and strive for the betterment of society.[14]

EXTERNAL OPPORTUNITIES AND THREATS   Other key terms in our study of strategic management are *external opportunities* and *external threats*. These terms refer to economic, social, cultural, demographic, environmental, political, legal, governmental, technological, and competitive trends and events that could significantly benefit or harm an organization in the future. Opportunities and threats are largely beyond the control of a single organization, thus the term *external*. The computer revolution, biotechnology, population shifts, changing work values and attitudes, space exploration, recyclable packages, and increased competition from foreign companies are examples of opportunities or threats for companies. These types of changes are creating a different type of consumer and consequently a need for different types of products, services, and strategies. As indicated in the Information Technology Perspective, the high investment in adding phone lines in underdeveloped countries is an opportunity for many companies.

Other opportunities and threats may include the passage of a new law, the introduction of a new product by a competitor, a national catastrophe, or the declining value of the dollar. A competitor's strength could be a threat. Unrest in Eastern Europe, rising interest rates, or the war against drugs could represent an opportunity or a threat.

A basic tenet of strategic management is that firms need to formulate strategies to take advantage of external opportunities and to avoid or reduce the impact of external threats. For this reason, identifying, monitoring, and evaluating external opportunities and threats is essential for success. This process of conducting research and gathering and assimilating external information is sometimes called *environmental scanning* or industry analysis.

INTERNAL STRENGTHS AND WEAKNESSES   *Internal strengths* and *internal weaknesses* are controllable activities within an organization that are performed especially well or poorly. Management, marketing, finance/accounting, production/operations, research and development, and computer information systems activities of a business are areas where internal strengths or weaknesses arise. The process of identifying and evaluating organizational strengths and weaknesses in the functional areas of a business is an essential strategic-management activity. Organizations strive to pursue strategies that capitalize on internal strengths and improve on internal weaknesses.

Strengths and weaknesses are determined relative to competitors. *Relative* deficiency or superiority is important information. Also, strengths and weaknesses can be determined by elements of being rather than performance. For example, a strength may involve ownership of natural resources or a historic reputation for quality. Strengths and weaknesses may be determined relative to a firm's own objectives. For example, high levels of inventory turnover may not be a strength to a firm that seeks never to stock-out.

Internal factors can be determined in a number of ways that include computing ratios, measuring performance, and comparing to past periods and industry averages. Various types of surveys can also be developed and administered to examine internal factors such as employee morale, production efficiency, advertising effectiveness, and customer loyalty. Robert H. Short, chief executive officer of Portland General Corporation, describes his firm's strategy in terms of strengths and weaknesses:

> First and foremost we are an energy company for the people of Oregon. Indeed, energy is our fundamental strength, and we intend to pursue growth aggressively in this business. To build on our strengths, however, we must mitigate or eliminate our weaknesses. I am proud of the way Portland General is drawing on its strengths to build for another century of success.[15]

LONG-TERM OBJECTIVES   *Objectives* can be defined as specific results that an organization seeks to achieve in pursing its basic mission. *Long-term* means more than one year. Objectives are essential for organizational success because they provide direction, aid in evaluation, create synergy, reveal priorities, allow coordination, and provide a basis for effective planning, organizing, motivating, and controlling activities. Objectives should be challenging, measurable, consistent, reasonable, and clear. In a multidimensional firm, ob-

INFORMATION TECHNOLOGY
Developing Countries Go Online

An integral component of any computer system is the telephone. A phone is essential for using a modem and a fax machine. As indicated in the following table, there is explosive telephone growth in many developing countries. Analysts expect computer growth in these countries to follow on the heels of the phone growth. Implications of these two trends for all kinds of companies is immense.

Recognize that when countries add phones, their people become potential consumers of many new products and services. The addition of phones thus opens whole new markets. For example, Brazil is the ninth-largest economy in the world and has 150 million people but a phone-line density of only 6.8 per 100 inhabitants. About 721,000 Brazilians have cellular phones in 1996, but that number is expected to reach 6 million by 1998. The

situation in Indonesia, a nation of 190 million, is similar. In Africa there are only 0.8 phone lines per 100 people.

MCI, Sprint, AT&T, Motorola, Nynex, BellSouth, U.S. West, Northern Telecom, and Bell Atlantic are competing aggressively with foreign phone companies to service developing countries. Note that the dollar infrastructure investment required to install phone lines in a country is huge.

COUNTRY	1992 # PHONE LINES PER 100 PEOPLE	2000 # PHONE LINES PER 100 PEOPLE	1992–2000 $ INVESTMENT FOR PHONES
China	0.98	3.50	$53.3
Thailand	3.10	9.35	6.6
India	0.77	1.52	13.7
Hungary	12.54	23.80	1.6
Poland	10.28	16.62	4.0
Russia	15.28	24.50	23.3
Chile	8.92	19.71	2.8
Brazil	6.83	9.49	10.2
Mexico	7.54	12.49	9.4
USA	56.49	65.92	55.8

Source: Adapted from Catherine Arnst, "The Last Frontier," *Business Week* (September 18, 1995): 106.

jectives should be established for the overall company and for each division. Minnesota Power's long-term objectives are to achieve a 13-percent return on equity (ROE) in their core electric utility, 14-percent ROE on water resource operations, and 15 percent on support businesses. Minnesota Power also strives to stay in the top 25 percent of electric utilities in the United States in terms of common stock's market-to-book ratio and to maintain an annual growth in earnings per share of 5 percent.

STRATEGIES   *Strategies* are the means by which long-term objectives will be achieved. Business strategies may include geographic expansion, diversification, acquisition, product development, market penetration, retrenchment, divestiture, liquidation, and joint venture. Strategies currently being pursued by Compaq Computer Company and Enron Corporation are described in Table 1–2.

ANNUAL OBJECTIVES   *Annual objectives* are short-term milestones that organizations must achieve to reach long-term objectives. Like long-term objectives, annual objectives should be measurable, quantitative, challenging, realistic, consistent, and prioritized. They should be established at the corporate, divisional, and functional levels in a large organization. Annual objectives should be stated in terms of management, marketing, finance/accounting, production/operations, research and development, and information systems accomplishments. A set of annual objectives is needed for each long-term objective. Annual objectives are especially important in strategy implementation, whereas long-term objectives are particularly important in strategy formulation. Annual objectives represent the basis for allocating resources.

Campbell Soup Corporation has an annual objective to achieve 20-percent growth in earnings, a 20 percent return on equity, and a 20-percent return on invested cash. The company calls this ERC, for earnings, returns, and cash.

The Tribune Company (the nation's fifth-largest publisher of newspapers and owner of the Chicago Cubs baseball team) is another firm that has clear annual objectives. Stanton

COMPAQ COMPUTER COMPANY
 	
  Headquartered in Houston, Texas, Compaq surpassed IBM in 1994 as the world's leading supplier of personal computers (PCs). Compaq's sales and profits for the second quarter of 1995 jumped 38 percent and 19 percent, respectively. But Compaq is not content just producing and selling PCs. Compaq's plans to move aggressively into computer networks with modems, routers, and switches. The first Compaq computer network system was introduced in 1996. The leading network system companies, 3M and Hewlett-Packard, are worried. Referring to Compaq's new networking strategy, Gary McWilliams says, "The arrival of this 800-pound gorilla could reshape the entire networking industry. As in the early years of the PC business, the networking market today consists of hundreds of specialized hardware makers." Compaq may dominate the computer networking market, or will this concentric diversification strategy lead to their demise? (adapted from Gary McWilliams, "Compaq: All Things to All Networks," *Business Week* [July 31, 1995]: 79).
 	
ENRON CORPORATION
 	
  Also headquartered in Houston, Texas, Enron is a $billion U.S. construction company aggressively expanding globally. Enron profits from international operations comprise 16.5 percent of total company profits in 1996 compared to only 4 percent in 1992. But Enron is finding political problems in foreign countries to be a nightmare. For example, the newly elected Maharashtra government of India abruptly cancelled Enron's contract to build a $2.8 billion utility plant in Dabhol even after construction had begun. Enron's $3 billion contract to build a natural gas pipeline between Bolivia and Brazil is delayed by a feud between the World Bank and Brazil over foreign ownership. Enron faces similar political nightmares over contracts it has in Indonesia, Qatar, Turkey, the Philippines, and China. (adapted from Gary McWilliams, "Enron: Maybe Megadeals Mean Megarisk," *Business Week* [September 4, 1995]: 52).
	TABLE 1–2
	Two Organizations'
	Strategies in 1996

Cook, president and chief executive officer of Tribune, emphasizes annual objectives. Tribune strives to have an 18-percent annual return on equity (net income divided by average stockholders' investment) and a 30-percent debt to total capital ratio.

POLICIES   The final key term to be highlighted here is *policies*—the means by which annual objectives will be achieved. Policies include guidelines, rules, and procedures established to support efforts to achieve stated objectives. Policies are guides to decision making and address repetitive or recurring situations.

Policies are most often stated in terms of management, marketing, finance/accounting, production/operations, research and development, and computer information systems activities. Policies can be established at the corporate level and apply to an entire organization, at the divisional level and apply to a single division, or at the functional level and apply to particular operational activities or departments. Policies, like annual objectives, are especially important in strategy implementation because they outline an organization's expectations of its employees and managers. Policies allow consistency and coordination within and between organizational departments.

Most firms have policies against drinking at work. The Centers for Disease Control recently reported that states with the highest alcohol consumption per employee were Wisconsin, New Hampshire, Minnesota, Montana, the Dakotas, Texas, and Hawaii.

Substantial research suggests that a healthier workforce can more effectively and efficiently implement strategies. The National Center for Health Promotion estimates that more than 80 percent of all American corporations have No Smoking policies. No Smoking policies are usually derived from annual objectives that seek to reduce corporate medical costs associated with absenteeism and to provide a healthy workplace. Pullman Company in Garden Grove, California, charges smokers $10 more each month for health insurance than it charges nonsmokers.

THE STRATEGIC-MANAGEMENT MODEL

The strategic-management process can best be studied and applied using a model. Every model represents some kind of process. The framework illustrated in Figure 1–1 is a widely accepted, comprehensive model of the strategic-management process.[16] This model does not guarantee success, but it does represent a clear and practical approach for formulating, implementing, and evaluating strategies. Relationships among major components of the strategic-management process are shown in the model, which appears in all subsequent chapters with appropriate areas shaped to show the particular focus of each chapter.

Identifying an organization's existing mission, objectives, and strategies is the logical starting point for strategic management because a firm's present situation and condition may preclude certain strategies and may even dictate a particular course of action. Every organization has a mission, objectives, and strategy, even if these elements are not consciously designed, written, or communicated. The answer to where an organization is going can be determined largely by where the organization has been!

The strategic-management process is dynamic and continuous. A change in any one of the major components in the model can necessitate a change in any or all of the other components. For instance, a shift in the economy could represent a major opportunity and require a change in long-term objectives and strategies; or a failure to accomplish annual objectives could require a change in policy; or a major competitor could announce a change in strategy that requires a change in the firm's mission. Therefore, strategy formulation, implementation, and evaluation activities should be performed on a continual basis, not just at the end of the year of semiannually. The strategic-management process never really ends.

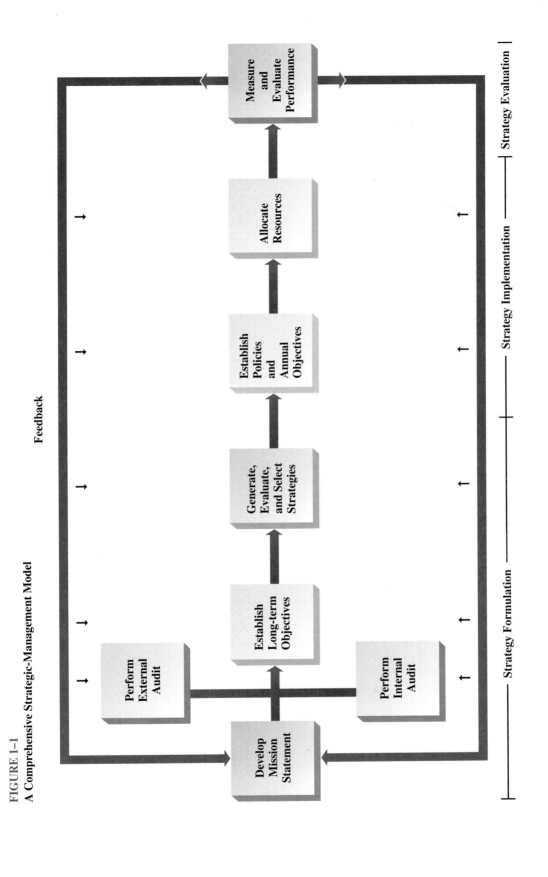

FIGURE 1–1
A Comprehensive Strategic-Management Model

Feedback

Perform
External
Audit

Develop
Mission
Statement

Establish
Long-term
Objectives

Generate,
Evaluate,
and Select
Strategies

Establish
Policies
and
Annual
Objectives

Allocate
Resources

Measure
and
Evaluate
Performance

Perform
Internal
Audit

Strategy Formulation

Strategy Implementation

Strategy Evaluation

The strategic-management process is not as cleanly divided and neatly performed in practice as the strategic-management model suggests. Strategists do not go through the process in lockstep fashion. Generally, there is give-and-take among hierarchical levels of an organization. Many organizations conduct formal meetings semiannually to discuss and update the firm's mission, opportunities/threats, strengths/weaknesses, strategies, objectives, policies, and performance. These meetings are commonly held off-premises and called *retreats.* The rationale for periodically conducting strategic-management meetings away

FIGURE 1–2
Forces Influencing Design of Strategic-Management Systems

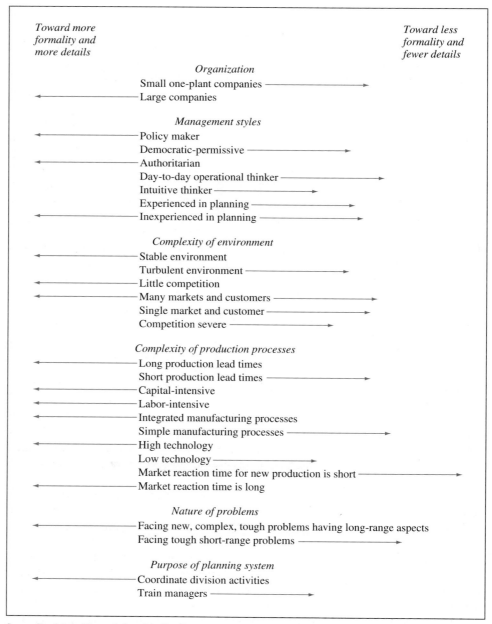

Source: Reprinted with permission of the Free Press, a Division of Macmillan, Inc., from *Strategic Planning: What Every Manager Must Know* by George A. Steiner (New York: Free Press, 1979): 54. Copyright 1979 by the Free Press.

from the work site is to encourage more creativity and candor among participants. Good communication and feedback are needed throughout the strategic-management process.

As shown in Figure 1–2, a number of different forces affect the formality of strategic management in organizations. Size of organization is a key factor; smaller firms are less formal in performing strategic-management tasks. Other variables that affect formality are management styles, complexity of environment, complexity of production process, nature of problems, and purpose of planning system.

BENEFITS OF STRATEGIC MANAGEMENT

Strategic management allows an organization to be more proactive than reactive in shaping its own future; it allows an organization to initiate and influence (rather than just respond to) activities, and thus to exert control over its own destiny. Small business owners, chief executive officers, presidents, and managers of many for-profit and nonprofit organizations have recognized and realized the benefits of strategic management.

Historically, the principal benefit of strategic management has been to help organizations make better strategies through the use of a more systematic, logical, and rational approach to strategic choice. This certainly continues to be a major benefit of strategic management, but research studies now indicate that the process, rather than the decision or document, is the more important contribution of strategic management.[17] *Communication is a key to successful strategic management.* Through involvement in the process, managers and employees become committed to supporting the organization. Dialogue and participation are essential ingredients. The chief executive officer of Rockwell International explains, "We believe that fundamental to effective strategic management is fully informed employees at all organizational levels. We expect every business segment to inform every employee about the business objectives, the direction of the business, the progress towards achieving objectives, and our customers, competitors and product plans."

The manner in which strategic management is carried out is thus exceptionally important. A major aim of the process is to achieve understanding and commitment from all managers and employees. Understanding may be the most important benefit of strategic management, followed by commitment. When managers and employees understand what the organization is doing and why, they often feel a part of the firm and become committed to assisting it. This is especially true if employees also understand linkages between their own compensation and organizational performance. Managers and employees become surprisingly creative and innovative when they understand and support the firm's mission, objectives, and strategies. A great benefit of strategic management, then, is the opportunity that the process provides to empower individuals. *Empowerment* is the act of strengthening an individual's sense of effectiveness. It means encouraging and rewarding employees to exercise initiative and imagination.[18]

More and more organizations are decentralizing the strategic-management process, recognizing that planning must involve lower-level managers and employees. The notion of centralized staff planning is being replaced in organizations by decentralized line manager planning. The process is a learning, helping, educating, and supporting activity, not merely a paper-shuffling activity among top executives. Strategic-management dialogue is more important than a nicely bound strategic-management document.[19] The worst thing strategists can do is develop strategic plans themselves and then present them to operating managers to execute. Through involvement in the process, line managers become "owners" of the strategy. Ownership of strategies by the people who have to execute them is a key to success!

Although making good strategic decisions is the major responsibility of an organization's owner or chief executive officer, managers and employees both must also be involved in strategy formulation, implementation, and evaluation activities. Participation is a key to gaining commitment for needed changes.

An increasing number of corporations and institutions are using strategic management to make effective decisions. Over 75 percent of all companies now use strategic-management techniques, compared to less than 25 percent in 1979.[20] But strategic management is not a guarantee for success; it can be dysfunctional if conducted haphazardly. The benefits of strategic management to Rockwell International Corporation, Columbia Gas System Service Corporation, and Ogden Corporation are evidenced in Table 1–3.

William Dearden of Hershey Foods Corporation attributes his company's success to strategic management:

> There is the strategic-management process. Planning for the long-term future has been entrenched as a way of life at Hershey, and we certainly plan to strengthen and rely on the process going forward.[21]

FINANCIAL BENEFITS   Research studies indicate that organizations using strategic-management concepts are more profitable and successful than those that do not. For example, a longitudinal study of 101 retail, service, and manufacturing firms over a 3-year period concluded that businesses using strategic-management concepts showed significant improvement in sales, profitability, and productivity compared to firms without systematic

---

TABLE 1–3
Top Managers Discuss Strategic Management in Their Firms

ROCKWELL INTERNATIONAL CORPORATION

We expect every business segment head to be responsible for the strategic direction of the business and the business team to be very knowledgeable about their business in the worldwide marketplace, to know where they are taking the business long term; and how they are going to position the business vis-à-vis worldwide competition, as well as the marketplace as a whole. We also expect every business to make full use of the corporation's resources in developing functionally integrated implementation strategies that will beat the best of the competition. We will distinguish ourselves as a strategically managed worldwide company through the care and thoroughness with which our strategic management is linked to operational decision making. (Donald Beall, chief executive officer of Rockwell International, *Internal Report,* 1990.)

COLUMBIA GAS SYSTEM SERVICE CORPORATION

Headquartered in Wilmington, Delaware, Columbia Gas System's Strategic Plan forms the basis of all other planning activities—marketing plans, capital programs, financial plans, and so forth. Strategic management goes far beyond operational planning that has been traditional throughout Columbia. We are not just looking at projections of how much gas we'll need and where it will come from. The first part of our Strategic Plan is the Mission Statement, which sets the direction for the company. All operating units have their own mission statements, defining their business and their corporate reason for existing. These in turn are followed by long-term objectives which are broad statements of what the company intends to do, followed by annual objectives which for the most part are quantified. (James D. Little, executive vice president of Columbia Gas System, *Columbia Today,* Winter 1985–86, p. 2.)

ODGEN CORPORATION

The best long-run results come from good strategic decisions, which ensure doing the right things (effectiveness), and the combination of design, technology, and automation, which ensure doing things right (efficiency). To predict . . . without the ability to adapt is simply to foresee one's own end! The strategic objectives Ogden has achieved have enabled the adaptation necessary to cope with the changing economic environment for the balance of this century. We are describing a classic example of evolution; in this case, corporate evolution. To survive, both organisms and corporations must adapt to new circumstances. (Ralph Ablon, chairman of the board, Ogden Corporation) planning activities; another study reported that up to 80 percent of the improvement possible in a firm's profitability is achieved through changes in a company's strategic direction; Cook and Ferris reported that the practices of high-performing firms reflect a more strategic orientation and longer-term focus.[22] High-performing firms tend to do systematic planning to prepare for future fluctuations in their external and internal environments. Firms with planning systems more closely resembling strategic-management theory generally exhibit superior long-term financial performance relative to their industry.

High-performing firms seem to make more informed decisions with good anticipation of both short- and long-term consequences. On the other hand, firms that perform poorly often engage in activities that are shortsighted and do not reflect good forecasting of future conditions. Michael Allen found that strategic management demonstrated impressive power by dramatically improving the performance of a number of major companies that had implemented it, including General Electric, American Express, Allied Corporation, Dun & Bradstreet, and Pitney Bowes.[23] Strategists of low-performing organizations are often preoccupied with solving internal problems and meeting paperwork deadlines. They typically underestimate their competitors' strengths and overestimate their own firm's strengths. They often attribute weak performance to uncontrollable factors such as poor economy, technological change, or foreign competition.

Dun & Bradstreet reports that more than 100,000 businesses in the United States fail annually. Business failures include bankruptcies, foreclosures, liquidations, and court-mandated receiverships. Although many factors besides a lack of effective strategic management obviously can lead to business failure, these statistics suggest that strategic-management concepts could yield substantial financial benefits for many organizations.

NONFINANCIAL BENEFITS   Besides helping firms avoid financial demise, strategic management offers other tangible benefits, such as an enhanced awareness of external threats, an improved understanding of competitors' strategies, increased employee productivity, reduced resistance to change, and a clearer understanding of performance-reward relationships. Strategic management enhances the problem-prevention capabilities of organizations because it promotes interaction among managers at all divisional and functional levels. Interaction can enable firms to turn on their managers and employees by nurturing them, sharing organizational objectives with them, empowering them to help improve the product or service, and recognizing their contributions. According to Tom Peters, the difference between a turned-on and a turned-off worker is not 5 percent or 10 percent, but 100 percent to 200 percent.[24]

In addition to empowering managers and employees, strategic management often brings order and discipline to an otherwise floundering firm. It can be the beginning of an efficient and effective managerial system. Strategic management may renew confidence in the current business strategy or point to the need for corrective actions. The strategic-management process provides a basis for identifying and rationalizing the need for change to all managers and employees of a firm; it helps them view change as an opportunity rather than a threat.

Greenley stresses that strategic management offers the following benefits:

1. It allows for identification, prioritization, and exploitation of opportunities.
2. It provides an objective view of management problems.
3. It represents a framework for improved coordination and control of activities.
4. It minimizes the effects of adverse conditions and changes.
5. It allows major decisions to better support established objectives.
6. It allows more effective allocation of time and resources to identified opportunities.
7. It allows fewer resources and less time to be devoted to correcting erroneous or ad hoc decisions.

8.   It creates a framework for internal communication among personnel.
9.   It helps to integrate the behavior of individuals into a total effort.
10. It provides a basis for the clarification of individual responsibilities.
11. It gives encouragement to forward thinking.
12. It provides a cooperative, integrated, and enthusiastic approach to tackling problems and opportunities.
13. It encourages a favorable attitude toward change.
14. It gives a degree of discipline and formality to the management of a business.[25]

BUSINESS ETHICS AND STRATEGIC MANAGEMENT

Business ethics can be defined as principles of conduct within organizations that guide decision making and behavior. Good business ethics is a prerequisite for good strategic management; good ethics is just good business!

A rising tide of consciousness about the importance of business ethics is sweeping America and the world. Strategists are the individuals primarily responsible for ensuring that high ethical principles are espoused and practiced in an organization. All strategy formulation, implementation, and evaluation decisions have ethical ramifications.

Newspapers and business magazines daily report legal and moral breaches of ethical conduct by both public and private organizations. As the Natural Environment Perspective indicates, harming the natural environment is unethical, illegal, and costly; as more and more countries and companies realize this fact, export opportunities for pollution control equipment abound.

A new wave of ethics issues related to product safety, employee health, sexual harassment, AIDS in the workplace, smoking, acid rain, affirmative action, waste disposal, foreign business practices, cover-ups, takeover tactics, conflicts of interest, employee privacy, inappropriate gifts, security of company records, and layoffs has accented the need for strategists to develop a clear code of business ethics. United Technologies Corporation recently revealed a 21-page Code of Ethics and named a new vice president of business ethics. Baxter Travenol Laboratories, IBM, Caterpillar Tractor, Chemical Bank, Exxon, Dow Corning, and Celanese are firms that have a formal code of business ethics. Note how clearly BellSouth's *code of business ethics* in Table 1–4 outlines the standards of behavior expected of all managers and employees.

A business code of ethics can provide a basis on which policies can be devised to guide daily behavior and decisions at the work site. Merely having a code of ethics, however, is not sufficient to ensure ethical business behavior. A code of ethics can be viewed as a public relations gimmick, or a set of platitudes, or window dressing. To ensure that the code is read, understood, believed, and remembered, organizations need to conduct periodic ethics workshops to sensitize people to workplace circumstances in which ethics issues may arise.[26] Chemical Bank, the nation's sixth-largest bank prior to being acquired by Chase Manhattan Bank in 1995, had an extensive ethics education program whereby all new employees attended sessions and signed Chemical's code of ethics. In a survey conducted by the national accounting firm Touche-Ross, 63 percent of corporate executives believe that high ethical standards strengthen, rather than weaken, a firm's competitive position.

An ethics "culture" needs to permeate organizations! To help create an ethics culture, Citicorp has developed a business ethics board game that is played by 40,000 employees in 45 countries. Called *The Work Ethic,* this game asks players business ethics questions, such as how to deal with a customer who offers you football tickets in exchange for a new, backdated IRA.

COUNT ON US!

We are committed to the highest ethical standards because we want people to know they can count on us. This commitment flows naturally from our responsibilities to our customers, our owners, our vendors and suppliers, our families, the communities where we live and work, and to each other. Trust is at the heart of these connections, and trust can only be built on honest and dependability—on ethical conduct.

OUR CUSTOMERS CAN COUNT ON US

We believe our first responsibility is to the people who count on us for their telecommunications needs—in the office, on the road, at home, wherever they might be. All else hinges on this. We will deal with customers straightforwardly and honestly. They will know they can depend not only on our products and services, but on our word and our character. We will promise only what we can deliver. When we err, we will make things right.

OUR OWNERS CAN COUNT ON US

We will provide the highest quality at a reasonable price. As we do so, we will earn a fair return on our owners' investment. Our aim is to increase the value of their investment over the years.

OUR VENDORS AND SUPPLIERS CAN COUNT ON US

Vendors and suppliers must know we will be fair. BellSouth's interests will dictate our decisions about what products and services to buy; our decisions will be based on factors such as quality, price, service, and reliability.

OUR FAMILIES CAN COUNT ON US

We want our families to be proud of our character as individuals in the jobs we do and proud that we work for a company known for its integrity. We seek a healthy balance between our work and our family life.

OUR COMMUNITIES CAN COUNT ON US

Beyond the quality, day-to-day service they expect from us in telecommunications, the cities and towns where we operate can also count on us for help in civic, charitable and other community activities.

WE CAN COUNT ON EACH OTHER

We take pride in the quality of our collective efforts as BellSouth; we take pride in the integrity of our company. A company's reputation is built on what its people do every day. BellSouth's reputation was built on the honest of hundreds of thousands of people over the years, and we recognize that we can diminish that reputation in one single instant. We also know, however, that we can reinforce it every day. And since you and I inherited a company with a reputation for honesty and integrity, we are obligated to pass the heritage on to the women and men who follow us.

We will be even-handed with everyone around us—in scheduling work, in assigning jobs, in awarding incentives and promotions and in the way we treat one another generally.

Each of us expects to be heard and we in turn pledge to listen. We want honesty and openness—about mistakes as well as successes.

We will speak out when we see ethical lapses. We expect that no one will ask us to do anything wrong. Likewise, we will not ask anyone else to do anything wrong.

Satisfying the letter of the law is not enough. Ours is a higher standard. BellSouth's obligations are for the long term—not just for this quarter or this year. These obligations demand this pledge of us on professional, industry and personal ethics: We will build on BellSouth's heritage of integrity so that people will have an abiding trust in the company and our employees; they will know they can count on us. This is our pledge.

TABLE 1–4
BellSouth's Code of Conduct

Source: BellSouth Corporation, *Internal Report,* 1993.

NATURAL ENVIRONMENT

Export Opportunities for Pollution Control Equipment

The global market for pollution control equipment is growing about 25 percent annually as people in more and more countries demand that companies quit polluting the natural environment. U.S. waste management technology is considered state-of-the-art and price-competitive internationally.

In India the market for pollution control equipment is growing 20 percent annually, exceeding $2 billion in 1997. U.S. exports of pollution control equipment to India are growing 30 percent annually to over $400 million in 1997.

Spain's imports of pollution control equipment are growing 16 percent annually, reaching nearly $1 billion in 1997. Spanish industry must invest an estimated $10 billion in the next decade to meet domestic environment requirements. U.S. firms plan to take the lead in this market.

The United Kingdom's imports of pollution control equipment from U.S. producers is growing 14 percent annually, reaching $4.3 billion in 1997. Laws are being passed daily requiring British heavy manufacturing companies to comply with strict emission limits or lose their operating licenses.

The air over countries and the water in countries permeates the entire globe over time, so new laws around the world requiring companies to quit polluting as a strategic management objective is encouraging.

Source: Adapted from *U.S. Global Trade Outlook: 1995–2000.* U.S. Department of Commerce: 38, 52, 85.

Diana Robertson at the Wharton School believes the game is effective because it is interactive. Many organizations, such as Prime Computer and Kmart, have developed a code-of-conduct manual outlining ethical expectations and giving examples of situations that commonly arise in their businesses. Harris Corporation's managers and employees are warned that failing to report an ethical violation by others could bring discharge.

One reason strategists' salaries are high compared to those of other individuals in an organization is that strategists must take the moral risks of the firm. Strategists are responsible for developing, communicating, and enforcing the code of business ethics for their organization. Although primary responsibility for ensuring ethical behavior rests with a firm's strategists, an integral part of the responsibility of all managers is to provide ethics leadership by constant example and demonstration. Managers hold positions that enable them to influence and educate many people. This makes managers responsible for the development and implementation of ethical decision making. Gellerman and Drucker respectively offer some good advice for managers:

> All managers risk giving too much because of what their companies demand from them. But the same superiors who keep pressing you to do more, or to do it better, or faster, or less expensively, will turn on you should you cross that fuzzy line between right and wrong. They will blame you for exceeding instructions or for ignoring their warnings. The smartest managers already know that the best answer to the question, "How far is too far?" is don't try to find out.[27]

A man (or woman) might know too little, perform poorly, lack judgment and ability, and yet not do too much damage as a manager. But if that person lacks character and integrity—no matter how knowledgeable, how brilliant, how successful—he destroys. He destroys people, the most valuable resource of the enterprise. He destroys spirit. And he destroys performance. This is particularly true of the people at the head of an enterprise. For the spirit of an organization is created from the top. If an organization is great in spirit, it is because the spirit of its top people is great. If it decays, it does so because the top rots, as the proverb has it, "Trees die from the top." No one should ever become a strategist unless he or she is willing to have his or her character serve as the model for subordinates.[28]

According to John Akers, ethics and competitiveness are inseparable.[29] No society anywhere in the world can compete very long or successfully with people stealing from one another or not trusting one another, with every bit of information requiring notarized confirmation, with every disagreement ending up in litigation, or with government having to regulate businesses to keep them honest. Akers says being unethical is a recipe for headaches, inefficiency, and waste. History has proven that the greater the trust and confidence of people in the ethics of an institution or society, the greater its economic strength. Business relationships are built mostly on mutual trust and reputation. Short-term decisions based on greed and questionable ethics will preclude the necessary self-respect to gain the trust of others. More and more firms believe that ethics training and an ethics culture create strategic advantage.

A recent *Business Horizons* article gives a number of business actions *always* considered to be unethical, including misleading advertising or labeling, causing environmental harm, poor product or service safety, padding expense accounts, insider trading, dumping banned or flawed products in foreign markets, lack of equal opportunities for women and minorities, overpricing, hostile takeovers, moving jobs overseas, and using nonunion labor in a union shop.[30] Recent research also suggests that Japanese firms are perceived by consumers to be more ethical than American firms.[31]

Ethics training programs should include messages from the CEO emphasizing ethical business practices, development and discussion of codes of ethics, and procedures for discussing and reporting unethical behavior. Firms can align ethical and strategic decision making by incorporating ethical considerations into long-term planning, integrating ethical decision making into the performance appraisal process, encouraging whistle-blowing or the reporting of unethical practices, and monitoring departmental and corporate performance regarding ethical issues.

In a final analysis, ethical standards come out of history and heritage. Our fathers and mothers and brothers and sisters of the past left to us an ethical foundation to build upon. Even the legendary football coach Vince Lombardi knew that some things were worth more than winning, and he required his players to have three kinds of loyalty: to God, to their families, and to the Green Bay Packers, "in that order."

COMPARING BUSINESS AND MILITARY STRATEGY

A strong military heritage underlies the study of strategic management. Terms such as *objectives, mission, strengths,* and *weaknesses* were first formulated to address problems on the battlefield. In many respects, business strategy is like military strategy, and military strategists have learned much over the centuries that can benefit business strategists today. Both business and military organizations try to use their own strengths to exploit competitors' weaknesses. If an organization's overall strategy is wrong (ineffective), then all the efficiency in the world may not be enough to allow success. Business or military success is generally not the happy result of accidental strategies. Rather, success is the product of continuous attention to changing external and internal conditions and the formulation and implementation of insightful adaptations to those conditions. The element of surprise provides great competitive advantages in both military and business strategy; information systems that provide data on opponents' or competitors' strategies and resources are also vitally important.

Of course, a fundamental difference between military and business strategy is that business strategy is formulated, implemented, and evaluated with an assumption of *competition,* whereas military strategy is based on an assumption of *conflict.* Nonetheless, military conflict and business competitors are so similar that many strategic-management techniques apply equally to both. Business strategists have access to valuable insights that military thinkers have refined over time. Superior strategy formulation and implementation can overcome an opponent's superiority in numbers and resources.

Both business and military organizations must adapt to change and constantly improve to be successful. Too often, firms do not change their strategies when their environment and competitive conditions dictate the need to change. Gluck offers a classic military example of this:

> When Napoleon won it was because his opponents were committed to the strategy, tactics, and organization of earlier wars. When he lost—against Wellington, the Russians, and the Spaniards—it was because he, in turn, used tried-and-true strategies against enemies who thought afresh, who were developing the strategies not of the last war, but of the next.[32]

CONCLUSION

All firms have a strategy, even if it is informal, unstructured, and sporadic. All organizations are heading somewhere, but unfortunately some organizations do not know where. The old saying "If you do not know where you are going, then any road will lead you there!" accents the need for organizations to use strategic-management concepts and techniques. The strategic-management process is becoming more and more widely used by small firms, large companies, nonprofit institutions, governmental organizations, and multinational conglomerates alike. The process of empowering managers and employees has almost limitless benefits.

Organizations should take a proactive rather than a reactive approach in their industry, and should strive to influence, anticipate, and initiate rather than just respond to events. The strategic-management process embodies this approach to decision making. It represents a logical, systematic, and objective approach for determining an enterprise's future direction. The stakes are generally too high for strategists to use intuition alone in choosing among alternative courses of action. Successful strategists take the time to think about their business, where they are with the business, and what they want to be as an organization, and then implement programs and policies to get from where they are to where they want to be in a reasonable period of time.

It is a known and accepted fact that people and organizations that plan ahead are much more likely to become what they want to become than those who do not plan at all. A good strategist plans and controls his plans, while a bad strategist never plans and then tries to control people! This textbook is devoted to providing you with the tools necessary to be a good strategist.

TAKE IT TO THE NET

We invite you to visit the DAVID page on the Prentice Hall Web site at:
http://www.prenhall.com/davidsm
for this chapter's World Wide Web exercises.

KEY TERMS AND CONCEPTS

America Online	(p. 4)	External Threats	(p. 9)	Strategic-management Process	(p. 5)
Annual Objectives	(p. 11)	Internal Strengths	(p. 9)	Strategies	(p. 11)
Business Ethics	(p. 18)	Internal Weaknesses	(p. 9)	Strategists	(p. 8)
Code of Business Ethics	(p. 18)	Internet	(p. 4)	Strategy Evaluation	(p. 5)
CompuServe	(p. 4)	Intuition	(p. 6)	Strategy Formulation	(p. 5)
E-mail	(p. 4)	Long-term Objectives	(p. 10)	Strategy Implementation	(p. 5)
Electronic Commerce	(p. 4)	Mission Statement	(p. 9)	Video Conferencing	(p. 4)
Empowerment	(p. 15)	Policies	(p. 12)	World Wide Web	(p. 4)
Environmental Scanning	(p. 9)	Prodigy	(p. 4)		
External Opportunities	(p. 9)	Strategic Management	(p. 4)		

ISSUES FOR REVIEW AND DISCUSSION

1. Explain why business policy is often called a *capstone course*.

2. Select one of the suggested readings at the end of this chapter. Go to your college library and find that article. Read the article. Prepare a one-page written summary that includes your personal thoughts on the subject.

3. What aspect of strategy formulation do you think requires the most time? Why?

4. Why is strategy implementation often considered the most difficult stage in the strategic-management process?

5. Why is it so important to integrate intuition and analysis in strategic management?

6. Explain the importance of a formal mission statement.

7. Discuss relationships among objectives, strategies, and policies.

8. Why do you think some chief executive officers fail to use a strategic-management approach to decision making? Can you identify and describe a good alternative approach?

9. Discuss the importance of feedback in the strategic-management model.

10. How can strategists best ensure that strategies formulated will be effectively implemented?

11. Give an example of a recent political development that changed the overall strategy of an organization.

12. Who are the major competitors of your college or university? What are their strengths and weaknesses? What are their strategies? How successful are these institutions compared to your college?

13. If you owned a small business, would you develop a code of business conduct? If yes, what variables would you include? If no, how would you ensure that ethical business standards were being followed by your employees?

14. Would strategic-management concepts and techniques benefit foreign businesses as much as domestic firms? Justify your answer.

15. What do you believe are some potential pitfalls or risks in using a strategic-management approach to decision making?

16. In your opinion, what is the single major benefit of using a strategic-management approach to decision making? Justify your answer.

17. Compare business strategy and military strategy.

18. What do you feel is the relationship between personal ethics and business ethics? Are they, or should they be, the same?

NOTES

1. Peter Drucker, *Management: Tasks, Responsibilities, and Practices* (New York: Harper & Row, 1974): 611.

2. Weston Agor, "How Top Executives Use Their Intuition to Make Important Decisions," *Business Horizons* 29, no. 1 (January–February 1986): 6. Also, see Andrew Campbell, "Brief Case: Strategy and Intuition—A Conversation with Henry Mintzberg," *Long Range Planning* 24, no. 2. (April 1991): 108–10.

3. Alfred Sloan, Jr., *Adventures of the White Collar Man* (New York: Doubleday, 1941): 104.

4. Quoted in Eugene Raudsepp, "Can You Trust Your Hunches?" *Management Review* 49, no. 4 (April 1960): 7.

5. Stephen Harper, "Intuition: What Separates Executives from Managers," *Business Horizons* 31, no. 5 (September–October 1988): 16.

6. Ron Nelson, "How to Be a Manager," *Success* (July–August 1985): 69.

7. Bruce Henderson, *Henderson on Corporate Strategy* (Boston: Abt Books, 1979): 6.

8. Robert Waterman, Jr., *The Renewal Factor: How the Best Get and Keep the Competitive Edge* (New York: Bantam, 1987). See also *Business Week* (14 September 1987): 100. Also, see *Academy of Management Executive III*, no. 2 (May 1989): 115.

9. Kenichi Ohmae, "Managing in a Borderless World," *Harvard Business Review* 67, no. 3 (May–June 1989): 153.

10. Harry Jonas III, Ronald Fry, and Suresh Srivastva, "The Office of the CEO: Understanding the Executive Experience," *Academy of Management Executive* 4, no. 3 (August 1990): 36.

11. Rosemary Brady, "World Class," *Forbes* (18 June 1984): 133. See also Harry S. Jonas III, Ronald E. Fry, and Suresh Srivastva, "The Person of the CEO: Understanding the Executive Experience," *Academy of Management Executive* III, no. 3 (August 1989): 205.

12. John Pearce II and Fred David, "The Bottom Line on Corporate Mission Statements," *Academy of Management Executive* 1, no. 2 (May 1987): 109.

13. Ibid., 112. See also John A. Pearce and Fred R. David, "Corporate Mission Statements: The Bottom Line," *Academy of Management Executive* 1, no. 2 (May 1987): 109; and Fred R. David, "How Companies Define Their Mission," *Long Range Planning* 22, no. 1 (February 1989): 90.

14. Adolph Coors Company, *Annual Report* (1988): 1.

15. Portland General Corporation, *Annual Report* (1986): 2, 3.

16. Fred R. David, "How Companies Define Their Mission," *Long Range Planning* 22, no. 1 (February 1989): 91.

17. Ann Langley, "The Roles of Formal Strategic Planning," *Long Range Planning* 21, no. 3 (June 1988): 40.

18. Robert Ford and Myron Fottler, "Empowerment: A Matter of Degree," *Academy of Management Executive* 9, no. 3 (August 1995): 21.

19. Bernard Reimann, "Getting Value from Strategic Planning," *Planning Review* 16, no. 3 (May–June 1988): 42.

20. Michael Allen, "Strategic Management Hits Its Stride," *Planning Review* 13, no. 5 (September–October 1985): 6.

21. Hershey Foods Corporation, *Annual Report,* 1983, 3.

22. Richard Robinson, Jr., "The Importance of Outsiders in Small Firm Strategic Planning," *Academy of Management Journal* 25, no. 1 (March 1982): 80. Also, S. Schoeffler, Robert Buzzell, and Donald Heany, "Impact of Strategic Planning on Profit Performance," *Harvard Business Review* (March 1974): 137; Lawrence Rhyne, "The Relationship of Strategic Planning to Financial Performance," *Strategic Management Journal* 7 (1986): 432; and Deborah Cook and Gerald Ferris, "Strategic Human Resource Management and Firm Effectiveness in Industries Experiencing Decline," *Human Resource Management* 25, no. 3 (Fall 1986): 454.

23. Allen, 6.

24. Tom Peters, "Passion for Excellence," Public Broadcasting System videotape, 1987.

25. Gordon Greenley, "Does Strategic Planning Improve Company Performance?" *Long Range Planning* 19, no. 2 (April 1986): 106.

26. Saul Gellerman, "Managing Ethics from the Top Down," *Sloan Management Review* (Winter 1989): 77.

27. Saul Gellerman, "Why 'Good' Managers Make Bad Ethical Choices," *Harvard Business Review* 64, no. 4 (July–August 1986): 88.

28. Drucker, 462, 463.

29. John Akers, "Ethics and Competitiveness—Putting First Things First," *Sloan Management Review* (Winter 1989): 69–71.

30. Gene Laczniak, Marvin Berkowitz, Russell Brooker, and James Hale, "The Ethics of Business: Improving or Deteriorating?" *Business Horizons* 38, no. 1 (January–February 1995): 43.

31. Ibid, p. 42.

32. Frederick Gluck, "Taking the Mystique out of Planning," *Across the Board* (July–August 1985): 59.

CURRENT READINGS

Ansoff, H Igor. "Comment on Henry Mintzberg's Rethinking Strategic Planning." *Long Range Planning* 27, no. 3 (June 1994): 31–32.

Argyris, Chris. "Good Communication That Blocks Learning." *Harvard Business Review* (July–August 1994): 77–86.

Badaracco, Joseph L., Jr., and Allen Webb. "Business Ethics: A View from the Trenches." *California Management Review* 37, no. 2 (Winter 1995): 8–28.

Barney, J.B. and M.H. Hansen. "Trustworthiness as a Source of Competitive Advantage." *Strategic Management Journal* 15, Special Issue (Winter 1994): 175–188.

Bettis, R.A. and M.A. Hitt. "The New Competitive Landscape." *Strategic Management Journal* 16, Special Issue (Summer 1995): 7–20.

Bluedorn, Allen C., Richard A. Johnson, Debra K. Cartwright, and Bruce R. Barringer. "The Interface and Convergence of the Strategic Management and Organizational Environment Domains." *Journal of Management* 20, no. 2 (Summer 1994): 201–262.

Bonifant, Benjamin C., Matthew B. Arnold, and Frederick J. Long. "Gaining Competitive Advantage Through Environmental Investments." *Business Horizons* 38, no. 4 (July–August 1995): 37–47.

Chen, Min. "Sun Tzu's Strategic Thinking and Contemporary Business." *Business Horizons* 37, no. 2 (March–April 1994): 42–48.

Collins, John W. "The Editor's Chair/Is Business Ethics an Oxymoron?" *Business Horizons* 37, no. 5 (September–October 1994): 1–8.

Daboub, Anthony J., Abdul M.A. Rasheed, Richard L. Priem, and David A. Gray. "Top Management Team Characteristics and Corporate Illegal Activity." *Academy of Management Review* 20, no. 1 (January 1995): 138–170.

Dawson, Leslie M. "Women and Men, Morality and Ethics." *Business Horizons* 38, no. 4 (July–August 1995): 61–68.

Dean, Thomas J. and Robert L. Brown. "Pollution Regulation as a Barrier to New Firm Entry: Initial Evidence and Implications for Future Research." *Academy of Management Journal* 38, no. 1 (February 1995): 288–303.

Dechant, Kathleen and Barbara Altman. "Environmental Leadership: From Compliance to Competitive Advantage." *Academy of Management Executive VIII*, no. 3 (August 1994): 7–27.

Dess, Gregory G., Anil Gupta, Jean-Francois Hennart, and Charles W.L. Hill. "Conducting and Integrating Strategy Research at the International, Corporate, and Business Levels: Issues and Directions." *Journal of Management* 21, no. 3 (Fall 1995): 357–394.

Dess, Gregory G., Abdul M.A. Rasheed, Kevin J. McLaughlin, and Richard L. Priem. "The New Corporate Architecture." *Academy of Management Executive IX*, no. 3 (August 1995): 7–20.

Dixon, J. Robb, Peter Arnold, Janelle Heineke, Jay S. Kim, and Paul Mulligan. "Business Process Reengineering: Improving in New Strategic Directions." *California Management Review* 36, no. 4 (Summer 1994): 93–108.

Donaldson, Thomas and Thomas W. Dunfee. "Toward a Unified Conception of Business Ethics: Integrative Social Contracts Theory." *Academy of Management Review* 19, no. 2 (April 1994): 252–284.

Elkington, John. "Towards the Sustainable Corporation: Win-Win-Win Business Strategies for Sustainable Development." *California Management Review* 36, no. 2 (Winter 1994): 90–100.

Ford, Robert C. and Myron D. Fottler. "Empowerment: A Matter of Degree." *Academy of Management Executive IX*, no. 3 (August 1995): 21–31.

Gersick, Connie J.G. "Pacing Strategic Change: The Case of a New Venture." *Academy of Management Journal* 37, no. 1 (February 1994): 9–45.

Hamel, G. "Strategy as a Field of Study: Why Search for a New Paradigm?" *Strategic Management Journal* 15, Special Issue (Summer 1994): 5–16.

Hart, S. and C. Banbury. "How Strategy-making Processes Can Make a Difference." *Strategic Management Journal* 15, no. 4 (May 1994): 251–270.

Hosmer, L.T. "Strategic Planning as If Ethics Mattered." *Strategic Management Journal* 15, Special Issue (Summer 1994): 17–34.

Houlden, Brian T. "How Corporate Planning Adapts and Survives." *Long Range Planning* 28, no. 4 (August 1995): 99–108.

Humble, John, David Jackson, and Alan Thomson. "The Strategic Power of Corporate Values." *Long Range Planning* 27, no. 6 (December 1994): 28–42.

Hunt, Shelby D. and Robert M. Morgan. "Organizational Commitment: One of Many Commitments or Key Mediating Construct?" *Academy of Management Journal* 37, no. 6 (December 1994): 1568–1587.

Inkpen, A. and N. Choudhury. "The Seeking of Strategy Where It Is Not: Towards a Theory of Strategy Absence." *Strategic Management Journal* 16, no. 4 (May 1995): 313–324.

Ketelhohn, Werner. "Re-engineering Strategic Management." *Long Range Planning* 28, no. 3 (June 1995): 68–75.

Korsgaard, M. Audrey, David M. Schweiger, and Harry J. Sapienza. "Building Commitment, Attachment, and Trust in Strategic Decision-Making Teams: The Role of Procedural Justice." *Academy of Management Journal* 38, no. 1 (February 1995): 60–84.

Laczniak, Gene R., Marvin W. Berkowitz, Russell G. Brooker, and James P. Hale. "The Ethics of Business: Improving or Deteriorating?" *Business Horizons* 38, no. 1 (January–February 1995): 39–47.

Lloyd, Glyn and Mike Phillips. "Inside IBM: Strategic Management in a Federation of Businesses." *Long Range Planning* 27, no. 5 (October 1994): 52–63.

MacMillan, I.C. and S. Venkataraman. "Defining and Developing Competence: A Strategic Process Paradigm." *Strategic Management Journal* 16, no. 4 (May 1995): 251–276.

Marlow, Hugh. "Intuition and Forecasting—A Holistic Approach." *Long Range Planning* 27, no. 6 (December 1994): 58–68.

Mayer, Roger C., James H. Davis, and F. David Schoorman. "An Integrative Model of Organizational Trust." *Academy of Management Review* (July 1995): 709–734.

Miceli, Marcia P. and Janet P. Near. "Relationships Among Value Congruence, Perceived Victimization, and Retaliation Against Whistle-blowers." *Journal of Management* 20, no. 4 (Winter 1994): 773–794.

Miceli, Marcia P. and Janet P. Near. "Whistleblowing: Reaping the Benefits." *Academy of Management Executive VIII*, no. 3 (August 1994): 65–72.

Miller, C. Chet and Laura B. Cardinal. "Strategic Planning and Firm Performance: A Synthesis of More than Two Decades of Research." *Academy of Management Journal* 37, no. 6 (December 1994): 1649–1665.

Mintzberg, Henry. "The Fall and Rise of Strategic Planning." *Harvard Business Review* (January–February 1994): 107–115.

Mintzberg, Henry. "Rethinking Strategic Planning. Part I: Pitfalls and Fallacies." *Long Range Planning* 27, no. 3 (June 1994): 12–21.

Mintzberg, Henry. "Rethinking Strategic Planning. Part II: New Roles for Planners." *Long Range Planning* 27, no. 3 (June 1994): 22–30.

Mintzberg, Henry. "The Pitfalls of Strategic Planning." *California Management Review* 36, no. 1 (Fall 1993): 32–47.

Near, Janet P. and Marcia P. Miceli. "Effective Whistle-blowing." *Academy of Management Review* (July 1995): 679–708.

Nevis, Edwin C., Anthony J. DiBella, and Janet M. Gould. "Understanding Organizations As Learning Systems." *Sloan Management Review* 36, no. 2 (Winter 1995): 73–86.

O'Neill, Hugh M., Special Editor. "Restructuring, Re-engineering, and Rightsizing: Do the Metaphors Make Sense?" *Academy of Management Executive VIII*, no. 4 (November 1994): 9–11.

Paine, Lynn Sharp. "Managing for Organizational Integrity." *Harvard Business Review* (March–April 1994): 106–118.

Porter, Michael E. and Claas van der Linde. "Green and Competitive: Ending the Stalemate." *Harvard Business Review* (September–October 1995): 120–137.

Powell, Gary N. and D. Anthony Butterfield. "Investigating the Glass Ceiling Phenomenon: An Empirical Study of Actual Promotions to Top Management." *Academy of Management Journal* 37, no. 1 (February 1994): 68–86.

Puffer, Sheila M. and Daniel J. McCarthy. "Finding the Common Ground in Russian and American Business Ethics." *California Management Review* 37, no. 2 (Winter 1995): 29–46.

Quinn, Dennis P. and Thomas M. Jones. "An Agent Morality View of Business Policy." *Academy of Management Review* 20, no. 1 (January 1995): 22–42.

Sanchez, R. "Strategic Flexibility in Product Competition." *Strategic Management Journal* 16, Special Issue (Summer 1995): 135–160.

Sarkis, Joseph and Abdul Rasheed. "Greening the Manufacturing Function." *Business Horizons* 38, no. 5 (September–October 1995): 17–27.

Simpson, Daniel (moderated by). "The Planning Process and the Role of the Planner." Chief Planning Officer Dialogue. *Planning Review* 23, no. 1 (January–February 1995): 20–23.

Singer, A.E. "Strategy as Moral Philosophy." *Strategic Management Journal* 15, no. 3 (March 1994): 191–214.

Smith, N. Craig. "Marketing Strategies for the Ethics Era." *Sloan Management Review* 36, no. 4 (Summer 1995): 85–95.

Stopford, J.M. and C.W.F. Baden-Fuller. "Creating Corporate Entrepreneurship." *Strategic Management Journal* 15, no. 7 (September 1994): 521–536.

Tharenou, Phyllis, Shane Latimer, and Denise Conroy. "How Do You Make It to the Top? An Examination of Influences on Women's and Men's Managerial Advancement." *Academy of Management Journal* 37, no. 4 (August 1994): 899–931.

Wally, Stefan and J. Robert Baum. "Personal and Structural Determinants of the Pace of Strategic Decision Making." *Academy of Management Journal* 37, no. 4 (August 1994): 932–956.

Wilson, Ian. "Strategic Planning Isn't Dead—It Changed." *Long Range Planning* 27, no. 4 (August 1994): 12–24.

THE COHESION CASE AND EXPERIENTIAL EXERCISES

Two special features of this text are introduced here: (1) the Cohesion Case and (2) the Experiential Exercises. As strategic-management concepts and techniques are introduced in this text, they are applied to the Cohesion Case through Experiential Exercises. The Cohesion Case centers on Hershey Foods Corporation in 1996. As the term *cohesion* implies, the Hershey Foods case and related exercises integrate material presented throughout the text. At least one exercise at the end of each chapter applies textual material to the Hershey Foods case. The Cohesion Case and Experiential Exercises thus work together to give students practice applying strategic-management concepts and tools as they are presented in the text. In this way, students become prepared to perform case analyses as the policy course progresses.

Based in Hershey, Pennsylvania, and a leading manufacturer of candy and pasta, Hershey Foods was selected as the Cohesion Case for several important reasons. First, Hershey is a multinational corporation, so global issues can be discussed in class. Second, Hershey is a multidivisional organization, thus allowing strategic-management concepts to be applied at the corporate, divisional, and functional levels. Third, Hershey is undergoing extensive strategic changes and recently was rumored to be a takeover target by a larger competitor, Nestlé. Fourth, you have probably eaten Hershey candy and pasta; this familiarity will help you learn this business. Fifth, Hershey is an exemplary organization in terms of business ethics and social responsibility; a significant part of Hershey Foods' profits go toward operating the Milton Hershey School for Orphaned Children. Finally, Hershey is very cooperative with students and professors; Hershey has a toll-free number (1-800-468-1714) that students or professors can call to obtain additional information about the company. Hershey's home page is: http://www.hersheys.com

Some Experiential Exercises in the text do not relate specifically to the Cohesion Case. At least one exercise at the end of each chapter applies textual material to your university. As a business administration student nearing graduation, you are quite knowledgeable about your university. Apply strategic-management concepts learned in this course to assist your institution. More and more colleges and universities are instituting strategic management.

After reading the text and applying concepts and tools to the Cohesion Case through Experiential Exercises, you should be well prepared to analyze business policy cases. The objectives of the case method are as follows:

1. To give you experience applying strategic-management concepts and techniques to different organizations
2. To give you experience applying and integrating the knowledge you have gained in prior courses and work experience
3. To give you decision-making experience in actual organizations

4. To improve your understanding of relationships among the functional areas of business and the strategic-management process
5. To improve your self-confidence; since there is no one right answer to a case, you will gain experience justifying and defending your own ideas, analyses, and recommendations
6. To improve your oral and written communication skills
7. To sharpen your analytical and intuitive skills

THE COHESION CASE
Fred R. David
Francis Marion University

HERSHEY FOODS CORPORATION—1996
http://www.hersheys.com

In June 1996, Hershey Foods introduced a new line of lower-fat chocolate confections called Sweet Escapes. This product differs from the company's previous attempts at lower-fat chocolates. It contains no fat substitutes and is essentially Hershey's chocolate processed in a different manner.

Sweet Escapes contains approximately 33 to 50 percent less fat and 33 percent fewer calories than leading candy bars and taps into a previously unreached market of fat avoiders who crave chocolate. Taste-test results have been strong enough that the company is confident in introducing the product via a national, rather than regional, rollout. Hershey anticipates $100 million in new revenues for 1996. This is not out of line with the company's other successful new product introductions: Nutrageous generated $90 million in its first full year of sales, and Hugs and Kisses with Almonds each generated about $90 million in sales within their first 6 to 9 months.

What is your favorite candy bar? Mr. Goodbar, Reese's, Kit Kat, Big Block, Whatchamacallit, Allsorts, Rolo, Krackel, BarNone, Mounds, Almond Joy, 5th Avenue, Snickers, or Baby Ruth? Did you know that all of these are made by Hershey Foods, except Snickers made by M&M Mars and Baby Ruth made by Nestlé? Mars and Nestlé are Hershey's two major competitors.

Have you ever been to Hershey, Pennsylvania? There you can walk down Chocolate Avenue, see sidewalks lit by lights in the shape of Hershey Kisses, visit the Hershey Zoo, and see the chocolate kiss tower in Hershey Park. Hershey is the home of Hershey Foods Corporation, which produces more than 38 million Hershey Kisses every day. Since 1893 Hershey Foods has grown from a one-product, one-plant operation to a $4 billion company with many U.S. and international plants providing an array of quality chocolate and confectionery products and services.

Hershey entered 1996 as the largest candy maker in the United States with 30.7-percent market share, ahead of M&M Mars' 22.6-percent market share. Hershey also is the largest pasta manufacturer in the United States with 28.4-percent market share, ahead of Borden's 23.1-percent market share. All but 11 percent of Hershey's sales are generated in domestic markets. Hershey's sales from international operations declined 10.2 percent in 1995 to $310 million. Hershey remains inexperienced and uncommitted in markets outside the United States, Mexico, and Canada, although both the candy and pasta industries are globalized. Hershey's confectionery losses in Mexico and Canada hit an all-time high in 1994. Can Hershey continue to survive as a domestic producer of candy and pasta, while its competitors gain economies of scale and learning in world markets? Shareholders are becoming concerned.

HISTORY

Milton Hershey's love for candy making began with a childhood apprenticeship under candy maker Joe Royer of Lancaster, Pennsylvania. Mr. Hershey was eager to own a candy-making business. After numerous attempts and even bankruptcy, he finally gained success in the caramel business. Upon seeing the first chocolate-making equipment at the Chicago Exhibition in 1893, Mr. Hershey envisioned endless opportunities for the chocolate industry.

By 1901, the chocolate industry in America was growing rapidly. Hershey's sales reached $662,000 that year, creating the need for a new factory. Mr. Hershey moved his company to Derry Church, Pennsylvania, a town that was renamed Hershey in 1906. The new Hershey factory provided a means of mass-producing a single chocolate product. In 1909 the Milton Hershey School for Orphans was founded. Mr. and Mrs. Hershey could not have children, so for years the Hershey Chocolate Company operated mainly to provide funds for the orphanage. Hershey's sales reached $5 million in 1911.

In 1927 the Hershey Chocolate Company was incorporated under the laws of the state of Delaware and listed on the New York Stock Exchange. That same year 20 percent of Hershey's stock was sold to the public. Between 1930 and 1960 Hershey went through rapid growth; the name *Hershey* became a household word. The legendary Milton Hershey died in 1945.

In the 1960s, Hershey acquired the H.B. Reese Candy Company, which makes Reese's Peanut Butter Cups, Reese's Peanut Butter Chips, and Reese's Pieces. Hershey also acquired San Giorgio Macaroni and Delmonico Foods, both pasta manufacturers. In 1968 Hershey Chocolate Corporation changed its name to Hershey Foods Corporation. Between 1976 and 1984 William Dearden served as Hershey's chief executive officer. An orphan who grew up in the Milton Hershey School for Orphans, Mr. Dearden diversified the company to reduce its dependence on fluctuating cocoa and sugar prices.

In the 1970s, Hershey acquired Y&S Candy Corporation, a manufacturer of licorice-type products, such as Y&S Twizzlers, Nibs, and Bassett's Allsorts. They purchased Procino-Rossi, a pasta company, and Skinner Macaroni Company and Friendly Ice Cream Corporation. Richard Zimmerman replaced William Dearden as chief executive officer of Hershey in 1984.

During the 1980s, Hershey acquired A. B. Marabou of Sweden, Franklin Restaurants, and the Dietrich Corporation, maker of Luden's Throat Drops, Luden's Mellomints, Queen Anne chocolate-covered cherries, and 5th Avenue candy bars. They also acquired the Canadian confectionery (chocolate and nonchocolate candy) and snack nut operations of Nabisco Brands Ltd. These businesses include bar and bagged candy items such as Oh Henry!, Eatmore, Cherry Blossom, Glosettes, Lowney, Life Savers, Breath Savers, Planters nuts, Beaver nuts, Chipits chocolate chips, Moirs boxed chocolates, Care*Free gum, and Bubble Yum gum. Hershey acquired Peter Paul/Cadbury's U.S. candy operations, which included plant facilities in Hazelton and York, Pennsylvania, and Naugatuck, Connecticut. This latter acquisition gave Hershey many new products in the United States, including Mounds, Almond Joy, York Peppermint Pattie, Cadbury Dairy Milk, Cadbury Fruit & Nut, Cadbury Caramello, and Cadbury Creme Eggs. Hershey received rights to market the Peter Paul products worldwide. The York facility was closed and those operations moved to Hershey's Reading, Pennsylvania, plant.

In the 1990s, Hershey acquired Ronzoni Foods Corporation from Kraft General Foods Corporation for $80 million. The purchase included the dry pasta, pasta sauces, and cheese businesses of Ronzoni Foods, which strengthened Hershey's position as a branded pasta supplier in the United States. Hershey also acquired Gubor Schokoladen, a German manufacturer and marketer of high-quality assorted pralines and seasonal chocolates. Gubor has two manufacturing plants in Germany and provides Hershey with increased European presence. Hershey purchased Nacional de Dulces (NDD) and renamed this company Hershey Mexico. It produces, imports, and markets chocolate products for the Mexican market under the Hershey brand name.

Kenneth Wolfe replaced Mr. Zimmerman as chief executive of Hershey Foods in 1993. Hershey Foods' mission statement in the 1980s was as follows:

> Hershey Foods Corporation's mission is to become a major diversified food company and a leading company in every aspect of our business as:
>
> The Number-one confectionery company in North America, moving toward worldwide confectionery market share leadership.
>
> A respected and valued supplier of high quality, branded consumer food products in North America and selected international markets.

Hershey's mission statement today has been modified and reads as follows: ". . . to be a focused food company in North America and selected international markets and a leader in every aspect of our business." Note that the current statement is shorter and backs off from aspiring to be a world leader in the confectionery industry. It also lacks a number of components generally included in a good mission statement.

Hershey spent most of 1994 and 1995 reorganizing and is today comprised of four divisions: Hershey Chocolate North America, Hershey Grocery, Hershey International, and Hershey Pasta Group. Hershey's current organizational chart is given in Case figure 1–1. Company sales, operating income, and operating margin information by division is provided in Case figure 1–2. Note that Hershey International has the lowest margins.

Case figure 1–3 gives Hershey's unit volume growth rates by division. Note that Hershey Chocolate North America and Hershey Grocery experienced declining sales in the first quarter of 1995. Confectionery sales are generally lowest during the second quarter of the year and highest during the third and fourth quarters, due largely to the holiday seasons. For example, in 1994 Hershey generated only 19 percent of annual sales during the second quarter. In contrast, 30 percent of annual sales were generated during the fourth quarter. Financial statements are given in Case figures 1–4 to 1–6.

HERSHEY CHOCOLATE NORTH AMERICA

This division was formed in late 1994 by combining Hershey's Mexico, Canadian, and U.S. operations, and now generates 71 percent of total company sales. Hershey's U.S. confectionery manufacturing operations are located in Hershey, Pennsylvania; Reading, Pennsylvania; Hazelton, Pennsylvania; Lancaster, Pennsylvania; Oakdale, California; Stuarts Draft, Virginia; and Naugatuck, Connecticut. Canadian operations are located in Smith Falls, Ontario; Montreal, Quebec; and Dartmouth, Nova Scotia. Mexican operations are located in Guadalajara, Mexico.

Hershey Chocolate North America produces an extensive line of chocolate and nonchocolate products sold in the form of single bars, bagged goods, and boxed items. These products are marketed under more than 50 brand names and sold in over 2 million retail outlets in the United States, including grocery wholesalers, chain stores, mass merchandisers, drug stores, vending companies, wholesale clubs, convenience stores, and food distributors. Sales to Wal-Mart Stores account for 10 percent of Hershey's total revenues.

Three new candies recently introduced in the United States were Reese's NutRageous, Twizzlers Pull-n-Peel, and Hershey's Nuggets. New products introduced into Canada were Hershey's Hugs, Peter Paul Mounds and Almond Joy, and Twizzlers Pull-n-Peel. Only one

CASE FIGURE 1–1
Hershey's Chain of Command

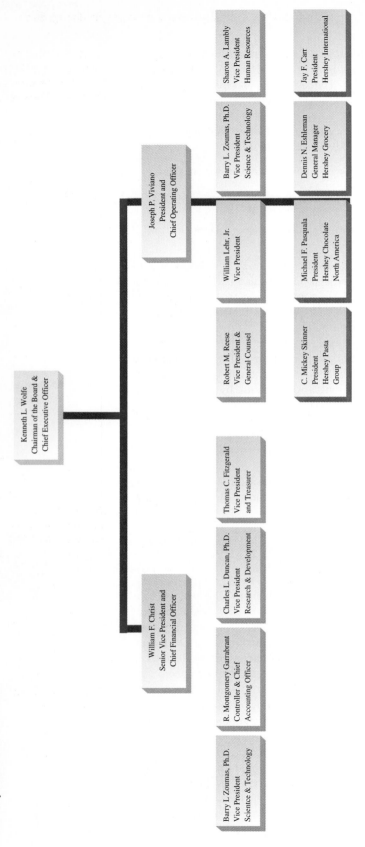

	1994	1995	5-YEAR AVERAGE	1995 VERSUS 1994
Sales				
Chocolate and Confectionery	$2,535.5	$2,635.7	1.8%	3.6%
Grocery Products	$ 310.5	$ 325.0	NM	4.7%
Hershey Pasta Group	415.0	430.0	6.3%	3.6%
International	345.3	310.0	NM	−10.2%
Total Sales	$3,606.3	$3,690.7	6.3%	2.3%
Operating Income				
Chocolate and Confectionery	$ 444.4	$ 489.0	6.3%	10.0%
Grocery Products	$ 38.0	$ 30.5	NM	−19.7%
Hershey Pasta Group	29.7	31.2	4.9%	5.1%
International	3.5	1.9	NM	−45.7%
Total Operating Income	$ 515.6	$ 552.6	7.5%	7.2%
General Corporate Expenses	41.0	42.0	4.3%	2.4%
Interest Expense	37.4	47.0	12.3%	25.7%
Interest Income	2.0	2.2	5.1%	10.0%
Interest Expense, Net	35.4	44.8	12.7%	26.6%
			6-YEAR AVERAGE	
Operating Margins				
Chocolate and Confectionery	17.5%	18.6%	16.5%	
Hershey Pasta Group	7.2%	7.3%	8.2%	
International	1.0%	0.6%	NM	
Total Operating Profit	14.3%	15.0%	14.5%	
Pretax Profit	12.2%	12.6%	12.4%	
Net Income	7.3%	7.6%	7.6%	

CASE FIGURE 1–2
Hershey Foods' Sales, Operating Income, and Operating Margins

	4Q 1995	3Q 1995	2Q 1995	1Q 1995
Chocolate	4%	4%	11%	−2%
Grocery	7%	−7%	−6%	−16%
Pasta	4%	2%	11%	2%
Canadian Operations	NA	NA	NA	NA
International	15%	5%	5%	4%
Total Corporate	6%	4%	10.0%	−1.5%

CASE FIGURE 1–3
Hershey Foods' Unit Volume Growth by Product Line

	4Q 1995	3Q 1995	2Q 1995	1Q 1995
Chocolate	0%	0%	0%	0%
Grocery	0%	0%	0%	0%
Pasta	0%	0%	1%	2%
Canadian Operations	NA	NA	NA	NA
International	0%	0%	−15%	5%
Total Corporate	0%	0%	−4%	1%

CASE FIGURE 1–4
Hershey Foods' Unit Pricing Growth by Product Line

CASE FIGURE 1–5
Hershey's Income Statements

FOR THE YEARS ENDED DECEMBER 31,	1995	1994	1993	1992
Net Sales	$3,690,667	$3,606,271	$3,488,249	$3,219,805
Costs and Expenses				
Cost of Sales	2,126,274	2,097,556	1,995,502	1,833,388
Selling, Marketing and Administrative	1,053,758	1,034,115	1,035,519	958,189
Total Costs and Expenses	3,180,032	3,131,671	3,031,021	2,791,577
Restructuring Charge	151	(106,105)	–	–
Gain on Sale of Investment Interest		–	80,642	–
Income Before Interest, Income Taxes and Accounting Changes	510,786	368,495	537,870	428,228
Interest Expense, Net	44,833	35,357	26,995	27,240
Income Before Income Taxes and Accounting Changes	465,953	333,138	510,875	400,988
Provision for Income Taxes	184,034	148,919	213,642	153,390
Income Before Cumulative Effect of Accounting Changes	281,919	184,219	297,233	242,598
Net Cumulative Effect of Accounting Changes		–	(103,908)	–
Net Income	$ 281,919	$ 184,219	$ 193,325	$ 242,598
Income per Share				
Before Accounting Changes	$ 3.40	$ 2.12	$ 3.31	$ 2.69
Net Cumulative Effect of Accounting Changes		–	(1.16)	–
Net Income	$ 3.40	$ 2.12	$ 2.15	$ 2.69
Cash Dividends Paid per Share				
Common Stock	$ 1.370	$ 1.250	$ 1.140	$ 1.030
Class B Common Stock	1.240	1.135	1.035	.935

new product was introduced in 1995: Super Fruit. Hershey's confectionery products are as follows:

Almond Joy candy bar
Amazin' Fruit gummy bears candy
Bar None candy bar
Cadbury's Creme Eggs candy
Cadbury's Dairy Milk chocolate bar
Cadbury's Fruit & Nut chocolate bar
Cadbury's Krisp chocolate bar
Cadbury's Mini Eggs candy
Cadbury's Roast Almond chocolate bar
Carmello candy bar
5th Avenue candy bar
Helps cough suppressant tablets
Hershey's Cookies 'n' Mint chocolate bar
Hershey's Golden Collection Almond
Hershey's Golden Collection Solitaires
Hershey's Kisses chocolates
Hershey's Kisses with Almonds chocolates
Hershey's milk chocolate bar
Hershey's milk chocolate bar with almonds
Hershey's Miniatures chocolate bars
Hugs

Kit Kat wafer bar
Krackel chocolate bar
Luden's throat drops
Mounds candy bar
Mr. Goodbar chocolate bar
Nibs candy
Reese's crunchy peanut butter cups
Reese's peanut butter chips
Reese's peanut butter cups
Reese's Pieces candy
Rolo caramels in milk chocolate
Skor toffee bar
Special Dark chocolate bar
Super Twizzlers candy
Symphony chocolate bar
Symphony chocolate bar with almonds
    and toffee chips
Twizzlers candy
Whatchamacallit candy bar
Y&S candy
York peppermint pattie

CASE FIGURE 1–6
Hershey's Balance Sheets

DECEMBER 31,	1995	1994	1993
Assets			
Current Assets			
Cash and Cash Equivalents	$ 32,346	$ 26,738	$ 15,959
Accounts Receivable—Trade	326,024	331,670	294,974
Inventories	397,570	445,702	453,442
Deferred Income Taxes	84,785	105,948	85,548
Prepaid Expenses and Other	81,598	38,608	39,073
Total Current Assets	922,323	948,666	888,996
Property, Plan and Equipment, Net	1,436,009	4,468,397	1,460,904
Intangibles Resulting from Business Acquisitions	428,714	453,582	473,408
Other Assets	43,577	20,336	31,783
Total Assets	$2,830,623	$2,890,981	$2,855,091
Liabilities and Stockholders' Equity			
Current Liabilities			
Accounts Payable	$ 127,067	$ 115,428	$ 125,658
Accrued Liabilities	300,549	265,283	301,989
Accrued Restructuring Reserves	7,574	82,055	–
Accrued Income Taxes	15,514	8,718	35,603
Short-term Debt	413,268	316,783	337,286
Current Portion of Long-term Debt	383	7,954	13,309
Total Current Liabilities	864,355	796,221	813,845
Long-term Debt	357,034	157,227	165,757
Other Long-term Liabilities	333,814	303,056	290,401
Deferred Income Taxes	192,461	193,377	172,744
Total Liabilities	1,747,664	1,449,881	1,442,747
Stockholders' Equity			
Preferred Stock, Share Issued: None in 1995, 1994, and 1993	–	–	–
Common Stock, Shares Issued: 74,679,357 in 1994 and 74,733,982 in 1995	74,734	74,679	74,669
Class B Common Stock, Shares Issued: 15,242,979 in 1994 and 15,241,454 in 1995	15,241	15,243	15,253
Additional Paid-in Capital	47,732	49,880	51,196
Cumulative Foreign Currency Translation Adjustments	(29,240)	(24,537)	(13,905)
Unearned ESOP Compensation	(35,128)	(38,321)	(41,515)
Retained Earnings	1,694,696	1,522,867	1,445,609
Treasury—Common Stock Shares, at Cost: 3,187,139 in 1994 and 12,709, 553 in 1995	(685,076)	(158,711)	(118,963)
Total Stockholders' Equity	1,082,959	1,441,100	1,412,344
Total Liabilities and Stockholders' Equity	$2,830,623	$2,890,981	$2,855,091

Reese's NutRageous
Twizzlers Pull-n-Peel
Hershey's Nuggets
Super Fruit
Almondillos chocolate
Breath Savers mints
Bridge Mixture candy
Cherry Blossom candy

Eat-More candy
Glosette candy
Goodies candy
Hershey almond bar
Hershey chocolate covered almonds
Hershey raisins and almonds bar
Life Savers candy

CASE FIGURE 1–7
**U.S. Candy Industry
Market Share Data**

COMPANY	1995	1994
Hershey	30.7%	30.6%
Mars	22.6%	23.0%
Nestlé	8.7%	8.3%
Brach & Brock	4.8%	5.9%
Leaf	4.0%	4.1%
RJR Nabisco (LifeSaver)	3.4%	3.4%
Russel Stover	7.4%	6.8%
Other	18.4%	17.9%

Lowney candy	Ovation chocolate covered sticks
Moirs chocolates	Planters nuts
Oh Henry! chocolate bar	Special Crisp candy bar

Declining value of Canada's currency coupled with a collapse of Mexico's currency hurt business in 1994 and 1995. Political and economic turmoil in Mexico also reduced profitability. Hershey does no business in, and does not export to, Latin America or South America although numerous countries there are rapidly growing. For the fourth quarter of 1995, sales of Hershey's North America Chocolate division rose 4 percent (5 percent due to volume and 1 percent less due to weak Canadian and Mexican currencies).

Conventional wisdom in the candy industry is that a person rarely selects the same candy bar twice in a row; consequently, product variety is crucial to success. Marketing issues relative to health, nutrition, and weight consciousness are important. The media Hershey uses most for advertising are network television, followed by syndicated television, spot television, magazines, and network and spot radio.

The U.S. confectionery market is growing only 2 percent annually in sales volume. The nonchocolate segment, which accounts for about one-third of the overall sweets market, is growing at 5 percent annually, while the chocolate segment is growing at 1 percent. Hershey has only 4 percent of the nonchocolate confectionery market, while the leader is RJR Nabisco with 18 percent. RJR's Life Savers and Gummy Life Savers compete with Hershey's Amazin' Fruit Gummy Bears. U.S. confectionery market share information for the seven leading competitors is given in Case figure 1–7. Note that Hershey has increased its market share recently at the expense of Mars and Brach & Brock.

HERSHEY GROCERY

This division generates 9 percent of Hershey's total sales and was formed to increase Hershey's emphasis on marketing its baking products, ice cream toppings, peanut butter, and other grocery items in North America. Hershey's chocolate milk is produced and sold under license by over 20 independent dairies throughout the United States. Hershey recently discontinued its line of chocolate bar flavor puddings because of falling demand. Hershey Grocery's revenues rose 7 percent while profits were flat during the fourth quarter of 1995, due largely to the puddings discontinuation and increased marketing expenses.

A list of Hershey's grocery products follows. The second half of the list contains products marketed in Canada rather than the United States or Mexico. Note that there are two names for several products, which from a marketing perspective perhaps is ineffective.

Hershey's baking chocolate	Hershey's vanilla chunks
Hershey's chocolate chips	Mini Chips semisweet chocolate
Hershey's chocolate drink	Reese's peanut butter
Hershey's chocolate milk	Brown Cow Chocolate Syrup
Hershey's chocolate milk mix	Chipits Chocolate Chips
Hershey's Chocolate Shoppe toppings	Hershey's Chocolate Chips
Hershey's cocoa	Hershey's Instant Chocolate Syrup
Hershey's fudge toppings	Strawberry Cow Strawberry Syrup
Hershey's mint chips	Chipits Baking Chocolate
Hershey's Premium baking bars	Chipits Cocoa
Hershey's Premium chocolate chunks	Hershey's Cocoa
Hershey's sweetened coconut flakes	Hershey's Syrup
Hershey's syrup	Top Scotch Butterscotch Syrup
Hershey's vanilla chips	

HERSHEY INTERNATIONAL

This division generates 8 percent of Hershey's total sales. Hershey exports confectionery and grocery products to more than 60 countries outside of North America. All company business outside of North America, including confectionery, grocery, and pasta, is handled under this division. Hershey recently divested of Petybon S.A., its pasta and biscuit manufacturer in Brazil.

In Europe, Hershey manufactures and markets confectionery products in Germany under the Gubor brand; in Italy under the Sperlari, Dondi, Galatine, Gnammy, and Scaramellini brands; and in Belgium and the Netherlands under the Jamin brand. Hershey has divested its stake in Freia Marabou, a Norwegian confectioner. Hershey recently paid $33 million for OZJ Jamin, which manufactures candy, cookies, biscuits, and ice cream for distribution to customers in the Netherlands and Belgium. Hershey just acquired the Italian candy maker Sperlari for $130 million. Europeans have the highest per-capita chocolate consumption rates in the world, but Hershey has no plans to overtake or even threaten Nestlé or Mars in Europe.

In the Far East, Hershey has signed licensing agreements with Selecta Dairy Products to manufacture Hershey's ice cream products in the Philippines and with Kuang Chuan Dairy in Taiwan to manufacture Hershey's beverages. Hershey introduced its products into Russia, the Philippines, and Taiwan for the first time in 1994. Overall in the Far East, however, Hershey is not planning sustained efforts due to perceived high political and economic risks coupled with their lack of experience.

Hershey International experienced a 1-percent sales and volume decline during the fourth quarter of 1995, but excluding the divestiture (in 3Q95) of its Dutch chocolate business. International sales and volume would have been up 15 percent year-over-year, Gabor (Germany) and Sperlari (Italy) both turned in strong quarters. Operating profit was off 30 percent year-over-year, due to the divestiture and to continued marketing investment in Russia.

HERSHEY PASTA

This division contributes 11 percent of Hershey's total company sales. Hershey's pasta sales grew 8.4 percent in 1993, 2.8 percent in 1994, and 3.6 percent in 1995. The popularity of pasta has increased over the last 10 years. Per-capita consumption of pasta has grown from 12.8 pounds per person in 1980 to almost 20 pounds today.

CASE FIGURE 1–8
U.S. Pasta Industry
Market Share Data

COMPANY	1995	1994
Hershey	28.4%	27.0%
Borden	23.1%	26.0%
Private Labels	15.2%	15.2%
CPC International	11.0%	11.4%
Imports	10.7%	9.9%
Quaker Oats	2.9%	2.9%
Archer Daniels Midland	1.0%	1.1%
Other	5.7%	6.5%
	100.0%	100.0%

For the fourth quarter of 1995, Hershey Pasta posted a 4-percent sales gain (2 percent volume and 2 percent price increase) and a 6-percent decrease in operating profit. However, pasta imports in the United States grew 30 percent in 1994 to 503 million pounds, while total U.S. consumption of pasta grew only 2 percent to 4 billion pounds. The flood of low-priced imported pasta into the United States is primarily coming from Italy and Turkey. This is a major threat facing Hershey.

Hershey's market share increased to 28.4 percent from 27.4 percent a year ago. While Borden, its closest rival, saw its market share decline to 23.1 percent from 24.9 percent over the same period. Tariffs levied on the inexpensive Turkish and Italian imports should eliminate some of their price advantage, and Hershey raised prices by 6 percent on two of its brands (accounting for roughly 33 percent of its pasta sales). U.S. pasta market share data is given in Case figure 1–8.

What is pasta anyway? Pasta is paste or dough made from semolina milled from durum wheat, a class of hard wheat grown in the United States, primarily in North Dakota. It is formed into shapes such as spaghetti and macaroni, then dried, boxed, and readied for sale. Hershey's pasta brands include San Giorgio, Skinner, Delmonico, P&R, Light 'n Fluffy, American Beauty, Perfection, Pastamania, and Ronzoni. Sales of these brands surpassed Borden's Creamette brand in 1993.

Hershey first expanded its business away from confectionery products into pasta with the acquisition in 1966 of San Giorgio Macaroni in Lebanon, Pennsylvania. Hershey has owned pasta facilities in Louisville, Kentucky; Auburn, New York; Omaha, Nebraska; Philadelphia, Pennsylvania; and Excellsior Springs, Missouri. Hershey recently expanded pasta production capacity at its main pasta manufacturing facility, the modern Winchester, Virginia, plant. Hershey Pasta manufactures and distributes pasta throughout the United States but does no exporting of pasta and has no plans to build pasta facilities anywhere outside the United States.

Hershey Pasta products are divided into four general categories: long goods, short cuts, egg products, and specialties. A brief listing of the major items in each category follows:

Long Goods

capellini	margherite	spaghettini
fettucine	perciatelli/long macaroni	vermicelli
linguine	spaghetti	angel hair

Short Cuts

alphabets	fideo cortado	rotini/twists
ditalini/salad macaroni	radiatore	shells
dumplings	occhi dilupo	ziti
ancini pepe	rigatoni	macarrones
elbows	rings/spaghetti rings	tubetti

fusilli	rotelle curly macaroni/twirls	mezzani rigati
orzo	mafalda	mezzani
ridged mostaccioli		

Egg Products

egg fettucini	noodles-fine, medium,	pot pie squares
kluski	extra-wide	spinach noodles
egg pastina	pot pie bows	

Specialties

long fusilli	lasagne	healthy ribbons
jumbo shells	manicotti	cannalloni

HERSHEY'S OPERATIONS

SOCIAL RESPONSIBILITY   Hershey Foods Corporation is committed to the values of its founder Milton S. Hershey—the highest standard of quality, honesty, fairness, integrity, and respect. The firm makes annual contributions of cash, products, and services to a variety of national and local charitable organizations. The corporation operates the Milton Hershey School for socially disadvantaged children and is the sole sponsor of the Hershey National Track and Field Youth Program. Hershey also makes contributions to the Children's Miracle Network, a national program benefiting children's hospitals across the United States.

RESEARCH AND DEVELOPMENT   Hershey engages in research and development activities to develop new products, improve the quality of existing products, and improve and modernize production processes. The company's recent research and development expenditures are listed in Case figure 1–9.

Hershey recently completed a test market of its Reduced Calorie and Fat candy bar. Test results suggest that consumers desire the real thing—calories, fat, and all—when they indulge in a candy bar. This finding is consistent with a general trend in the United States away from fitness, exercise, and nutrition to a more sedentary life style.

FINANCE   Hershey's 1995 financial statements are given at the end of this case. Note that revenues barely increased but that net income increased about 50 percent in 1994.

ADVERTISING AND PROMOTION   Hershey's recent expenditures on advertising and promotion have declined as given in Case figure 1–10.

YEAR	$ RESEARCH AND DEVELOPMENT
1984	$ 9.9 million
1985	11.2 million
1986	12.5 million
1987	12.9 million
1988	15.7 million
1989	16.1 million
1990	19.2 million
1991	22.8 million
1992	24.2 million
1993	26.2 million
1994	26.3 million

CASE FIGURE 1–9
Hershey's Annual R & D Expenditure Amounts

CASE FIGURE 1–10
**Hershey's Annual
Marketing Expenditures
($ in millions)**

Year	$ Advertising	$ Promotion
1987	$ 97	$171
1988	99	230
1989	121	256
1990	146	315
1991	117	325
1992	137	398
1993	130	444
1994	120	419

GLOBAL ISSUES

The chocolate/cocoa products industry is SIC 2066, while candy/confectionery is SIC 2064. The main distribution channels for chocolate are grocery, drug, and department stores as well as vending machine operators. Almost all of these distributors are local, regional, or national; only a few are multinational. While chocolate producers have not yet developed globally uniform marketing programs, the situation is changing. European unification extended grocery and department store channels of distribution. For example, Safeway, a U.S. grocer chain, now operates stores in Canada, Britain, Germany, and Saudi Arabia. As global channels of distribution become more available for chocolate manufacturers, global marketing uniformity will become more prevalent in the industry. Global cultural convergence is accelerating the need for more global marketing uniformity in the confectionery industry.

The confectionery industry is characterized by high manufacturing economies of scale. Hershey's main chocolate factory, for example, occupies more than 2 million square feet, is highly automated, and contains much heavy equipment, vats, and containers. It is the largest chocolate plant in the world. High manufacturing costs in any industry encourages global market expansion, globally standardized products, and globally centralized production.

The confectionery industry is also characterized by high transportation costs for moving milk and sugar, the primary raw materials. This fact motivates companies such as Hershey to locate near their sources of supply. Because milk can be obtained in large volumes in many countries, chocolate producers have many options in locating plants. This is also true because producing chocolate is not labor-intensive, nor does it require highly skilled labor.

Product development costs in the confectionery industry are relatively low, because the process largely involves mixing different combinations of the same ingredients. Whenever product development costs are low in an industry, firms are spurred to globalize existing brands rather than develop new ones for different countries.

Industry analysts expect the candy industry to continue to grow. Consumption of chocolate, according to industry analysts, is closely related to national income, although the Far East is an exception to this rule. Candy consumption varies in the major markets of the developed nations. Americans consume about 22 pounds of candy annually per person, and Europeans consume about 27 pounds of candy per person.

Chocolate accounts for about 54 percent of all candy consumed. Northern Europeans consume almost twice as much chocolate per capita as Americans. Among European countries, Switzerland, Norway, and United Kingdom citizens consume the most chocolate, whereas Finland, Yugoslavia, and Italy consume the least. The Japanese also consume very little chocolate—about 5 pounds per capita. Throughout Asia and Southern Europe, there is a preference for types of sweets other than chocolate, partly because of high incidence of lactose intolerance (difficulty in digesting dairy products).

Many consumers worldwide are becoming more and more weight conscious and health-oriented. Numerous organizations and individuals discourage candy consumption and promote the need for exercise and nutrition. The teenage customer base that historically has consumed so much chocolate is shrinking in the United States and most other countries. These persons are being replaced by older, wealthier consumers who prefer more sophisticated chocolates. In countries where birth rates and numbers of youth are still growing, disposable income tends to be low, and this is a barrier to entry. The confectionery industry overall is thus undergoing transition.

The most important raw material used in production of Hershey's products is cocoa beans. This commodity is imported from West Africa, South America, and Far Eastern equatorial regions. West Africa accounts for approximately 60 percent of the world's crop. Cocoa beans exhibit wide fluctuations in price, flavor, and quality, due to (1) weather and other conditions affecting crop size; (2) consuming countries' demand requirements; (3) producing countries' sales policies; (4) speculative influences; and (5) international economics and currency movements. Cocoa bean prices are determined by a provisional International Cocoa Agreement formed by certain producing and consuming countries. The average price of cocoa beans rose 25.8 percent in 1995, following a 28.9 percent rise in 1994. World production is not keeping pace with increased consumption. The price per pound in 1995 was $0.72 and is expected to continue increasing. This is a major problem for Hershey because even a small price increase at the retail level severely restricts consumer buying.

To minimize the effects of cocoa bean price fluctuations, Hershey purchases large inventories of cocoa beans and cocoa products. Hershey also purchases and sells cocoa future contracts. Hershey maintains West African and Brazilian crop-forecasting operations and continually monitors economic and political factors affecting market conditions.

Hershey's second-most-important raw material is sugar. Sugar is subject to price supports under domestic farm legislation. Due to import quotas and duties, sugar prices paid by U.S. users are substantially higher than prices on the world market. The average wholesale list price for refined sugar has remained stable at $0.30 per pound over recent years.

Other raw materials that Hershey Corporation purchases in substantial quantities include semolina milled from durum wheat, milk, peanuts, almonds, and coconut. The prices of milk and peanuts are affected by federal marketing orders and subsidy programs of the U.S. Department of Agriculture. Raising and lowering price supports on milk and peanuts greatly affect the cost of Hershey's raw materials. Market prices of peanuts and almonds are generally determined in the latter months of each year, following harvest time.

Tariffs imposed by different countries can greatly impede or promote globalization within an industry, especially where the product is manufactured. For example, U.S. tariffs on chocolate are very low, ranging from 35 cents for mass-produced chocolate to about $2.50 for some premium brands. Even a $0.10 difference in price among competing brands, however, makes a big difference to consumers.

Nationalistic tariffs as they impact candy are falling but still are high enough to be a concern. Japan, Korea, and Taiwan, for example, have reduced their tariff on imported chocolate from 20 percent to 10 percent. Europe is retaining its 12-percent tariff on chocolate imports from outside Europe. The United States has a 5-percent tariff on solid chocolate products and a 7-percent tariff on all other chocolate confectionery products. Technology standards across countries are similar to tariffs in that they vary and can impact global strategy plans. Japan, for example, prohibits the sale of chocolates that contain the additives BHT and TBHQ, which are approved by the U.S. Food & Drug Administration.

COMPETITORS

The $10 billion U.S. confectionery industry is composed of six major competitors who control nearly 70 percent of the market: Hershey, M&M Mars, Brach & Brock, Nestlé of Switzerland, RJR Nabisco, and Leaf, Inc. The remaining 30 percent is divided among many local and regional candy manufacturers.

Based in Switzerland, Nestlé clearly has an edge internationally, being the world leader in many food categories, including candy. Almost 98 percent of Nestlé's revenues come from international sales. Hershey's other competitors also do much of their business outside North America. For example, Cadbury-Schweppes obtains 50 percent from international sales, Mars 50 percent, while Hershey is the least with 10 percent. Hershey's two major candy competitors are Mars and Nestlé.

MARS   Mars was overtaken by Hershey in 1988 as the leading candy manufacturer in the United States, but Mars has a stronger presence than Hershey in Europe, Asia, Mexico, and Japan. Mars gained 12 percent of the market in Mexico after only one year of entering that market. Analysts estimate Mars' worldwide sales and profits to be more than $7 billion and $1 billion, respectively. Mars was successful introducing its Bounty chocolate candy into the United States without prior test marketing. Bounty was originally a European candy. Mars, unlike Hershey, uses uniform marketing globally. For example, the company's M&M candies slogan, "It melts in your mouth, not in your hands," is used worldwide. In contrast, Hershey's successful BarNone candy is named Temptation in Canada.

Mars is controlled by the Mars family through two brothers, John and Forrest, Jr. A marketing executive at Mars recently said, "Being No. 2 doesn't sit well with the brothers, and that's the biggest motivator." Mars was the first candy company to persuade merchants to put candy displays near cash registers in 1979. Mars is one of the world's largest private, closely held companies. It is a secretive company, unwilling to divulge financial information and corporate strategies. Recently, Mars has not been performing well, and there are reports of high turnover in their executive and sales rates.

Unlike Hershey, Mars has historically relied upon extensive marketing and advertising expenditures to gain market share, rather than on product innovation. Mars has been repackaging, restyling, and reformulating its leading brands, including Snickers, M&Ms, Milky Way, and 3 Musketeers, but that strategy is now being supplemented with extensive product development. New Mars products include Bounty, Balisto, and PB Max. It also successfully developed marketed frozen Snickers ice cream bars. The product was so successful that it dislodged Eskimo Pie and Original Klondike from the number-one ice cream snack slot without any assistance from promotional advertising. Mars has world-class production facilities in Hackettstown, New Jersey; from that plant it ships products worldwide. In addition, it has manufacturing plants in Mexico and in several European locations.

Mars entered Russia in 1992 and today virtually owns the chocolate market there. Kentave, one of the three Mars distributors in Moscow, sells $5 million monthly of Mars candy. Kentave estimates Mars's total monthly sales in Russia to be more than $30 million.

NESTLÉ   With annual sales of $7.3 billion in the United States and the recent acquisition of Carnation, Nestlé is the largest food company in the world. Nestlé's U.S. operations are headquartered in Glendale, California (818-549-6000). With corporate headquarters in Vevey, Switzerland (021-924-2111), Nestlé is a major competitor in Europe, the Far East, and South America. Nestlé sells products in more than 360 countries on all five continents, many in the Third World. It is the world's largest instant coffee manufacturer, with Nescafé the dominant product. Nestlé also produces and markets chocolate and malt drinks, and it is the world's largest producer of milk powder and condensed milk. Its coffee creamer product, Carnation Coffeemate, holds a sizeable portion of that market.

Nestlé's chocolate and confectionery products carry some popular brand names including Callier, Crunch, and Yes. With the acquisition of Rowntree, additional notable brands were added to the product line including Kit Kat, Smarties, After Eight, and Quality Street. The Perugina division produces Baci. Through the RJR Nabisco acquisition, Nestlé acquired Curtiss Brand, a U.S. confectionery producer with such products as Baby Ruth and Butterfinger. Nestlé manufactures chocolate in 23 countries, particularly in Switzerland and Latin America. Each factory is highly automated, employing an average of 250 people.

Another major product concentration for Nestlé is frozen foods and other refrigerated products. Findus in Europe and Stouffer in the United States represent the bulk of the group's frozen food sales with well-known brands such as Lean Cuisine. Nestlé also manufactures a fast-developing range of fresh pasta and sauces in Europe and the United States under the name Contadina. Through the Carnation division it also manufactures and sells pet foods including Friskies, Gourmet, and Fancy Feast.

Other Nestlé businesses include the Stouffer hotel chain in the United States and Mexico. Nestlé has some exposure in pharmaceuticals and cosmetics, including a majority interest in Alcon, a manufacturer of eye-care products in the United States; and a 28-percent interest in L'Oreal, the world's largest cosmetics manufacturer.

Since 25 percent of Nestlé's revenues and profits come from coffee, any adverse economic occurrences in South America, particularly Brazil, affect the company. Nestlé plans to continue to play to its strength, international markets outside the United States, to combat Hershey.

CONCLUSION

Hershey's global market share in the chocolate confectionery industry is only 10 percent, lowest among its competitors. A major strategic issue facing Hershey today is where, when, and how to best expand geographically. Perhaps Hershey should expand into the Far East because economies of those countries are growing so rapidly. China and India are huge untapped markets. Malaysia, Indonesia, Vietnam, and Thailand also are untapped. Should Hershey wait for Mars and Nestlé to gain a foothold in those countries?

More and more firms are becoming environmentally proactive in their manufacturing and service delivery processes. Environmentally responsible firms market themselves and their products as being green-sensitive. Concern for the natural environment is an issue Hershey should address before competitors seize the initiative. Developing environmentally safe products and packages, reducing industrial waste, recycling, and establishing an environmental audit process are strategies that could benefit Hershey.

Some analysts contend that Hershey International as a separate division producing and selling diverse products is an ineffective organizational design. Can you recommend an improved design that could improve Hershey's lackluster international operations?

Hershey's long-term debt more than doubled in 1995 to $357 million. Should Hershey use debt to acquire firms in other foreign countries? Analysis is needed to identify and value specific acquisition candidates. In developing an overall strategic plan, what recommendations would you present to CEO Kenneth Wolfe? What relative emphasis should Hershey place on chocolate versus pasta in 1996 through 1998? Should Hershey diversify more into nonchocolate candies because that segment is growing most rapidly? Should a new manufacturing plant be built in Asia or in Europe? Design a global marketing strategy that could enable Hershey to boost exports of both chocolate and pasta. Should Hershey increase their long-term debt or issue stock to raise the capital needed to implement your recommended strategies? Develop pro forma financial statements to fully assess and evaluate the impact of your proposed strategies.

EXPERIENTIAL EXERCISES

Experiential Exercise 1A

STRATEGY ANALYSIS FOR HERSHEY FOODS

PURPOSE

The purpose of this exercise is to give you experience identifying an organization's opportunities, threats, strengths, and weaknesses. This information is vital to generating and selecting among alternative strategies.

INSTRUCTIONS

Step 1 Identify what you consider to be Hershey's major opportunities, threats, strengths, weaknesses. On a separate sheet of paper, list these key factors under separate headings. Be sure to state each factor in specific terms.

Step 2 Through class discussion compare your external and internal factors to those developed by other students. From the discussion add to your list of factors. Keep this information for use in later exercises.

Experiential Exercise 1B

DEVELOPING A CODE OF BUSINESS ETHICS FOR HERSHEY FOODS

PURPOSE

This exercise can give you practice developing a code of business ethics. Research was recently conducted to examine codes of business ethics from large manufacturing and service firms in the United States. The 28 variables listed below were found to be included in a sample of more than 80 codes of business ethics. The variables are presented in order of how frequently they occurred. Thus, the first variable, "Conduct business in compliance with all laws," was the variable most often included in the sample documents; "Firearms at work are prohibited" was least often included.

1. Conduct business in compliance with all laws.
2. Payments for unlawful purposes are prohibited.
3. Avoid outside activities that impair duties.
4. Comply with all antitrust and trade regulations.
5. Comply with accounting rules and controls.
6. Bribes are prohibited.
7. Maintain confidentiality of records.
8. Participate in community and political activities.
9. Provide products and services of the highest quality.
10. Exhibit standards of personal integrity and conduct.
11. Do not propagate false or misleading information.
12. Perform assigned duties to the best of your ability.
13. Conserve resources and protect the environment.
14. Comply with safety, health, and security regulations.
15. Racial, ethnic, religious, and sexual harassment at work is prohibited.
16. Report unethical and illegal activities to your manager.
17. Convey true claims in product advertisements.
18. Make decisions without regard for personal gain.

19. Do not use company property for personal benefit.
20. Demonstrate courtesy, respect, honesty, and fairness.
21. Illegal drugs and alcohol at work are prohibited.
22. Manage personal finances well.
23. Employees are personally accountable for company funds.
24. Exhibit good attendance and punctuality.
25. Follow directives of supervisors.
26. Do not use abusive language.
27. Dress in businesslike attire.
28. Firearms at work are prohibited.[1]

INSTRUCTIONS

Step 1 On a separate sheet of paper, write a code of business ethics for Hershey. Include as many variables listed above as you believe appropriate to Hershey's business. Limit your document to 100 words or less.

Step 2 Read your code of ethics to the class. Comment on why you did or did not include certain variables.

Step 3 Explain why having a code of ethics is not sufficient for ensuring ethical behavior in an organization. What else does it take?

NOTES

1. Donald Robin, Michael Giallourakis, Fred R. David, and Thomas E. Moritz, "A Different Look at Codes of Ethics," *Business Horizons* 32, no. 1 (January–February 1989): 66–73.

Experiential Exercise 1C

THE ETHICS OF SPYING ON COMPETITORS

PURPOSE

This exercise gives you an opportunity to discuss ethical and legal issues in class as related to methods being used by many companies to spy on competing firms. Gathering and using information about competitors is an area of strategic management that Japanese firms do much better than American firms.

INSTRUCTIONS

On a separate sheet of paper, number from 1 to 18. For the 18 spy activities listed below, indicate whether or not you believe the activity is Ethical or Unethical and Legal or Illegal. Place an *E* for ethical or *U* for unethical and an *L* for legal or an *I* for illegal. Compare your answers to your classmates' answers and discuss any differences.

1. Buying competitors' garbage.
2. Dissecting competitors' products.
3. Taking plant tours anonymously.
4. Counting tractor-trailer trucks leaving competitors' loading bays.
5. Studying aerial photographs.
6. Analyzing labor contracts.
7. Analyzing help wanted ads.
8. Quizzing customers and buyers about the sales of competitors' products.
9. Infiltrating customers' and competitors' business operations.
10. Quizzing suppliers about competitors' level of manufacturing.
11. Using customers to buy out phony bids.

12. Encouraging key customers to reveal competitive information.
13. Quizzing competitors' former employees.
14. Interviewing consultants who may have worked with competitors.
15. Hiring key managers away from competitors.
16. Conducting phony job interviews to get competitors' employees to reveal information.
17. Sending engineers to trade meetings to quiz competitors' technical employees.
18. Quizzing potential employees who in the past may have worked with competitors.

Experiential Exercise 1D

STRATEGIC PLANNING FOR MY UNIVERSITY

PURPOSE

External and internal factors are the underlying bases of strategies formulated and implemented by organizations. Your college or university faces numerous external opportunities/threats and has many internal strengths/weaknesses. The purpose of this exercise is to illustrate the process of identifying critical external and internal factors.

External influences include trends in the following areas: economic, social, cultural, demographic, environmental, technological, political, legal, governmental, and competitive. External factors could include declining numbers of high school graduates; population shifts; community relations; increased competitiveness among colleges and universities; rising number of adults returning to college; decreased support from local, state, and federal agencies; and increasing number of foreign students attending American colleges.

Internal factors of a college or university include faculty, students, staff, alumni, athletic programs, physical plant, grounds and maintenance, student housing, administration, fundraising, academic programs, food services, parking, placement, clubs, fraternities, sororities, and public relations.

INSTRUCTIONS

Step 1 On a separate sheet of paper, make four headings: External Opportunities, External Threats, Internal Strengths, and Internal Weaknesses.

Step 2 As related to your college or university, list ten factors under each of the four headings.

Step 3 Discuss the factors as a class. Write the factors on the board.

Step 4 What new things did you learn about your university from the class discussion? How could this type of discussion benefit an organization?

Experiential Exercise 1E

STRATEGIC PLANNING AT A LOCAL COMPANY

PURPOSE

This activity is aimed at giving you practical knowledge about how organizations in your city are doing strategic planning. This exercise will also give you experience interacting on a professional basis with local business leaders.

INSTRUCTIONS

Step 1 Use the telephone to contact several business owners or top managers. Find an organization that does strategic planning. Make an appointment to visit with the president, chief executive officer, or owner of that business.

Step 2 Seek answers to the following questions during the interview:
   a. How does your firm actually conduct strategic planning? Who is involved in the process?
   b. Does your firm have a formal mission statement? How was the statement developed? When was the statement last changed?
   c. What are the benefits of engaging in strategic planning?
   d. What are the major costs or problems in doing strategic planning in your business?
   e. Do you anticipate making any changes in the strategic planning process at your company? If yes, please explain.

Step 3 Report your findings to the class.

Strategies in Action

CHAPTER OUTLINE

- ◆ TYPES OF STRATEGIES
- ◆ INTEGRATION STRATEGIES
- ◆ INTENSIVE STRATEGIES
- ◆ DIVERSIFICATION STRATEGIES
- ◆ DEFENSIVE STRATEGIES
- ◆ GUIDELINES FOR PURSUING STRATEGIES
- ◆ MERGERS AND LEVERAGED BUYOUTS
- ◆ MICHAEL PORTER'S GENERIC STRATEGIES
- ◆ STRATEGIC MANAGEMENT IN NONPROFIT AND GOVERNMENTAL ORGANIZATIONS
- ◆ STRATEGIC MANAGEMENT IN SMALL FIRMS

- ■ EXPERIENTIAL EXERCISE 2A
  What Happened at Hershey Foods in 1997?

- ■ EXPERIENTIAL EXERCISE 2B
  Examining Strategy Articles

- ■ EXPERIENTIAL EXERCISE 2C
  Classifying 1996 Strategies

- ■ EXPERIENTIAL EXERCISE 2D
  Strategic Management at the Dynamic Computer Company

- ■ EXPERIENTIAL EXERCISE 2E
  How Risky Are Various Alternative Strategies?

- ■ EXPERIENTIAL EXERCISE 2F
  Developing Alternative Strategies for My University

CHAPTER OBJECTIVES

After studying this chapter, you should be able to do the following:

1. Identify sixteen types of business strategies.
2. Identify numerous examples of organizations pursuing different types of strategies.
3. Discuss guidelines when generic strategies are most appropriate to pursue.
4. Discuss Porter's generic strategies.
5. Describe strategic management in nonprofit, governmental, and small organizations.

*A*lice said, "Would you please tell me which way to go from here?" The cat said, "That depends on where you want to get to."—LEWIS CARROLL

*T*omorrow always arrives. It is always different. And even the mightiest company is in trouble if it has not worked on the future. Being surprised by what happens is a risk that even the largest and richest company cannot afford, and even the smallest business need not run.—PETER DRUCKER

*P*lanning. Doing things today to make us better tomorrow. Because the future belongs to those who make the hard decisions today.—EATON CORPORATION

*B*y taking over companies and breaking them up, corporate raiders thrive on failed corporate strategies. Fueled by junk bond financing and growing acceptability, raiders can expose any company to takeover, no matter how large or blue chip.—MICHAEL PORTER

*W*hen organizations reach a fork in the road, forces are in motion that will, if not halted, drive a planning process towards the end-state of a self-perpetuating bureaucracy.—R. T. LENZ

*O*ne big problem with American business is that when it gets into trouble, it redoubles its effort. It's like digging for gold. If you dig down twenty feet and haven't found it, one of the strategies you could use is to dig twice as deep. But if the gold is twenty feet to the side, you could dig a long time and not find it.—EDWARD DE BONO

*I*f you don't invest for the long term, there is no short term.—GEORGE DAVID

*I*nnovate or evaporate. Particularly in technology-driven businesses, nothing quite recedes like success.—BILL SAPORITO

*T*he demise of strategic planning has been exaggerated. The process has simply moved from corporate staff down to operating managers.—BERNARD REIMANN

*T*his chapter brings strategic management to life with many contemporary examples. Sixteen types of strategies are defined and exemplified, including Michael Porter's generic strategies: cost leadership, differentiation, and focus. Guidelines are presented for determining when different types of strategies are most appropriate to pursue. An overview of strategic management in nonprofit organizations, governmental agencies, and small firms is provided.

TYPES OF STRATEGIES

The model illustrated in Figure 2–1 provides a conceptual basis for applying strategic management. Defined and exemplified in Table 2–1, alternative strategies that an enterprise could pursue can be categorized into thirteen actions: forward integration, backward integration, horizontal integration, market penetration, market development, product development, concentric diversification, conglomerate diversification, horizontal diversification, joint venture, retrenchment, divestiture, liquidation, and a combination strategy. Each alternative strategy has countless variations. For example, market penetration can include adding salespersons, increasing advertising expenditures, couponing, and using similar actions to increase market share in a given geographic area.

INTEGRATION STRATEGIES

Forward integration, backward integration, and horizontal integration are sometimes collectively referred to as *vertical integration* strategies. Vertical integration strategies allow a firm to gain control over distributors, suppliers, and/or competitors.

INFORMATION TECHNOLOGY
Do You Do Online Grocery Shopping?

More than 10,000 households in Chicago, San Francisco, and Boston today do their grocery shopping online from home. Peapod, with annual sales over $20 million, provides online grocery shopping through a network of 450 employees who fill orders and deliver goods to homes. Time is money, and online grocery shopping can save a lot of time. Peapod's cost is $29.95 start-up fee, $4.95 monthly service fee, and 5 percent of the grocery order. In return Peapod takes your order by computer, shops for the best prices, and delivers your groceries exactly when you desire delivery.

About 75 percent of Peapod's customers are women, in contrast to most competitors, 75 percent of whose online shoppers are men. Peapod's system allows grocery items to be chosen from menus organized by broad category (drinks), narrow category (beer), or brand name (Coors). Items can be sorted by cost per ounce or by what's on sale to figure out the best buys. This saves consumers money. Shoppers can also add comments, such as "I want green bananas." Shoppers see a running tally of their order. Peapod takes coupons, credit cards, checks or online payments. Online grocery buying reduces impulse buying, thus saving customers money.

Microsoft Chairman Bill Gates predicts that one-third of all grocery sales in the United States will be purchased electronically by the year 2005. This is an expected huge shift in the $400 billion U.S. grocery business, where only 1 percent of groceries are now bought from home, and that mostly by phone rather than computer. Strategic implications of this trend are immense for food wholesalers and retailers.

Source: Adapted from Susan Chandler, "The Grocery Cart in Your PC," *Business Week,* (September 11, 1995): 63–64.

FIGURE 2–1
A Comprehensive Strategic-Management Model

Feedback

Perform External Audit

Develop Mission Statement

Establish Long-term Objectives

Generate, Evaluate, and Select Strategies

Establish Policies and Annual Objectives

Allocate Resources

Measure and Evaluate Performance

Perform Internal Audit

Strategy Formulation

Strategy Implementation

Strategy Evaluation

TABLE 2–1
**Alternative Strategies
Defined and Exemplified**

STRATEGY	DEFINITION	EXAMPLE
Forward Integration	Gaining ownership or increased control over distributors or retailers	Slot-machine maker Alliance Gaming buys casino operator Bally Gaming.
Backward Integration	Seeking ownership or increased control of a firm's suppliers	Motel-8 acquires a furniture manufacturer.
Horizontal Integration	Seeking ownership or increased control over competitors	First Union Bank acquires First Fidelity Bancorp.
Market Penetration	Seeking increased market share for present products or services in present markets through greater marketing efforts	Johnson Insurance doubles its number of agents in Mexico.
Market Development	Introducing present products or services into new geographic area	Wal-Mart expands into Europe.
Product Development	Seeking increased sales by improving present products or services or developing new ones	Chrysler will soon offer Prowler, a hot-rod-styled sportscar.
Concentric Diversification	Adding new, but related, products or services	Gannet, the newspaper producer, acquires Multimedia, the television and cable company.
Conglomerate Diversification	Adding new, unrelated products or services	Westinghouse Electric acquires CBS Entertainment.
Horizontal Diversification	Adding new, unrelated products or services for present customers	MCI, the phone company, adds consulting and paging.
Joint Venture	Two or more sponsoring firms forming a separate organization for cooperative purposes	Ford Motor Company and Song Cong Diesel in Vietnam build an auto assembly plant near Hanoi.
Retrenchment	Regrouping through cost and asset reduction to reverse declining sales and profits	Glaxo Wellman is restructuring its U.S. operations, cutting 1,000 jobs.
Divestiture	Selling a division or part of an organization	Tenneco sells its Case Construction Corp.
Liquidation	Selling all of a company's assets, in parts, for their tangible worth	Ribol sells all its assets and ceases business.

FORWARD INTEGRATION   *Forward integration* involves gaining ownership or increased control over distributors or retailers. One company that is betting a large part of its future on forward integration is Coca-Cola. Coke continues to purchase domestic and foreign bottlers. Coke has been able to improve its acquired bottlers' efficiency in production and distribution. As indicated in the Information Technology Perspective, Peapod is an example company using a forward integration strategy by receiving grocery orders online and delivering goods to consumers' homes.

An effective means of implementing forward integration is *franchising.* Approximately 2,000 companies in about 50 different industries in the United States use franchising to distribute their products or services. Businesses can expand rapidly by franchising because costs and opportunities are spread among many individuals. Total sales by franchises in the United States are about $1 trillion annually.

BACKWARD INTEGRATION   Both manufacturers and retailers purchase needed materials from suppliers. *Backward integration* is a strategy of seeking ownership or increased control of a firm's suppliers. This strategy can be especially appropriate when a firm's current suppliers are unreliable, too costly, or cannot meet the firm's needs.

More and more, consumers are buying products according to environmental considerations, which include recyclability of the package. Some firms are thus using backward integration to gain control over suppliers of packages. Aluminum is still the most recyclable package, having a scrap value of $650 per ton versus plastic's $200, steel's $60, glass's $50, and paperboard's $30. Aluminum is recycled at a current rate of 64 percent, compared to steel at 25 percent, plastic at 15 percent, glass at 25 percent, and paperboard at 25 percent. Coca-Cola Company and PepsiCo are currently experimenting with bottles made completely from other recycled bottles.

Some industries in the United States (such as the automotive and aluminum industries) are reducing their historical pursuit of backward integration. Instead of owning their suppliers, companies negotiate with several outside suppliers. Ford and Chrysler buy over half of their components parts from outside suppliers such as TRW, Eaton, General Electric, and Johnson Controls. Deintegration makes sense in industries that have global sources of supply. *Outsourcing,* whereby companies use outside suppliers, shop around, play one seller against another, and go with the best deal, is becoming widely practiced.

Global competition is also spurring firms to reduce their number of suppliers and to demand higher levels of service and quality from those they keep. For example, Motorola recently reduced its number of suppliers from 10,000 to 3,000, Xerox cut its suppliers from 5,000 to 500, Digital Equipment cut from 9,000 to 3,000, General Motors from 10,000 to 5,500, and Texas Instruments from 22,000 to 14,000. Although traditionally relying on many suppliers to ensure uninterrupted supplies and low prices, American firms are now following the lead of Japanese firms, who have far fewer suppliers and closer, long-term relationships with those few. "Keeping track of so many suppliers is onerous," says Mark Shimelonis of Xerox.

HORIZONTAL INTEGRATION   *Horizontal integration* refers to a strategy of seeking ownership of or increased control over a firm's competitors. One of the most significant trends in strategic management today is the increased use of horizontal integration as a growth strategy. Mergers, acquisitions, and takeovers among competitors allow for increased economies of scale and enhanced transfer of resources and competencies. Kenneth Davidson makes the following observation about horizontal integration:

> The trend towards horizontal integration seems to reflect strategists' misgivings about their ability to operate many unrelated businesses. Mergers between direct competitors are more likely to create efficiencies than mergers between unrelated businesses, both because there is a greater potential for eliminating duplicate facilities and because the management of the acquiring firm is more likely to understand the business of the target.[1]

Horizontal integration has become the most favored growth strategy in many industries, including banking, where the number of U.S. banks has fallen from 14,000 in the late 1980s to under 9,000 in 1996. Nearly 500 bank mergers in the United States were announced in 1995 alone. The merger of Chase Manhattan Bank and Chemical Bank was one of those; the new Chase is cutting 12,000 employees and $1.5 billion in annual expenses by 1999. Analysts expect the horizontal integration strategy among banks to continue until the 25 largest banks hold 80 percent or more of the industry, up from 60 percent today. This could take another decade.

INTENSIVE STRATEGIES

Market penetration, market development, and product development are sometimes referred to as *"intensive strategies"* because they require intensive efforts to improve a firm's competitive position with existing products.

GLOBAL PERSPECTIVE
Global Issues in the Airline Industry

Have you ever flown with Aeroflot, the world's largest airline company? Probably not, because the airline industry has been slow to globalize, mainly because there is no overall system for regulating international aviation. Different countries have different agreements that promote air traffic regulation and protectionism. Germany and Japan, for example, commonly block discounting efforts by American carriers. Spain recently blocked American Airlines from flying to Madrid, but when the United States countered with threats to block Iberia Airlines of Spain from flying to Miami, Spain relented.

Increasing cooperation among countries today is spurring deregulation and globalization of the airline industry. The result is numerous airline ac-quisitions, mergers, and failures. By the year 2000, global passenger air traffic and revenues are expected to double, with industry revenues reaching $300 billion. But there will be far fewer carriers, probably just a few megacarriers and their subsidiaries.

Airline deregulation and globalization has the world's top carriers formulating new strategies. The world's top fourteen airlines ranked from the largest to smallest in passenger revenues generated are Aeroflot, American, United, Delta, Northwest, British Airways, Continental, US Air, TWA, Japan Airlines, Lufthansa, Air France, Air Nippon, and Singapore. These firms are already jockeying for space inside and outside of airports around the world and are formulating new strategies and alliances to position themselves for the emerging global airline industry.

English is the language of air-traffic controllers throughout the world, which aids U.S. carriers in globalizing. U.S. air carriers are sponsoring English training for Soviet air-traffic controllers in anticipation of getting permission to fly over Siberia on the way to Asia from Chicago, Seattle, and other northern U.S. cities.

MARKET PENETRATION   A *market-penetration* strategy seeks to increase market share for present products or services in present markets through greater marketing efforts. This strategy is widely used alone and in combination with other strategies. Market penetration includes increasing the number of salespersons, increasing advertising expenditures, offering extensive sales promotion items, or increasing publicity efforts. Procter & Gamble is an example of this, spending heavily on advertising to increase market share of Venezia, its upscale perfume. Its advertising campaign includes full-page ads with scent strips in glossy magazines. Microsoft's multimillion dollar advertising campaign to promote the new Windows 95 software is another example.

MARKET DEVELOPMENT   *Market development* involves introducing present products or services into new geographic areas. The climate for international market development is becoming more and more favorable, as illustrated in the Global Perspective. In many industries such as airlines, it is going to be hard to maintain a competitive edge by staying close to home.

Wal-Mart is an example firm that aggressively pursued a market development strategy throughout the 1980s and 1990s. Finally, with the opening of its store in Bennington, Vermont in late 1995, Wal-Mart could say it operated stores in all 50 states. The Wal-Mart in Bennington is located in a small downtown store rather than a huge suburb store, a concession to many local small businesspeople who vehemently opposed Wal-Mart expanding into Vermont.

PRODUCT DEVELOPMENT   *Product development* is a strategy that seeks increased sales by improving or modifying present products or services. Product development usually entails large research and development expenditures. An example firm betting its future on a product development strategy is FastShip Atlantic, which in 1998 plans to introduce the first transatlantic seagoing jet-powered freighter. This freighter will travel 38 knots in rough seas rather than 20 knots, which is normal for large cargo ships today. CEO David Giles says,

"This ship is going to do for the movement of things exactly what the Boeing 707 did for the movement of people."

Large expenditures in product development are a major reason why automotive and computer firms, such as General Motors, Ford, IBM, and Apple, do not own their distributors or dealers. Tandy is the only computer company that owns its distributors, which are Radio Shack stores. By the year 2000, GM plans to launch new car models monthly. The end of the fall new-car season is almost here.

DIVERSIFICATION STRATEGIES

There are three general types of *diversification strategies:* concentric, horizontal, and conglomerate. Overall, diversification strategies are becoming less and less popular as organizations are finding it more and more difficult to manage diverse business activities. In the 1960s and 1970s, the trend was to diversify so as not to be dependent on any single industry, but the 1980s saw a general reversal of that thinking. Diversification is now on the retreat. Michael Porter of the Harvard Business School says, "Management found they couldn't manage the beast." Hence, businesses are selling, or closing, less profitable divisions in order to focus on core businesses.

Peters and Waterman's advice to firms is to "stick to the knitting" and not to stray too far from the firm's basic areas of competence. However, diversification is still an appropriate and successful strategy sometimes. For example, Philip Morris derives 60 percent of its profits from sales of Marlboro cigarettes. Hamish Maxwell, Philip Morris's CEO, says, "We want to become a consumer-products company." Diversification makes sense for Philip Morris because cigarette consumption is declining, product liability suits are a risk, and some investors reject tobacco stocks on principle. In a diversification move Philip Morris spent $12.9 billion in a hostile takeover of Kraft General Foods, the world's second-largest food producer behind Nestlé.

CONCENTRIC DIVERSIFICATION   Adding new, but related, products or services is widely called *concentric diversification.* An example of this strategy is the recent entry of Bell Atlantic Corporation, a telephone company, into the video programming business. The cable industry had lobbied heavily against allowing telephone companies to sell programming.

MCI is an example company pursuing a concentric diversification strategy. The long-distance phone carrier is fast becoming a diversified communications conglomerate selling everything from consulting services to paging, software, Internet access, and cellular communications. CEO Bert Roberts, Jr., plans for half of MCI's revenues in the year 2000 to come from products that the company does not sell in 1995. Investors are not excited about MCI's strategy as evidenced by the firm's stock price falling 16 percent between 1993 and 1995 when the S&P 500 Index rose 27 percent.

HORIZONTAL DIVERSIFICATION   Adding new, unrelated products or services for present customers is called *horizontal diversification.* This strategy is not as risky as conglomerate diversification, because a firm should already be familiar with its present customers. For example, Motorola recently entered the cordless phone market by introducing a flip-top, 7.5-ounce cordless phone to be sold initially only through Sears Roebuck. AT&T dominates the $700 million U.S. cordless market with a 48-percent market share, followed by Panasonic with a 10-percent share and Sony with 8 percent. Motorola is producing the new phones in its Grayslake, Illinois, factory.

Another example of horizontal diversification is the 1995 Converse, Inc. acquisition of Apex One, Inc. Apex was a leading maker of specialty sports apparel for professional athletes, and Converse is the tennis shoe producer. Converse saw Apex as a cheap way to enter the apparel business and pick up valuable sponsorships. But the strategy failed for Converse, which, after owning Apex for only three months and being unable to solve their severe marketing and production problems, liquidated Apex and took a $41.6 million pre-tax loss on the initial investment.

CONGLOMERATE DIVERSIFICATION   Adding new, unrelated products or services is called *conglomerate diversification.* Some firms pursue conglomerate diversification based in part on an expectation of profits from breaking up acquired firms and selling divisions piecemeal. Richard West, dean of New York University's School of Business, says, "The stock market is rewarding deconglomerations, saying company assets are worth more separately than together. There is a kind of antisynergy, the whole being worth less than the parts."

Of the seven regional companies created by the breakup of AT&T, U.S. West has pursued the most risky diversification strategy. U.S. West, a telecommunications firm, now owns operations in industries such as cable TV, equipment financing, advertising services, real estate development, cellular telephones, and publishing. Based in Denver, U.S. West recently purchased Financial Security Assurance for $345 million, further diversifying into financial services.

General Electric is an example of a firm that is highly diversified. GE makes locomotives, lightbulbs, power plants, and refrigerators; GE manages more credit cards than American Express; GE owns more commercial aircraft than American Airlines.

DEFENSIVE STRATEGIES

In addition to integrative, intensive, and diversification strategies, organizations could also pursue joint venture, retrenchment, divestiture, or liquidation.

JOINT VENTURE   *Joint venture* is a popular strategy that occurs when two or more companies form a temporary partnership or consortium for the purpose of capitalizing on some opportunity. This strategy can be considered defensive only because the firm is not undertaking the project alone. Often, the two or more sponsoring firms form a separate organization and have shared equity ownership in the new entity. Other types of *cooperative arrangements* include research and development partnerships, cross-distribution agreements, cross-licensing agreements, cross-manufacturing agreements, and joint-bidding consortia.

Joint ventures and cooperative arrangements are being used increasingly because they allow companies to improve communications and networking, to globalize operations, and to minimize risk. Kathryn Rudie Harrigan, professor of strategic management at Columbia University, summarizes the trend toward increased joint venturing:

> In today's global business environment of scarce resources, rapid rates of technological change, and rising capital requirements, the important question is no longer, "Shall we form a joint venture?" Now the question is, "Which joint ventures and cooperative arrangements are most appropriate for our needs and expectations?" followed by, "How do we manage these ventures most effectively?"[2]

Cooperative agreements even between competitors are becoming popular. For example, Canon supplies photocopies to Kodak, France's Thomson and Japan's FVC manufacture videocassette recorders, Siemens and Fujitsu work together, and General Motors and Toyota assemble automobiles. For collaboration between competitors to succeed, both firms must contribute something distinctive, such as technology, distribution, basic research, or manufacturing capacity. But a major risk is that unintended transfers of important skills or technology may occur at organizational levels below where the deal was signed.[3] Information not covered in the formal agreement often gets traded in day-to-day interactions and dealings of engineers, marketers, and product developers. American firms often give away too much information to foreign firms when operating under cooperative agreements! Tighter formal agreements are needed, and Western companies must become better learners since leadership in many industries has shifted to the Far East and Europe.

RETRENCHMENT   *Retrenchment* occurs when an organization regroups through cost and asset reduction to reverse declining sales and profits. Sometimes called a turnaround or reorganizational strategy, retrenchment is designed to fortify an organization's basic distinctive competence. During retrenchment, strategists work with limited resources and face pressure from shareholders, employees, and the media. Retrenchment can entail selling off land and buildings to raise needed cash, pruning product lines, closing marginal businesses, closing obsolete factories, automating processes, reducing the number of employees, and instituting expense control systems.

In some cases, *bankruptcy* can be an effective type of retrenchment strategy. Bankruptcy can allow a firm to avoid major debt obligations and to void union contracts. There are five major types of bankruptcy: Chapter 7, Chapter 9, Chapter 11, Chapter 12, and Chapter 13.

Chapter 7 bankruptcy is a liquidation procedure used only when a corporation sees no hope of being able to operate successfully or to obtain the necessary creditor agreement. All the organization's assets are sold in parts for their tangible worth.

Chapter 9 bankruptcy applies to municipalities. The most recent municipality successfully declaring bankruptcy is Bridgeport, the largest city in Connecticut. Some states do not allow municipalities to declare bankruptcy.

Chapter 11 bankruptcy allows organizations to reorganize and come back after filing a petition for protection. Declaring Chapter 11 bankruptcy allowed the Manville Corporation and Continental Products to gain protection from liability suits filed over their manufacture of asbestos products. Million-dollar judgments against these companies would have required liquidation, so bankruptcy was a good strategy for these two firms. Similarly, Wang Laboratories recently emerged from Chapter 11 with one of the strongest balance sheets in the computer industry.

Chapter 12 bankruptcy was created by the Family Farmer Bankruptcy Act of 1986. This law became effective in 1987 and provides special relief to family farmers with debt equal to or less than $1.5 million.

Chapter 13 bankruptcy is a reorganization plan similar to Chapter 11 but available only to small businesses owned by individuals with unsecured debts of less than $100,000 and secured debts of less than $350,000. The Chapter 13 debtor is allowed to operate the business while a plan is being developed to provide for the successful operation of the business in the future.

DIVESTITURE   Selling a division or part of an organization is called *divestiture.* Divestiture is often used to raise capital for further strategic acquisitions or investments. Divestiture can be part of an overall retrenchment strategy to rid an organization of businesses that are unprofitable, that require too much capital, or that do not fit well with the firm's other activities.

Divestiture has become a very popular strategy as firms try to focus on their core strengths, lessening their level of diversification. In 1994, U.S. companies completed divestitures worth a record $22.6 billion. During the first half of 1995, more divestitures with a market value of $16.7 billion were closed and additional deals worth $18 billion were pending. In 1994 shares of spun-off companies appreciated an average of 20.2 percent in

TABLE 2–2
Some Example Divestitures in 1995

PARENT COMPANY	DIVESTED BUSINESS
U.S. Sprint	Cellular phone business
Union Pacific	Oil, gas, and mineral operations
Tenneco	Case Construction Co.
Viacom	Cable-TV operations
Anheuser-Busch	Campbell Taggart bakery
ITT	Broken into three public firms
W.R. Grace	National Medical Care dialysis
Travelers Insurance	Transport Holdings long-term care
Hilton Hotels	Casino operations
Kimberly-Clark	Tobacco-related businesses

their first year, compared with the S&P's rise of 1.5 percent. Brian Finn, cohead of mergers and acquisitions at First Boston Inc. says "divestitures are the last great opportunity for companies to dispose of a business tax-tree." Divestiture to shareholders is tax-free to both investors and the company; this is not true of divestitures to an individual or a company. Lee Hillman says, "The day of the conglomerate is a thing of the past."

A few divestitures consummated in 1995 are given in Table 2–2.

LIQUIDATION   Selling all of a company's assets, in parts, for their tangible worth is called *liquidation.* Liquidation is a recognition of defeat and consequently can be an emotionally difficult strategy. However, it may be better to cease operating than to continue losing large sums of money. Container-shipping pioneer Malcolm P. McLean liquidated McLean Industries, the 115-year-old shipping company. Reorganization under Chapter 11 bankruptcy had failed. Based in Charlotte, North Carolina, the company was 85-percent owned by Mr. McLean.

COMBINATION   Many, if not most, organizations pursue a combination of two or more strategies simultaneously, but a *combination strategy* can be exceptionally risky if carried too far. No organization can afford to pursue all the strategies that might benefit the firm. Difficult decisions must be made. Priorities must be established. Organizations, like individuals, have limited resources. Both organizations and individuals must choose among alternative strategies and avoid excessive indebtedness.

Organizations cannot do too many things well because resources and talents get spread thin and competitors gain advantage. In large diversified companies, a combination strategy is commonly employed when different divisions pursue different strategies. Also, organizations struggling to survive may employ a combination of several defensive strategies, such as divestiture, liquidation, and retrenchment, simultaneously.

GUIDELINES FOR PURSUING STRATEGIES

Table 2–3 reveals situations, conditions, and guidelines for when various alternative strategies are most appropriate to pursue. For example, note that a market development strategy is generally most appropriate when new channels of distribution are available that are reliable, inexpensive, and of good quality; when an organization is very successful at what it does; when new untapped or unsaturated markets exist; when an organization has the needed capital and human resources to manage expanded operations; and when an organization has excess production capacity; when an organization's basic industry is rapidly becoming global in scope.

TABLE 2–3
Guidelines for Situations When Particular Strategies Are Most Effective

FORWARD INTEGRATION

- When an organization's present distributors are especially expensive, or unreliable, or incapable of meeting the firm's distribution needs
- When the availability of quality distributors is so limited as to offer a competitive advantage to those firms that integrate forward
- When an organization competes in an industry that is growing and is expected to continue to grow markedly; this is a factor because forward integration reduces an organization's ability to diversify if its basic industry falters
- When an organization has both the capital and human resources needed to manage the new business of distributing its own products
- When the advantages of stable production are particularly high; this is a consideration because an organization can increase the predictability of the demand for its output through forward integration
- When present distributors or retailers have high profit margins; this situation suggests that a company could profitably distribute its own products and price them more competitively by integrating forward

BACKWARD INTEGRATION

- When an organization's present suppliers are especially expensive, or unreliable, or incapable of meeting the firm's needs for parts, components, assemblies, or raw materials
- When the number of suppliers is few and the number of competitors is many
- When an organization competes in an industry that is growing rapidly; this is a factor because integrative-type strategies (forward, backward, and horizontal) reduce an organization's ability to diversify in a declining industry
- When an organization has both the capital and human resources needed to manage the new business of supplying its own raw materials
- When the advantages of stable prices are particularly important; this is a factor because an organization can stabilize the cost of its raw materials and the associated price of its product through backward integration
- When present supplies have high profit margins, which suggests that the business of supplying products or services in the given industry is a worthwhile venture
- When an organization needs to acquire a needed resource quickly

HORIZONTAL INTEGRATION

- When an organization can gain monopolistic characteristics in a particular area or region without being challenged by the federal government for "tending substantially" to reduce competition
- When an organization competes in a growing industry
- When increased economies of scale provide major competitive advantages
- When an organization has both the capital and human talent needed to successfully manage an expanded organization
- When competitors are faltering due to a lack of managerial expertise or a need for particular resources that your organization possesses; note that horizontal integration would not be appropriate if competitors are doing poorly because overall industry sales are declining

MARKET PENETRATION

- When current markets are not saturated with your particular product or service
- When the usage rate of present customers could be significantly increased
- When the market shares of major competitors have been declining while total industry sales have been increasing
- When the correlation between dollar sales and dollar marketing expenditures has historically been high
- When increased economies of scale provide major competitive advantages

MARKET DEVELOPMENT

- When new channels of distribution are available that are reliable, inexpensive, and of good quality
- When an organization is very successful at what it does
- When new untapped or unsaturated markets exist
- When an organization has the needed capital and human resources to manage expanded operations
- When an organization has excess production capacity
- When an organization's basic industry is rapidly becoming global in scope

PRODUCT DEVELOPMENT

- When an organization has successful products that are in the maturity stage of the product life cycle; the idea here is to attract satisfied customers to try new (improved) products as a result of their positive experience with the organization's present products or services

continued

TABLE 2–3   continued

- When an organization competes in an industry that is characterized by rapid technological developments
- When major competitors offer better quality products at comparable prices
- When an organization competes in a high-growth industry
- When an organization has especially strong research and development capabilities

CONCENTRIC DIVERSIFICATION

- When an organization competes in a no-growth or a slow-growth industry
- When adding new, but related, products would significantly enhance the sales of current products
- When new, but related, products could be offered at highly competitive prices
- When new, but related, products have seasonal sales levels that counterbalance an organization's existing peaks and valleys
- When an organization's products are currently in the decline stage of the product life cycle
- When an organization has a strong management team

CONGLOMERATE DIVERSIFICATION

- When an organization's basic industry is experiencing declining annual sales and profits
- When an organization has the capital and managerial talent needed to compete successfully in a new industry
- When the organization has the opportunity to purchase an unrelated business that is an attractive investment opportunity
- When there exists financial synergy between the acquired and acquiring firm; note that a key difference between concentric and conglomerate diversification is that the former should be based on some commonality in markets, products, or technology, whereas the latter should be based more on profit considerations
- When existing markets for an organization's present products are saturated
- When antitrust action could be charged against an organization that has historically concentrated on a single industry

HORIZONTAL DIVERSIFICATION

- When revenues derived from an organization's current products or services would significantly increase by adding the new, unrelated products
- When an organization competes in a highly competitive and/or a no-growth industry, as indicated by low industry profit margins and returns
- When an organization's present channels of distribution can be used to market the new products to current customers
- When the new products have countercyclical sales patterns compared to an organization's present products

JOINT VENTURE

- When a privately owned organization is forming a joint venture with a publicly owned organization; there are some advantages of being privately held, such as close ownership; there are some advantages of being publicly held, such as access to stock issuances as a source of capital. Sometimes, the unique advantages of being privately and publicly held can be synergistically combined in a joint venture
- When a domestic organization is forming a joint venture with a foreign company; joint venture can provide a domestic company with the opportunity for obtaining local management in a foreign country, thereby reducing risks such as expropriation and harassment by host country officials
- When the distinctive competencies of two or more firms complement each other especially well
- When some project is potentially very profitable, but requires overwhelming resources and risks; the Alaskan pipeline is an example
- When two or more smaller firms have trouble competing with a large firm
- When there exists a need to introduce a new technology quickly

RETRENCHMENT

- When an organization has a clearly distinctive competence, but has failed to meet its objectives and goals consistently over time
- When an organization is one of the weaker competitors in a given industry
- When an organization is plagued by inefficiency, low profitability, poor employee morale, and pressure from stockholders to improve performance
- When an organization has failed to capitalize on external opportunities, minimize external threats, take advantage of internal strengths, and overcome internal weaknesses over time; that is, when the organization's strategic managers have failed (and possibly been replaced by more competent individuals)
- When an organization has grown so large so quickly that major internal reorganization is needed

continued

TABLE 2–3   continued

DIVESTITURE

- When an organization has pursued a retrenchment strategy and it failed to accomplish needed improvements
- When a division needs more resources to be competitive than the company can provide
- When a division is responsible for an organization's overall poor performance
- When a division is a misfit with the rest of an organization; this can result from radically different markets, customers, managers, employees, values, or needs
- When a large amount of cash is needed quickly and cannot be reasonably obtained from other sources
- When government antitrust action threatens an organization

LIQUIDATION

- When an organization has pursued both a retrenchment strategy and a divestiture strategy, and neither has been successful
- When an organization's only alternative is bankruptcy; liquidation represents an orderly and planned means of obtaining the greatest possible cash for an organization's assets. A company can legally declare bankruptcy first and then liquidate various divisions to raise needed capital
- When the stockholders of a firm can minimize their losses by selling the organization's assets

Source: Adapted from F. R. David, "How Do We Choose Among Alternative Growth Strategies?" *Managerial Planning* 33, no. 4 (January–February 1985): 14–17, 22.

MERGERS AND LEVERAGED BUYOUTS

Acquisition and merger are two commonly used ways to pursue strategies. An *acquisition* occurs when a large organization purchases (acquires) a smaller firm, or vice versa. A *merger* occurs when two organizations of about equal size unite to form one enterprise. When an acquisition or merger is not desired by both parties, it can be called a *takeover* or *hostile takeover.* There were 30 percent more mergers and acquisitions in 1994 than 1993. Regarding merger-mania restructuring in the United States, *Business Week* offers the following conclusion:

> It is clear now that restructurings are driven by a lot more than tax considerations, low stock prices, raiders' desire for a quick buck, and aggressive merger merchants on Wall Street. . . . Restructuring continues because U.S. industry needs it. Deregulation in industries from financial services to energy, from communications to transportation, has exposed managerial complacency and inefficient practices caused by years of shelter from market forces. . . . Plenty of companies have simply recognized that if they want to compete globally, they must slim down, toughen up, and focus on a narrower range of businesses.[4]

Among mergers, acquisitions, and takeovers in recent years, same-industry combinations have predominated. A general market consolidation is occurring in many industries, especially banking, insurance, defense, and health care, but also pharmaceuticals, food, airlines, accounting, publishing, computers, retailing, financial services, and biotechnology. Table 2–4 shows some mergers and acquisitions completed in 1995. There are many reasons for mergers and acquisitions, including the following:

- ◆ To provide improved capacity utilization
- ◆ To make better use of existing sales force
- ◆ To reduce managerial staff
- ◆ To gain economies of scale
- ◆ To smooth out seasonal trends in sales
- ◆ To gain access to new suppliers, distributors, customers, products, and creditors
- ◆ To gain new technology
- ◆ To reduce tax obligations

TABLE 2–4
Some Examples of Mergers and Acquisitions Completed in 1995

ACQUIRING FIRM	ACQUIRED FIRM
First Union	First Fidelity
Westinghouse Electric	CBS Entertainment
Walt Disney	Capital Cities/ABC
Chase Manhattan Bank	Chemical Bank
Time Warner	Turner Broadcasting
Union Electric	Cipsco
Upjohn Company	Pharmacia
Kimberly-Clark	Scott Paper
Crown Cork & Seal	Carnoud Metalbox
Norfolk Southern Corp.	Conrail Inc.
Bell Atlantic Corp.	Nynex Corp.
Union Pacific	Southern Pacific
Burlington Northern	Sante Fe Pacific
Boston Scientific	Heart Technology
Converse Inc.	Apex One Inc.
Interstate Bakeries	Continental Baking
CPC International	Entenmann's
Gannett	Multimedia
PNC Bank	MidAtlantic
First Chicago	NBD Bancorp
IBM	Lotus Development

Spurred by high stock prices, merger activity in 1995 outpaced that in 1994. Instead of being financed by junk-bond debt, the latest merger boom is being funded largely by stock.

LEVERAGED BUYOUTS (LBOs)   A *leveraged buyout* (LBO) occurs when a corporation's shareholders are bought out (hence *buyout*) by the company's management and other private investors using borrowed funds (hence *leveraged*).[5] Besides trying to avoid a hostile takeover, other reasons for initiating an LBO are senior management decisions that particular divisions do not fit into an overall corporate strategy or must be sold to raise cash, or receipt of an attractive offering price. An LBO takes a corporation private. There were nearly 2,000 LBOs consummated in the United States during the 1980s.

Borg-Warner, Owen-Illinois, and Jim Walter are companies that recently experienced leveraged buyouts. Under this arrangement the debt is paid back later through funds from operations and the sale of assets. Many banks, insurance companies, and other financial institutions are getting into the buyout business, sometimes called *merchant banking*.

Merchant bankers usually sell companies acquired in leveraged buyouts in pieces and at high profits. In the most profitable leveraged buyout ever recorded, Kohlberg, Kravis, Roberts (KKR) and Company acquired RJR Nabisco for $25 billion and then began selling divisions separately at premiums. RJR's divestitures included selling its fresh-fruit business for $875 million to Polly Peck, a London-based food company, and its Del Monte canned food business for about $1.48 billion to another leveraged buyout group led by Citicorp Venture Capital.

MICHAEL PORTER'S GENERIC STRATEGIES

Probably the three most widely read books on competitive analysis in the 1980s were Michael Porter's *Competitive Strategy* (Free Press, 1980), *Competitive Advantage* (Free Press, 1985), and *Competitive Advantage of Nations* (Free Press, 1989). According to Porter, strategies allow organizations to gain competitive advantage from three different bases: cost leadership, differentiation, and focus. Porter calls these bases *generic strategies. Cost leadership* emphasizes producing standardized products at very low per-unit cost for consumers who are price-sensitive. *Differentiation* is a strategy aimed at producing products and services considered unique industrywide and directed at consumers who are relatively price-insensitive. *Focus* means producing products and services that fulfill the needs of small groups of consumers.

Porter's strategies imply different organizational arrangements, control procedures, and incentive systems. Larger firms with greater access to resources typically compete on a cost leadership and/or differentiation basis, whereas smaller firms often compete on a focus basis.

Porter stresses the need for strategists to perform cost-benefit analyses to evaluate "sharing opportunities" among a firm's existing and potential business units. Sharing activities and resources enhances competitive advantage by lowering costs or raising differentiation. In addition to prompting sharing, Porter stresses the need for firms to "transfer" skills and expertise among autonomous business units effectively in order to gain competitive advantage. Depending upon factors such as type of industry, size of firm, and nature of competition, various strategies could yield advantages in cost leadership, differentiation, and focus.

COST LEADERSHIP STRATEGIES   A primary reason for pursuing forward, backward, and horizontal integration strategies is to gain cost leadership benefits. But cost leadership generally must be pursued in conjunction with differentiation. A number of cost elements affect the relative attractiveness of generic strategies, including economies or diseconomies of scale achieved, learning and experience curve effects, the percentage of capacity utilization achieved, and linkages with suppliers and distributors. Other cost elements to consider in choosing among alternative strategies include the potential for sharing costs and knowledge within the organization, R&D costs associated with new product development or modification of existing products, and labor costs, tax rates, energy costs, and shipping costs.

Striving to be the low-cost producer in an industry can be especially effective when the market is comprised of many price-sensitive buyers, when there are few ways to achieve product differentiation, when buyers do not care much about differences from brand to brand, or when there are a large number of buyers with significant bargaining power. The basic idea is to underprice competitors and thereby gain market share and sales, driving some competitors out of the market entirely.

A successful cost leadership strategy usually permeates the entire firm, as evidenced by high efficiency, low overhead, limited perks, intolerance of waste, intensive screening of budget requests, wide spans of control, rewards linked to cost containment, and broad employee participation in cost control efforts. Some risks of pursuing cost leadership are that competitors may imitate the strategy, thus driving overall industry profits down, technological breakthroughs in the industry may make the strategy ineffective, or buyer interest may swing to other differentiating features besides price. Several example firms that are well known for their low-cost leadership strategies are Wal-Mart, BIC, McDonald's, Black and Decker, Lincoln Electric, and Briggs and Stratton.

DIFFERENTIATION STRATEGIES   Different strategies offer different degrees of differentiation. Differentiation does not guarantee competitive advantage, especially if standard products sufficiently meet customer needs or if rapid imitation by competitors is possible. Durable products protected by barriers to quick copying by competitors are best. Successful differentiation can mean greater product flexibility, greater compatibility, lower costs, improved service, less maintenance, greater convenience, or more features. Product development is an example of a strategy that offers the advantages of differentiation.

A differentiation strategy should be pursued only after careful study of buyers' needs and preferences, to determine the feasibility of incorporating one or more differentiating features into a unique product that features the desired attributes. A successful differentiation strategy allows a firm to charge a higher price for its product and to gain customer loyalty since consumers may become strongly attached to the differentiation features. Special features to differentiate one's product can include superior service, spare parts availability, engineering design, product performance, useful life, gas mileage, or ease of use.

A risk of pursuing a differentiation strategy is that the unique product may not be valued highly enough by customers to justify the higher price. When this happens, a cost leadership strategy will easily defeat a differentiation strategy. Another risk of pursuing a differentiation strategy is that competitors may develop ways to quickly copy the differentiating features. Firms thus must find durable sources of uniqueness that cannot be quickly or cheaply imitated by rival firms.

Common organizational requirements for a successful differentiation strategy include strong coordination among the R&D and marketing functions and substantial amenities to attract scientists and creative people. Firms pursuing a differentiation strategy include Dr. Pepper, Jenn-Air, The Limited, BMW, Grady-White, Ralph Lauren, Maytag, and Cross. As indicated in this chapter's Natural Environment Perspective, an increasing number of firms are developing differentiation strategies that capitalize on consumer concern for preserving the natural environment.

FOCUS STRATEGIES   A successful focus strategy depends upon an industry segment that is of sufficient size, has good growth potential, and is not crucial to the success of other major competitors. Strategies such as market penetration and market development offer substantial focusing advantages. Midsize and large firms can effectively pursue focus-based strategies only in conjunction with differentiation or cost leadership-based strategies. All firms in essence follow a differentiated strategy. Since only one firm can differentiate itself with the lowest cost, the remaining firms in the industry must find other ways to differentiate their products.

NATURAL ENVIRONMENT
Profiting from Natural Environment Strategies

- ARCO introduced EC-1 Regular gasoline, a very clean emission control fuel. ARCO's sales of this product sky-rocketed and other oil companies are struggling to develop a similar or better product.
- Anheuser-Busch Companies recently converted nearly all of its breweries from fuel oil to natural gas. Natural gas is much less of a pollutant and is cheaper than fuel oil, thus allowing Anheuser to reap cost efficiencies and gain consumer loyalty.
- Ryder Truck Company recycles all the used crankcase oil from its 160,000 diesel trucks. The company reclaims about one million gallons of oil this way, saving over $1 million in purchase costs, taxes, and disposal costs.

- Sealy Mattress Company in Randolph, Massachusetts, recently installed new lighting in its manufacturing and warehouse facilities, gaining $40,000 a year in electricity savings. Lower demand for electricity means less pollution generated by power plants.
- Columbia University is spending $4 million to improve lighting across campus, realizing annual savings of $2.8 million.
- Merrill Lynch offers two Environmental Technology Trusts and a special Eco-Logical Fund. The latter is comprised of firms that are especially environmentally friendly. All three of these funds are selling exceptionally well.
- Samsung in South Korea has adopted environmental standards 50 percent

stricter than those of South Korean law. Samsung recently invested $71 million in antipollution and environmental preservation activities. The company gained consumer confidence and created advanced water and air decontamination technologies that are being marketed successfully worldwide.
- Lufthansa, the German airline company, cut its paper and plastic waste output by 3,700 tons annually by allowing passengers to select snacks prior to boarding instead of receiving pre-packaged snacks on board.

Focus strategies are most effective when consumers have distinctive preferences or requirements and when rival firms are not attempting to specialize in the same target segment. Firms pursuing a focus strategy include Midas, Red Lobster, Federal Express, US Sprint, MCI, Coors Brewers, and Schwinn.

Risks of pursuing a focus strategy include the possibility that numerous competitors recognize the successful focus strategy and copy the strategy, or that consumer preferences drift toward the product attributes desired by the market as a whole. An organization using a focus strategy may concentrate on a particular group of customers, geographic markets, or product line segments in order to serve a well-defined but narrow market better than competitors who serve a broader market.

THE VALUE CHAIN   According to Porter, the business of a firm can best be described as a *value chain* in which total revenues minus total costs of all activities undertaken to develop and market a product or service yields value. All firms in a given industry have a similar value chain, which includes activities such as obtaining raw materials, designing products, building manufacturing facilities, developing cooperative agreements, and providing customer service. A firm will be profitable as long as total revenues exceed the total costs incurred in creating and delivering the product or service. Firms should strive to understand not only their own value chain operations, but also their competitors', suppliers', and distributors' value chains.

THE COMPETITIVE ADVANTAGE OF NATIONS   Some countries around the world, such as Brazil, offer abundant natural resources, while others, such as Mexico, offer cheap labor. Others, such as Japan, offer a high commitment to education, while still others, such as the United States, offer innovativeness and entrepreneurship. Countries differ in what they have to offer businesses, and more and more firms are relocating various parts of their value chain operations to take advantage of what different countries have to offer.

Porter reveals in his most recent book that some countries seem to have a disproportionate share of successful firms in particular industries. Examples are the United States in entertainment, Italy in ceramic tile, Sweden in trucks, Japan in banking, Switzerland in candy, and Germany in cars. Porter attributes these differences to four decisive elements: (1) availability of strengths in certain narrow, technical fields; (2) high demand in the home country; (3) related and supporting industries in the home country; and (4) strong domestic rivals.[6] Local rivalry, for example, often stimulates growth in local distributors and suppliers. Organizations should strive to pursue strategies that effectively enable the firm to capitalize on the relative strengths of various nations. According to Porter, comparative differences among nations result in the following generalizations for strategic management: devaluation is bad for competitiveness; relaxing antitrust is bad; relaxing product safety and environmental regulations is bad; deregulation is good; promoting interfirm cooperation is bad; orderly marketing agreements are bad; and increasing defense contracts is bad.

STRATEGIC MANAGEMENT IN NONPROFIT AND GOVERNMENTAL ORGANIZATIONS

The strategic-management process is being used effectively by countless nonprofit and governmental organizations, such as the Girl Scouts and Boy Scouts, the Red Cross, chambers of commerce, educational institutions, medical institutions, public utilities, libraries, government agencies, and churches. The nonprofit sector, surprisingly, is by far America's largest employer, with 80 million Americans giving on average nearly 5 hours each week to one or more nonprofit organizations. Many nonprofit and governmental organizations outperform private firms and corporations on innovativeness, motivation, productivity, and strategic management. For example, the Salvation Army in Florida is able to rehabilitate 80 percent of persons convicted of their first offense. The Daisy Scouts, a Girl Scout program for 5-year-olds, has grown rapidly to more than 100,000 strong after being initiated only a few years ago.

Compared to for-profit firms, nonprofit and governmental organizations often function as a monopoly, produce a product or service that offers little or no measurability of performance, and are totally dependent on outside financing. Especially for these organizations, strategic management provides an excellent vehicle for developing and justifying requests for needed financial support.

EDUCATIONAL INSTITUTIONS   Educational institutions are using strategic-management techniques and concepts more frequently. Richard Cyert, president of Carnegie-Mellon University, says, "I believe we do a far better job of strategic management than any company I know." Population shifts nationally from the Northeast and Midwest to the Southeast and West are but one factor causing trauma for educational institutions that have not planned for changing enrollments. Ivy League schools in the Northeast are recruiting more heavily in the Southeast and West. This trend represents a significant change in the competitive climate for attracting the best high school graduates each year.

Schools of Business in more and more colleges and universities are developing and offering custom courses for individual companies. At Northwestern University's Kellogg School, for example, custom courses for companies such as Ernst & Young and Johnson & Johnson now comprise 40 percent of all executive education offerings. Custom courses account for 59 percent of executive education offerings at the University of Pennsylvania's Wharton School. "In the past, schools felt they were teaching the truth, and everyone would come kneel at their feet," says Nancy Hartigan at Kellogg. "Now companies are much more selective. Schools have to become more responsive to what organizations want." To become accredited by the American Association of Collegiate Schools of Business (AACSB), an elaborate strategic plan must be prepared by the applying school.

MEDICAL ORGANIZATIONS   The $200 billion American hospital industry is experiencing declining margins, excess capacity, bureaucratic overburdening, poorly planned and executed diversification strategies, soaring health care costs, reduced federal support, and high administrator turnover. The seriousness of this problem is accented by a 20- percent annual decline in inpatient use nationwide. Declining occupancy rates, deregulation, and accelerating growth of health maintenance organizations (HMOs), preferred provider organizations (PPOs), urgent care centers, outpatient surgery centers, diagnostic centers, specialized clinics, and group practices are other major threats facing hospitals today. Many private and state-supported medical institutions are in financial trouble as a result of traditionally taking a reactive rather than a proactive approach in dealing with their industry.

Hospitals—originally intended to be warehouses for people dying of tuberculosis, smallpox, cancer, pneumonia, and infectious diseases—are creating new strategies today as advances in the diagnosis and treatment of chronic diseases are undercutting that earlier mission. Hospitals are beginning to bring services to the patient as much as bringing the patient to the hospital; in 20 years health care will be concentrated in the home and in the residential community, not on the hospital campus. Chronic care will require day treatment facilities, electronic monitoring at home, user-friendly ambulatory services, decentralized service networks, and laboratory testing. A successful hospital strategy for the future will require renewed and deepened collaboration with physicians, who are central to hospitals' well-being, and a reallocation of resources from acute to chronic care in home and community settings.

Current strategies being pursued by many hospitals include creating home health services, establishing nursing homes, and forming rehabilitation centers. Backward integration strategies that some hospitals are pursuing include acquiring ambulance services, waste disposal services, and diagnostic services. The Stuart Circle Hospital in Richmond, Virginia, is using newspaper, radio, and outdoor advertising as part of a market penetration strategy. Archbold Memorial Hospital in Thomasville, Georgia, is pursuing a product development strategy by creating an outpatient mental health service, a nurse midwife service, and a substance abuse center. The Children's Memorial Hospital in Chicago has developed a new program called Pediatric Excellence that provides nursing care at home for medically fragile children. This strategy could be considered concentric diversification, as could the strategies of building fitness centers and diet centers. Desert Hospital in Palm Springs, California, has moved its noninvasive cardiac catheterization services out of the hospital and into a joint venture arrangement with physicians.

The ten most successful hospital strategies today are providing freestanding outpatient surgery centers, freestanding outpatient diagnostic centers, physical rehabilitation centers, home health services, cardiac rehabilitation centers, preferred provider services, industrial medicine services, women's medicine services, skilled nursing units, and psychiatric services.[7]

Due largely to increasing costs, more and more hospitals are contracting with outside companies to perform services such as providing 24-hour emergency room and life-support systems. Psicor in San Diego, for example, leases equipment and provides technicians for open-heart surgery in eighty hospitals across the country. At least 1,000 hospitals nationwide have contracted with firms such as Coastal Emergency Services in Durham, North Carolina, to provide emergency room services.

GOVERNMENTAL AGENCIES AND DEPARTMENTS   Federal, state, county, and municipal agencies and departments, such as police departments, chambers of commerce, forestry associations, and health departments, are responsible for formulating, implementing, and evaluating strategies that use taxpayers' dollars in the most cost-effective way to provide services and programs. Strategic-management concepts are increasingly being used to enable governmental organizations to be more effective and efficient.

But strategists in governmental organizations operate with less strategic autonomy than their counterparts in private firms. Public enterprises generally cannot diversify into unrelated businesses or merge with another firm. Governmental strategists usually enjoy little freedom in altering the organization's mission or redirecting objectives. Legislators and politicians often have direct or indirect control over major decisions and resources. Strategic issues get discussed and debated in the media and legislatures. Issues become politicized, resulting in fewer strategic choice alternatives. There is more predictability in the management of public sector enterprises.

On the surface, it may seem that strategic management is not applicable to government organizations, but the opposite is true. Government agencies and departments are finding that their employees get excited about the opportunity to participate in the strategic-management process and thereby have an effect on the organization's mission, objectives, strategies, and policies. In addition, government agencies are using a strategic-management approach to develop and substantiate formal requests for additional funding.

STRATEGIC MANAGEMENT IN SMALL FIRMS

Strategic management is vital for large firms' success, but what about small firms? The strategic-management process is just as vital for small companies. From their inception all organizations have a strategy, even if the strategy just evolves from day-to-day operations.

Even if conducted informally or by a single owner/entrepreneur, the strategic-management process can significantly enhance small firms' growth and prosperity. Recent data clearly show that an ever-increasing number of men and women in the United States are starting their own businesses. This means more individuals are becoming strategists. Widespread corporate layoffs have contributed to an explosion in small businesses and new ideas. For example, although less than 1 percent of the 900,000 auto mechanics in the United States are women, Janet Brown of Newport News, Virginia, recently opened and is successfully operating the Women's Auto Clinic, which features women mechanics.

Numerous magazine and journal articles have focused on applying strategic-management concepts to small businesses.[8] A major conclusion of these articles is that a lack of strategic-management knowledge is a serious obstacle for many small business owners. Other problems often encountered in applying strategic-management concepts to small businesses are a lack of sufficient capital to exploit external opportunities and a day-to-day cognitive frame of reference. Recent research also indicates that strategic management in small firms is more informal than in large firms, but small firms that engage in strategic management outperform those that do not.

CONCLUSION

The main appeal of any managerial approach is the expectation that it will enhance organizational performance. This is especially true of strategic management. Through involvement in strategic-management activities, managers and employees achieve a better understanding of an organization's priorities and operations. Strategic management allows organizations to be efficient, but more importantly, it allows them to be effective. Although strategic management does not guarantee organizational success, the process allows proactive rather than reactive decision making. Strategic management may represent a radical change in philosophy for some organizations, so strategists must be trained to anticipate and constructively respond to questions and issues as they arise. The sixteen strategies discussed in this chapter can represent a new beginning for many firms, especially if managers and employees in the organization understand and support the plan for action.

TAKE IT TO THE NET   We invite you to visit the DAVID page on the Prentice Hall Web site at:
http://www.prenhall.com/davidsm
for this chapter's World Wide Web exercises.

KEY TERMS AND CONCEPTS

Acquisition	(p. 59)	Focus	(p. 61)	Market Development	(p. 50)
Backward Integration	(p. 50)	Forward Integration	(p. 50)	Market Penetration	(p. 50)
Bankruptcy	(p. 55)	Franchising	(p. 50)	Merchant Banking	(p. 60)
Combination Strategy	(p. 50)	Generic Strategies	(p. 60)	Merger	(p. 59)
Concentric Diversification	(p. 50)	Horizontal Diversification	(p. 50)	Outsourcing	(p. 51)
Conglomerate Diversification	(p. 50)	Horizontal Integration	(p. 50)	Product Development	(p. 50)
Cooperative Arrangements	(p. 54)	Integration Strategies	(p. 48)	Retrenchment	(p. 50)
Cost Leadership	(p. 61)	Intensive Strategies	(p. 51)	Takeover	(p. 59)
Differentiation	(p. 61)	Joint Venture	(p. 50)	Value Chain	(p. 63)
Diversification Strategies	(p. 53)	Leveraged Buyout	(p. 60)	Vertical Integration	(p. 48)
Divestiture	(p. 50)	Liquidation	(p. 50)		

ISSUES FOR REVIEW AND DISCUSSION

1. How does strategy formulation differ for a small versus a large organization? For a for-profit versus a nonprofit organization?

2. Give recent examples of market penetration, market development, and product development.

3. Give recent examples of forward integration, backward integration, and horizontal integration.

4. Give recent examples of concentric diversification, horizontal diversification, and conglomerate diversification.

5. Give recent examples of joint venture, retrenchment, divestiture, and liquidation.

6. Select one of the suggested readings at the end of this chapter and find that article in your college library. Read the article and prepare a 5-minute oral report on the topic.

7. Do you think hostile takeovers are unethical? Why or why not?

8. What are the major advantages and disadvantages of diversification?

9. What are the major advantages and disadvantages of an integrative strategy?

10. How does strategic management differ in profit and nonprofit organizations?

11. Why is it not advisable to pursue too many strategies at once?

12. Explain Porter's value chain concept.

13. Describe the mechanics of a leveraged buyout.

14. What are the implications of Porter's "competitive advantage of nations" research?

NOTES

1. Kenneth Davidson, "Do Megamergers Make Sense?" *Journal of Business Strategy* 7, no. 3 (Winter 1987): 45.

2. Kathryn Rudie Harrigan, "Joint Ventures: Linking for a Leap Forward," *Planning Review* 14, no. 4 (July–August 1986):10.

3. Gary Hamel, Yves Doz, and C.K. Prahalad, "Collaborate with Your Competitors—and Win," *Harvard Business Review* 67, no. 1 (January–February 1989): 133.

4. "Why Nothing Seems to Make a Dent in Dealmaking," *Business Week* (20 July 1987): 75.

5. Dan Dalton, "The Ubiquitous Leveraged Buyout (LBO): Management Buyout or Management Sellout?" *Business Horizons* 32, no. 4 (July–August 1989): 36.

6. Bernard Reimann, "Selected Highlights of the 1988 Strategic Management Society Conference," *Planning Review* (January–February 1989): 26–7. See also Michael Porter, *Competitive Advantage of Nations* (New York: Free Press, 1989).

7. *Hospital,* May 5, 1991: 16.

8. Some of these articles are P.H. Thurston, "Should Smaller Companies Make Formal Plans?" *Harvard Business Review* 61, no. 5 (September–October 1983): 162–88; R. Robinson, J. Pearce, G. Vozikis, and T. Mescon, "The Relationship Between Stage of Development and Small Firm Planning and Performance," *Journal of Small Business Management* 22, no. 2 (April 1984): 45–52; L. Nagel, "Strategy Formulation for the Smaller Firm: A Practical Approach," *Long Range Planning* 14, no. 4 (August 1981): 115–20; P.G. Holland and W. Boulton, "Balancing the 'Family' and the 'Business' in Family Business," *Business Horizons* 27, no. 2 (March–April 1984): 16–21; F.R. David, "Computer Assisted Strategic Planning for Small Businesses," *Journal of Systems Management* 36, no. 7 (July 1985): 24–33.

CURRENT READINGS

Allio, Michael K. and Robert J. Allio. "Selective Insurance Corporation: Uniting Reengineering and Strategy." Case Study. *Planning Review* 23, no. 3(May–June 1995): 28–30.

Bahrami, Homa and Stuart Evans. "Flexible Re-Cycling and High-Technology Entrepreneurship." *California Management Review* 37, no. 3 (Spring 1995): 62–89.

Banbury, C.M. and W. Mitchell. "The Effect of Introducing Important Incremental Innovations on Market Share and Business Survival." *Strategic Management Journal* 16, Special Issue (Summer 1995): 161–182.

Barker, V.L., III and M.A. Mone. "Retrenchment: Cause of Turnaround or Consequence of Decline?" *Strategic Management Journal* 15, no. 5 (June 1994): 395–406.

Baron, David P. "Integrated Strategy: Market and Nonmarket Components." *California Management Review* 37, no. 2 (Winter 1995): 47–65.

Beamish, Paul W. and Andrew C. Inkpen. "Keeping International Joint Ventures Stable and Profitable." *Long Range Planning* 28, no. 3 (June 1995): 26–36.

Beaver, William. "Levi's Is Leaving China." *Business Horizons* 38, no. 2 (March–April 1995): 35–40.

Bleeke, Joel and David Ernst. "Is Your Strategic Alliance Really A Sale?" *Harvard Business Review* 73, no. 1 (January–February 1995): 97–106.

Brouthers, Keith D., Lane Eliot Brouthers, and Timothy J. Wilkinson. "Strategic Alliances: Choose Your Partners." *Long Range Planning* 28, no. 3 (June 1995): 18–25.

Brown, Shona L. and Kathleen M. Eisenhardt. "Product Development: Past Research, Present Findings, and Future Directions." *Academy of Management Review* 20, no. 2 (April 1995): 343–378.

Campbell, A., M. Goold, and M. Alexander. "Corporate Strategy: The Quest For Parenting Advantage." *Harvard Business Review* 73, no. 2 (March–April 1995): 120–132.

Chen, Ming-Jer and Donald C. Hambrick. "Speed, Stealth, and Selective Attack: How Small Firms Differ from Large Firms in Competitive Behavior." *Academy of Management Journal* 38, no. 2 (April 1995): 453–482.

Crockford, Doug. "Strategic Management in Privatized Businesses." *Long Range Planning* 27, no. 2 (April 1994): 111–118.

Daily, Catherine M. "Bankruptcy in Strategic Studies: Past and Promise." *Journal of Management* 20, no. 2 (Summer 1994): 263–296.

D'Aveni, Richard A. and David J. Ravenscraft. "Economies of Integration Versus Bureaucracy Costs: Does Vertical Integration Improve Performance?" *Academy of Management Journal* 37, no. 5 (October 1994): 1167–1206.

Emshoff, James R. "How to Increase Employee Loyalty While You Downsize." *Business Horizons* 37, no. 2 (March–April 1994): 49–57.

Gersick, Connie J.G. "Pacing Strategic Change: The Case of a New Venture." *Academy of Management Journal* 37, no. 1 (February 1994): 9–45.

Ghoshal, Sumantra and Henry Mintzberg. "Diversification and Diversifact." *California Management Review* 37, no. 1 (Fall 1994): 8–27.

Holland, Dutch and Sanjiv Kumar. "Getting Past the Obstacles to Successful Reengineering." *Business Horizons* 38, no. 3 (May–June 1995): 79–85.

Hoskisson, Robert E., Richard A. Johnson, and Douglas D. Moesel. "Corporate Divestiture Intensity in Restructuring Firms: Effects of Governance, Strategy, and Performance." *Academy of Management Journal* 37, no. 5 (October 1994): 1207–1251.

Ito, K. "Japanese Spinoffs: Unexplored Survival Strategies." *Strategic Management Journal* 16, no. 6 (September 1995): 431–446.

Kanter, Rosabeth Moss. "Collaborative Advantage: The Art of Alliances." *Harvard Business Review* (July–August 1994): 96–112.

Keser, W. Carl and Timothy A. Luehrman. "Rehabilitating The Leveraged Buyout." *Harvard Business Review* 73, no. 3 (May–June 1995): 119–131.

Kotha, S. "Mass Customization: Implementing the Emerging Paradigm for Competitive Advantage." *Strategic Management Journal* 16, Special Issue (Summer 1995): 21–42.

Kranove, D. and M. Shanley. "Cost Reductions or Reputation Enhancement as Motives for Mergers: The Logic of Multihospital Systems." *Strategic Management Journal* 16, no. 1 (January 1995): 55–74.

Kukalis, Sal and Mark Jungemann. "Strategic Planning for a Joint Venture." *Long Range Planning* 28, no. 3 (June 1995): 46–57.

Markides, C.C. "Diversification, Restructuring and Economic Performance." *Strategic Management Journal* 16, no. 2 (February 1995): 101–118.

Markides, C.C. and P.J. Williamson. "Related Diversification, Core Competencies and Corporate Performance." *Strategic Management Journal* 15, Special Issue (Summer 1994): 149–166.

Martinez, Erwin V. "Successful Reengineering Demands IS/Business Partnerships." *Sloan Management Review* 36, no. 4 (Summer 1995): 51–60.

McFarlan, F. Warren and Richard L. Nolan. "How to Manage an IT Outsourcing Alliance." *Sloan Management Review* 36, no. 2 (Winter 1995): 9–24.

McKinley, William, Carol M. Sanchez, and Allen G. Schick. "Organizational Downsizing: Constraining, Cloning, Learning." *Academy of Management Executive IX,* no. 3 (August 1995): 32–44.

Mertz, G.R. and M.H. Sauber. "Profiles of Managerial Activities in Small Firms." *Strategic Management Journal* 16, no. 7 (October 1995): 551–564.

Nosowski, Gerard. "Strategic Planning for a Public Service—The British Post Office." *Long Range Planning* 27, no. 3 (June 1994): 108–117.

Oviatt, Benjamin M. and Patricia Phillips McDougall. "Global Start-Ups: Entrepreneurs on a Worldwide Stage." *Academy of Management Executive IX,* no. 2 (May 1995): 30–44.

Pablo, Amy L. "Determinants of Acquisition Integration Level: A Decision-Making Perspective." *Academy of Management Journal* 37, no. 4 (August 1994): 803–836.

Pearce, J.A., II and D.K. Robbins. "Retrenchment Remains the Foundation of Business Turnaround." *Strategic Management Journal* 15, no. 5 (June 1994): 407–419.

Peel, Michael J. "The Impact of Corporate Restructuring: Mergers, Divestments and MBOs." *Long Range Planning* 28, no. 2 (April 1995): 92–101.

Peisch, Richard. "When Outsourcing Goes Awry." HBR Case Study. *Harvard Business Review* 73, no. 3 (May–June 1995): 24–39.

Pekar, Peter, Jr. and Robert Allio. "Making Alliances Work—Guidelines for Success." *Long Range Planning* 27, no. 4 (August 1994): 54–65.

Pennings, Johannes M., Harry Barkema, and Sytse Douma. "Organizational Learning and Diversification." *Academy of Management Journal* 37, no. 3 (June 1994): 608–640.

Quinn, James Brian and Frederick G. Hilmer. "Strategic Outsourcing." *Sloan Management Review* 35, no. 4 (Summer 1994): 43–56.

Shanklin, William L. "Offensive Strategies for Defense Companies." *Business Horizons* 38, no. 4 (July–August 1995): 53–60.

Shaughnessy, Haydn. "International Joint Ventures: Managing Successful Collaborations." *Long Range Planning* 28, no. 3 (June 1995): 10–17.

Sheppard, Jerry Paul. "Strategy and Bankruptcy: An Exploration Into Organizational Death." *Journal of Management* 20, no. 4 (Winter 1994): 795–834.

Stafford, Edwin R. "Using Co-operative Strategies to Make Alliances Work." *Long Range Planning* 27, no. 3 (June 1994): 64–74.

Suárez, F.F. and J.M. Utterback. "Dominant Designs and the Survival of Firms." *Strategic Management Journal* 16, no. 6 (September 1995): 415–430.

Towner, Simon J. "Four Ways to Accelerate New Product Development." *Long Range Planning* 27, no. 2 (April 1994): 57–65.

Walters, Bruce A., Steve Peters, and Gregory G. Dess. "Strategic Alliances and Joint Ventures: Making Them Work." *Business Horizons* 37, no. 4 (July–August 1994): 5–10.

Wiersema, M.F. and J.P. Liebeskind. "The Effects of Leveraged Buyouts on Corporate Growth and Diversification in Large Firms." *Strategic Management Journal* 16, no. 6 (September 1995): 447–460.

Wright, M., K. Robbie, S. Thompson, and K. Starkey. "Longevity and the Life-cycle of Management Buy-outs." *Strategic Management Journal* 15, no. 3 (March 1994): 215–228.

EXPERIENTIAL EXERCISES

Experiential Exercise 2A

WHAT HAPPENED AT HERSHEY FOODS IN 1997?

PURPOSE

In performing business policy case analysis, you will need to find epilogue information about the respective companies to determine what strategies were actually employed since the time of the case. Comparing *what actually happened* with *what you would have recommended and expected to happen* is an important part of business policy case analysis. Do not recommend what the firm actually did, unless in-depth analysis of the situation at the time reveals those strategies to have been best among all feasible alternatives. This exercise gives you experience conducting library research to determine what strategies Hershey, Mars, and Nestlé pursued in 1995–1997.

INSTRUCTIONS

Step 1 Go to your college library and look up Hershey Foods Corporation, Mars, and Nestlé Corporation in indexes such as the *Funk & Scott Index, Business Periodicals Index,* and *Wall Street Journal/Barron's Index.* Find some recent articles about firms in the confectionery industry. Scan Moody's, Dun & Bradstreet, and Standard & Poor's publications for information.

Step 2 Summarize your findings in a three-page report titled "Hershey Foods' Strategies in the mid-1990s." Include information about Mars and Nestlé. Also include your personal reaction to Hershey's strategies in terms of their attractiveness.

Experiential Exercise 2B

EXAMINING STRATEGY ARTICLES

PURPOSE

Strategy articles can be found weekly in journals, magazines, and newspapers. By reading and studying strategy articles, you can gain a better understanding of the strategic-management process. Several of the best journals in which to find corporate strategy articles are *Planning Review, Long Range Planning, Journal of Business Strategy,* and *Strategic Management Journal.* These journals are devoted to reporting the results of empirical research in strategic management. They apply strategic-management concepts to specific organizations and industries. They introduce new strategic-management techniques and provide short case studies on selected firms.

Other good journals in which to find strategic-management articles are *Harvard Business Review, Sloan Management Review, Business Horizons, California Management Review, Academy of Management Review, Academy of Management Journal, Academy of Management Executive, Journal of Management,* and *Journal of Small Business Management.*

In addition to journals, many magazines regularly publish articles that focus on business strategies. Several of the best magazines in which to find applied strategy articles are *Dun's Business Month, Fortune, Forbes, Business Week, Inc. Magazine,* and *Industry Week.* Newspapers such as *USA Today, The Wall Street Journal, The New York Times,* and *Barrons* cover strategy events when they occur—for example, a joint venture announcement, a bankruptcy declaration, a new advertising campaign start, acquisition of a company, divestiture of a division, a chief executive officer's hiring or firing, or a hostile takeover attempt.

In combination, journal, magazine, and newspaper articles can make the business policy course especially exciting. They allow current strategies of profit and nonprofit organizations to be identified and studied.

INSTRUCTIONS

Step 1 Go to your college library and find a recent journal article that focuses on a strategic-management topic. Select your article from one of the journals listed above. Copy the article and bring it to class.

Step 2 Give a three-minute oral report summarizing the most important information in your article. Include comments giving your personal reaction to the article. Pass your article around in class.

Experiential Exercise 2C
CLASSIFYING 1996 STRATEGIES

PURPOSE

This exercise can improve your understanding of various strategies by giving you experience classifying strategies. This skill will help you use the strategy-formulation tools presented later. Consider the following strategies being implemented in 1996 by various firms:

1. Cummins Engine, facing a weak truck market, cut 2,000 jobs, 7 percent of its total.
2. Monsanto received $580 million from selling its plastics division to Germany's Bayer.
3. German chemical giant Hoechst began huge new investments in China.
4. 3M closed its video and audiotape operations.
5. Aetna sold its property and casualty division to Travelers for $4 billion.
6. Reebok sold its Avia athletic shoe division.
7. Bank of Boston acquired BayBanks for $2.2 billion.
8. L'Oreal purchased Maybelline for $508 million, making it No. 2 in U.S. cosmetics.
9. British Petroleum began exploration of gas fields in the remote I-n-Salah region of the Sahara desert.
10. Boeing received a $4 billion order from Malaysian Airline System for 747 and 777 jets.

INSTRUCTIONS

Step 1 On a separate sheet of paper, number from 1 to 10. These numbers correspond to the strategies described above.

Step 2 What type of strategy best describes the 10 actions cited above? Indicate your answers on the separate sheet of paper.

Step 3 Exchange papers with a classmate and grade each other's paper as your instructor gives the right answers.

Experiential Exercise 2D
STRATEGIC MANAGEMENT AT THE DYNAMIC COMPUTER COMPANY

PURPOSE

This exercise can give you experience choosing among alternative growth strategies for a specific company. Remember that organizations cannot pursue all the strategies that potentially may benefit the firm. Difficult decisions have to be made to eliminate some options. Use the guidelines given in Table 2–3 to complete this exercise.

	1995	1996	1997
Sales	$ 13,000,000	$ 12,000,000	$ 10,000,000
Net Income	3,000,000	1,000,000	500,000
Total Assets	180,000,000	200,000,000	250,000,000
Market Share	15%	12%	10%

BACKGROUND

Dynamic Computer, Inc. (DCI) is a highly regarded personal computer manufacturer based in central California. DCI designs, develops, produces, markets, and services personal computer systems for individuals' needs in business, education, science, engineering, and the home. The company's main product is the Dynamic II personal computer system, complete with optional accessories and software. The company has recently announced a new system, the Dynamic III, that is aimed at large business firms. It is much more expensive than the Dynamic II. Dynamic's computer systems are distributed in the United States and Canada by 1,000 independent retail stores and internationally through 21 independent distributors, who resell to 850 foreign retail outlets. Approximately 700 of the retail outlets in the United States and Canada are authorized service centers for Dynamic products, but none of the outlets sell Dynamic products exclusively. Many of these outlets are not marketing Dynamic's products effectively.

The American computer industry grew at an inflation-adjusted, compound annual rate of about 20 percent from 1958 through the late 1980s. In the 1990s real annual growth in the computer industry is expected to average about 18 percent a year. The outlook for personal computers continues to be positive. However, this market is highly competitive and is characterized by rapid technological advances in both hardware and software. Margins on software are nearly double operating margins on hardware. New firms are entering the industry at an increasing rate, and this has resulted in a decline in Dynamic's sales, earnings, and market share in recent years. Many computer companies expect software sales and services to represent 50 percent of their total revenues by 1998. Dynamic is concerned about its future direction and competitiveness. Selected financial information for Dynamic is given in Table 2D–1.

INSTRUCTIONS

The owners of DCI have indicated a willingness to explore a number of alternative growth strategies for the future. They have hired you as a consultant to assist them in making strategic decisions regarding the future allocation of resources. The feeling is that to sustain growth, the company must make some critical decisions. Dynamic is financially capable of investing in several projects. The owners wish to use their resources wisely to produce the highest possible return on investment in the future. They are considering five alternative strategies:

1. Market penetration—establish a nationwide salesforce to market Dynamic products to large firms that do not buy through independent retailers.
2. Product development—develop an easier-to-use computer for small business firms.
3. Forward integration—offer major new incentives to distributors who sell and service Dynamic products.
4. Backward integration—purchase a major outside supplier of software.
5. Conglomerate diversification—acquire Toys Unlimited, a large and successful toy manufacturer.

Based on the strategy guidelines given in Chapter 2, your task is to offer specific recommendations to the strategists of DCI. Follow these steps:

Step 1   Across the top of a separate sheet of paper, set up five columns, with the following headings:

Individual Percentage Allocations	Group Percentage Allocations	Expert Percentage Allocations	The Absolute Difference Between Columns 1 and 3	The Absolute Difference Between Columns 2 and 3

Down the left side of your paper, number from 1 to 5. These numbers correspond to the five strategies listed above.

Step 2   Take 10 minutes to determine how you would allocate DCI's resources among the five alternative strategies. Record your answers by placing individual percentage values for strategies 1 through 5 under column 1. Your only constraint is that the total resources allocated must equal 100%. Distribute resources in the manner you think will offer the greatest future return on investment and profitability.

Step 3   Join with two other students in class. Develop a set of group percentage allocations and record these values for strategies 1 through 5 under column 2. Do not change your individual percentage allocations once discussion begins in your group.

Step 4   As your professor reveals the right answer and supporting rationale, record these values for strategies 1 through 5 under column 3.

Step 5   For each row, subtract column 3 values from column 1 values and record the absolute difference (ignore negatives) in column 4. Then, sum the column 4 values.

Step 6   For each row, subtract column 3 values from column 2 values and record the absolute difference (ignore negatives) in column 5. Then, sum the column 5 values.

Step 7   If the sum of column 4 values exceeds the sum of column 5 values, then your group allocation of DCI's resources was better than your individual allocation. However, if the sum of column 4 values is less than the sum of column 5 values, you were a better strategist than your group on this exercise.

Strategic-management research indicates that group strategic decisions are almost always better than individual strategic decisions. Did you do better than your group?

Experiential Exercise 2E

HOW RISKY ARE VARIOUS ALTERNATIVE STRATEGIES?

PURPOSE

This exercise focuses on how risky various alternative strategies are for organizations to pursue. Different degrees of risk are based largely on varying degrees of *externality,* defined as movement away from present business into new markets and products. In general, the greater the degree of externality, the greater the probability of loss resulting from unexpected events. High-risk strategies are generally less attractive than low-risk strategies.

INSTRUCTIONS

Step 1   On a separate sheet of paper, number vertically from 1 to 10. Think of 1 as "most risky," 2 as "next most risky," and so forth to 10, "least risky."

Step 2   Write the following strategies beside the appropriate number to indicate how risky you believe the strategy is to pursue: horizontal integration, horizontal diversification, liquidation, forward integration, backward integration, product development, market development, market penetration, joint venture, and conglomerate diversification.

Step 3 Grade your paper as your professor gives you the right answers and supporting rationale. Each correct answer is worth ten points. This exercise is based on a commonly accepted and published classification of strategies given in the footnote.[1]

NOTES

1. James Belohlav and Karen Giddens-Emig, "Selecting a Master Strategy," *Journal of Business Strategy* 7, no. 3 (Winter 1987): 77.

Experiential Exercise 2F

DEVELOPING ALTERNATIVE STRATEGIES FOR MY UNIVERSITY

PURPOSE

It is important for representatives from all areas of a college or university to identify and discuss alternative strategies that could benefit faculty, students, alumni, staff, and other constituencies. As you complete this exercise, notice the learning and understanding that occurs as people express differences of opinions. Recall that *the process of planning is more important than the document.*

INSTRUCTIONS

Step 1 Recall or locate the external opportunity/threat and internal strength/weakness factors that you identified as part of Experiential Exercise 1D. If you did not do that exercise, discuss now as a class important external and internal factors facing your college or university.

Step 2 Identify and put on the chalkboard alternative strategies that you feel could benefit your college or university. Your proposed actions should allow the institution to capitalize on particular strengths, improve upon certain weaknesses, avoid external threats, and/or take advantage of particular external opportunities. List at least twenty possible strategies on the board. Number the strategies as they are written on the board.

Step 3 On a separate sheet of paper, number from 1 to the total number of strategies listed on the board. Everyone in class should individually rate the strategies identified, using a 1 to 3 scale, where 1 = *I do not support implementation,* 2 = *I am neutral about implementation,* 3 = *I strongly support implementation.* In rating the strategies recognize that your institution cannot do everything desired or potentially beneficial.

Step 4 Go to the board and record your ratings in a row beside the respective strategies. Everyone in class should do this, going to the board perhaps by rows in the class.

Step 5 Sum the ratings for each strategy so that a prioritized list of recommended strategies is obtained. This prioritized list reflects the collective wisdom of your class. Strategies with the highest score are deemed best.

Step 6 Discuss how this process could enable organizations to achieve understanding and commitment from individuals.

Step 7 Share your class results with a university administrator and ask for comments regarding the process and top strategies recommended.

STRATEGY FORMULATION

The Business Mission

CHAPTER OUTLINE

CHAPTER OBJECTIVES

After studying this chapter, you should be able to do the following:

1. Describe the nature and role of mission statements in strategic management.

2. Discuss why the process of developing a mission statement is as important as the resulting document.

3. Identify the components of mission statement documents.

4. Discuss how a clear mission statement can benefit other strategic-management activities.

5. Evaluate mission statements of different organizations.

6. Write good mission statements.

NOTABLE QUOTES

A business is not defined by its name, statutes, or articles of incorporation. It is defined by the business mission. Only a clear definition of the mission and purpose of the organization makes possible clear and realistic business objectives.—PETER DRUCKER

A corporate vision can focus, direct, motivate, unify, and even excite a business into superior performance. The job of a strategist is to identify and project a clear vision.—JOHN KEANE

*W*here there is no vision, the people perish.—PROVERBS 29:18

*C*ustomers are first, employees second, shareholders third, and the community fourth. That's the credo at H. B. Fuller, the century-old adhesives maker in St. Paul.—PATRICIA SELLERS

*W*hat is especially difficult is getting different departments working together in the best interest of customers. Yet managers at all levels are the critical link to aligning the entire organization toward the customer.—RICHARD WHITELEY

*F*or strategists, there's a trade-off between the breadth and detail of information needed. It's a bit like an eagle hunting for a rabbit. The eagle has to be high enough to scan a wide area in order to enlarge his changes of seeing prey, but he has to be low enough to see the detail—the movement and features that will allow him to recognize his target. Continually making this trade-off is the job of a strategist—it simply can't be delegated.—FREDERICK GLUCK

*T*he best laid schemes of mice and men often go awry.—ROBERT BURNS *(paraphrased)*

A strategist's job is to see the company not as it is . . . but as it can become.—JOHN W. TEETS, CHAIRMAN OF GREYHOUND, INC.

*T*hat business mission is so rarely given adequate thought is perhaps the most important single cause of business frustration.—PETER DRUCKER

This chapter focuses on the concepts and tools needed to evaluate and write business mission statements. A practical framework for developing mission statements is provided. Actual mission statements from large and small organizations and for-profit and nonprofit enterprises are presented and critically examined. The process of creating a mission statement is discussed.

WHAT IS OUR BUSINESS?

Current thought on mission statements is based largely on guidelines set forth in the mid-1970s by Peter Drucker, often called "the father of modern management" for his pioneering studies at General Motors Corporation and for his 22 books and hundreds of articles. *Harvard Business Review* calls Drucker, age 79, "the preeminent management thinker of our time."

Drucker says asking the question, "What is our business?" is synonymous with asking the question, "What is our mission?" An enduring statement of purpose that distinguishes one organization from other similar enterprises, the *mission statement* is a declaration of an organization's "reason for being." It answers the pivotal question, "What is our business?" A clear mission statement is essential for effectively establishing objectives and formulating strategies.

Sometimes called a *creed statement,* a statement of purpose, a statement of philosophy, a statement of beliefs, a statement of business principles, a vision statement, or a statement "defining our business," a mission statement reveals the long-term vision of an organization in terms of what it wants to be and whom it wants to serve. All organizations have a reason for being, even if strategists have not consciously transformed this into writing. As illustrated in Figure 3–1, a carefully prepared statement of mission is widely recognized by both practitioners and academicians as the first step in strategic management.

> A business mission is the foundation for priorities, strategies, plans, and work assignments. It is the starting point for the design of managerial jobs and, above all, for the design of managerial structures. Nothing may seem simpler or more obvious than to know what a company's business is. A steel mill makes steel, a railroad runs trains to carry freight and passengers, an insurance company underwrites fire risks, and a bank lends money. Actually, "What is our business?" is almost always a difficult question and the right answer is usually anything but obvious. The answer to this question is the first responsibility of strategists. Only strategists can make sure that this question receives the attention it deserves and that the answer makes sense and enables the business to plot its course and set its objectives.[1]

We can perhaps best understand a business mission by focusing on a business when it is first started. In the beginning, a new business is simply a collection of ideas. Starting a new business rests on a set of beliefs that the new organization can offer some product or service, to some customers, in some geographic area, using some type of technology, at a profitable price. A new business owner typically believes that the management philosophy of the new enterprise will result in a favorable public image and that this concept of the business can be communicated to, and will be adopted by, important constituencies. When the set of beliefs about a business at its inception are put into writing, the resulting document mirrors the same basic ideas that compose a mission statement. As a business grows, owners or managers find it necessary to revise the founding set of beliefs, but those original ideas usually are reflected in the revised statement of mission.

Business mission statements can often be found in the front of annual reports. Mission statements often are displayed throughout a firm's premises, and they are distributed with company information sent to constituencies. The mission statement is a part of numerous internal reports, such as loan requests, supplier agreements, labor relations contracts, business plans, and customer service agreements. Barnett Bank's current mission statement is as follows:

FIGURE 3–1
A Comprehensive Strategic-Management Model

Feedback

Perform External Audit

Develop Mission Statement

Establish Long-term Objectives

Generate, Evaluate, and Select Strategies

Establish Policies and Annual Objectives

Allocate Resources

Measure and Evaluate Performance

Perform Internal Audit

Strategy Formulation

Strategy Implementation

Strategy Evaluation

Barnett's mission is to create value for its owners, customers and employees by creating and capitalizing on market leadership positions to sell and service a broad range of high quality, profitable financial services. Our sales emphasis will be full service to consumers and businesses in our communities and advisory and processing services to others. We will operate at the lowest possible cost consistent with maintaining high service quality and market leadership.[2]

A good mission statement describes an organization's purpose, customers, products or services, markets, philosophy, and basic technology. According to Vern McGinnis, a mission statement should (1) define what the organization is and what the organization aspires to be, (2) be limited enough to exclude some ventures and broad enough to allow for creative growth, (3) distinguish a given organization from all others, (4) serve as a framework for evaluating both current and prospective activities, and (5) be stated in terms sufficiently clear to be widely understood throughout the organization.[3]

Some strategists spend almost every moment of every day on administrative and tactical concerns, and strategists who rush quickly to establish objectives and implement strategies often overlook developing a mission statement. This problem is widespread even among large organizations. Approximately 40 percent of large corporations in America have not yet developed a formal mission statement, including Walt Disney Company, Grumman Corporation, and Wal-Mart Stores. However, 60 percent do have a formal mission document.[4] An increasing number of organizations every day are developing formal mission statements.

Some companies develop mission statements simply because they feel it is fashionable, rather than out of any real commitment. However, as will be described in this chapter, firms that develop and systematically revisit their mission, treat it as a living document, and consider it to be an integral part of the firms culture, realize great benefits. Johnson & Johnson (J&J) is an example firm. J&J managers meet regularly with employees to review, reword, and reaffirm the firm's mission. The entire J&J workforce recognizes the value that top management places on this exercise, and they respond accordingly.

THE IMPORTANCE OF A CLEAR MISSION

The importance of a mission statement to effective strategic management is well documented in the literature. A recent study comparing mission statements of Fortune 500 firms performing well and firms performing poorly concluded that high performers have more comprehensive mission statements than low performers.[5] King and Cleland recommend that organizations carefully develop a written mission statement for the following reasons:

1. To ensure unanimity of purpose within the organization.
2. To provide a basis, or standard, for allocating organizational resources.
3. To establish a general tone or organizational climate.
4. To serve as a focal point for individuals to identify with the organization's purpose and direction; and to deter those who cannot from participating further in the organization's activities.
5. To facilitate the translation of objectives into a work structure involving the assignment of tasks to responsible elements within the organization.
6. To specify organizational purposes and the translation of these purposes into objectives in such a way that cost, time, and performance parameters can be assessed and controlled.[6]

Reuben Mark, CEO of Colgate, maintains that a clear mission increasingly must make sense internationally. Colgate's mission can be summarized in five words: "We can be the best." Mark's thoughts on a mission statement are as follows:

When it comes to rallying everyone to the corporate banner, it's essential to push one vision globally rather than trying to drive home different messages in different cultures. The trick is to keep the vision simple but elevated: "We make the world's fastest computers" or "Telephone service for everyone." You're never going to get anyone to charge the machine guns only for financial objectives. It's got to be something that makes them feel better, feel a part of something.[7]

VISION VERSUS MISSION   Some organizations develop both a mission statement and a vision statement. Whereas the mission statement answers the question "What is our business?" the vision statement answers the question "What do we want to become?" Two example companies that have both a mission and vision statement are Amoco Corporation and Harley-Davidson Corporation, as given in Table 3–1.

It can be argued that profit, not mission or vision, is the primary corporate motivator. But profit alone is not enough to motivate people.[8] Profit is perceived negatively be some employees in companies. Employees may see profit as something that they earn and management then uses and even gives away—to shareholders. Although this perception is undesired

TABLE 3–1
Two Companies' Mission and Vision Statements

AMOCO CORPORATION

MISSION STATEMENT
Amoco is a worldwide integrated petroleum and chemical company. We find and develop petroleum resources and provide quality products and services for our customers. We conduct our business responsibly to achieve a superior financial return balanced with our long-term growth, benefiting shareholders and fulfilling our commitment to the community and the environment.

VISION STATEMENT
Amoco will be a global business enterprise, recognized throughout the world as preeminent by employees, customers, competitors, investors and the public. We will be the standard by which other businesses measure their performance. Our hallmarks will be the innovation, initiative and teamwork of our people and our ability to anticipate and effectively respond to change and to create opportunity.

HARLEY-DAVIDSON

MISSION STATEMENT
Stay true to the things that make a Harley-Davidson a Harley-Davidson. Keep the heritage alive. From the people in the front office to the craftsmen on our factory floor, that is what we do. And it's why each new generation of Harley-Davidson motorcycles, well refined, contains the best of the ones before it. We have a passion for our product few companies understand. But when you see the result, it all becomes clear. We're not just building motorcycles. We're carrying on a legend. Ask anyone who's ever owned a Harley-Davidson. It gets in your blood. Becomes a part of your life. And once it does, it never leaves. It's something you can't compare with anything else. We know because we've been there. That's why, for 90 years, we've remained firm in our commitment to building the kind of motorcycles that deserve the intense loyalty that Harley-Davidson enjoys. The styling is still pure. The engines still rumble. It's also why you'll see us at major rallies and rides throughout the year, listening and talking to our customers. Staying close to riders and to the sport is how we've kept alive the things that make a Harley-Davidson a Harley-Davidson. Our approach has always been different. But again, so has owning a Harley-Davidson. We wouldn't have it any other way.

VISION STATEMENT
Harley-Davidson, Inc. is an action oriented, international company—a leader in its commitment to continuously improve the quality of profitable relationships with stakeholders (customers, employees, suppliers, shareholders, governments, and society). Harley-Davidson believes the key to success is to balance stakeholders' interests through the empowerment of all employees to focus on value-added activities.
Our Vision is our corporate conscience and helps us to eliminate short-term thinking, such as cashing in on demand for our motorcycles by giving quantity precedence over quality or cutting corners in recreational or commercial vehicles to save a few dollars per unit. It also encourages every employee in our organization to be acutely aware of his or her role in satisfying our stakeholders.
Equally important to our Vision, we live by a Code of Business Conduct that is driven by a value system which promotes honesty, integrity, and personal growth in all our dealings with stakeholders. Our values are the rules by which we operate: Tell the truth; be fair; keep your promises; respect the individual; and encourage intellectual curiosity.
In addition, we never lose sight of the issues we feel must be addressed in order to be successful in the 1990s: Quality, participation, productivity, and cash flow. As a shareholder, you should expect no less from us.

and disturbing to management, it clearly indicates that both profit and vision are needed to effectively motivate a workforce.

When employees and managers together shape or fashion the vision or mission for a firm, the resultant document can reflect the personal visions that managers and employees have in their hearts and minds about their own future. Shared vision creates a commonality of interests that can lift workers out of the monotony of daily work and put them into a new world of opportunity and challenge.

THE PROCESS OF DEVELOPING A MISSION STATEMENT   As indicated in the strategic-management model, a clear mission statement is needed before alternative strategies can be formulated and implemented. It is important to involve as many managers as possible in the process of developing a mission statement, because through involvement, people become committed to an organization. Mark's comment above about machine guns accents the need for a good mission statement.

A widely used approach to developing a mission statement is to first select several articles about mission statements and ask all managers to read these as background information. Then ask managers to personally prepare a mission statement for the organization. A facilitator, or committee of top managers, then should merge these statements into a single document and distribute this draft mission statement to all managers. A request for modifications, additions, and deletions is needed next, along with a meeting to revise the document. To the extent that all managers have input into and support the final mission statement document, organizations can more easily obtain managers' support for other strategy formulation, implementation, and evaluation activities. Thus, the process of developing a mission statement represents a great opportunity for strategists to obtain needed support from all managers in the firm.

During the process of developing a mission statement, some organizations use discussion groups of managers to develop and modify the mission statement. Some organizations hire an outside consultant or facilitator to manage the process and help draft the language. Sometimes an outside person with expertise in developing mission statements and unbiased views can manage the process more effectively than an internal group or committee of managers. Decisions on how best to communicate the mission to all managers, employees, and external constituencies of an organization are needed when the document is in final form. Some organizations even develop a videotape to explain the mission statement and how it was developed.

A recent article by Campbell and Yeung emphasizes that the process of developing a mission statement should create an "emotional bond" and "sense of mission" between the organization and its employees.[9] Commitment to a company's strategy and intellectual agreement on the strategies to be pursued do not necessarily translate into an emotional bond; hence strategies that have been formulated may not be implemented. These researchers stress that an emotional bond comes when an individual personally identifies with the underlying values and behavior of a firm, thus turning intellectual agreement and commitment to strategy into a sense of mission. Campbell and Yeung also differentiate between the terms vision and mission, saying vision is "a possible and desirable future state of an organization" that includes specific goals, whereas mission is more associated with behavior and with the present.

THE NATURE OF A BUSINESS MISSION

A DECLARATION OF ATTITUDE   A mission statement is a declaration of attitude and outlook more than a statement of specific details. It is usually broad in scope for at least two major reasons. First, a good mission statement allows for the generation and consideration of a range of feasible alternative objectives and strategies without unduly stifling management creativity. Excess specificity would limit the potential of creative growth for the organization. On the other hand, an overly general statement that does not exclude any strategy alternatives could be dysfunctional. Apple Computer's mission statement, for example, should not open the possibility for diversification into pesticides, or Ford Motor Company's into food processing. As indicated in the Global Perspective, French mission statements are more general than British mission statements.

Second, a mission statement needs to be broad to effectively reconcile differences among and appeal to an organization's diverse stakeholders, the individuals and groups of persons who have a special stake or claim on the company. Stakeholders include employees, managers, stockholders, boards of directors, customers, suppliers, distributors, creditors, governments (local, state, federal, and foreign), unions, competitors, environmental groups, and the general public. Stakeholders affect and are affected by an organization's strategies, yet the claims and concerns of diverse constituencies vary and often conflict. For example, the general public is especially interested in social responsibility, whereas stockholders are more interested in profitability. Claims on any business may literally number in the thousands, and often include clean air, jobs, taxes, investment opportunities, career opportunities, equal employment opportunities, employee benefits, salaries, wages, clean water, and community services. All stakeholders' claims on an organization cannot be pursued with equal emphasis. A good mission statement indicates the relative attention that an organization will devote to meeting the claims of various stakeholders. More and more firms are becoming environmentally proactive in response to the concerns of stakeholders.

Reaching the fine balance between specificity and generality is difficult to achieve, but is well worth the effort. George Steiner offers the following insight on the need for a mission statement to be broad in scope:

> Most business statements of mission are expressed at high levels of abstraction. Vagueness nevertheless has its virtues. Mission statements are not designed to express concrete ends, but rather to provide motivation, general direction, an image, a tone, and a philosophy to guide the enterprise. An excess of detail could prove counterproductive since concrete specification

GLOBAL PERSPECTIVE

British Versus French Mission Statements

Researchers recently studied the mission statements of British and French firms. Results are summarized here.

Researchers found that a highly participative (French) approach to developing a mission statement is more effective in gaining employee commitment than a less participative (British) approach. Differences between British and French statements are rooted in or attributed to different culture, social, and economic factors in the two countries. For example, in Britain the predominance of equity financing has led to companies being frequently bought and sold like commodities. In contrast, the traditons of family ownership are stronger in France, providing a sense of community and a better basis for development of shared mission statements.

Source: Adapted from "Sharing the Vision: Company Mission Statements in Britain and France," *Long Range Planning* (February 1994): 84–94.

CHARACTERISTICS OF DOCUMENT	BRITAIN	FRANCE
Length	Short	Long
Specificity	Specific	General
Emphasis	Financial goals	Value to society
Architects	Top managers	All managers and employees
Durability	A year or less	Several years
Focus	Internal	Internal and external

NATURAL ENVIRONMENT

Is Your Firm Environmentally Proactive?

Conducting business in a way that preserves the natural environment is more than just good public relations; it is good business. Preserving the environment is a permanent part of doing business, for the following reasons:

1. Consumer demand for environmentally safe products and packages is increasing dramatically.

2. Public opinion demanding that firms conduct business in ways that preserve the natural environment is strong.

3. Environmental advocacy groups now have over 20 million Americans as members.

4. Federal and state environmental regulations are changing rapidly and becoming more complex.

5. More lenders are examining the environmental liabilities of businesses seeking loans.

6. Many consumers, suppliers, distributors, and investors shun doing business with environmentally weak firms.

7. Liability suits and fines against firms having environment problems are on the rise.

More and more firms are becoming environmentally proactive, which means taking the initiative to develop and implement strategies that preserve the environment while enhancing the firm's efficiency and effectiveness. The old undesirable alternative is to be environmentally reactive—waiting until environmental pressures are thrust upon the firm by law or consumer pressure. A reactive environmental policy often leads to high cleanup costs, numerous liability suits, loss in market share, reduced customer loyalty, and higher medical costs. In contrast, a proactive policy views environmental pressures as opportunities, and includes such actions as developing green products and packages, conserving energy, reducing waste, recycling, and creating a corporate culture that is environmentally sensitive.

A proactive policy forces a company to innovate and upgrade processes; this leads to reduced waste, improved efficiency, better quality, and greater profits. Successful firms today assess "the profit in preserving the environment" in decisions ranging from developing a mission statement to determining plant location, manufacturing technology, product design, packaging, and consumer relations. A proactive environmental policy is simply good business.

Source: Adapted from "The Profit in Preserving America," *Forbes* (November 11, 1991): 181–189.

could be the base for rallying opposition. Precision might stifle creativity in the formulation of an acceptable mission or purpose. Once an aim is cast in concrete it creates a rigidity in an organization and resists change. Vagueness leaves room for other managers to fill in the details, perhaps even to modify general patterns. Vagueness permits more flexibility in adapting to changing environments and internal operations. It facilitates flexibility in implementation.[10]

An effective mission statement arouses positive feelings and emotions about an organization; it is inspiring in the sense that it motivates readers to action. An effective mission statement generates the impression that a firm is successful, has direction, and is worthy of time, support, and investment. Japanese firms believe strongly in the emotional aspect of a mission statement, as revealed in this chapter's Natural Environment Perspective.

It reflects judgments about future growth directions and strategies based upon forward-looking external and internal analyses. A business mission should provide useful criteria for selecting among alternative strategies. A clear mission statement provides a basis for generating and screening strategic options. The statement of mission should be dynamic in orientation, allowing judgments about the most promising growth directions and those considered less promising.

A RESOLUTION OF DIVERGENT VIEWS   What are the reasons some strategists are reluctant to develop a statement of their business mission? First, the question, "What is our business?" can create controversy. Raising the question often reveals differences among strategists in the organization. Individuals who have worked together for a long time and who think they know each other may suddenly realize that they are in fundamental disagreement. For example, in a college or university, divergent views regarding the relative importance of teaching, research, and service are often expressed during the mission statement development process. Negotiation, compromise, and eventual agreement on important issues is needed before focusing on more specific strategy-formulation activities.

> "What is our mission?" is a genuine decision; and a genuine decision must be based on divergent views to have a chance to be a right and effective decision. Developing a business mission is always a choice between alternatives, each of which rests on different assumptions regarding the reality of the business and its environment. It is always a high-risk decision. A change in mission always leads to changes in objectives, strategies, organization, and behavior. The mission decision is far too important to be made by acclamation. Developing a business mission is a big step toward management effectiveness. Hidden or half-understood disagreements on the definition of a business mission underlie many of the personality problems, communication problems, and irritations that tend to divide a top-management group. Establishing a mission should never be made on plausibility alone, should never be made fast, and should never be made painlessly.[11]

Considerable disagreement among an organization's strategists over basic purpose and mission can cause trouble if not resolved. For example, unresolved disagreement over the business mission was one of the reasons for W. T. Grant's bankruptcy and eventual liquidation. As one executive reported,

> There was a lot of dissension within the company whether we should go the Kmart route or go after the Montgomery Ward and J. C. Penney position. Ed Staley and Lou Lustenberger (two top executives) were at loggerheads over the issue, with the upshot being we took a position between the two and that consequently stood for nothing.[12]

Too often, strategists develop a statement of business mission only when their organization is in trouble. Of course it is needed then. Developing and communicating a clear mission during troubled times may indeed have spectacular results and may even reverse decline. However, to wait until an organization is in trouble to develop a mission statement is a gamble that characterizes irresponsible management! According to Drucker, the most important time to ask seriously, "What is our business?" is when a company has been successful:

NATURAL ENVIRONMENT
Japanese Mission Statements

Japanese firms are actively including environmental affairs in their mission statements. Mr. Kouichi Yanagida, secretary-general of The Defense of Green Earth Foundation, says "almost every company in Japan with acumen at all has taken on the green (environmental) ideal." The green message is particularly effective in improving corporate images. The Japanese are strong on the importance of "mood" and "emotions" in developing mission statements. The idea is that no matter what the product or company, it is the good feeling associated with the mission statement that makes the difference. The green message is important not only in selling products but also in attracting new employees. Young Japanese are much more environmentally aware than their elders.

Industry surveys reveal that producing recycled paper requires 30 percent less water and 60 percent less electricity than conventional paper manufacturing. Nearly 50 percent of the 30 million tons of paper produced in Japan annually consists of recycled paper, mostly from discarded newspapers and paperboard. This contrasts with the United States, where 70 million tons of paper are produced annually, but only 22 million of that is recycled, a ratio of about 32 percent. Japanese firms are also designing products so that parts can be easily removed and recycled. The environmental dimension of Japanese firms' mission statements is thus not merely public relations; it is an integral part of strategic-management thought and action.

Success always obsoletes the very behavior that achieved it, always creates new realities, and always creates new and different problems. Only the fairy story ends, "They lived happily ever after." It is never popular to argue with success or to rock the boat. The ancient Greeks knew that the penalty of success can be severe. The management that does not ask, "What is our mission?" when the company is successful is, in effect, smug, lazy, and arrogant. It will not be long before success will turn into failure. Sooner or later, even the most successful answer to the question, "What is our business?" becomes obsolete.[13]

A CUSTOMER ORIENTATION

A good mission statement reflects the anticipations of customers. Rather than developing a product and then trying to find a market, the operating philosophy of organizations should be to identify customers' needs and then provide a product or service to fulfill those needs. Good mission statements identify the utility of a firm's products to its customers. This is why AT&T's mission statement focuses on communication rather than telephones, Exxon's mission statement focuses on energy rather than oil and gas, Union Pacific's mission statement focuses on transportation rather than railroads, and Universal Studios' mission statement focuses on entertainment instead of movies. The following utility statements are relevant in developing a mission statement:

Do not offer me things.

Do not offer me clothes. Offer me attractive looks.

Do not offer me shoes. Offer me comfort for my feet and the pleasure of walking.

Do not offer me a house. Offer me security, comfort, and a place that is clean and happy.

Do not offer me books. Offer me hours of pleasure and the benefit of knowledge.

Do not offer me records. Offer me leisure and the sound of music.

Do not offer me tools. Offer me the benefit and the pleasure of making beautiful things.

Do not offer me furniture. Offer me comfort and the quietness of a cozy place.

Do not offer me things. Offer me ideas, emotions, ambience, feelings, and benefits.

Please, do not offer me things.

A major reason for developing a business mission is to attract customers who give meaning to an organization. As indicated in the Information Technology Perspective, bank

INFORMATION TECHNOLOGY
Banks on the Brink

"Banking is vital to a healthy economy. Banks are not." This was the message a recent banking expert gave to a banking convention. Taking time to physically go to a bank is increasingly being seen as wasted time by consumers. Banking is a value-added information business; technology is making it continually easier for customers to manage their money anywhere, anytime. First Chicago now penalizes customers who use tellers by charging them $3 per visit. Security First, a savings bank, recently opened its doors on the Internet. "We'll be a one-branch bank in Kentucky with potential customers all over the U.S.," says CEO James Mahan III. Citibank has recently dropped all of its fees for electronic banking. William Randle warns that banks are becoming "buttons on a network operated by other entities."

There are over 40 million personal computers in the home in the United States. Four million of these computers did home banking in 1995, and this figure is expected to double annually in the 1990s. All the brick and mortar currently owned by banks is becoming a competitive disadvantage as home banking gains in popularity.

Banks are having to make strategic decisions regarding their electronic future. Should they sell some of their many office buildings? Should they form software partnerships, acquire software companies, or develop their own software? Should they merge with a competitor? Chase Manhattan and First Chicago recently formed partnerships with Intuit and Microsoft. NationsBank and Bank of America recently acquired software companies. First Union Corporation has created in Charlotte an electronic mall for Internet transactions.

Source: Adapted from Kelly Holland and Amy Cortese, "Faster Phone Networks? Any Decade Now," *Business Week* (June 12, 1995): 68–79.

customers increasingly desire online services and home banking. This change is requiring many banks to rethink their mission. A classic description of the purpose of a business reveals the relative importance of customers in a statement of mission:

> It is the customer who determines what a business is. It is the customer alone whose willingness to pay for a good or service converts economic resources into wealth and things into goods. What a business thinks it produces is not of first importance, especially not to the future of the business and to its success. What the customer thinks he/she is buying, what he/she considers value, is decisive—it determines what a business is, what it produces, and whether it will prosper. And what the customer buys and considers value is never a product. It is always utility, meaning what a product or service does for him. The customer is the foundation of a business and keeps it in existence.[14]

A DECLARATION OF SOCIAL POLICY   The words *social policy* embrace managerial philosophy and thinking at the highest levels of an organization. For this reason, social policy affects the development of a business mission statement. Social issues mandate that strategists consider not only what the organization owes its various stakeholders but also what responsibilities the firm has to consumers, environmentalists, minorities, communities, and other groups. After decades of debate on the topic of social responsibility, many firms still struggle to determine appropriate social policies.

The issue of social responsibility arises when a company establishes its business mission. The impact of society on business and vice versa, is becoming more pronounced each year. Social policies directly affect a firm's customers, products and services, markets, technology, profitability, self-concept, and public image. An organization's social policy should be integrated into all strategic-management activities, including the development of a mission statement. Carroll and Hoy assert that corporate social policy should be designed and articulated during strategy formulation, set and administered during strategy implementation, and reaffirmed or changed during strategy evaluation.[15] The emerging view of social responsibility holds that social issues should be attended to both directly and indirectly in determining strategies.

Firms should strive to engage in social activities that have economic benefits. For example, Merck & Company recently developed the drug ivermectin for treating river blindness, a disease caused by a fly-borne parasitic worm endemic in poor tropical areas of Africa, the Middle East, and Latin America. In an unprecedented gesture that reflected its corporate commitment to social responsibility, Merck then made ivermectin available at no cost to medical personnel throughout the world. Merck's action highlights the dilemma of orphan drugs, which offer pharmaceutical companies no economic incentive for development and distribution.

Despite differences in approaches, most American companies try to assure outsiders that they conduct business in a socially responsible way. The mission statement is an effective instrument for conveying this message. The Norton Company, for example, concludes its mission statement by saying:

> In order to fulfill this mission, Norton will continue to demonstrate a sense of responsibility to the public interest and to earn the respect and loyalty of its customers, employees, shareholders, and suppliers, and the communities in which it does business.[16]

COMPONENTS OF A MISSION STATEMENT

Mission statements can and do vary in length, content, format, and specificity. Most practitioners and academicians of strategic management consider an effective statement to exhibit nine characteristics or components. Since a mission statement is often the most visible and public part of the strategic-management process, it is important that it includes all of these essential components. Components and corresponding questions that a mission statement should answer are given here.

1. *Customers:* Who are the firm's customers?
2. *Products or services:* What are the firm's major products or services?
3. *Markets:* Geographically, where does the firm compete?
4. *Technology:* Is the firm technologically current?
5. *Concern for survival, growth, and profitability:* Is the firm committed to growth and financial soundness?
6. *Philosophy:* What are the basic beliefs, values, aspirations, and ethical priorities of the firm?
7. *Self-concept:* What is the firm's distinctive competence or major competitive advantage?
8. *Concern for public image:* Is the firm responsive to social, community, and environmental concerns?
9. *Concern for employees:* Are employees a valuable asset of the firm?

Excerpts from the mission statements of different organizations are provided in Table 3–2 to exemplify the nine essential components.

WRITING AND EVALUATING MISSION STATEMENTS

Perhaps the best way to develop a skill for writing and evaluating mission statements is to study actual company missions. Therefore, eleven mission statements are presented in Table 3–3. These statements are then evaluated in Table 3–4 based on the nine criteria presented in the previous section.

There is no one best mission statement for a particular organization, so good judgment is required in evaluating mission statements. In Table 3–4, a yes indicates that the given mission statement answers satisfactorily the question posed in Table 3–3 for the respective evaluative criteria. For example, the yes under customers for the Chase Manhattan mission statement means this statement answers "Who are our customers?" Notice that Chase Manhattan's customers are "individuals, industries, communities, and countries." A no would mean a particular mission statement does not answer or answers unsatisfactorily the key question associated with one of the nine evaluative criteria. For example, note that the Apple Computer, AT&T, BellSouth, and Corning mission statements do not identify the organization's customers. To determine whether a particular statement satisfactorily includes a given component, ask yourself the following question: "If I were responsible for writing a mission statement for this organization, would I have communicated this component better?" If your answer is yes, then record a no in the evaluation matrix. Generally, simple inclusion of the word *customers* or *employees* or *technology* is not adequately informative or inspiring in a statement.

Table 3–4 indicates that the Bancorp Hawaii mission statement is the "best" and the Corning mission statement is the "worst" of the examples. Overall, the example mission statements are weakest in the areas of technology, philosophy, and concern for survival, growth, and profitability. The statements are strongest in the areas of products or services, markets, and self-concept.

Let's focus specifically for a moment on the Apple Computer mission statement. Note that the statement does not include coverage of the Customer component, which could be individuals, businesses, educational institutions, and governmental agencies. Apple's statement does include the Product/Service component in saying, "We provide exceptional personal computing products and innovative customer services." The Apple statement includes coverage of the Market component in saying, "We help people around the world" and includes the tech-

TABLE 3–2
Examples of the Nine Essential Components of a Mission Statement

---

1. CUSTOMERS

We believe our first responsibility is to the doctors, nurses, and patients, to mothers and all others who use our products and services. (Johnson & Johnson)

---

2. PRODUCTS OR SERVICES

AMAX's principal products are molybdenum, coal, iron ore, copper, lead, zinc, petroleum and natural gas, potash, phosphates, nickel, tungsten, silver, gold, and magnesium. (AMAX)

Standard Oil Company (Indiana) is in business to find and produce crude oil, natural gas, and natural gas liquids; to manufacture high quality products useful to society from these raw materials; and to distribute and market those products and to provide dependable related services to the consuming public at reasonable prices. (Standard Oil Company)

---

3. MARKETS

We are dedicated to the total success of Corning Glass Works as a worldwide competitor. (Corning Glass Works)

Our emphasis is on North American markets, although global opportunities will be explored. (Blockway)

---

4. TECHNOLOGY

Control Data is in the business of applying micro-electronics and computer technology in two general areas: computer-related hardware; and computing-enhancing services, which include computation, information, education and finance (Control Data)

The common technology in these areas is discrete particle coatings. (Nashua)

---

5. CONCERN FOR SURVIVAL, GROWTH, AND PROFITABILITY

In this respect, the company will conduct its operations prudently, and will provide the profits and growth which will assure Hoover's ultimate success. (Hoover Universal)

To serve the worldwide need for knowledge at a fair profit by gathering, evaluating, producing and distributing valuable information in a way that benefits our customers, employees, authors, investors, and our society. (McGraw-Hill)

---

6. PHILOSOPHY

We believe human development to be the worthiest of the goals of civilization and independence to be the superior condition for nurturing growth in the capabilities of people. (Sun Company)

It's all part of the Mary Kay philosophy—a philosophy based on the golden rule. A spirit of sharing and caring where people give cheerfully of their time, knowledge, and experience. (Mary Kay Cosmetics)

---

7. SELF-CONCEPT

Crown Zellerbach is committed to leapfrogging competition within 1,000 days by unleashing the constructive and creative abilities and energies of each of its employees. (Crown Zellerbach)

---

8. CONCERN FOR PUBLIC IMAGE

To share the world's obligation for the protection of the environment. (Dow Chemical)

To contribute to the economic strength of society and function as a good corporate citizen on a local, state, and national basis in all countries in which we do business. (Pfizer)

---

9. CONCERN FOR EMPLOYEES

To recruit, develop, motivate, reward, and retain personnel of exceptional ability, character and dedication by providing good working conditions, superior leadership, compensation on the basis of performance, an attractive benefit program, opportunity for growth, and a high degree of employment security. (The Wachovia Corporation)

To compensate its employees with remuneration and fringe benefits competitive with other employment opportunities in its geographical area and commensurate with their contributions toward efficient corporate operations. (Public Service Electric and Gas Company)

---

nology component in saying, "We find innovative ways to use computing technology." No mention of Concern for Survival, Growth, and Profitability is given in the statement. Nor is coverage of the Philosophy, Concern for Public Image, or Concern for Employees components. The Apple mission statement includes coverage of Self-concept by mentioning education, which is

TABLE 3–3
Mission Statements of Eleven Organizations

AMERICAN HOME PRODUCTS

American Home Products Corporation makes a significant contribution to health care worldwide as a leader in researching, developing, manufacturing and marketing products that meet important health needs.

Our prescription drugs, nutritionals, over-the-counter medications, and medical devices, supplies and instrumentation benefit millions of people. We also produce and market well-known quality food brands in the United States and Canada.

We are focused on improving health care by finding and commercializing innovative, cost-effective therapies and technologies. Key to our efforts are efficient manufacturing, global distribution and marketing, and strict financial controls.

In 1992, American Home Products Corporation achieved record sales and earnings, and the company increased its dividend for the 41st consecutive year.

PFIZER, INC.

Pfizer, Inc. is a research-based, global health care company. Our principal mission is to apply scientific knowledge to help people around the world enjoy longer, healthier and more productive lives. The company has four business segments: health care, consumer health care, food science and animal health. We manufacture in 39 countries, and our products are available worldwide.

CHASE MANHATTAN CORPORATION

We provide financial services that enhance the well-being and success of individuals, industries, communities and countries around the world.

Through our shared commitment to those we serve, we will be the best financial services company in the world.

Customers will choose us first because we deliver the highest quality service and performance.

People will be proud and eager to work here.

Investors will buy our stock as a superior long-term investment.

To be the best for our customers, we are team players who show respect for our colleagues and commit to the highest standards of quality and professionalism.

    Customer focus
    Respect for each other
    Teamwork
    Quality
    Professionalism

FOOD LION, INC.

The Food Lion team will work hard to use our *talents* and *resourcefulness* to satisfy every customer by providing Extra Low Prices on a wide variety of quality products in a *clean, convenient,* and *friendly* environment.

APPLE COMPUTER

It is Apple's mission to help transform the way customers work, learn and communicate by providing exceptional personal computing products and innovative customer services.

We will pioneer new directions and approaches, finding innovative ways to use computing technology to extend the bounds of human potential.

Apple will make a difference: our products, services and insights will help people around the world shape the ways business and education will be done in the 21st century.

AT&T

We are dedicated to being the world's best at bringing people together—giving them easy access to each other and to the information and services they want—anytime, anywhere.

BANCORP HAWAII, INC.

The mission of Bancorp Hawaii is to be the finest, most effective financial services organization in the state of Hawaii and the Pacific markets we serve.

As a family of companies built around an outstanding regional bank, we will sell and deliver a broad range of services that meet the needs of our customers at prices which are competitive and consistent with our profit goals.

Our basic business strategy is to identify, understand and then satisfy the financial needs and wants of consumers, businesses, and governments. We will be alert to changes which impact our businesses and exercise initiative to capitalize on new opportunities.

continued

TABLE 3–3   continued

3 The geographic scope of our business will be expanded only to areas where our unique background, experience and capabilities will give us a competitive advantage and a reasonable opportunity for an adequate financial return. We will introduce only those new financial services which we can perform well.

4 Two primary goals are to achieve significant reductions in noninterest expense through enhanced productivity and automation and to increase noninterest income by marketing fee-based services.

5 We want to conduct our business under conditions largely determined by ourselves and will, therefore, always maintain a strong financial position. Our goal is to consistently rank among the top 10 percent of our peer group in terms of financial performance. This will ensure that we will fulfill our responsibility to increase the value of our shareholders' investment.

6 We will maintain a stimulating work environment—one that encourages, recognizes, and rewards high achievers, at all levels of the organization.

8 We will always conduct ourselves with integrity and endeavor to be a good neighbor and a responsible corporate citizen.

BELLSOUTH CORPORATION

BellSouth Corporation provides information services in local exchange and exchange access markets in its nine-state franchised territory. It also provides communications services and products such as advertising and publishing, mobile cellular telephone service, paging, and telecommunications and computer systems through its entities, in both the nine-state region and other major U.S. and international markets.

CORNING, INC.

Our purpose is to deliver superior, long-range economic benefits to our customers, our employees, our shareholders, and to the communities in which we operate. We accomplish this by living our corporate values.

NICHOLLS STATE UNIVERSITY (COLLEGE OF BUSINESS)

The principal mission of the College of Business is to prepare students to participate in society and the work force as educated individuals able to compete in a dynamic global economy. In order to enrich the learning process, the College also contributes to scholarship through applied research and instructional development. In addition to providing support to the employer community through the development of marketable skills in potential employees, the College also enhances the competitive capabilities of regional businesses by providing continuing education courses and consulting services through the Small Business Development Center (SBDC) and the individual efforts of faculty. The faculty advances the welfare of the University, the community, and academic and professional organizations through professional interactions.

SAM HOUSTON STATE UNIVERSITY (COLLEGE OF BUSINESS ADMINISTRATION)

The mission of the College of Business Administration is to support Sam Houston State University's mission by providing students with the educational experience in the field of business necessary to become productive citizens, to develop successful business-related careers and to provide interested students with the background necessary to pursue advanced studies in the field of business and related fields. The educational experience at the undergraduate and master's levels is designed to provide students with the intellectual flexibility to be successful in a dynamic business environment.

The highest priority of the College of Business Administration is teaching, primarily at the undergraduate level. In addition, the College encourages faculty professional development, scholarly productivity, and service to benefit all stakeholders: students, alumni, donors, regional businesses, and the State of Texas.

a segment of the industry that Apple does especially well. Overall, the Apple statement includes only three of the nine essential mission statement components.

In multidivisional organizations, strategists should ensure that divisional units perform strategic-management tasks, including the development of a statement of mission. Each division should involve its own managers and employees in developing a mission statement consistent with and supportive of the corporative mission. Anchor Hocking is an example of a multinational organization that has developed an overall corporate mission statement and a statement for each of its eight divisions. Notice that the Nicholls State and Sam Houston State mission statements that are given in Table 3–3 are for those in situations at the College of Business rather than in the university at large.

An organization that fails to develop a comprehensive and inspiring mission statement loses the opportunity to present itself favorably to existing and potential stakeholders.

TABLE 3–4
An Evaluation Matrix of Mission Statements

EVALUATIVE CRITERIA

COMPANY	CUSTOMERS	PRODUCTS/ SERVICES	MARKETS	CONCERN FOR SURVIVAL, GROWTH, AND PROFITABILITY	TECHNOLOGY
American Home Products	Yes	Yes	Yes	Yes	Yes
Pfizer, Inc.	Yes	Yes	Yes	No	No
Chase Manhattan Corporation	Yes	Yes	Yes	No	Yes
Food Lion, Inc.	Yes	No	No	No	No
Apple Computer	No	No	Yes	Yes	No
AT&T	No	No	Yes	No	No
Bancorp Hawaii, Inc.	Yes	Yes	Yes	No	Yes
BellSouth Corporation	No	Yes	Yes	No	No
Corning, Inc.	No	No	No	No	No
Nicholls State University	Yes	Yes	No	No	No
Sam Houston State University	Yes	Yes	Yes	No	No

COMPANY	PHILOSOPHY	SELF-CONCEPT	CONCERN FOR PUBLIC IMAGE	CONCERN FOR EMPLOYEES
American Home Products	No	Yes	No	No
Pfizer, Inc.	No	No	No	No
Chase Manhattan Corporation	Yes	Yes	Yes	Yes
Food Lion, Inc.	No	Yes	No	No
Apple Computer	No	Yes	No	No
AT&T	No	Yes	No	No
Bancorp Hawaii, Inc.	Yes	Yes	Yes	Yes
BellSouth Corporation	No	No	No	No
Corning, Inc.	Yes	No	Yes	Yes
Nicholls State University	No	Yes	Yes	Yes
Sam Houston State University	No	Yes	Yes	Yes

All organizations need customers, employees, and managers, and most firms need creditors, suppliers, and distributors. The business mission statement is an effective vehicle for communicating with important internal and external stakeholders. The principal value of a mission statement as a tool of strategic management is derived from its specification of the ultimate aims of a firm:

> It provides managers with a unity of direction that transcends individual, parochial, and transitory needs. It promotes a sense of shared expectations among all levels and generations of employees. It consolidates values over time and across individuals and interest groups. It projects a sense of worth and intent that can be identified and assimilated by company outsiders. Finally, it affirms the company's commitment to responsible action, which is symbiotic with its need to preserve and protect the essential claims of insiders for sustained survival, growth, and profitability of the firm.[17]

CONCLUSION

Every organization has a unique purpose and reason for being. This uniqueness should be reflected in a statement of mission. The nature of a business mission can represent either a competitive advantage or disadvantage for the firm. An organization achieves a heightened sense of purpose when strategists, managers, and employees develop and communicate a clear business mission. Drucker says developing a clear business mission is the "first responsibility of strategists." A good mission statement reveals an organization's customers, products or services, markets, technology, concern for survival, philosophy, self-concept, concern for public image, and concern for employees. These nine basic components serve as a practical framework for evaluating and writing mission statements. Being the first step in strategic-management, the mission statement provides direction for all planning activities.

A well-designed mission statement is essential for formulating, implementing, and evaluating strategy. Developing and communicating a clear business mission is one of the most commonly overlooked tasks in strategic management. Without a clear statement of mission, a firm's short-term actions can be counterproductive to long-term interests. A mission statement should always be subject to revision, but, if carefully prepared, it will require major changes only infrequently. Organizations usually reexamine their mission statement annually. Effective mission statements stand the test of time.

A mission statement is an essential tool for strategists, a fact illustrated in a short story told by Porsche CEO Peter Schultz:

> Three people were at work on a construction site. All were doing the same job, but when each was asked what his job was, the answers varied. "Breaking rocks," the first replied, "Earning a living," responded the second. "Helping to build a cathedral," said the third. Few of us can build cathedrals. But to the extent we can see the cathedral in whatever cause we are following, the job seems more worthwhile. Good strategists and a clear mission help us find those cathedrals in what otherwise could be dismal issues and empty causes.[18]

TAKE IT TO THE NET

We invite you to visit the DAVID page on the Prentice Hall Web site at:
http://www.prenhall.com/davidsm
for this chapter's World Wide Web exercises.

KEY TERMS AND CONCEPTS

Concern for Employees	(p. 88)	Markets	(p. 88)	Social Policy	(p. 87)
Concern for Public Image	(p. 88)	Mission Statement	(p.78)	Stakeholders	(p. 83)
Concern for Survival, Growth, and Profitability	(p. 88)	Mission Statement Components	(p. 88)	Technology	(p. 88)
		Philosophy	(p. 88)	Vision	(p. 81)
Creed Statement	(p. 78)	Products or Services	(p. 88)		
Customers	(p. 88)	Self-Concept	(p. 88)		

ISSUES FOR REVIEW AND DISCUSSION

1. Do local service stations need to have written mission statements? Why or why not?

2. Why do you think organizations that have a comprehensive mission tend to be high performers? Does having a comprehensive mission cause high performance?

3. Explain why a mission statement should not include strategies and objectives.

4. What is your college or university's self-concept? How would you state that in a mission statement?

5. Explain the principal value of a mission statement.

6. Why is it important for a mission statement to be reconciliatory?

7. In your opinion, what are the three most important components to include in writing a mission statement? Why?

8. How would the mission statements of a for-profit and a non-profit organization differ?

9. Write a business mission statement for an organization of your choice.

10. Go to your nearest library and look in the annual reports of corporations. Find a mission statement, make a photocopy of the document, bring the copy to class, and evaluate the document.

11. Who are the major stakeholders of the bank that you do business with locally? What are the major claims of those stakeholders?

12. Select one of the current readings at the end of this chapter. Look up that article in your college library and give a five-minute oral report to the class summarizing the article.

NOTES

1. Peter Drucker, *Management: Tasks, Responsibilities, and Practices* (New York: Harper & Row, 1974): 61.

2. Barnett Bank, Internal document, (1993).

3. Vern McGinnis, "The Mission Statement: A Key Step in Strategic Planning," *Business* 31, no. 6 (November–December 1981): 41.

4. Fred David, "How Companies Define Their Mission," *Long Range Planning* 22, no. 1 (February 1989): 90–92. Also, see John Pearce II and Fred David, "Corporate Mission Statements: The Bottom Line," *Academy of Management Executive* 1, no. 2 (May 1987): 110.

5. John Pearce II and Fred David, "Corporate Mission Statements: The Bottom Line," *Academy of Management Executive* 1, no. 2 (May 1987): 110.

6. W. R. King and D. I. Cleland, *Strategic Planning and Policy* (New York: Van Nostrand Reinhold, 1979): 124.

7. Brian Dumaine, "What the Leaders of Tomorrow See," *Fortune* (July 3, 1989): 50.

8. Joseph Quigley, "Vision: How Leaders Develop It, Share it and Sustain It," *Business Horizons* (September–October 1994): 39.

9. Andrew Campbell and Sally Yeung, "Creating a Sense of Mission," *Long Range Planning* 24, no. 4 (August 1991): 17.

10. George Steiner, *Strategic Planning: What Every Manager Must Know* (New York: The Free Press, 1979): 160.

11. Drucker, 78, 79.

12. "How W. T. Grant Lost $175 Million Last Year," *Business Week* (February 25, 1975): 75.

13. Drucker, 88.

14. Drucker, 61.

15. Archie Carroll and Frank Hoy, "Integrating Corporate Social Policy into Strategic Management," *Journal of Business Strategy* 4, no. 3 (Winter 1984): 57.

16. The Norton Company, *Annual Report* (1981).

17. John Pearce II, "The Company Mission as a Strategic Tool," *Sloan Management Review* 23, no. 3 (Spring 1982): 74.

18. Robert Waterman, Jr., *The Renewal Factor: How the Best Get and Keep the Competitive Edge* (New York: Bantam, 1987). Also, *Business Week* (September 14, 1987): 120.

CURRENT READINGS

Ackoff, Russell. "Mission Statements." *Planning Review* 15, no. 4 (July–August 1987): 30–32.

Bartlett, Christopher A. and Sumantra Ghoshal. "Changing the Role of Top Management: Beyond Strategy to Purpose." *Harvard Business Review* (November–December 1994): 79–90.

Bertodo, R. "The Role of Suppliers in Implementing a Strategic Vision." *Long Range Planning* 24, no. 3 (June 1991): 40–48.

Brabet, Julienne and Mary Klemm. "Sharing the Vision: Company Mission Statements in Britain and France." *Long Range Planning* 27, no. 1 (February 1994): 84–94.

Byars, Lloyd. "Organizational Philosophy and Mission Statements." *Planning Review* 15, no. 4 (July–August 1987): 32–36.

Campbell, Andrew. "The Power of Mission: Aligning Strategy and Culture." *Planning Review* 20, no. 5 (September–October 1992): 10–12.

Campbell, Andrew and Sally Yeung, "Brief Case: Mission, Vision and Strategic Intent." *Long Range Planning* 24, no. 4 (August 1991): 145–147.

Campbell, Andrew and Sally Yeung. "Creating a Sense of Mission." *Long Range Planning* 24, no. 4 (August 1991): 10–20.

Collins, James C. and Jerry I. Porras. "Building a Visionary Company." *California Management Review* 37, no. 2 (Winter 1995): 80–100.

Cummings, Stephen and John Davies. "Brief Case—Mission, Vision, Fusion." *Long Range Planning* 27, no. 6 (December 1994): 147–150.

David, Fred R. "How Companies Define Their Mission." *Long Range Planning* 22, no. 1 (February 1989): 90–97.

Dowling, G.R. "Developing Your Company Image into a Corporate Asset." *Long Range Planning* 26, no. 2 (April 1993): 101–109.

Graves, Samuel B. and Sandra A. Waddock. "Institutional Owners and Corporate Social Performance." *Academy of Management Journal* 37, no. 4 (August 1994): 1034–1046.

Ireland, R. Duane and Michael A. Hitt. "Mission Statements: Importance, Challenge, and Recommendations for Development." *Business Horizons* 35, no. 3 (May–June 1992): 34–42.

Kamfer, Louis. "Enscaling the Mission Statement as a Procedure for Organizational Diagnosis." *South African Journal of Business Management* 22, no. 1 (1991): 1–8.

Klemm, Mary, Stuart Sanderson, and George Luffman. "Mission Statements: Selling Corporate Values to Employees." *Long Range Planning* 24, no. 3 (June 1991): 73–78.

Kolesar, Peter J. "Vision, Values, and Milestones: TQM at Alcoa." *California Management Review* 35, no. 3 (Spring 1993): 133–165.

Larwood, Laurie, Cecelia M. Falbe, Mark P. Kriger, and Paul Miesing. "Structure and Meaning of Organizational Vision." *Academy of Management Journal* 38 no. 2 (April 1995): 740–769.

Lavin, Douglas. "Robert Eaton Thinks 'Vision' Is Overrated and He's Not Alone." *Wall Street Journal*, October 4, 1993: A1, A8.

McTavish, Ron. "One More Time: What Business are You In?" *Long Range Planning* 28, no. 2 (April 1995): 49–60.

Meyer, Christopher. "2020 Vision." *Planning Review* 20, no. 5 (September–October 1992): 39–41.

Osborne, Richard L. "Core Value Statements: The Corporate Compass." *Business Horizons* 34, no. 5 (September/October 1991): 28–34.

Oswald, S. L., K. W. Mossholder and S. G. Harris. "Vision Salience and Strategic Involvement: Implications for Psychological Attachment to Organization and Job." *Strategic Management Journal* 15, no. 6 (July 1994): 477–490.

Quigley, Joseph. "Vision: How Leaders Develop It, Share It, and Sustain It." *Business Horizons* 37, no. 5 (September–October 1994): 37–41.

Rogers, James E., Jr., "Adopting and Implementing a Corporate Environmental Charter." *Business Horizons* 35, no. 2 (March–April 1992): 29–33.

Schoemaker, Paul, J. H., "How to Link Strategic Vision to Core Capabilities." *Sloan Management Review* 34, no. 1 (Fall 1992): 67–82.

Snyder, Neil, and Michelle Graves. "Leadership and Vision." *Business Horizons* 37, no. 1 (January–February 1994): 1–7.

Swanson, Diane L. "Addressing a Theoretical Problem by Reorienting the Corporate Social Performance Model." *Academy of Management Review* 20, no. 1 (January 1995): 43–64.

Experiential Exercise 3A

EVALUATING MISSION STATEMENTS

PURPOSE

A business mission statement is an integral part of strategic management. It provides direction for formulating, implementing, and evaluating strategic activities. This exercise will give you practice evaluating mission statements, a skill that is prerequisite to writing a good mission statement.

INSTRUCTIONS

Step 1 Your instructor will select some or all of the following mission statements to evaluate. On a separate sheet of paper, construct an evaluation matrix like the one presented in Table 3–4. Evaluate the mission statements based on the nine criteria presented in the chapter.

Step 2 Record a *yes* in all cells of the evaluation matrix when the respective mission statement satisfactorily meets the desired criteria. Record a *no* in all cells when the respective mission statement does not meet the stated criteria.

MISSION STATEMENTS

Carolina Power & Light Company.   It is the mission of the Carolina Power & Light Company to provide the best service to present and future customers at the lowest rates consistent with fair compensation to employees. A fair return to those who have invested in the Company, safety for employees and the public, reasonable protection of the environment, and the development of technology to provide future service. Through the development and contribution of all employees, to the maximum of their potential, the Company will assure total quality performance that results in the highest achievable levels of customer satisfaction and recognition for excellence.

John B. Stetson University.   The mission of Stetson University is to provide students with an excellent education in an intellectually challenging and collaborative learning community. We pursue excellence through superior teaching, close student-faculty interaction, creative activity, and programs solidly grounded in liberal learning. We seek academically talented students with leadership potential and records of personal growth and community service. We prepare them for rewarding careers, selective graduate and professional programs, and a lifetime of learning. Stetson pursues truth in an open, caring, diverse environment, and encourages all members of its community to be morally sensitive and effective citizens committed to active forms of social responsibility. (*Stetson College Catalog,* 1993–1994, p. 5)

CSX Corporation.   CSX is a transportation company committed to being a leader in railroad, inland water and containerized distribution markets.

To attract the human and financial resources necessary to achieve this leadership position, CSX will support our three major constituencies:

For our customers, we will work as a partner to provide excellent service and meet all agreed-upon commitments.

For our employees, we will create a work environment that motivates and allows them to grow and develop and perform their jobs to the maximum of their capacity.

For our shareholders, we will meet our goals to provide them with sustainable superior returns.

University of North Carolina at Chapel Hill.   The University of North Carolina at Chapel Hill has been built by the people of the state and has existed for two centuries as the nation's first state university. Through its excellent undergraduate programs, it has provided higher education to ten generations of students, many of whom have become leaders of the State and the nation. Since the nineteenth century it has offered distinguished graduate and professional programs.

The university is a research university. Fundamental to this designation is a faculty actively involved in research, scholarship, and creative work, whose teaching is transformed by discovery and whose service is informed by current knowledge.

The mission of the university is to serve all the people of the state, and indeed the nation, as a center for scholarship and creative endeavor. The university exists to expand the body of knowledge; to teach students at all levels in an environment of research, free inquiry, and personal responsibility; to improve the condition of human life through service and publication; and to enrich our culture.

To fulfill this mission, the university must

Acquire, discover, preserve, synthesize, and transmit knowledge.

Provide high quality undergraduate instruction to students within a community engaged in original inquiry and creative expression, while committed to intellectual freedom, to personal integrity and justice, and to those values that foster enlightened leadership for the state and the nation.

Provide graduate and professional programs of national distinction at the doctoral and other advanced levels to future generations of research scholars, educators, professionals, and informed citizens.

Extend knowledge-based services and other resources of the university to the citizens of North Carolina and their institutions to enhance the quality of life for all people in the State.

Address, as appropriate, regional, national, and international needs.

This mission imposes special responsibilities upon the faculty, students, staff, administration, trustees, and other governance structures and constituencies of the university in their service and decision-making on behalf of the university. (*UNC College Catalog*, 1993–1994, p. 2)

Federal Express.   Federal Express is committed to our people-service-profit philosophy. We will produce outstanding financial returns by providing totally reliable, competitively superior global air-ground transportation of high-priority goods and documents that require rapid, time-certain delivery. Equally important, positive control of each package will be maintained utilizing real time electronic tracking and tracing systems. A complete record of each shipment and delivery will be presented with our request for payment. We will be helpful, courteous and professional to each other and the public. We will strive to have a satisfied customer at the end of each transaction.

Experiential Exercise 3B

WRITING A MISSION STATEMENT FOR HERSHEY FOODS

PURPOSE

There is no one best mission statement for a given organization. Analysts feel that the Hershey mission statement provided in the Cohesion Case can be improved. Writing a mission statement that includes desired components—and at the same time is inspiring and reconciliatory—requires careful thought. Mission statements should not be too lengthy; statements under 200 words are desirable.

INSTRUCTIONS

Step 1 Take 15 minutes to write a mission statement for Hershey Foods that does not exceed 200 words. Scan the case for needed details as you prepare your mission statement.

Step 2 Join with three other classmates to form a group of four people. Read each other's mission statements silently. As a group, select the best of your group's mission statements.

Step 3 Read that best mission statement to the class.

Experiential Exercise 3C

WRITING A MISSION STATEMENT FOR MY UNIVERSITY

PURPOSE

Most universities have a mission statement, as indicated by the examples provided in this chapter. The purpose of this exercise is to give you practice writing a mission statement for a nonprofit organization such as your own university.

INSTRUCTIONS

Step 1 Take 15 minutes to write a mission statement for your university. Your statement should not exceed 200 words.

Step 2 Read your mission statement to the class.

Step 3 Determine whether your institution has a mission statement. Look in the front of the college handbook. If your institution has a written statement, contact an appropriate administrator of the institution to inquire about how and when the statement was prepared. Share this information with the class. Analyze your college's mission statement in light of concepts presented in this chapter.

Experiential Exercise 3D

CONDUCTING MISSION STATEMENT RESEARCH

PURPOSE

This exercise gives you the opportunity to study the nature and role of mission statements in strategic management.

INSTRUCTIONS

Step 1 Call various organizations in your city or county to identify firms that have developed a formal mission statement. Contact nonprofit organizations and government agencies in addition to small and large businesses. Ask to speak with the director, owner, or chief executive officer of one organization. Explain that you are studying mission statements in class and are conducting research as part of a class activity.

Step 2 Ask several executives the following four questions and record their answers.
1. When did your organization first develop a formal mission statement? Who was primarily responsible for its development?
2. How long has your current mission statement existed? When was it last modified? Why was it modified at that point in time?
3. By what process is your firm's mission statement altered?
4. How is your mission statement used in the firm? How does it affect the firm's strategic-planning process?

Step 3 Provide an overview of your findings to the class.

ARE MISSION STATEMENTS ESOTERIC?[1]

PURPOSE

Some large American corporations have publicly denounced the importance of having a clear mission. Louis Gerstner, CEO of IBM, recently said, "The last thing IBM needs now is a vision." Robert Eaton, CEO of Chrysler, recently said, "Internally we don't use the word vision (mission). I believe in quantifiable short-term results—things we can all relate to—as opposed to some esoteric thing no one can quantify." Bill Gates, CEO of Microsoft Corporation, recently said, "Being a visionary (concerned with mission) is trivial." Douglas Lavin of *Wall Street Journal* recently said, "Vision (mission) may not exactly be dead in corporate America, but a surprising number of CEOs are casting aside their crystal balls to concentrate on the nuts-and-bolts of running their businesses in these leaner times; CEOs whose notion of vision (mission) is a sharp eye on the bottom line include John Sculley at Apple Computer, Ronald Compton at Aetna Life & Casualty; and John Smith, Jr., at General Motors."

INSTRUCTIONS

Step 1 Decide whether you agree or disagree with the CEO comments cited above. Do you agree with these persons that mission statements are esoteric or crystal ballish? Discuss this issue with several local business executives.

Step 2 Write a two-page essay explaining your personal views regarding the importance of mission statements.

Step 3 Summarize your views in a one-minute presentation to the class.

NOTES

1. This exercise is adapted from "Robert Eaton Thinks 'Vision' Is Overrated and He's Not Alone," *Wall Street Journal* (Oct. 4, 1993) pp. A1, A8.

USING THE *STRATEGY FORMULATOR* SOFTWARE

PURPOSE

The purpose of this exercise is to get you familiar with using the new *Strategy Formulator* strategic planning software that accompanies this text. Developing a mission statement is one of the first activities in the software program. At the end of Chapters 4, 5, and 6, there also will appear software exercises, so go ahead and begin to get familiar with this software. *Strategy Formulator* is useful in preparing case analyses and also is widely used by businesses actually doing strategic planning.

INSTRUCTIONS

Use the software to prepare a mission statement for your university. Do this in conjunction with Experiential Exercise 3C if possible. Bring a printout of your work to class.

The External Assessment

CHAPTER OUTLINE

CHAPTER OBJECTIVES

After studying this chapter, you should be able to do the following:

1. Describe how to conduct an external strategic-management audit.

2. Discuss ten major external forces that affect organizations: economic, social, cultural, demographic, environmental, political, governmental, legal, technological, and competitive.

3. Identify key sources of external information, including the Internet.

4. Discuss important forecasting tools used in strategic management.

5. Discuss the importance of monitoring external trends and events.

6. Explain how to develop an EFE Matrix.

7. Explain how to develop a Competitive Profile Matrix.

8. Discuss the importance of gathering competitive intelligence.

9. Describe the trend toward cooperation among competitors.

NOTABLE QUOTES

If you're not faster than your competitor, you're in a tenuous position, and if you're only half as fast, you're terminal.—GEORGE SALK

Positive trends in the environment breed complacency. That underscores a basic point: In change there is both opportunity and challenge.—CLIFTON GARVIN

The opportunities and threats existing in any situation always exceed the resources needed to exploit the opportunities or avoid the threats. Thus, strategy is essentially a problem of allocating resources. If strategy is to be successful, it must allocate superior resources against a decisive opportunity.—WILLIAM COHEN

Organizations pursue strategies that will disrupt the normal course of industry events and forge new industry conditions to the disadvantage of competitors.—IAN C. MACMILLAN

The idea is to concentrate our strength against our competitor's relative weakness.
—BRUCE HENDERSON

There was a time in America when business was easier. We set the pace for the rest of the world. We were immune to serious foreign competition. Many of us were regulated therefore protected. No longer. Today's leaders must recreate themselves and their ways of doing business in order to stay on top or stay competitive.—ROBERT H. WATERMAN, JR.

Competitive strategy must grow out of a sophisticated understanding of the rules of competition that determine an industry's attractiveness.—MICHAEL PORTER

The main reason for Japan's industrial might is that Japan leads the world in devising ways of creating products derived from basic technologies. America is by no means lacking in technology. But it does lack the creativity to apply new technologies commercially. This is America's biggest problem. On the other hand, it is Japan's strongest point.—AKIO MORITA

*T*his chapter examines the tools and concepts needed to conduct an external strategic-management audit (sometimes called *environmental scanning* or *industry analysis*). An *external audit* focuses on identifying and evaluating trends and events beyond the control of a single firm, such as increased foreign competition, population shifts to the Sunbelt, an aging society, information technology, and the computer revolution. An external audit reveals key opportunities and threats confronting an organization so that managers can formulate strategies to take advantage of the opportunities and avoid or reduce the impact of threats. This chapter presents a practical framework for gathering, assimilating, and analyzing external information.

THE NATURE OF AN EXTERNAL AUDIT

The purpose of an external audit is to develop a finite list of opportunities that could benefit a firm and threats that should be avoided. As the term *finite* suggests, the external audit is not aimed at developing an exhaustive list of every possible factor that could influence the business. Rather, it is aimed at identifying key variables that offer actionable responses. Firms should be able to respond either offensively or defensively to the factors by formulating strategies that take advantage of external opportunities or that minimize the impact of potential threats. Figure 4–1 illustrates how the external audit fits into the strategic-management process.

KEY EXTERNAL FORCES   *External forces* can be divided into five broad categories: (1) economic forces; (2) social, cultural, demographic, and environmental forces; (3) political, governmental, and legal forces; (4) technological forces; and (5) competitive forces. Relationships among these forces and an organization are depicted in Figure 4–2. External trends and events significantly affect all products, services, markets, and organizations in the world.

Changes in external forces translate into changes in consumer demand for both industrial and consumer products and services. External forces affect the types of products developed, the nature of positioning and market segmentation strategies, the types of services offered, and the choice of businesses to acquire or sell. External forces directly affect both suppliers and distributors. Identifying and evaluating external opportunities and threats enables organizations to develop a clear mission, to design strategies to achieve long-term objectives, and to develop policies to achieve annual objectives.

Some organizations survive solely because they recognize and take advantage of external opportunities. For example, Larson Company in Tucson, Arizona, has capitalized upon the growing concern for our natural environment by creating naturalistic environments for zoos, aquariums, shopping centers, amusement parks, and resort hotels. Larson's sales have grown dramatically to over $20 million annually. Larson contends that large, flashy nature exhibits are a big tourist draw. The new Mirage hotel and casino in Las Vegas, for example, attributes its success to the extensive use of artificial environments, ranging from a giant aquarium behind the registration desk to a 60-foot-high volcano outside the hotel.

The increasing complexity of business today is evidenced by more countries' developing the capacity and will to compete aggressively in world markets. Foreign businesses and countries are willing to learn, adapt, innovate, and invent to compete successfully in the marketplace. There are more competitive new technologies in Europe and the Far East today than ever before. American businesses can no longer beat foreign competitors with ease. For example, the world's four largest manufacturers of industrial and farm equipment are Mitsubishi

FIGURE 4-1
A Comprehensive Strategic-Management Model

Feedback

Develop Mission Statement

Perform External Audit

Perform Internal Audit

Establish Long-term Objectives

Generate, Evaluate, and Select Strategies

Establish Policies and Annual Objectives

Allocate Resources

Measure and Evaluate Performance

Strategy Formulation

Strategy Implementation

Strategy Evaluation

FIGURE 4–2
Relationships Between Key External Forces and an Organization

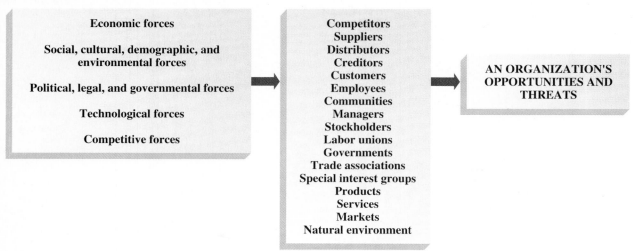

of Japan, INI of Spain, Mannesmann of Germany, and BTR of Britain; the world's two largest jewelry and silverware companies are Citizen Watch and Seiko, both of Japan. In publishing and printing, no U.S. company ranks among the six largest; in textiles no U.S. company ranks among the eight largest; in chemicals only two U.S. firms (Dupont and Dow Chemical) rank in the top 12; in metals, only one U.S. firm (Alcoa) ranks among the largest 16 firms globally.

Most organizations practice some form of external analysis as part of their planning process. Nearly 75 percent of chief executive officers of the Fortune 500 companies report that their firms perform external analysis and achieve numerous benefits from doing so.[1] Another 16 percent report that they do not have organized external analysis but probably should. Only 11 percent report that their firms do not conduct external audits and have no plans to begin.

THE PROCESS OF PERFORMING AN EXTERNAL AUDIT   The process of performing an external audit must involve as many managers and employees as possible. As emphasized in earlier chapters, involvement in the strategic-management process can lead to understanding and commitment from organizational members. Individuals appreciate having the opportunity to contribute ideas and to gain a better understanding of their firm's industry, competitors, and markets.

To perform an external audit, a company must first gather competitive intelligence and information about social, cultural, demographic, environmental, economic, political, legal, governmental, and technological trends. Individuals can be asked to monitor various sources of information such as key magazines, trade journals, and newspapers. These persons can submit periodic scanning reports to a committee of managers charged with performing the external audit. This approach provides a continuous stream of timely strategic information and involves many individuals in the external-audit process. *Online databases* provide another source for gathering strategic information, as does use of corporate, university, and public libraries. Suppliers, distributors, salespersons, customers, and competitors represent other sources of vital information.

Once information is gathered, it should be assimilated and evaluated. A meeting or series of meetings of up to 20 managers is needed to collectively identify the most important opportunities and threats facing the firm. Critical success factors should be listed on flip charts or a blackboard. A prioritized list of these factors could be obtained by requesting all managers to rank the factors identified, from 1 for the most important opportunity/threat to 20 for the least important opportunity/threat. *Critical success factors* can vary over time and by industry. Relationships with suppliers or distributors are often a critical success factor. Other variables commonly used include market share, breath of competing products, world economies, foreign affiliates, proprietary and key account advantages, price competitiveness, technological advancements, population shifts, interest rates, and pollution abatement.

Freund emphasizes that critical success factors should be (1) important to achieving long-term and annual objectives, (2) measurable, (3) relatively few in number, (4) applicable to all competing firms, and (5) hierarchical in the sense that some will pertain to the overall company and others will be more narrowly focused on functional or divisional areas.[2] A final list of the most important critical success factors should be communicated and distributed widely in the organization. Both opportunities and threats can be critical success factors.

INFORMATION TECHNOLOGY   *Information technology (IT)* has become a powerful tool for conducting an external audit. The quantity and quality of industry and competitive information available to organizations has increased dramatically in recent years. Advanced computer technology, telecommunications, data access and storage devices, fax machines, online databases, graphics, and software represent efficient and effective vehicles for identifying and evaluating opportunities and threats. Effective use of the *Internet* as the information superhighway is becoming more and more essential for business success.

The World Wide Web is a global network available via the Internet whereby an individual or firm can place information or advertisements for consumption by others around the world—or just within a corporation. Unlike other cyberspace services, Web pages can contain both text and nontext items, including sound clips, graphics, and even movies. Having a Web site in *cyberspace* can allow large savings in paper, copying, phone, and postage. The savings in advertising can be even higher. A Web browser such as Netscape Communications Navigator on a personal computer can allow anyone to look at what is stored on any Web server in the world.

Getting on the Web is quite simple and inexpensive, and it can be the difference between formulationg strategies based on up-to-date, rather than out-of-date, information. Consultants are readily available to provide assistance. Books such as *HTML for Fun and Profit* (Prentice-Hall/SunSoft Press) are available. If you design your Web pages so well that consumer demand increases for your product or service, you may decide to add to your information and/or advertisements and move them out of your Web site and over the Internet. Doing this begins to be costly, but the additional revenues may more than offset the costs.

By the year 2000, millions of people and businesses will each own a small part of cyberspace; they will own their own Web site. Shouldn't your company have its own Web site and peruse the sites of competing companies, suppliers, distributors, and customers? The answer, increasingly, is *yes*. The proliferation of people and companies worldwide using the Web, however, is raising questions about invasion of privacy and breaches of security.

As the year 1996 began, more than 30 million people worldwide were using the Web, a tenfold increase from 1990. Included in this figure are close to 25,000 businesses, up from just over 1,000 in 1990. Web users are located in more than 100 countries worldwide. Nearly 10,000 people are signing up each day for U.S. consumer online services.

With both private and corporate connections to the Web proliferating, firms must take for granted that every computer on the planet can reach and interact with almost any other. Security and privacy are becoming more and more of a concern. Linking a firm's computer to cyberspace opens it to potentially millions of largely unidentified visitors, some of whom may have malicious, criminal, or otherwise unethical intent. Verification that senders or receivers on the Internet are who they say they are can be a challenge. A competitor could bombard your system with false messages and information.

The range of products and measures designed to enhance computer security is increasing daily. Software is now available that can generate a new password every few minutes, encrypt all outgoing messages with secret codes or keystrokes, or even block unwanted traffic arriving to your computer from the Internet. Yet, electronic commerce creates vast opportunities for tax evasion, money laundering, and other financial crime. "There is an imaginable potential for a serious challenge to the whole political and social order," says Nathaniel Borenstein. "I'm not that sanguine that the government has the control they think they do."

Information technology (IT) itself is changing the very nature of opportunities and threats by altering the life cycles of products, increasing the speed of distribution, creating new products and services, erasing limitations of traditional geographic markets, and changing the historical trade-off between production standardization and flexibility. IT is altering economies of scale, changing entry barriers, and redefining the relationship between industries and various suppliers, creditors, customers, and competitors. As an example, consider the airline industry's business travel market:

> Given the current rate of development in telecommunications and office technology, video conferences may become a major substitute for some business air travel soon. This would significantly affect the airline industry's business travel market. Strategists today must address a crucial question: What impact will IT have on our industry over the next five to ten years in terms of products and services, markets, and production economies?[3]

The era of the mainframe computer is giving way to a proliferation of affordable microcomputers that are almost as powerful. This trend is creating a new basis for competition in virtually all industries and has generated new buyers, suppliers, products, and services. The microcomputer revolution especially represents an opportunity for innovative young companies. Entrenched industrial leaders face more competition than ever from small firms using advanced microcomputer technology.

To effectively capitalize on information technology, a number of organizations are establishing two new positions in their firms: *Chief Information Officer (CIO)* and *Chief Technology Officer (CTO)*. This trend reflects the growing importance of information technology in strategic management. A CIO and CTO work together to assure that information needed to formulate, implement, and evaluate strategies is available where and when it is needed. These persons are responsible for developing, maintaining, and updating a company's information database. The CIO is more a manager, managing the overall external-audit process; the CTO is more a technician, focusing on technical issues such as data acquisition, data processing, decision support systems, and software and hardware acquisition.

ECONOMIC FORCES

Low inflation and high unemployment in the 1990s have caused sweeping changes in the buying patterns of consumers. As consumers perceive that more money is buying them less, many adopt a buy-now-save-later motto. Both consumer debt and governmental debt levels have soared at the expense of future security. As a percent of disposable income, consumer savings have fallen to below 4 percent. Interest rates have dropped to the lowest levels in decades. Banks are hesitant to lend money and businesses are reluctant to obtain additional debt; consumers are reluctant to make purchases. Many states are increasing taxes. Four states already have a state income tax higher than 10 percent: Massachusetts, North Dakota, Vermont, and California. Nine states have no state income tax: Alaska, Florida, Nevada, New Hampshire, South Dakota, Tennessee, Texas, Washington, and Wyoming.

Shift to a service economy in the United States	Import/export factors
Availability of credit	Demand shifts for different categories of goods
Level of disposable income	and services
Propensity of people to spend	Income differences by region and consumer
Interest rates	groups
Inflation rates	Price fluctuations
Economies of scale	Exportation of labor and capital from the
Money market rates	United States
Federal government budget deficits	Monetary policies
Gross national product trend	Fiscal policies
Consumption patterns	Tax rates
Unemployment trends	European Economic Community (ECC) policies
Worker productivity levels	Organization of Petroleum Exporting Countries
Value of the dollar in world markets	(OPEC) policies
Stock market trends	Coalitions of Lesser Developed Countries
Foreign countries' economic conditions	(LDC) policies

TABLE 4–1
Key Economic Variables to Be Monitored

Increasing numbers of two-income households is an economic trend in America. As affluence increases, individuals place a premium on time. Improved customer service, immediate availability, trouble-free operation of products, and dependable maintenance and repair services are becoming more important. Americans today are more willing than ever to pay for good service if it limits inconvenience.

Economic factors have a direct impact on the potential attractiveness of various strategies. For example, if interest rates rise, then funds needed for capital expansion become more costly or unavailable. Also, as interest rates rise, discretionary income declines, and the demand for discretionary goods falls. As stock prices increase, the desirability of equity as a source of capital for market development increases. Also, as the market rises, consumer and business wealth expands. A summary of economic variables that often represent opportunities and threats for organizations is provided in Table 4–1.

Trends in the dollar's value have significant and unequal effects on companies in different industries and in different locations. For example, the pharmaceutical, tourism, entertainment, motor vehicle, aerospace, and forest products industries benefit greatly with the dollar's fall against the yen, franc, and mark. Agricultural and petroleum industries are hurt by the dollar's rise against the currencies of Mexico, Brazil, Venezuela, and Australia. Generally, a strong or high dollar makes American goods more expensive on overseas markets. This worsens America's trade deficit. When the value of the dollar falls, tourism-oriented firms benefit, because Americans do not travel abroad as much when the value of the dollar is low; rather, foreigners visit and vacation more in the United States.

A low value of the dollar means lower imports and higher exports; it helps U.S. companies' competitiveness in world markets. The years 1995 and 1996 have seen the U.S. dollar gaining against virtually every other currency. One benefit of this trend is that consumers pay less for imported goods such as cars and computer memory chips. Domestic firms that manufacture extensively outside the United States also benefit from the rising value of the dollar. If the U.S. budget deficit is cut further, the value of the dollar will almost surely continue to rise, to 150 yen perhaps.

America's eight largest exporting firms are Boeing, General Motors, General Electric, IBM, Ford Motor, Chrysler, McDonnell Douglas, and Philip Morris. The top ten countries that receive U.S. exports, in rank order, are Canada, Japan, Mexico, Britain, Germany, South Korea, Taiwan, France, The Netherlands, and Singapore, as indicated in the Global Perspective. Note that the United States imports more goods from China than any other country, except Canada, Japan, and Mexico.

GLOBAL PERSPECTIVE

Top 25 Purchasers of U.S. Goods Exports, 1993–95 (Dollars in millions)

COUNTRY	1993	1994	1995
Canada	100,444	114,441	126,024
Japan	47,891	53,481	64,298
Mexico	41,581	50,840	45,401
United Kingdom	26,438	26,833	28,827
South Korea	14,782	18,028	25,413
Germany	18,932	19,237	22,376
Taiwan	16,168	17,078	19,295
Netherlands	12,839	13,591	16,559
Singapore	11,678	13,022	15,318
France	13,267	13,622	14,241
Hong Kong	9,874	11,445	14,220
Belgium/Luxembourg	9,439	10,944	12,459
China	8,763	9,287	11,748
Brazil	6,058	8,118	11,444
Australia	8,276	9,781	10,789
Italy	6,464	7,193	8,862
Malaysia	6,064	6,965	8,818
Thailand	3,766	4,861	6,402
Switzerland	6,806	5,614	6,241
Saudi Arabia	6,661	6,010	6,085
Israel	4,429	5,006	5,593
Spain	4,168	4,625	5,529
Philippines	3,529	3,888	5,294
Venezuela	4,590	4,042	4,641
Colombia	3,235	4,070	4,628

Top 25 Purchasers of U.S. Goods Exports, 1993–95 (Dollars in millions)

COUNTRY	1993	1994	1995
Canada	111,216	128,948	145,118
Japan	107,246	119,149	123,577
Mexico	39,917	49,493	61,704
China	31,540	38,781	45,555
Germany	28,562	31,749	36,846
Taiwan	25,101	26,711	28,975
United Kingdom	21,730	25,063	26,891
South Korea	17,118	19,658	24,184
Singapore	12,798	15,360	18,563
Malaysia	10,563	13,977	17,484
France	15,279	16,755	17,177
Italy	13,216	14,711	16,498
Thailand	8,542	10,307	11,350
Hong Kong	9,554	9,698	10,293
Venezuela	8,140	8,378	9,711
Brazil	7,479	8,708	8,815
Saudi Arabia	7,708	7,687	8,232
Switzerland	5,973	6,376	7,596
Indonesia	5,435	6,523	7,437
Philippines	4,894	5,720	7,007
Netherlands	5,443	6,015	6,378
Sweden	4,534	5,044	6,246
Belgium/Luxembourg	5,402	6,342	6,050
India	4,554	5,302	5,736
Israel	4,420	5,223	5,723

Every business day an average of 2,389 American workers learn that they will lose their jobs. More than 500,000 annual employee layoffs by U.S. firms in the 1990s has led to terms such as *downsizing, rightsizing,* and *decruiting* becoming common. The U.S. and world economies face a sustained period of slow, low-inflationary expansion, global over-capacity, high unemployment, price wars, and increased competitiveness. Thousands of laid-off workers are being forced to become entrepreneurs to make a living. The United States is becoming more entrepreneurial every day.

SOCIAL, CULTURAL, DEMOGRAPHIC, AND ENVIRONMENTAL FORCES

Social, cultural, demographic, and environmental changes have a major impact upon virtually all products, services, markets, and customers. Small, large, for-profit and nonprofit organizations in all industries are being staggered and challenged by the opportunities and threats arising from changes in social, cultural, demographic, and environmental variables. In every way, the United States is much different in 1997 than it was in 1987, and the year 2007 promises even greater changes.

Social, cultural, demographic, and environmental trends are shaping the way Americans live, work, produce, and consume. New trends are creating a different type of consumer and, consequently, a need for different products, different services, and different strategies. There are now more American households with people living alone or with unrelated people than there are households consisting of married couples with children. Census data suggest that Americans are not returning to traditional lifestyles. Church membership fell substantially during the 1980s for nearly all religious denominations, except Southern Baptists and Mormons.

Significant trends for the 1990s include consumers becoming more educated, the population aging, narcissism replacing the Protestant work ethic, minorities becoming more influential, people looking for local rather than federal solutions to problems, fixation on youth decreasing, more emphasis being placed on preserving the natural environment, and more women entering the workforce. The United States Census Bureau projects that the number of Hispanics will increase from 10 percent of the population in 1996 to 15 percent by 2021, when they will become a larger minority group than blacks in America. The percentage of blacks in America will increase from 12 percent to 14 percent between 1996 and 2021. Eight states currently have more than 500,000 Hispanics as registered voters: California, New Mexico, Arizona, Texas, Florida, New York, Illinois, and New Jersey.

During the 1990s, the number of individuals aged 50 and over will increase 18.5 percent, to 76 million. In contrast, the number of Americans under age 50 will grow by just 3.5 percent. The trend toward an older America is good news for restaurants, hotels, airlines, cruise lines, tours, resorts, theme parks, luxury products and services, recreational vehicles, home builders, furniture producers, computer manufacturers, travel services, pharmaceutical firms, automakers, and funeral homes. Older Americans are especially interested in health care, financial services, travel, crime prevention, and leisure.

The aging American population affects the strategic orientation of nearly all organizations. Apartment complexes for the elderly, with one meal a day, transportation, and utilities included in the rent, have increased to more than 200,000 units nationwide. Called *lifecare facilities,* the number of complexes is expected to increase to exceed 1 million by 1998. Some well-known companies building these facilities include Avon, Marriott, and Hyatt. By the year 2005, individuals aged 65 and older in the United States will rise to 13 percent of the total population; Japan's elderly population ratio will rise to 17 percent, and West Germany's to 19 percent.

Americans are on the move in a population shift to the South and West (Sunbelt) and away from the Northeast and Midwest (Frostbelt). The Internal Revenue Service provides the Census Bureau with massive computer files of demographic data. By comparing individual address changes from year to year, the Census Bureau now publishes extensive information about population shifts across the country. For example, Arizona will be the fastest growing state during the 1990s as its population increases 23 percent. Nevada, New Mexico, and Florida are close behind with projected growth rates above 20 percent. Wyoming will remain the nation's least populated state and California the most populated state. Texas will replace New York as the most populous state. States incurring the greatest loss of people for the 1990s are North Dakota, Wyoming, Pennsylvania, Iowa, and West Virginia. This type of information can be essential for successful strategy formulation, including where to locate new plants and distribution centers and where to focus marketing efforts.

Americans are becoming less and less interested in fitness and exercise. Fitness participants declined in the United States by 3.5 percent annually in the 1990s. Makers of fitness products, such as Nike, Reebok International, and CML Group—which makes NordicTrack—are experiencing declines in sales growth. American Sports Data in Hartsdale, New York, reports that "the one American in five who exercises regularly is now outnumbered by three couch potatoes."

Mark Starik at George Washington University argues that with the thawing of the Cold War, no greater threat to business and society exists than the voracious, continuous decimation and degradation of our natural environment. The U.S. Clean Air Act went into effect in 1994. The U.S. Clean Water Act went into effect in 1984. As indicated in the Natural Environment Perspective, American firms planning to begin or expand operations in Mexico face immense pollution and health problems. A summary of important social, cultural, demographic, and environmental variables that represent opportunities or threats for virtually all organizations is given in Table 4–2.

TABLE 4–2
Key Social, Cultural, Demographic, and Environmental Variables

Childbearing rates	Attitudes toward retirement
Number of special interest groups	Attitudes toward leisure time
Number of marriages	Attitudes toward product quality
Number of divorces	Attitudes toward customer service
Number of births	Pollution control
Number of deaths	Attitudes toward foreign peoples
Immigration and emigration rates	Energy conservation
Social security programs	Social programs
Life expectancy rates	Number of churches
Per-capita income	Number of church members
Location of retailing, manufacturing, and service businesses	Social responsibility
Attitudes toward business	Attitudes toward careers
Lifestyles	Population changes by race, age, sex, and level of affluence
Traffic congestion	Attitudes toward authority
Inner-city environments.	Population changes by city, county, state, region, and country
Average disposable income	Value placed on leisure time
Trust in government	Regional changes in tastes and preferences
Attitudes toward government	Number of women and minority workers
Attitudes toward work	Number of high school and college graduates by geographic area
Buying habits	Recycling
Ethical concerns	Waste management
Attitudes toward saving	Air pollution
Sex roles	Water pollution
Attitudes toward investing	Ozone depletion
Racial equality	Endangered species
Use of birth control	
Average level of education	
Government regulation	

POLITICAL, GOVERNMENTAL, AND LEGAL FORCES

Federal, state, local, and foreign governments are major regulators, deregulators, subsidizers, employers, and customers of organizations. Political, governmental, and legal factors can therefore represent key opportunities or threats for both small and large organizations. For industries and firms that depend heavily on government contracts or subsidies, political forecasts can be the most important part of an external audit. Changes in patent laws, antitrust legislation, tax rates, and lobbying activities can affect firms significantly.

Irvine Companies, Baldwin Company, and Santa Margarita Company in California were recently forced to abandon strategies to further develop the southern California coastline because the federal government added the California coastal gnatcatcher to the endangered species list. This tiny California songbird faces possible extinction because its habitat, the low scrub and sagebrush that dots the southern California coast, was being destroyed by the firms cited.

Firms such as Chambers Development, Waste Management, and Browning-Ferris, which build and operate large private dumps, are poised for the Environmental Protection Agency (EPA) to close about 6,000 municipal, public solid-waste landfills operating below standards in the United States. New EPA landfill rules set standards for location, design, operation, and closure of public landfills, as well as groundwater-monitoring procedures.

The increasing global interdependence among economies, markets, governments, and organizations makes it imperative that firms consider the possible impact of political variables on the formulation and implementation of competitive strategies. A number of nationally known firms forecast political, governmental, and legal variables, including Frost

NATURAL ENVIRONMENT

Mexico's Natural Environment

Mexico is one of the most polluted countries in the world, and this situation was a stumbling block in the North American Free Trade Agreement (NAFTA) that recently became law. The natural environment presents both opportunities and threats for American firms doing business in Mexico.

Numerous Mexican cities have no sewage system; they dump millions of gallons of raw sewage daily into rivers and dumping sites. Ciudad Juarez, for example, is a large city near the U.S. border that has no sewage system, and that dumps 22 million gallons of raw sewage a day. Air pollution is another huge problem in Mexico. The ozone levels in Mexico City recently hit 342, a poisonous level far exceeding the less-than-100 satisfactory level. All Mexico City schools closed, children stayed in-

doors, hundreds of people wore face masks, scores of businesses closed, and all hospital incinerators shut down. Smokestack industries in Mexico City, a metropolis of nearly 20 million inhabitants, emit tons of sulfur and heavy metals daily into the air.

President Zedillo of Mexico is committed to reversing Mexico's natural environment record, but many analysts say his programs of environmental reform are too little too late. Hundreds of species of Mexican fauna and flora have become extinct in the last two decades; 80 percent of Mexico's huge Lacandona jungle has been destroyed. The incidence of lung cancer, heart disease, typhoid fever, polio, hepatitis, cholera, and numerous other diseases is more than 10 times higher in Mexico than in the United States. The 2,000-mile U.S.-Mexico bor-

der is a polluted industrial corridor of assembly factories known as *maquilas*.

What effect is NAFTA having on the monumental natural environment problems that plague Mexico? More U.S. companies are locating facilities in Mexico. U.S. firms are exporting more products to Mexico, such as pollution control equipment, Mexico is exporting more products to the United States, such as lettuce and tomatoes. Is NAFTA mutually benefiting both countries?

Source: Adapted from Stephen Mumme, "Clearing the Air: Environmental Reform in Mexico." *Environment* 33, no. 10 (December 1991): 7–30.

TABLE 4–3
Risk Forecast for 101 Countries for 1996–2000

COUNTRY	REGIME	INFLATION	TURMOIL	TRANSFER	INVESTMENT	EXPORT	GROWTH
U.S.	Clinton	3.3%	Low	A	A	A	3.0%
China	Pragmatists	12.0%	Low	A−	B+	B+	8.5%
Libya	Qaddafi	15.0%	Moderate	B	C+	B−	2.8%
France	Balladoe	2.5%	Low	A+	A	A	3.0%
Sudan	Moderate Military	60.0%	High	C	C−	C−	5.0%
Russia	Yeltsin	50.0%	Moderate	B−	C	C	2.0%
Israel	Labor Coalition	10.5%	Moderate	C+	A−	B−	4.5%
Brazil	Cordozo	800.0%	High	C	B	B−	2.5%

Source: William Coplin and Michael O'Leary, "On the Threshold of the 21st Century: A Surprising Wealth of Business Opportunities," *Planning Review* (March/April 1995): 36–43. (Note: Only 8 of 101 countries are included here.)

& Sullivan, Probe International, and Arthur D. Little (ADL). ADL forecasts the political climate in foreign countries by examining five criteria: (1) social development, (2) technological advancement, (3) abundance of natural resources, (4) level of domestic tranquility, and (5) type of political system. ADL has found that political unrest follows whenever a country's development in any one of these areas gets too far ahead of the others. Ford, DuPont, Singer, and PepsiCo are among the many companies that use forecasts developed by outside firms to identify key political and governmental opportunities and threats.

Political forecasting can be especially critical and complex for multinational firms that depend on foreign countries for natural resources, facilities, distribution of products, special assistance, or customers. *Planning Review* publishes an extensive political risk forecast for 101 countries worldwide; an excerpt from a recent political forecast is given in Table 4–3.

Strategists today must possess skills to deal more legalistically and politically than previous strategists, whose attention was directed more to economic and technical affairs of the firm. Strategists today are spending more time anticipating and influencing public policy actions. They spend more time meeting with government officials, attending important hearings and government-sponsored conferences, giving public speeches, and meeting with trade groups, industry associations, and government agency directors. Before entering or expanding international operations, strategists need a good understanding of the political and decision-making processes in countries where their firm may conduct business. For example, the republics that comprise the former Soviet Union differ greatly in wealth, resources, language, and lifestyle.

Increasing global competition toward the year 2000 accents the need for accurate political, governmental, and legal forecasts. Many strategists will have to become familiar with political systems in Europe and Asia and with trading currency futures. East Asian countries have already become world leaders in labor-intensive industries. Frederick Gluck, director of McKinsey & Company, concludes that a world market is emerging from what previously was a multitude of distinct national markets, and that the climate for international business in the 1990s is much more favorable than in the 1980s. Mass communication and high technology are creating similar patterns of consumption in diverse cultures worldwide! This means that many companies may find it difficult to survive by relying solely on domestic markets.

It is no exaggeration that in an industry that is, or is rapidly becoming, global, the riskiest possible posture is to remain a domestic competitor. The domestic competitor will watch as more aggressive companies use this growth to capture economies of scale and learning. The domestic competitor will then be faced with an attack on domestic markets using different (and possibly

Government regulations or deregulations	Sino-American relationships	**TABLE 4–4**
Changes in tax laws	Russian-American relationships	**Important Political,**
Special tariffs	European-American relationships	**Governmental, and Legal**
Political action committees	African-American relationships	**Variables**
Voter participation rates	Import-export regulations	
Number, severity, and location of government protests	Government fiscal and monetary policy changes	
Number of patents	Political conditions in foreign countries	
Changes in patent laws	Special local, state, and federal laws	
Environmental protection laws	Lobbying activities	
Level of defense expenditures	Size of government budgets	
Legislation on equal employment	World oil, currency, and labor markets	
Level of government subsidies	Location and severity of terrorist activities	
Antitrust legislation	Local, state, and national elections	

superior) technology, product design, manufacturing, marketing approaches, and economies of scale. A few examples suggest how extensive the phenomenon of world markets has already become. Hewlett-Packard's manufacturing chain reaches halfway around the globe, from well-paid, skilled engineers in California to low-wage assembly workers in Malaysia. General Electric has survived as a manufacturer of inexpensive audio products by centralizing its world production in Singapore.[4]

Local, state, and federal laws, regulatory agencies, and special interest groups can have a major impact on the strategies of small, large, for-profit, and nonprofit organizations. Many companies have altered or abandoned strategies in the past because of political or governmental actions. For example, many nuclear power projects have been halted and many steel plants shut down because of pressure from the Environmental Protection Agency (EPA). Other federal regulatory agencies include the Food and Drug Administration (FDA), the National Highway Traffic and Safety Administration (NHTSA), the Occupational Safety and Health Administration (OSHA), the Consumer Product Safety Commission (CPSC), the Federal Trade Commission (FTC), the Securities Exchange Commission (SEC), the Equal Employment Opportunity Commission (EEOC), the Federal Communications Commission (FCC), the Federal Maritime Commission (FMC), the Interstate Commerce Commission (ICC), the Federal Energy Regulatory Commission (FERC), the National Labor Relations Board (NLRB), and the Civil Aeronautics Board (CAB). A summary of political, governmental, and legal variables that can represent key opportunities or threats to organizations is provided in Table 4–4.

TECHNOLOGICAL FORCES

Revolutionary technological changes and discoveries such as superconductivity, computer engineering, thinking computers, robotics, unmanned factories, miracle drugs, space communications, space manufacturing, lasers, cloning, satellite networks, fiber optics, biometrics, and electronic funds transfer are having a dramatic impact on organizations. Superconductivity advancements alone, which increase the power of electrical products by lowering resistance to current, are expected to revolutionize business operations in the 1990s, especially in the transportation, utility, healthcare, electrical, and computer industries.

New microprocesser-based equipment and process technologies, such as *computer-aided design and manufacturing (CAD/CAM),* direct numerical control (DNC), computer-centralized numerical control (CNC), flexible production centers (FPC), equipment and process technology (EPT), and computer-integrated manufacturing (CIM), are burgeoning.

INFORMATION TECHNOLOGY
Developing Countries Want to Call Home

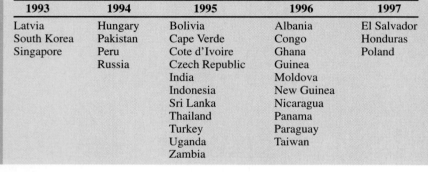

In a movie, ET tried to call home. In 1996 only 15 percent of the world's population has 71 percent of the world's phones. More than 50 percent of the world's people have never even used a phone. Over two-thirds of households around the world have no telephone. Cambodia has about the fewest phones of any country, only 0.06 phone lines per 100 inhabitants.

The United States has close to 60 phone lines per 100 inhabitants. There are 47 countries with less than 1 phone line per 100 people.

Developing countries now realize they cannot develop their own economies or compete in world markets without phones. They must be able to communicate to survive. So, third-world countries are quickly adding phone lines. Underdeveloped countries are increasing their number of phone lines by an average 11.7 percent a year for the next five years, compared to 3.7 percent for the world's 24 highest-income countries. For example, China will install 100 million phones between 1996 and 1999.

To spur phone line development and installation, underdeveloped countries usually privitize their telephone companies. The table gives telephone company privitizations in developing countries through 1997.

Sources: Adapted from Catherine Arnst, "The Last Frontier," *Business Week* (September 18, 1995): 98–114.

1993	1994	1995	1996	1997
Latvia	Hungary	Bolivia	Albania	El Salvador
South Korea	Pakistan	Cape Verde	Congo	Honduras
Singapore	Peru	Cote d'Ivoire	Ghana	Poland
	Russia	Czech Republic	Guinea	
		India	Moldova	
		Indonesia	New Guinea	
		Sri Lanka	Nicaragua	
		Thailand	Panama	
		Turkey	Paraguay	
		Uganda	Taiwan	
		Zambia		

As indicated in the Information Technology Perspective, simply gaining access to a telephone line is a technological problem in many countries around the world.

Technological forces represent major opportunities and threats that must be considered in formulating strategies. Technological advancements can dramatically affect organizations' products, services, markets, suppliers, distributors, competitors, customers, manufacturing processes, marketing practices, and competitive position. Technological advancements can create new markets, result in a proliferation of new and improved products, change the relative competitive cost positions in an industry, and render existing products and services obsolete. Technological changes can reduce or eliminate cost barriers between businesses, create shorter production runs, create shortages in technical skills, and result in changing values and expectations of employees, managers, and customers. Technological advancements can create new *competitive advantages* that are more powerful than existing advantages. No company or industry today is insulated against emerging technological developments. In high-tech industries identification and evaluation of key technological opportunities and threats can be the most important part of the external strategic-management audit.

Organizations that have traditionally limited technology expenditures to what they can fund after meeting marketing and financial requirements urgently need a reversal in thinking. The pace of technological change is increasing and literally wiping out more and more businesses every day. An emerging consensus holds that technology management is one of the key responsibilities of strategists. Firms should pursue strategies that take advantage of technological opportunities to achieve sustainable, competitive advantages in the marketplace.

Technology-based issues will underlie nearly every important decision that strategists make. Crucial to those decisions will be the ability to approach technology planning analytically and strategically. . . . technology can be planned and managed using formal techniques similar to those used in business and capital investment planning. An effective technology strategy is built on a penetrating analysis of technology opportunities and threats, and an assessment of the relative importance of these factors to overall corporate strategy.[5]

In practice, critical decisions about technology are too often delegated to lower organizational levels or are made without an understanding of their strategic implications. Many strategists spend countless hours determining market share, positioning products in terms of features and price, forecasting sales and market size, and monitoring distributors; yet too often technology does not receive the same respect:

The impact of this oversight is devastating. Firms not managing technology to ensure their futures may eventually find their futures managed by technology. Technology's impact reaches far beyond the "high-tech" companies. Although some industries may appear to be relatively technology-insensitive in terms of products and market requirements, they are not immune from the impact of technology; companies in smokestack as well as service industries must carefully monitor emerging technological opportunities and threats.[6]

Not all sectors of the economy are equally affected by technological developments. The communications, electronics, aeronautics, and pharmaceutical industries are much more volatile than the textile, forestry, and metals industries. For strategists in industries affected by rapid technological change, identifying and evaluating technological opportunities and threats can represent the most important part of an external audit. Key questions about technology that should be asked during the external audit are presented in Table 4–5.

Some technological advancements expected before the year 2000 in the computer and medical industry are computers that recognize handwriting; voice-controlled computers; gesture-controlled computers; color fax; picture phones; and defeat of heart disease, AIDS, rheumatoid arthritis, multiple sclerosis, leukemia, and lung cancer. New technological advancements from Japan include tape recorders the size of a matchbox, television sets with flat screens that can be hung on a wall, translation telephones, microminiaturized personal computers, robots that wash windows, and sports cars that rival Lamborghinis but cost only half as much.

Electronic data interchange (EDI) is an information technology that has changed the way America does business. EDI allows companies to lower inventory levels, improve customer service, and reduce payroll expenses by sending specially formatted documents such as invoices and purchase orders from one company's computer to another's. EDI is enabling organizations to perform external audits more effectively and to gain competitive advantages in world markets. *Business Week* gives the following example of EDI in use:

In businesses such as the $55 billion textile industry, which has suffered as retailers doubled their purchases of cheap Asian apparel over the past five years, adopting EDI has become a way to get an edge over foreign rivals. Led by textile magnate Roger Milliken, 220 top retail and clothing executives convened earlier this year to back industry-standard formats for purchase orders, shipping documents, and other forms. Their purpose is to beat Asian rivals by making it easier for retailers to deal with U.S. suppliers. "This is the beginning of a revolution in our industry," says Milliken.[7]

COMPETITIVE FORCES

The top five competitors in four different industries are identified in Table 4–6. An important part of an external audit is to identify rival firms and to determine their strengths, weaknesses, capabilities, opportunities, threats, objectives, and strategies.

TABLE 4–5
Key Questions to Ask in Assessing the Technological Environment

- What are the technologies within the corporation?
- Which technologies are utilized in the firm's business? products? components and parts?
- How critical is each technology to each of these products and businesses?
- Which technologies are contained in purchased parts and material?
- Which of these external technologies might become critical and why? Will they remain available outside the firm?
- What was the evolution of these technologies over time? In which companies were these technological changes initiated?
- What is the likely evolution of these technologies in the future?
- What have been the firm's investments in critical technologies over time?
- What were the investments and investment patterns of its leading technological competitors? Historical? Planned?
- What has been the investment in the product and in the process side of these technologies? For the firm and for its competitors? Design? Production? Implementation and service?
- What is the subjective ranking of different firms in each of these technologies?
- What are the firm's businesses and products?
- What are the parts and components of these products?
- What is the cost and value-added structure of these parts, components, products, and businesses?
- What has been the historical financial and strategic performance of the business, and what are the implications of these trends? In terms of cash generation and earnings characteristics? Investment requirements? Growth? Market position and market share?
- What are the applications of the firm's technologies?
- In which does the firm currently participate and why? In which does the firm not participate and why?
- How attractive is each of these applications as an investment opportunity in terms of its market growth, its potential for profit improvement, and/or its potential for increasing technological leadership?
    Underlying growth charateristics
    Evolution of customer needs and requirements
    Current and emeging market segments; segment growth rates
    Competitive positioning and likely strategies of key competitors
- How critical are the firm's technologies to each of these applications?
- What other technologies are critical to the external applications?
- How do the technologies differ in each of these applications?
- What are the competing technologies in each application? What are the determinations of substitution dynamics?
- What is and will be the degree of technological change in each of these technologies?
- What are the applications that the firm should consider entering?
- What should be the priorities of technological resource investment?
- What technological resources are required for the firm to achieve its current business objectives?
- What should be the level and rate of corporate technology investments?
- Which technological investments should be curtailed or eliminated?
- What additional technologies will be required in order to achieve the current corporate business objectives?
- What are the implications of the technology and business portfolios for corporate strategy?

Source: Boris Petrov, "The Advent of the Technology Portfolio." Reprinted by permission from the *Journal of Business Strategy,* Fall 1982. Published by Warren, Gorham & Lamont, Inc. Boston, Mass. Copyright © 1982. All rights reserved.

Collecting and evaluating information on competitors is essential for successful strategy formulation. Identifying major competitors is not always easy because many firms have divisions that compete in different industries. Most multidivisional firms generally do not provide sales and profit information on a divisional basis for competitive reasons. Also, privately held firms do not publish any financial or marketing information.

Despite the problems mentioned above, financial information on leading competitors in particular industries can be found in publications such as *Moody's Manuals, Standard Corporation Descriptions, Value Line Investment Surveys, Ward's Business Directory,*

	1995 SALES IN $ MILLIONS	PERCENTAGE CHANGE FROM 1994	1995 PROFITS IN $ MILLIONS	PERCENTAGE CHANGE FROM 1994
AEROSPACE				
Lockheed Martin	22,853	+74	682	+53
United Technologies	22,802	+8	750	+28
Boeing	19,515	−11	393	−54
Allied Signal	14,346	+12	875	+15
McDonnell Douglas	14,332	+9	−416	−170
FOREST PRODUCTS				
International Paper	19,797	+32	1,153	+223
Georgia Pacific	14,292	+12	1,018	+228
Kimberly-Clark	13,789	+13	799	+36
Weyerhaeuser	11,788	+87	33	−94
Stone Container	7,351	+28	256	−
COMPUTERS				
IBM	71,940	+12	4,178	+38
Hewlett-Packard	31,519	+26	2,433	+52
Compaq	14,755	+36	789	−09
Digital Computer	13,813	+03	122	−
Apple	11,062	+20	424	+37
PUBLISHING				
R. R.Donnelley	6,513	+33	299	+11
Gannett	4,007	+05	477	+03
Times Mirror	3,491	−09	1,227	+609
Reader's Digest	3,069	+09	264	+07
McGraw-Hill	2,935	+06	227	+12

TABLE 4–6
The Top Five U.S. Competitors in Four Different Industries in 1995

Dun's Business Rankings, Standard and Poor's Industry Surveys, Industry Week, Forbes, Fortune, Business Week, and *Inc.* In addition, the *Million Dollar Directory* lists key personnel, products, divisions, and SIC codes for over 160,000 U.S. public and private companies whose revenues exceed $500,000. *Standard and Poor's Register of Corporate Directors and Executives* and the *Directory of Corporate Affiliations* are other excellent sources of competitive information. Questions about competitors such as those presented in Table 4–7 are important to address in performing an external audit.

Competition in virtually all industries can be described as intense, and sometimes cutthroat. For example, when RJR Nabisco was seriously wounded by management changes and a record $25 billion leveraged buyout, its major competitor, Philip Morris, did everything it could to take advantage of the situation. Philip Morris used pricing tactics and expanded its salesforce in a direct effort to muscle RJR out of the market. "I can assure you that we plan to take advantage of any opportunities the changed situation at RJR may bring," said Philip Morris's William Murray. One analyst commented, "These are war games."

In a recent article seven characteristics were given that describe the most competitive companies in America: (1) Market share matters; the 90th share point isn't as important as the 91st, and nothing is more dangerous than falling to 89; (2) Understand and remember precisely what business you are in; (3) Whether it's broke or not, fix it—make it better; not just products, but the whole company if necessary; (4) Innovate or evaporate; particularly in technology-driven businesses, nothing quite recedes like success; (5) Acquisition is essential to

TABLE 4–7
Key Questions About Competitors

1. What are the major competitors' strengths?
2. What are the major competitors' weaknesses?
3. What are the major competitors' objectives and strategies?
4. How will the major competitors most likely respond to current economic, social, cultural, demographic, geographic, political, governmental, technological, and competitive trends affecting our industry?
5. How vulnerable are the major competitors to our alternative company strategies?
6. How vulnerable are our alternative strategies to successful counterattack by our major competitors?
7. How are our products or services positioned relative to major competitors?
8. To what extent are new firms entering and old firms leaving this industry?
9. What key factors have resulted in our present competitive position in this industry?
10. How have the sales and profit rankings of major competitors in the industry changed over recent years? Why have these rankings changed that way?
11. What is the nature of supplier and distributor relationships in this industry?
12. To what extent could substitute products or services be a threat to competitors in this industry?

growth; the most successful purchases are in niches that add a technology or a related market; (6) People make a difference; tired of hearing it? Too bad; (7) There is no substitute for quality and no greater threat than failing to be cost competitive on a global basis; these are complementary concepts, not mutually exclusive ones.[8]

COMPETITIVE INTELLIGENCE PROGRAMS   Good competitive intelligence in business, as in the military, is one of the keys to success. The more information and knowledge a firm can obtain about its competitors, the more likely it can formulate and implement effective strategies. Major competitors' weaknesses can represent external opportunities; major competitors' strengths may represent key threats.

Firms need an effective *competitive intelligence (CI)* program. The three basic missions of a CI program are (1) to provide a general understanding of an industry and its competitors, (2) to identify areas in which competitors are vulnerable and to asseses the impact strategic actions would have on competitors, and (3) to identify potential moves that a competitor might make that would endanger a firm's position in the market.[9] Competitive information is equally applicable for strategy formulation, implementation, and evaluation decisions. An effective CI program allows all areas of a firm to access consistent and verifiable information in making decisions. All members of an organization, from the chief executive officer to custodians, are valuable intelligence agents and should feel a part of the CI process. Special characteristics of a successful CI program include flexibility, usefulness, timeliness, and cross-functional cooperation.

The increasing emphasis on competitive analysis in the United States is evidenced by more and more corporations putting this function on their organizational charts under job titles such as Director of Competitive Analysis, Competitive Strategy Manager, Director of Information Services, or Associate Director of Competitive Assessment. The responsibilities of a *Director of Competitive Analysis* include planning, collecting data, analyzing data, facilitating the process of gathering and analyzing data, disseminating intelligence on a timely basis, researching special issues, and recognizing what information is important and who needs to know. Competitive intelligence is not corporate espionage, because 95 percent of the information a company needs to make strategic decisions is available and accessible to the public. Dialog, for example, is a large database that offers an exclusive menu of competitive intelligence information. Other excellent sources of competitive information include trade journals, want ads, newspaper articles, and government filings, as well as customers, suppliers, distributors, and competitors themselves.

TABLE 4–8
New Ways to Battle Corporate Spooks

Though the vast majority of companies don't resort to James Bond tactics when gathering information on competitors, a few just can't resist. Hitachi tried to pay $525,000 to IBM employees for some of Big Blue's trade secrets in the early 1980s but was caught in a sophisticated sting operation. Before that, a competitor flew a plane over a DuPont plant and snapped pictures to help figure out the factory's capacity. More recently, Procter & Gamble has charged that a number of companies used spies to get hold of its secret recipe for soft cookies.

How can you avoid being victimized? Educating employees about the seriousness of leaking sensitive information is a good place to start. Warn your workers about companies that hire head-hunting firms to grill unwitting job candidates on business plans and R&D secrets. Assume that any consulting firm or organization that calls and says it is doing an industry study is digging up nuggets for the competition. Ben Zour, a senior analyst for business research at Eastman Kodak, says, "You have to make employees sensitive to the fact that if they leak, they will lose their jobs." Or worse—if the breach is serious enough—an employee could face criminal prosecution.

Every company tries to keep competitors from hiring away its best employees. But be careful too about pulling that trick yourself. In a recent case in Scotland, an American electronics firm hired an accomplished marketing manager from a competing multinational. A month later he returned to his old company—with some of the firm's European business plans.

Next to leaks, electronic eavesdropping poses the biggest threat to your trove of secrets. Unless you've done a thorough electronic sweep recently, assume anything you communicate by telex, electronic mail, fax, or phone is up for grabs. An estimated 70 foreign governments have the ability to read what multinationals transmit into their countries. Jan Herring, a consultant with Futures Group of Glastonbury, Connecticut, warns that often an American executive will attend an important meeting in, say, Japan and have the conference room swept for electronic bugs, then will return to his hotel and tell his U.S. colleagues the results of the meeting—over a phone line tapped by a competitor. Says Herring, "You find companies that lose by $600 on a $6 million bid, and you wonder why."

Electronic eavesdropping devices are getting ever more sophisticated. At Spy Shops International in Miami, a particularly popular device is a laser gun that can hear conversations up to a half mile away by measuring sound vibrations in an office window. Another gadget can read your computer screen some two blocks away by picking up radio waves emitted by the machine. Naturally, the store also sells countermeasures: an apparent cigarette pack that vibrates in your pocket when someone who's wired walks in, for example, or a computer that foils wiretaps by scrambling messages.

If you discover a bug, don't despair. Companies that resort to illegal or unethical spying are very likely in desperate straits. If you can pinpoint what they're trying to learn by spying on your company, chances are you have spotted a weakness and can strike back.

Source: Brian Dumaine, "Corporate Spies Snoop to Conquer," used by permission of *Fortune* (November 7, 1988): 72.

Computer-based filing systems are often used to assimilate newspaper clippings, annual reports, and similar information about competitors. The *Thomas Register* and *Directory of American Firms Operating in Foreign Countries* are helpful for identifying suppliers, distributors, and potential competitors. Telephone interviews can also be an efficient and effective means of gathering competitive intelligence. For example, to learn details about expansion of a competitor's facility, strategists could call the local tax assessor. The Occupational Safety and Health Administration could be called to obtain information about production capacity and utilization in a given industry. It is important to study an organization's competitors carefully when preparing a business policy case analysis.

Marriott is an American company that does an excellent job of gathering and using competitive intelligence. Before building Fairfield Inns, a team of Marriott employees spent 6 months traveling the country staying in rival hotels/motels and gathering information about service, quality, walls, beds, food, and service. This team identified rival firms' strengths and weaknesses in nearly every aspect of hotel/motel operations, from soap to soundproof rooms. Intelligence officers agree that unethical tactics should never be used to obtain information. However, poorly performing firms sometimes resort to this practice. Table 4–8 reveals some new ways to battle unethical information-gathering tactics.

Some CI activities are illegal and/or unethical, but determining which is often a matter of opinion for a jury to decide. Mindy Kotler, president of Search Associates, says, "If you talk to a Japanese executive, he says, 'Of course, information gathering is part of the job.' If you ask a typical Harvard MBA, he or she says, 'It's the company librarian's job.' " Gathering competitive intelligence should be a part of everyone's job in an organization. Marriott and Motorola—another American company that does a particularly good job of gathering competitive intelligence—agree that all the information you could wish for can be collected without resorting to unethical tactics. They keep their intelligence staffs small, usually under five people, and spend less than $200,000 per year on gathering competitive intelligence.

COOPERATION AMONG COMPETITORS   Strategies that stress cooperation among competitors are being used more and more. Three of Europe's largest computer firms recently changed from foe to friend as they agreed to work together on a strategy to link Europe's diverse computer systems. The three companies—Germany's Siemens-Nixdorf Information Systems AG, France's Cie des Machines Bull, and Italy's Ing. C. Olivetti & Co.—excluded the United Kingdom firm ICL Ltd., which is 80-percent owned by Fujitsu.

Corning has successfully formed 15 joint ventures with foreign rival firms, including agreements with BICC in Britain, Ciba-Geigy in Switzerland, Cie Financiere des Fibres Optiques in France, Siemens in West Germany, Finimi in Belgium, Asahi Glass in Japan, Beijing Electronic Glass Engineering Technology in China, NGK Insulators in Japan, Samsung Group in South Korea, and Australian Consolidated Industries in Australia. The perceived need for cooperation between competitors has turned even bitter enemies into friends. For example, Warner-Lambert Inc. of the United States recently agreed to pool all of its nonprescription drug operations with the United Kingdom drug makers Wellcome PLC and Galaxo Holdings PLC.

The idea of joining forces with a competitor is not easily accepted by Americans, who often view cooperation and partnerships with skepticism and suspicion. Indeed, joint ventures and cooperative arrangements among competitors demand a certain amount of trust to combat paranoia about whether one firm will injure the other. However, multinational firms are becoming more globally cooperative, and increasing numbers of domestic firms are joining forces with competitive foreign firms to reap mutual benefits.

Intel and Texas Instruments recently agreed to a *cooperative mutual-gain strategy* whereby the two firms will swap semiconductor designs and manufacturing technologies for developing computer chips and act as alternate suppliers for each other. This technology exchange will allow both companies to gain market share in the burgeoning market for application-specific integrated circuits (ASICs), the fastest growing segment of the semiconductor industry. Kathryn Harrigan at Columbia University says, "Within a decade most companies will be members of teams that compete against each other."

American companies often enter alliances primarily to avoid investments, being more interested in reducing the costs and risks of entering new businesses or markets than in acquiring new skills. In contrast, *learning from the partner* is a major reason why Asian and European firms enter into cooperative agreements. American firms, too, should place *learning* high on the list of reasons to cooperate with competitors. American companies often form alliances with Asian firms to gain an understanding of their manufacturing excellence, but Asian competence in this area is not easily transferable. Manufacturing excellence is a complex system that includes employee training and involvement, integration with suppliers, statistical process controls, value engineering, and design. In contrast, American know-how in technology and related areas can more easily be imitated. American firms thus need to be careful not to give away more intelligence than they receive in cooperative agreements with rival Asian firms.

SOURCES OF EXTERNAL INFORMATION

A wealth of strategic information is available to organizations from both published and unpublished sources. Unpublished sources include customer surveys, market research, speeches at professional and shareholders' meetings, television programs, interviews, and conversations with stakeholders. Published sources of strategic information include periodicals, journals, reports, government documents, abstracts, books, directories, newspapers, and manuals. Computerization has made it easier today for firms to gather, assimilate, and evaluate information. For example, the *National Trade Data Bank (NTDB)* is a complete source of international business information published monthly by the U.S. Department of Commerce. NTDB is available on CD Rom and is also accessible via Internet at the following sites:

- ◆ FTP: ftp.stat.usagov
- ◆ Gopher: gopher.stat.usagov
- ◆ Mosaic: www.stat.usagov

To order the NTDB or learn more about the service, call 202-482-1986.

INDEXES A number of excellent indexes reveal the location of strategic information by subject, topic, source, author, company, and industry. Indexes can save managers considerable time and effort in identifying and evaluating opportunities and threats. A description of major indexes available for locating information is provided in Table 4–9.

ONLINE DATABASES Millions of people today use online services for both business and personal purposes. *America Online* and *CompuServe* are the two leading commercial online services. Together they have over 7 million subscribers in 1996. Both of these companies are expanding their menu of available services to include everything from online access to most major television networks, newspapers, and magazines to online interviewing of celebrities, to access to the furthermost boundaries of the Internet. Both companies are harnessing the power of multimedia, combining sound, video, and graphics with text.

Nearly 10,000 people are signing up each day as online subscribers in the United States. At the end of 1996, more than 10 million paying subscribers use online services in the United States. Complementing the commercial online industry is the Internet, which has become the worldwide online network of networks. More than 30 million people in more than 100 countries use the Internet, and this number is growing explosively.

Two of the premier Internet access providers are Netcom and PSI. Both companies offer consumers and businesses a widening range of services and information resources from all over the world. Interactive services are soon to offer users not only access to information worldwide but also the ability to communicate with the person or company that created the information. The historical barriers to personal and business success—time zones and diverse cultures—are being eliminated. Online services are poised to become as important to our society by the end of this decade as television and newspapers. Visit the EDGAR SEC database at http://www.sec.gov

LIBRARY PUBLICATIONS Important published sources of strategic information are provided in Tables 4–10 through 4–14. Some of the most widely used sources are described in Table 4–15.

TABLE 4–9
Major Indexes That Reference Economic, Social, Political, Technological, and Competitive Information

NAME OF INDEX	TYPE OF INFORMATION	DESCRIPTION
Applied Science & Technology Index	Technological	A subject index that covers more than 200 selected journals in the fields of aeronautics and space science, automation, chemistry, construction, earth sciences, electricity and electronics, engineering, industrial and mechanical arts, materials, mathematics, metallurgy, physics, telecommunication, transportation, and related subjects. *ASTI* is published monthly.
Business Periodicals Index	Economic Social Political Technological Competitive	This is probably the best known index for its overall subject coverage of selected periodicals in the following fields of business: accounting, advertising and public relations, automation, banking, communications, economics, finance and investments, insurance, labor, management, marketing, taxation, and also specific businesses, industries, and trades. This index also includes a review of books appearing in the journals it indexes, listed together under the heading "Book Reviews." *BPI* is published monthly.
Funk & Scott Index of Corporations & Industries	Competitive	This is the best index for current information on companies and industries. It covers a wide selection of business, industrial, and financial periodicals and also a few brokerage house reports. The yellow pages in the weeklies and the green pages in cumulated issues list articles (or data in articles) on all SIC (Standard Industrial Classification) industries; the white pages list articles on companies. Since many of the entries refer to very brief citations, it is important to note that major articles are designated by a black dot that precedes the abbreviated title of the journal. *F&S* is published weekly.
F&S Index International	Competitive Political	A companion of the index above, covering articles on foreign companies and industries that have appeared in some 1,000 foreign and domestic periodicals and other documents. It is arranged in three parts: (1) by SIC number or product; (2) by region and country; (3) by company. *F&SI* is published monthly.
Public Affairs Information Service Bulletin	Social[a] Political	This is a selective listing in the areas of economic and social conditions, public administration, and international relations, published in English throughout the world. The important differences in this index are (1) it only selectively indexes journals to cover those articles pertinent to its subject coverage; (2) it covers not only periodical articles but also selected books, pamphlets, government publications, and reports of public and private agencies. There is a companion index called *Public Affairs Information Service: Foreign Language Index*. The *PAIS* is published weekly.
Readers' Guide to Periodical Literature	Economic Social Political Technological Competitive	A very popular author and subject index to periodicals published in the United States. The *RGPL* is published bimonthly.
Social Sciences Index	Social Economic Political	A subject and author index to articles in over 260 journals that cover the fields of anthropology, area studies, economics, environmental science, geography, law and criminology, medical sciences, political science, psychology, public administration, sociology, and related subjects. At the back of each issue is an author listing of book reviews that appear in the indexed journals. The *SSI* is published quarterly.
New York Times Index	Economic Social Political Technological Competitive	This is an excellent and very detailed index of articles published by the *New York Times* newspaper. The index is arranged alphabetically and includes many helpful cross-references. The *NYTI* is published bimonthly.
Wall Street Journal/ Barron's Index	Economic Social Political Technological Competitive	A valuable index of *Wall Street Journal* and *Barron's* articles. Each issue is in two parts; corporate news and general news. The index includes a list of book reviews. The *WSJI* is published monthly.

[a]"Social" includes cultural, demographic, and environmental information; "Political" includes governmental and legal information.
Source: Adapted from Lorna M. Daniells, *Business Information Sources* (Los Angeles: University of California Press, 1976), 14–17.

Economic Outlook
American Register of Exporters and Importers
Worldcasts
Federal Reserve Bank of St. Louis, *Rate of Change in Economic Data for Ten Industrial Countries*
Handbook of Basic Economic Statistics
National Bureau of Economic Research publications
Marketing Economic Guide
U.S. Council of Economic Advisors, *Economic Indicators*
Chase Econometric Associates' publications
U.S. Bureau of Labor Statistics, *Monthly Labor Review*
U.S. Bureau of Labor Statistics, *Handbook of Labor Statistics*
U.S. Bureau of the Census, *Statistical Abstract of the United States*
Survey of Business
Business Conditions Digest

Survey of Manufacturers
U.S. Department of Commerce, *Survey of Current Business*
U.S. Department of Commerce, *Business Statistics*
U.S. Department of Commerce, *Long-Term Economic Growth*
U.S. Department of Commerce, *Foreign Economic Trends and Their Implications for the United States*
U.S. Industrial Outlook
Securities and Exchange Commission, *Survey of Buying Power*
United Nations, *Yearbook of International Trade Statistics*
U.S. Board of Governors of the Federal Reserve System, *Federal Reserve Bulletin*
Kiplinger Washington Letter
Guide to Foreign Trade Statistics
Census of Retail Trade
Census of Wholesale Trade
Index of Economic Articles

TABLE 4–10
Sources of Economic Information

American Statistics Index
Demographic Yearbook
Social Indicators and Social Reporting
Brookings Institute Report
Ford Foundation Report
World Bank Atlas
Annals of the American Academy of Political and Social Sciences
Conference Board, *Business Outlook*
Yearbook of International Organizations
Chamber of Commerce publications
Great Britain Central Statistical Office, *Social Trends*
County Business Patterns

Census of Populations
Census of Housing
Census of Agriculture
Census of Manufacturers
Guide to Consumer Markets
County and City Data Book
United Nations Educational, Scientific, and Cultural Organization, *Statistical Yearbook*
Dun & Bradstreet, *Principal International Business*
Telephone directories
City directories
Public opinion polls

TABLE 4–11
Sources of Social, Cultural, Demographic, and Environmental Information

---

Monthly *Catalog of United States Government Publications*
Federal Register
Directory of American Firms Operating in Foreign Countries
Code of Federal Regulations
Congressional Information Service publications
Bureau of National Affairs publications

Chamber of Commerce publications
Kiplinger Washington Letter
Lobbyists
U.S. Congress, *Official Congressional Directory*
Census of Governments
American Statistics Index
Congressional Information Service Annual

TABLE 4–12
Sources of Political, Governmental, and Legal Information

Scientific and Technical Information Source
Trade journals and industrial reports
Department of Defense Annual Reports
Research and Development Directory
Proceedings to professional meetings
Annual Report of the National Science Foundation

World Guide to Trade Associations
University reports
Congressional reports
Patent records

TABLE 4–13
Sources of Technological Information

TABLE 4–14
Sources of Information on Competitors

Annual reports of companies	Trade association publications
Directory of Corporate Affiliations	*County Business Patterns*
Securities and Exchange Commission, 10K Reports	*County and City Data Book*
U.S. Industrial Outlook	*Fortune*
Value Line Investment Survey	*Dun's Business Month*
Moody's Industrial Manual	*Industry Week*, "Trends and Forecasts"
Moody's Investors Service	*Industry Week*, "Financial Analysis of Industry"
Moody's Handbook of Common Stocks	*Business Week*, "Survey of Capital Requirements of Nonfinancial Corporations"
Moody's Bank and Finance Manual	
Moody's Municipal & Government Manual	*Business Week*, "Annual Survey of International Corporate Performance"
Moody's Public Utilities Manual	
Moody's Transportation Manual	*Business Week*, "Survey of Corporate Performance"
Dun & Bradstreet, *Million Dollar Directory*	
Dun & Bradstreet, *Reference Book*	*Business Week*, "Investment Outlook"
Dun & Bradstreet, *Key Business Ratios*	*Business Week*, "Annual Survey of Bank Performance"
Standard & Poor's Corp., *Industry Surveys*	
Standard & Poor's Corp., *Standard Corporation Records*	*Barron's*
	Forbes, "Annual Report on American Industry"
Standard & Poor's Corp., *Analyst's Handbook*	
Standard & Poor's Corp., *Earnings Forecast*	*Nation's Business*, "Lesson of Leadership"
Standard & Poor's Corp., *Bond Guide*	*Census of Manufacturers*
Standard & Poor's Corp., *Security Owners Stock Guide*	*Encyclopedia of Associations*
	Facts on File
Standard & Poor's Corp., *The Outlook*	U.S. Department of Commerce, *Overseas Business Reports*
Standard & Poor's *Register of Corporations, Directors and Executives*	
	Conference Board, *Business Outlook*
Barometer of Small Business	*Starch Marketing*
Dow Jones & Co., *Dow Jones Investor's Handbook*	*U.S. Industrial Directory*
	Fortune 500 Directory
U.S. Internal Revenue Service, *Statistics of Income: Corporation Income Tax Returns*	*Wall Street Transcript*
	F & S Index of Corporate Change
Robert Morris Associates, *Annual Statement Studies*	*Investment Dealers' Digest*
	Conference Board Record
Leo Troy, *Almanac of Business and Industrial Financial Ratios*	Local newspapers
U.S. Department of Commerce, *International Economic Indicators and Competitive Trends*	

FORECASTING TOOLS AND TECHNIQUES

Forecasts are educated assumptions about future trends and events. Forecasting is a complex activity due to factors such as technological innovation, cultural changes, new products, improved services, stronger competitors, shifts in government priorities, changing social values, unstable economic conditions, and unforeseen events. Managers often must rely upon published forecasts to identify key external opportunities and threats effectively.

Many of the publications cited in Tables 4–10 through 4–14 forecast external variables. Several examples include *Industry Week's* "Trends and Forecasts," *Business Week's* "Investment Outlook," and Standard & Poor's *Industry Surveys*. The reputation and continued success of these publications depend to some extent upon accurate forecasts, so published sources of information can offer the best projections available for some variables.

When published forecasts of key external or internal variables are not available, organizations must develop their own projections. Most organizations forecast (project) their

TABLE 4–15
Key Sources of External Information

SOURCE	BRIEF DESCRIPTION
Statistical Abstract of the U.S. (published annually)	Provides social, demographic, environmental, political, and economic information about the United States
United States Industrial Outlook (published annually)	Provides industry forecasts, profiles, data, trends, and projections. Industries are classified by type of business and by SIC Code
Survey of Business (published quarterly)	Provides information concerning the economic outlook of specific industries. Many graphs are given
Business Conditions Digest (published monthly)	Provides charts and graphs of past, present, and forecasted unemployment rates, productivity and income data, consumption patterns, and prices of products and services
Survey of Manufacturers (published annually)	Provides manufacturing data for many industries, including the value of inventories, plant and equipment expenditures, book value of assets, rental payments, etc.
Predicasts (published quarterly)	A guide to corporate organization developments, including liquidations, name changes, new companies, joint ventures, bankruptcies, and divestitures
Survey of Buying Power (published annually)	Provides information on households, population shifts, disposable income, and retail sales by geographic area
Federal Reserve Bulletin (published monthly)	Includes congressional reports, staff studies, announcements, legal developments in the monetary and banking systems
Forbes (published weekly)	A magazine that focuses on current business issues and topics
Business Week (published weekly)	A magazine that contains current business news, including corporate strategy articles
Fortune (published biweekly)	A popular magazine that reports news and events in the business world
Federal Register (published daily)	Gives all public regulations and legal notices issued by federal agencies
Trade journals	Provide news, forecasts, changes, and developments in particular industries. Examples are *Hardware Ace* and *The Underwriter.*
Securities and Exchange Commission's *10K Reports* (published annually)	Gives detailed descriptive and financial information on a specific company
Annual reports (published annually)	Published by corporations for shareholders and interested parties. Reveals company plans, organization, and financial condition
Moody's Industrial Manual (published annually)	Provides information on firms' capital structures, histories, financial conditions, and bond ratings
The Dun & Bradstreet Corporation	Publishes many reference indexes, including *Market Profile Analysis, Dun's Business Rankings, The Billion Dollar Directory, Who Owns Whom,* and *Principal International Businesses*
United States Census of Manufacturers (published annually)	Presents manufacturing data by state and area within states. Includes data on employment, payroll, number of workers, hours, wages, capital expenditures, and the like.
Value Line (published weekly)	Provides investment information on companies and industries. Evaluates companies and industries on financial criteria.
Guide to Consumer Markets (published annually)	Provides detailed consumer information on the distribution and prices of goods and services, labor force changes, and other key areas
Chambers of Commerce	Provide valuable local business information such as traffic patterns, locations of particular businesses, household income levels, etc.
Facts on File (published weekly)	Weekly summaries of world business news are provided.

own revenues and profits annually. Organizations sometimes forecast market share or customer loyalty in local areas. Since forecasting is so important in strategic management and since the ability to forecast (in contrast to the ability to use a forecast) is essential, selected forecasting tools are examined further here.

Forecasting tools can be broadly categorized into two groups: quantitative techniques and qualitative techniques. Quantitative forecasts are most appropriate when historical data are available and when the relationships among key variables are expected to remain the same in the future. The three basic types of quantitative forecasting techniques are econometric models, regression, and trend extrapolation. *Econometric models* are based on simultaneous systems of regression equations that forecast variables such as interest rates and money supply. With the advent of sophisticated computers, econometric models have become the most widely used approach for forecasting economic variables.

All quantitative forecasts, regardless of statistical sophistication and complexity, are based on historical relationships among key variables. *Linear regression,* for example, is based on the assumption that the future will be just like the past—which, of course, it never is. As historical relationships become less stable, quantitative forecasts becomes less accurate.

The six basic qualitative approaches to forecasting are (1) salesforce estimate, (2) juries of executive opinion, (3) anticipatory surveys or market research, (4) scenario forecasts, (5) delphi forecasts, and (6) brainstorming. Qualitative or judgmental forecasts are particularly useful when historical data are not available or when constituent variables are expected to change significantly in the future.

Due to advancements in computer technology, quantitative forecasting techniques are usually cheaper and faster than qualitative methods. Quantitative techniques such as multiple regression can generate measures of error that allow a manager to estimate the degree of confidence associated with a given forecast. Forecasting tools must be used carefully or the results can be more misleading than helpful, but qualitative techniques require more intuitive judgment than do quantitative ones. Managers sometimes erroneously forecast what they would like to occur.

No forecast is perfect, and some forecasts are even wildly inaccurate. This fact accents the need for strategists to devote sufficient time and effort to study the underlying bases for published forecasts and to develop internal forecasts of their own. Key external opportunities and threats can be effectively identified only through good forecasts. Accurate forecasts can provide major competitive advantages for organizations. Forecasts are vital to the strategic-management process and to the success of organizations.

MAKING ASSUMPTIONS   Planning would be impossible without assumptions. McConkey defines assumptions as "best present estimates of the impact of major external factors, over which the manager has little if any control, but which may exert a significant impact on performance or the ability to achieve desired results.[10] Strategists are faced with countless variables and imponderables that can be neither controlled nor predicted with 100-percent accuracy.

By identifying future occurrences that could have a major effect on the firm and making reasonable assumptions about those factors, strategists can carry the strategic-management process forward. Assumptions are needed only for future trends and events that are most likely to have a significant effect on the company's business. Based on the best information at the time, assumptions serve as checkpoints on the validity of strategies. If future occurrences deviate significantly from assumptions, strategists know that corrective actions may be needed. Without reasonable assumptions, the strategy-formulation process could not proceed effectively. Firms that have the best information generally make the most accurate assumptions, which can lead to major competitive advantages.

COMPETITIVE ANALYSIS: PORTER'S FIVE-FORCES MODEL

Illustrated in Figure 4–3, Porter's *five-forces model* of competitive analysis is a widely used approach for developing strategies in many industries. The intensity of competition among firms varies widely across industries. Table 4–16 reveals the average return on assets for

FIGURE 4–3
The Five-forces Model of Competition

firms in 31 different industries in 1994. Intensity of competition is highest in lower-return industries. According to Porter, the nature of competitiveness in a given industry can be viewed as a composite of five forces:

1. Rivalry among competitive firms
2. Potential entry of new competitors
3. Potential development of substitute products
4. Bargaining power of suppliers
5. Bargaining power of consumers

RIVALRY AMONG COMPETING FIRMS Rivalry among competing firms is usually the most powerful of the five competitive forces. The strategies pursued by one firm can be successful only to the extent that they provide competitive advantage over the strategies

INDUSTRY MEDIAN RANK	ROA %	INDUSTRY MEDIAN RANK	ROA %
1 Pharmaceuticals	12.3	17 Forest and Paper Products	2.0
2 Beverages	5.1	18 Wholesalers	2.0
3 Telecommunications	4.9	19 General Merchandisers	1.7
4 Soaps, Cosmetics	4.8	20 Motor Vehicles and Parts	1.6
5 Food	4.7	21 Industrial and Farm Equipment	1.5
6 Specialist Retailers	4.4	22 Electric and Gas Utilities	1.3
7 Aerospace	4.0	23 Metal Products	1.2
8 Scientific, Photo, Control Equipment	3.7	24 Engineering, Construction	0.7
		25 Diversified Financials	0.6
9 Food and Drug Stores	3.6	26 Insurance	0.5
10 Publishing, Printing	3.4	27 Airlines	0.4
11 Petroleum Refining	3.1	28 Railroads	0.3
12 Tobacco	3.0	29 Trading	0.2
13 Computers, Office Equipment	2.5	30 Commercial Banks	0.2
14 Chemicals	2.4	31 Metals	(0.1)
15 Mail, Pkg., and Freight Delivery	2.1		
16 Electronics, Electrical Equipment	2.1	The Global 500 Median	1.2

TABLE 4–16
Intensity of Competition Among Firms in 31 Different Industries (1994) *Return on Assets*

Source: Adapted from *Fortune*, "It Was a Banner Year for Profits," (August 7, 1995): F-28.

being pursued by rival firms. Changes in strategy by one firm may be met with retaliatory countermoves, such as lowering price, enhancing quality, adding features, providing services, extending warranties, and increasing advertising.

The intensity of rivalry among competing firms tends to increase as the number of competitors increases, as competitors become more equal in size and capability, as demand for the industry's products declines, and as price cutting becomes common. Rivalry also increases when consumers can switch brands easily, when barriers to leaving the market are high, when fixed costs are high, when the product is perishable, when rival firms are diverse in strategies, origins, and culture, and when mergers and acquisitions are common in the industry. As rivalry among competing firms intensifies, industry profits decline, in some cases to the point where an industry becomes inherently unattractive.

POTENTIAL ENTRY OF NEW COMPETITORS   Whenever new firms can easily enter a particular industry, the intensity of competitiveness among firms increases. Barriers to entry, however, can include the need to gain economies of scale quickly, the need to gain technology and specialized know-how, the lack of experience, strong customer loyalty, strong brand preferences, large capital requirements, lack of adequate distribution channels, government regulatory policies, tariffs, lack of access to raw materials, possession of patents, undesirable locations, counterattack by entrenched firms, and potential saturation of the market.

Despite numerous barriers to entry, new firms sometimes enter industries with higher-quality products, lower prices, and substantial marketing resources. Compaq's entering the personal computer market and Wal-Mart's entering the discount market are examples. The strategist's job is, therefore, to identify potential new firms entering the market, to monitor the new rival firms' strategies, to counterattack as needed, and to capitalize on existing strengths and opportunities.

DEVELOPMENT OF SUBSTITUTE PRODUCTS   In many industries, firms are in close competition with producers of substitute products in other industries. Examples are plastic container producers competing with glass, paperboard, and aluminum can producers, or acetaminophen manufacturers competing with other manufacturers of pain and headache remedies. The presence of substitute products puts a ceiling on the price that can be charged before the consumers will switch to the substitute product.

Competitive pressures arising from substitute products increase as the relative price of substitute products declines and as consumers' switching costs decrease. The competitive strength of substitute products is best measured by the inroads into market share those products obtain, as well as those firms' plans for increased capacity and market penetration.

BARGAINING POWER OF SUPPLIERS   The bargaining power of suppliers affects the intensity of competition in an industry, especially when there is a large number of suppliers, when there are only a few good substitute raw materials, or when the cost of switching raw materials is especially costly. It is often in the best interest of both suppliers and producers to assist each other with reasonable prices, improved quality, development of new services, just-in-time deliveries, and reduced inventory costs, thus enhancing long-term profitability for all concerned.

Firms may pursue a backward integration strategy to gain control or ownership of suppliers. This strategy is especially effective when suppliers are unreliable, too costly, or not capable of meeting the firm's needs on a consistent basis. Firms can generally negotiate more favorable terms with suppliers when backward integration is a commonly used strategy among rival firms in an industry.

BARGAINING POWER OF CONSUMERS   When customers are concentrated, large, or buy in volume, their bargaining power represents a major force affecting intensity of competition in an industry. Rival firms may offer extended warranties or special services to gain customer loyalty whenever the bargaining power of consumers is substantial. Bargaining power of consumers is also higher when the products being purchased are standard or undifferentiated. When this is the case, consumers can often negotiate selling price, warranty coverage, and accessory packages to a greater extent.

INDUSTRY ANALYSIS: THE EXTERNAL FACTOR EVALUATION (EFE) MATRIX

An *External Factor Evaluation (EFE) Matrix* allows strategists to summarize and evaluate economic, social, cultural, demographic, environmental, political, governmental, legal, technological, and competitive information. There are five steps in developing an EFE Matrix:

1. List key external factors as identified in the external-audit process. Include a total of from 10 to 20 factors, including both opportunities and threats affecting the firm and its industry. List the opportunities first and then the threats. Be as specific as possible, using percentages, ratios, and comparative numbers whenever possible.

2. Assign to each factor a weight that ranges from 0.0 (not important) to 1.0 (very important). The weight indicates the relative importance of that factor to being successful in the firm's industry. Opportunities often receive higher weights than threats, but threats too can receive high weights if they are especially severe or threatening. Appropriate weights can be determined by comparing successful with unsuccessful competitors or by discussing the factor and reaching a group consensus. The summation of all weights assigned to the factors must equal 1.0.

3. Assign a 1-to-4 rating to each critical success factor to indicate how effectively the firm's current strategies respond to the factor, where 4 = *the response is superior,* 3 = *the response is above average,* 2 = *the response is average,* and 1 = *the response is poor.* Ratings are based on effectiveness of the firm's strategies. Ratings are thus company-based, whereas the weights in Step 2 are industry-based.

4. Multiply each factor's weight by its rating to determine a weighted score.

5. Sum the weighted scores for each variable to determine the total weighted score for the organization.

Regardless of the number of key opportunities and threats included in an EFE Matrix, the highest possible *total weighted score* for an organization is 4.0 and the lowest possible total weighted score is 1.0. The average total weighted score is 2.5. A total weighted score of 4.0 indicates that an organization is responding in an outstanding way to existing opportunities and threats in its industry. In other words, the firm's strategies effectively take advantage of existing opportunities and minimize the potential adverse effect of external threats. A total score of 1.0 indicates that the firm's strategies are not capitalizing on opportunities or avoiding external threats.

An example of an EFE Matrix is provided in Table 4–17. Note that "Consumers are more willing to pay for biodegradable packages" is the most important factor affecting this industry, as indicated by the weight of 0.14. The firm in this example is pursuing strategies that effectively capitalize on this opportunity, as indicated by the rating of 4. The total weighted score of 2.64 indicates that this firm is just above average in its effort to pursue strategies that capitalize on external opportunities and avoid threats. It is important to note here that a thorough understanding of the factors being used in the EFE Matrix is more important than the actual weights and ratings assigned.

THE COMPETITIVE PROFILE MATRIX (CPM)

The *Competitive Profile Matrix (CPM)* identifies a firm's major competitors and their particular strengths and weaknesses in relation to a sample firm's strategic position. The weights and total weighted scores in both a CPM and EFE have the same meaning. However, the factors in a CPM include both internal and external issues; the ratings refer to strengths and weaknesses. There are some important differences between the EFE and CPM. First of all, the critical success factors in a CPM are broader; they do not include specific or factual data and may even focus on internal issues. The critical success factors in a CPM also are not grouped into opportunities and threats as they are in an EFE. In a CPM the ratings and total weighted scores for rival firms can be compared to the sample firm. This comparative analysis provides important internal strategic information.

A sample Competitive Profile Matrix is provided in Table 4–18. In this example, Financial Position is the most important critical success factor, as indicated by a weight of 0.40. The sample company's "product quality" is superior, as evidenced by a rating of 4; competitor 1's Financial Position is poor, as indicated by a rating of 1; competitor 2 is the strongest firm overall, as indicated by a total weighted score of 2.8.

A word on interpretation: Just because one firm receives a 3.2 rating and another receives a 2.8 rating in a Competitive Profile Matrix, it does not follow that the first firm is 20 percent better than the second. Numbers reveal the relative strength of firms, but their implied precision is an illusion. Numbers are not magic. The aim is not to arrive at a single magic number, but rather to assimilate and evaluate information in a meaningful way that aids in decision making.

TABLE 4–17
A Sample External Factor Evaluation Matrix

KEY EXTERNAL FACTORS	WEIGHT	RATING	WEIGHTED SCORE
OPPORTUNITIES			
1. The U.S./Canadian Free Trade Agreement is spurring growth.	.08	3	.24
2. Equity markets are healthy.	.06	2	.12
3. Disposable income is increasing 3 percent annually.	.11	1	.11
4. Consumers are more willing to pay for biodegradable packages.	.14	4	.56
5. New software can shorten product life cycle.	.09	4	.36
THREATS			
1. Japanese markets are closed to many U.S. products.	.10	2	.20
2. The European Community has imposed new tariffs.	.12	4	.48
3. The Russian Republic is unstable politically.	.07	3	.21
4. Federal and state support for business is declining.	.13	2	.26
5. Unemployment rates are increasing.	.10	1	.10
Total	1.00		2.64

Note: (1) The ratings indicate how effectively the firm's strategies respond to each factor, where 4 = the response is superior, 3 = the response is above average, 2 = the response is average, and 1 = the response is poor. (2) The total weighted score of 2.64 is above the average of 2.50.

TABLE 4-18
A Competitive Profile Matrix

CRITICAL SUCCESS FACTORS	SAMPLE COMPANY			COMPETITOR 1		COMPETITOR 2	
	WEIGHT	RATING	WEIGHTED SCORE	RATING	WEIGHTED SCORE	RATING	WEIGHTED SCORE
Market Share	0.20	3	0.6	2	0.4	2	0.4
Price Competitiveness	0.20	1	0.2	4	0.8	1	0.2
Financial Position	0.40	2	0.8	1	0.4	4	1.6
Product Quality	0.10	4	0.4	3	0.3	3	0.3
Customer Loyalty	0.10	3	0.3	3	0.3	3	0.3
Total	1.00		2.3		2.2		2.8

Note: (1) The ratings values are as follows: 1 = major weakness, 2 = minor weakness, 3 = minor strength, 4 = major strength. (2) As indicated by the total weighted score of 2.8, Competitor 2 is strongest. (3) Only five critical success factors are included for simplicity; this is too few in actuality.

CONCLUSION

Due to increasing turbulence in markets and industries around the world, the external audit has become an explicit and vital part of the strategic-management process. This chapter provides a framework for collecting and evaluating economic, social, cultural, demographic, environmental, political, governmental, legal, technological, and competitive information. Firms that do not mobilize and empower their managers and employees to identify, monitor, forecast, and evaluate key external forces may fail to anticipate emerging opportunities and threats and, consequently, may pursue ineffective strategies, miss opportunities, and invite organizational demise. Firms not taking advantage of the World Wide Web, America Online, and the Internet are falling behind technologically.

A major responsibility of strategists is to ensure development of an effective external-audit system. This includes using information technology to devise a competitive intelligence system that works. The external-audit approach described in this chapter can be effectively used by any size or type of organization. Typically the external-audit process is more informal in small firms, but the need to understand key trends and events is no less important for these firms. The EFE Matrix and five-forces model can help strategists evaluate the market and industry, but these tools must be accompanied by good intuitive judgment. Multinational firms especially need a systematic and effective external-audit system because external forces vary so greatly among foreign countries.

We invite you to visit the DAVID page on the Prentice Hall Web site at:
http://www.prenhall.com/davidsm
for this chapter's World Wide Web exercises.

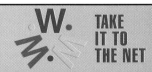

KEY TERMS AND CONCEPTS

America Online	(p. 121)	Chief Technology Officer (CTO)	(p. 106)	Competitive-Information System	(p. 118)
Business Periodicals Index	(p. 122)	Competitive Advantage	(p. 126)	Competitive Intelligence (CI)	(p. 118)
Chief Information Officer (CIO)	(p. 106)	Competitive Analysis	(p. 126)	Competitive Profile Matrix (CPM)	(p. 130)

ISSUES FOR REVIEW AND DISCUSSION

1. Explain how to conduct an external strategic-management audit.

2. Identify a recent economic, social, political, or technological trend that significantly affects financial institutions.

3. Discuss the following statement: Major opportunities and threats usually result from an interaction among key environmental trends rather than from a single external event or factor.

4. Identify two industries experiencing rapid technological changes and three industries that are experiencing little technological change. How does the need for technological forecasting differ in these industries? Why?

5. Use Porter's five-forces model to evaluate competitiveness within the U.S. banking industry.

6. What major forecasting techniques would you use to identify (1) economic opportunities and threats and (2) demographic opportunities and threats? Why are these techniques most appropriate?

7. How does the external audit affect other components of the strategic-management process?

8. As the owner of a small business, explain how you would organize a strategic-information scanning system. How would you organize such a system in a large organization?

9. Construct an EFE Matrix for an organization of your choice.

10. Make an appointment with a librarian at your university to learn how to use online databases. Report your findings in class.

11. Give some advantages and disadvantages of cooperative versus competitive strategies.

12. As a local bank strategist, explain when you would use qualitative versus quantitative forecasts.

13. What is your forecast for interest rates and the stock market in the next several months? As the stock market moves up, do interest rates always move down? Why? What are the strategic implications of these trends?

14. Explain how information technology affects strategies of the organization where you most recently worked.

15. Let's say your boss develops an EFE Matrix that includes 62 factors. How would you suggest reducing the number of factors to 20?

16. Select one of the current readings at the end of this chapter. Prepare a one-page written summary that includes your personal opinion of the article.

17. Discuss the ethics of gathering competitive intelligence.

18. Discuss the ethics of cooperating with rival firms.

NOTES

1. John Diffenbach, "Corporate Environmental Analysis in Large U.S. Corporations," *Long Range Planning* 16, no. 3 (June 1983): 109.

2. York Freund, "Critical Success Factors," *Planning Review* 16, no. 4 (July–August 1988): 20.

3. Gregory Parsons, "Information Technology: A New Competitive Weapon," *Sloan Management Review* 25, no. 1 (Fall 1983): 5.

4. Frederick Gluck, "Global Competition in the 1990s," *Journal of Business Strategy* (Spring 1983): 22, 24.

5. John Harris, Robert Shaw, Jr., and William Sommers, "The Strategic Management of Technology," *Planning Review* 11, no. 1 (January–February 1983): 28, 35.

6. Susan Levine and Michael Yalowitz, "Managing Technology: The Key to Successful Business Growth," *Management Review* 72, no. 9 (September 1983): 44.

7. Susan Gelford, "An Electronic Pipeline That's Changing the Way America Does Business," *Business Week* 3, no. 4 (August 1987): 80.

8. Bill Saporito, "Companies That Compete Best," *Fortune* (May 22, 1989): 36.

9. John Prescott and Daniel Smith, "The Largest Survey of 'Leading-Edge' Competitor Intelligence Managers," *Planning Review* 17, no. 3 (May–June 1989): 6–13.

10. Dale McConkey, "Planning in a Changing Environment," *Business Horizons* 31, no. 5 (September–October 1988): 67.

CURRENT READINGS

Benjamin, Robert and Rolf Wigand. "Electronic Markets and Virtual Value Chains on the Information Superhighway." *Sloan Management Review* 36, no. 2 (Winter 1995): 62–72.

Berman, Evan, Eduardo Vasconcellos, and William B. Werther, Jr. "Executive Levers for the Strategic Management of Technology." *Business Horizons* 37, no. 1 (January–February 1994): 33–39.

Bernhardt, Douglas C. "'I Want It Fast, Factual, Actionable'—Tailoring Competitive Intelligence to Executives' Needs." Executive Summaries. *Long Range Planning* 27 (February 1994): 1.

Buggie, Frederick D. "Expert Innovation Teams: A New Way to Increase Productivity Dramatically." *Planning Review* 23, no. 4 (July–August 1995): 26–31.

Carlin, Barbara A., Michael J. Dowling, William D. Roering, John Wyman, John Kalinoglou, and Greg Clyburn. "Sleeping with the Enemy: Doing Business with a Competitor." *Business Horizons* 37, no. 5 (September–October 1994): 9–15

Chen, M. and D. Miller. "Competitive Attack, Retaliation and Performance: An Expectancy-Valence Framework." *Strategic Management Journal* 15, no. 2 (February 1994): 85–102.

Clarkson, Max B. E. "A Stakeholder Framework for Analyzing and Evaluation Corporate Social Performance." *Academy of Management Review* 20, no. 1 (January 1995): 92–117.

Coplin, William D., and Michael K. O'Leary. "On the Threshold of the 21st Century: A Surprising Wealth of Business Opportunities." The 1995–2000 world Political Risk Forecast. *Planning Review* 23, no. 2 (March–April 1995): 36–44.

Drucker, Peter F. "The Information Executives Truly Need." *Harvard Business Review* 73, no. 1 (January–February 1995): 54–63.

Early, Michael J. and David F. Feeny. "Is Your CIO Adding Value?" *Sloan Management Review* (September 1994): 11–20.

Fink, Dieter. "Information Systems Planning in a Volatile Environment." *Long Range Planning* 27, no. 6 (December 1994): 108–114.

Gibbs, Barrie. "The Effects of Environment and Technology on Managerial Roles." *Journal of Management* 20, no. 3 (Fall 1994): 581–604.

Hagedorn, J. and J. Schakenraad. "The Effect of Strategic Technology Alliances on Company Performance." *Strategic Management Journal* 15, no. 4 (May 1994): 291–310.

Hamel, Gary, C. K. Prahald. "Competing for the Future." *Harvard Business Review* (July–August 1995): 122–130.

McGee, J. E., M. J. Dowling, and W. L. Megginson. "Cooperative Strategy and New Venture Performance: The Role of Business Strategy and Management Experience." *Strategic Management Journal* 16, no. 7 (October 1995): 565–581.

McLeod, Raymond, Jr., Jack William Jones, and Carol Saunders. "The Difficulty in Solving Strategic Problems: The Experiences of Three CIOs." *Business Horizons* 38, no. 1 (January–February 1995): 28–38.

Organ, Dennis W. and Joseph H. Foegen. "The Editor's Chair/(Inter)Net Gain?" *Business Horizons* 38, no. 5 (September–October 1995): 1–3.

Pfeffer, Jeffrey. "Competitive Advantage Through People." *California Management Review* 36, no. 2 (Winter 1994): 9–28.

Powell, T. C. "Total Quality Management as Competitive Advantage: A Review and Empirical Study." *Strategic Management Journal* 16, no. 1 (January 1995): 15–38.

Quinn, James Brian and Martin Neil Baily. "Information Technology: Increasing Productivity in Services." *Academy of Management Executive VIII,* no. 3 (August 1994): 28–51.

Ramaswamy, K., A. S. Thomas, and R. J. Litschert. "Organizational Performance in a Regulated Environment: The Role of Strategic Orientation." *Strategic Management Journal* 15, no. 1 (January 1994): 63–74.

Shrivastava, P. "Environmental Technologies and Competitive Advantage." *Strategic Management Journal* 16, Special Issue (Summer 1995): 183–200.

Smith, K. G., C. M. Grimm, and M. J. Gannon. "Dynamics of Competitive Strategy." *Academy of Management Review* 19, no. 4 (October 1994): 829–832.

Tan, J. Justin and R. J. Litschert. "Environment-Strategy Relationship and Its Performance Implications: An Empirical Study of the Chinese Electronics Industry." *Strategic Management Journal* 15, no. 1 (January 1994): 1–20.

Teng, James T. C., Varun Grover, and Kirk D. Fiedler. "Business Process Reengineering: Charting a Strategic Path for the Information Age." *California Management Review* 36, no. 3 (Spring 1994): 9–31.

Tyler, B. B. and H. K. Steensma. "Evaluating Technological Collaborative Opportunities: A Cognitive Modeling Perspective." *Strategic Management Journal* 16, Special Issue (Summer 1995): 43–70.

Tyre, Marcie J. and Wanda J. Orlikowsi. "Exploiting Opportunities for Technological Improvement in Organizations." *Sloan Management Review* 35 no. 1 (Fall 1993): 13–26.

Watanabe, Kiyohiko and Yukichi Arao. "Omron's Creative Information System." *Long Range Planning* 28, no. 2 (April 1995): 39–48.

Werther, William B., Jr. and Jeffrey L. Kerr. "The Shifting Sands of Competitive Advantage." *Business Horizons* 38, no. 3 (May–June 1995): 11–17.

Zahra, Shaker A., Sarah Nash, and Deborah J. Bickford. "Transforming Technological Pioneering into Competitive Advantage." *Academy of Management Executive IX*, no. 1 (February 1995): 17–31.

DEVELOPING AN EFE MATRIX FOR HERSHEY FOODS

PURPOSE

This exercise will give you practice developing an EFE Matrix. An EFE Matrix summarizes the results of an external audit. This is an important tool widely used by strategists.

INSTRUCTIONS

Step 1 Join with two other students in class and jointly prepare an EFE Matrix for Hershey Foods. Refer back to the Cohesion Case and to Experiential Exercise 1A if needed to identify external opportunities and threats.

Step 2 All three-person teams participating in this exercise should record their team's EFE total weighted score on the board. Put your initials after your score to identify it as your team's.

Step 3 Compare the total weighted scores. Which team's score came closest to the instructor's answer? Discuss reasons for variation in the scores reported on the board.

THE LIBRARY SEARCH

PURPOSE

This exercise will help you become familiar with important sources of external information available in your college library. A key part of preparing an external audit is to examine published sources of information for relevant economic, social, cultural, demographic, environmental, political, governmental, technological, and competitive trends and events. External opportunities and threats must be identified and evaluated before strategies can be formulated effectively.

INSTRUCTIONS

Step 1 Select a company or business located in your county. Go to your college library and conduct an external audit for this company. Find opportunities and threats in recent issues of the local newspaper. Also check magazines. Search for information using the Internet.

Step 2 On a separate sheet of paper, list ten opportunities and ten threats that face this company. Be specific in stating each factor by including percentages and numbers wherever possible.

Step 3 Include a bibliography page to reveal where you found the information.

Step 4 Share your information with a manager of that company. Ask for his or her comments and additions.

Step 5 Write a three-page summary of your findings and submit it to your professor.

Experiential Exercise 4C

DEVELOPING AN EFE MATRIX FOR MY UNIVERSITY

PURPOSE

More and more colleges and universities are embarking upon the strategic-management process. Institutions are consciously and systematically identifying and evaluating external opportunities and threats facing higher education in your state, the nation, and the world.

INSTRUCTIONS

Step 1 Join with two other individuals in class and jointly prepare an EFE Matrix for your institution.

Step 2 Go to the board and record your total weighted score in a column that includes the scores for all three-person teams participating. Put your initials after your score to identify it as your team's.

Step 3 Which team viewed your college's strategies most positively; which team viewed your college's strategies most negatively? Discuss the nature of the differences.

Experiential Exercise 4D

USING THE *STRATEGY FORMULATOR* SOFTWARE

PURPOSE

The purpose of this exercise is to give you experience using the *Strategy Formulator* software that is available with this text. This software can make it easier for you to develop, revise, update, and print various strategy-formulation analyses.

INSTRUCTIONS

Step 1 Use the *Strategy Formulator* software to develop a list of opportunities and threats facing your university (Experiential Exercise 4C).

Step 2 Bring a printout of your work to class. Discuss any problems or questions you encountered in using this software.

Experiential Exercise 4E

DEVELOPING A COMPETITIVE PROFILE MATRIX FOR HERSHEY FOODS

PURPOSE

Monitoring competitors' performance and strategies is a key aspect of an internal audit. This exercise is designed to give you practice evaluating the competitive position of organizations in a given industry, and assimilating that information in the form of a Competitive Profile Matrix.

INSTRUCTIONS

Step 1 Turn back to the Cohesion Case and review the section on competitors.

Step 2 On a separate sheet of paper, prepare a Competitive Profile Matrix that includes Hershey Foods, Nestlé, and Mars.

Step 3 Turn in your Competitive Profile Matrix for a classwork grade.

Experiential Exercise 4F

DEVELOPING A COMPETITIVE PROFILE MATRIX FOR MY UNIVERSITY

PURPOSE

Your college or university competes with all other educational institutions in the world, especially those in your own state. Competition for state funds, students, faculty, staff, endowments, gifts, and federal funds are areas of competitiveness. The purpose of this exercise is to give you practice thinking competitively about the business of education in your state.

INSTRUCTIONS

Step 1 Identify two colleges or universities in your state that compete directly with your institution for students. Interview several persons who are aware of particular strengths and weaknesses of those universities. Record information about the two competing universities.

Step 2 Prepare a Competitive Profile Matrix that includes your institution and the two competing institutions. Include the following factors in your analysis:
1. Tuition costs
2. Quality of faculty
3. Academic reputation
4. Average class size
5. Campus landscaping
6. Athletic programs
7. Quality of students
8. Graduate programs
9. Location of campus
10. Campus culture

Step 3 Submit your Competitive Profile Matrix to your professor for evaluation.

The Internal Assessment

CHAPTER OUTLINE

CHAPTER OBJECTIVES

After studying this chapter, you should be able to do the following:

1. Describe how to perform an internal strategic-management audit.

2. Discuss key interrelationships among the functional areas of business.

3. Identify the basic functions or activities that comprise management, marketing, finance/accounting, production/operations, research and development, and computer information systems.

4. Explain how to determine and prioritize a firm's internal strengths and weaknesses.

5. Explain the importance of financial ratio analysis.

6. Discuss the nature and role of computer information systems in strategic management.

7. Develop an Internal Factor Evaluation (IFE) Matrix.

Like a product or service, the planning process itself must be managed and shaped, if it is to serve executives as a vehicle for strategic decision-making.—ROBERT LENZ

The difference between now and five years ago is that information systems had limited function. You weren't betting your company on it. Now you are.—WILLIAM GRUBER

Weak leadership can wreck the soundest strategy.—SUN ZI

A firm that continues to employ a previously successful strategy eventually and inevitably falls victim to a competitor.—William Cohen

It is the ability of an organization to move information and ideas from the bottom to the top and back again in continuous dialogue that the Japanese value above all things. As this dialogue is pursued, strategy evolves.—ROSENBERG AND SCHEWE

An organization should approach all tasks with the idea that they can be accomplished in a superior fashion.—THOMAS WATSON, JR.

World class information technologies are proving to be a significant strategic advantage, helping North American companies maintain and expand their position in the global marketplace.—Y. NAKAMURA

By 2010, managers will have to handle greater cultural diversity. Managers will have to understand that employees don't think alike about such basics as "handling confrontation" or even what it means "to do a good day's work."—JEFFREY SONNENFELD

There is no substitute for quality and no greater threat than failing to be cost competitive on a global basis. These are complementary concepts, not mutually exclusive ones.—BILL SAPORITO

*T*his chapter focuses on identifying and evaluating a firm's strengths and weaknesses in the functional areas of business, including management, marketing, finance/accounting, production/operations, research and development, and computer information systems. Relationships among these areas of business are examined. Strategic implications of important functional area concepts are examined. The process of performing an internal audit is described.

THE NATURE OF AN INTERNAL AUDIT

All organizations have strengths and weaknesses in the functional areas of business. No enterprise is equally strong or weak in all areas. Maytag, for example, is known for excellent production and product design, whereas Procter & Gamble is known for superb marketing. Internal strengths/weaknesses, coupled with external opportunities/threats and a clear statement of mission, provide the basis for establishing objectives and strategies. Objectives and strategies are established with the intention of capitalizing upon internal strengths and overcoming weaknesses! The internal-audit part of the strategic-management process is emphasized in Figure 5–1.

KEY INTERNAL FORCES   It is not possible in a business policy text to review in depth all the material presented in courses such as marketing, finance, accounting, management, computer information systems, and production/operations; there are many subareas within these functions, such as customer service, warranties, advertising, packaging, and pricing under marketing.

For different types of organizations, such as hospitals, universities, and government agencies, the functional business areas, of course, differ. In a hospital, for example, functional areas may include cardiology, hematology, nursing, maintenance, physician support, and receivables. Functional areas of a university can include athletic programs, placement services, housing, fund-raising, academic research, counseling, and intramural programs. Within large organizations, each division has certain strengths and weaknesses. For example, AT&T is strong in communications and weak in computers.

A firm's strengths that cannot be easily matched or imitated by competitors are called *distinctive competencies*. Building competitive advantages involves taking advantage of distinctive competencies. For example, 3M exploits its distinctive competence in research and development by producing a wide range of innovative products. Strategies are designed in part to improve on a firm's weaknesses, turning them into strengths, and maybe even into distinctive competencies.

Some researchers emphasize the importance of the internal audit part of the strategic-management process by comparing it to the external audit. Robert Grant concludes that the internal audit is more important, saying:

> In a world where customer preferences are volatile, the identity of customers is changing, and the technologies for serving customer requirements are continually evolving, an externally focused orientation does not provide a secure foundation for formulating long-term strategy. When the external environment is in a state of flux, the firm's own resources and capabilities may be a much more stable basis on which to define its identity. Hence, a definition of a business in terms of what it is capable of doing may offer a more durable basis for strategy than a definition based upon the needs which the business seeks to satisfy.[1]

THE PROCESS OF PERFORMING AN INTERNAL AUDIT   The process of performing an *internal audit* closely parallels the process of performing an external audit. Representative managers and employees from throughout the firm need to be involved in

FIGURE 5–1

A Comprehensive Strategic-Management Model

Feedback

Perform
External
Audit

Develop
Mission
Statement

Perform
Internal
Audit

Establish
Long-term
Objectives

Generate,
Evaluate,
and Select
Strategies

Establish
Policies
and
Annual
Objectives

Allocate
Resources

Measure
and
Evaluate
Performance

Strategy Formulation

Strategy Implementation

Strategy Evaluation

141

determining a firm's strengths and weaknesses. The internal audit requires gathering and assimilating information about the firm's management, marketing, finance/accounting, production/operations, research and development, and computer information systems operations. Key factors should be prioritized as described in Chapter 4 so that the firm's most important strengths and weaknesses can be collectively determined.

Compared to the external audit, the process of performing an internal audit provides more opportunity for participants to understand how their jobs, departments, and divisions fit into the whole organization. This is a great benefit because managers and employees perform better when they understand how their work affects other areas and activities of the firm. For example, when marketing and manufacturing managers jointly discuss issues related to internal strengths and weaknesses, they gain a better appreciation of issues, problems, concerns, and needs in all the functional areas. In organizations that do not use strategic management, marketing, finance, and manufacturing managers often do not interact with each other in significant ways. Performing an internal audit thus is an excellent vehicle or forum for improving the process of communication in the organization. *Communication* may be the most important word in management.

Performing an internal audit requires gathering, assimilating, and evaluating information about the firm's operations. Critical success factors, consisting of both strengths and weaknesses, can be identified and prioritized in the manner discussed in Chapter 4. According to William King, a task force of managers from different units of the organization, supported by staff, should be charged with determining the 10 to 20 most important strengths and weaknesses that should influence the future of the organization:

> The development of conclusions on the 10 to 20 most important organizational strengths and weaknesses can be, as any experienced manager knows, a difficult task, when it involves managers representing various organizational interests and points of view. Developing a 20-page list of strengths and weaknesses could be accomplished relatively easily, but a list of the 10 to 15 most important ones involves significant analysis and negotiation. This is true because of the judgments that are required and the impact which such a list will inevitably have as it is used in the formulation, implementation, and evaluation of strategies.[2]

RELATIONSHIPS AMONG THE FUNCTIONAL AREAS OF BUSINESS

Strategic management is a highly interactive process that requires effective coordination among management, marketing, finance/accounting, production/operations, R&D, and computer information systems managers. Although the strategic-management process is overseen by strategists, success requires that managers and employees from all functional areas work together to provide ideas and information. Financial managers, for example, may need to restrict the number of feasible options available to operations managers, or R&D managers may develop such good products that marketing managers need to set higher objectives. A key to organizational success is effective coordination and understanding among managers from all functional business areas! Through involvement in performing an internal strategic-management audit, managers from different departments and divisions of the firm come to understand the nature and effect of decisions in other functional business areas in their firm. Knowledge of these relationships is critical for effectively establishing objectives and strategies.

A failure to recognize and understand relationships among the functional areas of business can be detrimental to strategic management, and the number of those relationships that must be managed increases dramatically with a firm's size, diversity, geographic dispersion, and the number of products or services offered. Governmental and nonprofit enterprises have traditionally not placed sufficient emphasis on relationships among the business functions. For example, some state governments, utilities, universities, and hospitals have only recently begun to establish marketing objectives and policies that are consistent with their financial capabilities and limitations. Some firms place too great an emphasis on one function at the expense of others. Ansoff explains:

> During the first fifty years, successful firms focused their energies on optimizing the performance of one of the principal functions: production/operations, R&D, or marketing. Today, due to the growing complexity and dynamism of the environment, success increasingly depends on a judicious combination of several functional influences. This transition from a single function focus to a multifunction focus is essential for successful strategic management.[3]

Financial ratio analysis exemplifies the complexity of relationships among the functional areas of business. A declining return on investment or profit margin ratio could be the result of ineffective marketing, poor management policies, research and development errors, or a weak computer information system. The effectiveness of strategy formulation, implementation, and evaluation activities hinges upon a clear understanding of how major business functions affect one another. For strategies to succeed, a coordinated effort among all the functional areas of business is needed. In the case of planning, George says:

> We may conceptually separate planning for the purpose of theoretical discussion and analysis, but in practice, neither is it a distinct entity nor is it capable of being separated. The planning function is mixed with all other business functions and, like ink once mixed with water, it cannot be set apart. It is spread throughout and is a part of the whole of managing an organization.[4]

INTEGRATING STRATEGY AND CULTURE   Relationships among a firm's functional business activities can perhaps be exemplified best by focusing on organizational culture, an internal phenomenon that permeates all departments and divisions of an organization. *Organizational culture* can be defined as "a pattern of behavior developed by an organization as it learns to cope with its problem of external adaptation and internal integration, that has worked well enough to be considered valid and to be taught to new members as the correct way to perceive, think, and feel."[5] This definition emphasizes the importance of matching external with internal factors in making strategic decisions.

Organizational culture captures the subtle, elusive, and largely unconscious forces that shape a workplace. Remarkably resistant to change, culture can represent a major strength or weakness for the firm. It can be an underlying reason for strengths or weaknesses in any of the major business functions.

Defined in Table 5–1, *cultural products* include values, beliefs, rites, rituals, ceremonies, myths, stories, legends, sagas, language, metaphors, symbols, heroes, and heroines. These products or dimensions are levers that strategists can use to influence and direct strategy formulation, implementation, and evaluation activities. An organization's culture compares to an individual's personality in the sense that no organization has the same culture and no individual has the same personality. Both culture and personality are fairly enduring and can be warm, aggressive, friendly, open, innovative, conservative, liberal, harsh, or likable.

Dimensions of organizational culture permeate all the functional areas of business. It is something of an art to uncover the basic values and beliefs that are buried deeply in an organization's rich collection of stories, language, heroes, and rituals, but cultural products can represent important strengths and weaknesses. Culture is an aspect of organizations that can no longer be taken for granted in performing an internal strategic-management audit, because culture and strategy must work together.

The strategic-management process takes place largely within a particular organization's culture. Lorsch found that executives in successful companies are emotionally committed to

TABLE 5–1
Cultural Products and Associated Definitions

Rites	Relatively elaborate, dramatic, planned sets of activities that consolidate various forms of cultural expressions into one event, carried out through social interactions, usually for the benefit of an audience
Ceremonial	A system of several rites connected with a single occasion or event
Ritual	A standardized, detailed set of techniques and behaviors that manage anxieties, but seldom produce intended, technical consequences of practical importance
Myth	A dramatic narrative of imagined events, usually used to explain origins or transformations of something. Also, an unquestioned belief about the practical benefits of certain techniques and behaviors that is not supported by facts
Saga	An historical narrative describing the unique accomplishments of a group and its leaders, usually in heroic terms
Legend	A handed-down narrative of some wonderful event that is based on history but has been embellished with fictional details
Story	A narrative based on true events, sometimes a combination of truth and fiction
Folktale	A completely fictional narrative
Symbol	Any object, act, event, quality, or relation that serves as a vehicle for conveying meaning, usually by representing another thing
Language	A particular form or manner in which members of a group use sounds and written signs to convey meanings to each other
Metaphors	Shorthand words used to capture a vision or to reinforce old or new values
Values	Life-directing attitudes that serve as behavioral guidelines
Belief	An understanding of a particular phenomenon
Heroes/Heroines	Individuals whom the organization has legitimized to model behavior for others

Source: Adapted from H. M. Trice and J. M. Beyer, "Studying Organizational Cultures Through Rites and Ceremonials," *Academy of Management Review* 9, no. 4 (October 1984): 655.

the firm's culture, but he concluded that culture can inhibit strategic management in two basic ways. First, managers frequently miss the significance of changing external conditions because they are blinded by strongly held beliefs. Second, when a particular culture has been effective in the past, the natural response is to stick with it in the future, even during times of major strategic change.[6] An organization's culture must support the collective commitment of its people to a common purpose. It must foster competence and enthusiasm among managers and employees.

Organizational culture significantly affects business decisions and thus must be evaluated during an internal strategic-management audit. If strategies can capitalize on cultural strengths, such as a strong work ethic or highly ethical beliefs, then management can often implement changes swiftly and easily. However, if the firm's culture is not supportive, strategic changes may be ineffective or even counterproductive. A firm's culture can become antagonistic to new strategies, with the result being confusion and disorientation. An organization's culture should infuse individuals with enthusiasm for implementing strategies. Allarie and Firsirotu emphasize the need to understand culture:

> Culture provides an explanation for the insuperable difficulties a firm encounters when it attempts to shift its strategic direction. Not only has the "right" culture become the essence and foundation of corporate excellence, it is also claimed that success or failure of reforms hinges on management's sagacity and ability to change the firm's driving culture in time and in tune with required changes in strategies.[7]

The potential value of organizational culture has not been fully realized in the study of strategic management. Ignoring the effect that culture can have on relationships among the functional areas of business can result in barriers to communication, lack of coordination, and an inability to adapt to changing conditions. Some tension between culture and a firm's strategy is inevitable, but the tension should be monitored so that it does not reach a point at which relationships are severed and the culture becomes antagonistic. The resulting disarray among members of the organization would disrupt strategy formulation, implementation, and evaluation. On the other hand, a supportive organizational culture can make managing much easier.

Internal strengths and weaknesses associated with a firm's culture are sometimes overlooked due to the interfunctional nature of this phenomenon. It is important, therefore, for strategists to understand their firm as a sociocultural system. Success is often determined by linkages between a firm's culture and strategies. The challenge of strategic management today is to bring about the changes in organizational culture and individual mind-sets necessary to support the formulation, implementation, and evaluation of strategies. As indicated in the Global Perspective, this challenge becomes greater as a firm initiates or expands multinational operations. Note how managers in the Far East differ from U.S. and European managers in style and behavior.

OPERATING AS IF THE NATURAL ENVIRONMENT MATTERS   Both employees and consumers are becoming especially resentful of firms that take more than they give from the natural environment; likewise, people today are especially appreciative of firms that conduct operations in a way that mends rather than harms the environment.

The U.S. Justice Department recently issued new guidelines for companies to uncover environmental wrongdoing among their managers and employees without exposing themselves to potential criminal liability. The new guidelines give nine hypothetical examples to illustrate the new legal requirements. The examples include Company A, which regularly

GLOBAL PERSPECTIVE
How Cultures of Countries Vary

There are two basic types of cultures in the world—high-context and low-context. High-context cultures are oral cultures where what a person says in writing is *less important* than who a person is and what the social context is surrounding a business agreement. In low-context cultures, what a person says in writing is *more important* than who a person is and what the social context is surrounding a business agreement. The following diagram gives an arrangement of high-context and low-context cultures worldwide:

Chinese   High-Context Culture
Korean
Japanese
Vietnamese   ▲
Arab   │
Greek   │
Spanish   │
Italian   │
English   │
North American   │
Scandinavian   ▼
Swiss
German   Low-Context Culture

There are numerous implications of the high-context/low-context culture analysis that should be considered in doing business globally. For example:

1. In high-context countries casual conversations have a level of business significance far beyond the content being discussed. High-context foreign nationals want to know a lot about people personally and about their companies before making business commitments.

2. Businesspeople in high-context cultures expect a presentation to be in short, separate segments to allow time for questions and digestion of what has been presented. Frequent deviations from the major business topic are expected. High-context persons are not time- or efficiency-oriented and thus like to relax some during business meetings.

3. In high-context cultures, age, seniority, and experience are very important, so sending a young expert to conduct a meeting or close a sale would often be interpreted negatively.

4. A passive, impersonal style of communication is best with low-context cultures. Avoid exaggeration, hyperbole, superlatives, and egocentrism.

Source: Adapted from Ronald Dulek, John Fielden, and John Hill, "International Communication: An Executive Primer," *Business Horizons* (January–February 1991): 19–25. Also, Edward Hall, "How Cultures Collide," *Psychology Today* (July 1976): 67–74.

conducts a comprehensive environmental audit, goes straight to the government as soon as something wrong is turned up, disciplines the responsible people in the company, and gives their names as well as all relevant documentation to the government. The Justice Department will prosecute but be lenient in this case. The extreme example is Company K, which tries to cover up an environmental violation and does not cooperate with the government or provide names. Its audit is narrow, and its compliance program is "no more than a collection of paper." No leniency is likely for this firm. United Technologies Corporation, for example, recently was a Company K and incurred a $5.3 million fine for abuses in handling and discharging hazardous wastes.

MANAGEMENT

The *functions of management* consist of five basic activities: planning, organizing, motivating, staffing, and controlling. An overview of these activities is provided in Table 5–2.

PLANNING   The only thing certain about the future of any organization is change, and *planning* is the essential bridge between the present and the future that increases the likelihood of achieving desired results. Planning is the cornerstone of effective strategy formulation. But even though it is considered the foundation of management, it is commonly the task that managers neglect most. Planning is essential for successful strategy implementation and strategy evaluation, largely because organizing, motivating, staffing, and controlling activities are dependent upon good planning.

The process of planning must include involvement of managers and employees throughout an organization. As noted in Figure 5–2, the time horizon for planning decreases

TABLE 5–2
The Basic Functions of Management

FUNCTION	DESCRIPTION	MOST IMPORTANT AT WHICH STAGE OF THE STRATEGIC-MANAGEMENT PROCESS?
Planning	Planning consists of all those managerial activities related to preparing for the future. Specific tasks include forecasting, establishing objectives, devising strategies, developing policies, and setting goals.	Strategy Formulation
Organizing	Organizing includes all those managerial activities that result in a structure of task and authority relationships. Specific areas include organizational design, job specialization, job descriptions, job specifications, span of the control, unity of command, coordination, job design, and job analysis.	Strategy Implementation
Motivating	Motivating involves efforts directed toward shaping human behavior. Specific topics include leadership, communication, work groups, behavior modification, delegation of authority, job enrichment, job satisfaction, needs fulfillment, organizational change, employee morale, and managerial morale.	Strategy Implementation
Staffing	Staffing activities are centered on personnel or human resource management. Included are wage and salary administration, employee benefits, interviewing, hiring, firing, training, management development, employee safety, affirmative action, equal employment opportunity, union relations, career development, personnel research, discipline policies, grievance procedures, and public relations.	Strategy Implementation
Controlling	Controlling refers to all those managerial activities directed toward assuring that actual results are consistent with planned results. Key areas of concern include quality control, financial control, sales control, inventory control, expense control, analysis of variances, rewards, and sanctions.	Strategy Evaluation

from two to five years for top-level to less than six months for lower-level managers. The important point is that all managers do planning and should involve subordinates in the process to facilitate employee understanding and commitment.

Planning can have a positive impact on organizational and individual performance. Planning allows an organization to identify and take advantage of external opportunities and minimize the impact of external threats. Planning is more than extrapolating from the past and present into the future. It also includes developing a mission, forecasting future events and trends, establishing objectives, and choosing strategies to pursue.

An organization can develop synergy through planning. *Synergy* exists when everyone pulls together as a team that knows what it wants to achieve; synergy is the 2 + 2 = 5 effect. By establishing and communicating clear objectives, employees and managers can work together toward desired results. Synergy can result in powerful competitive advantages. The strategic-management process itself is aimed at creating synergy in an organization.

Planning allows a firm to adapt to changing markets and thus shape its own destiny. Strategic management can be viewed as a formal planning process that allows an organization to pursue proactive rather than reactive strategies. Successful organizations strive to

FIGURE 5–2
The Three Levels of Planning

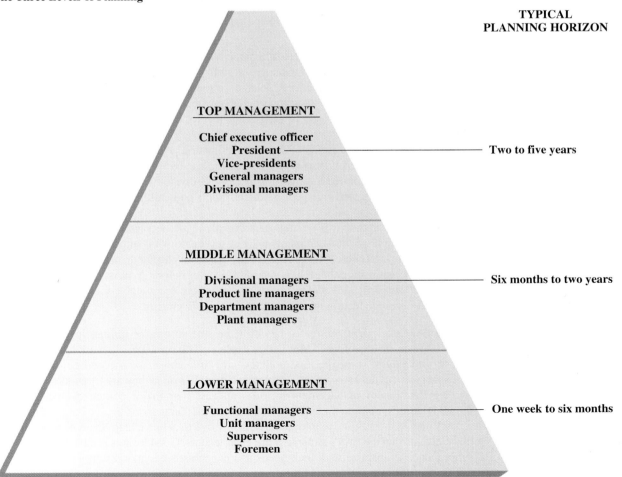

control their own futures rather than merely react to external forces and events as they occur. Historically, organisms and organizations that have not adapted to changing conditions have become extinct. Swift adaptation is needed today more than ever before because changes in markets, economies, and competitors worldwide are accelerating.

ORGANIZING   The purpose of *organizing* is to achieve coordinated effort by defining task and authority relationships. Organizing means determining who does what and who reports to whom. There are countless examples in history of well-organized enterprises successfully competing against, and in some cases defeating, much stronger but less well-organized firms. A well-organized firm generally has motivated managers and employees who are committed to seeing the organization succeed. Resources are allocated more effectively and used more efficiently in a well-organized firm than in a disorganized firm.

The organizing function of management can be viewed as consisting of three sequential activities: breaking tasks down into jobs (work specialization), combining jobs to form departments (departmentalization), and delegating authority. Breaking tasks down into jobs requires development of job descriptions and job specifications. These tools clarify for both managers and employees what particular jobs entail. In *Wealth of Nations* published in 1776, Adam Smith cited the advantages of work specialization in the manufacture of pins:

> One man draws the wire, another straightens it, a third cuts it, a fourth points it, a fifth grinds it at the top for receiving the head. Ten men working in this manner can produce 48,000 pins in a single day, but if they had all wrought separately and independently, each might at best produce twenty pins in a day.[8]

Combining jobs to form departments results in an organizational structure, span of control, and a chain of command. Changes in strategy often require changes in structure because new positions may be created, deleted, or merged. Organizational structure dictates how resources are allocated and how objectives are established in a firm. Allocating resources and establishing objectives geographically, for example, is much different from doing so by product or customer.

The most common forms of departmentalization are functional, divisional, strategic business unit, and matrix. These types of structure are discussed further in Chapter 7. Sears recently reorganized its 825 stores into six broad divisions: electronics and appliances, home fashions, home improvement products, men's and children's products, women's apparel, and automotive and recreational products.

Delegating authority is an important organizing activity, as evidenced in the old saying "You can tell how good a manager is by observing how his or her department functions when he or she isn't there." Employees today are more educated and more capable of participating in organizational decision making than ever before. In most cases, they expect to be delegated authority and responsibility, and to be held accountable for results. Delegation of authority is embedded in the strategic-management process.

MOTIVATING   *Motivating* can be defined as the process of influencing people to accomplish specific objectives.[9] Motivation explains why some people work hard and others do not. Objectives, strategies, and policies have little chance of succeeding if employees and managers are not motivated to implement strategies once they are formulated. The motivating function of management includes at least four major components: leadership, group dynamics, communication, and organizational change.

When managers and employees of a firm strive to achieve high levels of productivity, this indicates that the firm's strategists are good leaders. Good leaders establish rapport with subordinates, empathize with their needs and concerns, set a good example, and are trustworthy and fair. Leadership includes developing a vision of the firm's future and inspiring people to work hard to achieve that vision. Kirkpatrick and Locke recently reported that certain traits also characterize effective leaders: knowledge of the business, cognitive ability, self-confidence, honesty, integrity, and drive.[10]

Research suggests that democratic behavior on the part of leaders results in more positive attitudes toward change and higher productivity than does autocratic behavior. Drucker says:

> Leadership is not a magnetic personality. That can just as well be demagoguery. It is not "making friends and influencing people." That is flattery. Leadership is the lifting of a person's vision to higher sights, the raising of a person's performance to a higher standard, the building of a person's personality beyond its normal limitations.[11]

Group dynamics play a major role in employee morale and satisfaction. Informal groups or coalitions form in every organization. The norms of coalitions can range from being very positive to very negative toward management. It is important, therefore, that strategists identify the composition and nature of informal groups in an organization to facilitate strategy formulation, implementation, and evaluation. Leaders of informal groups are especially important in formulating and implementing strategy changes.

Communication, perhaps the most important word in management, is a major component in motivation. An organization's system of communication determines whether strategies can be implemented successfully. Good two-way communication is vital for gaining support for departmental and divisional objectives and policies. Top-down communication encourages bottom-up communication. The strategic-management process becomes a lot easier when subordinates are encouraged to discuss their concerns, reveal their problems, provide recommendations, and give suggestions. A primary reason for instituting strategic management is to build and support effective communication networks throughout the firm.

> The manager of tomorrow must be able to get his people to commit themselves to the business, whether they are machine operators or junior vice presidents. Ah, you say, participative management. Have a cigar. But just because most managers tug a forelock at the P word doesn't mean they know how to make it work. In the 1990s, throwing together a few quality circles won't suffice. The key issue will be empowerment, a term whose strength suggests the need to get beyond merely sharing a little information and a bit of decision making.[12]

STAFFING   The management function of *staffing*, also called *personnel management* or *human resource management*, includes activities such as recruiting, interviewing, testing, selecting, orienting, training, developing, caring for, evaluating, rewarding, disciplining, promoting, transferring, demoting, and dismissing employees. Staffing activities play a major role in strategy-implementation efforts, and for this reason human resource managers are becoming more actively involved in the strategic-management process. Strengths and weaknesses in the staffing area are important to identify.

The complexity and importance of human resource activities have increased to such a degree that all but the smallest organizations now need a full-time human resource manager. Numerous court cases that directly affect staffing activities are decided each day. Organizations and individuals can be penalized severely for not following federal, state, and local laws and guidelines related to staffing.[13] Line managers simply cannot stay abreast of all the legal developments and requirements regarding staffing. The human resources department coordinates staffing decisions in the firm so that an organization as a whole meets legal requirements. This department also provides needed consistency in administering company rules, wages, and policies.

Human resources management is particularly challenging for international companies. For example, the inability of spouses and children to adapt to new surroundings has become a major staffing problem in overseas transfers. The problems include premature returns, job performance slumps, resignation, discharge, low morale, marital discord, and general discontent. Firms such as Ford Motor and Exxon have begun screening and interviewing spouses and children before assigning persons to overseas positions. 3M Corporation introduces children to peers in the target country and offers spouses educational benefits.

Strategists are becoming increasingly aware of how important human resources are to effective strategic management. Human resource managers are becoming more involved and more proactive in formulating and implementing strategies. They provide leadership for organizations that are restructuring or allowing employees to work at home as suggested in the Information Technology Perspective.

Waterman describes staffing activities among successful companies:

> Successful (renewing) companies are busy taking out layers of management, cutting staff, and pushing decisions down. Nucor Corporation runs a successful, near billion-dollar steel enterprise from a headquarters office and complement of seven people in a Charlotte, N.C., shopping mall. At Dana Corporation, President Woody Morcott and others take extraordinary pride in the fact that today there are only five layers between the chief executive's office and the person on the factory floor. In the mid-1970s there were 14 . . . Leaner organizations set the stage for success (renewal). They make each one of us more important. They empower the individual.[14]

CONTROLLING   The *controlling* function of management includes all those activities undertaken to assure that actual operations conform to planned operations. All managers in an organization have controlling responsibilities, such as conducting performance evaluations and taking necessary action to minimize inefficiencies. The controlling function of management is particularly important for effective strategy evaluation. Controlling consists of four basic steps:

1. Establishing performance standards
2. Measuring individual and organizational performance
3. Comparing actual performance to planned performance standards
4. Taking corrective actions

INFORMATION TECHNOLOGY
The Officeless Office

In many firms information technology is doing away with the workplace and allowing employees to work at home or anywhere, anytime. The number of work-at-home employees and managers is expected to exceed 13 million by 1998 in the United States. "There is nothing I can do in an office that I can't do at home," says William Holtz, vice president for global enterprise services with Northern Telecom. From his home in Philadelphia, Holtz supervises a staff of 1,000 in Nashville, Tennessee. More and more managers are moving away from the mind-set of having to see their employees and watch them work.

The mobile concept of work allows employees to work the traditional 9-to-5 workday across any of the 24 time zones around the globe. Affordable desktop videoconferencing software developed by AT&T, Intel, Lotus, or Vivo Software allows employees to beam in whenever needed. Any manager or employee who travels a lot away from the office may be a good candidate for working at home rather than in an office provided by the firm. Salespersons and consultants are good examples, but any person whose job largely involves talking to others or handling information could easily operate at home with the proper computer system and software. The accounting firm Ernst & Young has reduced its office space requirements

by 2 million square feet over the past three years by allowing employees to work at home.

Many people see the officeless office trend as leading to a resurgence of family togetherness in American society. Even the design of homes may change from having large open areas to having more private small areas conducive to getting work done.

Source: Adapted from Edward Baig, "Welcome to the Officeless Office," *Business Week* (June 26, 1995): 104.

Measuring individual performance is often conducted ineffectively or not at all in organizations. Some reasons for this shortcoming are that evaluation can create confrontations that most managers prefer to avoid, can take more time than most managers are willing to give, and can require skills that many managers lack. No single approach to measuring individual performance is without limitations. For this reason, an organization should examine various methods, such as the graphic rating scale, the behaviorally anchored rating scale, and the critical incident method, and then develop or select a performance appraisal approach that best suits the firm's needs. Increasingly, firms are striving to link organizational performance with managers' and employees' pay. This topic is discussed further in Chapter 7.

MARKETING

Marketing can be described as the process of defining, anticipating, creating, and fulfilling customers' needs and wants for products and services. Joel Evans and Barry Bergman suggest that there are nine basic *functions of marketing*: (1) customer analysis, (2) buying supplies, (3) selling products/services, (4) product and service planning, (5) pricing, (6) distribution, (7) marketing research, (8) opportunity analysis, and (9) social responsibility.[15] Understanding these functions helps strategists identify and evaluate marketing strengths and weaknesses.

CUSTOMER ANALYSIS   *Customer analysis*—the examination and evaluation of consumer needs, desires, and wants—involves administering customer surveys, analyzing consumer information, evaluating market positioning strategies, developing customer profiles, and determining optimal market segmentation strategies. The information generated by customer analysis can be essential in developing an effective mission statement. Customer profiles can reveal the demographic characteristics of an organization's customers. Buyers, sellers, distributors, salespeople, managers, wholesalers, retailers, suppliers, and creditors can all participate in gathering information to identify customers' needs and wants successfully. Successful organizations continually monitor present and potential customers' buying patterns.

BUYING SUPPLIES   The second function of marketing is buying supplies needed to produce and sell a product or service. *Buying* consists of evaluating alternative suppliers or vendors, selecting the best suppliers, arranging acceptable terms with suppliers, and procuring the supplies. The buying process can be complicated by such factors as price controls, recession, foreign trade restrictions, strikes, walkouts, and machine breakdowns. Even the weather can significantly disrupt procurement of needed supplies. Quite often, the question arises whether to make or buy needed supplies and services. Recall that backward integration, gaining control over suppliers, is a particularly attractive strategy when suppliers are unreliable, costly, or incapable of meeting company needs.

SELLING PRODUCTS/SERVICES   Successful strategy implementation generally rests upon the ability of an organization to sell some product or service. *Selling* includes many marketing activities such as advertising, sales promotion, publicity, personal selling, sales-force management, customer relations, and dealer relations. These activities are especially critical when a firm pursues a market penetration strategy. The effectiveness of various selling tools for consumer and industrial products varies. Personal selling is most important for industrial goods companies, and advertising is most important for consumer goods companies. Determining organizational strengths and weaknesses in the selling function of marketing is an important part of performing an internal strategic-management audit.

PRODUCT AND SERVICE PLANNING   *Product and service planning* includes activities such as test marketing; product and brand positioning; devising warranties; packaging; determining product options, product features, product style, and product quality; deleting old products; and providing for customer service. Product and service planning is particularly important when a company is pursuing product development or diversification.

One of the most effective product and service planning techniques is *test marketing*. Test markets allow an organization to test alternative marketing plans and to forecast future sales of new products. In conducting a test market project, an organization must decide how many cities to include, which cities to include, how long to run the test, what information to collect during the test, and what action to take after the test has been completed. Test marketing is more frequently used by consumer goods companies than by industrial goods companies. Test marketing can allow an organization to avoid substantial losses by revealing weak products and ineffective marketing approaches before large-scale production begins.

PRICING   Five major stakeholders affect *pricing* decisions: consumers, governments, suppliers, distributors, and competitors. Sometimes an organization will pursue a forward integration strategy primarily to gain better control over prices charged to consumers. Governments can impose constraints on price-fixing, price discrimination, minimum prices, unit pricing, price advertising, and price controls. For example, the Robinson-Patman Act prohibits manufacturers and wholesalers from discriminating in price among channel member purchasers (suppliers and distributors) if competition is injured.

Competing organizations must be careful not to coordinate discounts, credit terms, or condition of sale; not to discuss prices, markups, and costs at trade association meetings; and not to arrange to issue new price lists on the same date, to rotate low bids on contracts, or to uniformly restrict production to maintain high prices. Strategists should view price from both a short-run and a long-run perspective, because competitors can copy price changes with relative ease. Often a dominant firm will aggressively match all price cuts by competitors.

DISTRIBUTION   *Distribution* includes warehousing, distribution channels, distribution coverage, retail site locations, sales territories, inventory levels and location, transportation carriers, wholesaling, and retailing. Most producers today do not sell their goods directly to consumers. Various marketing entities act as intermediaries; they bear a variety of names such as wholesalers, retailers, brokers, facilitators, agents, middlemen, vendors, or simply distributors.

Distribution becomes especially important when a firm is striving to implement a market development or forward integration strategy. Some of the most complex and challenging decisions facing a firm concern product distribution. Intermediaries flourish in our economy because many producers lack the financial resources and expertise to carry out direct marketing. Manufacturers who could afford to sell directly to the public often can gain greater returns by expanding and improving their manufacturing operations. Even General Motors would find it very difficult to buy out its more than 18,000 independent dealers.

Successful organizations identify and evaluate alternative ways to reach their ultimate market. Possible approaches vary from direct selling to using just one or many wholesalers and retailers. Strengths and weaknesses of each channel alternative should be determined according to economic, control, and adaptive criteria. Organizations should consider the costs and benefits of various wholesaling and retailing options. They must consider the need to motivate and control channel members and the need to adapt to changes in the future. Once a marketing channel is chosen, an organization usually must adhere to it for an extended period of time.

MARKETING RESEARCH   *Marketing research* is the systematic gathering, recording, and analyzing of data about problems relating to the marketing of goods and services. Marketing research can uncover critical strengths and weaknesses, and marketing researchers employ numerous scales, instruments, procedures, concepts, and techniques to gather information. Marketing research activities support all of the major business functions of an organization. Organizations that possess excellent marketing research skills have a definite strength in pursuing generic strategies.

> The President of PepsiCo says, "Looking at the competition is the company's best form of market research. The majority of our strategic successes are ideas that we borrow from the marketplace, usually from a small regional or local competitor. In each case, we spot a promising new idea, improve on it, and then out-execute our competitor."[16]

About 20,000 new products are introduced by U.S. companies annually, but 85 percent of these fail within three years. Many CEOs continue to trust their own best judgment over market research; this mind-set can be detrimental to a business. For example, the Greyhound Bus company first pursued the African-American market by placing advertising on black radio stations. However, instead of creating a new commercial, Greyhound used its popular country-western music ad. Black Americans generally dislike country music, so Greyhound's strategy failed.

OPPORTUNITY ANALYSIS   The eighth function of marketing is *opportunity analysis*, which involves assessing the costs, benefits, and risks associated with marketing decisions. Three steps are required to perform a *cost/benefit analysis:* (1) compute the total costs associated with a decision, (2) estimate the total benefits from the decision, and (3) compare the total costs with the total benefits. As expected benefits exceed total costs, an opportunity becomes more attractive. Sometimes the variables included in a cost/benefit analysis cannot be quantified or even measured, but usually reasonable estimates can be made to allow the analysis to be performed. One key factor to be considered is risk. Cost/benefit analyses should also be performed when a company is evaluating alternative ways to be socially responsible.

SOCIAL RESPONSIBILITY   The final function of marketing, according to Evans and Bergman, is to determine how best to meet the firm's social responsibility obligations. *Social responsibility* can include offering products and services that are safe and reasonably priced. Demands by special interest groups on business organizations greatly increased during the 1980s. Arguments still rage today, though, about how socially responsible firms should be. A clear social policy can represent a major strength for organizations, whereas a poor social policy can be a weakness.

Some strategists view social responsibility as a focus that detracts from, or is counter to, their profit-minded pursuits. Although there may be some clearly distinct economic versus social concerns, there is a rather broad area in which economic and social concerns are consistent with one another. Many corporate activities are profitable, and at the same time are socially responsible. When a firm engages in social activities, it must do so in a way that receives economic advantages.

FINANCE/ACCOUNTING

Financial condition is often considered the single best measure of a firm's competitive position and overall attractiveness to investors. Determining an organization's financial strengths and weaknesses is essential to formulating strategies effectively. A firm's liquidity, leverage, working capital, profitability, asset utilization, cash flow, and equity can eliminate some strategies as being feasible alternatives. Financial factors often alter existing strategies and change implementation plans.

FINANCE/ACCOUNTING FUNCTIONS   According to James Van Horne, the *functions of finance/accounting* comprise three decisions: the investment decision, the financing decision, and the dividend decision.[17] Financial ratio analysis is the most widely used method for determining an organization's strengths and weaknesses in the investment, financing, and dividend areas. Because the functional areas of business are so closely related, financial ratios can signal strengths or weaknesses in management, marketing, production, research and development, and computer information systems activities.

The *investment decision*, also called *capital budgeting*, is the allocation and reallocation of capital and resources to projects, products, assets, and divisions of an organization. Once strategies are formulated, capital budgeting decisions are required to implement strategies successfully. The *financing decision* concerns determining the best capital structure for the firm and includes examining various methods by which the firm can raise capital (for example, by issuing stock, increasing debt, selling assets, or using a combination of these approaches). The financing decision must consider both short-term and long-term needs for working capital. Two key financial ratios that indicate whether a firm's financing decisions have been effective are the debt-to-equity ratio and the debt-to-total-assets ratio.

Dividend decisions concern issues such as the percentage of earnings paid to stockholders, the stability of dividends paid over time, and the repurchase or issuance of stock. Dividend decisions determine the amount of funds that are retained in a firm compared to the amount paid out to stockholders. Three financial ratios that are helpful in evaluating a firm's dividend decisions are the earnings-per-share ratio, the dividends-per-share ratio, and the price-earnings ratio. The benefits of paying dividends to investors must be balanced against the benefits of retaining funds internally, and there is no set formula on how to balance this trade-off. For the reasons listed here, dividends are sometimes paid out even when funds could be better reinvested in the business or when the firm has to obtain outside sources of capital:

1. Paying cash dividends is customary. Failure to do so could be thought of as a stigma. A dividend change is considered a signal about the future.
2. Dividends represent a sales point for investment bankers. Some institutional investors can buy only dividend-paying stocks.
3. Shareholders often demand dividends, even in companies with great opportunities for reinvesting all available funds.
4. A myth exists that paying dividends will result in a higher stock price.

BASIC TYPES OF FINANCIAL RATIOS   Financial ratios are computed from an organization's income statement and balance sheet. Computing financial ratios is like taking a picture, because the results reflect a situation at just one point in time. Comparing ratios over time and to industry averages is more likely to result in meaningful statistics that can be used to identify and evaluate strengths and weaknesses. Trend analysis, illustrated in Figure 5–3, is a useful technique that incorporates both the time and industry average dimensions of financial ratios. Note that the dotted lines reveal projected ratios. Four major sources of industry-average financial ratios follow:

1. Dun & Bradstreet's *Industry Norms and Key Business Ratios*—Fourteen different ratios are calculated in an industry-average format for 800 different types of businesses. The ratios are presented by Standard Industrial Classification (SIC) number and are grouped by annual sales into three size categories.
2. Robert Morris Associates' *Annual Statement Studies*—Sixteen different ratios are calculated in an industry-average format. Industries are referenced by SIC numbers published

FIGURE 5–3
A Financial Ratio Trend Analysis

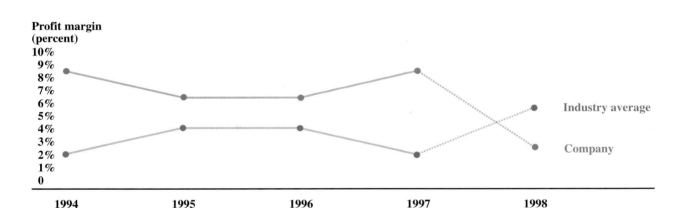

by the Bureau of the Census. The ratios are presented in four size categories by annual sales for all firms in the industry.

3. Troy Leo's *Almanac of Business & Industrial Financial Ratios*—Twenty-two financial ratios and percentages are provided in an industry-average format for all major industries. The ratios and percentages are given for 12 different company-size categories for all firms in a given industry.

4. Federal Trade Commission Reports—The FTC publishes quarterly financial data, including ratios on manufacturing companies. FTC reports include analyses by industry group and asset size.

Table 5–3 provides a summary of key financial ratios showing how each ratio is calculated and what each ratio measures. However, all the ratios are not significant for all industries and companies. For example, accounts receivable turnover and average collection period are not very meaningful to a company that does primarily a cash receipts business. Key financial ratios can be classified into the following five types:

1. *Liquidity ratios* measure a firm's ability to meet maturing short-term obligations.
   Current ratio
   Quick or acid-test ratio
2. *Leverage ratios* measure the extent to which a firm has been financed by debt.
   Debt-to-total-assets ratio
   Debt-to-equity ratio
   Long-term debt-to-equity ratio
   Times-interest-earned (or coverage) ratio

TABLE 5–3
A Summary of Key Financial Ratios

Ratio	How Calculated	What It Measures
LIQUIDITY RATIOS		
Current Ratio	$$\frac{\text{Current assets}}{\text{Current liabilities}}$$	The extent to which a firm can meet its short-term obligations
Quick Ratio	$$\frac{\text{Current assets minus inventory}}{\text{Current liabilities}}$$	The extent to which a firm can meet its short-term obligations without relying upon the sale of its inventories
LEVERAGE RATIOS		
Debt-to-total-assets Ratio	$$\frac{\text{Total debt}}{\text{Total assets}}$$	The percentage of total funds that are provided by creditors
Debt-to-equity Ratio	$$\frac{\text{Total debt}}{\text{Total stockholders' equity}}$$	The percentage of total funds provided by creditors versus by owners
Long-term Debt-to-equity Ratio	$$\frac{\text{Long-term debt}}{\text{Total stockholders' equity}}$$	The balance between debt and equity in a firm's long-term capital structure
Times-interest-earned Ratio	$$\frac{\text{Profits before interest and taxes}}{\text{Total interest charges}}$$	The extent to which earnings can decline without the firm becoming unable to meet its annual interest costs
ACTIVITY RATIOS		
Inventory Turnover	$$\frac{\text{Sales}}{\text{Inventory of finished goods}}$$	Whether a firm holds excessive stocks of inventories and whether a firm is selling its inventories slowly compared to the industry average
Fixed-assets Turnover	$$\frac{\text{Sales}}{\text{Fixed assets}}$$	Sales productivity and plant and equipment utilization
Total-assets Turnover	$$\frac{\text{Sales}}{\text{Total assets}}$$	Whether a firm is generating a sufficient volume of business for the size of its asset investment
Accounts-receivable Turnover	$$\frac{\text{Annual credit sales}}{\text{Accounts receivable}}$$	The average length of time it takes a firm to collect credit sales (in percentage terms)
Average Collection Period	$$\frac{\text{Accounts receivable}}{\text{Total credit sales}/365 \text{ days}}$$	The average length of time it takes a firm to collect on credit sales (in days)
PROFITABILITY RATIOS		
Gross Profit Margin	$$\frac{\text{Sales minus cost of goods sold}}{\text{Sales}}$$	The total margin available to cover operating expenses and yield a profit
Operating Profit Margin	$$\frac{\text{Earnings before interest and taxes (EBIT)}}{\text{Sales}}$$	Profitability without concern for taxes and interest
Net Profit Margin	$$\frac{\text{Net income}}{\text{Sales}}$$	After-tax profits per dollar of sales
Return on Total Assets (ROA)	$$\frac{\text{Net income}}{\text{Total assets}}$$	After-tax profits per dollar of assets; this ratio is also called return on investment (ROI)
Return on Stockholders' Equity (ROE)	$$\frac{\text{Net income}}{\text{Total stockholders' equity}}$$	After-tax profits per dollar of stockholders' investment in the firm
Earning Per Share (EPS)	$$\frac{\text{Net income}}{\text{Number of shares of common stock outstanding}}$$	Earnings available to the owners of common stock
GROWTH RATIOS		
Sales	Annual percentage growth in total sales	Firm's growth rate in sales
Income	Annual percentage growth in profits	Firm's growth rate in profits
Earnings Per Share	Annual percentage growth in EPS	Firm's growth rate in EPS
Dividends Per Share	Annual percentage growth in dividends per share	Firm's growth rate in dividends per share
Price-earning Ratio	$$\frac{\text{Market price per share}}{\text{Earnings per share}}$$	Faster-growing and less risky firms tend to have higher price-earnings ratios

3. *Activity ratios* measure how effectively a firm is using its resources.

> Inventory-turnover ratio
> Total-assets turnover
> Fixed-assets turnover
> Average collection period

4. *Profitability ratios* measure management's overall effectiveness as shown by the returns generated on sales and investment.

> Gross profit margin
> Operating profit margin
> Net profit margin
> Return on total assets (ROA)
> Return on stockholders' equity (ROE)
> Earnings per share

5. *Growth ratios* measure the firm's ability to maintain its economic position in the growth of the economy and industry.

> Sales
> Net income
> Earnings per share
> Dividends per share
> Price-earnings ratio

Financial ratio analysis is not without some limitations. First of all, financial ratios are based on accounting data, and firms differ in their treatment of such items as depreciation, inventory valuation, research and development expenditures, pension plan costs, mergers, and taxes. Also, seasonal factors can influence comparative ratios. Therefore, conformity to industry composite ratios does not establish with certainty that a firm is performing normally or that it is well managed. Likewise, departures from industry averages do not always indicate that a firm is doing especially well or badly. For example, a high inventory-turnover ratio could indicate efficient inventory management and a strong working capital position, but it could also indicate a serious inventory shortage and a weak working capital position.

It is important to recognize that a firm's financial condition depends not only on the functions of finance, but also on many other factors that include (1) management, marketing, production/operations, research and development, and computer information systems decisions; (2) actions by competitors, suppliers, distributors, creditors, customers, and shareholders; and (3) economic, social, demographic, political, governmental, and technological trends. Even natural environment liabilities can affect financial ratios, as indicated in the Natural Environment Perspective. So, financial ratio analysis, like all other analytical tools, should be used wisely.

PRODUCTION/OPERATIONS

The *production/operations functions* of a business consists of all those activities that transform inputs into goods and services. Production/operations management deals with inputs, transformations, and outputs that vary across industries and markets. A manufacturing operation transforms or converts inputs such as raw materials, labor, capital, machines, and facilities into finished goods and services. As indicated in Table 5–4, Roger Schroeder suggests that production/operations management comprises five functions or decision areas: process, capacity, inventory, workforce, and quality.

Production/operations activities often represent the largest part of an organization's human and capital assets. In most industries, the major costs of producing a product or service

TABLE 5–4
**The Basic Functions of
Production Management**

FUNCTION	DESCRIPTION
1. Process	Process decisions concern the design of the physical production system. Specific decisions include choice of technology, facility layout, process flow analysis, facility location, line balancing, process control, and transportation analysis.
2. Capacity	Capacity decisions concern determination of optimal output levels for the organization—not too much and not too little. Specific decisions include forecasting, facilities planning, aggregate planning, scheduling, capacity planning, and queuing analysis.
3. Inventory	Inventory decisions involve managing the level of raw materials, work in process, and finished goods. Specific decisions include what to order, when to order, how much to order, and materials handling.
4. Workforce	Workforce decisions are concerned with managing the skilled, unskilled, clerical, and managerial employees. Specific decisions include job design, work measurement, job enrichment, work standards, and motivation techniques.
5. Quality	Quality decisions are aimed at assuring that high-quality goods and services are produced. Specific decisions include quality control, sampling, testing, quality assurance, and cost control.

Source: Adapted from R. Schroeder, *Operations Management* (New York: McGraw-Hill Book Co., 1981): 12.

are incurred within operations, so production/operations can have great value as a competitive weapon in a company's overall strategy. Strengths and weaknesses in the five functions of production can mean the success or failure of an enterprise.

Many production/operations managers are finding that cross-training of employees can help their firms respond to changing markets faster. Cross-training of workers can increase efficiency, quality, productivity, and job satisfaction. For example, at General Motors' Detroit Gear & Axle plant, costs related to product defects were reduced 400 percent in two years as a result of cross-training workers. A shortage of qualified labor in America is another reason cross-training is becoming a common management practice.

There is much reason for concern that many organizations have not taken sufficient account of the capabilities and limitations of the production/operations function in formulating strategies. Scholars contend that this neglect has had unfavorable consequences on corporate performance in America. In Table 5–5, James Dilworth outlines several types of strategic decisions that a company might make and considers production/operations implications of those decisions. Production capabilities and policies can also greatly affect strategies:

> Given today's decision-making environment with shortages, inflation, technological booms, and government intervention, a company's production/operations capabilities and policies may not be able to fulfill the demands dictated by strategies. In fact, they may dictate corporate strategies. It is hard to imagine that an organization can formulate strategies today without first considering the constraints and limitations imposed by its existing production/operations structure.[18]

RESEARCH AND DEVELOPMENT

The fifth major area of internal operations that should be examined for specific strengths and weaknesses is research and development (R&D). Many firms today conduct no R&D, and yet many other companies depend on successful R&D activities for survival. Firms pursuing a product development strategy especially need to have a strong R&D orientation. Table 5–6 gives R&D information for ten American industries in 1994. Note that health-care firms on

TABLE 5–5
Impact of Strategy Elements on Production Management

POSSIBLE ELEMENTS OF STRATEGY	CONCOMITANT CONDITIONS THAT MAY AFFECT THE OPERATIONS FUNCTION AND ADVANTAGES AND DISADVANTAGES
1. Compete as low-cost provider of goods or services	Discourages competition Broadens market Requires longer production runs and fewer product changes Requires special-purpose equipment and facilities
2. Compete as high-quality provider	Often possible to obtain more profit per unit, and perhaps more total profit from a smaller volume of sales Requires more quality-assurance effort and higher operating cost Requires more precise equipment, which is more expensive Requires highly skilled workers, necessitating higher wages and greater training efforts
3. Stress customer service	Requires broader development of service people and service parts and equipment Requires rapid response to customer needs or changes in customer tastes, rapid and accurate information system, careful coordination Requires a higher inventory investment
4. Provide rapid and frequent introduction of new products	Requires versatile equipment and people Has higher research and development costs Has high retraining costs and high tooling and changeover in manufacturing Provides lower volumes for each product and fewer opportunities for improvements due to the learning curve
5. Strive for absolute growth	Requires accepting some projects or products with lower marginal value, which reduces ROI Diverts talents to areas of weakness instead of concentrating on strengths
6. Seek vertical integration	Enables company to control more of the process May not have economies of scale at some stages of process May require high capital investment as well as technology and skills beyond those currently available within the organization
7. Maintain reserve capacity for flexibility	Provides ability to meet peak demands and quickly implement some contingency plans if forecasts are too low Requires capital investment in idle capacity Provides capability to grow during the lead time normally required for expansion
8. Consolidate processing (Centralize)	Can result in economies of scale Can locate near one major customer or supplier Vulnerability: one strike, fire, or flood can halt the entire operation
9. Disperse processing of service (Decentralize)	Can be near several market territories Requires more complex coordination network: perhaps expensive data transmission and duplication of some personnel and equipment at each location If each location produces one product in the line, then other products still must be transported to be available at all locations If each location specializes in a type of component for all products, the company is vulnerable to strike, fire, flood, etc. If each location provides total product line, then economies of scale may not be realized
10. Stress the use of mechanization, automation, robots	Requires high capital investment Reduces flexibility May affect labor relations Makes maintenance more crucial
11. Stress stability of employment	Serves the security needs of employees and may develop employee loyalty Helps to attract and retain highly skilled employees May require revisions of make-or-buy decisions, use of idle time, inventory, and subcontractors as demand fluctuates

Source: Production and Operations Management: Manufacturing and Nonmanufacturing, Second Edition, by J. Dilworth. Copyright © 1983 by Random House, Inc. Reprinted by permission of Random House, Inc.

TABLE 5–6
R&D Expenditure
Information for U.S.
Firms

INDUSTRY	TOTAL R&D EXPENDITURES 1994 VERSUS 1993 (PERCENT CHANGE)	TOTAL R&D EXPENDITURES AS A PERCENT OF SALES
Chemicals	−02	3.7
Health care	+05	9.8
Electrical	+14	5.7
Manufacturing	+10	2.8
Food	+09	0.8
Leisure Time	+05	4.3
Office Equipment	−01	7.1
Automotive	−11	3.8
Aerospace	−05	4.2
Telecommunications	+04	3.3
All Industries in 1994	+04	3.5

Source: Adapted from *Business Week,* July 3, 1995, p. 78.

average spend the most money on R&D as a percentage of revenues, while food companies spend the least. Also, on average, U.S. firms spent 4 percent more on R&D in 1994 than 1993.

Organizations invest in R&D because they believe that such investment will lead to superior product or services and give them competitive advantages. Research and development expenditures are directed at developing new products before competitors do, improving product quality, or improving manufacturing processes to reduce costs.[19]

A recent article emphasizes that effective management of the R&D function today requires a strategic and operational partnership between R&D and the other vital business functions. A spirit of partnership and mutual trust between general and R&D managers is evident in the best-managed firms today. Managers in these firms jointly explore, assess, and decide the what, when, why, and how much of R&D. Priorities, costs, benefits, risks, and rewards associated with R&D activities are discussed openly and shared. The overall mission of R&D has thus become broad-based, including supporting existing businesses, helping launch new businesses, developing new products, improving product quality, improving manufacturing efficiency, and deepening or broadening the company's technological capabilities.[20]

The best-managed firms today seek to organize R&D activities in a way that breaks the isolation of R&D from the rest of the company and promotes a spirit of partnership between R&D managers and other managers in the firm. R&D decisions and plans must be integrated and coordinated across departments and divisions by sharing experiences and information. The strategic-management process facilitates this new cross-functional approach to managing the R&D function.

When companies are acquired, R&D departments are often pared down or eliminated due to redundancy. For example, when General Electric acquired RCA, it sold RCA's research laboratories to SRI International. The proliferation of mergers, acquisitions, and takeovers in the United States is one reason for forecasters' fears that total R&D spending in the United States is poised for a downturn. Other worrisome trends are burgeoning trade deficits, waning competitiveness, and the rapidly rising cost of R&D. Declines in R&D would hurt virtually all the types of strategies described in Chapter 2, especially product development. There was an 8-percent decline in 1994 in DuPont's R&D spending.

INTERNAL AND EXTERNAL R&D   Cost distributions among R&D activities vary by company and industry, but total R&D costs generally do not exceed manufacturing and

NATURAL ENVIRONMENT

Environmental Liability on the Balance Sheet

Environmental liability may be the largest recognized or unrecognized liability on a company's balance sheet. More and more American firms are finding themselves liable for cleanup costs and damages stemming from waste disposal practices of the past, in some cases going back 100 years. Environmental liabilities associated with air and water pollution, habitat destruction, deforestation, and medical problems can be immense. For this reason, many financial institutions now inquire about environmental liabilities as part of their commercial lending procedures. Firms such as American Insurance Company specialize in providing environmental liability insurance to companies.

Environmental Protection Agency (EPA) regulations comprise more than 11,000 pages; they vary with location and size of firm and are being added to daily. The complexity of these regulations can translate into liabilities for the environmentally reactive firm. Proactive firms, on the other hand, are adding a green executive and department to oversee management of environmental policies and practices of the firm. The responsibility of "green executives" includes thinking through environmental regulations, marketing needs, public attitudes, consumer demands, and potential problems. Ideally, green executives should promote development of a corporate culture where all managers and employees become "green," or environmentally sensitive. Such a culture would represent an internal strength to the firm.

marketing start-up costs. Four approaches to determining R&D budget allocations are commonly used: (1) financing as many project proposals as possible, (2) using a percentage-of-sales method, (3) budgeting about the same amount that competitors spend for R&D, or (4) deciding how many successful new products are needed and working backward to estimate the required R&D investment.

R&D in organizations can take two basic forms: (1) internal R&D, in which an organization operates its own R&D department, and/or (2) contract R&D, in which a firm hires independent researchers or independent agencies to develop specific products. Many companies use both approaches to develop new products. A widely used approach for obtaining outside R&D assistance is to pursue a joint venture with another firm. R&D strengths (capabilities) and weaknesses (limitations) play a major role in strategy formulation and strategy implementation.

Most firms have no choice but to continually develop new and improved products because of changing consumer needs and tastes, new technologies, shortened product life cycles, and increased domestic and foreign competition. A shortage of ideas for new products, increased global competition, increased market segmentation, strong special interest groups, and increased government regulation are several factors making the successful development of new products more and more difficult, costly, and risky. In the pharmaceutical industry, for example, only one out of every 10,000 drugs created in the laboratory ends up on pharmacists' shelves. Scarpello, Boulton, and Hofer emphasize that different strategies require different R&D capabilities:

> The focus of R&D efforts can vary greatly depending on a firm's competitive strategy. Some corporations attempt to be market leaders and innovators of new products, while others are satisfied to be market followers and developers of currently available products. The basic skills required to support these strategies will vary, depending on whether R&D becomes the driving force behind competitive strategy. In cases where new product introduction is the driving force for strategy, R&D activities must be extensive. The R&D unit must then be able to advance scientific and technological knowledge, exploit that knowledge, and manage the risks associated with ideas, products, services, and production requirements.[21]

COMPUTER INFORMATION SYSTEMS

Information ties all business functions together and provides the basis for all managerial decisions. It is the cornerstone of all organizations. Information represents a major source of competitive advantage or disadvantage. Assessing a firm's internal strengths and weaknesses in information systems is a critical dimension of performing an internal audit. The company motto of Mitsui, a large Japanese trading company, is "Information is the lifeblood of the company." A satellite network connects Mitsui's 200 worldwide offices.

A computer information system's purpose is to improve the performance of an enterprise by improving the quality of managerial decisions. An effective information system thus collects, codes, stores, synthesizes, and presents information in such a manner that it answers important operating and strategic questions. The heart of an information system is a data base containing the kinds of records and data important to managers.

A *computer information system* receives raw material from both the external and internal evaluation of an organization. It gathers data about marketing, finance, production, and personnel matters internally, and social, cultural, demographic, environmental, economic, political, government, legal, technological, and competitive factors externally. Data are integrated in ways needed to support managerial decision making.

There is a logical flow of material in a computer information system, whereby data are input to the system and transformed into output. Outputs include computer printouts, written reports, tables, charts, graphs, checks, purchase orders, invoices, inventory records, payroll accounts, and a variety of other documents. Payoffs from alternative strategies can be calculated and estimated. *Data* become *information* only when they are evaluated, filtered, condensed, analyzed, and organized for a specific purpose, problem, individual, or time.

An effective computer information system utilizes computer hardware, software, models for analysis, and a database. Some people equate information systems with the advent of the computer, but historians have traced recordkeeping and noncomputer data processing to Babylonian merchants living in 3500 B.C. Benefits of an effective information system include an improved understanding of business functions, improved communications, more informed decision making, analysis of problems, and improved control.

Because organizations are becoming more complex, decentralized, and globally dispersed, the function of information systems is growing in importance. Spurring this advance is the falling cost and increasing power of computers. There are costs and benefits associated with obtaining and evaluating information, just as with equipment and land. Like equipment, information can become obsolete and may need to be purged from the system. An effective information system is like a library, collecting, categorizing, and filing data for use by managers throughout the organization. Information systems are a major strategic resource, monitoring environment changes, identifying competitive threats, and assisting in the implementation, evaluation, and control of strategy.

We are truly in an information age. Firms whose information-system skills are weak are at a competitive disadvantage. On the other hand, strengths in information systems allow firms to establish distinctive competencies in other areas. Low-cost manufacturing and good customer service, for example, can depend on a good information system.

Watson and Rainer recently found that executive information systems provide managerial support in six key areas: electronic mail, access to external news, access to external data bases, word processing, spreadsheet, and automated filing.[22] A good executive information system provides graphic, tabular, and textual information. Graphic capabilities are needed so current conditions and trends can be examined quickly; tables provide greater detail and enable variance analyses; textual information adds insight and interpretation to data.

STRATEGIC PLANNING SOFTWARE   The computer revolution today is being compared in magnitude to the industrial revolution. Computers are now common at the desks of almost every professional and administrative employee of industry, government, and academia. The proliferation of computers has aided strategic management because software products can be designed to enhance participation and to provide integration, uniformity, analysis, and economy. Strategic planning software can allow firms to tap the knowledge base of everyone in the firm. There are a number of commercially available strategic planning software products designed to train and assist managers in strategic planning, including *Business Advantage, Business Simulator, SUCCESS, ANS-PLAN-A, Strategy!, CheckMATE, EXCEL, STRATPAC, SIMPLAN, REVEAL, COSMOS,* and *BASICS P-C.*[23]

Some strategic decision support systems, however, are too sophisticated, expensive, or restrictive to be used easily by managers in a firm. This is unfortunate because the strategic-management process must be a people process to be successful. People make the difference! Strategic planning software thus should be simple and unsophisticated. Simplicity allows wide participation among managers in a firm and participation is essential for effective strategy implementation.

One strategic planning software product that parallels this text and offers managers and executives a simple yet effective approach for developing organizational strategies is CheckMATE. This IBM-compatible, personal computer software performs planning analyses and generates strategies a firm could pursue. CheckMATE, a Windows-based program, incorporates the most modern strategic planning techniques. No previous experience with computers or knowledge of strategic planning is required of the user. CheckMATE thus promotes communication, understanding, creativity, and forward thinking among users.

CheckMATE is not a spreadsheet or database program; it is an expert system that carries a firm through strategy formulation and implementation. A major strength of the new CheckMATE strategic planning software is its simplicity and participative approach. The user is asked approptiate questions, responses are recorded, information is assimilated, and results are printed. Individuals can work through the software independently and then meet to develop joint recommendations for the firm.

The CheckMATE software utilizes the most modern strategic planning analytical matrices to generate alternative strategies firms could pursue. Specific analytical procedures included in the CheckMATE program are Strategic Planning and Action Evaluation (SPACE) analysis, Threats-Opportunities-Weaknesses-Strengths (TOWS) analysis, Internal-External (IE) analysis, and Grand Strategy Matrix analysis. These widely used strategic planning analyses are described in Chapter 6.

Twenty-three customized industry applications of CheckMATE are available in a new Windows format. An individual license costs $95. More information about CheckMATE can be obtained at 803-669-6960 (phone) or 803-673-9460 (fax). FDavid@FMarion.edu (e-mail).

INTERNAL-AUDIT CHECKLISTS

The checklists of questions provided in this section can be helpful in determining specific strengths and weaknesses in the functional area of business. An answer of *no* to any question could indicate a potential weakness, although the strategic significance and implications of negative answers will of course vary by organization, industry, and severity of the weakness. Positive or *yes* answers to the checklist questions suggest potential areas of strength. The questions provided in Table 5–7 are not all-inclusive, but they can facilitate internal-audit efforts.

TABLE 5–7
Internal Audit Checklist of Questions

MANAGEMENT

1. Does the firm use strategic-management concepts?
2. Are company objectives and goals measurable and well communicated?
3. Do managers at all hierarchical levels plan effectively?
4. Do managers delegate authority well?
5. Is the organization's structure appropriate?
6. Are job descriptions and job specifications clear?
7. Is employee morale high?
8. Is employee turnover and absenteeism low?
9. Are organizational reward and control mechanisms effective?

MARKETING

1. Are markets segmented effectively?
2. Is the organization positioned well among competitors?
3. Has the firm's market share been increasing?
4. Are present channels of distribution reliable and cost-effective?
5. Does the firm have an effective sales organization?
6. Does the firm conduct market research?
7. Is product quality and customer service good?
8. Are the firm's products and services priced appropriately?
9. Does the firm have an effective promotion, advertising, and publicity strategy?
10. Is marketing planning and budgeting effective?
11. Do the firm's marketing managers have adequate experience and training?

FINANCE

1. Where is the firm financially strong and weak as indicated by financial ratio analyses?
2. Can the firm raise needed short-term capital?
3. Can the firm raise needed long-term capital through debt and/or equity?
4. Does the firm have sufficient working capital?
5. Are capital budgeting procedures effective?
6. Are dividend payout policies reasonable?
7. Does the firm have good relations with its investors and stockholders?
8. Are the firm's financial managers experienced and well trained?

PRODUCTION

1. Are suppliers of raw materials, parts, and subassemblies reliable and reasonable?
2. Are facilities, equipment, machinery, and offices in good condition?
3. Are inventory-control policies and procedures effective?
4. Are quality-control policies and procedures effective?
5. Are facilities, resources, and markets strategically located?
6. Does the firm have technological competencies?

RESEARCH AND DEVELOPMENT

1. Does the firm have R&D facilities? Are they adequate?
2. If outside R&D firms are used, are they cost-effective?
3. Are the organization's R&D personnel well qualified?
4. Are R&D resources allocated effectively?
5. Are management information and computer systems adequate?
6. Is communication between R&D and other organizational units effective?
7. Are present products technologically competitive?

COMPUTER INFORMATION SYSTEMS

1. Do all managers in the firm use the information system to make decisions?
2. Is there a chief information officer or director of information systems position in the firm?
3. Are data in the information system updated regularly?
4. Do managers from all functional areas of the firm contribute input to the information system?
5. Are there effective passwords for entry into the firm's information system?
6. Are strategists of the firm familiar with the information systems of rival firms?
7. Is the information system user-friendly?
8. Do all users of the information system understand the competitive advantages that information can provide firms?
9. Are computer training workshops provided for users of the information system?
10. Is the firm's information system continually being improved in content and user-friendliness?

THE INTERNAL FACTOR EVALUATION (IFE) MATRIX

A summary step in conducting an internal strategic-management audit is to construct an *Internal Factor Evaluation (IFE) Matrix.* This strategy-formulation tool summarizes and evaluates the major strengths and weaknesses in the functional areas of a business, and it also provides a basis for identifying and evaluating relationships among those areas. Intuitive judgments are required in developing an IFE Matrix, so the appearance of a scientific approach should not be interpreted to mean this is an all-powerful technique. A thorough understanding of the factors included is more important than the actual numbers. Similar to the EFE Matrix and Competitive Profile Matrix described in Chapter 4, an IFE Matrix can be developed in five steps:

1. List critical success factors as identified in the internal-audit process. Use a total of from 10 to 20 internal factors, including both strengths and weaknesses. List strengths first and then weaknesses. Be as specific as possible, using percentages, ratios, and comparative numbers.

2. Assign a weight that ranges from 0.0 (not important) to 1.0 (all-important) to each factor. The weight assigned to a given factor indicates the relative importance of the factor to being successful in the firm's industry. Regardless of whether a key factor is an internal strength or weakness, factors considered to have the greatest effect on organizational performance should be assigned the highest weights. The summation of all weights must total 1.0.

3. Assign a 1-to-4 rating to each factor to indicate whether that factor represents a major weakness (rating = 1), a minor weakness (rating = 2), a minor strength (rating = 3), or a major strength (rating = 4). Ratings are thus company-based, whereas the weights in Step 2 are industry-based.

4. Multiply each factor's weight by its rating to determine a weighted score for each variable.

5. Sum the weighted scores for each variable to determine the total weighted score for the organization.

Regardless of how many factors are included in an IFE Matrix, the total weighted score can range from a low of 1.0 to a high of 4.0, with the average score being 2.5. Total weighted scores well below 2.5 characterize organizations that are weak internally, whereas scores significantly above 2.5 indicate a strong internal position. Like the EFE Matrix, an IFE Matrix should include from 10 to 20 key factors. The number of factors has no effect upon the range of total weighted scores because the weights always sum to 1.0.

When a key internal factor is both a strength and a weakness, the factor should be included twice in the IFE Matrix, and a weight and rating should be assigned to each statement. For example, the Playboy logo both helps and hurts Playboy Enterprises; the logo attracts customers to the *Playboy* magazine, but it keeps the Playboy cable channel out of many markets.

An example of IFE Matrix is provided in Table 5–8. Note that the firm's major strengths are its current ratio, profit margin, and employee morale as indicated by the rating of 4. The major weaknesses are lack of a strategic-management system, rising R&D expenses, and ineffective dealer incentives. The total weighted score of 2.80 indicates that the firm is above average in its overall internal strategic position.

In multidivisional firms each autonomous division or strategic business unit should construct an IFE Matrix. Divisional matrices can then be integrated to develop an overall corporate IFE Matrix.

KEY INTERNAL FACTORS	WEIGHT	RATING	WEIGHTED SCORE
STRENGTHS			
1. Current ratio increased to 2.52.	.06	4	.24
2. Profit margin increased to 6.94.	.16	4	.64
3. Employee morale is high.	.18	4	.72
4. New computer information system.	.08	3	.24
5. Market share has increased to 24 percent.	.12	3	.36
WEAKNESSES			
1. Legal suits have not been resolved.	.05	2	.10
2. Plant capacity has fallen to 74 percent.	.15	2	.30
3. Lack of a strategic management system.	.06	1	.06
4. R&D expenses have increased 31 percent.	.08	1	.08
5. Dealer incentives have not been effective.	.06	1	.06
Total	1.00		2.80

TABLE 5–8
A Sample Internal Factor Evaluation Matrix

Note: The ratings values are as follows: 1 = major weakness, 2 = minor weakness, 3 = minor strength, 4 = major strength.

CONCLUSION

Management, marketing, finance/accounting, production/operations, research and development, and computer information systems represent the core operations of most businesses. A strategic-management audit of a firm's internal operations is vital to organizational health. Many companies still prefer to be judged solely on their bottom-line performance. However, an increasing number of successful organizations are using the internal audit to gain competitive advantages over rival firms.

Systematic methodologies for performing strength-weakness assessments are not well developed in the strategic-management literature, but it is clear that strategists must identify and evaluate internal strengths and weaknesses in order to formulate and choose among alternative strategies effectively. The EFE Matrix, Competitive Profile Matrix, IFE Matrix, and a clear statement of mission provide the basic information needed to formulate competitive strategies successfully. The process of performing an internal audit represents an opportunity for managers and employees throughout the organization to participate in determining the future of the firm. Involvement in the process can energize and mobilize managers and employees.

TAKE IT TO THE NET

We invite you to visit the DAVID page on the Prentice Hall Web site at:
http://www.prenhall.com/davidsm
for this chapter's World Wide Web exercises.

KEY TERMS AND CONCEPTS

Buying	(p. 151)	Functions of Finance/Accounting	(p. 154)	Opportunity Analysis	(p. 153)
Capital Budgeting	(p. 154)	Functions of Management	(p. 146)	Organizational Culture	(p. 143)
Computer Information Systems	(p. 162)	Functions of Marketing	(p. 151)	Organizing	(p. 148)
Controlling	(p. 150)	Functions of Production/	(p. 157)	Personnel Management	(p. 149)
Cost/Benefit Analysis	(p. 153)	Operations		Planning	(p. 146)
Cultural Products	(p. 143)	Human Resource Management	(p. 149)	Pricing	(p. 152)
Customer Analysis	(p. 151)	Internal Audit	(p. 163)	Selling	(p. 151)
Distinctive Competencies	(p. 140)	Internal Factor Evaluation (IFE)	(p. 164)	Social Responsibility	(p. 153)
Distribution	(p. 152)	Matrix		Staffing	(p. 149)
Dividend Decision	(p. 154)	Investment Decision	(p. 154)	Synergy	(p. 147)
Financial Ratio Analysis	(p. 143)	Marketing Research	(p. 153)	Test Marketing	(p. 152)
Financing Decision	(p. 154)	Motivating	(p. 148)		

ISSUES FOR REVIEW AND DISCUSSION

1. Explain why prioritizing the relative importance of strengths and weaknesses to include in an IFE Matrix is an important strategic-management activity.

2. How can delegation of authority contribute to effective strategic management?

3. Diagram a formal organizational chart that reflects the following positions: a president, two executive officers, four middle managers, and eighteen lower-level managers. Now, diagram three overlapping and hypothetical informal group structures. How can this information be helpful to a strategist in formulating and implementing strategy?

4. How could a strategist's attitude toward social responsibility affect a firm's strategy? What is your attitude toward social responsibility?

5. Which of the three basic functions of finance/accounting do you feel is most important in a small electronics manufacturing concern? Justify your position.

6. Do you think aggregate R&D expenditures for American firms will increase or decrease next year? Why?

7. Explain how you would motivate managers and employees to implement a major new strategy.

8. Why do you think production/operations managers are often not directly involved in strategy-formulation activities? Why can this be a major organizational weakness?

9. Give two examples of staffing strengths and two examples of staffing weaknesses of an organization with which you are familiar.

10. Would you ever pay out dividends when your firm's annual net profit is negative? Why? What effect could this have on a firm's strategies?

11. If a firm has zero debt in its capital structure, is that always an organizational strength? Why or why not?

12. Describe the production/operations system in a police department.

13. After conducting an internal audit, a firm discovers a total of one hundred strengths and one hundred weaknesses. What procedures could then be used to determine the most important of these? Why is it important to reduce the total number of key factors?

14. Select one of the suggested readings at the end of this chapter. Look that article up in your college library. Give a five-minute oral report to the class summarizing the article and your views on the topic.

15. Why do you believe cultural products affect all the functions of business?

16. Do you think cultural products affect strategy formulation, implementation, or evaluation the most? Why?

17. Identify cultural products at your college or university. Do these products, viewed collectively or separately, represent a strength or weakness for the organization?

18. Describe the computer information system at your college or university.

19. Explain the difference between data and information in terms of each being useful to strategists.

20. What are the most important characteristics of an effective computer information system?

NOTES

1. Robert Grant, "The Resource-Based Theory of Competitive Advantage: Implications for Strategy Formulation." *California Management Review* (Spring 1991): 116.

2. Reprinted by permission of the publisher from "Integrating Strength-Weakness Analysis into Strategic Planning," by William King, *Journal of Business Research II*, no. 4: p. 481. Copyright 1983 by Elsevier Science Publishing Co., Inc.

3. Igor Ansoff, "Strategic Management of Technology," *Journal of Business Strategy* 7, no. 3 (Winter 1987): 38.

4. Claude George, Jr. *The History of Management Thought*, 2nd ed. (Englewood Cliffs, N.J.: Prentice-Hall, 1972): 174.

5. Edgar Schein, *Organizational Culture and Leadership* (San Francisco: Jossey-Bass, 1985): 9.

6. John Lorsch, "Managing Culture: The Invisible Barrier to Strategic Change," *California Management Review* 28, no. 2 (1986): 95–109.

7. Y. Allarie and M. Firsirotu, "How to Implement Radical Strategies in Large Organizations," *Sloan Management Review* (Spring 1985): 19.

8. Adam Smith, *Wealth of Nations* (New York: Modern Library, 1937): 3–4.

9. Daft, Richard, *Management*, 3rd ed. (Orlando, Fla.: Dryden Press, 1993): 512.

10. Shelley Kirkpatrick and Edwin Locke, "Leadership: Do Traits Matter?" *Academy of Management Executive* 5, no. 2 (May 1991): 48.

11. Peter Drucker, *Management Tasks, Responsibilities, and Practice* (New York: Harper & Row, 1973): 463.

12. Brian Dumaine, "What the Leaders of Tomorrow See," *Fortune* (July 3, 1989): 51.

13. J. M. Bryson and P. Bromiley, "Critical Factors Affecting the Planning and Implementation of Major Products," *Strategic Management Journal* 14, no. 5 (July 1993): 319.

14. Robert Waterman, Jr. "The Renewal Factor," *Business Week* (September 14, 1987): 104.

15. J. Evans and B. Berman, *Marketing* (New York: Macmillan, 1982): 17.

16. Quoted in Robert Waterman, Jr., "The Renewal Factor," *Business Week* (September 14, 1987): 108.

17. J. V. Horne, *Financial Management and Policy* (Englewood Cliffs, N.J.: Prentice-Hall, 1974): 10.

18. W. Boulton and B. Saladin, "Let's Make Production-Operations Management Top Priority for Strategic Planning in the 1980s," *Managerial Planning* 32, no. 1 (July–August 1983): 19.

19. Vida Scarpello, William Boulton, and Charles Hofer, "Reintegrating R&D into Business Strategy," *Journal of Business Strategy* 6, no. 4 (Spring 1986): 50.

20. Philip Rouseel, Kamal Saad, and Tamara Erickson, The Evolution of Third Generation R&D," *Planning Review* 19, no. 2 (March–April 1991): 18–26.

21. Ibid., 50, 51.

22. Hugh Watson and Kelly Rainer, Jr., "A Manager's Guide to Executive Support Systems," *Business Horizons* (March–April 1991): 49.

23. Robert Mockler, "A Catalog of Commercially Available Software for Strategic Planning," *Planning Review* 19, no. 3 (May/June 1991): 28. John Sterling, "Strategic Management Software Review," *Planning Review* (January–February 1992): 29–33.

CURRENT READINGS

Abrahamson, Eric and Charles J. Fombrun. "Macrocultures: Determinants and Consequences." *Academy of Management Review* 19, no. 4 (October 1994): 728–755.

Amburgey, Terry L. and Tina Dacin. "As the Left Foot Follows the Right? The Dynamics of Strategic and Structural Change." *Academy of Management Journal* 37, no. 6 (December 1994): 1427–1452.

Anderson, L. McTier. "Marketing Science: Where's the Beef?" *Business Horizons* 37, no. 1 (January–February 1994): 8–16.

"Are Women Set up for Failure on the Road to the Executive Suite?" Research Translations. *Academy of Management Executive VIII*, no. 4 (November 1994): 84–85.

Azzone, G. and U. Bertelé. "Exploiting Green Strategies for Competitive Advantage." *Long Range Planning* 27, no. 6 (December 1994): 69–81.

Blum, Terry C., Dail L. Fields, and Jodi S. Goodman. "Organization-level Determinants of Women in Management." *Academy of Management Journal* 37, no. 2 (April 1994): 241–268.

Bonvillian, Gary and William A. Nowlin. "Cultural Awareness: An Essential Element of Doing Business Abroad." *Business Horizons* 37, no. 6 (November–December 1994): 44–50.

Bowen, David E. and Edward E. Lawler III. "Empowering Service Employees." *Sloan Management Review* 36, no. 4 (Summer 1995): 73–84.

Chatman, Jennifer A. and Karen A. Jehn. "Assessing the Relationship Between Industry Characteristics and Organizational Culture: How Different Can You Be? *Academy of Management Journal* 37, no. 3 (June 1994): 522–553.

Clement, Ronald W. "Culture, Leadership, and Power: The Keys to Organizational Change." *Business Horizons* 37, no. 1 (January–February 1994): 33–39.

Collis, David J. and Cynthia A. Montgomery. "Competing on Resources: Strategy in the 1990s." *Harvard Business Review* 73, no. 4 (July–August 1995): 118.

Caily, Catherine M. and Dan R. Dalton. "Bankruptcy and Corporate Governance: The Impact of Board Composition and Structure." *Academy of Management Journal* 37, no. 6 (December 1994): 1603–1617.

Davidson, Alistar and Mary Chung. "Strategic Management Technology." *Planning Review* 23, no. 2 (March–April): 28–31.

Earley, P. Christopher and Harbir Singh. "International and Intercultural Management Research: What's Next?" *Academy of Management Journal* 38, no. 2 (April 1995): 327–340.

Floyd, Steven W. and Bill Wooldridge. "Dinosaurs or Dynamos? Recognizing Middle Management's Strategic Role." *Academy of Management Executive VIII*, no. 4 (November 1994): 47–57.

Freid, Connie and Stan Freid. "Beyond Relationship Marketing: Anticipating What Customers Want." *Planning Review* 23, no. 4 (July–August 1995): 40.

Gale, Bradley T. "Quality Profiling: The First Step in Reengineering and Benchmarking." *Planning Review* 23, no. 3 (May–June 1995): 37–38.

Garud, R. and A. Kumaraswamy. "Technological and Organizational Designs for Realizing Economies of Substitution." *Strategic Management Journal* 16, Special Issue (Summer 1995): 93–110.

Gilmore, James. "How to Make Reengineering Truly Effective." Reader Response. *Planning Review* 23, no. 3 (May–June 1995): 39.

Goodstein, Jerry D. "Institutional Pressures and Strategic Responsiveness: Employer Involvement in Work-Family Issues." *Academy of Management Journal* 37, no. 2 (April 1994): 350–382.

Hambrick, Donald C. "Fragmentation and the Other Problems CEOs Have with Their Top Management Teams." *California Management Review* 37, no. 3 (Spring 1995): 110–127.

Hanson, Randall, Rebecca I. Porterfield, and Kathleen Ames. "Employee Empowerment at Risk: Effects of Recent NLRB Rulings." *Academy of Management Executive IX*, no. 2 (May 1995): 45–56.

Hutt, Michael D., Beth A. Walker, and Gary L. Frankwick. "Hurdle the Cross-functional Barriers to Strategic Change." *Sloan Management Review* 36, no. 3 (Spring 1995): 22–30.

Jennings, D. F. and S. L. Seaman. "High and Low Levels of Organizational Adaptation: An Empirical Analysis of Strategy, Structure, and Performance." *Strategic Management Journal* 15, no. 60 (July 1994) 459–476.

Kono, Toyohiro. "Changing a Company's Strategy and Culture." *Long Range Planning* 27, no. 5 (October 1994): 85–97.

Kotter, John P. "Leading Change: Why Transformation Efforts Fail." *Harvard Business Review* 73, no. 2 (March–April 1995): 59–67.

Leemon, Daniel O. "Marketing's Core Role in Strategic Reengineering." *Planning Review* 23, no. 2 (March–April 1995): 8–13.

Longenecker, Clinton O. and William K. Meade II. "Marketing as a Management Style." *Business Horizons* 38, no. 4 (July–August 1995): 77–83.

Mangaliso, Mzamo P. "The Strategic Usefulness of Management Information as Perceived by Middle Managers." *Journal of Management* 21, no. 2 (Summer 1995): 231–250.

Organ, Dennis W. and Tom Fuller. "The Editor's Choir/Does Business Need Leaders?" *Business Horizons* 38, no. 4 (July–August 1995): 1–4.

Peppers, Don and Martha Rogers. "A New Marketing Paradigm: Share of Customer, Not Market Share." *Planning Review* 23, no. 2 (March–April 1995): 14–19.

Pfeffer, Jeffrey. "Producing Sustainable Competitive Advantage through the Effective Management of People." *Academy of Management Executive XI,* no. 1 (February 1995): 55–72.

Pisano, Gary P. and Steven C. Wheelwright. "The New Logic of High-Tech R&D." *Harvard Business Review* (September–October 1995): 93–107.

Randall, Robert M. "Putting the 'Wow!' Back in Strategy and Marketing." A Conversation with Tom Peters. *Planning Review* 23, no. 2 (May–June 1995): 20–23.

Rao, Akshay R. and Robert W. Ruekert. "Brand Alliances as Signals of Product Quality." *Sloan Management Review* 36, no. 1 (Fall 1995): 87–98.

Reeves, Carol A. and David A. Bednar. "Defining Quality: Alternatives and Implications." *Academy of Management Review* 19, no. 2 (April 1994): 419–445.

Reger, Rhonda K., Loren T. Gustafson, Samuel, M. DeMarie, and John V. Mullane. "Reframing the Organization: Why Implementing Total Quality Is Easier Said Than Done." *Academy of Management Review* 19, no. 2 (April 1994): 565–584.

Sanchez, R. "Strategic Flexibility in Product Competition." *Strategic Management Journal* 16, Special Issue (Summer 1995): 135–160.

Schendel, D. "Introduction to 'Competitive Organizational Behavior: Toward an Organizationally-based Theory of Competitive Advantage'." *Strategic Management Journal* 15, Special Issue (Winter 1994): 1–4.

Shea, John and David Gobeli. "TQM: The Experiences of Ten Small Businesses." *Business Horizons* 38, no. 1 (January–February 1995): 71–77.

Sitkin, Sim B., Kathleen M. Sutcliffe, and Roger G. Schroeder. "Distinguishing Control From Learning in Total Quality Management; A Contingency Perspective." *Academy of Management Review* 19, no. 2 (April 1994): 537–564.

Skyrme, David J. "Flexible Working: Building a Lean and Responsive Organization." *Long Range Planning* 27, no. 5 (October 1994): 98–110.

Smith, N. Craig. "Marketing Strategies for the Ethics Era." *Sloan Management Review* 36, no. 4 (Summer 1995): 85–95.

Spencer, Barbara A.. "Models of Organization and Total Quality Management: A Comparison and Critical Evaluation." *Academy of Management Review* 19, no. 2 (April 1994): 446–471.

Stone, Romuald A. "AIDS in the Workplace: An Executive Update." *Academy of Management Executive VIII,* no. 3 (August 1994): 52–64.

Tharenou, Phyllis, Shane Latimer, and Denise Conroy. "How Do You Make It to the Top? An Examination of Influences on Women's and Men's Managerial Advancement." *Academy of Management Journal* 37, no. 4 (August 1994): 899–931.

"The Strategist's Software Directory." *Journal of Business Review* 15, no. 1 (January/February 1994): 54–58.

Veiga, John F., John N. Yanouzas, and Ann K. Buchholtz. "Emerging Cultural Values Among Russian Managers: What Will Tomorrow Bring?" *Business Horizons* 38, no. 4 (July–August 1995): 20–27.

Van de Ven, Andrew H. and Marshall Scott Poole. "Explaining Development and Change in Organizations." *Academy of Management Review* (July 1995): 510–540.

Waldman, David A. "The Contributions of Total Quality Management to a Theory of Work Performance." *Academy of Management Review* 19, no. 2 (April 1994): 510–536.

Waterman, R. H., Jr., J. A. Waterman, B. A. Collard. "Toward a Career-resilient Workforce." *Harvard Business Review* (July–August 1994): 87–95.

Zabriskie, Noel B. and Alan B. Huellmentel. "Marketing Research as a Strategic Tool." *Long Range Planning* 27, no. (February 1994): 107–118.

Experiential Exercise 5A

PERFORMING A FINANCIAL RATIO ANALYSIS FOR HERSHEY FOODS

PURPOSE

Financial ratio analysis is one of the best techniques for identifying and evaluating internal strengths and weaknesses. Potential investors and current shareholders look closely at firms' financial ratios, making detailed comparisons to industry averages and to previous periods of time. Financial ratio analyses provide vital input information for developing an IFE Matrix.

INSTRUCTIONS

Step 1 On a separate sheet of paper, number from 1 to 20. Referring to Hershey's income statement and balance sheet (pp. 32–33), calculate 20 1995 financial ratios for the company. Use Table 5–3 as a reference.

Step 2 Go to your college library and find industry average financial ratios for the confectionery industry. Record the industry average values in a second column on your paper.

Step 3 In a third column, indicate whether you consider each ratio to be a strength, a weakness, or a neutral factor for Hershey.

Experiential Exercise 5B

CONSTRUCTING AN IFE MATRIX FOR HERSHEY FOODS

PURPOSE

This exercise will give you experience developing an IFE Matrix. Identifying and prioritizing factors to include in an IFE Matrix fosters communication among functional and divisional managers. Preparing an IFE Matrix allows human resource, marketing, production/operations, finance/accounting, R&D, and computer information systems managers to vocalize their concerns and thoughts regarding the business condition of the firm. This results in an improved collective understanding of the business.

INSTRUCTIONS

Step 1 Join with two other individuals to form a three-person team. Develop a team IFE Matrix for Hershey Foods.

Step 2 Compare your team's IFE Matrix to other teams' IFE Matrices. Discuss any major differences.

Step 3 What strategies do you think would allow Hershey to capitalize on its major strengths? What strategies would allow Hershey to improve upon its major weaknesses?

CONSTRUCTING AN IFE MATRIX FOR MY UNIVERSITY

PURPOSE

This exercise gives you the opportunity to evaluate your university's major strengths and weaknesses. As will become clearer in the next chapter, an organization's strategies are largely based upon striving to take advantage of strengths and improving upon weaknesses.

INSTRUCTIONS

Step 1 Join with two other individuals to form a three-person team. Develop a team IFE Matrix for your university. You may use the strength/weaknesses determined in Experiential Exercise 1D.

Step 2 Go to the board and diagram your team's IFE Matrix.

Step 3 Compare your team's IFE Matrix to other teams' IFE Matrices. Discuss any major differences.

Step 4 What strategies do you think would allow your university to capitalize on its major strengths? What strategies would allow your university to improve upon its major weaknesses?

USING THE *STRATEGY FORMULATOR* SOFTWARE

PURPOSE

The purpose of this exercise is to enhance your skills using the *Strategy Formulator* software that is available with this text. This software can make it easier for you to develop, revise, update, and print various strategy-formulation analyses.

INSTRUCTIONS

Step 1 Use the *Strategy Formulator* software to develop a list of strengths and weaknesses for your university (Experiential Exercise 5C).

Step 2 Bring a printout of your work to class. Discuss any problems or questions you encountered in using this software.

Strategy Analysis and Choice

CHAPTER OUTLINE

CHAPTER OBJECTIVES

After studying this chapter, you should be able to do the following:

1. Describe a three-stage framework for choosing among alternative strategies.

2. Explain how to develop a TOWS Matrix, SPACE Matrix, BCG Matrix, IE Matrix, and QSPM.

3. Identify important behavioral, political, ethical, and social responsibility considerations in strategy analysis and choice.

4. Discuss the role of intuition in strategic analysis and choice.

5. Discuss the role of organizational culture in strategic analysis and choice.

6. Discuss the role of a board of directors in choosing among alternative strategies.

NOTABLE QUOTES

Strategic management is not a box of tricks or a bundle of techniques. It is analytical thinking and commitment of resources to action. But quantification alone is not planning. Some of the most important issues in strategic management cannot be quantified at all.—PETER DRUCKER

Objectives are not commands; they are commitments. They do not determine the future; they are the means to mobilize resources and energies of an organization for the making of the future.
—PETER DRUCKER

Life is full of lousy options.—GENERAL P. X. KELLEY

When a crisis forces choosing among alternatives, most people will choose the worse possible one
—RUDIN'S LAW

Strategy isn't something you can nail together in slap-dash fashion by sitting around a conference table.—TERRY HALLER

Planning is often doomed before it ever starts, either because too much is expected of it or because not enough is put into it.—T. J. CARTWRIGHT

To acquire or not to acquire, that is the question.—ROBERT J. TERRY

Corporate boards need to work to stay away from the traps that force every member to go along with the majority. Devil's advocates represent one easy-to-implement solution.—CHARLES SCHWENK

Whether it's broke or not, fix it—make it better. Not just products, but the whole company if necessary.—BILL SAPORITO

*S*trategic analysis and choice largely involves making subjective decisions based on objective information. This chapter introduces important concepts that can help strategists generate feasible alternatives, evaluate those alternatives, and choose a specific course of action. Behavioral aspects of strategy formulation are described, including politics, culture, ethics, and social responsibility considerations. Modern tools for formulating strategies are described, and the appropriate role of a board of directors is discussed.

THE NATURE OF STRATEGY ANALYSIS AND CHOICE

As indicated by Figure 6–1, this chapter focuses on establishing long-term objectives, generating alternative strategies, and selecting strategies to pursue. Strategy analysis and choice seeks to determine alternative courses of action that could best enable the firm to achieve its mission and objectives. The firm's present strategies, objectives, and mission, coupled with the external and internal audit information, provide a basis for generating and evaluating feasible alternative strategies.

Unless a desperate situation faces the firm, alternative strategies will likely represent incremental steps to move the firm from its present position to a desired future position. For example, Kindercare Learning Centers has a strategy to open 100 new centers per year, thus expanding from current markets into new areas. Alternative strategies do not come out of the wild blue yonder; they are derived from the firm's mission, objectives, external audit, and internal audit; they are consistent with, or build upon, past strategies that have worked well! Strategies do not come from thinking computers, although computers are becoming more and more helpful, as evidenced in the Information Technology Perspective.

THE PROCESS OF GENERATING AND SELECTING STRATEGIES   Strategists never consider all feasible alternatives that could benefit the firm, because there are an infinite number of possible actions and an infinite number of ways to implement those actions. Therefore, a manageable set of the most attractive alternative strategies must be developed. The advantages, disadvantages, trade-offs, costs, and benefits of these strategies

INFORMATION TECHNOLOGY
Thinking Computers Are Almost Here

Artificial Intelligence (AI) is the most common term in business and industry that refers to thinking computers. Other terms are *fuzzy logic, expert system, data mining, genetic algorithm,* and *neural network.* More than 70 percent of America's top 500 companies are using AI, according to a recent Commerce Department survey. AI sales worldwide are over $1.5 billion and growing rapidly.

Banks use AI extensively to detect fraud; banks call AI neural networks that mimic the circuitry of brain cells by learning from its own mistakes.

Companies use AI to develop and improve products ranging from home appliances and airplanes to office equipment and factory machinery. Firms such as Deere & Company use AI for factory floor scheduling. AI programs search through huge amounts of data and discover unnoticed relationships that often amount to new knowledge.

The goal of AI researchers is to produce a computer and software that can emulate the human brain and think. Dr. Simon at Carnegie Mellon University says, "Within ten years, computers will become more intelligent than humans.

Why people feel threatened by that, I don't know. We all know someone who's smarter than we are, and cars run faster than we do. Why is this so different? Our species can stand some improvement—and we can use all the assistance we can get.

Source: Adapted from Otis Port, "Computers That Think Are Almost Here," *Business Week* (July 17, 1995): 68–72.

FIGURE 6–1

A Comprehensive Strategic-Management Model

Feedback

Develop
Mission
Statement

Perform
External
Audit

Perform
Internal
Audit

Establish
Long-term
Objectives

Generate,
Evaluate,
and Select
Strategies

Establish
Policies
and
Annual
Objectives

Allocate
Resources

Measure
and
Evaluate
Performance

Strategy Formulation ——— Strategy Implementation ——— Strategy Evaluation should be determined. This section discusses the process that many firms use to determine an appropriate set of alternative strategies.

Identifying and evaluating alternative strategies should involve many of the managers and employees who earlier assembled the organizational mission statement, performed the external audit, and conducted the internal audit. Representatives from each department and division of the firm should be included in this process, as was the case in previous strategy-formulation activities. Recall that involvement provides the best opportunity for managers and employees to gain an understanding of what the firm is doing and why, and to become committed to helping the firm accomplish its objectives.

All participants in the strategy analysis and choice activity should have the firm's external and internal audit information by their sides. This information, coupled with the firm's mission statement, will help participants crystallize in their own minds particular strategies that they believe could benefit the firm most. Creativity should be encouraged in this thought process.

Alternative strategies proposed by participants should be considered and discussed in a meeting or series of meetings. Proposed strategies should be listed in writing. When all feasible strategies identified by participants are given and understood, the strategies should be ranked in order of attractiveness by all participants, with 1 = *should not be implemented,* 2 = *should possibly be implemented,* 3 = *should probably be implemented,* and 4 = *should definitely be implemented.* This process will result in a prioritized list of best strategies that reflects the collective wisdom of the group.

As indicated in the Natural Environment Perspective, the success of some strategies can depend on environmental attitudes.

LONG-TERM OBJECTIVES

Long-term objectives represent the results expected from pursuing certain strategies. Strategies represent the actions to be taken to accomplish long-term objectives. The time frame for objectives and strategies should be consistent, usually from two to five years.

THE NATURE OF LONG-TERM OBJECTIVES
Objectives should be quantitative, measurable, realistic, understandable, challenging, hierarchical, obtainable, and congruent among organizational units. Each objective should also be associated with a time line. Objectives are commonly stated in terms such as growth in assets, growth in sales, profitability, market share, degree and nature of diversification, degree and nature of vertical integration, earnings per share, and social responsibility. Clearly established objectives offer many benefits. They provide direction, allow synergy, aid in evaluation, establish priorities, reduce uncertainty, minimize conflicts, stimulate exertion, and aid in both the allocation of resources and the design of jobs.

Long-term objectives are needed at the corporate, divisional, and functional levels in an organization. They are an important measure of managerial performance. Many practitioners and academicians attribute a significant part of U.S. industry's competitive decline to the short-term, rather than long-term, strategy orientation of managers in the United States. Arthur D. Little argues that bonuses or merit pay for managers today must be based to a greater extent on long-term objectives and strategies. A general framework for relating objectives to performance evaluation is provided in Table 6–1. A particular organization could tailor these guidelines to meet its own needs, but incentives should be attached to both long-term and annual objectives.

Clearly stated and communicated objectives are vital to success for many reasons. First, objectives help stakeholders understand their role in an organization's future. They also provide a basis for consistent decision making by managers whose values and attitudes differ.

NATURAL ENVIRONMENT
Formulating Strategies Based on Environmental Attitudes

Americans can be grouped into categories based on their attitudes, actions, and concern toward natural environment deterioration and preservation.

CHARACTERISTICS	HIGH CONCERN FOR THE NATURAL ENVIRONMENT	LOW CONCERN FOR THE NATURAL ENVIRONMENT
Sex		
Male	34%	55%
Female	66	45
Education		
Less than High School	11	30
High School Graduate	39	39
Some College	22	20
College Graduate Or More	28	11
Occupation		
Executive/Professional	25	11
White Collar	18	15
Blue Collar	19	36
Marital Status		
Married	69	59
Not Married	30	41
Political/Social Ideology		
Conservative	43	36
Middle of the Road	26	41
Liberal	28	16
Region		
Northeast	31	17
Midwest	27	22
South	18	48
West	24	13
Median Income (in thousands)	$32.1	$21.2

Note in the table that persons most concerned about the natural environment tend to be more educated, have higher household income, live in the West or Northeast, and live in cities. These persons especially engage in activities such as not purchasing products from companies that are environmentally irresponsible, avoiding purchasing aerosol products, recycling paper and bottles, using biodegradable products, and contributing money to environmental groups. This information can be helpful to companies in formulating strategies such as market development (where to locate new facilities), product development (manufacturing new equipment or developing green products), and market penetration (whom to focus advertising efforts upon).

Source: Adapted from the Roper Organization, 205 East 42nd Street, New York, NY 10017. Also from Joe Schwartz and Thomas Miller, "The Earth's Best Friends," *American Demographics* (February 1991): 28.

By reaching a consensus on objectives during strategy-formulation activities, an organization can minimize potential conflicts later during implementation. Objectives set forth organizational priorities and stimulate exertion and accomplishment. They serve as standards by which individuals, groups, departments, divisions, and entire organizations can be evaluated. Objectives provide the basis for designing jobs and organizing activities to be performed in an organization. They also provide direction and allow for organizational synergy.

ORGANIZATIONAL LEVEL	BASIS FOR ANNUAL BONUS OR MERIT PAY
Corporate	75% based on long-term objectives 25% based on annual objectives
Divisional	50% based on long-term objectives 50% based on annual objectives
Functional	25% based on long-term objectives 75% based on annual objectives

TABLE 6–1
Varying Performance Measures by Organizational Level

Without long-term objectives, an organization would drift aimlessly toward some unknown end! It is hard to imagine an organization or individual being successful without clear objectives. Success only rarely occurs by accident; rather, it is the result of hard work directed toward achieving certain objectives.

NOT MANAGING BY OBJECTIVES   An unknown educator once said, "If you think education is expensive, try ignorance." The idea behind this saying also applies to establishing objectives. Strategists should avoid the following alternative ways to "not managing by objectives."

◆ Managing by Extrapolation—adheres to the principle "If it ain't broke, don't fix it." The idea is to keep on doing about the same things in the same ways, because things are going well.

◆ Managing by Crisis—based on the belief that the true measure of a really good strategist is the ability to solve problems. Because there are plenty of crises and problems to go around for every person and every organization, strategists ought to bring their time and creative energy to bear on solving the most pressing problems of the day. Managing by crisis is actually a form of reacting rather than acting and of letting events dictate the whats and whens of management decisions.

◆ Managing by Subjectives—built on the idea that there is no general plan for which way to go and what to do; just do the best you can to accomplish what you think should be done. In short, "Do your own thing, the best way you know how" (sometimes referred to as *the mystery approach to decision making* because subordinates are left to figure out what is happening and why).

◆ Managing by Hope—based on the fact that the future is laden with great uncertainty, and that if we try and do not succeed, then we hope our second (or third) attempt will succeed. Decisions are predicted on the hope that they will work and that good times are just around the corner, especially if luck and good fortune are on our side.[1]

A COMPREHENSIVE STRATEGY-FORMULATION FRAMEWORK

Important strategy-formulation techniques can be integrated into a three-stage decision-making framework, as shown in Figure 6–2. The tools presented in this framework are applicable to all sizes and types of organizations and can help strategists identify, evaluate, and select strategies.

Stage 1 of the formulation framework consists of the EFE Matrix, the IFE Matrix, and the Competitive Profile Matrix. Called the *Input Stage,* Stage 1 summarizes the basic input information needed to formulate strategies. Stage 2, called the *Matching Stage,* focuses upon generating feasible alternative strategies by aligning key external and internal factors. Stage 2 techniques include the Threats-Opportunities-Weaknesses-Strengths (TOWS) Matrix, the Strategic Position and Action Evaluation (SPACE) Matrix, the Boston Consulting Group (BCG) Matrix, the Internal-External (IE) Matrix, and the Grand Strategy Matrix. Stage 3, called the *Decision Stage,* involves a single technique, the Quantitative Strategic Planning Matrix (QSPM). A QSPM uses input information from Stage 1 to objectively evaluate feasible alternative strategies identified in Stage 2. A QSPM reveals the relative attractiveness of alternative strategies and thus provides an objective basis for selecting specific strategies.

All nine techniques included in the *strategy-formulation framework* require integration of intuition and analysis. Autonomous divisions in an organization commonly use strategy-formulation techniques to develop strategies and objectives. Divisional analyses provide a basis for identifying, evaluating, and selecting among alternative corporate-level strategies.

Strategists themselves, not analytic tools, are always responsible and accountable for strategic decisions. Lenz emphasizes that the shift from a words-oriented to a numbers-oriented planning process can give rise to a false sense of certainty; it can reduce dialogue,

FIGURE 6–2
The Strategy-Formulation Analytical Framework

STAGE 1: THE INPUT STAGE				
External Factor Evaluation (EFE) Matrix		Competitive Profile Matrix		Internal Factor Evaluation (IFE) Matrix
STAGE 2: THE MATCHING STAGE				
Threats-Opportunities-Weaknesses-Strengths (TOWS) Matrix	Strategic Position and Action Evaluation (SPACE) Matrix	Boston Consulting Group (BCG) Matrix	Internal-External (IE) Matrix	Grand Strategy Matrix
STAGE 3: THE DECISION STAGE				
Quantitative Strategic Planning Matrix (QSPM)				

discussion, and argument as a means to explore understandings, test assumptions and foster organizational learning.[2] Strategists therefore must be wary of this possibility and use analytical tools to facilitate, rather than diminish, communication. Without objective information and analysis, personal biases, politics, emotions, personalities, and *halo error* (the tendency to put too much weight on a single factor) unfortunately may play a dominant role in the strategy-formulation process.

THE INPUT STAGE

Procedures for developing an EFE Matrix, an IFE Matrix, and a Competitive Profile Matrix were presented in the previous two chapters. The information derived from these three matrices provides basic input information for the matching and decision stage matrices described later in this chapter.

The input tools require strategists to quantify subjectivity during early stages of the strategy-formulation process. Making small decisions in the input matrices regarding the relative importance of external and internal factors allows strategists to generate and evaluate alternative strategies more effectively. Good intuitive judgment is always needed in determining appropriate weights and ratings.

THE MATCHING STAGE

Strategy is sometimes defined as the match an organization makes between its internal resources and skills . . . and the opportunities and risks created by its external factors.[3] The *matching stage* of the strategy-formulation framework consists of five techniques that can be used in any sequence: the TOWS Matrix, the SPACE Matrix, the BCG Matrix, the IE Matrix, and the Grand Strategy Matrix. These tools rely upon information derived from the *input stage* to match external opportunities and threats with internal strengths and weaknesses. Matching external and internal critical success factors is the key to effectively

TABLE 6–2
Matching Key External and Internal Factors to Formulate Alternative Strategies

KEY INTERNAL FACTOR		KEY EXTERNAL FACTOR		RESULTANT STRATEGY
Excess working capacity (an internal strength)	+	20% annual growth in the cablevision industry (an external opportunity)	=	Acquire Visioncable, Inc.
Insufficient capacity (an internal weakness)	+	Exit of two major foreign competitors from the industry (an external opportunity)	=	Pursue horizontal integration by buying competitors' facilities
Strong R & D expertise (an internal strength)	+	Decreasing numbers of young adults (an external threat)	=	Develop new products for older adults
Poor employee morale (an internal weakness)	+	Strong union activity (an external threat)	=	Develop a new employee-benefits package

generating feasible alternative strategies! For example, a firm with excess working capital (an internal strength) could take advantage of the cablevision industry's 20-percent annual growth rate (an external opportunity) by acquiring a firm in the cablevision industry. This example portrays simple one-to-one matching. In most situations, external and internal relationships are more complex, and the matching requires multiple alignments for each strategy generated. The basic concept of matching is illustrated in Table 6–2.

Any organization, whether military, product-oriented, service-oriented, governmental, or even athletic, must develop and execute good strategies to win. A good offense without a good defense, or vice versa, usually leads to defeat. Developing strategies that use strengths to capitalize on opportunities could be considered an offense, whereas strategies designed to improve upon weaknesses while avoiding threats could be termed defensive. Every organization has some external opportunities and threats and internal strengths and weaknesses that can be aligned to formulate feasible alternative strategies. As indicated in the Global Perspective, the net effect of U.S. firms' strategies in 1994 was to create a negative U.S. trade balance with most foreign countries.

THE THREATS-OPPORTUNITIES-WEAKNESSES-STRENGTHS (TOWS) MATRIX

The *Threats-Opportunities-Weaknesses-Strengths (TOWS) Matrix* is an important matching tool that helps managers develop four types of strategies: SO Strategies, WO Strategies, ST Strategies, and WT Strategies.[4] Watching key external and internal factors is the most difficult part of developing a TOWS Matrix and requires good judgment, and there is no one best set of matches. Note in Table 6–2 that the first, second, third, and fourth strategies are SO, WO, ST, and WT Strategies, respectively.

SO Strategies use a firm's internal strengths to take advantage of external opportunities. All managers would like their organizations to be in a position where internal strengths can be used to take advantage of external trends and events. Organizations generally will pursue WO, ST, or WT Strategies in order to get into a situation where they can apply SO Strategies. When a firm has major weaknesses, it will strive to overcome them and make them strengths. When an organization faces major threats, it will seek to avoid them in order to concentrate on opportunities.

WO Strategies aim at improving internal weaknesses by taking advantage of external opportunities. Sometimes key external opportunities exist, but a firm has internal weaknesses that prevent it from exploiting those opportunities. For example, there may be a high demand for electronic devices to control the amount and timing of fuel injection in automobile engines (opportunity), but a certain auto parts manufacturer may lack the technology required for producing these devices (weakness). One possible WO Strategy would be to acquire this technology by forming a joint venture with a firm having competency in this

GLOBAL PERSPECTIVE

U.S. Bilateral Trade Balances, 1993–1995 ($ Billion)

	1993	1994	1995
BIG EMERGING MARKETS			
Argentina			
Exports	3.8	4.5	4.2
Imports	1.2	1.7	1.8
Balance	2.6	2.7	2.4
Brazil			
Exports	6.1	8.1	11.4
Imports	7.5	8.7	8.8
Balance	−1.4	−0.6	2.6
China			
Exports	8.8	9.3	11.7
Imports	31.5	38.8	45.5
Balance	−22.8	−29.5	−33.8
Hong Kong			
Exports	9.9	11.5	14.2
Imports	9.6	9.7	10.3
Balance	0.3	1.8	−3.9
Taiwan			
Exports	16.2	17.1	19.3
Imports	25.1	26.7	29.0
Balance	−8.9	−9.6	−9.7
India			
Exports	2.8	2.3	3.3
Imports	4.6	5.3	5.7
Balance	−1.8	−3.0	−2.7
Indonesia			
Exports	2.8	2.8	3.4
Imports	5.4	6.5	7.4
Balance	−2.7	−3.7	−4.0
Mexico			
Exports	41.6	50.8	45.4
Imports	39.9	49.5	61.7
Balance	1.7	1.3	−16.3

	1993	1994	1995
Poland			
Exports	0.9	0.6	0.8
Imports	0.5	0.7	0.7
Balance	0.5	0.0	0.1
South Africa			
Exports	2.2	2.2	2.8
Imports	1.8	2.0	2.2
Balance	0.3	0.1	0.6
South Korea			
Exports	14.8	18.0	25.4
Imports	17.1	19.7	24.2
Balance	−2.3	−1.6	1.2
Turkey			
Exports	3.4	2.8	2.7
Imports	1.2	1.6	1.8
Balance	2.2	1.2	0.9
INDUSTRIAL COUNTRIES			
European Union			
Exports	97.0	102.8	123.8
Imports	97.9	110.9	129.8
Balance	−1.0	−8.1	−6.0
United Kingdom			
Exports	26.4	26.8	28.8
Imports	21.7	25.1	26.9
Balance	4.7	1.8	1.9
Germany			
Exports	18.9	19.2	22.4
Imports	28.6	31.8	36.8
Balance	−9.6	−12.5	−14.4
France			
Exports	13.3	13.6	14.2
Imports	15.3	16.8	17.2
Balance	−2.0	−3.2	−3.0

	1993	1994	1995
Italy			
Exports	6.5	7.2	8.9
Imports	13.2	14.7	16.5
Balance	−6.8	−7.5	−7.6
Spain			
Exports	4.2	4.6	5.5
Imports	3.0	3.6	3.9
Balance	1.2	1.1	1.6
Canada			
Exports	100.4	114.4	126.0
Imports	111.2	129.0	145.0
Balance	−10.8	−14.5	−19
Japan			
Exports	47.9	53.5	64.3
Imports	107.2	119.1	123.6
Balance	−59.4	−65.7	−59.3
ECONOMIES IN TRANSITION			
Russia			
Exports	3.0	2.6	2.8
Imports	1.7	3.2	4.0
Balance	1.2	−0.7	−1.2

Source: Department of Commerce.
Note: Some totals may not add due to rounding.

area. An alternative WO Strategy would be to hire and train people with the required technical capabilities.

ST Strategies use a firm's strengths to avoid or reduce the impact of external threats. This does not mean that a strong organization should always meet threats in the external environment head-on. A recent example of ST Strategy occurred when Texas Instruments used an excellent legal department (a strength) to collect nearly $700 million in damages and royalties from nine Japanese and Korean firms that infringed on patents for semiconductor memory chips (threat). Rival firms that copy ideas, innovations, and patented products are a major threat in many industries. This is a major problem for U.S. firms selling products in China.

WT Strategies are defensive tactics directed at reducing internal weaknesses and avoiding environmental threats. An organization faced with numerous external threats and internal weaknesses may indeed be in a precarious position. In fact, such a firm may have to fight for its survival, merge, retrench, declare bankruptcy, or choose liquidation.

FIGURE 6–3
The TOWS Matrix

	STRENGTHS—S	WEAKNESSES—W
Always leave blank	1. 2. 3. 4. 5. 6. 7. 8. 9. 10. **List strengths**	1. 2. 3. 4. 5. 6. 7. 8. 9. 10. **List weaknesses**
OPPORTUNITIES—O 1. 2. 3. 4. 5. **List opportunities** 6. 7. 8. 9. 10.	**SO STRATEGIES** 1. 2. 3. 4. **Use strengths to take** 5. **advantage of opportunities** 6. 7. 8. 9. 10.	**WO STRATEGIES** 1. 2. 3. 4. **Overcome weaknesses by** 5. **taking advantage of** 6. **opportunities** 7. 8. 9. 10.
THREATS—T 1. 2. 3. 4. 5. **List threats** 6. 7. 8. 9. 10.	**ST STRATEGIES** 1. 2. 3. 4. **Use strengths to avoid** 5. **threats** 6. 7. 8. 9. 10.	**WT STRATEGIES** 1. 2. 3. 4. **Minimize weaknesses and** 5. **avoid threats** 6. 7. 8. 9. 10.

A schematic representation of the TOWS Matrix is provided in Figure 6–3. Note that a TOWS Matrix is composed of nine cells. As shown, there are four key factor cells, four strategy cells, and one cell that is always left blank (the upper left cell). The four strategy cells, labeled *SO, WO, ST,* and *WT,* are developed after completing four key factor cells, labeled *S, W, O,* and *T.* There are eight steps involved in constructing a TOWS Matrix:

1. List the firm's key external opportunities.
2. List the firm's key external threats.
3. List the firm's key internal strengths.
4. List the firm's key internal weaknesses.
5. Match internal strengths with external opportunities and record the resultant SO Strategies in the appropriate cell.
6. Match internal weaknesses with external opportunities and record the resultant WO Strategies.

FIGURE 6–4
The TOWS Matrix for a Food Company

	STRENGTHS—S	WEAKNESSES—W
	1. Current ratio increased to 2.52	1. Legal suits have not been resolved
	2. Profit margin increased to 6.94	2. Plant capacity has fallen to 74%
	3. Employee morale is high	3. Lack of a strategic-management system
	4. New computer information system	4. R&D expenses have increased 31%
	5. Market share has increased to 24%	5. Dealer incentives have not been effective
OPPORTUNITIES—O	**SO STRATEGIES**	**WO STRATEGIES**
1. Western European unification	1. Acquire food company in Europe (S1, S5, O1)	1. Form a joint venture to distribute soup in Europe (W3, O1)
2. Rising health consciousness in selecting foods	2. Build a manufacturing plant in Mexico (S2, S5, O5)	2. Develop new Pepperidge Farm products (W1, O2, O4)
3. Free market economies arising in Asia	3. Develop new healthy soups (S3, O2)	
4. Demand for soups increasing 10% annually	4. Form a joint venture to distribute soup in Asia (S1, S5, O3)	
5. U.S./Mexico Free Trade Agreement		
THREATS—T	**ST STRATEGIES**	**WT STRATEGIES**
1. Food revenues increasing only 1% annually	1. Develop new microwave TV dinners (S1, S5, T2)	1. Close unprofitable European operations (W3, T3, T5)
2. ConAgra's Banquet TV dinners lead market with 27.4% share	2. Develop new biodegradable soup containers (S1, T4)	2. Diversify into nonsoup foods (W5, T1)
3. Unstable economies in Asia		
4. Tin cans are not biodegradable		
5. Low value of the dollar		

7. Match internal strengths with external threats and record the resultant ST Strategies.
8. Match internal weaknesses with external threats and record the resultant WT Strategies.

The purpose of each Stage 2 matching tool is to generate feasible alternative strategies, not to select or determine which strategies are best! Not all of the strategies developed in the TOWS Matrix, therefore, will be selected for implementation. A sample TOWS Matrix for a food company is provided in Figure 6–4.

The strategy-formulation guidelines provided in Chapter 2 can enhance the process of matching key external and internal factors. For example, when an organization has both the capital and human resources needed to distribute its own products (internal strength) and distributors are unreliable, costly, or incapable of meeting the firm's needs (external threat), then forward integration can be an attractive ST Strategy. When a firm has excess production capacity (internal weakness) and its basic industry is experiencing declining annual sales and profits (external threat), then concentric diversification can be an effective WT Strategy. It

FIGURE 6–5
The SPACE Matrix

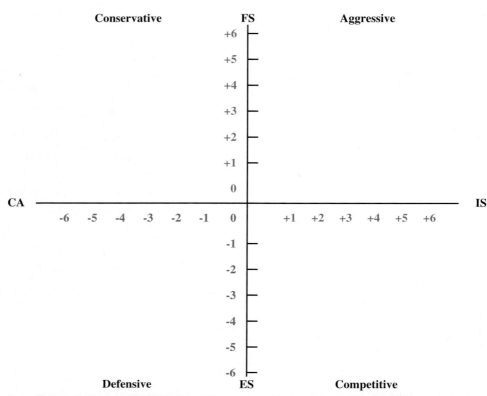

Source: H. Rowe, R. Mason, and K. Dickel, *Strategic Management and Business Policy: A Methodological Approach* (Reading, Massachusetts: Addison-Wesley Publishing Co. Inc., © 1982): 155. Reprinted with permission of the publisher.

is important to use specific, rather than general, strategy terms when developing a TOWS Matrix. In addition, it is important to include the "S1,O2" type notation after each strategy in the TOWS Matrix. This notation reveals the rationale for each alternative strategy.

THE STRATEGIC POSITION AND ACTION EVALUATION (SPACE)
MATRIX   The *Strategic Position and Action Evaluation (SPACE) Matrix,* another important Stage 2 *matching* tool, is illustrated in Figure 6–5. Its four-quadrant framework indicates whether aggressive, conservative, defensive, or competitive strategies are most appropriate for a given organization. The axes of the SPACE Matrix represent two internal dimensions *(financial strength* [FS] and *competitive advantage* [CA]) and two external dimensions *(environmental stability* [ES] and *industry strength* [IS]). These four factors are the most important determinants of an organization's overall strategic position.[5]

Depending upon the type of organization, numerous variables could comprise each of the dimensions represented on the axes of the SPACE Matrix. Factors earlier included in the firm's EFEM and IFEM should be considered in developing a SPACE Matrix. Other variables commonly included are given in Table 6–3. For example, return on investment, leverage, liquidity, working capital, and cash flow are commonly considered determining factors of an organization's financial strength. Like the TOWS Matrix, the SPACE Matrix should be tailored to the particular organization being studied and based on factual information as much as possible.

The steps required to develop a SPACE Matrix are as follows:

1. Select a set of variables to comprise financial strength (FS), competitive advantage (CA), environmental stability (ES), and industry strength (IS).

INTERNAL STRATEGIC POSITION	EXTERNAL STRATEGIC POSITION
FINANCIAL STRENGTH (FS)	*ENVIRONMENTAL STABILITY (ES)**
Return on investment	Technological changes
Leverage	Rate of inflation
Liquidity	Demand variability
Working capital	Price range of competing products
Cash flow	Barriers to entry into market
Ease of exit from market	Competitive pressure
Risk involved in business	Price elasticity of demand
COMPETITIVE ADVANTAGE (CA)	*INDUSTRY STRENGTH (IS)*
Market share	Growth potential
Product quality	Profit potential
Product life cycle	Financial stability
Customer loyalty	Technological know-how
Competition's capacity utilization	Resource utilization
Technological know-how	Capital intensity
Control over suppliers and distributors	Ease of entry into market
	Productivity, capacity utilization

TABLE 6–3
Example Factors That Comprise the SPACE Matrix Axes

Source: H. Rowe, R. Mason, and K. Dickel, *Strategic Management and Business Policy: A Methodological Approach* (Reading, Massachusetts: Addison-Wesley Publishing Co. Inc., 1982): 155–156. Reprinted with permission of the publisher.
*A stable environment represents a better strategic position than an unstable environment.

2. Assign a numerical value ranging from +1 (worst) to +6 (best) to each of the variables that comprise the FS and IS dimensions. Assign a numerical value ranging from −1 (best) to −6 (worst) to each of the variables that comprise the ES and CA dimensions.

3. Compute an average score for FS, CA, IS, and ES by summing the values given to the variables of each dimension and dividing by the number of variables included in the respective dimension.

4. Plot the average scores for FS, IS, ES, and CA on the appropriate axis in the SPACE Matrix.

5. Add the two scores on the *x*-axis and plot the resultant point on *X*. Add the two scores on the *y*-axis and plot the resultant point on *Y*. Plot the intersection of the new *xy* point.

6. Draw a *directional vector* from the origin of the SPACE Matrix through the new intersection point. This vector reveals the type of strategies recommended for the organization: aggressive, competitive, defensive, or conservative.

Some examples of strategy profiles that can emerge from a SPACE analysis are shown in Figure 6–6. The directional vector associated with each profile suggests the type of strategies to pursue: aggressive, conservative, defensive, or competitive. When a firm's directional vector is located in the *aggressive quadrant* of the SPACE Matrix, an organization is in an excellent position to use its internal strengths to (1) take advantage of external opportunities, (2) overcome internal weaknesses, and (3) avoid external threats. Therefore, market penetration, market development, product development, backward integration, forward integration, horizontal integration, conglomerate diversification, concentric diversification, horizontal diversification, or a combination strategy can all be feasible, depending on the specific circumstances that face the firm.

The directional vector may appear in the *conservative quadrant* (upper left quadrant) of the SPACE Matrix, which implies staying close to the firm's basic competencies and not taking excessive risks. Conservative strategies most often include market penetration, market development, product development, and concentric diversification. The directional vector may be located in the lower left or *defensive quadrant* of the SPACE Matrix, which suggests that the firm should focus on improving internal weaknesses and avoiding external

FIGURE 6–6
Example Strategy Profiles

Aggresssive Profiles

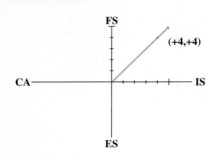

A financially strong firm that has achieved major competitive advantages in a growing and stable industry

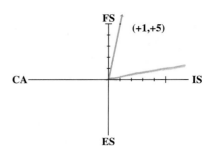

A firm whose financial strength is a dominating factor in the industry

Conservative Profiles

A firm that has achieved financial strength in a stable industry that is not growing; the firm has no major competitive advantages

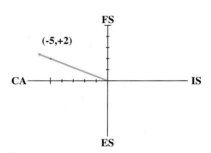

A firm that suffers from major competitive disadvantages in an industry that is technologically stable but declining in sales

Competitive Profiles

A firm with major competitive advantages in a high-growth industry

An organization that is competing fairly well in an unstable industry

Defensive Profiles

A firm that has a very weak competitive position in a negative growth, stable industry

A financially troubled firm in a very unstable industry

Source: H. Rowe, R. Mason, and K Dickel, *Strategic Management and Business Policy: A Methodological Approach* (Reading, Massachusetts: Addison-Wesley Publishing Co. Inc., © 1982): 155. Reprinted with permission of the publisher.

TABLE 6–4
**A SPACE Matrix for a
Bank**

FINANCIAL STRENGTH	RATINGS
The bank's primary capital ratio is 7.23 percent, which is 1.23 percentage points over the generally required ratio of 6 percent.	1.0
The bank's return on assets is negative 0.77, compared to a bank industry average ratio of positive 0.70.	1.0
The bank's net income was $183 million, down 9 percent a year earlier.	3.0
The bank's revenues increased 7 percent to $3.46 billion.	4.0
	9.0

INDUSTRY STRENGTH	
Deregulation provides geographic and product freedom.	4.0
Deregulation increases competition in the banking industry.	2.0
Pennsylvania's interstate banking law allows the bank to acquire other banks in New Jersey, Ohio, Kentucky, The District of Columbia, and West Virginia.	4.0
	10.0

ENVIRONMENTAL STABILITY	
Lesser developed countries are experiencing high inflation and political instability.	-4.0
Headquartered in Pittsburgh, the bank has historically been heavily dependent on the steel, oil, and gas industries. These industries are depressed.	-5.0
Banking deregulation has created instability throughout the industry.	-4.0
	-13.0

COMPETITIVE ADVANTAGE	
The bank provides data processing services for more than 450 institutions in 38 states.	-2.0
Superregional banks, international banks, and nonbanks are becoming increasingly competitive.	-5.0
The bank has a large customer base.	-2.0
	-9.0

CONCLUSION
ES Average is $-13.0 \div 3 = -4.33$ IS Average is $+10.0 \div 3 = 3.33$
CA Average is $-9.0 \div 3 = -3.00$ FS Average is $+9.0 \div 4 = 2.25$
Directional Vector Coordinates: x-axis: $-3.00 + (+3.33) = +0.33$
y-axis: $-4.33 + (+2.25) = -2.08$
The bank should pursue Competitive Type Strategies

threats. Defensive strategies include retrenchment, divestiture, liquidation, and concentric diversification. Finally, the directional vector may be located in the lower right or *competitive quadrant* of the SPACE Matrix, indicating competitive strategies. Competitive strategies include backward, forward, and horizonal integration, market penetration, market development, product development, and joint venture.

SPACE Matrix analysis for a bank is provided in Table 6–4. Note that competitive strategies are recommended.

THE BOSTON CONSULTING GROUP (BCG) MATRIX   Autonomous divisions (or profit centers) of an organization make up what is called a *business portfolio*. When a firm's divisions compete in different industries, a separate strategy often must be developed for each business. The *Boston Consulting Group (BCG) Matrix* and the *Internal-External (IE) Matrix* are designed specifically to enhance a multidivisional firm's efforts to formulate strategies.

The BCG Matrix graphically portrays differences among divisions in terms of relative market share position and industry growth rate. The BCG Matrix allows a multidivisional organization to manage its portfolio of businesses by examining the relative market share position and the industry growth rate of each division relative to all other divisions in the organization. *Relative market share position* is defined as the ratio of a division's own

FIGURE 6–7
The BCG Matrix

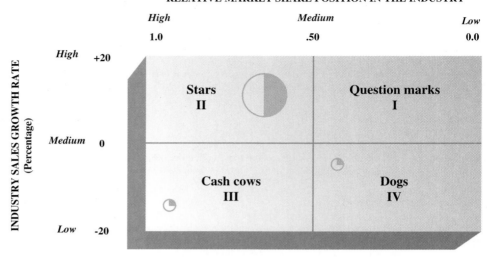

market share in a particular industry to the market share held by the largest rival firm in that industry. Relative market share position is given on the *x*-axis of the BCG Matrix. The midpoint on the *x*-axis is usually set at .50, corresponding to a division that has half the market share of the leading firm in the industry. The *y*-axis represents the industry growth rate in sales, measured in percentage terms. The growth rate percentages on the *y*-axis could range from −20 to +20 percent, with 0.0 being the midpoint. These numerical ranges on the *x*- and *y*-axes are often used, but other numerical values could be established as deemed appropriate for particular organizations.

An example of a BCG Matrix appears in Figure 6–7. Each circle represents a separate division. The size of the circle corresponds to the proportion of corporate revenue generated by that business unit, and the pie slice indicates the proportion of corporate profits generated by that division. Divisions located in Quadrant I of the BCG Matrix are called Question Marks, those located in Quadrant II are called Stars, those located in Quadrant III are called Cash Cows, and finally those divisions located in Quadrant IV are called Dogs.

◆ Question Marks—Divisions in Quadrant I have a low relative market share position, yet compete in a high-growth industry. Generally, these firms' cash needs are high and their cash generation is low. These businesses are called *Question Marks* because the organization must decide whether to strengthen them by pursuing an intensive strategy (market penetration, market development, or product development) or to sell them.

◆ Stars—Quadrant II businesses (often called *Stars*) represent the organization's best long-run opportunities for growth and profitability. Divisions with a high relative market share and a high industry growth rate should receive substantial investment to maintain or strengthen their dominant positions. Forward, backward, and horizontal integration; market penetration; market development; product development; and joint ventures are all appropriate strategies for these divisions to consider.

◆ Cash Cows—Divisions positioned in Quadrant III have a high relative market share position but compete in a low-growth industry. Called *Cash Cows* because they generate cash in excess of their needs, they are often milked. Many of today's Cash Cows were yesterday's Stars. Cash Cow divisions should be managed to maintain their strong position for as long as possible. Product development or concentric diversification may be attractive strategies for strong Cash Cows. However, as a Cash Cow division becomes weak, retrenchment or divestiture can become more appropriate.

◆ Dogs—Quadrant IV divisions of the organization have a low relative market share position and compete in a slow-or-no-market-growth industry; they are *Dogs* in the firm's portfolio.

FIGURE 6–8
An Example BCG Matrix

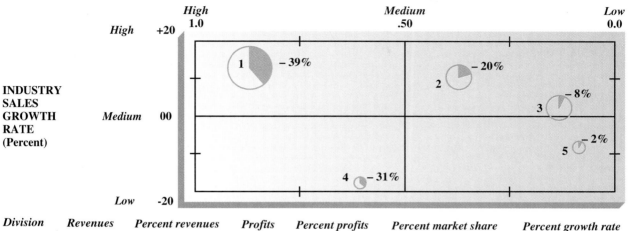

Division	Revenues	Percent revenues	Profits	Percent profits	Percent market share	Percent growth rate
1	$60,000	37	$10,000	39	80	+15
2	40,000	24	5,000	20	40	+10
3	40,000	24	2,000	8	10	1
4	20,000	12	8,000	31	60	-20
5	5,000	3	500	2	5	-10
Total	$165,000	100	$25,500	100		

Because of their weak internal and external position, these businesses often are liquidated, divested, or trimmed down through retrenchment. When a division first becomes a Dog, retrenchment can be the best strategy to pursue because many Dogs have bounced back, after strenuous asset and cost reduction, to become viable, profitable divisions.

The major benefit of the BCG Matrix is that it draws attention to the cash flow, investment characteristics, and needs of an organization's various divisions. The divisions of many firms evolve over time: Dogs become Question Marks, Question Marks become Stars, Stars become Cash Cows, and Cash Cows become Dogs, in an ongoing counterclockwise motion. Less frequently, Stars become Question Marks, Question Marks become Dogs, Dogs become Cash Cows, and Cash Cows become Stars (in a clockwise motion). In some organizations no cyclical motion is apparent. Over time, organizations should strive to achieve a portfolio of divisions that are Stars.

One example of a BCG Matrix is provided in Figure 6–8, which illustrates an organization composed of five divisions with annual sales ranging from $5,000 to $60,000. Division I has the greatest sales volume, so the circle representing that division is the largest one in the Matrix. The circle corresponding to Division 5 is the smallest, because its sales volume ($5,000) is least among all the divisions. The pie slices within the circles reveal the percent of corporate profits contributed by each division. As shown, Division 1 contributes the highest profit percentage, 39 percent. Notice in the diagram that Division 1 is considered a Star, Division 2 is a Question Mark, Division 3 is also a Question Mark, Division 4 is a Cash Cow, and Division 5 is a Dog.

The BCG Matrix, like all analytical techniques, has some limitations. For example, viewing every business as either a Star, Cash Cow, Dog, or Question Mark is an oversimplification; many businesses fall right in the middle of the BCG Matrix and are thus not easily classified.

FIGURE 6–9
The Internal-External (IE) Matrix

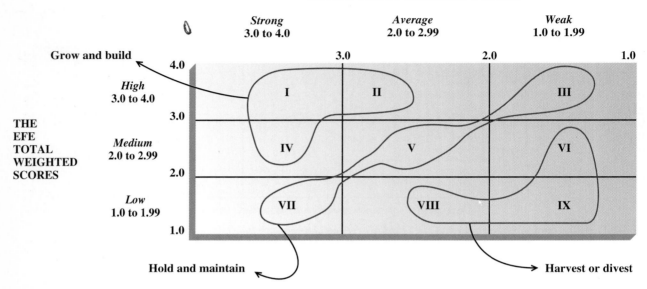

Note: The IE was developed from the General Electric (GE) Business Screen Matrix. For a description of the GE Matrix, see: Michael Allen, "Diagramming GE's Planning for What's WATT," in *Corporate Planning: Techniques and Applications*, eds. R. Allio and M. Pennington (New York: AMACOM, 1979).

Furthermore, the BCG Matrix does not reflect whether or not various divisions or their industries are growing over time; that is, the matrix has no temporal qualities, but rather is a snapshot of an organization at a given point in time. Finally, other variables besides relative market share position and industry growth rate in sales, such as size of the market and competitive advantages, are important in making strategic decisions about various divisions.

THE INTERNAL-EXTERNAL (IE) MATRIX   The *Internal-External (IE) Matrix* positions an organization's various divisions in a nine-cell display illustrated in Figure 6–9. The IE Matrix is similar to the BCG Matrix in that both tools involve plotting organization divisions in a schematic diagram; this is why they are both called portfolio matrices. Also, the size of each circle represents the percentage sales contribution of each division, and pie slices reveal the percentage profit contribution of each division in both the BCG and IE Matrix.

But there are some important differences between the BCG Matrix and IE Matrix. First, the axes are different. Also, the IE Matrix requires more information about the divisions than the BCG Matrix. Further, the strategic implications of each matrix are different. For these reasons, strategists in multidivisional firms often develop both the BCG Matrix and the IE Matrix in formulating alternative strategies. A common practice is to develop a BCG Matrix and an IE Matrix for the present and then develop projected matrices to reflect the future. This before-and-after analysis forecasts the expected effect of strategic decisions on an organization's portfolio of divisions.

The IE Matrix is based on two key dimensions: the IFE total weighted scores on the *x*-axis and the EFE total weighted scores on the *y*-axis. Recall that each division of an organization should construct an IFE Matrix and an EFE Matrix for its part of the organization. The total weighted scores derived from the divisions allow construction of the corporate-level IE Matrix. On the *x*-axis of the IE Matrix, an IFE total weighted score of 1.0 to 1.99 represents a weak internal position, a score of 2.0 to 2.99 is considered average, and a score

FIGURE 6–10
An Example IE Matrix

THE IFE TOTAL WEIGHTED SCORES

Division	Sales	Percent sales	Profits	Percent profits	IFE scores	EFE scores
1	$100	25	10	50	3.6	3.2
2	200	50	5	25	2.1	3.5
3	50	12.5	4	20	3.1	2.1
4	50	12.5	1	5	1.8	2.5
Total	400	100	20	100		

of 3.0 to 4.0 is strong. Similarly, on the *y*-axis, an EFE total weighted score of 1.0 to 1.99 is considered low, a score of 2.0 to 2.99 is medium, and a score of 3.0 to 4.0 is high.

The IE Matrix can be divided into three major regions that have different strategy implications. First, the prescription for divisions that fall into cells I, II, or IV can be described as *grow and build*. Intensive (market penetration, market development, and product development) or integrative (backward integration, forward integration, and horizontal integration) strategies can be most appropriate for these divisions. Second, divisions that fall into cells III, V, or VII can best be managed with *hold and maintain* strategies; market penetration and product development are two commonly employed strategies for these types of divisions. Third, a common prescription for divisions that fall into cells VI, VIII, or IX is *harvest or divest*. Successful organizations are able to achieve a portfolio of businesses positioned in or around cell I in the IE Matrix.

An example of a completed IE Matrix is given in Figure 6–10, which depicts an organization composed of four divisions. As indicated by the positioning of the circles, *grow and build* strategies are appropriate for Division 1, Division 2, and Division 3. Division 4 is a candidate for *harvest or divest*. Division 2 contributes the greatest percentage of company sales and thus is represented by the largest circle. Division 1 contributes the greatest proportion of total profits; it has the largest percentage pie slice.

THE GRAND STRATEGY MATRIX   In addition to the TOWS Matrix, SPACE Matrix, BCG Matrix, and IE Matrix, the *Grand Strategy Matrix* has become a popular tool for formulating alternative strategies. All organizations can be positioned in one of the Grand Strategy Matrix's four strategy quadrants. A firm's divisions could likewise be positioned. As illustrated in Figure 6–11, the Grand Strategy Matrix is based on two evaluative dimensions: competitive

FIGURE 6–11
The Grand Strategy Matrix

RAPID MARKET GROWTH

Quadrant II

1. Market development
2. Market penetration
3. Product development
4. Horizontal integration
5. Divestiture
6. Liquidation

Quadrant I

1. Market development
2. Market penetration
3. Product development
4. Forward integration
5. Backward integration
6. Horizontal integration
7. Concentric diversification

WEAK COMPETITIVE POSITION

STRONG COMPETITIVE POSITION

Quadrant III

1. Retrenchment
2. Concentric diversification
3. Horizontal diversification
4. Conglomerate diversification
5. Divestiture
6. Liquidation

Quadrant IV

1. Concentric diversification
2. Horizontal diversification
3. Conglomerate diversification
4. Joint ventures

SLOW MARKET GROWTH

Source: Adapted from Roland Christensen, Norman Berg, and Malcolm Salter, *Policy Formulation and Administration* (Homewood, Ill.: Richard D. Irwin, 1976): 16–18.

position and market growth. Appropriate strategies for an organization to consider are listed in sequential order of attractiveness in each quadrant of the matrix.

Firms located in Quadrant I of the Grand Strategy Matrix are in an excellent strategic position. For these firms, continued concentration on current markets (market penetration and market development) and products (product development) are appropriate strategies. It is unwise for a Quadrant I firm to shift notably from its established competitive advantages. When a Quadrant I organization has excessive resources, then backward, forward, or horizontal integration may be effective strategies. When a Quadrant I firm is too heavily committed to a single product, then concentric diversification may reduce the risks associated with a narrow product line. Quadrant I firms can afford to take advantage of external opportunities in many areas: they can aggressively take risks when necessary. As indicated in the Natural Environment Perspective, Quadrant I firms often take the lead in developing green products and advocating environmental preservation.

Firms positioned in Quadrant II need to evaluate their present approach to the marketplace seriously. Although their industry is growing, they are unable to compete effectively, and they need to determine why the firm's current approach is ineffectual and how the company can best change to improve its competitiveness. Since Quadrant II firms are in a rapid-market-growth industry, an intensive strategy (as opposed to integrative or diversification) is usually the first option that should be considered. However, if the firm is lacking a distinctive competence or competitive advantage, then horizontal integration is often a desirable alternative. As a last result, divestiture or liquidation should be considered. Divestiture can provide funds needed to acquire other businesses or buy back shares of stock.

Quadrant III organizations compete in slow-growth industries and have weak competitive positions. These firms must make some drastic changes quickly to avoid further demise and possible liquidation. Extensive cost and asset reduction (retrenchment) should be pursued first. An alternative strategy is to shift resources away from the current business into different areas. If all else fails, the final options for Quadrant III businesses are divestiture or liquidation.

Finally, Quadrant IV businesses have a strong competitive position but are in a slow-growth industry. These firms have the strength to launch diversified programs into more promising growth areas. Quadrant IV firms have characteristically high cash flow levels and limited internal growth needs and can often pursue concentric, horizontal, or conglomerate diversification successfully. Quadrant IV firms may also pursue joint ventures.

THE DECISION STAGE

Analysis and intuition provide a basis for making strategy-formulation decisions. The matching techniques just discussed reveal feasible alternative strategies. Many of these strategies will likely have been proposed by managers and employees participating in the strategy analysis and choice activity. Any additional strategies resulting from the matching analyses could be discussed and added to the list of feasible alternative options. As indicated earlier in this chapter, participants could rate these strategies on a 1 to 4 scale so that a prioritized list of the best strategies could be achieved.

THE QUANTITATIVE STRATEGIC PLANNING MATRIX (QSPM)   Other than ranking strategies to achieve the prioritized list, there is only one analytical technique in the literature designed to determine the relative attractiveness of feasible alternative actions. This technique is the *Quantitative Strategic Planning Matrix (QSPM),* which comprises Stage 3 of the strategy-formulation analytical framework.[5] This technique objectively indicates which alternative strategies are best. The QSPM uses input from Stage 1 analyses and matching results from Stage 2 analyses to decide objectively among alternative strategies. That is, the EFE Matrix, IFE Matrix, and Competitive Profile Matrix that comprise Stage 1, coupled with the TOWS Matrix, SPACE Analysis, BCG Matrix, IE Matrix, and Grand Strategy Matrix that make up Stage 2, provide the needed information for setting up the QSPM (Stage 3). The QSPM is a tool that allows strategists to evaluate alternative strategies objectively, based on previously identified external and internal critical success factors. Like other strategy-formulation analytical tools, the QSPM requires good intuitive judgment.

The basic format of the QSPM is illustrated in Table 6–5. Note that the left column of a QSPM consists of key external and internal factors (from Stage 1), and the top row consists of feasible alternative strategies (from Stage 2). Specifically, the left column of a QSPM consists of information obtained directly from the EFE Matrix and IFE Matrix. In a column adjacent to the critical success factors, the respective weights received by each factor in the EFE Matrix and the IFE Matrix are recorded.

The top row of a QSPM consists of alternative strategies derived from the TOWS Matrix, SPACE Matrix, BCG Matrix, IE Matrix, and Grand Strategy Matrix. These matching tools usually generate similar feasible alternatives. However, not every strategy suggested by the matching techniques has to be evaluated in a QSPM. Strategists should use good intuitive judgment in selecting strategies to include in a QSPM.

Conceptually, the QSPM determines the relative attractiveness of various strategies based on the extent to which key external and internal critical success factors are capitalized

TABLE 6–5
The Quantitative Strategic Planning Matrix—QSPM

| | | STRATEGIC ALTERNATIVES | | |
KEY FACTORS	WEIGHT	STRATEGY 1	STRATEGY 2	STRATEGY 3
KEY EXTERNAL FACTORS				
Economy				
Political/Legal/Governmental				
Social/Cultural/Demographic/Environmental				
Technological				
Competitive				
KEY INTERNAL FACTORS				
Management				
Marketing				
Finance/Accounting				
Production/Operations				
Research and Development				
Computer Information Systems				

upon or improved. The relative attractiveness of each strategy within a set of alternatives is computed by determining the cumulative impact of each external and internal critical success factor. Any number of sets of alternative strategies can be included in the QSPM, and any number of strategies can comprise a given set. But only strategies within a given set are evaluated relative to each other. For example, one set of strategies may include concentric, horizontal, and conglomerate diversification, whereas another set may include issuing stock and selling a division to raise needed capital. These two sets of strategies are totally different, and the QSPM evaluates strategies only within sets. Note in Table 6–5 that three strategies are included and they comprise just one set.

A QSPM for a food company is provided in Table 6–6. This example illustrates all the components of the QSPM: Key Factors, Strategic Alternatives, Weights, Attractiveness Scores, Total Attractiveness Scores, and Sum Total Attractiveness Score. The three new terms just introduced—(1) Attractiveness Scores, (2) Total Attractiveness Scores, and (3) Sum Total Attractiveness Score—are defined and explained below as the six steps required to develop a QSPM are discussed.

Step 1 **List the firm's key external opportunities/threats and internal strengths/weaknesses in the left column of the QSPM**. This information should be taken directly from the EFE Matrix and IFE Matrix. A minimum of 10 external critical success factors and 10 internal critical success factors should be included in the QSPM.

Step 2 **Assign weights to each external and internal critical success factor**. These Weights are identical to those in the EFE Matrix and the IFE Matrix. The Weights are presented in a straight column just to the right of the external and internal critical success factors.

Step 3 **Examine the Stage 2 (matching) matrices and identify alternative strategies that the organization should consider implementing**. Record these strategies in the top row of the QSPM. Group the strategies into mutually exclusive sets if possible.

Step 4 **Determine the Attractiveness Scores (AS),** defined as numerical values that indicate the relative attractiveness of each strategy in a given set of alternatives. *Attractiveness Scores* are determined by examining each external or internal critical success factor, one at a time, and asking the question, "Does this factor affect the choice of strategies being made?" If the answer to this question is *yes,* then the strategies should be compared relative to that key factor. Specifically, Attractiveness Scores should be assigned to each strategy to indicate the relative attractiveness of one strategy over others, considering the particular factor. The range for Attractiveness Scores is 1 = *not attractive,* 2 = *somewhat attractive,* 3 = *reasonably attractive,* and 4 = *highly attractive.* If the answer to the above question is *no,* indicating that the respective critical success factor has no effect upon the specific choice being made, then do not assign Attractiveness Scores to the strategies in that set.

Step 5 **Compute the Total Attractiveness Scores.** Total Attractiveness Scores are defined as the product of multiplying the Weights (Step 2) by the Attractiveness Scores (Step 4) in each row. The Total Attractiveness Scores indicate the relative attractiveness of each alternative strategy, considering only the impact of the adjacent external or internal critical success factor. The higher the Total Attractiveness Score, the more attractive the strategic alternative (considering only the adjacent critical success factor).

Step 6 **Compute the Sum Total Attractiveness Score.** Add Total Attractiveness Scores in each strategy column of the QSPM. *Sum Total Attractiveness Scores* reveal which strategy is most attractive in each set of alternatives. Higher scores indicate more attractive strategies, considering all the relevant external and internal factors that could affect the strategic decisions. The magnitude of the difference between the Sum Total Attractiveness Scores in a given set of strategic alternatives indicates the relative desirability of one strategy over another.

In Table 6–6, two alternative strategies—establishing a joint venture in Europe and establishing a joint venture in Asia—are being considered by a food company.

Note that NAFTA has no impact on the choice being made between the two strategies, so dashes (–) appear across that row. Several other factors also have no effect on the choice being made, so dashes are recorded in those rows as well. If a particular factor affects one strategy but not the other, it affects the choice being made, so attractiveness scores should be recorded. The *sum total attractiveness score* of 5.30 in Table 6–6 indicates that the joint venture in Europe is a more attractive strategy, compared to the joint venture in Asia.

You should have a rationale for each AS score assigned. In Table 6–6, the rationale for the AS scores in the first row is that the unification of Western Europe creates more stable business conditions in Europe than Asia. The AS score of 4 for the joint venture in Europe and 2 for the joint venture in Asia indicates that the European venture is most acceptable and the Asian venture is possibly acceptable, considering only the first critical success factor. AS scores, therefore, are not mere guesses; they should be rational, defensible, and reasonable.

POSITIVE FEATURES AND LIMITATIONS OF THE QSPM   A positive feature of the QSPM is that sets of strategies can be examined sequentially or simultaneously. For example, corporate-level strategies could be evaluated first, followed by divisional-level strategies, and then functional-level strategies. There is no limit to the number of strategies that can be evaluated or the number of sets of strategies that can be examined at once using the QSPM.

Another positive feature of the QSPM is that it requires strategists to integrate pertinent external and internal factors into the decision process. Developing a QSPM makes it less likely that key factors will be overlooked or weighted inappropriately. A QSPM draws attention to important relationships that affect strategy decisions. Although developing a QSPM requires a number of subjective decisions, making small decisions along the way enhances the probability that the final strategic decisions will be best for the organization. A QSPM can be adapted for use by small and large for-profit and nonprofit organizations and can be applied to virtually any type of organization. A QSPM can especially enhance strategic choice in multinational firms because many key factors and strategies can be considered at once. It also has been applied successfully by a number of small businesses.[6]

The QSPM is not without some limitations. First, it always requires intuitive judgments and educated assumptions. The ratings and attractiveness scores require judgmental

TABLE 6–6
A QSPM for a Food Company

		JOINT VENTURE IN EUROPE		JOINT VENTURE IN ASIA	
CRITICAL SUCCESS FACTORS	WEIGHT	AS	TAS	AS	TAS
OPPORTUNITIES					
1. Western European unification	.10	4	.40	2	.20
2. Rising health consciousness in selecting foods	.15	4	.60	3	.45
3. Free market economies arising in Asia	.10	2	.20	4	.40
4. Demand for soups increasing 10 percent annually	.15	3	.45	4	.60
5. NAFTA	.05	–	–	–	–
THREATS					
1. Food revenues increasing only 1 percent annually	.10	3	.30	4	.40
2. ConAgra's Banquet TV Dinners lead market with 27.4 percent share	.05	–	–	–	–
3. Unstable economies in Asia	.10	4	.40	1	.10
4. Tin cans are not biodegradable	.05	–	–	–	–
5. Low value of the dollar	.15	4	.60	2	.30
STRENGTHS					
1. Profits rose 30 percent	.10	4	.40	2	.20
2. New North American division	.10	–	–	–	–
3. New health conscious soups are successful	.10	4	.40	2	.20
4. Swanson TV dinners' market share has increased to 25.1 percent	.05	4	.20	3	.15
5. One fifth of all managers' bonuses is based on overall corporate performance	.05	–	–	–	–
6. Capacity utilization increased from 60 percent to 80 percent	.15	3	.45	4	.60
WEAKNESSES					
1. Pepperidge Farm sales have declined 7 percent	.05	–	–	–	–
2. Restructuring cost $302 million	.05	–	–	–	–
3. The company's European operation is losing money	.15	2	.30	3	.45
4. The company is slow in globalizing	.15	4	.60	3	.45
5. Pretax profit margin of 8.4 percent is only one-half industry average	.05	–	–	–	–
TOTAL			5.30		4.50

AS = Attractiveness Score; TAS = Total Attractiveness Score
Attractiveness Score: 1 = not acceptable; 2 = possibly acceptable; 3 = probably acceptable; 4 = most acceptable.

decisions, even though they should be based on objective information. Discussion among strategists, managers, and employees throughout the strategy-formulation process, including development of a QSPM, is constructive and improves strategic decisions. Constructive discussion during strategy analysis and choice may arise because of genuine differences of interpretation of information and varying opinions. Another limitation of the QSPM is that it can be only as good as the prerequisite information and matching analyses upon which it is based.

CULTURAL ASPECTS OF STRATEGY CHOICE

All organizations have a culture. Culture includes the set of shared values, beliefs, attitudes, customs, norms, personalities, and heroes that describe a firm. Culture is the unique way an organization does business. It is the human dimension that creates solidarity and meaning, and inspires commitment and productivity in an organization when strategy changes are made. All human beings have a basic need to make sense of their world, to feel in control, and to make meaning. When events threaten meaning, individuals react defensively. Managers and employees may even sabotage new strategies in an effort to recapture the status quo.

It is beneficial to view strategic management from a cultural perspective because success often rests upon the degree of support that strategies receive from a firm's culture. If a firm's strategies are supported by cultural products such as values, beliefs, rites, rituals, ceremonies, stories, symbols, language, and heroes, then managers can often implement changes swiftly and easily. However, if a supportive culture does not exist and is not cultivated, then strategy changes may be ineffective or even counterproductive. A firm's culture can become antagonistic to new strategies, and the result of that antagonism may be confusion and disarray.

Strategies that require fewer cultural changes may be more attractive because extensive changes can take considerable time and effort. Whenever two firms merge, culture-strategy linkages become especially important to evaluate and consider. For example, Walt Disney Company is actively integrating the culture of Capital Cities/ABC with its own, and Westinghouse is trying to integrate its culture with CBS Inc.

When two or three companies from different countries form a joint venture, such as the recent venture among Honeywell, NEC Corporation of Japan, and Compagnie des Machines Bull of France, merging corporate cultures can be a problem. Jerome Meyer, a Honeywell executive, is president and CEO of the new organization, the first multinational computer company. "We've not had an alliance of these dimensions before, with its geographic diversity and cultural conflict," said Michael Geran, an analyst with E. F. Hutton. "The skill to run it will be a tremendous challenge." He predicted that Meyer would become primarily "a referee."

Culture provides an explanation for the difficulties a firm encounters when it attempts to shift its strategic direction, as the following statement explains:

> Not only has the "right" corporate culture become the essence and foundation of corporate excellence, but success or failure of needed corporate reforms hinges on management's sagacity and ability to change the firm's driving culture in time and in tune with required changes in strategies.[7]

THE POLITICS OF STRATEGY CHOICE

All organizations are political. Unless it is managed, political maneuvering consumes valuable time, subverts organizational objectives, diverts human energy, and results in the loss of some valuable employees. Sometimes political biases and personal preferences get unduly embedded in strategy choice decisions. Internal politics affect the choice of strategies in all organizations. The hierarchy of command in an organization, combined with the career aspirations of different people and the need to allocate scarce resources, guarantees the formation of coalitions of individuals who strive to take care of themselves first and the organization second, third, or fourth. Coalitions of individuals often form around key strategy issues that face an enterprise. A major responsibility of strategists is to guide the development of coalitions, to nurture an overall team concept, and to gain the support of key individuals and groups of individuals.

In the absence of objective analyses, strategy decisions are too often based on the politics of the moment. With development of improved strategy-formation tools, political factors become less important in making strategic decisions. In the absence of objectivity, political factors sometimes dictate strategies, and this is unfortunate. Managing political relationships is an integral part of building enthusiasm and esprit de corps in an organization. Don Beeman and Tom Sharkey offer the following guidelines for minimizing the negative aspects of organizational politics:

1. Make clear the bases and processes for performance evaluation.
2. Differentiate rewards among high and low performers.
3. Make sure rewards are as immediately and directly related to performance as possible.
4. Minimize resource competition among managers.
5. Replace resource competition among managers.
6. Where highly cohesive political empires exist, break them apart by removing or splitting the most dysfunctional subgroups.
7. Be keenly sensitive to managers whose mode of operation is personalization of political patronage. Approach these persons with a directive to "stop political maneuvering." If it continues, remove them from the position and preferably the company.[8]

A classic study of strategic management in nine large corporations examined the political tactics of successful and unsuccessful strategists.[9] Successful strategists were found to let weakly supported ideas and proposals die through inaction and to establish additional hurdles or tests for strongly supported ideas considered unacceptable but not openly opposed. Successful strategists kept a low political profile on unacceptable proposals and strived to let most negative decisions come from subordinates or a group consensus, thereby reserving their personal vetoes for big issues and crucial moments. Successful strategists did a lot of chatting and informal questioning to stay abreast of how things were progressing and to know when to intervene. They led strategy but did not dictate it. They gave few orders, announced few decisions, depended heavily on informal questioning, and sought to probe and clarify until a consensus emerged.

Successful strategists generously and visibly rewarded key thrusts that succeeded. They assigned responsibility for major new thrusts to *champions,* the individuals most strongly identified with the idea or product and whose futures were linked to its success. They stayed alert to the symbolic impact of their own actions and statements so as not to send false signals that could stimulate movements in unwanted directions.

Successful strategists ensured that all major power bases within an organization were represented in, or had access to, top management. They interjected new faces and new views into considerations of major changes. (This is important because new employees and managers generally have more enthusiasm and drive than employees who have been with the firm a long time. New employees do not see the world the same old way nor act as screens against changes.) Successful strategists minimized their own political exposure on highly controversial issues and in circumstances where major opposition from key power centers was likely. In combination, these findings provide a basis for managing political relationships in an organization.

Since strategies must be effective in the marketplace and capable of gaining internal commitment, the following tactics used by politicians for centuries can aid strategists:

◆ *Equifinality:* It is often possible to achieve similar results using different means or paths. Strategists should recognize that achieving a successful outcome is more important than imposing the method of achieving it. It may be possible to generate new alternatives that give equal results but with far greater potential for gaining commitment.

◆ *Satisfying:* Achieving satisfactory results with an acceptable strategy is far better than failing to achieve optimal results with an unpopular strategy.

◆ *Generalization:* Shifting focus from specific issues to more general ones may increase strategists' options for gaining organizational commitment.

◆ *Focus on Higher-order Issues:* By raising an issue to a higher level, many short-term interests can be postponed in favor of long-term interests. For instance, by focusing on issues of survival, the auto and steel industries were able to persuade unions to make concessions on wage increases.

◆ *Provide Political Access on Important Issues:* Strategy and policy decisions with significant negative consequences for middle managers will motivate intervention behavior from them. If middle managers do not have an opportunity to take a position on such decisions in appropriate political forums, they are capable of successfully resisting the decisions after they are made. Providing such political access provides strategists with information that might otherwise not be available and that could be useful in managing intervention behavior.[10]

THE ROLE OF A BOARD OF DIRECTORS

The widespread lack of involvement by *boards of directors* in the strategic-management process is changing in America. Historically, boards of directors have mostly been insiders who would not second-guess top executives on strategic issues. It has generally been understood that strategists are responsible and accountable for implementing strategy, so they, not board members, should formulate strategy. Consequently, chief executive officers usually avoided discussions of overall strategy with directors because the results of those discussions often restricted their freedom of action. The judgments of board members were seldom used on acquisitions, divestitures, large capital investments, and other strategic matters. Often the board would meet only annually to fulfill its minimum legal requirements; in many organizations, boards served merely a traditional legitimizing role.

Today, boards of directors are composed mostly of outsiders who are becoming more involved in organizations' strategic management. In a recent study of 1,300 large corporations in the United States, nearly 40 percent of the boards of directors reported that they were actively involved in their firms' strategic-management process.[11] The trend in America is toward smaller boards, now averaging 12 members rather than 18 as they did a few years ago. Smaller boards can discuss issues more easily; individuals in small groups take responsibility more personally.

Just as directors are beginning to place more emphasis on staying informed about an organization's health and operations, they are also taking a more active role in assuring that publicly issued documents are accurate representations of a firm's status. It is becoming widely recognized that a board of directors has legal responsibilities to stockholders and society for all company activities, for corporate performance, and for assuring that a firm has an effective strategy. Failure to accept responsibility for auditing or evaluating a firm's strategy is considered a serious breach of a director's duties. Stockholders, government agencies, and customers are filing legal suits against directors for fraud, omissions, inaccurate disclosures, lack of due diligence, and culpable ignorance about a firm's operations with increasing frequency. Liability insurance for directors has become exceptionally expensive and has caused numerous directors to resign.

Two recent rulings have particulary affected the role of boards of directors in the strategy-formulation process. First, the Supreme Court of Delaware ruled that the directors of the Trans Union Corporation violated the interests of shareholders when they hastily accepted a takeover bid from the Marmon Group; that ruling erodes the so-called business judgment rule, which protects directors from liability as long as their decisions represent a good-faith effort to serve the best interests of the corporation. One clear signal from the Trans Union case is that haste can be costly for board members.

In another landmark ruling that illustrates how boards of directors are increasingly being held responsible for the overall performance of organizations, the Federal Deposit Insurance Corporation forced Continental Illinois to accept the resignations of 10 of the troubled bank's outside directors. The impact of increasing legal pressures on board members is that directors are demanding greater and more regular access to financial performance information.

Kesner and Johnson recently identified some boardroom reforms that are lessening the likelihood of lawsuits today. These reforms include increasing the percentage of outsiders on the board, separating the positions of CEO and chairperson, requiring directors to hold substantial amounts of stock in the firm, and decreasing the board size. Outsiders now outnumber insiders at 90 percent of all American firms, and the average number of outsiders is three times that of insiders.

A direct response of increased pressure on directors to stay informed and execute their responsibilities is that audit committees are becoming commonplace. Milton Lauenstein proposes that a board of directors should conduct an annual strategy audit in much the same fashion that it reviews the annual financial audit. In performing such an audit, a board could work jointly with operating management and/or seek outside counsel. The questions provided in Table 6–7 illustrate the areas that a strategy audit might encompass, but, of course, not all of these questions apply to every situation and organization.

The trend among corporations toward decreased diversification, increased takeover activity, increased legal pressures, multidivisional structures, and multinational operations augments the problem of keeping directors informed. Boards should play a role beyond that of performing a strategic audit. They should provide greater input and advice in the strategy-formulation process to assure that strategists are providing for the long-term needs of the firm. This is being done through the formation of three particular board committees: nominating committees to propose candidates for the board and senior officers of the firm; compensation committees to evaluate the performance of top executives and determine the terms and conditions of their employment; and public policy committees to give board-level attention to company policies and performance on subjects of concern such as business ethics, consumer affairs, and political activities.

Nearly 41 percent of all firms that have a board of directors have developed a mission statement for the board.[12] A board of directors' mission statement outlines the purpose and intent of the board and defines to whom, or for what, the board is held accountable. A board mission statement also indicates company expectations about the quality of preparation for and the process for conducting board meetings. Overall, the mission of boards of directors must be expanded in the 1990s. Companies should assign managers to join directors on board committees, rather than limit the board's contact with only a few top managers. Directors must assume a more activist stance in management development, rather than just react to management initiatives.

Powerful boards of directors are associated with high organizational performance. Powerful boards participate in corporate decisions more fully, share their experiences with the CEO regarding certain strategies, and are actively involved in industry analysis. Firms can develop more powerful boards by regularly reviewing board committee activities, evaluating board meetings, and involving the board more extensively in strategic issues. More and more companies are paying board members partly or totally in stock, which gives outside directors more and more reason to identify with the shareholders they represent rather than the CEO they oversee.

CONCLUSION

The essence of strategy formulation is an assessment of whether an organization is doing the right things and how it can be more effective in what it does. Every organization should be wary of becoming a prisoner of its own strategy, because even the best strategies become obsolete sooner or later. Regular reappraisal of strategy helps management avoid compla-

TABLE 6–7
A Board of Directors Strategy-Audit Framework

- Is the company adequately informed about its markets? What further information would be worth the cost of getting? How should it be obtained?
- How well informed is the company about its competitors? How well is it able to forecast what competitors will do under various circumstances? Is there a sound basis for such competitive appraisals? Is the company underestimating or overestimating its competitors?
- Has management adequately explored various ways of segmenting its market? To what extent is it addressing market segments in which the company's strengths provide meaningful advantages?
- Are the products and services the company proposes to sell ones that it can provide more effectively than competitors? What is the basis for such a belief?
- Do the various activities proposed in the strategy provide synergistic advantages? Are they compatible?
- Does the proposed strategy adequately address questions of corporate objectives, financial policy, scope of operations, organization, and integration?
- What specific resources (personnel, skills, information, facilities, technology, finances, relationships) will be needed to execute the strategy? Does the company already possess these resources? Has management established programs for building these resources and overall competence which will provide telling competitive advantages over the long run?
- To what extent does the strategy define a unique and appropriate economic role for the company? How different is it from the competitors' strategy?
- Has the issue of growth rate been raised? Are there good reasons to believe that investment in growth will pay off? Does the company's track record support such a conclusion?
- Does the proposed dividend policy reflect the company's growth policy, based on a demonstrated ability or inability to reinvest cash flow advantageously? Or is it just a "safe" compromise, conforming to what others usually do?
- Is management capable of implementing the strategy effectively? What leads to this conclusion?
- How and to what extent is the strategy to be communicated to the organization? Is it to be distributed in written form? If competitors are aware of the company's strategy, will that help or hurt?
- What provision is to be made for employing the strategy as a guide to operating decisions? To what extent is it to be used by the board? How?
- How is it to be kept up to date? Are there to be regular reviews? How often and by whom?
- Has a set of long-range projections of operations following the strategy been prepared? Have the possible results of following alternative strategies been prepared?
- Does the strategy focus on the few really important key issues? Is it too detailed? Does it address genuine business questions (as opposed to "motherhood" statements)?
- In its strategic thinking, has management avoided the lure of simplistic approaches such as the following:
  Growth for growth's sake
  Diversification for diversification's sake
  Aping the industry leader
  Broadening the scope in order to secure incremental earnings
  Assuming it can execute better than competitors without objective evidence that such is the case
- Are there other issues, trends, or potential events that should have been taken into account?

Source: Milton Lauenstein, "Boards of Directors: The Strategy Audit," *Journal of Business Strategy 4,* no. 3 (Winter 1984): 90, 91. Reprinted with permission.

cency. Objectives and strategies should be consciously developed and coordinated and should not merely evolve out of day-to-day operating decisions.

An organization with no sense of direction and no coherent strategy precipitates its own demise. When an organization does not know where it wants to go, it usually ends up some place it does not want to be! Every organization needs to consciously establish and communicate clear objectives and strategies.

Modern strategy-formulation tools and concepts are described in this chapter and integrated into a practical three-stage framework. Tools such as the TOWS Matrix, SPACE Matrix, BCG Matrix, IE Matrix, and QSPM can significantly enhance the quality of strategic decisions, but they should never be used to dictate the choice of strategies. Behavioral, cultural, and political aspects of strategy generation and selection are always important to consider and manage. Due to increased legal pressure from outside groups, boards of directors are assuming a more active role in strategy analysis and choice. This is a positive trend for organizations.

TAKE IT TO THE NET   **.W. .M.**   We invite you to visit the DAVID page on the Prentice Hall Web site at:
http://www.prenhall.com/davidsm
for this chapter's World Wide Web exercises.

KEY TERMS AND CONCEPTS

Aggressive Quadrant	(p. 185)	Dogs	(p. 188)	Relative Market Share Position	(p. 187)
Artificial Intelligence (AI)	(p. 174)	Environmental Stability (ES)	(p. 184)	SO Strategies	(p. 180)
Attractiveness Scores (AS)	(p. 194)	Expert System	(p. 174)	ST Strategies	(p. 181)
Boards of Directors	(p. 199)	Financial Strength (FS)	(p. 184)	Stars	(p. 188)
Boston Consulting Group (BCG) Matrix	(p. 187)	Grand Strategy Matrix	(p. 191)	Strategic Position and Action Evaluation (SPACE)Matrix	(p. 184)
		Halo Error	(p. 179)		
Business Portfolio	(p. 187)	Industry Strength (IS)	(p. 184)	Strategy-Formulation Framework	(p. 178)
Cash Cows	(p. 188)	Input Stage	(p. 178)	Sum Total Attractiveness Scores	(p. 195)
Champions	(p. 198)	Internal-External (IE) Matrix	(p. 190)	Threats-Opportunities-Weaknesses-Strengths (TOWS) Matrix	(p. 180)
Competitive Advantage (CA)	(p. 184)	Long-term Objectives	(p. 176)		
Competitive Quadrant	(p. 187)	Matching	(p. 179)	Total Attractiveness Score (TAS)	(p. 195)
Conservative Quadrant	(p. 185)	Matching Stage	(p. 178)		
Decision Stage	(p. 178)	Quantitative Strategic Planning Matrix (QSPM)	(p. 193)	WO Strategies	(p. 180)
Defensive Quadrant	(p. 185)			WT Strategies	(p. 181)
Directional Vector	(p. 185)	Question Marks	(p. 188)		

ISSUES FOR REVIEW AND DISCUSSION

1. How would application of the strategy-formulation framework differ from a small to a large organization?

2. What types of strategies would you recommend for an organization that achieves total weighted scores of 3.6 on the IFE and 1.2 on the EFE Matrix?

3. Given the following information, develop a SPACE Matrix for the XYZ Corporation: FS = +2; ES = −6; CA = −2; IS = +4.

4. Given the information in the table below, develop a BCG Matrix and an IE Matrix:

Divisions	1	2	3
Profits	$10	$15	$25
Sales	$100	$50	$100
Relative Market Share	0.2	0.5	0.8
Industry Growth Rate	+.20	+.10	−.10
IFE Total Weighted Scores	1.6	3.1	2.2
EFE Total Weighted Scores	2.5	1.8	3.3

5. Explain the steps involved in developing a QSPM.

6. How would you develop a set of objectives for your school of business?

7. What do you think is the appropriate role of a board of directors in strategic management? Why?

8. Discuss the limitations of various strategy-formulation analytical techniques.

9. Explain why cultural factors should be an important consideration in analyzing and choosing among alternative strategies.

10. How are the TOWS Matrix, SPACE Matrix, BCG Matrix, IE Matrix, and Grand Strategy Matrix similar? How are they different?

11. How would profit and nonprofit organizations differ in their applications of the strategy-formulation framework?

12. Select an article from the suggested readings at the end of this chapter and prepare a report on that article for your class.

NOTES

1. Steven C. Brandt, *Strategic Planning in Emerging Companies* (Reading, Massachusetts: Addison-Wesley, 1981). Reprinted with permission of the publisher.

2. R. T. Lenz, "Managing the Evolution of the Strategic Planning Process," *Business Horizons* 30, no. 1 (January–February 1987): 37.

3. Robert Grant. The Resource-Based Theory of Competitive Advantage: Implications for Strategy Formulation. *California Management Review* (Spring 1991): 114.

4. Heinz Weihrich, "The TOWS Matrix: A Tool for Situational Analysis," *Long Range Planning* 15, no. 2 (April 1982): 61.

5. Fred David, "The Strategic Planning Matrix—A Quantitative Approach," *Long Range Planning* 19, no. 5 (October 1986): 102. Andre Gib and Robert Margulies, "Making Competitive Intelligence Relevant to the User." *Planning Review* 19, no. 3 (May/June 1991): 21.

6. Fred David, "Computer-Assisted Strategic Planning in Small Businesses," *Journal of Systems Management* 36, no. 7 (July 1985): 24–34.

7. Y. Allarie and M. Firsirotu, "How to Implement Radical Strategies in Large Organizations," *Sloan Management Review* 26, no. 3 (Spring 1985): 19. Another excellent article is P. Shrivastava, "Integrating Strategy Formulation with Organizational Culture," *Journal of Business Strategy* 5, no. 3 (Winter 1985): 103–111.

8. Ibid.

9. James Brian Quinn, *Strategies for Change: Logical Incrementalism* (Homewood, Ill.: Richard D. Irwin, 1980), 128–145. These political tactics are listed in A. Thompson and A. Strickland, *Strategic Management: Concepts and Cases* (Plano, Tex.: Business Publications, 1984): 261.

10. William Guth and Ian MacMillan, "Strategy Implementation Versus Middle Management Self-Interest," *Strategic Management Journal* 7, no. 4 (July–August 1986): 321.

11. John Henke, Jr., "Involving the Board of Directors in Strategic Planning," *Journal of Business Strategy* 7, no. 2 (Fall 1986): 89.

12. Ada Demb, Danielle Chouet, Tom Lossius, and Fred Neubauer, "Defining the Role of the Board," *Long Range Planning* 22, no. 1 (February 1989): 61–68.

CURRENT READINGS

Bilimoria, Diana and Sandy Kristin Piderit. "Board Committee Membership: Effects of Sex-based Bias." *Academy of Management Journal* 37, no. 6 (December 1994): 1453–1477.

Boyd, B. K. "Board Control and CEO Compensation." *Strategic Management Journal* 15, no. 5 (June 1994): 335–344.

Boyd, B. K. "CEO Duality and Firm Performance: A Contingency Model." *Strategic Management Journal* 16, no. 4 (May 1995): 301–312.

Brandenburger, Adam M. and Barry J. Nalebuff. "The Right Game: Use Game Theory to Shape Strategy." *Harvard Business Review* 73, no. 4 (July–August 1995): 57–73.

Brooks, G. R. "Defining Market Boundaries." *Strategic Management Journal* 16, no. 7 (October 1995): 535–550.

Clemons, Eric K. "Using Scenario Analysis to Manage the Strategic Risks of Reengineering." *Sloan Management Review* 36, no. 4 (Summer 1995): 61–72.

Finkelstein, Sydney and Richard A. D'Aveni. "CEO Duality as a Double-edged Sword: How Boards of Directors Balance Entrenchment Avoidance and Unity of Command." *Academy of Management Journal* 37, no. 5 (October 1994): 1079–1108.

Firstenberg, Paul B. and Burton G. Malkiel. "The Twenty-First Century Boardroom: Who Will Be in Charge?" *Sloan Management Review* 36, no. 1 (Fall 1994): 27–36.

Goodstein, K. Gautam, and W. Boeker. "The Effects of Board Size and Diversity on Strategic Change." *Strategic Management Journal* 15, no. 3 (March 1994): 241–258.

Ilinitch, Anne Y. and Stefan C. Schaltegger. "Developing a Green Business Portfolio." *Long Range Planning* 28, no. 2 (April 1995): 29–38.

Judge, William Q., Jr. and Gregory H. Dobbins. "Antecedents and Effects of Outside Director's Awareness of CEO Decision Style." *Journal of Management* 21, no. 1 (Spring 1995): 43–64.

Keeney, Ralph L. "Creativity In Decision Making With Value-Focused Thinking." *Sloan Management Review* 35, no. 4 (Summer 1994): 33–42.

Kesner, Idalene and Terrence C. Sebora. "Executive Succession: Past, Present and Future." *Journal of Management* 20, no. 2 (Summer 1994): 327–372.

Lorsch, Jay W. "Empowering the Board." *Harvard Business Review* 73, no. 1 (January–February 1995): 107–118.

Lubatkin, Michael and Sayan Chatterjee. "Extending Modern Portfolio Theory into the Domain of Corporate Diversification: Does It Apply?" *Academy of Management Journal* 37, no. 1 (February 1994): 109–136.

Nath, D. and D. Sudharshan. "Measuring Strategy Coherence Through Patterns of Strategic Choices." *Strategic Management Journal* 15, no. 1 (January 1994): 42–62.

Park, Jae C. "Reengineering Boards of Directors." *Business Horizons* 38, no. 2 (March–April 1995): 63–69.

Rediker, K. J. and A. Seth. "Boards of Directors and Substitution Effects of Alternative Governance Mechanisms." *Strategic Management Journal* 16, no. 2 (February 1995): 85–100.

Schwenk, Charles R. "Strategic Decision Making." *Journal of Management* 21, no. 3 (Fall 1995): 471–494.

Shoemaker, Paul J. H. "Scenario Planning: A Tool for Strategic Thinking." *Sloan Management Review* 36, no. 2 (Winter 1995): 25–40.

Smale, John G., Alan J. Patricof, Denys Henderson, Bernard Marcus, and David W. Johnson. "Redraw the Line Between the Board and the CEO." Perspectives. *Harvard Business Review* 73, no. 2 (March–April 1995): 153–160.

Sterling, John. "Portfolio-Plus: An Analysis Tool for Strategic Planners." Strategic Management Software. *Planning Review* 23, no. 3 (May–June 1995): 224–27.

Wally, Stefan and J. Robert Baum. "Personal and Structural Determinants of the Pace of Strategic Decision Making." *Academy of Management Journal* 37, no. 4 (August 1994): 932–956.

DEVELOPING A TOWS MATRIX FOR HERSHEY FOODS

PURPOSE

The most widely used strategy-formulation technique among American firms is the TOWS Matrix. This exercise requires development of a TOWS Matrix for Hershey. Matching key external and internal factors in a TOWS Matrix requires good intuitive and conceptual skills. You will improve with practice in developing a TOWS Matrix.

INSTRUCTIONS

Recall from Experiential Exercise 1A that you already may have determined Hershey's external opportunities/threats and internal strengths/weaknesses. This information could be used in completing this exercise. Follow the steps outlined below:

Step 1 On a separate sheet of paper, construct a large nine-cell diagram that will represent your TOWS Matrix. Label the cells appropriately.

Step 2 Record Hershey's opportunities/threats and strengths/weaknesses appropriately in your diagram.

Step 3 Match external and internal factors to generate feasible alternative strategies for Hershey. Record SO, WO, ST, and WT Strategies in appropriate cells of the TOWS Matrix. Use the proper notation to indicate the rationale for the strategies. You do not necessarily have to have strategies in all four strategy cells.

Step 4 Compare your TOWS Matrix to another student's TOWS Matrix. Discuss any major differences.

DEVELOPING A SPACE MATRIX FOR HERSHEY FOODS

PURPOSE

Should Hershey pursue aggressive, conservative, competitive, or defensive strategies? Develop a SPACE Matrix for Hershey to answer this question. Elaborate on the strategic implications of your directional vector. Be specific in terms of strategies that could benefit Hershey.

INSTRUCTIONS

Step 1 Join with two other persons in class and develop a joint SPACE Matrix for Hershey.

Step 2 Diagram your SPACE Matrix on the board. Compare your matrix with other teams' matrices.

Step 3 Discuss the implications of your SPACE analysis.

DEVELOPING A BCG MATRIX FOR HERSHEY FOODS

PURPOSE

Portfolio matrices are widely used by multidivisional organizations to help identify and select strategies to pursue. A BCG analysis identifies particular divisions that should receive fewer resources than others. It may identify some divisions to be divested. This exercise can give you practice developing a BCG Matrix.

INSTRUCTIONS

Step 1 Place the following five column headings at the top of a separate sheet of paper: Divisions, Revenues, Profits, Relative Market Share Position, Industry Growth Rate.

Step 2 Complete a BCG Matrix for Hershey.

Step 3 Compare your BCG Matrix to other students' matrices. Discuss any major differences.

Experiential Exercise 6D

DEVELOPING A QSPM FOR HERSHEY FOODS

PURPOSE

This exercise can give you practice developing a Quantitative Strategic Planning Matrix to determine the relative attractiveness of various strategic alternatives.

INSTRUCTIONS

Step 1 Join with two other students in class to develop a joint QSPM for Hershey.

Step 2 Go to the blackboard and record your strategies and their Sum Total Attractiveness Scores. Compare your team's strategies and total attractiveness scores to those of other teams.

Step 3 Discuss any major differences.

Experiential Exercise 6E

FORMULATING INDIVIDUAL STRATEGIES

PURPOSE

Individuals and organizations are alike in many ways. Each has competitors and each should plan for the future. Every individual and organization faces some external opportunities and threats and has some internal strengths and weaknesses. Both individuals and organizations establish objectives and allocate resources. These and other similarities make it possible for individuals to use many strategic-management concepts and tools. This exercise is designed to demonstrate how the TOWS Matrix can be used by individuals to plan their futures. As one nears completion of a college degree and begins interviewing for jobs, planning can be particularly important.

INSTRUCTIONS

On a separate sheet of paper, construct a TOWS Matrix. Include what you consider to be your major external opportunities, your major external threats, your major strengths, and your major weaknesses. An internal weakness may be a low grade point average. An external opportunity may be that your university offers a graduate program that interests you. Match key external and internal factors by recording in the appropriate cell of the matrix alternative strategies or actions that would allow you to capitalize upon your strengths, overcome your weaknesses, take advantage of your external opportunities, and minimize the impact of external threats. Be sure to use the appropriate matching notation in the strategy cells of the matrix. Since every individual (and organization) is unique, there is no one right answer to this exercise.

Experiential Exercise 6F

THE MACH TEST

PURPOSE

The purpose of this exercise is to enhance your understanding and awareness of the impact that behavioral and political factors can have on strategy analysis and choice.

INSTRUCTIONS

Step 1 On a separate sheet of paper, number from 1 to 10. For each of the ten statements given below, record a *1, 2, 3, 4,* or *5* to indicate your attitude, where

1 = I disagree a lot.
2 = I disagree a little.
3 = My attitude is neutral.
4 = I agree a little.
5 = I agree a lot.

1. The best way to handle people is to tell them what they want to hear.
2. When you ask someone to do something for you, it is best to give the real reason for wanting it, rather than giving a reason that might carry more weight.
3. Anyone who completely trusts anyone else is asking for trouble.
4. It is hard to get ahead without cutting corners here and there.
5. It is safest to assume that all people have a vicious streak, and it will come out when they are given a chance.
6. One should take action only when it is morally right.
7. Most people are basically good and kind.
8. There is no excuse for lying to someone else.
9. Most people forget more easily the death of their father than the loss of their property.
10. Generally speaking, people won't work hard unless they're forced to do so.

Step 2 Add up the numbers you recorded beside statements 1, 3, 4, 5, 9, and 10. This sum is Subtotal One. For the other four statements, reverse the numbers you recorded, so a *5* becomes a *1, 4* becomes 2, 2 becomes *4, 1* becomes *5,* and *3* remains *3.* Then add those four numbers to get Subtotal Two. Finally, add Subtotal One and Subtotal Two to get your Final Score.

YOUR FINAL SCORE

Your Final Score is your Machiavellian Score. Machiavellian principles are defined in a dictionary as "manipulative, dishonest, deceiving, and favoring political expediency over morality." These tactics are not desirable, are not ethical, and are not recommended in the strategic-management process! You may, however, encounter some highly Machiavellian individuals in your career, so beware. It is important for strategists not to manipulate others in the pursuit of organizational objectives. Individuals today recognize and resent manipulative tactics more than ever before. J. R. Ewing (on *Dallas*) is a good example of someone who is a high Mach (score over 30). The National Opinion Research Center used this short form in a random sample of American adults and found the national average Final Score to be 25.[1] The higher your score, the more Machiavellian (manipulative) you tend to be. The following scale is descriptive of individual scores on this test:

- ◆ Below 16: Never uses manipulation as a tool.
- ◆ 16 to 20: Rarely uses manipulation as a tool.
- ◆ 21 to 25: Sometimes uses manipulation as a tool.
- ◆ 26 to 30: Often uses manipulation as a tool.
- ◆ Over 30: Always uses manipulation as a tool.

TEST DEVELOPMENT

The Mach (Machiavellian) test was developed by Dr. Richard Christie, whose research suggests the following tendencies:

1. Men are generally more Machiavellian than women.
2. There is no significant difference between high Machs and low Machs on measures of intelligence or ability.
3. Although high Machs are detached from others, they are detached in a pathological sense.
4. Machiavellian Scores are not statistically related to authoritarian values.
5. High Machs tend to be in professions that emphasize the control and manipulation of individuals; for example, law, psychiatry, and behavioral science.
6. Machiavellianism is not significantly related to major demographic characteristics, such as educational level or marital status.
7. High Machs tend to come from a city or have urban backgrounds.
8. Older adults tend to have lower Mach scores than younger adults.[2]

A classic book on power relationships, *The Prince,* was written by Niccolo Machiavelli. Several excerpts from *The Prince* are given below:

Men must either be cajoled or crushed, for they will revenge themselves for slight wrongs, while for grave ones they cannot. The injury therefore that you do to a man should be such that you need not fear his revenge.

We must bear in mind . . . that there is nothing more difficult and dangerous, or more doubtful of success, than an attempt to introduce a new order of things in any state. The innovator has for enemies all those who derived advantages from the old order of things, while those who expect to be benefitted by the new institution will be but lukewarm defenders.

A wise prince, therefore, will steadily pursue such a course that the citizens of his state will always and under all circumstances feel the need for his authority, and will therefore always prove faithful to him.

A prince should seem to be merciful, faithful, humane, religious, and upright, and should even be so in reality; but he should have his mind so trained that, when occasion requires it, he may know how to change to the opposite.[3]

NOTES

1. Richard Christie and Florence Geis, *Studies in Machiavellianism* (Academic Press, 1970). Material in this exercise adapted with permission of the authors and the Academic Press.
2. Ibid., 82–83.
3. Niccolo Machiavelli, *The Prince* (New York: The Washington Press, 1963).

Experiential Exercise 6G
DEVELOPING A BCG MATRIX FOR MY UNIVERSITY

PURPOSE

A BCG Matrix is useful to develop for many nonprofit organizations, including colleges and universities. Of course there are no profits for each division or department and in some cases no revenues. However, you can be creative in performing a BCG Matrix. For example, the pie slice in the circles can represent the number of majors receiving jobs upon graduation, or the number of faculty teaching in that area, or some other variable that you believe is important to consider. The size of the circles can represent the number of students majoring in particular departments or areas.

INSTRUCTIONS

Step 1 On a separate sheet of paper, develop a BCG Matrix for your university. Include all academic schools, departments, or colleges.

Step 2 Diagram your BCG Matrix on the blackboard.

Step 3 Discuss differences among the BCG Matrices on the board.

Experiential Exercise 6H

USING THE *STRATEGY FORMULATOR* SOFTWARE

PURPOSE

The purpose of this exercise is to give you practice using the *Strategy Formulator* software to generate and prioritize strategies.

INSTRUCTIONS

Step 1 Gather the work that you have developed for your university in earlier Experiential Exercises.

Step 2 Using the *Strategy Formulator* software, develop the following matrices: TOWS, SPACE, IE, Grand Strategy. Generate and prioritize strategies for your university.

Step 3 Bring a printout of your work to class. Discuss any problems or questions that you encountered.

Experiential Exercise 6I

THE ROLE OF BOARDS OF DIRECTORS

PURPOSE

The widespread lack of involvement by boards of directors in the strategic-management process is changing in America! Historically, boards of directors have mostly been "insiders" who would not second-guess top executives on strategic issues. It has generally been understood that strategists are responsible and accountable for implementing strategy, so they should formulate strategy, not board members. Consequently, chief executive officers usually avoided discussions of overall strategy with directors because the results often restricted their freedom of action. The judgments of board members was seldom used on acquisitions, divestitures, large capital investments, and other strategic matters. Often the board would meet only annually to fulfill its minimum legal requirements. Boards just served a traditional legitimizing role in many organizations.

This exercise will give you a better understanding of the role of boards of directors in formulating, implementing, and evaluating strategies.

INSTRUCTIONS

Identify a person in your community who serves on a board of directors. Make an appointment to interview that person and seek answers to the questions given below. Summarize your findings in a five minute oral report to the class.

On what board are you a member?
How often does the board meet?
How long have you served on the board?

What role does the board play in this company?
How has the role of the board changed in recent years?
What changes would you like to see in the role of the board?
To what extent do you prepare for the board meeting?
To what extent are you involved in strategic management of the firm?

Experiential Exercise 6J

LOCATING COMPANIES IN A GRAND STRATEGY MATRIX

PURPOSE

The Grand Strategy Matrix is a popular tool for formulating alternative strategies. All organizations can be positioned in one of the Grand Strategy Matrix's four strategy quadrants. The divisions of a firm could likewise be positioned. The Grand Strategy Matrix is based on two evaluative dimensions: competitive position and market growth. Appropriate strategies for an organization to consider are listed in sequential order of attractiveness in each quadrant of the matrix. This exercise gives you experience using a Grand Strategy Matrix.

INSTRUCTIONS

Using the year-end 1994 financial information given below, prepare a Grand Strategy Matrix on a separate sheet of paper. Write the respective company names in the appropriate quadrant of the matrix. Based on this analysis, what strategies are recommended for each company?

COMPANY	COMPANY SALES/PROFIT GROWTH (%)	INDUSTRY	INDUSTRY SALES/PROFITS GROWTH (%)
Eaton	+38/+85	Automotive Parts	+19/+7
Cummins Engine	+12/+39	Automotive Parts	+19/+7
Pennzoil	0/Neg	Oil, Gas, & Coal	+2/+4
Chevron	+4/+79	Oil, Gas, & Coal	+2/+4
Microsoft	+28/+26	Computer Software	+21/+29
Lotus Development	−1/Neg	Computer Software	+21/+29
Boise Cascade	+5/Neg	Forest Products	+8/Neg
Weyerhaeuser	+9/+12	Forest Products	+8/Neg

Part 3

STRATEGY IMPLEMENTATION

Implementing Strategies: Management Issues

CHAPTER OUTLINE

- ◆ THE NATURE OF STRATEGY IMPLEMENTATION
- ◆ ANNUAL OBJECTIVES
- ◆ POLICIES
- ◆ RESOURCE ALLOCATION
- ◆ MANAGING CONFLICT
- ◆ MATCHING STRUCTURE WITH STRATEGY
- ◆ RESTRUCTURING AND REENGINEERING
- ◆ LINKING PERFORMANCE AND PAY TO STRATEGIES
- ◆ MANAGING RESISTANCE TO CHANGE
- ◆ MANAGING THE NATURAL ENVIRONMENT

- ◆ CREATING A STRATEGY-SUPPORTIVE CULTURE
- ◆ PRODUCTION/OPERATIONS CONCERNS WHEN IMPLEMENTING STRATEGIES
- ◆ HUMAN RESOURCE CONCERNS WHEN IMPLEMENTING STRATEGIES

- ■ EXPERIENTIAL EXERCISE 7A
  Revising Hershey Foods' Organizational Chart
- ■ EXPERIENTIAL EXERCISE 7B
  Matching Managers with Strategy
- ■ EXPERIENTIAL EXERCISE 7C
  Do Organizations Really Establish Objectives?
- ■ EXPERIENTIAL EXERCISE 7D
  Understanding My University's Culture

CHAPTER OBJECTIVES

After studying this chapter, you should be able to do the following:

1. Explain why strategy implementation is more difficult than strategy formulation.

2. Discuss the importance of annual objectives and policies in achieving organizational commitment for strategies to be implemented.

3. Explain why organizational structure is so important in strategy implementation.

4. Compare and contrast restructuring and reengineering.

5. Describe the relationships between production/operations and strategy implementation.

6. Explain how a firm can effectively link performance and pay to strategies.

7. Discuss Employee Stock Ownership Plans (ESOPs) as a strategic-management concept.

8. Describe how to modify an organizational culture to support new strategies.

You want your people to run the business as if it were their own.—WILLIAM FULMER

The ideal organizational structure is a place where ideas filter up as well as down, where the merit of ideas carries more weight than their source, and where participation and shared objectives are valued more than executive orders.—EDSON SPENCER

A management truism says structure follows strategy. However, this truism is often ignored. Too many organizations attempt to carry out a new strategy with an old structure.—DALE McCONKEY

Poor Ike; when he was a general, he gave an order and it was carried out. Now, he's going to sit in that office and give an order and not a damn thing is going to happen.—HARRY TRUMAN

Changing your pay plan is a big risk, but not changing it could be a bigger one.—NANCY PERRY

I find a tendency for management to speak in stern, macho tones when adopting incentives. Then in a few quarters down the road, they turn into Father Christmas.—MARC WALLACE

In Japan, workers receive an average 25 percent of total pay in the form of a flexible bonus. In America, the average is still only 1 percent.—NANCY PERRY

Of course objectives are not a railroad timetable. They can be compared to a compass bearing by which a ship navigates. A compass bearing is firm, but in actual navigation, a ship may veer off its course for many miles. Without a compass bearing, a ship would neither find its port nor be able to estimate the time required to get there.—PETER DRUCKER

The best game plan in the world never blocked or tackled anybody.—VINCE LOMBARDI

In most organizations, the top performers are paid too little and the worst performers too much.—CASS BETTINGER

The strategic-management process does not end when the firm decides what strategy or strategies to pursue. There must be a translation of strategic thought into strategic action. This translation is much easier if managers and employees of the firm understand the business, feel a part of the company, and through involvement in strategy-formulation activities have become committed to helping the organization succeed. Without understanding and commitment, strategy-implementation efforts face major problems.

Implementing strategy affects an organization from top to bottom; it impacts all the functional and divisional areas of a business. It is beyond the purpose and scope of this text to examine all the business administration concepts and tools important in strategy implementation. This chapter focuses on management issues most central to implementing strategies in the 1990s, and Chapter 8 focuses on important marketing, finance/accounting, R&D, and computer information systems issues.

THE NATURE OF STRATEGY IMPLEMENTATION

The strategy-implementation stage of strategic management stands out in Figure 7–1. Successful strategy formulation does not guarantee successful strategy implementation. It is always more difficult to do something (strategy implementation) than to say you are going to do it (strategy formulation)! Although inextricably linked, strategy implementation is fundamentally different from strategy formulation. Strategy formulation and implementation can be contrasted in the following ways:

- ◆ Strategy formulation is positioning forces before the action.
- ◆ Strategy implementation is managing forces during the action.
- ◆ Strategy formulation focuses on effectiveness.
- ◆ Strategy implementation focuses on efficiency.
- ◆ Strategy formulation is primarily an intellectual process.
- ◆ Strategy implementation is primarily an operational process.
- ◆ Strategy formulation requires good intuitive and analytical skills.
- ◆ Strategy implementation requires special motivation and leadership skills.
- ◆ Strategy formulation requires coordination among a few individuals.
- ◆ Strategy implementation requires coordination among many persons.

Strategy-formulation concepts and tools do not differ greatly for small, large, for-profit, or nonprofit organizations. However, strategy implementation varies substantially among different types and sizes of organizations. Implementing strategies requires such actions as altering sales territories, adding new departments, closing facilities, hiring new employees, changing an organization's pricing strategy, developing financial budgets, developing new employee benefits, establishing cost-control procedures, changing advertising strategies, building new facilities, training new employees, transferring managers among divisions, and building a better computer information system. These types of activities obviously differ greatly between manufacturing, service, and governmental organizations.

MANAGEMENT PERSPECTIVES   In all but the smallest organizations, the transition from strategy formulation to strategy implementation requires a shift in responsibility from strategists to divisional and functional managers. Implementation problems can arise because of this shift in responsibility, especially if strategy-formulation decisions come as a surprise to middle- and lower-level managers. Managers and employees are motivated more by perceived self-interests than by organizational interests, unless the two coincide. Therefore, it is essential that divisional and functional managers be involved as much as possible in strategy-formulation activities. Of equal importance, strategists should be involved as much as

FIGURE 7–1
A Comprehensive Strategic-Management Model

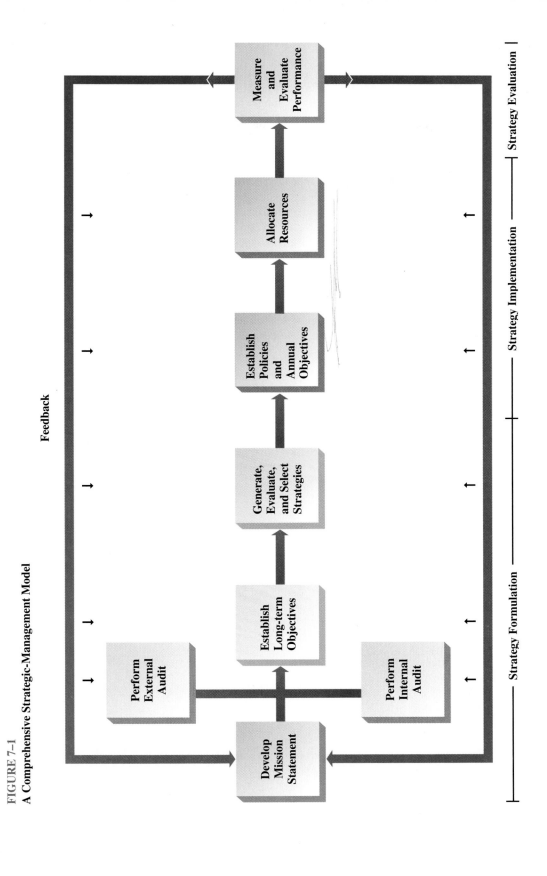

Feedback

Strategy Formulation — Strategy Implementation — Strategy Evaluation possible in strategy-implementation activities. As indicated in the Information Technology Perspective, gathering global information by fax can be an effective and efficient strategy-implementation activity.

Management issues central to strategy implementation include establishing annual objectives, devising policies, allocating resources, altering an existing organizational structure, restructuring and reengineering, revising reward and incentive plans, minimizing resistance to change, matching managers with strategy, developing a strategy-supportive culture, adapting production/operations processes, developing an effective human resource function and downsizing. Management changes are necessarily more extensive when strategies to be implemented move a firm in a major new direction.

Managers and employees throughout an organization should participate early and directly in strategy-implementation decisions. Their role in strategy implementation should build upon prior involvement in strategy-formulation activities. Strategists' genuine personal commitment to implementation is a necessary and powerful motivational force for managers and employees. Too often, strategists are too busy to actively support strategy-implementation efforts, and their lack of interest can be detrimental to organizational success. The rationale for objectives and strategies should be understood and clearly communicated throughout an

INFORMATION TECHNOLOGY
International Trade Administration Automated Fax Retrieval Services

To serve our customers better, the International Trade Administration is currently working to consolidate all of its fax retrieval systems on the **1-800-USA-TRAD(E)** number. At the opening voice prompt, select 1 to be connected to the fax retrieval systems, then follow the voice instructions to request your document:

1-800-USA-TRAD(E)

Press 1 for the Trade Information Center

Press 2 for the Central and Eastern Europe Business Information Center (CEEBIC)

Press 3 for the Business Information Service for Russia and the Newly Independent States (BISNIS)

Press 4 for the Offices of NAFTA and the Americas (Mexico, Canada, Latin America and the Caribbean)
    For information on North America (Mexico and Canada), press 1.

Main Menu document number:	0101
Tariff Menu document number for Mexico:	6000
Tariff Menu document number for Canada:	7000
Rules of Origin Menu document number:	5000
Certificate of Origin document numbers:	5002 or 5003

    For information on Latin America and the Caribbean, press 2.

Main Menu document number:	0100

    For information on Haiti, press 3.

Main Menu document number:	Choose option 1

Press 5 for the Japan Export Information Center

Press 6 for the Asia Business Center

Press 8 for the Business Information Center for Northern Ireland and the Border Counties of the Republic of Ireland

Press 9 for the Uruguay Round and the World Trade Organization

OFFICES OF AFRICA, NEAR EAST AND SOUTH ASIA

Fax Number:	(202) 482-1064
Main Menu document number for Africa:	3000
Main Menu document number for Near East:	0100
Main Menu document number for South Asia:	4000

organization. Major competitors' accomplishments, products, plans, actions, and performance should be apparent to all organizational members. Major external opportunities and threats should be clear, and managers' and employees' questions should be answered. Top-down flow of communication is essential for developing bottom-up support.

Firms need to develop a competitor focus at all hierarchical levels by gathering and widely distributing competitive intelligence; every employee should be able to benchmark her or his efforts against best-in-class competitors so that the challenge becomes personal. This is a challenge for strategists of the firm. Firms should provide training for both managers and employees to ensure they have and maintain the skills necessary to be world-class performers.

ANNUAL OBJECTIVES

Establishing annual objectives is a decentralized activity that directly involves all managers in an organization. Active participation in establishing annual objectives can lead to acceptance and commitment. *Annual objectives* are essential for strategy implementation because they (1) represent the basis for allocating resources; (2) are a primary mechanism for evaluating managers; (3) are the major instrument for monitoring progress toward achieving long-term objectives; and (4) establish organizational, divisional, and departmental priorities. Considerable time and effort should be devoted to ensuring that annual objectives are well conceived, consistent with long-term objectives, and supportive of strategies to be implemented. Approving, revising, or rejecting annual objectives is much more than a rubber-stamp activity. The purpose of annual objectives can be summarized as follows:

> Annual objectives serve as guidelines for action, directing and channeling efforts and activities of organization members. They provide a source of legitimacy in an enterprise by justifying activities to stakeholders. They serve as standards of performance. They serve as an important source of employee motivation and identification. They give incentives for managers and employees to perform. They provide a basis for organizational design.[1]

Clearly stated and communicated objectives are critical to success in all types and sizes of firms. Annual objectives, stated in terms of profitability, growth, and market share by business segment, geographic area, customer groups, and product, are common in organizations. Figure 7–2 illustrates how the Stamus Company could establish annual objectives based on long-term objectives. Table 7–1 reveals associated revenue figures that correspond to the objectives outlined in Figure 7–2. Note that, according to plan, the Stamus Company will slightly exceed its long-term objective of doubling company revenues between 1996 and 1998.

Figure 7–2 also reflects how a hierarchy of annual objectives can be established based on an organization's structure. Objectives should be consistent across hierarchical levels and form a network of supportive aims. *Horizontal consistency of objectives* is as important as *vertical consistency*. For instance, it would not be effective for manufacturing to achieve more than its annual objective of units produced if marketing could not sell the additional units.

	1996	1997	1998
Division I Revenues	1.0	1.400	1.960
Division II Revenues	0.5	0.700	0.980
Division III Revenues	0.5	0.750	1.125
Total Company Revenues	2.0	2.850	4.065

TABLE 7–1
The Stamus Company's Revenue Expectations (in millions of dollars)

FIGURE 7–2
The Stamus Company's Hierarchy of Aims

Annual objectives should be measurable, consistent, reasonable, challenging, clear, communicated throughout the organization, characterized by an appropriate time dimension, and accompanied by commensurate rewards and sanctions. Too often, objectives are stated in generalities, with little operational usefulness. Annual objectives such as "to improve communication" or "to improve performance" are not clear, specific, or measurable.

Objectives should state quantity, quality, cost, and time and also be verifiable. Terms such as *maximize, minimize, as soon as possible,* and *adequate* should be avoided.

Annual objectives should be compatible with employees' and managers' values and should be supported by clearly stated policies. More of something is not always better! Improved quality or reduced cost may, for example, be more important than quantity. It is important to tie rewards and sanctions to annual objectives so that employees and managers understand that achieving objectives is critical to successful strategy implementation. Clear annual objectives do not guarantee successful strategy implementation but they do increase the likelihood that personal and organizational aims can be accomplished. Overemphasis on achieving objectives can result in undesirable conduct, such as faking the numbers, distorting the records, and letting objectives become ends in themselves. Managers must be alert to these potential problems.

POLICIES

Changes in a firm's strategic direction do not occur automatically. On a day-to-day basis, policies are needed to make a strategy work. Policies facilitate solving recurring problems and guide the implementation of strategy. Broadly defined, *policy* refers to specific guidelines, methods, procedures, rules, forms, and administrative practices established to support and encourage work toward stated goals. Policies are instruments for strategy implementation. Policies set boundaries, constraints, and limits on the kinds of administrative actions that can be taken to reward and sanction behavior; they clarify what can and cannot be done in pursuit of an organization's objectives.

Policies let both employees and managers know what is expected of them, thereby increasing the likelihood that strategies will be implemented successfully. They provide a basis for management control, allow coordination across organizational units, and reduce the amount of time managers spend making decisions. Policies also clarify what work is to be done by whom. They promote delegation of decision making to appropriate managerial levels where various problems usually arise. Many organizations have a policy manual that serves to guide and direct behavior. About 80 percent of all corporations in the United States have instituted "no smoking" policies.

Policies can apply to all divisions and departments (for example, "We are an equal opportunity employer"). Some policies apply to a single department ("Employees in this department must take at least one training and development course each year"). Whatever their scope and form, policies serve as a mechanism for implementing strategies and obtaining objectives. Policies should be stated in writing whenever possible. They represent the means for carrying out strategic decisions. Examples of policies that support a company strategy, a divisional objective, and a departmental objective are given in Table 7–2.

Some example issues that may require a management policy are as follows:

- ◆ To offer extensive or limited management-development workshops and seminars
- ◆ To centralize or decentralize employee-training activities
- ◆ To recruit through employment agencies, college campuses, and/or newspapers
- ◆ To promote from within or hire from the outside
- ◆ To promote on the basis of merit or on the basis of seniority
- ◆ To tie executive compensation to long-term and/or annual objectives
- ◆ To offer numerous or few employee benefits
- ◆ To negotiate directly or indirectly with labor unions
- ◆ To delegate authority for large expenditures or to retain this authority centrally
- ◆ To allow much, some, or no overtime work

TABLE 7–2
A Hierarchy of Policies

Company Strategy: Acquire a chain of retail stores to meet our sales growth and profitability objectives.
Supporting policies:

1. "All stores will be open from 8 A.M. to 8 P.M. Monday through Saturday." (This policy could increase retail sales if stores currently are open only 40 hours a week.)
2. "All stores must submit a Monthly Control Data Report." (This policy could reduce expense-to-sales ratios.)
3. "All stores must support company advertising by contributing 5 percent of their total monthly revenues for this purpose." (This policy could allow the company to establish a national reputation.)
4. "All stores must adhere to the uniform pricing guidelines set forth in the Company Handbook." (This policy could help assure customers that the company offers a consistent product in terms of price and quality in all its stores.)

Divisional Objective: Increase the division's revenues from $10 million in 1996 to $15 million in 1997.
Supporting policies:

1. "Beginning in January 1996, this division's salespersons must file a weekly activity report that includes the number of calls made, the number of miles traveled, the number of units sold, the dollar volume sold, and the number of new accounts opened." (This policy could assure that salespersons do not place too great an emphasis in certain areas.)
2. "Beginning in January 1996, this division will return to its employees 5 percent of its gross revenues in the form of a Christmas bonus." (This policy could increase employee productivity.)
3. "Beginning in January 1996, inventory levels carried in warehouses will be decreased by 30 percent in accordance with a Just-in-Time manufacturing approach." (This policy could reduce production expenses and thus free funds for increased marketing efforts.)

Production Department Objective: Increase production from 20,000 units in 1996 to 30,000 units in 1997.
Supporting policies:

1. "Beginning in January 1996, employees will have the option of working up to 20 hours of overtime per week." (This policy could minimize the need to hire additional employees.)
2. "Beginning in January 1996, perfect attendance awards in the amount of $100 will be given to all employees who do not miss a workday in a given year." (This policy could decrease absenteeism and increase productivity.)
3. "Beginning in January 1996, new equipment must be leased rather than purchased." (This policy could reduce tax liabilities and thus allow more funds to be invested in modernizing production processes.)

- ◆ To establish a high- or low-safety stock of inventory
- ◆ To use one or more suppliers
- ◆ To buy, lease, or rent new production equipment
- ◆ To stress quality control greatly or not
- ◆ To establish many or only a few production standards
- ◆ To operate one, two, or three shifts
- ◆ To discourage using insider information for personal gain
- ◆ To discourage sexual harassment
- ◆ To discourage smoking at work
- ◆ To discourage insider trading
- ◆ To discourage moonlighting

RESOURCE ALLOCATION

Resource allocation is a central management activity that allows for strategy execution. In organizations that do not use a strategic-management approach to decision making, resource allocation is often based on political or personal factors. Strategic management enables resources to be allocated according to priorities established by annual objectives. Nothing could be more detrimental to strategic management and to organizational success than for resources to be allocated in ways not consistent with priorities indicated by approved annual objectives.

All organizations have at least four types of resources that can be used to achieve desired objectives: financial resources, physical resources, human resources, and technological resources. Allocating resources to particular divisions and departments does not mean that strategies will be successfully implemented. A number of factors commonly prohibit effective resource allocation, including an overprotection of resources, too great an emphasis on short-run financial criteria, organizational politics, vague strategy targets, a reluctance to take risks, and a lack of sufficient knowledge.

Below the corporate level, there often exists an absence of systematic thinking about resources allocated and strategies of the firm. Yavitz and Newman explain why:

> Managers normally have many more tasks than they can do. Managers must allocate time and resources among these tasks. Pressure builds up. Expenses are too high. The CEO wants a good financial report for the third quarter. Strategy formulation and implementation activities often get deferred. Today's problems soak up available energies and resources. Scrambled accounts and budgets fail to reveal the shift in allocation away from strategic needs to currently squeaking wheels.[2]

The real value of any resource-allocation program lies in the resulting accomplishment of an organization's objectives. Effective resource allocation does not guarantee successful strategy implementation because programs, personnel, controls, and commitment must breathe life into the resources provided. Strategic management itself is sometimes referred to as a "resource-allocation process."

MANAGING CONFLICT

Interdependency of objectives and competition for limited resources often leads to conflict. *Conflict* can be defined as a disagreement between two or more parties on one or more issues. Establishing annual objectives can lead to conflict because individuals have different expectations and perceptions, schedules create pressure, personalities are incompatible, and misunderstandings between line and staff occur. For example, a collection manager's objective of reducing bad debts by 50 percent in a given year may conflict with a divisional objective to increase sales by 20 percent.

Establishing objectives can lead to conflict because managers and strategists must make trade-offs, such as whether to emphasize short-term profits or long-term growth, profit margin or market share, market penetration or market development, growth or stability, high risk or low risk, and social responsiveness or profit maximization. Conflict is unavoidable in organizations, so it is important that conflict be managed and resolved before dysfunctional consequences affect organizational performance. Conflict is not always bad. An absence of conflict can signal indifference and apathy. Conflict can serve to energize opposing groups into action and may help managers identify problems.

Various approaches for managing and resolving conflict can be classified into three categories: avoidance, defusion, and confrontation. *Avoidance* includes such actions as ignoring the problem in hopes that the conflict will resolve itself or physically separating the conflicting individuals (or groups). *Defusion* can include playing down differences between conflicting parties while accentuating similarities and common interests, compromising so that there is neither a clear winner nor loser, resorting to majority rule, appealing to a higher authority, or redesigning present positions. *Confrontation* is exemplified by exchanging members of conflicting parties so that each can gain an appreciation of the other's point of view, focusing on superordinate goals such as company survival, or holding a meeting at which conflicting parties present their views and work through their differences.

MATCHING STRUCTURE WITH STRATEGY

Changes in strategy often require changes in the way an organization is structured for two major reasons. First, structure largely dictates how objectives and policies will be established. For example, the format for objectives and policies established under a geographic organizational structure is couched in geographic terms. Objectives and policies are stated largely in terms of products in an organization whose structure is based on product groups. The structural format for developing objectives and policies can significantly impact all other strategy-implementation activities.

The second major reason why changes in strategy often require changes in structure is that structure dictates how resources will be allocated. If an organization is structured based on customer groups, then resources will be allocated in that manner. Similarly, if an organization's structure is set up along functional business lines, then resources are allocated by functional areas. Unless new or revised strategies place emphasis in the same areas as old strategies, structural reorientation commonly becomes a part of strategy implementation.

Changes in strategy lead to changes in organizational structure. Structure should be designed to facilitate the strategic pursuit of a firm and, therefore, follows strategy. Without a strategy or reasons for being (mission), structure is not important. Chandler found a particular structure sequence to be often repeated as organizations grow and change strategy over time; this sequence is depicted in Figure 7–3.

There is no one optimal organizational design or structure for a given strategy or type of organization. What is appropriate for one organization may not be appropriate for a similar firm, although successful firms in a given industry do tend to organize themselves in a similar way. For example, consumer-goods companies tend to emulate the divisional structure-by-product form of organization. Small firms tend to be functionally structured (centralized). Medium-size firms tend to be divisionally structured (decentralized). Large firms tend to use an SBU (strategic business unit) or matrix structure. As organizations grow, their structures generally change from simple to complex as a result of concatenation, or the linking together of several basic strategies.

Numerous external and internal forces affect an organization; no firm could change its structure in response to every one of these forces, because to do so would lead to chaos. However, when a firm changes its strategy, the existing organizational structure may become ineffective. Symptoms of an ineffective organizational structure include too many levels of management, too many meetings attended by too many people, too much atten-

FIGURE 7–3
Chandler's Strategy-Structure Relationship

tion being directed toward solving interdepartmental conflicts, too large a span of control, and too many unachieved objectives. Changes in structure can facilitate strategy-implementation efforts, but changes in structure should not be expected to make a bad strategy good, or to make bad managers good, or to make bad products sell.

Structure undeniably can and does influence strategy. Strategies formulated must be workable, so if a certain new strategy required massive structural changes it would not be an attractive choice. In this way, structure can shape the choice of strategies. But a more important concern is determining what types of structural changes are needed to implement new strategies and how these changes can best be accomplished. We examine this issue by focusing on seven basic types of organizational structure: functional, divisional by geographic area, divisional by product, divisional by customer, divisional by process, strategic business unit (SBU), and matrix.

THE FUNCTIONAL STRUCTURE   ~centralized   The most widely used structure is the functional or centralized type, because this structure is the simplest and least expensive of the seven alternatives. A *functional structure* groups tasks and activities by business function such as production/operations, marketing, finance/accounting, research and development, and computer information systems. A university may structure its activities by major functions that include academic affairs, student services, alumni relations, athletics, maintenance, and accounting. Besides being simple and inexpensive, a functional structure also promotes specialization of labor, encourages efficiency, minimizes the need for an elaborate control system, and allows rapid decision making. Some disadvantages of a functional structure are that it forces accountability to the top, minimizes career development opportunities, and is sometimes characterized by low employee morale, line/staff conflicts, poor delegation of authority, and inadequate planning for products and markets.

The 1980s and 1990s witnessed most large companies abandoning the functional structure in favor of decentralization and improved accountability. A company that still adheres to a functional design, however, is Food Lion, Inc., as shown in Figure 7–4.

THE DIVISIONAL STRUCTURE   The *divisional* or *decentralized structure* is the second most common type used by American businesses. As a small organization grows, it has more and more difficulty managing different products and services in different markets. Some form of divisional structure generally becomes necessary to motivate employees, control operations, and compete successfully in diverse locations. The divisional structure can be organized in one of four ways: by geographic area, by product or service, by customer, or by process. Within a divisional structure, functional activities are performed both centrally and in each separate division.

A divisional structure has some clear advantages. First and perhaps foremost, accountability is clear. That is, divisional managers can be held responsible for sales and profit levels. Since a divisional structure is based on extensive delegation of authority, managers and employees can easily see the results of their good or bad performances. As a result, employee morale is generally higher in a divisional structure than it is in a centralized structure. Other advantages of the divisional design are that it creates career development opportunities for managers, allows local control of local situations, leads to a competitive climate within an organization, and allows new businesses and products to be added easily. AT&T recently restructured by breaking large businesses into smaller, focused units, totaling 24 divisions and 19 subsidiaries.

The divisional design is not without some limitations, however. Perhaps the most important limitation is that a divisional structure is costly, for a number of reasons. First, each division requires functional specialists who must be paid. Second, there exists some duplication of staff services, facilities, and personnel; for instance, functional specialists are also

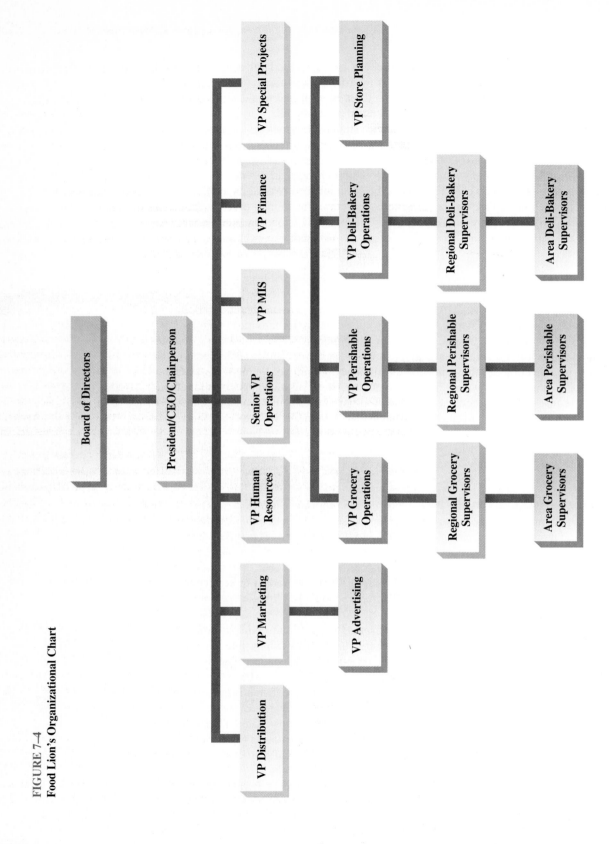

FIGURE 7–4
Food Lion's Organizational Chart

- Board of Directors
- President/CEO/Chairperson
- VP Distribution
- VP Marketing
  - VP Advertising
- VP Human Resources
- Senior VP Operations
  - VP Grocery Operations
    - Regional Grocery Supervisors
      - Area Grocery Supervisors
  - VP Perishable Operations
    - Regional Perishable Supervisors
      - Area Perishable Supervisors
  - VP Deli-Bakery Operations
    - Regional Deli-Bakery Supervisors
      - Area Deli-Bakery Supervisors
- VP MIS
- VP Finance
- VP Special Projects
- VP Store Planning

224

needed centrally (at headquarters) to coordinate divisional activities. Third, managers must be well-qualified, since the divisional design forces delegation of authority; better-qualified individuals require higher salaries. A divisional structure can also be costly because it requires an elaborate, headquarters-driven control system. Finally, certain regions, products, or customers may sometimes receive special treatment, and it may be difficult to maintain consistent, companywide practices. Nonetheless, for most large organizations and many small firms, the advantages of a divisional structure more than offset the potential limitations.

A *divisional structure by geographic area* is appropriate for organizations whose strategies need to be tailored to fit the particular needs and characteristics of customers in different geographic areas. This type of structure can be most appropriate for organizations that have similar branch facilities located in widely dispersed areas. A divisional structure by geographic area allows local participation in decision making and improved coordination within a region. ABB (Asia Brown Bover Ltd.) reorganized its management structure into three large geographic regions: Europe, the Americas, and Asia-Pacific. Percy Barnevik, ABB's chief executive officer, says the growing unification of Europe requires that the continent be treated as one market, and the opening up of markets under the North American Free Trade Agreement made establishment of one region for the Americas a logical step. Treating the Asia-Pacific region as one division ensures focused attention in the area of the world with the greatest growth potential.

The *divisional structure by product* is most effective for implementing strategies when specific products or services need special emphasis. Also, this type of structure is widely used when an organization offers only a few products or services, or when an organization's products or services differ substantially. The divisional structure allows strict control and attention to product lines, but it may also require a more skilled management force and reduced top-management control. General Motors, Du Pont, and Procter & Gamble use a divisional structure by product to implement strategies. Huffy, the largest bicycle company in the world, is another firm that is highly decentralized based on a divisional-by-product structure. Based in Ohio, Huffy's divisions are the Bicycle division, the Gerry Baby Products division, Huffy Sports division, YLC Enterprises, and Washington Inventory Service. Harry Shaw, Huffy's chairman, believes decentralization is one of the keys to Huffy's success.

When a few major customers are of paramount importance and many different services are provided to these customers, then a *divisional structure by customer* can be the most effective way to implement strategies. This structure allows an organization to cater effectively to the requirements of clearly defined customer groups. For example, book publishing companies often organize their activities around customer groups such as colleges, secondary schools, and private commercial schools. Some airline companies have two major customer divisions: passengers and freight or cargo services. Merrill Lynch is organized into separate divisions that cater to different groups of customers, including wealthy individuals, institutional investors, and small corporations.

A *divisional structure by process* is similar to a functional structure, because activities are organized according to the way work is actually performed. However, a key difference between these two designs is that functional departments are not accountable for profits or revenues, whereas divisional process departments are evaluated on these criteria. An example of a divisional structure by process is a manufacturing business organized into six divisions: electrical work, glass cutting, welding, grinding, painting, and foundry work. In this case, all operations related to these specific processes would be grouped under the separate divisions. Each process (division) would be responsible for generating revenues and profits. The divisional structure by process can be particularly effective in achieving objectives when distinct production processes represent the thrust of competitiveness in an industry.

THE STRATEGIC BUSINESS UNIT (SBU) STRUCTURE   As the number, size, and diversity of divisions in an organization increase, controlling and evaluating divisional operations become increasingly difficult for strategists. Increases in sales often are not accompanied by similar increases in profitability. The span of control becomes too large at top levels of the firm. For example, in a large conglomerate organization composed of ninety divisions, the chief executive officer could have difficulty even remembering the first names of divisional presidents. In multidivisional organizations an SBU structure can greatly facilitate strategy-implementation efforts.

The *SBU structure* groups similar divisions into strategic business units and delegates authority and responsibility for each unit to a senior executive who reports directly to the chief executive officer. This change in structure can facilitate strategy implementation by improving coordination between similar divisions and channeling accountability to distinct business units. In the ninety-division conglomerate just mentioned, the ninety divisions could perhaps be regrouped into ten SBUs according to certain common characteristics such as competing in the same industry, being located in the same area, or having the same customers.

Two disadvantages of an SBU structure are that it requires an additional layer of management, which increases salary expenses, and the role of the group vice-president is often ambiguous. However, these limitations often do not outweigh the advantages of improved coordination and accountability. Atlantic Richfield and Fairchild Industries are examples of firms that successfully uses an SBU-type structure.

THE MATRIX STRUCTURE   A *matrix structure* is the most complex of all designs because it depends upon both vertical and horizontal flows of authority and communication (hence the term *matrix*). In contrast, functional and divisional structures depend primarily on vertical flows of authority and communication. A matrix structure can result in higher overhead because it creates more management positions. Other characteristics of a matrix structure that contribute to overall complexity include dual lines of budget authority (a violation of the unity-of-command principle), dual sources of reward and punishment, shared authority, dual reporting channels, and a need for an extensive and effective communication system.

Despite its complexity, the matrix structure is widely used in many industries, including construction, health care, research, and defense. Some advantages of a matrix structure are that project objectives are clear, there are many channels of communication, workers can see visible results of their work, and shutting down a project can be accomplished relatively easily.

In order for a matrix structure to be effective, organizations need participative planning, training, clear mutual understanding of roles and responsibilities, excellent internal communication, and mutual trust and confidence. The matrix structure is being used more frequently by American businesses because firms are pursuing strategies that add new products, customer groups, and technology to their range of activities. Out of these changes are coming product managers, functional managers, and geographic-area managers, all of whom have important strategic responsibilities. When several variables, such as product, customer, technology, geography, functional area, and line of business, have roughly equal strategic priorities, a matrix organization can be an effective structural form.

RESTRUCTURING AND REENGINEERING

Restructuring and reengineering are becoming commonplace on the corporate landscape across the U.S. and Europe. *Restructuring*—also called *downsizing, rightsizing,* or *delayering*—involves reducing the size of the firm in terms of number of employees, number of divisions or units, and in the number of hierarchical levels in the firm's organizational structure. This reduction in size in intended to improve both efficiency and effectiveness. Restructuring is concerned primarily with shareholder well-being, rather than employee well-being.

In contrast, *reengineering* is concerned more with employee and customer well-being than shareholder well-being. Reengineering—also called process management, process innovation, or process redesign—involves reconfiguring or redesigning work, jobs, and processes for the purpose of improving cost, quality, service, and speed. Reengineering does not usually affect the organizational structure or chart, nor does it imply job loss or employee layoffs. Whereas restructuring is concerned with eliminating, shrinking, and moving organizational departments and divisions, the focus of reengineering is changing the way work is actually carried out.

Reengineering is characterized by many tactical (short-term; business-function-specific) decision, whereas restructuring is better described as strategic (long-term; affects all business functions) decisions.

RESTRUCTURING   Firms often employ restructuring when various ratios appear out of line with competitors as determined through benchmarking exercises. Benchmarking simply involves comparing a firm against the best firms in the industry on a wide variety of performance-related criteria. Some benchmarketing ratios commonly used in rationalizing the need for restructuring are headcount to sales volume, or corporate staff to operating employees, or span of control figures.

The primary benefit sought from restructuring is cost reduction. For some highly bureaucratic firms, restructuring can actually rescue the firm from global competition and demise. But the downside of restructuring can be reduced employee commitment, creativity, and innovation that accompanies the uncertainty and trauma associated with pending the actual employee layoffs.

Between 1991 and 1994, 25 U.S. firms laid off over 700,000 employees as part of restructuring activities, including, for example, Sears Roebuck, which laid off 50,000 employees during that time.

REENGINEERING   The argument for a firm engaging in reengineering usually goes as follows: Many companies historically have been organized vertically by business function. This arrangement has led over time to managers' and employees' mind-sets being defined by their particular function, rather than by overall customer service, product quality, or corporate performance. The logic is that all firms tend to bureaucratize over time. As routines become entrenched, turf becomes delineated and defended, and politics takes precedence over performance. Walls that exist in the physical workplace are reflections of our mental walls.

In reengineering, a firm uses information technology to break down functional barriers and create a work system based on business processes, products, or outputs, rather than on functions or inputs. Cornerstones of reengineering are decentralization, reciprocal interdependence, and information sharing. A firm that exemplifies complete information sharing is Springfield ReManufacturing Corporation, which provides to all employees a weekly income statement of the firm, as well as extensive other company performance information.

There are numerous examples of firms that benefited in the 1990s from reengineering—including Union Carbide, which reduced its fixed costs by $400 million; Taco Bell, which raised its restaurant peak capacity form $400 per hour to $1,500 per hour; and AT&T which created a new business telephone system called PBX.

A benefit of reengineering is that it offers employees the opportunity to see more clearly how their particular job impacts the final product or service being marketed by the firm. However, reengineering also can raise manager and employee anxiety, which unless managed can lead to corporate trauma.

LINKING PERFORMANCE AND PAY TO STRATEGIES

Most companies today are practicing some form of pay-for-performance for employees and managers other than top executives. The average employee performance bonus is 6.8 percent of pay for individual performance, 5.5 percent of pay for group productivity, and 6.4 percent of pay for companywide profitability.

Staff control of pay systems, often prevents line managers from using financial compensation as a strategic tool. Flexibility regarding managerial and employee compensation is needed to allow short-term shifts in compensation that can stimulate efforts to achieve long-term objectives. NBC recently unveiled a new method for paying its affiliated stations. The compensation formula is 50-percent based on audience viewing of shows from 4 P.M. to 8 P.M. and 50-percent based on how many adults aged 25 to 54 watch NBC over the course of a day.

How can an organization's reward system be more closely linked to strategic performance? How can decisions on salary increases, promotions, merit pay, and bonuses be more closely aligned to support the long-term strategic objectives of the organization? There are no widely accepted answers to these questions, but a dual bonus system based on both annual objectives and long-term objectives is becoming common. The percentage of a manager's annual bonus attributable to short-term versus long-term results should vary by hierarchical level in the organization. A chief executive officer's annual bonus could, for example, be determined on a 75-percent short-term and 25-percent long-term basis. It is important that bonuses not be based solely on short-term results, because such a system ignores long-term company strategies and objectives.

Du Pont Canada has a 16-percent return on equity objective. If this objective is met, the company's 4,000 employees receive a "performance sharing cash award" equal to 4 percent of pay. If return on equity falls below 11 percent, employees get nothing. If return on equity exceeds 28 percent, workers receive a 10-percent bonus.

Profit sharing is another widely used form of incentive compensation. More than 30 percent of American companies have profit-sharing plans, but critics emphasize that too many factors affect profits for this to be a good criterion. Taxes, pricing, or an acquisition would wipe out profits, for example. Also, firms try to minimize profits in a sense to reduce taxes.

Still another criterion widely used to link performance and pay to strategies is gain sharing. *Gain sharing* requires employees or departments to establish performance targets; if actual results exceed objectives, all members get bonuses. More than 26 percent of American companies use some form of gain sharing; about 75 percent of gain-sharing plans have been adopted since 1980. Carrier, a subsidiary of United Technologies, has had excellent success with gain sharing in its six plants in Syracuse, New York; Firestone's tire plant in Wilson, North Carolina, has experienced similar success with gain sharing.

Criteria such as sales, profit, production efficiency, quality, and safety could also serve as bases for an effective *bonus system.* If an organization meets certain understood, agreed-upon profit objectives, every member of the enterprise should share in the harvest. A bonus system can be an effective tool for motivating individuals to support strategy-implementation efforts. BankAmerica, for example, recently overhauled its incentive system to link pay to sales of the bank's most profitable products and services. Branch managers receive a base salary plus a bonus based on the number of new customers and on sales of bank products. Every employee in each branch is also eligible for a bonus if the branch exceeds its goals. Thomas Peterson, a top BankAmerica executive, says, "We want to make people responsible for meeting their goals, so we pay incentives on sales, not on controlling costs or on being sure the parking lot is swept."

Five tests are often used to determine whether a performance-pay plan will benefit an organization:

1. *Does the plan capture attention?* Are people talking more about their activities and taking pride in early successes under the plan?
2. *Do employees understand the plan?* Can participants explain how it works and what they need to do to earn the incentive?
3. *Is the plan improving communications?* Do employees know more than they used to about the company's mission, plans, and objectives?
4. *Does the plan pay out when it should?* Are incentives being paid for desired results—and being *withheld* when objectives are not met?
5. *Is the company or unit performing better?* Are profits up? Has market share grown? Have gains resulted in part from the incentives?[3]

In addition to a dual bonus system, a combination of reward-strategy incentives such as salary raises, stock options, fringe benefits, promotions, praise, recognition, criticism, fear, increased job autonomy, and awards can be used to encourage managers and employees to push hard for successful strategic implementation. The range of options for getting people, departments, and divisions to actively support strategy-implementation activities in a particular organization is almost limitless. Merck, for example, recently gave each of its 37,000 employees a 10-year option to buy 100 shares of Merck stock at a set price of $127. Steven Darien, Merck's vice president of human resources, says, "We needed to find ways to get everyone in the workforce on board in terms of our goals and objectives. Company executives will begin meeting with all Merck workers to explore ways in which employees can contribute more."

Increasing criticism aimed at chief executive officers for their high pay has resulted in executive compensation being linked to performance of their firm more closely than ever before. CEO Deryck Maughan of Salomon saw an 87-percent drop in his pay in 1994 when his firm incurred a $963 million in pretax losses. CEO Charles Sanford of Bankers Trust saw a 57-percent drop in his pay as his firm's return-on-equity dropped nearly half to 13.5 percent. Although the linkage between CEO pay and corporate performance is getting closer each day, the magnitude of CEO pay in the United States is still astronomical, as indicated in Table 7–3. A close pay-performance linkage does not imply less pay. In fact, the opposite is true when

	1995 SALARY AND BONUS THOUSANDS OF DOLLARS	LONG-TERM COMPENSATION	TOTAL PAY
1. Lawrence Coss Green Tree Financial	$65,580	NONE	$65,580
2. Sanford Weill Travelers Group	5,607	$44,233	49,840
3. John Welch Jr. General Electric	5,321	16,741	22,062
4. Gordon Binder Amgen	1,513	19,992	21,505
5. James Donald DSC Communications	5,595	13,588	19,183
6. Casey Cowell U.S. Robotics	2,799	15,770	18,569
7. Floyd English Andrew Corp.	1,739	15,927	17,666
8. Howard Solomon Forest Laboratories	611	16,416	17,026
9. Stanley Gault Goodyear Tire & Rubber	2,207	14,343	16,550
10. Edward Brennan Sears, Roebuck	3,098	13,252	16,350

TABLE 7–3
The Top-Paid U.S. CEOs in 1995

GLOBAL PERSPECTIVE
CEO Pay in Europe—Coming to Light

Total pay for CEOs in Europe in 1994 averaged $389,711, far less than the $1.4 million average in the United States. European laws do not require disclosure of CEO pay, but this is changing. More and more European countries and companies are following the U.S. pattern of full disclosure of executive compensation to shareholders, which is causing unrest and discontent in the boardrooms and on the shop floor of numerous European firms. European CEOs argue for comparable pay to their U.S. counterparts, but their employees and board members are angered and offended to learn of current pay levels in light of harsh times.

British Gas PLC in 1994 awarded CEO Cedric Brown a 76-percent salary increase at a time when the firm was laying off 25,000 workers. At the company's annual meeting, employees and shareholders marched a 350-pound pig named Cedric to the podium to protest the CEO's pay. Protests such as this are not limited to firms in England—the European country which requires executive compensation disclosure most. CEOs in France and Sweden and Germany also are being criticized as their pay is being more and more disclosed and a topic of discussion.

Perhaps the key to resolving the rising level of discord in Europe regarding executive pay is to link CEO pay directly, and perhaps exclusively, to performance of the firm.

Source: Adapted from Julia Flynn, "Continental Divide Over Executive Pay," *Business Week* (July 3, 1995): 40–1.

the firm does well. Overall corporate profits among U.S. corporations rose 34 percent in 1994, while average CEO salary and bonus rose 10 percent to $1,399,698.[4] In 1995, profits grew 16 percent while the average CEO salary and bonus climbed 18 percent to $1,653,670. But throw in gains from stock options, and the average CEO's pay rose 30 percent in 1995 to $3,746,392.

As indicated in the Global Perspective, CEO pay in Europe is low compared to U.S. CEOs.

MANAGING RESISTANCE TO CHANGE

No organization or individual can escape change. But the thought of change raises anxieties because people fear economic loss, inconvenience, uncertainty, and a break in normal social patterns. Almost any change in structure, technology, people, or strategies has the potential to disrupt comfortable interaction patterns. For this reason, people resist change. The strategic-management process itself can impose major changes on individuals and processes. Reorienting an organization to get people to think and act strategically is not an easy task.

> The level of familiarity with strategic thinking in the U.S. is high, but acceptance is low. U.S. management has to undergo a cultural change, and it's difficult to force people to change their thinking; it's like ordering them to use personal computers. One obstacle is that top executives are often too busy fighting fires to devote time to developing managers who can think strategically. Yet, the best-run companies recognize the need to develop managers who can fashion and implement strategy.[5]

Resistance to change can be considered the single greatest threat to successful strategy implementation. Resistance in the form of sabotaging production machines, absenteeism, filing unfounded grievances, and an unwillingness to cooperate regularly occurs in organizations. People often resist strategy implementation because they do not understand what is happening or why changes are taking place. In that case, employees may simply need accurate information. Successful strategy implementation hinges upon managers' ability to develop an organizational climate conducive to change. Change must be viewed as an opportunity rather than as a threat by managers and employees.

Resistance to change can emerge at any stage or level of the strategy-implementation process. Although there are various approaches for implementing changes, three commonly used strategies are a force change strategy, an educative change strategy, and a rational or self-interest change strategy. A *force change strategy* involves giving orders and enforcing those orders; this strategy has the advantage of being fast, but it is plagued by low commitment and high resistance. The *educative change strategy* is one that presents information to convince people of the need for change; the disadvantage of an educative change strategy is that implementation becomes slow and difficult. However, this type of strategy evokes greater commitment and less resistance than does the force strategy. Finally, a *rational* or *self-interest change strategy* is one that attempts to convince individuals that the change is to their personal advantage. When this appeal is successful, strategy implementation can be relatively easy. However, implementation changes are seldom to everyone's advantage.

The rational change strategy is the most desirable, so this approach is examined a bit further. Managers can improve the likelihood of successfully implementing change by carefully designing change efforts. Jack Duncan describes a rational or self-interest change strategy as consisting of four steps. First, employees are invited to participate in the process of change and the details of transition; participation allows everyone to give opinions, to feel a part of the change process, and to identify their own self-interests regarding the recommended change. Second, some motivation or incentive to change is required; self-interest can be the most important motivator. Third, communication is needed so that people can understand the purpose for the changes. Giving and receiving feedback is the fourth step; everyone enjoys knowing how things are going and how much progress is being made.[6]

Igor Ansoff summarizes the need for strategists to manage resistance to change as follows:

> Observation of the historical transitions from one orientation to another shows that, if left unmanaged, the process becomes conflict-laden, prolonged, and costly in both human and financial terms. Management of resistance involves anticipating the focus of resistance and its intensity. Second, it involves eliminating unnecessary resistance caused by misperceptions and insecurities. Third, it involves mustering the power base necessary to assure support for the change. Fourth, it involves planning the process of change. Finally, it involves monitoring and controlling resistance during the process of change. . . .[7]

Due to diverse external and internal forces, change is a fact of life in organizations. The rate, speed, magnitude, and direction of changes vary over time by industry and organization. Strategists should strive to create a work environment in which change is recognized as necessary and beneficial so that individuals can adapt to change more easily. Adopting a strategic-management approach to decision making can itself require major changes in the philosophy and operations of a firm.

Strategists can take a number of positive actions to minimize managers' and employees' resistance to change. For example, individuals who will be affected by a change should be involved in the decision to make the change and in decisions about how to implement change. Strategists should anticipate changes and develop and offer training and development workshops so managers and employees can adapt to those changes. They also need to communicate the need for changes effectively. The strategic-management process can be described as a process of managing change. Robert Waterman describes how successful (renewal) organizations involve individuals to facilitate change:

> Implementation starts with, not after, the decision. When Ford Motor Company embarked on the program to build the highly successful Taurus, management gave up the usual, sequential design process. Instead they showed the tentative design to the workforce and asked their help in devising a car that would be easy to build. Team Taurus came up with no less than 1,401

items suggested by Ford employees. What a contrast from the secrecy that characterized the industry before! When people are treated as the main engine rather than interchangeable parts, motivation, creativity, quality, and commitment to implementation go up.[8]

MANAGING THE NATURAL ENVIRONMENT

Monsanto, a large U.S. chemical company, is an excellent example of a firm that protects the natural environment. Monsanto's motto is "Zero Spills, Zero Releases, Zero Incidents, and Zero Excuses."

The 1990s may well be remembered as the decade of the environment. Earth itself has become a stakeholder for all business firms. Consumer interest in businesses' preserving nature's ecological balance and fostering a clean, healthy environment is high and growing. Evidence of this growing interest is that circulation of the top three natural environmental magazines, *Audubon, Greenpeace,* and *Sierra,* is soaring. Advertising revenues from these three magazines increased nearly 25 percent annually in the early 1990s, when the magazine industry in general experienced slow or no growth in advertising revenues. This consumer interest is spurring companies to reconcile environmental and economic considerations.

The ecological challenge facing all organizations requires managers to formulate strategies that preserve and conserve natural resources and control pollution. Special natural environmental issues include ozone depletion, global warming, depletion of rain forests, destruction of animal habitats, protecting endangered species, developing biodegradable products and packages, waste management, clean air, clean water, erosion, destruction of natural resources, and pollution control. More and more firms are developing green product lines that are biodegradable and/or are made from recycled products. Green products sell well.

The Environmental Protection Agency recently reported that U.S. citizens and organizations spend more than about $200 billion annually on pollution abatement. Environmental concerns touch all aspects of a business's operations, including workplace risk exposures, packaging, waste reduction, energy use, alternative fuels, environmental cost accounting, and recycling practices. As indicated in the Natural Environment Perspective, preserving the natural environment makes good business sense.

Managing as if the earth matters requires an understanding of how international trade, competitiveness, and global resources are connected. Environmental affairs can no longer be simply a technical function performed by specialists in a firm; more emphasis must be placed on developing an environmental perspective among all employees and managers of the firm. Many companies are moving environmental affairs from the staff side of the organization to the line side, to make the corporate environmental group report directly to the chief operating officer. Some firms are also including environmental factors on their performance appraisal instruments and tying environmental performance directly to raises, bonuses, and promotions. For example, Conoco ties compensation of all its top managers to environmental action plans, and Occidental Chemical includes environmental responsibilities in all job descriptions.

Societies have been plagued by environmental disasters to such an extent recently that firms failing to recognize the importance of environmental issues and challenges could suffer severe consequences. Managing environmental affairs can no longer be an incidental or secondary function of company operations. Hooper and Rocca emphasize that "Product design, manufacturing, transportation, customer use, and ultimate disposal of a product should not merely reflect environmental considerations, but be driven by them. Firms that excel in the management of environmental affairs will benefit from constructive relations with consumers, regulators, vendors, and other industry players—substantially improving their prospects of success."

Firms should formulate and implement strategies from an environmental perspective. Environmental strategies could include developing or acquiring green businesses, divesting or altering environment-damaging businesses, striving to become a low-cost producer through waste minimization and energy conservation, or pursuing a differentiation strategy through green product features. In addition to creating strategies, firms could include an environmental representative on the board of directors, conduct regular environmental audits, implement bonuses for favorable environmental results, become involved in environmental issues and programs, incorporate environmental values in mission statements, establish environmentally oriented objectives, acquire environmental skills, and provide environmental training programs for company employees and managers.

CREATING A STRATEGY-SUPPORTIVE CULTURE

Strategists should strive to preserve, emphasize, and build upon aspects of an existing *culture* that support proposed new strategies. Aspects of an existing culture that are antagonistic to a proposed strategy should be identified and changed. Substantial research indicates that new strategies are often market driven and dictated by competitive forces. For this reason, changing a firm's culture to fit a new strategy is usually more effective than changing a strategy to fit an existing culture. Numerous techniques are available to alter an organization's culture, including recruitment, training, transfer, promotion, restructure of an organization's design, role modeling, and positive reinforcement.

In a recent article, Jack Duncan described *triangulation* as an effective, multi-method technique for studying and altering a firm's culture.[9] Triangulation includes the combined use of obtrusive observation, self-administered questionnaires, and personal interviews to determine the nature of a firm's culture. The process of triangulation reveals needed changes in a firm's culture that could benefit strategy.

Schein indicates that the following elements are most useful in linking culture to strategy:

1. Formal statements of organizational philosophy, charters, creeds, materials used for recruitment and selection, and socialization
2. Designing of physical spaces, facades, buildings
3. Deliberate role modeling, teaching, and coaching by leaders
4. Explicit reward and status system, promotion criteria
5. Stories, legends, myths, and parables about key people and events
6. What leaders pay attention to, measure, and control
7. Leader reactions to critical incidents and organizational crises
8. How the organization is designed and structured
9. Organizational systems and procedures
10. Criteria used for recruitment, selection, promotion, leveling off, retirement, and "excommunication" of people.[10]

In the personal and religious side of life, the impact of loss and change is easy to see.[11] Memories of loss and change often haunt individuals and organizations for years. Ibsen says, "Rob the average man of his life illusion and you rob him of his happiness at the same stroke."[12] When attachments to a culture are severed in an organization's attempt to change direction, employees and managers often experience deep feelings of grief. This phenomenon commonly occurs when external conditions dictate the need for a new strategy.

Managers and employees often struggle to find meaning in a situation that changed many years before. Some people find comfort in memories; others find solace in the present. Weak linkages between strategic management and organizational culture can jeopardize performance and success. Deal and Kennedy emphasize that making strategic changes in an organization always threatens a culture:

> . . . people form strong attachments to heroes, legends, the rituals of daily life, the hoopla of extravaganza and ceremonies, and all the symbols of the workplace. Change strips relationships and leaves employees confused, insecure, and often angry. Unless something can be done to provide support for transitions from old to new, the force of a culture can neutralize and emasculate strategy changes.[13]

The old corporate culture at AT&T could be described as consisting of lifetime careers, intense loyalty to the company, up-from-the-ranks management succession, dedication to the service ethos, and management by consensus. As AT&T moved from a regulated monopoly to a highly competitive environment in the 1980s, the company made numerous changes to create a culture that supported the new strategy; it redesigned its organizational structure, articulated its value system explicitly, provided management training to modify behavior in support of new values, revised recruiting aims and practices, and modified old symbols. AT&T abandoned its familiar logo, a bell with a circle, and adopted a new logo, a globe encircled by electronic communications, that symbolizes its new strategies to compete with Sprint and MCI.

PRODUCTION/OPERATIONS CONCERNS WHEN IMPLEMENTING STRATEGIES

Production/operations capabilities, limitations, and policies can significantly enhance or inhibit attainment of objectives. Production processes typically constitute more than 70 percent of a firm's total assets. A major part of the strategy-implementation process takes place at the production site. Production-related decisions such as plant size, plant location, product design, choice of equipment, kind of tooling, size of inventory, inventory control, quality control, cost control, use of standards, job specialization, employee training, equipment and resource utilization, shipping and packaging, and technological innovation can have a dramatic impact on the success or failure of strategy-implementation efforts.

> There was a time when people were "factors of production," managed little differently from machines or capital. No more. The best people will not tolerate it. And if that way of managing ever generated productivity, it has the reverse effect today. While capital and machines either are or can be managed toward sameness, people are individuals. They must be managed that way. When companies encourage individual expression, it is difficult for them not to be successful (renew). The only true source of success in a company is the individual.[14]

Examples of adjustments in production systems that could be required to implement various strategies are provided in Table 7–4 for both for-profit and nonprofit organizations. For instance, note that when a bank formulates and selects a strategy to add ten new branches, a production-related implementation concern is site location. As indicated in the Natural Environment Perspective, pollution control can also be an important concern in production decisions.

Just in Time (JIT) production approaches can significantly reduce the costs of implementing strategies. With JIT, parts and materials are delivered to a production site just as

TABLE 7–4
Production Management and Strategy Implementation

TYPE OF ORGANIZATION	STRATEGY BEING IMPLEMENTED	PRODUCTION SYSTEM ADJUSTMENTS
Hospital	Adding a cancer center (Product Development)	Purchase specialized equipment and add specialized people.
Bank	Adding ten new branches (Market Development)	Perform site location analysis.
Beer brewery	Purchasing a barley farm operation (Backward Integration)	Revise the inventory control system.
Steel manufacturer	Acquiring a fast-food chain (Conglomerate Diversification)	Improve the quality control system.
Computer company	Purchase a retail distribution chain (Forward Integration)	Alter the shipping, packaging, and transportation systems.

they are needed, rather than being stockpiled as a hedge against later deliveries. Harley-Davidson reports that at one plant alone, JIT freed $22 million previously tied up in inventory and greatly reduced reorder lead time. *Industry Week* made the following observation about JIT:

> Most of the nation's 1,000 largest industrial companies are experimenting with, or preparing to implement, "Just in Time" manufacturing schemes. Suppliers who can't, or won't, play by the new rules are finding themselves on the sidelines. "Just in Case" just isn't good enough any more.[15]

Factors that should be studied before locating production facilities include the availability of major resources, the prevailing wage rates in the area, transportation costs related to shipping and receiving, the location of major markets, political risks in the area or country, and the availability of trainable employees.

For high-technology companies, production costs may not be as important as production flexibility, because major product changes can be needed often. Industries such as biogenetics and plastics rely on production systems that must be flexible enough to allow frequent changes and rapid introduction of new products. An article in *Harvard Business Review* explains why some organizations get into trouble:

> They too slowly realize that a change in product strategy alters the tasks of a production system. These tasks, which can be stated in terms of requirements for cost, product flexibility, volume flexibility, product performance, and product consistency, determine which manufacturing policies are appropriate. As strategies shift over time, so must production policies covering the location and scale of manufacturing facilities, the choice of manufacturing process, the degree of vertical integration of each manufacturing facility, the use of R&D units, the control of the production system, and the licensing of technology.[16]

A common management practice, cross-training of employees, can facilitate strategy implementation and can yield many benefits. Employees gain a better understanding of the whole business and can contribute better ideas in planning sessions. Production/operations managers need to realize, however, that cross-training employees can create problems related to the following issues:

1. It can thrust managers into roles that emphasize counseling and coaching over directing and enforcing.
2. It can necessitate substantial investments in training and incentives.
3. It can be very time-consuming.
4. Skilled workers may resent unskilled workers who learn their jobs.
5. Older employees may not want to learn new skills.

HUMAN RESOURCE CONCERNS WHEN IMPLEMENTING STRATEGIES

The job of human resource manager is changing rapidly as companies downsize and reorganize in the 1990s. Strategic responsibilities of the human resource manager include assessing the staffing needs and costs for alternative strategies proposed during strategy formulation and developing a manpower plan for effectively implementing strategies. This plan must consider how best to manage spiraling health-care insurance costs. Employers' health-coverage expenses consume an average 26 percent of firms' net profits, even though most companies now require employees to pay part of their health-insurance premiums. The plan must also include how to motivate employees and managers during a time when layoffs are common and work loads are high.

The human resource department must develop performance incentives that clearly link performance and pay to strategies. The process of empowering managers and employees through involvement in strategic-management activities yields the greatest benefits when all organizational members understand clearly how they will benefit personally if the firm does well. Linking company and personal benefits is a major new strategic responsibility of human resource managers. Other new responsibilities for human resource managers may include establishing and administering an *Employee Stock Ownership Plan (ESOP),* instituting an effective child-care policy, and providing leadership for managers and employees to balance work and family.

A well-designed strategic-management system can fail if insufficient attention is given to the human resource dimension. Human resource problems that arise when businesses implement strategies can usually be traced to one of three causes: (1) disruption of social and political structures, (2) failure to match individuals' aptitudes with implementation tasks, and (3) inadequate top management support for implementation activities.[17]

Strategy implementation poses a threat to many managers and employees in an organization. New power and status relationships are anticipated and realized. New formal and informal groups are formed whose values, beliefs, and priorities may be largely unknown. Managers and employees may become engaged in resistance behavior as their roles, prerogatives, and power in the firm change. Disruption of social and political structures that accompany strategy execution must be anticipated and considered during strategy formulation and managed during strategy implementation.

A concern in matching managers with strategy is that jobs have specific and relatively static responsibilities, while people are dynamic in their personal development. Commonly used methods that match managers with strategies to be implemented include transferring managers, developing leadership workshops, offering career development activities, promotions, job enlargement, and job enrichment.

A number of other guidelines can help ensure that human relationships facilitate rather than disrupt strategy-implementation efforts. Specifically, managers should do a lot of chatting and informal questioning to stay abreast of how things are progressing and to know when to intervene. Managers can build support for strategy-implementation efforts by giving few orders, announcing few decisions, depending heavily on informal questioning, and seeking to probe and clarify until a consensus emerges. Key thrusts that succeed should be rewarded generously and visibly. A sense of humor is important, too. According to Adia Personnel Services, 72 percent of personnel executives nationwide say that humor is appropriate in discussions with colleagues; 63 percent say humor is appropriate in job interviews; 58 percent say humor is appropriate in performance reviews; and 53 percent say humor is appropriate in tense meetings.

It is suprising that so often during strategy formulation, individual values, skills, and abilities needed for successful strategy implementation are not considered. It is rare that a firm selecting new strategies or significantly altering existing strategies possesses the right line and staff personnel in the right positions for successful strategy implementation. The need to match individual aptitudes with strategy-implementation tasks should be considered in strategy choice.

Inadequate support from strategists for implementation activities often undermines organizational success. Chief executive officers, small business owners, and government agency heads must be personally committed to strategy implementation and express this commitment in highly visible ways. Strategists' formal statements about the importance of strategic management must be consistent with actual support and rewards given for activities completed and objectives reached. Otherwise, stress created by inconsistency can cause uncertainty among managers and employees at all levels.

Perhaps the best method for preventing and overcoming human resource problems in strategic management is to actively involve as many managers and employees as possible in the process. Although time-consuming, this approach builds understanding, trust, commitment, and ownership and reduces resentment and hostility. The true potential of strategy formulation and implementation resides in people.

EMPLOYEE STOCK OWNERSHIP PLANS (ESOPs) An ESOP is a tax-qualified, defined-contribution employee-benefit plan whereby employees purchase stock of the company through borrowed money or cash contributions. ESOPs empower employees to work as owners; this is a primary reason why the number of ESOPs grew dramatically throughout the 1980s and 1990s to more than 10,000 plans covering more than 11.5 million employees. ESOPs now control more than $60 billion in corporate stock in the United States.

Besides reducing worker alienation and stimulating productivity, ESOPs allow firms other benefits, such as substantial tax savings. Principal, interest, and dividend payments on ESOP-funded debt are tax deductible. Banks lend money to ESOPs at interest rates below prime. This money can be repaid in pretax dollars, lowering the debt service as much as 30 percent in some cases.

If an ESOP owns more than 50 percent of the firm, those who lend money to the ESOP are taxed on only 50 percent of the income received on the loans. ESOPs are not for every firm, however, because the initial legal, accounting, actuarial, and appraisal fees to set up an ESOP are about $50,000 for a small or mid-sized firm, with annual expenses of about $15,000. Analysts say ESOPs also do not work well in firms that have fluctuating payrolls and profits. Human resource managers in many firms conduct preliminary research to determine the desirability of an ESOP, and then facilitate its establishment and administration if benefits outweigh the costs.

To establish an ESOP, a firm sets up a trust fund and purchases shares of its stock, which are allocated to individual employee accounts. All full-time employees over age 21 usually participate in the plan. Allocations of stock to the trust are made on the basis of relative pay, seniority, or some other formula. When an ESOP borrows money to purchase stock, the debt is guaranteed by the company and thus appears on the firm's balance sheet. On average, ESOP employees get $1,300 worth of stock per year, but cannot take physical possession of the shares until they quit, retire, or die. The median level of employee ownership in ESOP plans is 30 to 40 percent, although the range is from about 10 percent to 100 percent.

Research confirms that ESOPs can have a dramatic positive effect on employee motivation and corporate performance, especially if ownership is coupled with expanded employee participation and involvement in decision making. Market surveys indicate that customers prefer to do business with firms that are employee-owned.

Many companies are following the lead of Polaroid, which established an ESOP as a tactic for preventing a hostile takeover. Polaroid's CEO, MacAllister Booth, says, "Twenty years from now we'll find that employees have a sizable stake in every major American corporation." (It is interesting to note here that Polaroid is chartered in the state of Delaware, which requires corporate suitors to acquire 85 percent of a target company's shares to complete a merger; over 50 percent of all American corporations are incorporated in Delaware for this reason.) Wyatt Cafeterias, a Southwestern U.S. operator of 120 cafeterias, also adopted the ESOP concept to prevent a hostile takeover. Employee productivity at Wyatt has greatly increased since the ESOP began, as illustrated in the following quotes:

> The key employee in our entire organization is the person serving the customer on the cafeteria line. In the past, because of high employee turnover and entry-level wages for many line jobs, these employees received far less attention and recognition than managers. We now tell the tea cart server, "You own the place. Don't wait for the manager to tell you how to do your job better or how to provide better service. You take care of it." Sure, we're looking for productivity increases, but since we began pushing decisions down to the level of people who deal directly with customers, we've discovered an awesome side effect—suddenly the work crews have this "happy to be here" attitude that the customers really love.[18]

Companies such as Avis, Procter & Gamble, BellSouth, ITT, Xerox, Delta, Austin Industries, Health Trust, The Parsons Corporation, Dyncorp, and Charter Medical have established ESOPs to assist strategists in divesting divisions, going private, and consummating leveraged buyouts. ESOPs can be found today in all kinds of firms, from small retailers to large manufacturers. Employees can own anywhere from 1 percent to 100 percent of the company. Nearly all ESOPs are established in healthy firms, not failing firms.

BALANCING WORK LIFE AND HOME LIFE   Human resource managers need to foster more effective balancing of professional and private lives, because nearly 50 million people in the United States are now part of two-career families. A corporate objective to become more lean and mean must today include consideration for the fact that a good home life contributes immensely to a good work life.

> You can count on baby-boomers to force the issue of family versus work onto the corporate agenda. Fully 73 percent of all women age 25 to 34 now work for pay, as do half of all women with babies under a year old. For them and their husbands, child care, flexible hours, and job sharing are pressing concerns.[19]

The work/family issue is no longer just a woman's problem. Some specific measures that firms are taking to address this issue are providing spouse relocation assistance as an employee benefit, providing company resources for family recreational and educational use, establishing employee country clubs, such as those at IBM and Bethlehem Steel, and creating family/work interaction opportunities. A recent study by Joseph Pleck of Wheaton College found that in companies that do not offer paternity leave for fathers as a benefit, most men take short informal paternity leaves anyway by combining vacation time and sick days.

Some organizations have developed family days, when family members are invited into the workplace, taken on plant or office tours, dined by management, and given a chance to see exactly what other family members do each day. Family days are inexpensive and increase the employee's pride in working for the organization. Flexible working hours during the week is another human resource response to the need for individuals to balance work life and home life. The work/family topic is being made part of the agenda at meetings and thus is becoming discussable in many organizations.

Research indicates that employees who are dissatisfied with child-care arrangements are most likely to be absent or unproductive.[20] Lack of adequate child care in a community can be a deterrent in recruiting and retaining good managers and employees. Some benefits of on-site child-care facilities are improved employee relations, reduced absenteeism and turnover, increased productivity, enhanced recruitment, and improved community relations.

A recent survey of women managers revealed that one-third would leave their present employer for another employer offering child-care assistance. The Conference Board recently reported that more than 500 firms in the United States had created on-site or near-site child-care centers for their employees, including Merck, Campbell Soup, Hoffman–La Roche, Stride-Rite, Johnson Wax, CIGNA, Champion International, Walt Disney World, and Playboy Resorts.

Other common child-care service arrangements include employer-sponsored day care, child-care information, and referral services. IBM, Steelcase, Honeywell, Citibank, 3M, and Southland have established contracts with third-party child-care information and referral services.

The nation's largest employer-sponsored day-care center is operated by Intermedics, a Texas-based medical instruments firm. Employee turnover declined 23 percent the first year Intermedics instituted the center. Due to the high cost of child care, numerous firms are forming partnerships to build and manage child-care facilities. The largest collaboration so far is the new $2 million, 194-child day-care center in Charlotte, financed and operated by IBM, American Express, Allstate, Duke Power, and University Research Park. The teacher-child ratio at this center is 50 percent lower than required by North Carolina law. Other large partnership child-care centers have recently been built in Minneapolis, Rochester, Dallas–Fort Worth, and New York City. In Virginia, 22 companies recently pooled $100,000 to establish a parent-run child-care cooperative. Other companies that effectively address child-care concerns of managers and employees include Clorox and Nyloncraft. Even small businesses are beginning to offer child-care benefits for employees. Some small firms that now offer an on-site day-care center for employees' children include Bowles Corporation in North Ferrisburg, Vermont; Byrne Electrical Specialists in Rockford, Michigan; Chalet Dental Clinic in Yakima, Washington; and Stackpole Ltd. in Brownsville, Tennessee.

CORPORATE FITNESS PROGRAMS   At least 10,000 U.S. employers now offer programs to improve or maintain their employees' health, such as programs to stop smoking, reduce cholesterol, promote regular exercise, and control high blood pressure. Another 1,000 American firms offer on-site, fully equipped fitness centers to promote good employee health. Perhaps the leader in this area is Johnson & Johnson, which provides an 11,000-square-foot fitness center, aerobics and other exercise classes, seminars on AIDS and alcohol abuse, and an indoor track. J & J's program is called Live for Life.

CONCLUSION

Successful strategy formulation does not at all guarantee successful strategy implementation. Although inextricably interdependent, strategy formulation and strategy implementation are characteristically different. In a single word, strategy implementation means *change*. It is widely agreed that "the real work begins after strategies are formulated." Successful strategy implementation requires support, discipline, motivation, and hard work from all managers and employees. It is sometimes frightening to think that a single individual can sabotage strategy-implementation efforts irreparably.

Formulating the right strategies is not enough, because managers and employees must be motivated to implement those strategies. Management issues considered central to strategy implementation include matching organizational structure with strategy, linking performance and pay to strategies, creating an organizational climate conducive to change, managing political relationships, creating a strategy-supportive culture, adapting production/operations processes, and managing human resources. Establishing annual objectives, devising policies, and allocating resources are central strategy-implementation activities common to all organizations. Depending on the size and type of organization, other management issues could be equally important to successful strategy implementation.

TAKE IT TO THE NET

We invite you to visit the DAVID page on the Prentice Hall Web site at:
http://www.prenhall.com/davidsm
for this chapter's World Wide Web exercises.

KEY TERMS AND CONCEPTS

Avoidance	(p. 221)	Employee Stock Ownership Plans (ESOPs)	(p. 237)	Rational Change Strategy	(p. 231)
Conflict	(p. 221)			Reengineering	(p. 227)
Confrontation	(p. 221)	Establish Annual Objectives	(p. 217)	Resistance to Change	(p. 230)
Culture	(p. 233)	Force Change Strategy	(p. 231)	Resource Allocation	(p. 220)
Defusion	(p. 221)	Functional Structure	(p. 223)	Restructuring	(p. 226)
Delayering	(p. 226)	Gain Sharing	(p. 228)	Annual Objectives	(p. 217)
Devise Policies	(p. 219)	Horizontal Consistency of Objectives	(p. 217)	Rightsizing	(p. 226)
Divisional Structure by Geographic Area, Product, Customer, or Process	(p. 223)			Strategic Business Unit (SBU) Structure	(p. 226)
		Just in Time	(p. 234)		
		Matrix Structure	(p. 226)	Triangulation	(p. 233)
Downsizing	(p. 226)	Policies	(p. 219)	Vertical Consistency of Objectives	(p. 217)
Educative Change Strategy	(p. 231)	Profit Sharing	(p. 228)		

ISSUES FOR REVIEW AND DISCUSSION

1. Allocating resources can be a political and an ad hoc activity in firms that do not use strategic management. Why is this true? Does adopting strategic management assure easy resource allocation? Why?

2. Compare strategy formulation with strategy implementation in terms of each being an art or a science.

3. Describe the relationship between annual objectives and policies.

4. Identify a long-term objective and two supporting annual objectives for a familiar organization.

5. Identify and discuss three policies that apply to your present business policy class.

6. Explain the following statement: Horizontal consistency of goals is as important as vertical consistency.

7. Describe several reasons why conflict may occur during objective-setting activities.

8. In your opinion, what approach to conflict resolution would be best for resolving a disagreement between a personnel manager and a sales manager over the firing of a particular salesperson? Why?

9. Describe the organizational culture of your college or university.

10. Explain why organizational structure is so important in strategy implementation.

11. In your opinion, how many separate divisions could an organization reasonably have without using an SBU-type organizational structure? Why?

12. Would you recommend a divisional structure by geographic area, product, customer, or process for a medium-sized bank in your local area? Why?

13. What are the advantages and disadvantages of decentralizing the wage and salary function of an organization? How could this be accomplished?

14. Consider a college organization with which you are familiar. How did management issues affect strategy implementation in that organization?

15. As production manager of a local newspaper, what problems would you anticipate in implementing a strategy to increase the average number of pages in the paper by 40 percent?

16. Select an article from the suggested readings at the end of this chapter. Read the article and give a summary report to the class revealing your thoughts on the topic.

17. Do you believe expenditures for child-care or fitness facilities are warranted from a cost/benefit perspective? Why or why not?

18. Explain why successful strategy implementation often hinges on whether the strategy-formulation process empowers managers and employees.

NOTES

1. A. G. Bedeian and W. F. Glueck, *Management,* 3rd. ed. (Chicago: The Dryden Press, 1983): 212.

2. Ibid., 200.

3. Ibid., 58.

4. John Byrne and Lori Bongiorno, "CEO Pay: Ready for Takeoff," *Business Week* (April 24, 1995): 88–94.

5. Perry Pascarella, "The Toughest Turnaround of All," *Industry Week* (April 2, 1984): 33. Reprinted with permission from *Industry Week,* April 2, 1984. Copyright Renton Publishing Inc., Cleveland, Ohio.

6. Jack Duncan, *Management* (New York: Random House, 1983): 381–390.

7. H. Igor Ansoff, "Strategic Management of Technology," *Journal of Business Strategy* 7, no. 3 (Winter 1987): 38.

8. Robert Waterman, Jr., "How the Best Get Better," *Business Week* (September 14, 1987): 104.

9. Jack Duncan, "Organizational Culture: Getting a Fix on an Elusive Concept," *Academy of Management Executives III,* no. 3 (August 1989): 229.

10. E. H. Schein, "The Role of the Founder in Creating Organizational Culture," *Organizational Dynamics* (Summer 1983): 13–28.

11. T. Deal and A. Kennedy, "Culture: A New Look Through Old Lenses," *Journal of Applied Behavioral Science* 19, no. 4 (1983): 498–504.

12. H. Ibsen, "The Wild Duck," in O. G. Brochett and L. Brochett (Eds.), *Plays for the Theater* (New York: Holt, Rinehart & Winston, 1967). Also, R. Pascale, "The Paradox of "Corporate Culture": Reconciling Ourselves to Socialization," *California Management Review* 28, 2 (1985): 26, 37–40.

13. T. Deal and A. Kennedy, *Corporate Cultures: The Rites and Rituals of Corporate Life* (Reading, Mass: Addison-Wesley, 1982).

14. Robert Waterman, Jr., "The Renewal Factor," *Business Week* (September 14, 1987): 100.

15. "Just in Time: Putting the Squeeze on Suppliers," *Industry Week* (July 9, 1984): 59.

16. Robert Stobaugh and Piero Telesio, "Match Manufacturing Policies and Product Strategy," *Harvard Business Review* 61, no. 2 (March–April 1983): 113.

17. R. T. Lenz and Marjorie Lyles, "Managing Human Resource Problems in Strategy Planning Systems," *Journal of Business Strategy* 60, no. 4 (Spring 1986): 58.

18. J. Warren Henry, "ESOPs with Productivity Payoffs," *Journal of Business Strategy* (July–August 1989): 33.

19. Ronald Henkoff, "Is Greed Dead?" *Fortune* (August 14, 1989): 49.

20. Richard Levine, "Childcare: Inching Up the Corporate Agenda," *Management Review* 78, no. 1 (January 1989): 43.

CURRENT READINGS

Barney, J. B. and E. J. Zajac. "Competitive Organizatinal Behavior: Toward an Organizationally-based Theory of Competitive Advantage." *Strategic Management Journal* 15, Special Issue (Winter 1994): 5–10.

Belasco, James A. and Ralph C. Stayer. "Why Empowerment Doesn't Empower: The Bankruptcy of Current Paradigms." *Business Horizons* 37, no. 2 (March–April 1994): 29–41.

Birkinshaw, Julian. "Encouraging Entrepreneurial Activity in Multinational Corporations. " *Business Horizons* 38, no. 3 (May–June 1995): 32–38.

Bowen, David E. and Edward E. Lawler III. "Empowering Service Employees." *Sloan Management Review* 36, no. 4 (Summer 1995): 73–84.

Brown, Kenneth and Lyle Sussman. "Phong Siu-Ming vs. Burgers-R-Us: Cultural Diversity or Cultural Discrimination?" *Business Horizons* 38, no. 2 (March–April 1995): 51–58.

Bucholtz, Ann K. and Barbara A. Ribbens. "Role of Chief Executive Officers in Takeover Resistance: Effects of CEO Incentives and Individual Characteristics." *Academy of Management Journal* 37, no. 3 (June 1994): 554–579.

Byron, S. J. and J. William "Coming to Terms with the New Corporate Contract." *Business Horizons* 38, no. 1 (January–February 1995): 8–15.

Corbett, Charles and Luk Van Wassenhove. "The Green Fee: Internalizing and Operationalizing Environmental Issues." *Cali-fornia Management Review* 36, no. 1 (Fall 1993): 116–135.

Daily, C. M. and D. R. Dalton. "CEO and Director Turnover in Failing Firms: An Illusion of Change?" *Strategic Management Journal* 16, no. 5 (June 1995): 393–400.

Dougherty, Deborah and Edward H. Bowman. "The Effects of Organizational Downsizing on Product Innovation." *California Management Review* 37, no. 4 (Summer 1995): 28–44.

Ford Jeffrey D. and Laurie W. Ford. "The Role of Conversations in Producing Intentional Change in Organization." *Academy of Management Review* (July 1995): 541–570.

Fram, Eugene H. and Riad Ajami. "Globalization of Markets and Shopping Stress: Cross-Country Comparisons." *Business Horizons* 37, no. 1 (January–February 1994): 17–23.

Ghorpade, Jai and Milton M. Chen. "Creating Quality-driven Performance Appraisal Systems." *Academy of Management Executive IX,* no. 1 (February 1995): 32–41.

Ghoshal, Sumantra. "Changing the Role of Top Management: Beyond Structure to Processes." *Harvard Business Review* 73, no. 1 (January–February 1995): 86–96.

Glew, David J., Anne M. O'Leary-Kelly, and Ricky W. Griffen. "Participation in Organizations: A Preview of the Issues and Proposed Framework for Future Analysis." *Journal of Management* 21, no. 3 (Fall 1995): 395–421.

Goodstein, Jerry D. "Institutional Pressures and Strategic Responsiveness: Employer Involvement in Work-Family Issues." *Academy of Management Review* 37, no. 2 (April 1994): 350–382.

Greenberg, Paul E., Stan N. Finkelstein, and Ernst R. Berndt. "Economic Consequences of Illness in the Workplace." *Sloan Management Review* 36, no. 4 (Summer 1995): 26–38.

Hambrick, D. C. and S. Finkelstein. "The Effects of Ownership Structure on Conditions at the Top: The Case of CEO Pay Raises." *Strategic Management Journal* 16, no. 3 (March 1995): 175–194.

Huntsman, Stephen. "Using Strategic Planning to Drive Organizational Change." *Long Range Planning* 27, no. 1 (February 1994): 50–55.

Huselid, Mark A. "The Impact of Human Resource Management Practices on Turnover, Productivity, and Corporate Financial Performance." *Academy of Management Journal* 38, no. 3 (June 1995): 635–672.

Keidel, Robert W. "Rethinking Organizational Design." *Academy of Management Executive VIII,* no. 4 (November 1994): 12–30.

Lado, Augustine A. and Mary C. Wilson. "Human Resource Systems and Sustained Competitive Advantage: A Competency-based Perspective." *Academy of Management Review* 19, no. 2 (April 1994): 699–727.

Lau, Chung-Ming and Richard W. Woodman. "Understanding Organizational Change: A Schematic Perspective." *Academy of Management Journal* 38, no. 2 (April 1995): 537–554.

Lorenz, Christopher. "Harnessing Design as a Strategic Resource." *Long Range Planning* 27, no. 5 (October 1994): 73–84.

Majumdar, S. K. and V. Ramaswamy. "Going Direct to Market: The Influence of Exchange Conditions." *Strategic Management Journal* 16, no. 5 (June 1995): 333–352.

Miles, Raymond E., Henry J. Coleman, Jr., and W. E. Douglas Creed. "Keys to Success in Corporate Redesign." *California Management Review* 37, no. 3 (Spring 1995): 128–145.

Mohr, J. and R. Spekman. "Characteristics of Partnership Success: Partnership Attributes, Communication Behavior, and Conflict Resolution Techniques." *Strategic Management Journal* 15, no. 2 (February 1994): 135–152.

Platz, Donald L. "On the Horizon/Supporting Employees Who Are Parents: A Worksite Child-rearing Program." *Business Horizons* 38, no. 2 (March–April 1995): 81–82.

Powell, Gary N. and D. Anthony Butterfield. "Investigating the 'Glass Ceiling' Phenomenon: An Empirical Study of Actual Promotions to Top Management." *Academy of Management Journal* 37, no. 1, (February 1994): 68–86.

Priem, Richard L., David A. Harrison, and Nan Kanoff Muir. "Structured Conflict and Consensus Outcomes in Group Decision Making." *Journal of Management* 21, no. 4 (1995): 691– 710.

Ranney, Joyce and Mark Deck. "Making Teams Work: Lessons from the Leaders in New Product Development." *Planning Review* 23, no. 4 (July–August 1995): 6–13.

Reynierse, James H. "Ten Commandments for CEOs Seeking Organizational Change." *Business Horizons* 37, no. 1 (January–February 1994): 40–45.

Scheibal, William. "When Cultures Clash: Applying Title VII Abroad." *Business Horizons* 38, no. 5 (September–October 1995): 4–8.

Shadur, Mark A. "Total Quality—Systems Survive, Cultures Change." *Long Range Planning* 28, no. 2 (April 1995): 115–125.

Shea, John and David Gobeli. "TQM: The Experiences of Ten Small Businesses." *Business Horizons* 38, no. 1 (January–February 1995): 71–77.

Snell, Scott A. and James W. Dean, Jr. "Strategic Compensation for Intergrated Manufacturing: The Moderating Effects of Jobs and Organizatinal Inertia." *Academy of Management Journal* 37, no. 5 (October 1994): 1109–1140.

Snell, Scott A. and Mark A. Youndt. "Human Resource Management and Firm Performance: Testing a Contingency Model of Executive Controls." *Journal of Management* 21, no. 4 (Journal of Management (1995): 711–738.

Sonnenfeld, Sandi. "The Challenge of Going Green." Perspectives. *Harvard Business Review* (July–August 1994): 37–51.

Stacey, R. D. "The Science of Complexity: An Alternative Perspective for Strategic Change Processes." *Strategic Management Journal* 16, no. 6 (September 1995): 477–491.

Stewart, J. M. "Empowering Multinational Subsidiaries." *Long Range Planning* 28, no. 4 (August 1995): 63–73.

Tichy, Noel M., and Ram Charan. "The CEO As Coach: An Interview With Allied Signal's Lawrence A. Bossidy." *Harvard Business Review* 73, no. 2 (March–April 1995): 68–79.

Toombs, Ken and George Bailey. " How to Redesign Your Organization to Match Customer Needs." *Planning Review* 23, no. 2 (March–April 1995): 20–24.

Wall, James A., Jr. and Ronda Roberts Callister. "Conflict and its Management." *Journal of Management* 21, no. 3 (Fall 1995): 515–558.

Walley, Noah and Bradley Whitehead. "It's not Easy Being Green." *Harvard Business Review* (May–June 1994): 46–53.

Welbourne, Theresa, M. and Luis R. Gomez Mejia. "Gainsharing: A Critical Review and A Future Research Agenda." *Journal of Management* 21, no. 3 (Fall 1995): 559–570.

Welbourne, Theresa, David B. Balkin, and Luis R. Gomez-Mejia. "Gainsharing and Mutual Monitoring: A Combined Agency–

Organizational Justice Interpretation." *Academy of Management Journal* 38, no. 3 (June 1995): 881–899.

Wolfe, Richard A. and Donald F. Parker. "Employee Health Management: Challenges and Opportunities." *Academy of Management Executive VIII,* no. 2 (May 1994): 22–31.

REVISING HERSHEY FOODS' ORGANIZATIONAL CHART

PURPOSE

Developing and altering organizational charts is an important skill for strategists to possess. This exercise can improve your skill in altering an organization's hierarchical structure in response to new strategies being formulated.

INSTRUCTIONS

Step 1 Turn back to Hershey's organizational chart given in the Cohesion Case (p. 30).

Step 2 On a separate sheet of paper, diagram an organizational chart that you believe would best suit Hershey's needs if the company decided to form a divisional structure by product.

Step 3 Provide as much detail in your chart as possible, including the names of individuals and the titles of positions.

MATCHING MANAGERS WITH STRATEGY

PURPOSE

For many years, strategists believed that good managers could adapt to handle any situation. Consequently, strategists rarely replaced or transferred managers as the need arose to implement new strategies. Today, this situation is changing. Research supports the notion that certain management characteristics are needed for certain strategic situations.[1] Chase Manhattan Bank, Heublein, Texas Instruments, Corning Glass, and General Electric are examples of companies that match managers to strategic requirements.

This exercise can improve your awareness and understanding of particular managerial characteristics that have been found to be most desirable for implementing certain types of strategies. Having the right managers in the right jobs can determine the success or failure of strategy-implementation efforts. This exercise is based on a recently published framework that has proved to be useful in "matching managers to strategy."[2]

INSTRUCTIONS

Your task is to match specific managerial characteristics with particular generic strategies. Four broad types of strategies are examined:

1. Retrenchment/Turnaround
2. Intensive (market penetration, market development, and product development)
3. Liquidation/Divestiture
4. Integration (backward, forward, and horizontal)

Five managerial characteristics have been found to be associated with each of these strategies. On a separate sheet of paper, list the four types of strategies. Beside each strategy, record the appropriate letter of the five managerial characteristics that you believe are most needed to successfully implement those strategies. Each of the managerial characteristics in the following list should be used only once in completing this exercise.

A. Is technically knowledgeable—"knows the business"
B. Is "callous"—tough-minded, determined, willing to be the bad guy
C. Is "take charge"—oriented—strong leader
D. Is a good negotiator
E. Wants to be respected, not necessarily liked
F. Has good analytical ability
G. Is low glory-seeking—willing to do dirty jobs; does not want glamour
H. Has excellent staffing skills
I. Handles pressure well
J. Is a risk taker
K. Has good relationship-building skills
L. Has good organizational and team-building skills
M. Is oriented to getting out the most efficiency, not growth
N. Anticipates problems—"Problem Finder"
O. Has strong analytical and diagnostic skills, especially financial
P. Is an excellent business strategist
Q. Has good communication skills
R. Has personal magnetism
S. Is highly analytical—focuses on costs/benefits, does not easily accept current ways of doing things
T. Has good interpersonal influence

NOTES

1. Marc Gerstein and Heather Reisman, "Strategic Selection: Matching Executives to Business Conditions," *Sloan Management Review* 24, no. 2(Winter 1983): 33–47.

2. Ibid., 37.

Experiential Exercise 7C
DO ORGANIZATIONS REALLY ESTABLISH OBJECTIVES?

PURPOSE

Objectives provide direction, allow synergy, aid in evaluation, establish priorities, reduce uncertainty, minimize conflicts, stimulate exertion, and aid in both the allocation of resources and the design of jobs. This exercise will enhance your understanding of how organizations use or misuse objectives.

INSTRUCTIONS

Step 1   Join with one other person in class to form a two-person team.

Step 2   Contact by telephone the owner or manager of an organization in your city or town. Request a 30-minute personal interview or meeting with that person for the purpose of discussing "business objectives." During your meeting, seek answers to the following questions:

1. Do you believe it is important for a business to establish and clearly communicate long-term and annual objectives? Why or why not?
2. Does your organization establish objectives? If yes, what type and how many? How are the objectives communicated to individuals? Are your firm's objectives in written form or simply communicated orally?
3. To what extent are managers and employees involved in the process of establishing objectives?
4. How often are your business objectives revised and by what process?

Step 3 Take good notes during the interview. Let one person be the note taker and one person do most of the talking. Have your notes typed up and ready to turn in to your professor.

Step 4 Prepare a 5-minute oral presentation for the class, reporting the results of your interview. Turn in your typed report.

Experiential Exercise 7D

UNDERSTANDING MY UNIVERSITY'S CULTURE

PURPOSE

It is something of an art to uncover the basic values and beliefs that are buried deeply in an organization's rich collection of stories, language, heroes, and rituals. Yet culture can be the most important factor in implementing strategies.

INSTRUCTIONS

Step 1 On a separate sheet of paper, list the following terms: hero/heroine, belief, metaphor, language, value, symbol, story, legend, saga, folktale, myth, ceremonial, rite, and ritual.

Step 2 For your college or university, give examples of each term. If necessary, speak with faculty, staff, alumni, administration, or fellow students of the institution to identify examples of each term. Refer back to p. 144 for definitions of the terms if needed.

Step 3 Report your findings to the class. Tell the class how you feel regarding cultural products being consciously used to help implement strategies.

Implementing Strategies: Marketing, Finance/ Accounting, R&D, and CIS Issues

CHAPTER OUTLINE

CHAPTER OBJECTIVES

After studying this chapter, you should be able to do the following:

1. Explain market segmentation and product positioning as strategy-implementation tools.

2. Discuss procedures for determining the worth of a business.

3. Explain why pro forma financial analysis is a central strategy-implementation tool.

4. Explain how to evaluate the attractiveness of debt versus stock as a source of capital to implement strategies.

5. Discuss the nature and role of research and development in strategy implementation.

6. Explain how computer information systems can determine the success of strategy-implementation efforts.

The greatest strategy is doomed if it's implemented badly.—BERNARD REIMANN

Organizations should approach all tasks with the idea that they can be accomplished in a superior fashion.—THOMAS WATSON, JR.

There is no "perfect" strategic decision. One always has to pay a price. One always has to balance conflicting objectives, conflicting opinions, and conflicting priorities. The best strategic decision is only an approximation—and a risk.—PETER DRUCKER

The real question isn't how well you're doing today against your own history, but how you're doing against your competitors.—DONALD KRESS

Effective organizational responses are retarded not so much by failing to recognize what needs to be done, but by not doing what ought to be done.—JOHN KEANE

As market windows open and close more quickly, it is important that R&D be tied more closely to corporate strategy.—WILLIAM SPENSER

Market share matters. The 90th share point isn't as important as the 91st, and nothing is more dangerous than falling to 89.—BILL SAPORITO

Most of the time, strategists should not be formulating strategy at all; they should be getting on with implementing strategies they already have.—HENRY MINTZBERG

The best plan is only a plan, that is, good intentions. Unless commitment is made, there are only promises and hopes, but no plan.—PETER DRUCKER

*S*trategies have no chance of being implemented successfully in organizations that do not market goods and services well, in firms that cannot raise needed working capital, in firms that produce technologically inferior products, or in firms that have a weak information system. This chapter examines marketing, finance/accounting, R&D, and computer information systems issues that are central to effective strategy implementation. Special topics include market segmentation, market positioning, evaluating the worth of a business, determining to what extent debt and/or stock should be used as a source of capital, developing pro forma financial statements, contracting R&D outside the firm, and creating an information support system. Manager and employee involvement and participation are essential for success in marketing, finance/accounting, R&D, and CIS activities.

THE NATURE OF STRATEGY IMPLEMENTATION

The quarterback can call the best play possible in the huddle, but that does not mean the play will go for a touchdown. The team may even lose yardage unless the play is executed (implemented) well. Less than 10 percent of strategies formulated are successfully implemented! There are many reasons for this low success rate, including failing to segment markets appropriately, paying too much for a new acquisition, falling behind competitors in R&D, and not recognizing the benefit of computers in managing information.

Strategy implementation directly affects the lives of plant managers, division managers, department managers, sales managers, product managers, project managers, personnel managers, staff managers, supervisors, and all employees. In some situations, individuals may not have participated in the strategy-formulation process at all and may not appreciate, understand, or even accept the work and thought that went into strategy formulation. There may even be foot-dragging or resistance on their part. Managers and employees who do not understand the business and are not committed to the business may attempt to sabotage strategy-implementation efforts in hopes that the organization will return to its old ways. The strategy-implementation stage of the strategic-management process is emphasized in Figure 8–1.

MARKETING ISSUES

Countless marketing variables affect the success or failure of strategy implementation, and the scope of this text does not allow addressing all those issues. However, two variables are of central importance to strategy implementation: *market segmentation* and *product positioning*. Market segmentation and product positioning rank as marketing's most important contributions to strategic management. Some examples of marketing decisions that may require policies are as follows:

1. To use exclusive dealerships or multiple channels of distribution
2. To use heavy, light, or no TV advertising
3. To limit (or not) the share of business done with a single customer
4. To be a price leader or a price follower
5. To offer a complete or limited warranty
6. To reward salespeople based on a straight commission or a combination salary/commission

FIGURE 8–1

A Comprehensive Strategic-Management Model

Feedback

Develop Mission Statement

Perform External Audit

Perform Internal Audit

Establish Long-term Objectives

Generate, Evaluate, and Select Strategies

Establish Policies and Annual Objectives

Allocate Resources

Measure and Evaluate Performance

Strategy Formulation

Strategy Implementation

Strategy Evaluation

TABLE 8–1
The Marketing Mix Component Factors

PRODUCT	PLACE	PROMOTION	PRICE
Quality	Distribution channels	Advertising	Level
Features and Options	Distribution coverage	Personal selling	Discounts and
Style	Outlet location	Sales promotion	allowances
Brand Name	Sales territories	Publicity	Payment terms
Packaging	Inventory levels and		
Product Line	locations		
Warranty	Transportation carriers		
Service Level			
Other Services			

Source: E. Jerome McCarthy, *Basic Marketing: A Managerial Approach,* 9th ed. (Homewood, Ill: Richard D. Irwin, Inc., 1987): 37–44 (1st ed., 1960).

MARKET SEGMENTATION   Market segmentation is widely used in implementing strategies, especially for small and specialized firms. *Market segmentation* can be defined as the subdividing of a market into distinct subsets of customers according to needs and buying habits. Market segmentation is an important variable in strategy implementation for at least three major reasons. First, strategies such as market development, product development, market penetration, and diversification require increased sales through new markets and products. To implement these strategies successfully, new or improved market-segmentation approaches are required. Second, market segmentation allows a firm to operate with limited resources, because mass production, mass distribution, and mass advertising are not required. Market segmentation can enable a small firm to compete successfully with a large firm by maximizing per-unit profits and per-segment sales. Finally, market segmentation decisions directly affect *marketing-mix variables:* product, place, promotion, and price, as indicated in Table 8–1.

Geographic and demographic bases for segmenting markets are the most commonly employed, as illustrated in Table 8–2. Beer producers, for example, have generally divided the light beer market into three segments:

> The light beer market can be meaningfully separated into three motivation segments: those who are calorie-conscious, those who prefer less alcohol, and those who prefer a lighter taste. In fact, it is possible for one person to consume light beer on three separate occasions for three different reasons. The situation may therefore dictate the segment the consumer falls into.[1]

Evaluating potential market segments requires strategists to determine the characteristics and needs of consumers, analyze consumer similarities and differences, and develop consumer group profiles. Segmenting consumer markets is generally much simpler and easier than segmenting industrial markets, because industrial products, such as electronic circuits and forklifts, have multiple applications and appeal to diverse customer groups. Royal Crown Cola Company recently shifted its market segmentation strategy from teenagers to adults. To make this switch the company spent $20 million on a new advertising campaign. RC Cola Company says it has not given up on teens, but will now go after teens through parents.

Market segmentation matrices and decision trees can facilitate implementing strategies effectively. An example of a matrix for segmenting the lawn fertilizer market is provided in Figure 8–2. Similar matrices could be developed for almost any market, product, or service. Market segmentation strategies in the men's fragrance business are described as follows:

> The men's fragrance business breaks into four segments based on price. At the bottom are Mennen's Skin Bracer, Brut 33, and Aqua Velva that are sold mainly in food and drug stores and are priced below $4 for a 3 ounce bottle. The next tier, at about $4 to $5 for 4

TABLE 8–2
Alternative Bases for Market Segmentation

VARIABLE	TYPICAL BREAKDOWNS
GEOGRAPHIC	
Region	Pacific, Mountain, West North Central, West South Central, East North Central, East South Central, South Atlantic, Middle Atlantic, New England
County Size	A, B, C, D
City or SMSA Size	Under 5,000; 5,000–20,000; 20,000–50,000; 50,000–100,000; 100,000–250,000; 250,000–500,000; 500,000–1,000,000; 1,000,000–4,000,000; 4,000,000 or over
Density	Urban, suburban, rural
Climate	Northern, southern
DEMOGRAPHIC	
Age	Under 6, 6–11, 12–19, 20–34, 35–49, 50–64, 65+
Sex	Male, female
Family Size	1–2, 3–4, 5+
Family Life Cycle	Young, single; young, married, no children; young, married, youngest child under 6; young, married, youngest child 6 or over; older, married, with children; older, married, no children under 18; older, single; other
Income	Under $2,500; $2,500–$5,000; $5,000–$7,500; $7,500–$10,000; $10,000–$15,000; $15,000–$20,000; $20,000–$30,000; $30,000–$50,000; $50,000 and over
Occupation	Professional and technical; managers, officials, and proprietors; clerical, sales; craftsmen, foremen; operatives; farmers; retired; students; housewives; unemployed
Education	Grade school or less; some high school; high school graduate; some college; college graduate
Religion	Catholic, Protestant, Jewish, other
Race	White, black, Oriental
Nationality	American, British, French, German, Scandinavian, Italian, Latin American, Middle Eastern, Japanese
PSYCHOGRAPHIC	
Social Class	Lower lowers, upper lowers, lower middles, upper middles, lower uppers, upper uppers
Lifestyle	Straights, swingers, long hairs
Personality	Compulsive, gregarious, authoritarian, ambitious
BEHAVIORAL	
Use Occasion	Regular occasion, special occasion
Benefits Sought	Quality, service, economy
User Status	Nonuser, ex-user, potential user, first-time user, regular user
Usage Rate	Light user, medium user, heavy user
Loyalty Status	None, medium, strong, absolute
Readiness Stage	Unaware, aware, informed, interested, desirous, intending to buy
Attitude Toward Product	Enthusiastic, positive, indifferent, negative, hostile

Source: Philip Kotler, *Marketing Management: Analysis, Planning and Control,* © 1984: 256. Reprinted by permission of Prentice-Hall, Inc., Englewood Cliffs, New Jersey.

ounces, is Old Spice and English Leather. Next, are the mass prestige brands, with twice the amount of scent as after-shaves, led by Chaps and Stetson at $10 and up. Above that are expensive department store brands, such as Obsession for Men, Aramis, Polo, Giorgio, and beyond. Old Spice is the best selling men's fragrance in the world, with sales above $180 million annually.[2]

   Segmentation is a key to matching supply and demand, which is one of the thorniest problems in customer service. Segmentation often reveals that large, random fluctuations in demand actually consist of several small, predictable, and manageable patterns. Matching supply and demand allows factories to produce desirable levels without extra shifts, overtime, and subcontracting. Matching supply and demand also minimizes the number and severity of stockouts. The demand for hotel rooms, for example, can be dependent on foreign tourists, businesspersons, and vacationers. Focusing on these three

FIGURE 8–2
Tools for Segmenting the Lawn Fertilizer Market

Heavy users	**High income**	Central city
		Suburban
		Rural
	Low income	Central city
		Suburban
		Rural
Light users	**High income**	Central city
		Suburban
		Rural
	Low income	Central city
		Suburban
		Rural
Nonusers	**High income**	Central city
		Suburban
		Rural
	Low income	Central city
		Suburban
		Rural

Source: Fred Winter, "Market Segmentation: A Tactical Approach," *Business Horizons* (January–February 1984): 60, 61.

market segments separately, however, can allow hotel firms to predict overall supply and demand more effectively.

More and more, banks are segmenting markets to increase effectiveness. "You're dead in the water if you aren't segmenting the market," says Anne Moore, president of a bank consulting firm in Atlanta. NCNB Corporation recently announced its Financial Connections program for young adults starting careers. Barnett Banks in Florida offers its Senior Partners Program for different segments of the elderly, based on various lifestyles.

PRODUCT POSITIONING   After segmenting markets so that the firm can target particular customer groups, the next step is to find out what customers want and expect. This takes analysis and research. A severe mistake is to assume the firm knows what customers want and expect. Countless research studies reveal large differences between how customers define service and rank the importance of different service activities and how producers view services. Many firms have become successful by filling the gap between what customers and producers see as good service. What the customer believes is good service is paramount, not what the producer believes service should be.

Identifying target customers upon whom to focus marketing efforts sets the stage for deciding how to meet the needs and wants of particular consumer groups. *Product positioning* is widely used for this purpose. Positioning entails developing schematic representations that reflect how your products or services compare to competitors' on dimensions most important to success in the industry. The following steps are required in product positioning:

1. Select key criteria that effectively differentiate products or services in the industry.
2. Diagram a two-dimensional product positioning map with specified criteria on each axis.
3. Plot major competitors' products or services in the resultant four-quadrant matrix.
4. Identify areas in the positioning map where the company's products or services could be most competitive in the given target market. Look for vacant areas (niches).
5. Develop a marketing plan to position the company's products or services appropriately.

FIGURE 8–3
Examples of Product Positioning Maps

A. **A PRODUCT POSITIONING MAP FOR BANKS**

B. **A PRODUCT POSITIONING MAP FOR PERSONAL COMPUTERS**

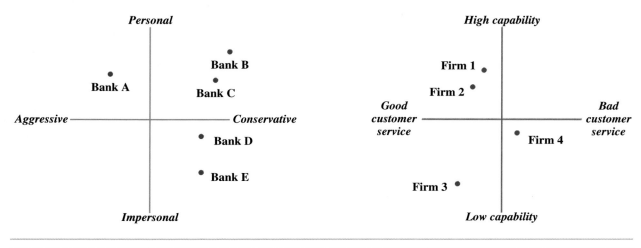

C. **A PRODUCT POSITIONING MAP FOR MENSWEAR RETAIL STORES**

D. **A PRODUCT POSITIONING MAP FOR THE RENTAL CAR MARKET**

Because just two criteria can be examined on a single product positioning map, multiple maps are often developed to assess various approaches to strategy implementation. *Multidimensional scaling* could be used to examine three or more criteria simultaneously, but this technique requires computer assistance and is beyond the scope of this text. Some examples of product positioning maps are illustrated in Figure 8–3.

Some rules of thumb for using product positioning as a strategy-implementation tool are the following:

1. Look for the hole or *vacant niche*. The best strategic opportunity might be an unserved segment.

2. Don't squat between segments. Any advantage from squatting (such as a larger target market) is offset by a failure to satisfy one segment. In decision-theory terms, the intent here is to avoid suboptimization by trying to serve more than one objective function.

3. Don't serve two segments with the same strategy. Usually, a strategy successful with one segment cannot be directly transferred to another segment.

4. Don't position yourself in the middle of the map. The middle usually means a strategy that is not clearly perceived to have any distinguishing characteristics. This rule can vary with the number of competitors. For example, when there are only two competitors, as in U.S. presidential elections, the middle becomes the preferred strategic position.[3]

One firm that uses product positioning effectively is Bristol-Myers Squibb Japan. This pharmaceutical giant recently began marketing Paraplatin, an anticancer drug that has few or no side effects, in Japan. Medical doctors in Japan usually conceal knowledge of a cancer diagnosis from a patient; therefore, Paraplatin is a favored cancer drug among the Japanese.

An effective product positioning strategy meets two criteria: (1) it uniquely distinguishes a company from the competition, and (2) it leads customers to expect slightly less service than a company can deliver. Firms should not create expectations that exceed the service the firm can or will deliver. Network Equipment Technology is an example of a company that keeps customer expectations slightly below perceived performance. This is a constant challenge for marketers. Firms need to inform customers about what to expect and then exceed the promise; underpromise and then overdeliver! For multinational firms, this rule of thumb often requires considerable time on the telephone. An alternative to the telephone is the Internet, as evidenced in the Information Technology Perspective.

INFORMATION TECHNOLOGY
Three Ways to Advertise on the Internet

1. ESTABLISH A WORLD WIDE WEB SITE

Example: Aspen Skiing Company (ASC) in Colorado has established a *World Wide Web* page to inform potential customers about its prices and the specifics of rooms and tour packages. ASC's Web page includes weather reports updated daily or even hourly. ASC plans to use the Web's graphical power to show each of its customers the actual room he or she is reserving and the view from that room. Thus, a Web site is an excellent marketing tool for continually updating information (data, text, pictures) available to customers.

2. USE NEWSGROUPS

Example: Harvard Business Service (HBS) is a $2 million firm that provides companies with incorporation services and helps them find venture capital. HBS promotes itself by posting catchy one-page advertisements in scores of Internet newsgroups, especially business and entrepreneurial *newsgroups*. Some Internet newsgroups do not accept advertisements, but many do, such as the ones found at alt.business.misc and biz.misc. HBS also finds clients by reading posted inquiries in newsgroups on the Internet. HBS's fees to use the Internet newsgroups are about $300 monthly, paid to Prodigy, CompuServe, America Online, and NetCom. HBS's top manager says, "Is it worth it? Yes. Our volume has doubled in a year. The Internet is a way to reach millions of people, and it's very cost-effective. I don't know how we ever did things before." You may visit HBS by e-mail at hbs@reply.net.

3. USE E-MAIL

Example: Sending *e-mail* is free, except for online time, typically about $2 an hour. In contrast, regular mail can be tremendously expensive. An adventure-travel company named Mountain Travel-Sobek (MTS) uses e-mail to distribute its four-page brochure called *Hot News*. This is a weekly online publication developed and sent by MTS via e-mail to 1,500 subscribers. About 77,000 Internet users see *Hot News* monthly at MTS's web site. With $15 million in annual revenues, MTS has offices and guides all over the world. Founding partner Richard Bangs says, "Can you imagine the costs if we tried to send our brochure every week by regular mail? I just push one button, and *Hot News* goes to everybody." Subscribers get MTS's brochure in their e-mail box each week. You can read *Hot News* at http://www.mtspbek.com.

Source: Adapted from Rusty Weston, "Five Ways to do Business on the Internet," *Inc. Technology* (1995), no. 3: 75–7.

FINANCE/ACCOUNTING ISSUES

In this section, we examine several finance/accounting concepts considered to be central to strategy implementation: acquiring needed capital, developing pro forma financial statements, preparing financial budgets, and evaluating the worth of a business. Some examples of decisions that may require finance/accounting policies are:

1. To raise capital with short-term debt, long-term debt, preferred stock, or common stock.
2. To lease or buy fixed assets.
3. To determine an appropriate dividend payout ratio.
4. To use LIFO, FIFO, or a market-value accounting approach.
5. To extend the time of accounts receivable.
6. To establish a certain percentage discount on accounts within a specified period of time.
7. To determine the amount of cash that should be kept on hand.

ACQUIRING CAPITAL TO IMPLEMENT STRATEGIES   Successful strategy implementation often requires additional capital. Besides net profit from operations and the sale of assets, two basic sources of capital for an organization are debt and equity. Determining an appropriate mix of debt and equity in a firm's capital structure can be vital to successful strategy implementation. *An Earnings Per Share/Earnings Before Interest and Taxes (EPS/EBIT)* analysis is the most widely used technique for determining whether debt, stock, or a combination of debt and stock is the best alternative for raising capital to implement strategies. This technique involves an examination of the impact that debt versus stock financing has on earnings per share, under various assumptions as to EBIT.

Theoretically, an enterprise should have enough debt in its capital structure to boost its return on investment by applying debt to products and projects earning more than the cost of the debt. In low earning periods too much debt in the capital structure of an organization can endanger stockholders' return and jeopardize company survival. Fixed debt obligations generally must be met, regardless of circumstances. This does not mean that stock issuances are always better than debt for raising capital. Some special concerns with stock issuances are dilution of ownership, effect on stock price, and the need to share future earnings with all new shareholders.

In the 1990s, interest rates were low, yet stock issuances remained very popular for the purpose of paying off corporate debt. Kmart is one firm that issued new stock worth over $1 billion to reduce its debt. Sony Corporation also raised nearly $3 billion by selling new shares of stock to reduce the company's debt. The lingerie maker Warnaco Group, which accounts for 30 percent of the women's bra market in the United States, recently sold 6 million shares to the public to reduce its debt.

Without going into detail on other institutional and legal issues related to the debt versus stock decision, EPS/EBIT may be best explained by working through an example. Let's say the Brown Company needs to raise $1 million to finance implementation of a market-development strategy. The company's common stock currently sells for $50 per share, and 100,000 shares are outstanding. The prime interest rate is 10 percent and the company's tax rate is 50 percent. The company's earnings before interest and taxes (EBIT) next year are expected to be $2 million if a recession occurs, $4 million if the economy stays as is, and $8 million if the economy significantly improves. *EPS/EBIT analysis* can be used to determine if all stock, all debt, or some combination of stock and debt is the best capital financing alternative. The EPS/EBIT analysis for this example is provided in Table 8–3.

FIGURE 8–4

An EPS/EBIT Chart for the Brown Company

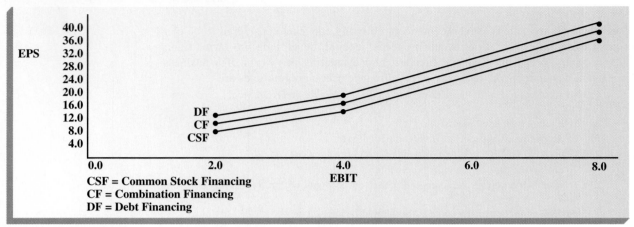

CSF = Common Stock Financing
CF = Combination Financing
DF = Debt Financing

TABLE 8–3

EPS/EBIT Analysis for the Brown Company (in millions)

	COMMON STOCK FINANCING			DEBT FINANCING			COMBINATION FINANCING		
	RECESSION	**NORMAL**	**BOOM**	**RECESSION**	**NORMAL**	**BOOM**	**RECESSION**	**NORMAL**	**BOOM**
EBIT	$2.0	$ 4.0	$ 8.0	$2.0	$ 4.0	$ 8.0	$2.0	$ 4.0	$ 8.0
Interest[a]	0.0	0.0	0.0	.10	.10	.10	.05	.05	.05
EBT	2.0	4.0	8.0	1.9	3.9	7.9	1.95	3.95	7.95
Taxes	1.0	2.0	4.0	.95	1.95	3.95	.975	1.975	3.975
EAT	1.0	2.0	4.0	.95	1.95	3.95	.975	1.975	3.975
#Shares[b]	.12	.12	.12	.10	.10	.10	.11	.11	.11
EPS[c]	8.33	16.66	33.33	9.5	19.50	39.50	8.86	17.95	36.14

[a]The annual interest charge on $1 million at 10% is $100,000 and on $0.5 million is $50,000. This row is in $, not %.
[b]To raise all of the needed $1 million with stock, 20,000 new shares must be issued, raising the total to 120,000 shares outstanding. To raise one-half of the needed $1 million with stock, 10,000 new shares must be issued, raising the total to 110,000 shares outstanding.
[c]EPS = Earnings After Taxes (EAT) divided by (Number of shares outstanding).

As indicated by the EPS values of 9.5, 19.50, and 39.50 in Table 8–3, debt is the best financing alternative for the Brown Company if a recession, boom, or normal year is expected. An EPS/EBIT chart can be constructed to determine the break-even point, where one financing alternative becomes more attractive than another. Figure 8–4 indicates that issuing common stock is the least attractive financing alternative for the Brown Company.

EPS/EBIT analysis is a valuable tool for making capital financing decisions needed to implement strategies, but several considerations should be made whenever using this technique. First, profit levels may be higher for stock or debt alternatives when EPS levels are lower. For example, looking only at the earnings after taxes (EAT) values in Table 8–3, the common stock option is the best alternative, regardless of economic conditions. If the Brown Company's mission includes strict profit maximization, as opposed to the maximization of stockholders' wealth or some other criterion, then stock rather than debt is the best choice of financing.

Another consideration when using EPS/EBIT analysis is flexibility. As an organization's capital structure changes, so does its flexibility for considering future capital needs. Using all debt or all stock to raise capital in the present may impose fixed obligations, restrictive covenants, or other constraints that could severely reduce a firm's ability to raise additional capital in the future. Control is also a concern. When additional stock is issued to finance strategy implementation, ownership and control of the enterprise are diluted. This can be a serious concern in today's business environment of hostile takeovers, mergers, and acquisitions. Also, dilution of ownership can be an overriding concern in closely held corporations, where stock issuances affect the decision-making power of majority stockholders. For example, the Smucker family owns 30 percent of the stock in Smucker's, a well-known jam and jelly company. When Smucker's acquired Dickson Family, Inc., the company used mostly debt rather than stock in order not to dilute the family ownership.

When using EPS/EBIT analysis, timing in relation to movements of stock prices, interest rates, and bond prices becomes important. In times of depressed stock prices, debt may prove to be the most suitable alternative from both a cost and a demand standpoint. However, when cost of capital (interest rates) is high, stock issuances become more attractive. In fact, even when interest rates are low, as in 1993, stock issuances can be very popular. The explosion of new mergers and acquisitions in 1993–1997 was fueled by equity, a time when stock prices were high. Using stock for acquisitions rather than debt enhances a firm's reported earnings because, unlike debt acquirers, stock acquirers do not have to deduct goodwill from their earnings for years to come.

PRO FORMA FINANCIAL STATEMENTS *Pro forma (projected) financial statement analysis* is a central strategy-implementation technique because it allows an organization to examine the expected results of various actions and approaches. This type of analysis can be used to forecast the impact of various implementation decisions (for example, to increase promotion expenditures by 50 percent to support a market-development strategy, to increase salaries by 25 percent to support a market-penetration strategy, to increase research and development expenditures by 70 percent to support product development, or to sell $1 million of common stock to raise capital for diversification). Nearly all financial institutions require at least three years of projected financial statements whenever a business seeks capital. A pro forma income statement and balance sheet allow an organization to compute projected financial ratios under various strategy-implementation scenarios. When compared to prior years and to industry averages, financial ratios provide valuable insights into the feasibility of various strategy-implementation approaches.

A 1998 pro forma income statement and balance sheet for the Litten Company are provided in Table 8–4. The pro forma statements for Litten are based on five assumptions: (1) The company needs to raise $45 million to finance expansion into foreign markets; (2) $30 million of this total will be raised through increased debt and $15 million through common stock; (3) sales are expected to increase 50 percent; (4) three new facilities, costing a total of $30 million, will be constructed in foreign markets; and (5) land for the new facilities is already owned by the company. Note in Table 8–4 that Litten's strategies and their implementation are expected to result in a sales increase from $100 million to $150 million and in a net increase in income from $6 million to $9.75 million, in the forecasted year.

There are six steps in performing pro forma financial analysis:

1. Prepare the pro forma income statement before the balance sheet. Start by forecasting sales as accurately as possible.
2. Use the percentage-of-sales method to project cost-of-goods-sold (CGS) and the expense items in the income statement. For example, if CGS is 70 percent of sales in the prior year (as it is in Table 8–4), then use that same percentage to calculate CGS in the future year— unless there is a reason to use a different percentage. Items such as interest, dividends, and taxes must be treated independently and cannot be forecasted using the percentage-of-sales method.
3. Calculate the projected net income.

TABLE 8–4

A Pro Forma Income Statement and Balance Sheet for the Litten Company (in millions)

	PRIOR YEAR 1997	PROJECTED YEAR 1998	REMARKS
PRO FORMA INCOME STATEMENT			
Sales	100	150.00	50% increase
Cost of Goods Sold	70	105.00	70% of sales
Gross Margin	30	45.00	
Selling Expense	10	15.00	10% of sales
Administrative Expense	5	7.50	5% of sales
Earnings Before Interest and Taxes	15	22.50	
Interest	3	3.00	
Earnings Before Taxes	12	19.50	
Taxes	6	9.75	50% rate
Net Income	6	9.75	
Dividends	2	5.00	
Retained Earnings	4	4.75	
PRO FORMA BALANCE SHEET			
Assets			
Cash	5	7.75	Plug figure
Accounts Receivable	2	4.00	Incr. 100%
Inventory	20	45.00	
Total Current Assets	27	56.75	
Land	15	15.00	
Plant and Equipment	50	80.00	Add 3 new plants at $10 million each
Less Depreciation	10	20.00	
Net Plant and Equipment	40	60.00	
Total Fixed Assets	55	75.00	
Total Assets	82	131.75	
Liabilities			
Accounts Payable	10	10.00	
Notes Payable	10	10.00	
Total Current Liabilities	20	20.00	
Long-term Debt	40	70.00	Borrowed $30 million
Additional Paid-in Capital	20	35.00	Issued 100,000 shares at $150 each
Retained Earnings	2	6.75	2 + 4.75
Total Liabilities and New Worth	82	131.75	

4. Subtract from the net income any dividends to be paid and add the remaining net income to Retained Earnings. Reflect the Retained Earnings total on both the income statement and balance sheet, because this item is the key link between the two projected statements.

5. Project the balance sheet items, beginning with *retained earnings* and then forecasting stockholders' equity, long-term liabilities, current liabilities, total liabilities, total assets, fixed assets, and current assets (in that order). Use the cash account as the plug figure; that is, use the cash account to make the assets total the liabilities. Then, make appropriate adjustments. For example, if the cash needed to balance the statements is too small (or too large), make appropriate changes to borrow more (or less) money than planned.

6. List comments (remarks) on the projected statements. Any time a significant change is made in an item from a prior year to the projected year, an explanation (remark) should be provided. Remarks are essential because otherwise pro formas are meaningless.

TABLE 8–5
A Six-month Cash Budget for the Toddler Toy Company in 1998

CASH BUDGET (IN THOUSANDS)	JULY	AUG	SEPT.	OCT.	NOV.	DEC.	JAN.
Receipts							
Collections	$12,000	$21,000	$31,000	$35,000	$22,000	$18,000	$11,000
Payments							
Purchases	14,000	21,000	28,000	14,000	14,000	7,000	
Wages and Salaries	1,500	2,000	2,500	1,500	1,500	1,000	
Rent	500	500	500	500	500	500	
Other Expenses	200	300	400	200	200	100	
Taxes	–	8,000	–	–	–	–	
Payment on Machine	–	–	10,000	–	–	–	
Total Payments	$16,200	$31,800	$41,400	$16,200	$16,200	$ 8,600	
Net Cash Gain (Loss) During Month	−4,200	−10,800	−10,400	18,800	5,800	9,400	
Cash at Start of Month If No Borrowing Is Done	6,000	1,800	−9,000	−19,400	−600	5,200	
Cumulative Cash (Cash at start plus gains or minus losses)	1,800	−9,000	−19,400	−600	5,200	14,600	
Less Desired Level of Cash	−5,000	−5,000	−5,000	−5,000	−5,000	−5,000	
Total Loans Outstanding to Maintain $5,000 Cash Balance	$3,200	$14,000	$24,400	$ 5,600	–	–	
Surplus Cash	–	–	–	–	$ 200	$ 9,600	

FINANCIAL BUDGETS A *financial budget* is a document that details how funds will be obtained and spent for a specified period of time. Annual budgets are most common, although the period of time for a budget can range from one day to more than 10 years. Fundamentally, financial budgeting is a method for specifying what must be done to complete strategy implementation successfully. Financial budgeting should not be thought of as a tool for limiting expenditures but rather as a method for obtaining the most productive and profitable use of an organization's resources. Financial budgets can be viewed as the planned allocation of a firm's resources, based on forecasts of the future.

There are almost as many different types of financial budgets as there are types of organizations. Some common types of budgets include cash budgets, operating budgets, sales budgets, profit budgets, factory budgets, capital budgets, expense budgets, divisional budgets, variable budgets, flexible budgets, and fixed budgets. When an organization is experiencing financial difficulties, budgets are especially important in guiding strategy implementation.

Perhaps the most common type of financial budget is the *cash budget*. The Financial Accounting Standards Board has mandated that every publicly held company in the United States must issue an annual cash-flow statement in addition to the usual financial reports. The statement includes all receipts and disbursements of cash in operations, investments, and financing. It supplements the Statement on Changes in Financial Position formerly included in the annual reports of all publicly held companies. A 1998 cash budget for the Toddler Toy Company is provided in Table 8–5. Note that Toddler is not expecting to have surplus cash until November of 1998.

Financial budgets have some limitations. First, budgetary programs can become so detailed that they are cumbersome and overly expensive. Overbudgeting or underbudgeting can cause problems. Second, financial budgets can become a substitute for objectives. A budget is a tool and not an end in itself. Third, budgets can hide inefficiencies if based solely on precedent rather than periodic evaluation of circumstances and standards. Finally, budgets are sometimes used as instruments of tyranny that result in frustration, resentment, absenteeism, and high turnover. To minimize the effect of this last concern, managers should increase the participation of subordinates in preparing budgets.

EVALUATING THE WORTH OF A BUSINESS   Evaluating the worth of a business is central to strategy implementation because integrative, intensive, and diversification strategies are often implemented by acquiring other firms. Other strategies, such as retrenchment and divestiture, may result in the sale of a division of an organization, or of the firm itself. Approximately 12,000 transactions occur each year in which businesses are bought or sold in the United States. In all these cases, it is necessary to establish the financial worth or cash value of a business to successfully implement strategies.

All the various methods for determining a business's worth can be grouped into three main approaches: what a firm owns, what a firm earns, or what a firm will bring in the market. But it is important to realize that valuation is not an exact science. The valuation of a firm's worth is based on financial facts, but common sense and intuitive judgment must enter into the process. It is difficult to assign a monetary value to such factors as a loyal customer base, a history of growth, legal suits pending, dedicated employees, a favorable lease, a bad credit rating, or good patents, which may not be reflected in a firm's financial statements. Also, different valuation methods will yield different totals for a firm's worth, and no prescribed approach is best for a certain situation. Evaluating the worth of a business truly requires both qualitative and quantitative skills.

The first approach in evaluating the worth of a business is determining its net worth or stockholders' equity. Net worth represents the sum of common stock, additional paid-in capital, and retained earnings. After calculating net worth, add or subtract an appropriate amount for goodwill (such as high customer loyalty) and overvalued or undervalued assets. This total provides a reasonable estimate of a firm's monetary value. If a firm has goodwill, it will be listed on the balance sheet, perhaps being called intangibles.

The second approach to measuring the value of a firm grows out of the belief that the worth of any business should be based largely on the future benefits its owners may derive through net profits. A conservative rule of thumb is to establish a business's worth as five times the firm's current annual profit. A five-year average profit level could also be used. When using this approach, remember that firms normally suppress earnings in their financial statements to minimize taxes.

The third approach, letting the market determine a business's worth, involves three methods. First, base the firm's worth on the selling price of a similar company. A potential problem, however, is that sometimes comparable figures are not easy to locate, even though substantial information on firms that buy or sell to other firms is available in major libraries. The second approach is called the *price-earnings ratio method.* To use this method, divide the market price of the firm's common stock by the annual earnings per share and multiply this number by the firm's average net income for the past five years. The third approach can be called the *outstanding shares method.* To use this method, simply multiply the number of shares outstanding by the market price per share and add a premium. The premium is simply a per share dollar amount that a person or firm is willing to pay to control (acquire) the other company.

Business evaluations are becoming routine in many situations. Businesses have many strategy-implementation reasons for determining their worth in addition to preparing to be sold or to buy other companies. Employee plans, taxes, retirement, mergers, acquisitions, expansion plans, banking relationships, death of a principal, divorce, partnership agreements, and IRS audits are other reasons for a periodic valuation. It is just good business to have a reasonable understanding of what your firm is worth. This knowledge protects the interests of all parties involved.

DECIDING WHETHER TO GO PUBLIC   Going public means selling off a percentage of your company to others in order to raise capital; consequently, it dilutes the owners' control of the firm. Going public is not recommended for companies with less than $10 million in sales because the initial costs can be too high for the firm to generate sufficient cash flow to make going public worthwhile. One dollar in four is the average total cost paid to lawyers, accountants, and underwriters when an initial stock issuance is under $1 million; one dollar in twenty will go to cover these costs for issuances over $20 million.

In addition to initial costs involved with a stock offering, there are additional costs and obligations associated with reporting and management in a publicly held firm. For firms larger than $10 million in sales, going public can provide major advantages; it can allow the firm to raise capital to develop new products, build plants, expand, grow, and market products and services more effectively.

Before going public, a firm must have quality management with a proven track record for achieving quality earnings and positive cash flow. The company also should enjoy growing demand for its products. Sales growth of about 5 or 6 percent a year is good for a private firm, but shareholders expect public companies to grow around 10 to 15 percent per year.

RESEARCH AND DEVELOPMENT (R&D) ISSUES

Research and development (R&D) personnel can play an integral part in strategy implementation. These individuals are generally charged with developing new products and improving old products in a way that will allow effective strategy implementation. R&D employees and managers perform tasks that include transferring complex technology, adjusting processes to local raw materials, adapting processes to local markets, and altering products to particular tastes and specifications. Strategies such as product development, market penetration, and concentric diversification require that new products be successfully developed and that old products be significantly improved. But the level of management support for R&D is often constrained by resource availability:

> If U.S. business is to maintain its position in the global business environment, then R&D support will have to become a major U.S. commitment. U.S. managers cannot continue to ignore it or take funds away from it for short-term profits and still have long-term strategic options. If one runs away from more aggressive product and process strategies, one should not be surprised by the fact that competitive advantages are lost to foreign competitors.[4]

Technological improvements that affect consumer and industrial products and services shorten product life cycles. Companies in virtually every industry are relying more and more on the development of new products and services to fuel profitability and growth. Table 8–6 provides a breakdown of R&D expenditures in 1994 for the eight American companies that spent the most on R&D. American companies in 1994 increased their R&D expenditures only 4.0 percent.

U.S. companies spend 3.5 percent of sales on R&D, compared to 5.5 percent for Japanese firms, 5.4 percent for German firms, 5.2 percent for Canadian firms, 6.3 percent for Swiss firms, and 5.8 percent for Swedish firms. Although U.S. R&D expenditures are below those in many other industrialized countries, there are wide variations among companies.

Surveys suggest that the most successful organizations use an R&D strategy that ties external opportunities to internal strength and is linked with objectives. Well-formulated R&D policies match market opportunities with internal capabilities and provide an initial screen to all ideas generated. R&D policies can enhance strategy-implementation efforts to

TABLE 8–6
Ranking the Top Eight American Companies in R&D Spending in 1994

COMPANY	IN TOTAL DOLLARS (MILLIONS)
1. General Motors	$7,036
2. Ford Motor	5,214
3. IBM	3,382
4. AT&T	3,110
5. Hewlett-Packard	2,027
6. Motorola	1,860
7. Boeing	1,704
8. Digital Equipment	1,301

Source: Adapted from *Business Week* (July 3, 1995): 79.

1. Emphasize product or process improvements.
2. Stress basic or applied research.
3. Be leaders or followers in R&D.
4. Develop robotics or manual-type processes.
5. Spend a high, average, or low amount of money on R&D.
6. Perform R&D within the firm or to contract R&D to outside firms.
7. Use university researchers or private-sector researchers.

There must be effective interactions between R&D departments and other functional departments in implementing different types of generic business strategies. Conflicts between marketing, finance/accounting, R&D, and information systems departments can be minimized with clear policies and objectives. Table 8–7 gives some examples of R&D activities that could be required for successful implementation of various strategies.

Many firms wrestle with the decision to acquire R&D expertise from external firms or to develop R&D expertise internally. The following guidelines can be used to help make this decision:

1. If the rate of technical progress is slow, the rate of market growth is moderate, and there are significant barriers to possible new entrants, then in-house R&D is the preferred solution. The reason is that R&D, if successful, will result in a temporary product or process monopoly that the company can exploit.
2. If technology is changing rapidly and the market is growing slowly, then a major effort in R&D may be very risky, because it may lead to development of an ultimately obsolescent technology or one for which there is no market.
3. If technology is changing slowly but the market is growing fast, there generally is not enough time for in-house development. The prescribed approach is to obtain R&D expertise on an exclusive or nonexclusive basis from an outside firm.
4. If both technical progress and market growth are fast, R&D expertise should be obtained through acquisition of a well-established firm in the industry.[5]

There are at least three major R&D approaches for implementing strategies. The first strategy is to be the first firm to market new technological products. This is a glamorous and exciting strategy but also a dangerous one. Firms such as 3M, Polaroid, and General Electric have been successful with this approach, but many other pioneering firms have fallen, with rival firms seizing the initiative. Two firms also using this first R&D strategy are Global Ozone Solutions and American Thermalfo; these firms manufacture machines that extract ozone-depleting chlorofluorocarbons, or CFCs, from the air. As indicated in the Natural Environment Perspective, Eastern European cities such as Prague could use these products.

A second R&D approach is to be an innovative imitator of successful products, thus minimizing the risks and costs of start-up. This approach entails allowing a pioneer firm to develop the first version of the new product and to demonstrate that a market exists. Then,

NATURAL ENVIRONMENT

Doing Business in Eastern Europe and the Former Soviet Republics

The new democratic governments of Eastern Europe and the former Soviet Union recently discovered and reported that decades of atrocities have been committed against the natural environments in their countries. Polluted air and water know no country boundaries, so Western Europe, and indeed the whole earth, has suffered and continues to suffer from environmental destruction in Eastern Europe and Asia.

U.S. firms planning expansion into Eastern Europe and Asia must be careful not to further harm the natural environment in those countries. Firms also must be careful where they locate within these countries because the incidence of diseases such as cancer, typhoid fever, asthma, leukemia, hypertension, pneumonia, bronchitis, and tuberculosis is especially high in some areas.

U.S. firms must make the natural environment a strategic issue and concern when doing business internationally (and domestically). Consider the following facts regarding the natural environment in Eastern Europe and the former Soviet republics:

- Ninety percent of the Black Sea is biologically dead due to industrial wastes pouring in from the Danube and Dnieper rivers.
- Eighty percent of the Baltic Sea is biologically dead due to organic wastes being dumped by Poland, Eastern Germany, and the former Soviet republics.
- The Caspian Sea receives 40 percent of 28.6 cubic kilometers of polluted wastewater annually, most of it from the Volga River.
- Many large cities in the former Soviet republics, including Kaunasin, Lithuania, and Riga, have no sewage treatment facilities at all.
- The largest body of fresh water in the world, Lake Baikal in Asia, is nearly biologically dead after years of industrial pollution and agricultural runoff.

- In Prague, Czechoslovakia, the average annual concentration of sulfur dioxide in the air is 155 micrograms per cubic meter; any level over 40 is dangerous, according to the World Health Organization (WHO); no U.S. city has a level over 20.
- Pesticide poisonings in the former Soviet republics kill 14,000 people annually and cause an additional 700,000 illnesses.
- The Elbe River carries 10 tons of mercury, 24 tons of cadmium, and 142 tons of lead to the North Sea annually.

Source: Adapted from Hilary French, "Green Revolutions: Environmental Reconstruction in Eastern Europe and the Soviet Union," *Columbia Journal of World Business* (Spring 1991): 28–46.

laggard firms develop a similar product. This strategy requires excellent R&D personnel and an excellent marketing department.

A third R&D strategy is to be a low-cost producer by mass-producing products similar to but less expensive than products recently introduced. Far Eastern countries used this approach effectively during the 1980s to crush the $8 billion U.S. consumer electronics industry. As a new product is accepted by more and more customers, price becomes increasingly important in the buying decision. Also, mass marketing replaces personal selling as the dominant selling strategy. This R&D strategy requires substantial investment in plant and equipment, but fewer expenditures in R&D than the two approaches described earlier.

TABLE 8–7

Research and Development Involvement in Selected Strategy-implementation Situations

TYPE OF ORGANIZATION	STRATEGY BEING IMPLEMENTED	R&D ACTIVITY
Pharmaceutical Company	Product development	Develop a procedure for testing the effects of a new drug on different subgroups.
Boat Manufacturer	Concentric diversification	Develop a procedure to test the performance of various keel designs under various conditions.
Plastic Container Manufacturer	Market penetration	Develop a biodegradable container.
Electronics Company	Market development	Develop a telecommunications system in a foreign country.

R&D activities among American firms need to be more closely aligned to business objectives. There needs to be expanded communication between R&D managers and strategists. Corporations are experimenting with various methods to achieve this improved communication climate, including different roles and reporting arrangements for managers and new methods to reduce the time it takes research ideas to become reality.[6]

COMPUTER INFORMATION SYSTEMS (CIS) ISSUES

Although no firm would use the same marketing or management approach for 20 years, many companies have 20-year-old *information systems* that threaten their very existence. Nevertheless, developing new user applications often takes a backseat to keeping an old system running. This unfortunate situation is happening at a time when the quantity and quality of information available to firms and their competitors is increasing exponentially.

Firms that gather, assimilate, and evaluate external and internal information most effectively are gaining competitive advantages over other firms. Recognizing the importance of having an effective computer information system will not be an option in the future; it will be a requirement. Information is the basis for understanding in a firm. Robert Kavner, president of AT&T Data Systems Group, says, "Modern corporations are organizing around information flow. With the growth of communications networks such as the Internet, the barriers of time and place have been breached. By mirroring people's work needs and habits, networked computing systems have made new modes of work possible."

It is estimated that the quantity of human knowledge is doubling every decade. In many industries, information is becoming the most important factor differentiating successful and unsuccessful firms. The process of strategic management is facilitated immensely in firms that have an effective information system. Many companies are establishing a new approach to information systems, one that blends the technical knowledge of the computer

GLOBAL PERSPECTIVE
Country Commercial Guides

YOUR BEST SOURCE FOR OVERSEAS BUSINESS INFORMATION

The facts you need

Country Commercial Guides (CCGs) provide the facts you need to succeed in more than 100 foreign markets. They are prepared overseas by the agencies of the U.S. Government Trade Promotion Coordinating Committee. Each CCG presents a comprehensive view of a selected country's commercial environment, with up-to-date information on topics of crucial interest to you:

- Market conditions
- Economic situation
- Political environment

- Best export sectors
- Trade regulations
- Business travel
- Investment
- Financing
- Upcoming trade events
- Marketing strategies
- Services for exporters
- U.S. and country contracts

How to order yours

CCGs are available on the National Trade Data Bank (NTDB), the government's complete source of international business information. The NTDB is published monthly on CD ROM and is also accessible via Internet on the World Wide Web at www.stat-usa.gov. To order the NTDB or learn more about the service, call 202-482-1986.

CCGs are also available through the National Technical Information Service (NTIS) electronically and in hard copy. Call 1-800-553-NTIS to order or to request information.

U.S. Department of Commerce •
International Trade Administration

experts with the vision of senior management. Some guidelines that allow computer information systems to enhance strategy implementation are as follows:

1. Computer hardware and software should facilitate global information consistency.
2. All component parts should be accessible through a common order-processing system.
3. All divisions should be self-sufficient yet compatible in their information systems capabilities.
4. A basic purpose of information systems is to support cross-functional integration of the business functions.
5. Integration of voice and data communications is a goal of information systems.
6. Data and information obtained within the firm should be available to any department or person in the firm who can demonstrate a need for it, except for reasons of security or integrity of the database.
7. Information systems design should stress effectiveness in the business environment rather than efficiency in the technical environment.[7]

Information collection, retrieval, and storage can be used to create competitive advantages in ways such as cross-selling to customers, monitoring suppliers, keeping managers and employees informed, coordinating activities among divisions, and managing funds. Like inventory and human resources, information is becoming recognized as a valuable organizational asset that can be controlled and managed. Firms that implement strategies using the best information will reap competitive advantages in the 1990s. John Young, president and CEO of Hewlett-Packard Company, says, "There really isn't any right amount to spend on information systems. Many management teams spend too much time thinking about how to beat down the information system's cost, instead of thinking about how to get more value out of the information they could have available and how to link that to strategic goals of the company."

A good information system can allow a firm to reduce costs. For example, on-line orders from salespersons to production facilities can shorten materials ordering costs and reduce inventory costs. Direct communications between suppliers, manufacturers, marketers, and customers can link elements of the value chain together as though they were one organization. Improved quality and service often result from an improved information system.

Dun & Bradstreet is an example of a company that has an excellent information system. Every D & B customer and client in the world has a separate nine-digit number. The data base of information associated with each number has become so widely used that it is like a business social security number. D & B reaps great competitive advantages from its information system.

As indicated in the Global Perspective, a good information system for a global company should include use of the online Country Commercial Guides (CCGs).

CONCLUSION

Successful strategy implementation depends upon cooperation among all functional and divisional managers in an organization. Marketing departments are commonly charged with implementing strategies that require significant increases in sales revenues in new areas and with new or improved products. Finance and accounting managers must devise effective strategy-implementation approaches at low cost and minimum risk to that firm. R&D managers have to transfer complex technologies or develop new technologies to successfully implement strategies. Information systems managers are being called upon more and more to provide leadership and training for all individuals in the firm. The nature and role of marketing, finance/accounting, R&D, and computer information systems activities, coupled with management activities described in Chapter 7, largely determine organizational success.

TAKE IT TO THE NET

We invite you to visit the DAVID page on the Prentice Hall Web site at:
http://www.prenhall.com/davidsm
for this chapter's World Wide Web exercises.

KEY TERMS AND CONCEPTS

Cash Budget	(p. 260)	Marketing-mix Variables	(p. 252)	Product Positioning	(p. 254)
E-mail	(p. 256)	Multidimensional Scaling	(p.255)	Research and Development	(p. 262)
EPS/EBIT Analysis	(p. 257)	Newsgroups	(p. 256)	Retained Earnings	(p. 260)
Financial Budget	(p. 260)	Outstanding Shares Method	(p. 262)	Vacant Niche	(p. 255)
Information Systems	(p. 265)	Price-earnings Ratio Method	(p. 262)	World Wide Web	(p. 256)
Market Segmentation	(p. 252)	Pro Forma Financial Statement Analysis	(p. 258)		

ISSUES FOR REVIEW AND DISCUSSION

1. Suppose your company has just acquired a firm that produces battery-operated lawn mowers, and strategists want to implement a market-penetration strategy. How would you segment the market for this product? Justify your answer.

2. Explain how you would estimate the total worth of a business.

3. Diagram and label clearly a product positioning map that includes six fast-food restaurants.

4. Explain why EPS/EBIT analysis is a central strategy-implementation technique.

5. How would the R&D role in strategy implementation differ in small versus large organizations?

6. Discuss the limitations of EPS/EBIT analysis.

7. Explain how marketing, finance/accounting, R&D, and computer information systems managers' involvement in strategy formulation can enhance strategy implementation.

8. Is the following statement true or false: "Retained earnings on the balance sheet are not monies available to finance strategy implementation"? Explain.

9. Explain why pro forma financial statement analysis is considered both a strategy-formulation and a strategy-implementation tool.

10. Describe some marketing, finance/accounting, R&D, and computer information systems activities that a small restaurant chain might undertake to expand into a neighboring state.

11. Select one of the suggested readings at the end of this chapter, find that article in your college library, and summarize it in a five-minute oral report for the class.

12. Discuss the computer information systems at your college or university.

NOTES

1. Fred Winter, "Market Segmentation: A Tactical Approach," *Business Horizons* 27, no. 1 (January–February 1984): 59.

2. Jeff Trachtenberg, "The Sweet Smell of Success," *Forbes* (August 10, 1987): 92.

3. Biggadike, 627.

4. Vida Scarpello, William Boulton, and Charles Hofer, "Reintegrating R&D into Business Strategy," *Journal of Business Strategy* 6, no. 4 (Spring 1986): 55.

5. Pier Abetti, "Technology: A Key Strategic Resource," *Management Review* 78, no. 2 (February 1989): 38.

6. William Spencer and Deborah Triant, "Strengthening the Link Between R&D and Corporate Strategy," *Journal of Business Strategy* 10, no. 1 (January/February 1989): 42.

7. Thomas Davenport, Michael Hammer, and Tauno Metsisto, "How Executives Can Shape Their Company's Information Systems," *Harvard Business Review* 67, no. 2 (March–April 1989): 131.

CURRENT READINGS

Anderson, L. McTier. "Marketing Science: Where's the Beef?" *Business Horizons* 37, no. 1 (January–February 1994): 8–16.

Black, J. A. and K. B. Boal. "Strategic Resources: Traits, Configurations and Paths to Sustainable Competitive Advantage." *Strategic Management Journal* 15, Special Issue (Summer 1994): 131–148.

Chi, T. "Trading in Strategic Resources: Necessary Conditions, Transaction Cost Problems, and Choice of Exchange Structure." *Strategic Management Journal* 15, no. 4 (May 1994): 271–290.

Fletcher, Keith, Colin Wheeler and Julia Wright. "Strategic Implementation of Database Marketing: Problems and Pitfalls." *Long Range Planning* 27, no. 00 (February 1994): 133–141.

Kotha, S. "Mass Customization: Implementing the Emerging Paradigm for Competitive Advantage." *Strategic Management Journal* 16, Special Issue (Summer 1995): 21–42.

Markus, M. Lynne and Mark Keil. "If We Build It, They Will Come: Designing Information Systems That People Want to Use." *Sloan Management Review* 35, no. 4 (Summer 1994): 11–26.

McKenna, Regis. "Real-Time Marketing." *Harvard Business Review* 73, no. 4 (July–August 1995): 87–98.

Morris, Michael H. and Leyland F. Pitt. "Implementing Marketing Strategies in the U.S. and South Africa." *Long Range Planning* 27 (February 1994): 56–71.

Pellegrinelli, Sergio and Cliff Bowman. "Implementing Strategy Through Projects." *Long Range Planning* 27, no. 4 (August 1994): 112–124.

Robins, J. and M. F. Wiersema. "A Resource-based Approach to the Multibusiness Firm: Empirical Analysis of Portfolio Interrelationships and Corporate Financial Performance." *Strategic Management Journal* 16, no. 4 (May 1995): 277–300.

Spekman, Robert E., John W. Kamauff, and Deborah J. Salmond. "At Last Purchasing Is Becoming Strategic." *Long Range Planning* 27, no. 2 (April 1994): 76–84.

Topfer, Armin. "New Products—Cutting the Time to Market." *Long Range Planning* 28, no. 2 (April 1995): 61–78.

EXPERIENTIAL EXERCISES

Experiential Exercise 8A

DEVELOPING A PRODUCT POSITIONING MAP FOR HERSHEY FOODS

PURPOSE

Organizations continually monitor how their products and services are positioned relative to competitors.[1] This information is especially useful for marketing managers, but is also used by other managers and strategists.

INSTRUCTIONS

Step 1 On a separate sheet of paper, develop a product positioning map for Hershey. Include Nestlé, Mars, and Hershey in your map.

Step 2 Go to the blackboard and diagram your product positioning map.

Step 3 Compare your product positioning map with those diagrammed by other students. Discuss any major differences.

Experiential Exercise 8B

PERFORMING AN EPS/EBIT ANALYSIS FOR HERSHEY FOODS

PURPOSE

An EPS/EBIT analysis is one of the most widely used techniques for determining the extent that debt and/or stock should be used to finance strategies to be implemented. This exercise can give you practice performing EPS/EBIT analysis.

INSTRUCTIONS

Let's say Hershey considered raising $2 billion to introduce Hershey products in 20 new countries around the world in 1995. Determine whether Hershey should have used all debt, all stock, or a 50–50 combination of debt and stock to finance this market-development strategy. Assume a 44-percent tax rate and an 8-percent interest rate. Hershey's stock price was $50 per share. Hershey paid an annual dividend of $1.25 per share of common stock. The EBIT range for 1995 was between $300 and $500 million. A total of 90 million shares of common stock were outstanding. Develop an EPS/EBIT chart to reflect your analysis.

Experiential Exercise 8C

USING *CASE ANALYST* TO PREPARE PRO FORMA FINANCIAL STATEMENTS FOR HERSHEY FOODS

PURPOSE

This exercise is designed to give you experience preparing pro forma financial statements. Use the *Case Analyst* software if possible. Pro forma analysis is a central strategy-implementation technique because it allows managers to anticipate and evaluate the expected results of various strategy-implementation approaches. This service will give you practice using the *Case Analyst* software.

INSTRUCTIONS

Step 1 Work with a classmate. Develop a 1996 pro forma income statement and balance sheet for Hershey. Assume that Hershey plans to raise $100 million in 1995 to introduce Hershey products in 20 new countries and plans to obtain 50-percent financing from a bank and 50-percent financing from a stock issuance. Make other assumptions as needed, and state them clearly in written form.

Step 2 Load the *Case Analyst* software and develop your pro forma analysis.

Step 3 Compute Hershey's current ratio, debt-to-equity ratio, and return-on-investment ratio for 1993, 1994, and 1995. How do your 1996 projected ratios compare to the 1994 and 1995 ratios? Why is it important to make this comparison?

Step 4 Bring your pro forma printout to class and discuss any problems or questions you encountered in using *Case Analyst*.

Step 5 Compare your pro forma statements to the statements of other students. What major differences exist between your analysis and the work of other students?

Experiential Exercise 8D

DETERMINING THE CASH VALUE OF HERSHEY FOODS

PURPOSE

It is simply good business practice to periodically determine the financial worth or cash value of your company. This exercise gives you practice determining the total worth of a company using several methods. Use 1994 as the sample year.

INSTRUCTIONS

Step 1 Calculate the financial worth of Hershey based on three methods: (1) the net worth or stockholders' equity, (2) the future value of Hershey's earnings, and (3) the price-earnings ratio.

Step 2 In a single dollar amount, how much is Hershey worth?

Step 3 Compare your analyses and conclusions with the work of other students.

Experiential Exercise 8E

DEVELOPING A PRODUCT POSITIONING MAP FOR MY UNIVERSITY

PURPOSE

The purpose of this exercise is to give you practice developing product positioning maps. Nonprofit organizations, such as universities, are more and more using product positioning maps to determine effective ways to implement strategies.

INSTRUCTIONS

Step 1 Join with two other persons in class to form a group of three.

Step 2 Jointly prepare a product positioning map that includes your institution and four other colleges or universities in your state.

Step 3 Go to the blackboard and diagram your product positioning map.

Step 4 Discuss differences among the maps diagrammed on the board.

Experiential Exercise 8F

DO BANKS REQUIRE PRO FORMA STATEMENTS?

PURPOSE

The purpose of this exercise is to explore the practical importance and use of projected financial statements in the banking business.

INSTRUCTIONS

Contact two local bankers by phone and seek answers to the questions listed below. Record the answers you receive and report your findings to the class.

1. Does your bank require projected financial statements as part of a business loan application?
2. How does your bank use projected financial statements when they are part of a business loan application?
3. What special advice do you give potential business borrowers in preparing projected financial statements?

Part 4

STRATEGY
EVALUATION

Strategy Review, Evaluation, and Control

CHAPTER OBJECTIVES

After studying this chapter, you should be able to do the following:

1. Describe a practical framework for evaluating strategies.

2. Explain why strategy evaluation is complex, sensitive, and yet essential for organizational success.

3. Discuss the importance of contingency planning in strategy evaluation.

4. Discuss the role of auditing in strategy evaluation.

5. Explain how computers can aid in evaluating strategies.

Complicated controls do not work. They confuse. They misdirect attention from what is to be controlled to the mechanics and methodology of the control.—SEYMOUR TILLES

Strategic thinking lives through dialogue or dies through writer's cramp.—DAVID MOORE

Although Plan A may be selected as the most realistic . . . the other major alternatives should not be forgotten. They may well serve as contingency plans.—DALE McCONKEY

Organizations are most vulnerable when they are at the peak of their success.—R. T. LENZ

As spans of control widen, computers will become even more necessary.—BRIAN DUMAINE

Strategy evaluation must make it as easy as possible for managers to revise their plans and reach quick agreement on the changes.—DALE McCONKEY

While strategy is a word that is usually associated with the future, its link to the past is no less central. Life is lived forward but understood backward. Managers may live strategy in the future, but they understand it through the past.—HENRY MINTZBERG

Unless strategy evaluation is performed seriously and systematically, and unless strategists are willing to act on the results, energy will be used up defending yesterday. No one will have the time, resources, or will to work on exploiting today, let alone to work on making tomorrow.—PETER DRUCKER

I have a duty to the soldiers, their parents, and the country, to remove immediately any commander who does not satisfy the highest performance demands. It is a mistake to put a person in a command that is not the right command. It is therefore my job to think through where that person belongs.
—GEORGE C. MARSHALL

*T*he best-formulated and -implemented strategies become obsolete as a firm's external and internal environments change. It is essential, therefore, that strategists systematically review, evaluate, and control the execution of strategies. This chapter presents a framework that can guide managers' efforts to evaluate strategic-management activities, to make sure they are working, and to make timely changes. Computer information systems being used to evaluate strategies are discussed. Guidelines are presented for formulating, implementing, and evaluating strategies.

THE NATURE OF STRATEGY EVALUATION

The strategic-management process results in decisions that can have significant, long-lasting consequences. Erroneous strategic decisions can inflict severe penalties and can be exceedingly difficult, if not impossible, to reverse. Most strategists agree, therefore, that strategy evaluation is vital to an organization's well-being; timely evaluations can alert management to problems or potential problems before a situation becomes critical. Strategy evaluation includes three basic activities: (1) examining the underlying bases of a firm's strategy, (2) comparing expected results with actual results, and (3) taking corrective actions to ensure that performance conforms to plans. The strategy-evaluation stage of the strategic-management process is illustrated in Figure 9–1.

Adequate and timely feedback is the cornerstone of effective strategy evaluation. Strategy evaluation can be no better than the information on which it operates. Too much pressure from top managers may result in lower managers contriving numbers they think will be satisfactory.

Strategy evaluation can be a complex and sensitive undertaking. Too much emphasis on evaluating strategies may be expensive and counterproductive. No one likes to be evaluated too closely! The more managers attempt to evaluate the behavior of others, the less control they have. Yet, too little or no evaluation can create even worse problems. Strategy evaluation is essential to ensure that stated objectives are being achieved.

In many organizations, strategy evaluation is simply an appraisal of how well an organization has performed. Have the firm's assets increased? Has there been an increase in profitability? Have sales increased? Have productivity levels increased? Have profit margin, return on investment, and earnings-per-share ratios increased? Some firms argue that their strategy must have been correct if the answers to these types of questions are affirmative. Well, the strategy or strategies may have been correct, but this type of reasoning can be misleading, because strategy evaluation must have both a long-run and short-run focus. Strategies often do not affect short-term operating results until it is too late to make needed changes.

It is impossible to demonstrate conclusively that a particular strategy is optimal or even to guarantee that it will work. One can, however, evaluate it for critical flaws. Richard Rumelt offers four criteria that could be used to evaluate a strategy: consistency, consonance, advantage, and feasibility. Described in Table 9–1, *consonance* and *advantage* are mostly based on a firm's external assessment, whereas *consistency* and *feasibility* are largely based on an internal assessment.

Strategy evaluation is important because organizations face dynamic environments in which key external and internal factors often change quickly and dramatically. Success today is no guarantee for success tomorrow! An organization should never be lulled into complacency with success. Countless firms have thrived one year only to struggle for survival the following year. For example, Digital Equipment's profits dropped in 1994 to negative $2.16 billion. Other companies that experienced net profit losses in excess of $1 billion in

FIGURE 9-1

A Comprehensive Strategic-Management Model

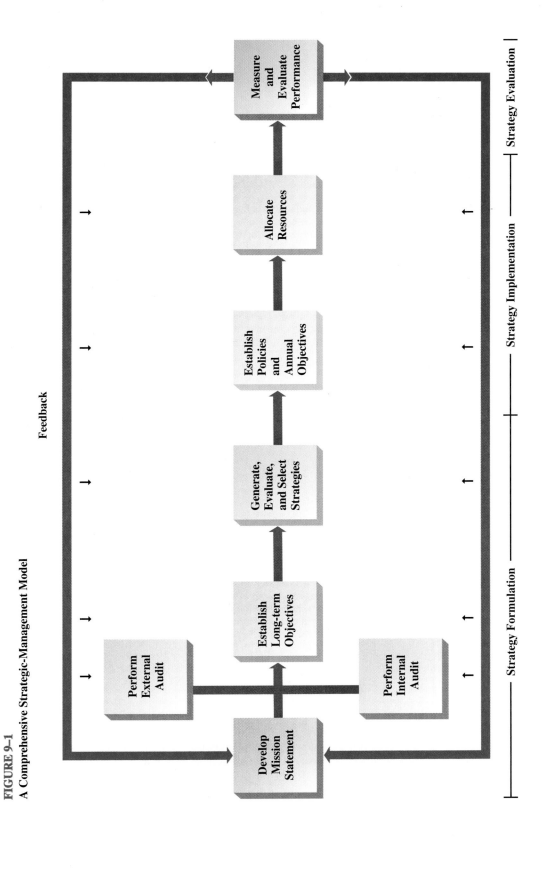

TABLE 9–1
Rumelt's Criteria for Evaluating Strategies

CONSISTENCY

A strategy should not present inconsistent goals and policies. Organizational conflict and interdepartmental bickering are often symptoms of a managerial disorder, but these problems may also be a sign of strategic inconsistency. Rumelt offers three guidelines to help determine if organizational problems are due to inconsistencies in strategy.

- If managerial problems continue despite changes in personnel, and if they tend to be issue-based rather than people-based, then strategies may be inconsistent.
- If success for one organizational department means, or is interpreted to mean, failure for another department, then strategies may be inconsistent.
- If policy problems and issues continue to be brought to the top for resolution, then strategies may be inconsistent.

CONSONANCE

Consonance refers to the need for strategies to examine *sets of trends* as well as individual trends in evaluating strategies. A strategy must represent an adaptive response to the external environment and to the critical changes occurring within it. One difficulty in matching a firm's key internal and external factors in the formulation of strategy is that most trends are the result of interactions among other trends. For example, the day care explosion came about as a combined result of many trends that included a rise in the average level of education, increased inflation, and an increase in women in the work force. Thus, while single economic or demographic trends might appear steady for many years, there are waves of change going on at the interaction level.

FEASIBILITY

A strategy must neither overtax available resources nor create unsolvable subproblems. The final broad test of strategy is its feasibility; that is, can the strategy be attempted within the physical, human, and financial resources of the enterprise? The financial resources of a business are the easiest to quantify and are normally the first limitation against which strategy is evaluated. It is sometimes forgotten, however, that innovative approaches to financing are often possible. Devices such as captive finance subsidiaries, sale-leaseback arrangements, and tying plant mortgages to long-term contracts have all been used effectively to help win key positions in suddenly expanding industries. A less quantifiable, but actually more rigid, limitation on strategic choice is that imposed by individual and organizational capabilities. In evaluating a strategy, it is important to examine whether an organization has demonstrated in the past that it possesses the abilities, competencies, skills, and talents needed to carry out a given strategy.

ADVANTAGE

A strategy must provide for the creation and/or maintenance of a competitive advantage in a selected area of activity. Competitive advantages normally are the result of superiority in one of three areas: 1) resources, 2) skills, or 3) position. The idea that the positioning of one's resources can enhance their combined effectiveness is familiar to military theorists, chess players, and diplomats. Position can also play a crucial role in an organization's strategy. Once gained, a good position is defensible—meaning so costly to capture that rivals are deterred from full-scale attacks. Positional advantage tends to be self-sustaining, as long as the key internal and environmental factors that underlie it remain stable. This is why entrenched firms can be almost impossible to unseat, even if their raw skill levels are only average. Although not all positional advantages are associated with size, it is true that larger organizations tend to operate in markets and use procedures that turn their size into advantage, while smaller firms seek product/ market positions that exploit other types of advantage. The principal characteristics of good position is that it permits the firm to obtain advantage from policies that would not similarly benefit rivals without the same position. Therefore, in evaluating strategy, organizations should examine the nature of positional advantages associated with a given strategy.

Source: Adapted from Richard Rumelt, "The Evaluation of Business Strategy," in W. F. Glueck, ed., *Business Policy and Strategic Management* (New York: McGraw-Hill, 1980): 359–367.

1994 were Prudential Insurance and Ameritech. Organizational demise can come swiftly, as further evidenced by the examples described in Table 9–2.

Strategy evaluation is becoming increasingly difficult with the passage of time, for many reasons. Domestic and world economies were more stable in years past, product life cycles were longer, product development cycles were shorter, technological advancement was slower, change occurred less often, there were fewer competitors, foreign companies were weak, and there were more regulated industries. Other reasons why strategy evaluation is more difficult today include the following trends:

1. A dramatic increase in the environment's complexity
2. The increasing difficulty of predicting the future with accuracy

The following Fortune 500 companies experienced more than a 20-percent decline in revenues for 1994:

General Dynamics	Actava
Salomon	Westinghouse Electric
Bank of Boston	Emcor Group
Maxtor	Charter Medical
American Express	Conseco
Ethyl	Kemper
John Handcock	

These Fortune 500 companies experienced more than a 100-percent decline in profits in 1994:

Gencorp	PlyGem Industries
Thiokol	Gaylord Container
Salomon	Host Mariott
Trans World Airlines	Ornda Healthcorp.
Continental Airlines	National Medical Enterprises
Maxtor	Continental Medical Systems
Occidental Petroleum	Continental Insurance
Litton Industries	Twentieth Century Ind.
Central Maine Power	Mascotech
Alexander or Alex Svcs.	Prudential Insurance
Cooper Industries	Louisiana Land & Explorers
Zurn Industries	Unocal
General American Life	EG & G
State Farm Group	Price/Costco
Pennzoil	Compusa
Arvin Industries	Standard Commercial
Pinkerton's	Dibrell Brothers
Hechinger	Ldds Communications
Morrison Knudsen	Ameritech
3Com	Bell Atlantic
Tyson Foods	Yellow

TABLE 9–2
Examples of Organizational Demise

3. The increasing number of variables
4. The rapid rate of obsolescence of even the best plans
5. The increase in the number of both domestic and world events affecting organizations
6. The decreasing time span for which planning can be done with any degree of certainty[1]

A fundamental problem facing managers today is how to effectively control employees in light of modern organizational demands for greater flexibility, innovation, creativity, and initiative from employees.[2] How can managers today assure that empowered employees acting in an entrepreneurial manner do not put the well-being of the business at risk? Recall that Kidder, Peabody, & Company recently lost $350 million when one of their traders allegedly booked fictitious profits; Sears, Roebuck and Company took a $60 million charge against earnings after admitting that its automobile service businesses were performing unnecessary repairs. The costs to companies such as these in terms of damaged reputations, fines, missed opportunities, and diversion of management's attention are enormous.

When empowered employees are held accountable for and pressured to achieve specific goals and are given wide latitude in their actions to achieve them, there can be dysfunctional behavior. For example, Nordstrom, the upscale fashion retailer known for outstanding customer services, recently was subjected to lawsuits and fines when employees underreported hours worked in order to increase their sales per hour—the company's primary performance criterion. Nordstrom's customer service and earnings were enhanced, until the misconduct was reported, at which time severe penalties were levied against the firm.

THE PROCESS OF EVALUATING STRATEGIES

Strategy evaluation is necessary for all sizes and kinds of organizations. Strategy evaluation should initiate managerial questioning of expectations and assumptions, should trigger a review of objectives and values, and should stimulate creativity in generating alternatives and formulating criteria of evaluation.[3] Regardless of the size of the organization, a certain amount of *management by wandering around* at all levels is essential to effective strategy evaluation. Strategy-evaluation activities should be performed on a continuing basis, rather than at the end of specified periods of time or just after problems occur. Waiting until the end of the year, for example, could result in a firm closing the barn door after the horses have already escaped.

Evaluating strategies on a continuous rather than a periodic basis allows benchmarks of progress to be established and more effectively monitored. Some strategies take years to implement; consequently, associated results may not become apparent for years. Successful strategists combine patience with a willingness to take corrective actions promptly when necessary. There always comes a time when corrective actions are needed in an organization! Centuries ago, a writer (perhaps Solomon) made the following observations about change:

> There is a time for everything,
> A time to be born and a time to die,
> A time to plant and a time to uproot,
> A time to kill and a time to heal,
> A time to tear down and a time to build,
> A time to weep and a time to laugh,
> A time to mourn and a time to dance,
> A time to scatter stones and a time to gather them,
> A time to embrace and a time to refrain,
> A time to search and a time to give up,
> A time to keep and a time to throw away,
> A time to tear and a time to mend,
> A time to be silent and a time to speak,
> A time to love and a time to hate,
> A time for war and a time for peace.[4]

In a study that examined the timing of strategy evaluation in many organizations, Lindsay and Rue hypothesized that strategy-evaluation activities would be conducted more frequently as environmental complexity and instability increased.[5] However, the researchers found a surprising inverse relationship between planning review frequency and organizational environment. Top managers in dynamic environments performed strategy-evaluation activities less frequently than those in stable environments. Lindsay and Rue concluded that forecasting is more difficult under complex and unstable environmental conditions, so strategists may see less need for frequent evaluation of their long-range plans. Evidence for this conclusion was stronger for large firms than for small ones.

Managers and employees of the firm should be continually aware of progress being made toward achieving the firm's objectives. As critical success factors change, organizational members should be involved in determining appropriate corrective actions. If assumptions and expectations deviate significantly from forecasts, then the firm should renew strategy-formulation activities, perhaps sooner than planned. In strategy evaluation, like strategy formulation and strategy implementation, people make the difference.

Through involvement in the process of evaluating strategies, managers and employees become committed to keeping the firm moving steadily toward achieving objectives.

A STRATEGY-EVALUATION FRAMEWORK

Table 9–3 summarizes strategy-evaluation activities in terms of key questions that should be addressed, alternative answers to those questions, and appropriate actions for an organization to take. Notice that corrective actions are almost always needed except when (1) external and internal factors have not significantly changed and (2) the firm is progressing satisfactorily toward achieving stated objectives. Relationships among strategy-evaluation activities are illustrated in Figure 9–2.

REVIEWING BASES OF STRATEGY   As shown in Figure 9–2, *reviewing the underlying bases of an organization's strategy* could be approached by developing a revised EFE Matrix and IFE Matrix. A *revised IFE Matrix* should focus on changes in the organization's management, marketing, finance/accounting, production/operations, R&D, and computer information systems strengths and weaknesses. A *revised EFE Matrix* should indicate how effective a firm's strategies have been in response to key opportunities and threats. This analysis could also address such questions as the following:

1. How have competitors reacted to our strategies?
2. How have competitors' strategies changed?
3. Have major competitors' strengths and weaknesses changed?
4. Why are competitors making certain strategic changes?
5. Why are some competitors' strategies more successful than others?
6. How satisfied are our competitors with their present market positions and profitability?
7. How far can our major competitors be pushed before retaliating?
8. How could we more effectively cooperate with our competitors?

Numerous external and internal factors can prohibit firms from achieving long-term and annual objectives. Externally, actions by competitors, changes in demand, changes in technology, economic changes, demographic shifts, and governmental actions may prohibit objectives from being accomplished. Internally, ineffective strategies may have been chosen, or implementation activities may have been poor.

TABLE 9–3
A Strategy-evaluation Assessment Matrix

HAVE MAJOR CHANGES OCCURRED IN THE FIRM'S INTERNAL STRATEGIC POSITION?	HAVE MAJOR CHANGES OCCURRED IN THE FIRM'S EXTERNAL STRATEGIC POSITION?	HAS THE FIRM PROGRESSED SATISFACTORILY TOWARD ACHIEVING ITS STATED OBJECTIVES?	RESULT
No	No	No	Take corrective actions
Yes	Yes	Yes	Take corrective actions
Yes	Yes	No	Take corrective actions
Yes	No	Yes	Take corrective actions
Yes	No	No	Take corrective actions
No	Yes	Yes	Take corrective actions
No	Yes	No	Take corrective actions
No	No	Yes	Continue present strategic course

FIGURE 9–2
A Strategy-evaluation Framework

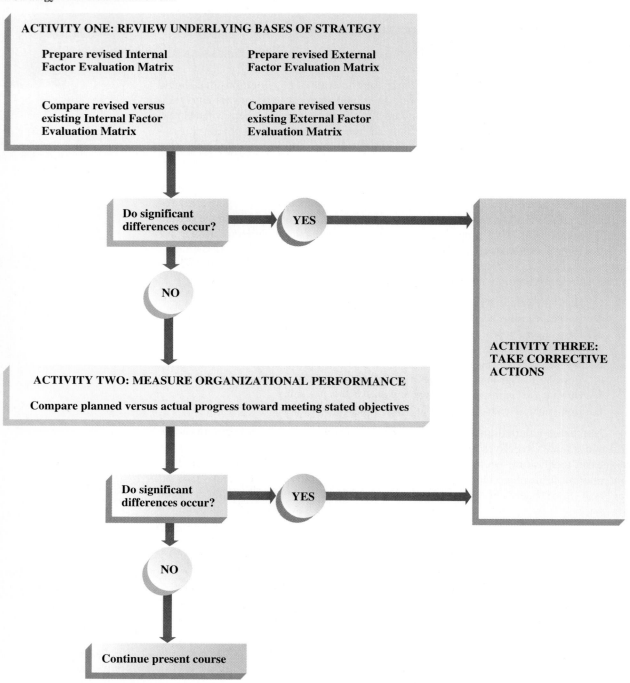

ACTIVITY ONE: REVIEW UNDERLYING BASES OF STRATEGY

Prepare revised Internal
Factor Evaluation Matrix

Prepare revised External
Factor Evaluation Matrix

Compare revised versus
existing Internal Factor
Evaluation Matrix

Compare revised versus
existing External Factor
Evaluation Matrix

Do significant
differences occur?   YES

NO

ACTIVITY THREE:
TAKE CORRECTIVE
ACTIONS

ACTIVITY TWO: MEASURE ORGANIZATIONAL PERFORMANCE

Compare planned versus actual progress toward meeting stated objectives

Do significant
differences occur?   YES

NO

Continue present course

Objectives may have been too optimistic. Thus, failure to achieve objectives may not be the result of unsatisfactory work by managers and employees. All organizational members need to know this to encourage their support for strategy-evaluation activities. Organizations desperately need to know as soon as possible when their strategies are not effective. Sometimes managers and employees on the front line discover this well before strategists.

External opportunities and threats and internal strengths and weaknesses that represent the bases of current strategies should continually be monitored for change. It is not really a question of whether these factors will change, but rather when they will change and in what ways. Some key questions to address in evaluating strategies are given here.

1. Are our internal strengths still strengths?
2. Have we added other internal strengths? If so, what are they?
3. Are our internal weaknesses still weaknesses?
4. Do we now have other internal weaknesses? If so, what are they?
5. Are our external opportunities still opportunities?
6. Are there now other external opportunities? If so, what are they?
7. Are our external threats still threats?
8. Are there now other external threats? If so, what are they?
9. Are we vulnerable to a hostile takeover?

MEASURING ORGANIZATIONAL PERFORMANCE   Another important strategy-evaluation activity is *measuring organizational performance.* This activity includes comparing expected results to actual results, investigating deviations from plans, evaluating individual performance, and examining progress being made toward meeting stated objectives. Both long-term and annual objectives are commonly used in this process. Criteria for evaluating strategies should be measurable and easily verifiable. Criteria that predict results may be more important than those that reveal what already has happened. For example, strategists do not want to find out that sales last quarter were 20 percent under what were expected. More importantly, they need to know that sales next quarter may be 20 percent below standard unless some action is taken to counter the trend. Really effective control requires accurate forecasting.

Failure to make satisfactory progress toward accomplishing long-term or annual objectives signals a need for corrective actions. Many factors, such as unreasonable policies, unexpected turns in the economy, unreliable suppliers or distributors, or ineffective strategies, can result in unsatisfactory progress toward meeting objectives. Problems can result from ineffectiveness (not doing the right things) or inefficiency (doing the right things poorly).

Determining which objectives are most important in the evaluation of strategies can be difficult. Strategy evaluation is based on both quantitative and qualitative criteria. Selecting the exact set of criteria for evaluating strategies depends on a particular organization's size, industry, strategies, and management philosophy. An organization pursuing a retrenchment strategy, for example, could have an entirely different set of evaluative criteria from an organization pursuing a market-development strategy. Quantitative criteria commonly used to evaluate strategies are financial ratios, which strategists use to make three critical comparisons: (1) comparing the firm's performance over different time periods, (2) comparing the firm's performance to competitors', and (3) comparing the firm's performance to industry averages. Some key financial ratios that are particularly useful as criteria for strategy evaluation are as follows:

1. Return on investment	5. Debt to equity
2. Return on equity	6. Earnings per share
3. Profit margin	7. Sales growth
4. Market share	8. Asset growth

But there are some potential problems associated with using quantitative criteria for evaluating strategies. First, most quantitative criteria are geared to annual objectives rather than long-term objectives. Also, different accounting methods can provide different results on many quantitative criteria. Third, intuitive judgments are almost always involved in deriving quantitative criteria. For these and other reasons, qualitative criteria are also important in evaluating strategies. Human factors such as high absenteeism and turnover rates, poor production quality and quantity rates, or low employee satisfaction can be underlying causes of declining performance. Marketing, finance/accounting, R&D, or computer information systems factors can also cause financial problems. Seymour Tilles identifies six qualitative questions that are useful in evaluating strategies:

1. Is the strategy internally consistent?
2. Is the strategy consistent with the environment?
3. Is the strategy appropriate in view of available resources?
4. Does the strategy involve an acceptable degree of risk?
5. Does the strategy have an appropriate time framework?
6. Is the strategy workable?[6]

Some additional key questions that reveal the need for qualitative or intuitive judgments in strategy evaluation are as follows:

1. How good is the firm's balance of investments between high-risk and low-risk projects?
2. How good is the firm's balance of investments between long-term and short-term projects?
3. How good is the firm's balance of investments between slow-growing markets and fast-growing markets?
4. How good is the firm's balance of investments among different divisions?
5. To what extent are the firm's alternative strategies socially responsible?
6. What are the relationships among the firm's key internal and external strategic factors?
7. How are major competitors likely to respond to particular strategies?

TAKING CORRECTIVE ACTIONS   The final strategy-evaluation activity, *taking corrective actions,* requires making changes to reposition a firm competitively for the future. As indicated in the Global Perspective, expanding globally is a popular corrective action used by retailing firms. Other examples of changes that may be needed are altering an organization's structure, replacing one or more key individuals, selling a division, or revising

GLOBAL PERSPECTIVE

Global Retailing in 1996

Mass retailers such as Toys "Я" Us, Wal-Mart, Kmart, and Miami-based Sunglass Hut International are transforming their store names into global brands, much like Coke and Pepsi. From Singapore to Santiago, customer wants, tastes, preferences, and needs are converging, not just for products but also for convenience, wider selection, and sharper pricing. The pace of global expansion in the retail industry is explosive, frenzied, and furious. Consumer preferences in the United States (and the world) are rapidly changing to a more casual lifestyle and dress. Even IBM in 1994 relaxed its fabled corporate dress code. Europeans crave American jeans and sneakers.

A few retailing facts from 1996 are as follows:

1. Office Depot, Saks Fifth Avenue, and J. C. Penney launched major Mexican expansion strategies.
2. Foot Locker opened its 800th store in Europe.
3. Wal-Mart opened its 80th store in Mexico and added 3 stores in Brazil, 2 in Argentina, and 3 in Hong Kong.
4. Sunglass Hut International, the largest retailer of sunglasses in the United States, added 56 stores in airports around the world.
5. The largest Japanese retailer, Yaohan, opened hundreds of new stores in China.

Source: Adapted from Carla Rapoport and Justin Martin, "Retailers Go Global," *Business Week* (February 20, 1995): 102–7.

a business mission. Other changes could include establishing or revising objectives, devising new policies, issuing stock to raise capital, adding additional salespersons, allocating resources differently, or developing new performance incentives. Taking corrective actions does not necessarily mean that existing strategies will be abandoned or even that new strategies must be formulated.

> The probabilities and possibilities for incorrect or inappropriate actions increase geometrically with an arithmetic increase in personnel. Any person directing an overall undertaking must check on the actions of the participants as well as the results, that they have achieved. If either the actions or results do not comply with preconceived or planned achievements, then corrective actions are needed.[7]

No organization can survive as an island; no organization can escape change. Taking corrective actions is necessary to keep an organization on track toward achieving stated objectives. In his thought-provoking books, *Future Shock* and *The Third Wave,* Alvin Toffler argues that business environments are becoming so dynamic and complex that they threaten people and organizations with *future shock,* which occurs when the nature, types, and speed of changes overpower an individual's or organization's ability and capacity to adapt. Strategy evaluation enhances an organization's ability to adapt successfully to changing circumstances. Brown and Agnew refer to this notion as *corporate agility.*[8] As indicated in the Natural Environment Perspective, Taiwan is one country that experienced future shock in the 1980s and almost overnight required all of its business firms to use corporate agility to preserve the country's beauty and resources.

Taking corrective actions raises employees' and managers' anxieties. Research suggests that participation in strategy-evaluation activities is one of the best ways to overcome individuals' resistance to change. According to Erez and Kanfer, individuals accept change best when they have a cognitive understanding of the changes, a sense of control over the situation, and an awareness that necessary actions are going to be taken to implement the changes.[9]

NATURAL ENVIRONMENT

Taiwan's Natural Environment

Only a little larger than the state of Maryland, Taiwan has a population of over 21,000,000 people, making it the most densely populated country in the world except for Bangladesh. Manufacturing is Taiwan's principal type of business, and the country was stifling in bad air, awash in contaminated water, and blanketed in its own waste by the mid-1980s.

In late 1988, Taiwan passed the Solid Waste Management Act, which gave the Taiwan Environmental Protection Agency (EPA) strict authority to enforce laws requiring all businesses to manage disposal of their products. Fifteen categories of commercial products and materials became subject to mandatory recycling, and manufactur-

ers were required to take cradle-to-grave responsibility for their products. Soft-drink bottlers funded a collection system and plastics producers funded a processing plant to ensure adequate supplies of post-consumer plastics.

Taiwanese firms are now responsible for retrieving and disposing of their own packages and containers that are nondegradable, not easily reused, or composed of hazardous elements. Firms must collect and recycle or abandon use of their packages distributed in Taiwan.

Taiwan recycles nearly 50 percent of all its soft-drink bottles today through a system that is both efficient and profitable. Primary credit for the "greening" of Taiwan's natural envi-

ronment goes to Dr. Eugene Chien, who took charge of the country's EPA in 1987 and designed a national solid-waste management policy based on recycling. The EPA's program includes an extensive education program in the nation's grade schools. The Taiwanese today generally do business only with firms that are committed to reversing the decades of natural environment destruction in their country—which the Portuguese sailors in 1590 called Ilha Formosa, meaning beautiful island.

Strategy evaluation can lead to strategy-formulation changes, strategy-implementation changes, both formulation and implementation changes, or no changes at all. Strategists cannot escape having to revise strategies and implementation approaches sooner or later. Hussey and Langham offer the following insight on taking corrective actions:

> Resistance to change is often emotionally based and not easily overcome by rational argument. Resistance may be based on such feelings as loss of status, implied criticism of present competence, fear of failure in the new situation, annoyance at not being consulted, lack of understanding of the need for change, or insecurity in changing from well-known and fixed methods. It is necessary, therefore, to overcome such resistance by creating situations of participation and full explanation when changes are envisaged.[10]

Corrective actions should place an organization in a better position to capitalize upon internal strengths; to take advantage of key external opportunities; to avoid, reduce, or mitigate external threats; and to improve internal weaknesses. Corrective actions should have a proper time horizon and an appropriate amount of risk. They should be internally consistent and socially responsible. Perhaps most importantly, corrective actions strengthen an organization's competitive position in its basic industry. Continuous strategy evaluation keeps strategists close to the pulse of an organization and provides information needed for an effective strategic-management system. Carter Bayles describes the benefits of strategy evaluation as follows:

> Evaluation activities may renew confidence in the current business strategy or point to the need for actions to correct some weaknesses, such as erosion of product superiority or technological edge. In many cases, the benefits of strategy evaluation are much more far-reaching, for the outcome of the process may be a fundamentally new strategy that will lead, even in a business that is already turning a respectable profit, to substantially increased earnings. It is this possibility that justifies strategy evaluation, for the payoff can be very large.[11]

PUBLISHED SOURCES OF STRATEGY-EVALUATION INFORMATION

A number of publications are helpful in evaluating a firm's strategies. For example, in its May and June issue each year, *Fortune* identifies and evaluates the Fortune 1,000 (the largest manufacturers) and the Fortune 50 (the largest retailers, transportation companies, utilities, banks, insurance companies, and diversified financial corporations in the United States). In these issues *Fortune* also ranks the best and worst performers on various factors such as return on investment, sales volume, and profitability.

Fortune annually evaluates organizations in 25 industries. Eight key attributes serve as evaluative criteria: quality of management; innovativeness; quality of products or services; long-term investment value; financial soundness; community and environmental responsibility; ability to attract, develop, and keep talented people; and use of corporate assets. *Fortune's* 1995 evaluation in Table 9–4 reveals the firms considered best in their respective industries.[12]

Another excellent evaluation of corporations in America, "The Annual Report on American Industry," is published annually in the January issue of *Forbes.* It provides a detailed and comprehensive evaluation of hundreds of American companies in many different industries. *Business Week, Industry Week,* and *Dun's Business Month* also periodically publish detailed evaluations of American businesses and industries. Although published sources of strategy-evaluation information focus primarily on large, publicly held businesses, the comparative ratios and related information are widely used to evaluate small businesses and privately owned firms as well.

COMPANY	INDUSTRY
Boeing	Aerospace
Penske Truck Leasing	Trucking
Ford Motor	Motor vehicles and parts
McDonald's	Food service
United Parcel Service	Package & freight delivery
Merrill Lynch	Brokerage
Microsoft	Computers and data services
Deere	Industrial and farm equipment
Intel	Electronics
Hewlett-Packard	Computers and office equipment
Dow Jones	Publishing, printing
3M	Scientific and photo equipment
Norfolk Southern	Railroads
Southwest Airlines	Airlines
Walt Disney	Entertainment
Fluor	Engineering and construction
United HealthCare	Health care
Enron	Pipelines
SBC Communications	Telecommunications
Berkshire Hathaway	Diversified financial
American International Group	Insurance
J.P. Morgan	Commercial banking
Leggett & Platt	Furniture
Procter & Gamble	Soaps, cosmetics
Wal-Mart Stores	General merchandise
Levi Strauss Associates	Apparel
American Brands	Tobacco
Coca-Cola	Beverages
General Mills	Food
Alcoa	Metals
Gillette	Metal products
Corning	Building materials, glass
Rubbermaid	Rubber and plastic products
Kimberly-Clark	Forest products
Unifi	Textiles
Johnson & Johnson	Pharmaceuticals
DuPont	Chemicals
Burlington Resources	Mining, crude oil
Shell Oil	Petroleum refining
Southern	Electric and gas utilities
Sysco	Wholesalers
Albertson's	Food and drug stores
Home Depot	Specialist retailers
CUC International	Advertising, marketing
Mirage Resorts	Hotels, casinos, resorts
Microsoft	Computer and data services

TABLE 9–4
Fortune's 1995 Top Industry Performers

CHARACTERISTICS OF AN EFFECTIVE EVALUATION SYSTEM

Strategy evaluation must meet several basic requirements to be effective. First, strategy-evaluation activities must be economical; too much information can be just as bad as too little information, and too many controls can do more harm than good. Strategy-evaluation activities also should be meaningful; they should specifically relate to a firm's objectives. They should provide managers with useful information about tasks over which they have control and influence. Strategy-evaluation activities should provide timely information; on occasion and in some areas, managers may need information daily. For example, when a firm has diversified by acquiring another firm, evaluative information may be needed frequently. However, in an R&D department, daily or even weekly evaluative information could be dysfunctional. Approximate information that is timely is generally more desirable as a basis for strategy evaluation than accurate information that does not depict the present. Frequent measurement and rapid reporting may frustrate control rather than give better control. The time dimension of control must coincide with the time span of the event being measured.

Strategy evaluation should be designed to provide a true picture of what is happening. For example, in a severe economic downturn, productivity and profitability ratios may drop alarmingly, while employees and managers are actually working harder. Strategy evaluations should portray this type of situation fairly. Information derived from the strategy-evaluation process should facilitate action and should be directed to those individuals in the organization who need to take action based on it. Managers commonly ignore evaluative reports that are provided for informational purposes only; not all managers need to receive all reports. Controls need to be action-oriented rather than information-oriented.

The strategy-evaluation process should not dominate decisions; it should foster mutual understanding, trust, and common sense! No department should fail to cooperate with another in evaluating strategies. Strategy evaluations should be simple, not too cumbersome, and not too restrictive. Complex strategy-evaluation systems often confuse people and accomplish little. The test of an effective evaluation system is its usefulness, not its complexity.

Large organizations require a more elaborate and detailed strategy-evaluation system because it is more difficult to coordinate efforts among different divisions and functional areas. Managers in small companies often communicate with each other and their employees daily and do not need extensive evaluative reporting systems. Familiarity with local environments usually makes gathering and evaluating information much easier for small organizations than for large businesses. But the key to an effective strategy-evaluation system may be the ability to convince participants that failure to accomplish certain objectives within a prescribed time is not necessarily a reflection of their performance.

There is no one ideal strategy-evaluation system. The unique characteristics of an organization, including its size, management style, purpose, problems, and strengths, can determine a strategy-evaluation and control system's final design. Robert Waterman offers the following observation about successful organizations' strategy-evaluation and control systems:

> Successful companies treat facts as friends and controls as liberating. Morgan Guaranty and Wells Fargo not only survive but thrive in the troubled waters of bank deregulation, because their strategy evaluation and control systems are sound, their risk is contained, and they know themselves and the competitive situation so well. Successful companies have a voracious hunger for facts. They see information where others see only data. They love comparisons, rankings, anything that removes decision-making from the realm of mere opinion. Successful companies maintain tight, accurate financial controls. Their people don't regard controls as an imposition of autocracy, but as the benign checks and balances that allow them to be creative and free.[13]

CONTINGENCY PLANNING

A basic premise of good strategic management is that firms plan ways to deal with unfavorable and favorable events before they occur. Too many organizations prepare contingency plans just for unfavorable events; this is a mistake, because both minimizing threats and capitalizing on opportunities can improve a firm's competitive position.

Regardless of how carefully strategies are formulated, implemented, and evaluated, unforeseen events such as strikes, boycotts, natural disasters, arrival of foreign competitors, and government actions can make a strategy obsolete. To minimize the impact of potential threats, organizations should develop contingency plans as part of the strategy-evaluation process. *Contingency plans* can be defined as alternative plans that can be put into effect if certain key events do not occur as expected. Only high-priority areas require the insurance of contingency plans. Strategists cannot and should not try to cover all bases by planning for all possible contingencies. But in any case, contingency plans should be as simple as possible.

Some contingency plans commonly established by firms include the following:

1. If a major competitor withdraws from particular markets as intelligence reports indicate, what actions should our firm take?
2. If our sales objectives are not reached, what actions should our firm take to avoid profit losses?
3. If demand for our new product exceeds plans, what actions should our firm take to meet the higher demand?
4. If certain disasters occur, such as loss of computer capabilities, a hostile takeover attempt, loss of patent protection, or destruction of manufacturing facilities due to earthquakes, tornados, or hurricanes, what actions should our firm take?
5. If a new technological advancement makes our new product obsolete sooner than expected, what actions should our firm take?

Too many organizations discard alternative strategies not selected for implementation, when the work devoted to analyzing these options is valuable information. Alternative strategies not selected for implementation can serve as contingency plans, in case the strategy or strategies selected do not work.

When strategy-evaluation activities reveal the need for a major change quickly, an appropriate contingency plan can be executed in a timely way. Contingency plans can promote a strategist's ability to respond quickly to key changes in the internal and external bases of an organization's current strategy. For example, if underlying assumptions about the economy turn out to be wrong and contingency plans are ready, then managers can make appropriate changes promptly.

In some cases, external or internal conditions present unexpected opportunities. When such opportunities occur, contingency plans could allow an organization to capitalize on them quickly. Linneman and Chandran report that contingency planning gives users such as Du Pont, Dow Chemical, Consolidated Foods, and Emerson Electric three major benefits: It permits quick response to change, it prevents panic in crisis situations and it makes managers more adaptable by encouraging them to appreciate just how variable the future can be. They suggest that effective contingency planning involves a seven-step process as follows:

1. Identify both beneficial and unfavorable events that could possibly derail the strategy or strategies.
2. Specify trigger points. Calculate about when contingent events are likely to occur.
3. Assess the impact of each contingent event. Estimate the potential benefit or harm of each contingent event.
4. Develop contingency plans. Be sure that contingency plans are compatible with current strategy and are economically feasible.
5. Assess the counterimpact of each contingency plan. That is, estimate how much each contingency plan will capitalize on or cancel out its associated contingent event. Doing this will quantify the potential value of each contingency plan.
6. Determine early warning signals for key contingent events. Monitor the early warning signals.
7. For contingent events with reliable early warning signals, develop advance action plans to take advantage of the available lead time.[14]

AUDITING

A frequently used tool in strategy evaluation is the audit. *Auditing* is defined by the American Accounting Association (AAA) as "a systematic process of objectively obtaining and evaluating evidence regarding assertions about economic actions and events to ascertain the degree of correspondence between those assertions and established criteria, and communicating the results to interested users."[15] People who perform audits can be divided into three groups: independent auditors, government auditors, and internal auditors. Independent auditors basically are certified public accountants (CPAs) who provide their services to organizations for a fee; they examine the financial statements of an organization to determine whether they have been prepared according to generally accepted accounting principles (GAAP) and whether they fairly represent the activities of the firm. Independent auditors use a set of standards called generally accepted auditing standards (GAAS). Public accounting firms often have a consulting arm that provides strategy-evaluation services.

Two government agencies—the General Accounting Office (GAO) and the Internal Revenue Service (IRS)—employ government auditors responsible for making sure that organizations comply with federal laws, statutes, and policies. GAO and IRS auditors can audit any public or private organization. The third group of auditors are employees within an organization who are responsible for safeguarding company assets, for assessing the efficiency of company operations, and for ensuring that generally accepted business procedures are practiced. To evaluate the effectiveness of an organization's strategic-management system, internal auditors often seek answers to the questions posed in Table 9–5. Aaron Kelly developed the *Planning Process Audit (PPA)* presented in Table 9–6.

THE ENVIRONMENTAL AUDIT   For an increasing number of firms, overseeing environmental affairs is no longer a technical function performed by specialists; it rather has become an important strategic-management concern. Product design, manufacturing, transportation, customer use, packaging, product disposal, and corporate rewards and sanc-

TABLE 9–5
Key Strategy-evaluation Questions

1. Do you feel that the strategic-management system exists to provide service to you in your day-to-day work? How has it helped you in this respect?
2. Has the strategic-management system provided the service that you feel was promised at the start of its design and implementation? In which areas has it failed and exceeded, in your opinion?
3. Do you consider that the strategic-management system has been implemented with due regard to costs and benefits? Are there any areas in which you consider the costs to be excessive?
4. Do you feel comfortable using the system? Could more attention have been paid to matching the output of the system to your needs and, if so, in what areas?
5. Is the system flexible enough in your opinion? If not, where should changes be made?
6. Do you still keep a personal store of information in a notebook or elsewhere? If so, will you share that information with the system? Do you see any benefits in so doing?
7. Is the strategic-management system still evolving? Can you influence this evolution and, if not, why not?
8. Does the system provide timely, relevant, and accurate information? Are there any areas of deficiency ?
9. Do you think that the strategic-management system makes too much use of complex procedures and models? Can you suggest areas in which less 'smplicated techniques might be used to advantage?
10. Do you consider that there has been sufficient attention paid to the confidentiality and security of the information in the system? Can you suggest areas for improvement of these aspects of its operation?

Source: K. J. Radford, *Information Systems for Strategic Decision.* © 1978: 220–221. Reprinted by permission of Prentice-Hall, Inc., Englewood Cliffs, N.J. Also, Lloyd Byars, *Strategic Management* (New York: Harper & Row, 1984): 237.

TABLE 9–6
The Planning Process Audit

1.	To what extent do you feel top management has been committed to the pursuit of stated corporate strategy?
2.	To what extent do you feel committed to the pursuit of stated corporate strategy?
3.	Has top management's decision making been consistent with stated corporate strategy?
4.	Has decision making been more or less centralized than anticipated?
5.	Do you feel you have received sufficient resource support (financial and human) to pursue your stated plans?
6.	Do everyday, operational plans seem to support the overall corporate strategy?
7.	How would you rate the extent and quality of the coordination of plans among functional areas/departments/divisions?
8.	How would you rate the extent and quality of the communication of plans to lower organizational levels?
9.	Does the reward system (pay, promotions, etc.) seem to be tied to your planning efforts?
10.	Do the written plans seem to adequately represent the actual goals toward which managers seem to be working?
11.	How complex is the present planning process?
12.	How formal is the present planning process?
13.	Do you feel you have the right types and amounts of external information to fulfill your planning responsibilities?
14.	Do you feel you have the right types and amounts of internal information to fulfill your planning responsibilities? If not, what other internal information do you feel you need?
15.	Would any other training help you do a better job of planning? If yes, what other specific training would help?
16.	What are the major problems of the current planning system?
17.	How might the planning process be improved upon?

Source: C. Aaron Kelly, "Auditing the Planning Process," *Managerial Planning* 32, no. 4 (January–February 1984): 13. Used with permission.

tions should reflect environmental considerations. Firms that effectively manage environmental affairs are benefiting from constructive relations with employees, consumers, suppliers, and distributors.

In a recent article, Shimell emphasizes the need for organizations to conduct environmental audits of their operations and to develop a Corporate Environmental Policy (CEP).[16] Shimell contends that an environmental audit should be as rigorous as a financial audit and should include training workshops in which staff can help design and implement the policy. The CEP should be budgeted and requisite funds allocated to ensure that it is not a public relations facade. A Statement of Environmental Policy should be published periodically to inform shareholders and the public of environmental actions taken by the firm.

Instituting an environmental audit can include moving environmental affairs from the staff side of the organization to the line side. Some firms are also introducing environmental criteria and objectives in their performance appraisal instruments and systems. Conoco, for example, ties compensation of all its top managers to environmental action plans. Occidental Chemical includes environmental responsibilities in all its job descriptions for positions.

USING COMPUTERS TO EVALUATE STRATEGIES

The usefulness of computers in facilitating strategy evaluation cannot be overestimated. When properly designed, installed, and operated, a computer network can efficiently acquire information promptly and accurately. Computers can allow diverse strategy-evaluation reports to be generated for different levels and types of managers. For example, strategists will want reports concerned with whether the mission, objectives, and strategies of the enterprise are being achieved. Middle managers could require strategy-implementation information, such as whether construction of a new facility is on schedule or a product's development is proceeding as expected. Lower-level managers could need evaluation reports that focus on operational concerns such as absenteeism and turnover rates, productivity rates, and the number and nature of grievances. Computers are being used more and more to integrate reports and enhance strategy evaluation at all levels in organizations.

For more than a decade, we have been reading about the senior executive war room and the office of the future, a room containing a number of computer terminals with graphic displays. There the chief executive officer of an organization spends most of the day monitoring the firm's internal and external condition and formulating, implementing, and evaluating strategies. The corporate war room may never become a reality, but computers are becoming an integral part of strategic-management systems. Computers now offer strategists integration, uniformity, analysis, and economy in evaluating strategic-management activities. Use of the Internet, World Wide Web, e-mail, America Online, and Prodigy can make the difference today between a firm that is up to date or out of date in the currentness of information the firm uses to make strategic decisions.

Business today has become so competitive that strategists are being forced to extend planning horizons and to make decisions under greater and greater degrees of uncertainty. As a result, more information has to be obtained and assimilated to formulate, implement, and evaluate strategic decisions. In any competitive situation, the side with the best intelligence (information) usually wins; computers enable managers to evaluate vast amounts of information quickly and accurately. Xerox president Paul Allaire and Paul Lego, chairman of Westinghouse, are examples of top executives who use a personal computer daily to make faster and better decisions. As indicated in the Information Technolgy Perspective, computers today can even enable the firm to change its location.

A limitation of computer-based systems to evaluate and monitor strategy execution is that personal values, attitudes, morals, preferences, politics, personalities, and emotions are not programmable. This limitation accents the need to view computers as tools, rather than as actual decision-making devices. Computers can significantly enhance the process of effectively integrating intuition and analysis in strategy evaluation. The General Accounting Office of the United States Government offers the following conclusions regarding the appropriate role of computers in strategy evaluation:

INFORMATION TECHNOLOGY
How to Change Your Business Location Using the Internet

ESTABLISH A WORLD WIDE WEB SITE

Example: Mail-order company, Hello Direct Inc., in San Jose, California, has put much of its telecommunications products catalog on the Web and uses a toll-free phone number to take orders. Its e-mail inquiries are up to nearly 1,000 monthly. Hello Direct's top manager says it would take 5,000 catalog mailings to get 300 inquiries, so the Web site is unbelievably economical, considering the cost of paper and postage. Establishing a Web site is analogous to opening a retail store downtown for your business. You can visit Hello Direct at http:www.hello direct.com.

JOIN A CYBERMALL

Example: A coffee-bean store named Hawaii's Best Espresso Company (HBEC) and located in Maui recently created a homepage with color photographs describing their gourmet products. Not many Internet users visited their site, so owners, Bob and Arminda Alexander linked their homepage to six different cybermalls for a few hundred dollars. A cybermall is a group of businesses that have a single World Wide Web site. Now HBEC gets over 1,000 visits by Web shoppers each day, producing $15,000 a month in orders. Business has been so good that the owners have closed their actual shop in Maui. Bob says, "It's a gas to

turn on a computer in the morning and have hundreds of dollars of business be there waiting. We are now open 24 hours a day and we don't have to be there." Joining a cybermall is analogous to opening a retail store in a local mall (as opposed to downtown). You can visit HBEC at http://planet-hawaii.com/bec.

Source: Adapted from Steven Dickman, "Catching Customers on the Web," *Inc. Technology* (Summer 1995): 56–9 and Rusty Weston, "Five Ways to do Business on the Internet," *Inc. Technology.* (1995) no. 3:75–7.

The aim is to enhance and extend judgment. Computers should be looked upon not as a provider of solutions, but rather as a framework which permits science and judgment to be brought together and made explicit. It is the explicitness of this structure, the decision-maker's ability to probe, modify, and examine "What if?" alternatives, that is of value in extending judgment.[17]

GUIDELINES FOR EFFECTIVE STRATEGIC MANAGEMENT

Failing to follow certain guidelines in conducting strategic management can foster criticisms of the process and create problems for the organization. An integral part of strategy evaluation must be to evaluate the quality of the strategic-management process. Issues such as, "Is strategic management in our firm a people process or paper process?" should be addressed.

> Even the most technically perfect strategic plan will serve little purpose if it is not implemented. Many organizations tend to spend an inordinate amount of time, money, and effort on developing the strategic plan, treating the means and circumstances under which it will be implemented as afterthoughts! Change comes through implementation and evaluation, not through the plan. A technically imperfect plan that is implemented well will achieve more than the perfect plan that never gets off the paper on which it is typed.[18]

Strategic management must not become a self-perpetuating bureaucratic mechanism. Rather, it must be a self-reflective learning process that familiarizes managers and employees in the organization with key strategic issues and feasible alternatives for resolving those issues. Strategic management must not become ritualistic, stilted, orchestrated, or too formal, predictable, and rigid. Words supported by numbers, rather than numbers supported by words, should represent the medium for explaining strategic issues and organizational responses. A key role of strategists is to facilitate continuous organizational learning and change. Robert Waterman emphasizes this, saying:

> Successful companies know how to keep things moving. If they share a habit pattern, it's the habit of habit breaking. Sometimes they seem to like change for its own sake. IBM's chief executive, John Akers, says, "IBM never reorganizes except for a good business reason, but if they haven't reorganized in a while, that's a good business reason." Successful companies are deliberate bureaucracy-busters. They delight in smashing pettifogging encumbrances that Harry Quadracci calls "playing office."[19]

R.T. Lenz offers some important guidelines for effective strategic management:

> Keep the strategic-management process as simple and nonroutine as possible. Eliminate jargon and arcane planning language. Remember, strategic management is a process for fostering learning and action, not merely a formal system for control. To avoid routinized behavior, vary assignments, team membership, meeting formats, and the planning calendar. The process should not be totally predictable, and settings must be changed to stimulate creativity. Emphasize word-oriented plans with numbers as back-up material. If managers cannot express their strategy in a paragraph or so, they either do not have one or do not understand it. Stimulate thinking and action that challenge the assumptions underlying current corporate strategy. Welcome bad news. If strategy is not working, managers desperately need to know it. Further, no pertinent information should be classified as inadmissable merely because it cannot be quantified. Build a corporate culture in which the role of strategic management and its essential purposes are understood. Do not permit "technicians" to co-opt the process. It is ultimately a process for learning and action. Speak of it in these terms. Attend to psychological, social, and political dimensions, as well as the information infrastructure and administrative procedures supporting it.[20]

An important guideline for effective strategic management is open-mindedness. A willingness and eagerness to consider new information, new viewpoints, new ideas, and new possibilities is essential; all organizational members must share a spirit of inquiry and learning. Strategists such as chief executive officers, presidents, owners of small businesses, and heads of government agencies must commit themselves to listen to and understand managers' positions well enough to be able to restate those positions to the managers' satisfaction. In addition, managers and employees throughout the firm should be able to describe the strategists' positions to the satisfaction of the strategists. This degree of discipline will promote understanding and learning.

No organization has unlimited resources. No firm can take on an unlimited amount of debt or issue an unlimited amount of stock to raise capital. Therefore, no organization can pursue all the strategies that potentially could benefit the firm. Strategic decisions thus always have to be made to eliminate some courses of action and to allocate organizational resources among others. Most organizations can afford to pursue only a few corporate-level strategies at any given time. It is a critical mistake for managers to pursue too many strategies at the same time, thereby spreading the firm's resources so thin that all strategies are jeopardized. Joseph Charyk, CEO of The Communication Satellite Corporation (COMSAT), said, "We have to face the cold fact that Comsat may not be able to do all it wants. We must make hard choices on which ventures to keep and which to fold."

Strategic decisions require trade-offs such a long-range versus short-range considerations or maximizing profits versus increasing shareholders' wealth. There are ethics issues too. Strategy trade-offs require subjective judgments and preferences. In many cases, a lack of objectivity in formulating strategy results in a loss of competitive posture and profitability. Most organizations today recognize that strategic-management concepts and techniques can enhance the effectiveness of decisions. Subjective factors such as attitudes toward risk, concern for social responsibility, and organizational culture will always affect strategy-formulation decisions, but organizations need to be as objective as possible in considering qualitative factors.

CONCLUSION

This chapter presents a strategy-evaluation framework that can facilitate accomplishment of annual and long-term objectives. Effective strategy evaluation allows an organization to capitalize on internal strengths as they develop, to exploit external opportunities as they emerge, to recognize and defend against threats, and to improve internal weaknesses before they become detrimental.

Strategists in successful organizations take the time to formulate, implement, and then evaluate strategies deliberately and systematically. Good strategists move their organization forward with purpose and direction, continually evaluating and improving the firm's external and internal strategic position. Strategy evaluation allows an organization to shape its own future rather than allowing it to be constantly shaped by remote forces that have little or no vested interest in the well-being of the enterprise.

Although not a guarantee for success, strategic management is allowing more and more organizations to make effective long-term decisions, to execute those decisions more efficiently, and to take corrective actions as needed to assure success. Computers are being used increasingly to coordinate strategic-management activities and to assure that decisions are based on good information. A key to effective strategy evaluation and to successful strategic management is an integration of intuition and analysis.

> A potentially fatal problem is the tendency for analytical and intuitive issues to polarize. This polarization leads to strategy evaluation that is dominated by either analysis or intuition, or to strategy evaluation that is discontinuous, with a lack of coordination among analytical and intuitive issues.[21]

Strategists in successful organizations realize that strategic management is first and foremost a people process. It is an excellent vehicle for fostering organizational communication. People are what make the difference in organizations.

> The real key to effective strategic management is to accept the premise that the planning process is more important than the written plan, that the manager is continuously planning and does not stop planning when the written plan is finished. The written plan is only a snapshot as of the moment it is approved. If the manager is not planning on a continuous basis—planning, measuring, and revising—the written plan can become obsolete the day it is finished. This obsolescence becomes more of a certainty as the increasingly rapid rate of change makes the business environment more uncertain.[22]

We invite you to visit the DAVID page on the Prentice Hall Web site at:

http://www.prenhall.com/davidsm

for this chapter's World Wide Web exercises.

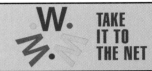

TAKE IT TO THE NET

KEY TERMS AND CONCEPTS

Advantage	(p. 278)	Future Shock	(p. 285)	Reviewing the Underlying Bases of an Organization's Strategy	(p. 281)
Auditing	(p. 290)	Management by Wandering Around	(p. 280)		
Consistency	(p. 278)				
Consonance	(p. 278)	Measuring Organizational Performance	(p. 283)	Revised EFE Matrix	(p. 281)
Contingency Plans	(p. 289)			Revised IFE Matrix	(p. 281)
Corporate Agility	(p. 285)	Planning Process Audit (PPA)	(p. 291)	Taking Corrective Actions	(p. 284)
Feasibility	(p. 278)				

ISSUES FOR REVIEW AND DISCUSSION

1. Why has strategy evaluation become so important in business today?

2. BellSouth Services is considering putting divisional EFE and IFE matrices on line for continual updating. How would this affect strategy evaluation?

3. What types of quantitative and qualitative criteria do you think David Glass, CEO of Wal-Mart, uses to evaluate the company's strategy?

4. As owner of a local, independent supermarket, explain how you would evaluate the firm's strategy.

5. Under what conditions are corrective actions not required in the strategy-evaluation process?

6. Identify types of organizations that may need to evaluate strategy more frequently than others. Justify your choices.

7. As executive director of the state forestry commission, in what way and how frequently would you evaluate the organization's strategies?

8. Identify some key financial ratios that would be important in evaluating a bank's strategy.

9. As owner of a chain of hardware stores, describe how you would approach contingency planning.

10. Strategy evaluation allows an organization to take a proactive stance toward shaping its own future. Discuss the meaning of this statement.

11. Select an article listed in the suggested readings for this chapter. Give a five-minute oral report to the class summarizing the article and your thoughts on the particular topic.

12. Identify guidelines that you think are most important for using strategic management effectively in organizations. Justify your answer.

NOTES

1. Dale McConkey, "Planning in a Changing Environment," *Business Horizons* (September–October 1988): 64.

2. Robert Simons, "Control in an Age of Empowerment," *Harvard Business Review* (March–April 1995): 80.

3. Dale Zand, "Reviewing the Policy Process," *California Management Review* 21, no. 1 (Fall 1978): 37.

4. Eccles. 3: 1–8.

5. W. Lindsay and L. Rue, "Impact of the Organization Environment on the Long-Range Planning Process: A Contingency View," *Academy of Management Journal* 23, no. 3 (September 1980): 402.

6. Seymour Tilles, "How to Evaluate Corporate Strategy," *Harvard Business Review* 41 (July–August 1963): 111–21.

7. Claude George, Jr., *The History of Management Thought* (Englewood Cliffs, N.J.: Prentice-Hall, 1968), 165–66.

8. John Brown and Neil Agnew, "Corporate Agility," *Business Horizons* 25, no. 2 (March–April 1982): 29.

9. M. Erez and F. Kanfer, "The Role of Goal Acceptance in Goal Setting and Task Performance," *Academy of Management Review* 8, no. 3 (July 1983): 457.

10. D. Hussey and M. Langham, *Corporate Planning: The Human Factor* (Oxford, England: Pergamon Press, 1979): 138.

11. Carter Bayles, "Strategic Control: The President's Paradox," *Business Horizons* 20, no. 4 (August 1977):18.

12. Anne Fisher, "Where Companies Rank in Their Own Industries," *Fortune* (March 4, 1996): 100–115.

13. Robert Waterman, Jr., "How the Best Get Better," *Business Week* (September 14, 1987): 105.

14. Robert Linneman and Rajan Chandran, "Contingency Planning: A Key to Swift Managerial Action in the Uncertain Tomorrow," *Managerial Planning* 29, no. 4 (January–February 1981): 23–27.

15. American Accounting Association, *Report of Committee on Basic Auditing Concepts* (1971): 15–74.

16. Pamela Shimell, "Corporate Environmental Policy in Practice," *Long Range Planning* 24, no. 3 (June 1991): 10.

17. GAO *Report* PAD—80–21, 17.

18. McConkey, 66.

19. Robert H. Waterman, Jr., *The Renewal Factor: How the Best Get and Keep the Competitive Edge* (New York: Bantam, 1987).

20. R.T. Lenz, "Managing the Evolution of the Strategic Planning Process," *Business Horizons* 30, no. 1 (January–February 1987): 39.

21. Michael McGinnis, "The Key to Strategic Planning: Integrating Analysis and Intuition," *Sloan Management Review* 26, no. 1 (Fall 1984): 49.

22. McConkey, 72.

CURRENT READINGS

Alexander, Marcus, Andrew Campbell, and Michael Goold. "A New Model for Reforming the Planning Review Process." *Planning Review* 23, no. 1 (January–February 1995): 12–19.

Band, David C. and Gerald Scanlan. "Strategic Control Through Core Competencies." *Long Range Planning* 28, no. 2 (April 1995): 102–114.

Donaldson, Gordon. "A New Tool for Boards: The Strategic Audit." *Harvard Business Review* 73, no. 4 (July–August 1995): 99–108.

Houlden, Brian T. "How Corporate Planning Adapts and Survives." *Long Range Planning* 28, no. 4 (August 1995): 99–108.

Housel, Tom and Valery Kanevsky. "A New Methodology for Business Process Auditing." The Innovative Manager. *Planning Review* 23, no. 3 (May–June 1995): 31–36.

Kaufmann, Jeffrey B., Idalene F. Kesner, and Thomas Lee Hazen. "The Myth of Full Disclosure: A Look at Organizational Communications During Crises." *Business Horizons* 37, no. 4 (July–August 1994): 29–39.

Lacity, M. C., L. P. Willcocks, and D. F. Feeny. "Maximize Flexibility and Control." *Harvard Business Review* 73, no. 3 (May–June 1995): 84–93.

Mitroff, Ian I., Richard O. Mason, and Christine M. Pearson. "Radical Surgery: What Will Tomorrow's Organizations Look Like?" *Academy of Management Executive VIII*, no. 2 (May 1994): 11–21.

Simons, Robert. "Control in an Age of Empowerment." *Harvard Business Review* 73, no. 2 (March–April 1995): 80–88.

Simons, R. "How New top Managers Use Control Systems as Levers of Strategic Renewal." *Strategic Management Journal* 15, no. 3 (March 1994): 169–190.

Taylor, William C. "Control in an Age of Chaos." *Harvard Business Review* (November–December 1994) Books in Review: 64–90.

Yan, Aimin and Barbara Gray. "Bargaining Power, Management Control, and Performance in United States—China Joint Ventures: A Comparative Case Study." *Academy of Management Journal* 37, no. 6 (December 1994): 1478–1517.

Zajac, E. J. and J. D. Westphal. "The Costs and Benefits of Managerial Incentives and Monitoring in Large U.S. Corporations: When Is More Not Better?" *Strategic Management Journal* 15, Special Issue (Winter 1994): 121–142.

*Paper accepted by Michael Hitt.

PREPARING A STRATEGY-EVALUATION REPORT FOR HERSHEY FOODS

PURPOSE

This exercise can give you experience locating strategy-evaluation information in your college library. Published sources of information can significantly enhance the strategy-evaluation process. Performance information on competitors, for example, can help put into perspective a firm's own performance.

INSTRUCTIONS

Step 1 Use *F & S Index of Corporations and Industries, Business Periodicals Index,* and the *Wall Street Journal Index* in your college library to locate strategy-evaluation information on Hershey, Mars, and Nestlé. List 5 to 10 articles written in the last 6 months that discuss these firms or the confectionery industry.

Step 2 Summarize your research findings by preparing a strategy-evaluation report for your professor. Include in your report a summary of Hershey's strategies and performance in 1996 and a summary of your conclusions regarding the effectiveness of Hershey's strategies.

Step 3 Based on your analysis do you feel Hershey is pursuing effective strategies? What recommendations would you offer Richard Zimmerman, Hershey's chief executive officer?

EVALUATING MY UNIVERSITY'S STRATEGIES

PURPOSE

An important part of evaluating strategies is determining the nature and extent of changes in an organization's external opportunities/threats and internal strengths/weaknesses. Changes in these underlying critical success factors can indicate a need to change or modify the firm's strategies.

INSTRUCTIONS

As a class discuss positive and negative changes in your university's external and internal factors during your college career. Begin by listing on the board new or emerging opportunities and threats. Then identify strengths and weaknesses that have changed significantly during your college career. In light of the external and internal changes identified, discuss whether your university's strategies need modifying. Are there any new strategies that you would recommend? Make a list to recommend to your department chairperson, dean, or chancellor.

WHO PREPARES AN ENVIRONMENTAL AUDIT?

PURPOSE

The purpose of this activity is to determine the nature and prevalence of environmental audits among companies in your state.

INSTRUCTIONS

Contact by phone at least five different plant managers or owners of large businesses in your area. Seek answers to the questions listed below. Present your findings in a written report to your professor.

1. Does your company conduct an environmental audit? If yes, please describe the nature and scope of the audit.
2. Are environmental criteria included in the performance evaluation of managers? If yes, please specify the criteria.
3. Are environmental affairs more a technical function or management function in your company?
4. Does your firm offer any environmental workshops for employees? If yes, please describe them.

Part 5

GLOBAL ISSUES IN STRATEGIC MANAGEMENT

International Strategic Management

CHAPTER OUTLINE

- ◆ THE NATURE OF GLOBAL COMPETITION
- ◆ CULTURES AROUND THE WORLD
- ◆ THE GLOBAL CHALLENGE
- ◆ MEXICO
- ◆ RUSSIA
- ◆ CHINA
- ◆ JAPAN
- ◆ THE EUROPEAN UNION

- ◆ GUIDELINES FOR SUCCESS AS A GLOBAL COMPETITOR

- ■ EXPERIENTIAL EXERCISE 10A
  Determining the Competitive Environment for Hershey's Products in Other Countries

- ■ EXPERIENTIAL EXERCISE 10B
  Determining My University's Recruiting Efforts in Foreign Countries

- ■ EXPERIENTIAL EXERCISE 10C
  Lessons in Doing Business Globally

CHAPTER OBJECTIVES

After studying this chapter, you should be able to do the following:

1. Describe the effects of a world economy and global competitors on strategic management.

2. Discuss the nature and strategic implications of diverse cultures around the world.

3. Discuss ramifications of the North American Free Trade Agreement (NAFTA).

4. Discuss changes in Japan as they affect strategy decisions.

5. Discuss changes in Mexico as they affect strategy decisions.

6. Discuss changes in Russia as they affect strategy decisions.

7. Discuss changes in Europe as they affect strategy decisions.

8. Discuss changes in China as they affect strategy decisions.

9. Provide guidelines for firms interested in initiating, continuing, or expanding international operations.

In the 1990s, globalization will mature from a buzzword to a pervasive reality. Companies will have to meet global standards for quality, design, pricing, and service.—BRIAN DUMAINE

Market research is unfamiliar. The closest thing to a market survey that many East Europeans have experienced is a government interrogation.—JOHN QUELCH

Sad but true, U.S. buisnesspeople have the lowest foreign language proficiency of any major trading nation. U.S. business schools do not emphasize foreign languages, and students traditionally avoid them.—RONALD DULEK

Japan is not going to change. We love to work hard and Americans don't. . . . The result is that we'll continue to work hard and amass huge surpluses of money. We'll buy up your land and you'll live there and pay rent.—WATARU HIRAIZUMI

The inclination of Japanese, Taiwanese, and Korean workers to sacrifice themselves for the good of the firm, in ways that we may find strange, surely bears some relation to their performance and rising competitiveness.—PHILIP WEST

For Americans in the Southwest U.S., the major foreign country that affects business operations is clear. It's Mexico.—KEN THURSTON

One can master a few phrases of Chinese or Japanese, learn that Seoul is west of Tokyo, buy the proper gifts, learn to eat with chopsticks, and still be far from understanding what is really going on in the Far East.—PHILIP WEST

Americans can be more successful if they recognize that foreign managers see them differently than they see themselves.—ARTHUR WHITEHILL

This chapter focuses on international strategic-management issues. Each day, more and more U.S. businesses enter global markets and more and more rival foreign firms enter U.S. markets. One-third of all college students in the United States who receive advanced degrees in science, math, and engineering are foreign citizens.

> Recently, I heard a story about former President George Bush being in a coma for three years and waking to find Dan Quayle standing at his bedside. Upon seeing the Vice President, the President began asking questions. "How long have I been asleep?" The President then inquires about the state of the U.S. economy. To his surprise, Quayle tells him that the budget and the trade deficits have been reduced to zero. Then, the President asks about inflation, which he figures must be at an all-time high. Again, to his surprise, Quayle says that inflation is not a problem. Having his doubts, the President asks for specifics. "How much," he asks "does a first class stamp cost?" "Very reasonable," Quayle responds, "only 30 Yen."[1]

THE NATURE OF GLOBAL COMPETITION

For centuries before Columbus discovered America and surely for centuries to come, businesses have searched and will continue to search for new opportunities beyond their national boundaries. There has never been a more internationalized and economically competitive society than today's. Some American industries, such as textiles, semiconductors, and consumer electronics, are in complete disarray as a result of the international challenge.

Organizations that conduct business operations across national borders are called *international firms* or *multinational corporations (MNCs)*. The term *parent company* refers to a firm investing in international operations, while *host country* is the country where that business is conducted. As illustrated in Figure 10–1, the strategic-management process is conceptually the same for multinational firms as for purely domestic firms; however, the process is more complex for international firms due to the presence of more variables and relationships. Social, cultural, demographic, environmental, political, governmental, legal, technological, and competitive opportunities and threats that face a multinational corporation are almost limitless, and the number and complexity of these factors increase dramatically with the number of products produced and the number of geographic areas served.

More time and effort are required to identify and evaluate external trends and events in multinational corporations. Geographical distance, cultural and national differences, and variations in business practices often make communication between domestic headquarters and overseas operations difficult. Strategy implementation can be more difficult because different cultures have different norms, values, and work ethics.

The fall of communism and advancements in telecommunications are drawing countries, cultures, and organizations worldwide closer together. Foreign revenue as a percent of total company revenues already exceeds 50 percent in hundreds of U.S. firms, including Exxon, Gillette, Dow Chemical, Citicorp, Colgate-Palmolive, and Texaco. Joint ventures and partnerships between domestic and foreign firms are becoming the rule rather than the exception!

World trade centers are proliferating in the United States and abroad because of growing interest in foreign trade. Trade centers were recently built in Cedar Rapids, Iowa; Santa Ana, California; Hartford, Connecticut; Pomona, California; Long Beach, California; St. Paul, Minnesota; Toledo, Ohio; and Wichita, Kansas. These new world trade centers offer many specialized services, such as assisting small businesses in exporting or importing, and housing foreign banks, export firms, and law offices.

Fully 95 percent of the world's population lives outside the United States, and this group is growing 70 percent faster than the American population! The lineup of competitors in virtually all industries today is global. Six of the world's 10 largest public companies (in annual revenues) are based in Japan, including Mitsubishi, the largest corporation

FIGURE 10–1
A Comprehensive Strategic-Management Model

Feedback

| Develop Mission Statement | Perform External Audit | Perform Internal Audit | Establish Long-term Objectives | Generate, Evaluate, and Select Strategies | Establish Policies and Annual Objectives | Allocate Resources | Measure and Evaluate Performance |

Strategy Formulation

Strategy Implementation

Strategy Evaluation

in the world. Global competition is more than a management fad. General Motors, Ford, and Chrysler compete with Toyota, Daimler Benz, and Hyundai. General Electric and Westinghouse battle Siemens and Mitsubishi. Caterpillar and Deere compete with Komatsu. Goodyear battles Michelin, Bridgestone, and Pirelli. Boeing and McDonnell Douglas compete with Airbus. Only a few U.S. industries, such as furniture, printing, retailing, consumer packaged goods, and retail banking, are not yet greatly challenged by foreign competitors. But many products and components in these industries too are now manufactured in foreign countries.

International operations can be as simple as exporting a product to a single foreign country, or as complex as operating manufacturing, distribution, and marketing facilities in many countries. More and more U.S. firms are acquiring foreign companies and forming joint ventures with foreign firms, and more and more foreign firms are acquiring U.S. companies and forming joint ventures with U.S. firms. This trend is accelerating dramatically. AT&T's Chief Executive Robert Allen says, "The phrase *global markets* is not empty rhetoric. Foreign competitors are here. And we must be there." Many U.S. firms have been spoiled by the breadth and plenty of home markets and remain ignorant of foreign languages and culture. As indicated in Table 10–1, U.S. exports increased 10.8 percent in 1994 to $9.2 billion.

ADVANTAGES AND DISADVANTAGES OF INTERNATIONAL OPERATIONS

Firms have numerous reasons to formulate and implement strategies that initiate, continue, or expand involvement in business operations across national borders. Perhaps the greatest advantage is that firms can gain new customers for their products and services, thus increasing revenues. Growth in revenues and profits is a common organizational objective and often an expectation of shareholders, because it is a measure of organizational success.

In addition to seeking growth, firms have the following potentially advantageous reasons to initiate, continue, and expand international operations:

1. Foreign operations can absorb excess capacity, reduce unit costs, and spread economic risks over a wider number of markets.

TABLE 10–1

U.S. Foreign Trade

World export growth rates climb steadily

		VALUE ($ BILLION)			AVERAGE ANNUAL PERCENTAGE CHANGE	
		1989	**1993**	**1994**	**1989–1993**	**1993–1994**
World	Exports	4.6	8.3	9.2	15.9	10.8
	Imports	3.0	4.9	4.9	13.0	–
Japan	Exports	0.8	1.2	1.4	10.7	16.7
	Imports	0.7	1.1	1.1	12.0	–
Canada	Exports	0.5	1.0	1.0	18.9	–
	Imports	0.1	0.2	0.2	18.9	–
Germany	Exports	0.6	0.9	1.0	10.7	11.1
	Imports	0.8	1.1	1.0	8.3	−9.1
France	Exports	0.3	0.5	0.6	13.6	20.0
	Imports	0.1	0.3	0.2	31.6	−33.3
UK	Exports	0.3	0.5	0.5	13.6	–
	Imports	0.2	0.3	0.3	10.7	–
BEMs	Exports	0.7	1.3	1.4	16.7	7.7
	Imports	0.3	0.7	0.8	23.6	14.3
Rest of World	Exports	1.4	2.9	3.1	20.0	6.9
	Imports	0.8	1.2	1.2	10.7	–

Note: BEMs are big emerging markets comprised of Argentina, Brazil, China, Hong Kong, Taiwan, India, Indonesia, Mexico, and South Africa.

Sources: U.S. Department of Commerce: Bureau of the Census; International Trade Administration (ITA).

2. Foreign operations can allow firms to establish low-cost production facilities in locations close to raw materials and/or cheap labor.

3. Competitors in foreign markets may not exist, or competition may be less intense than in domestic markets.

4. Foreign operations may result in reduced tariffs, lower taxes, and more favorable political treatment.

5. Joint ventures can enable firms to learn the technology, culture, and business practices of other people and to make contacts with potential customers, suppliers, creditors, and distributors in foreign countries.

There are also numerous potential disadvantages of initiating, continuing, or expanding business across national borders. One risk is that foreign operations could be seized by nationalistic factions, which occurred in Kuwait during the Gulf War. Other disadvantages include the following:

1. Firms confront different and often little-understood social, cultural, demographic, environmental, political, governmental, legal, technological, economic, and competitive forces when doing business internationally. These forces can make communication difficult between the parent firm and subsidiaries.

2. Weaknesses of competitors in foreign lands are often overestimated, and strengths are often underestimated. Keeping informed about the number and nature of competitors is more difficult when doing business internationally.

3. Language, culture, and value systems differ among countries, and this can create barriers to communication and problems managing people.

4. Gaining an understanding of regional organizations such as the *European Economic Community,* the Latin American Free Trade Area, the International Bank for Reconstruction and Development, and the International Finance Corporation is difficult and often required in doing business internationally.

5. Dealing with two or more monetary systems can complicate international business operations.

CULTURES AROUND THE WORLD

To successfully compete in world markets, U.S. managers must obtain a better knowledge of historical, cultural, and religious forces that motivate and drive people in other countries. In Japan, for example, business relations operate within the context of *Wa,* which stresses group harmony and social cohesion. In China, business behavior revolves around *Guanxi,* or personal relations. In Korea, activities involve concern for *Inhwa,* or harmony based on respect of hierarchical relationships, including obedience to authority.[2]

In Europe, it is generally true that the farther north on the continent, the more participatory the management style. Most European workers are unionized and enjoy more frequent vacations and holidays than U.S. workers. A 90-minute lunch break plus 20-minute morning and afternoon breaks are common in European firms. Guaranteed permanent employment is commonly a part of employment contracts in Europe. In socialist countries such as France, Belgium, and the United Kingdom, the only ground for immediate dismissal from work is a criminal offense. A six-month trial period at the beginning of employment is usually part of the contract with a European firm. Many Europeans resent pay-for-performance, commission salaries, and objective measurement and reward systems. This is true especially of workers in southern Europe. Many Europeans also find the notion of *team spirit* difficult to grasp, because the unionized environment has dichotomized worker-management relations throughout Europe.

A weakness that U.S. firms have in competing with Pacific Rim firms is a lack of understanding of Far Eastern cultures, including how Asians think and behave. Spoken

TABLE 10–2
Cultural Pitfalls That
You Need To Know

Waving is a serius insult in Greece and Nigeria, particularly if the hand is near someone's face.
Making a "goodbye" wave in Europe can mean "no," but means "come here" in Peru.
In China, last names are written first. In Latin America, a man named Carlos Lopez-Garcia should be addressed as Mr. Lopez, but should be addressed as Mr. Garcia in Brazil.
Breakfast meetings are considered uncivilized in most foreign countries.
Latin Americans average being twenty minutes late to business appointments.
Direct eye contact is impolite in Japan.
Don't cross your legs in Arab or many Asian countries—it's rude to show the sole of your shoe.
In Brazil, touching your thumb and first finger—an American "OK" Sign—is the equivalent of raising your middle finger.
Nodding or tossing your head back in southern Italy, Malta, Greece, and Tunisia means "no." In India, this body motion means "yes."
Snapping your fingers is vulgar in France and Belgium.
Folding your arms across your chest is a sign of annoyance in Finland.
In China, leave some food on your plate to show that your host was so generous that you couldn't finish.
Do not eat with your left hand when dining with clients from Malaysia or India.
One form of communication works the same worldwide. It's the smile, so take that along wherever you go.

Chinese, for example, has more in common with spoken English than with spoken Japanese or Korean. Managers around the world face the responsibility of having to exert authority while at the same time trying to be liked by subordinates. U.S. managers consistently put more weight on being friendly and liked, whereas Asian and European managers exercise authority often without this concern. Americans tend to use first names instantly in business dealings with foreigners, but foreigners find this presumptuous. In Japan, for example, first names are used only among family members and intimate friends; even long-time business associates and coworkers shy away from the use of first names. Other cultural differences or pitfalls that U.S. managers need to know are given in Table 10–2.

AMERICAN VERSUS FOREIGN CULTURES   U.S. managers have a low tolerance for silence, whereas Asian managers view extended periods of silence as important for organizing and evaluating one's thoughts. U.S. managers are much more action-oriented than their counterparts around the world; they rush to appointments, conferences, and meetings, and then feel the day has been productive. But for foreign managers, resting, listening, meditating, and thinking is considered productive. Sitting through a conference without talking is unproductive in the United States, but it is viewed as positive in Japan if one's silence helps preserve unity.

U.S. managers also put greater emphasis on short-term results than foreign managers. In marketing, for example, Japanese managers strive to achieve "everlasting customers," whereas many Americans strive to make a one-time sale. Marketing managers in Japan see making a sale as the beginning, not the end, of the selling process. This is an important distinction. Japanese managers often criticize U.S. managers for worrying more about shareholders, whom they do not know, than employees, whom they do know. Americans refer to "hourly employees," whereas Japanese refer to "lifetime employees." As indicated in the Global Perspective, German and Mexican managers have an autocratic management style, whereas U.S. and British managers are more participative.

Rose Knotts recently summarized some important cultural differences between U.S. and foreign managers:[3]

1. Americans place an exceptionally high priority on time, viewing time as an asset. Many foreigners place more worth on relationships. This difference results in foreign managers often viewing U.S. managers as "more interested in business than people."

GLOBAL PERSPECTIVE
Comparing Management Styles Across Countries

Management styles vary across countries. Managers in some countries rank high on conformity, and authoritarian management styles are commonly used in these cultures. Managers in other countries rank high on individualism; participative management styles are more common and effective in these countries. Knowledge of these differences can be useful in selecting managers for overseas assignments and for enhancing effectiveness of foreign operations.

The following diagram gives the relative ranking of various countries' beliefs about conformity and individualism.

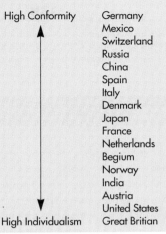

High Conformity

Germany
Mexico
Switzerland
Russia
China
Spain
Italy
Denmark
Japan
France
Netherlands
Begium
Norway
India
Austria
United States
Great Britian

High Individualism

Source: Adapted from R. Klauss and B. M. Bass, "Group Influence on Individual Behavior Across Cultures," *Journal of Cross-Cultural Psychology* (June 1974): 236–46.

2. Personal touching and distance norms differ around the world. Americans generally stand about 3 feet from each other in carrying on business conversations, but Arabs and Africans stand about one foot apart. Touching another person with the left hand in business dealings is taboo in some countries. American managers need to learn the personal space rules of foreign managers with whom they interact in business.

3. People in some cultures do not place the same significance on material wealth as American managers often do. Lists of the "largest corporations" and "highest paid" executives abound in the United States. "More is better" and "bigger is better" in the United States, but not everywhere. This can be a consideration in trying to motivate individuals in other countries.

4. Family roles and relationships vary in different countries. For example, males are valued more than females in some cultures, and peer pressure, work situations, and business interactions reinforce this phenomenon.

5. Language differs dramatically across countries, even countries that speak the same language. Words and expressions commonly used in one country may be greedy or disrespectful in another. For example: "While an American would say that he put some gas in his truck, drove to his girlfriend's apartment, took the elevator to her floor, and rang the doorbell, an Englishman would say that he put some petrol in his lorry, drove to his girlfriend's flat, took the lift to her floor, and then knocked her up."[4]

6. Business and daily life in some societies is governed by religious factors. Prayer times, holidays, daily events, and dietary restrictions, for example, need to be respected by American managers not familiar with these practices in some countries.

7. Time spent with the family and quality of relationships are more important in some cultures than personal achievement and accomplishments, which is espoused by the traditional American manager. For example, where a person is in the hierarchy of a firm's organizational structure, how large the firm is, and where the firm is located are much more important factors to American managers than to many foreign managers.

8. Many cultures around the world value modesty, team spirit, collectivity, and patience much more than competitiveness and individualism, which are so important in America.

9. Punctuality is a valued personal trait when conducting business in America, but it is not revered in many of the world's societies. Eating habits also differ dramatically across cultures. For example, belching is acceptable in many countries as evidence of satisfaction with the food that has been prepared. Chinese cultures consider it good manners to sample a portion of each food served.

10. To prevent social blunders when meeting with managers from other lands, one must learn and respect the rules of etiquette of others. Sitting on a toilet seat is viewed as unsanitary in most countries, but not the United States. Leaving food or drink after dining is considered impolite in some countries. Bowing instead of shaking hands is customary in many countries. Many cultures view Americans as unsanitary for locating toilet and bathing facilities in the same area, while Americans view people of some cultures as unsanitary for not taking a bath or shower every day.

11. Americans often do business with individuals they do not know, but this practice is not accepted in many other cultures. In Mexico and Japan, for example, an amicable relationship is often mandatory before conducting business.

THE GLOBAL CHALLENGE

Foreign competitors are battering U.S. firms in many industries. In its simplest sense, the international challenge faced by U.S. business is twofold: (1) how to gain and maintain exports to other nations and (2) how to defend domestic markets against imported goods. Few companies can afford to ignore the presence of international competition. Firms that seem insulated and comfortable today may be vulnerable tomorrow; for example, foreign banks do not yet compete or operate in most of the United States.

America's economy is becoming much less American. A world economy and monetary system is emerging. Corporations in every corner of the globe are taking advantage of the opportunity to share in the benefits of worldwide economic development. Markets are shifting rapidly and in many cases converging in tastes, trends, and prices. Innovative transport systems are accelerating the transfer of technology, and shifts in the nature and location of production systems are reducing the response time to changing market conditions.

More and more countries around the world are welcoming foreign investment and capital. As a result, labor markets have steadily become more international. East Asian countries have become market leaders in labor-intensive industries, Brazil offers abundant natural resources and rapidly developing markets, and Germany offers skilled labor and technology. The drive to improve the efficiency of global business operations is leading to greater functional specialization. This is not limited to a search for the familiar low-cost labor in Latin America or Asia. Other considerations include the cost of energy, availability of resources, inflation rates, existing tax rates, and the nature of trade regulations. Yang Shangkun insists that China's door is still open to foreign capital and technology, despite the massacre in Tiananmen Square and continued strength of the Communist Party.

The ability to identify and evaluate strategic opportunities and threats in an international environment is a prerequisite competency for strategists. The nuances of competing in international markets are seemingly infinite. Language, culture, politics, attitudes, and economies differ significantly across countries. The availability, depth, and reliability of economic and marketing information in different countries varies extensively, as does industrial structures, business practices, and the number and nature of regional organizations. Differences between domestic and multinational operations that affect strategic management are summarized in Table 10–3.

THE IMPACT OF DIVERSE INDUSTRIAL POLICIES   Some *industrial policies* include providing government subsidies, promoting exports, restructuring industries, nationalizing businesses, imposing regulations, changing tax laws, instituting pollution standards, and establishing import quotas. The vicissitudes of foreign affairs make identifying and selecting among alternative strategies more challenging for MNCs than for their domestic counterparts.

TABLE 10–3
Differences Between U.S. and Multinational Operations that Affect Strategic Management

FACTOR	U.S. OPERATIONS	INTERNATIONAL OPERATIONS
Language	English used almost universally	Local language must be used in many situations
Culture	Relatively homogeneous	Quite diverse, both between countries and within a country
Politics	Stable and relatively unimportant	Often volatile and of decisive importance
Economy	Relatively uniform	Wide variations among countries and between regions within countries
Government Interference	Minimal and reasonably predictable	Extensive and subject to rapid change
Labor	Skilled labor available	Skilled labor often scarce, requiring training or redesign of production methods
Financing	Well-developed financial markets	Poorly developed financial markets Capital flows subject to government control
Market Research	Data easy to collect	Data difficult and expensive to collect
Advertising	Many media available; few restrictions	Media limited; many restrictions; low literacy rates rule out print media in some countries
Money	U.S. dollar used universally	Must change from one currency to another; changing exchange rates and government restrictions are problems
Transportation/ Communication	Among the best in the world	Often inadequate
Control	Always a problem Centralized control will work	A worse problem. Centralized control won't work. Must walk a tightrope between overcentralizing and losing control through too much decentralizing
Contracts	Once signed, are binding on both parties, even if one party makes a bad deal	Can be voided and renegotiated if one party becomes dissatisfied
Labor Relations	Collective bargaining; can lay off workers easily	Often cannot lay off workers; may have mandatory worker participation in management; workers may seek change through political process rather than collective bargaining
Trade Barriers	Nonexistent	Extensive and very important

Source: R. G. Murdick, R. C. Moor, R. H. Eckhouse, and T. W. Zimmerer, *Business Policy: A Framework for Analysis,* 4th ed. (Columbus, Ohio: Grid Publishing Company, 1984): 275.

Strategic management has proven to be a valuable tool in the successful firm's repertoire. Firms traveling on the path of international business face more risks than their domestic counterparts, but also may reap greater rewards. Properly done, strategic management offers these firms a map to guide them on their journey through the perilous paths of international business.[5]

Perhaps the greatest threat to domestic firms engaged in international operations is the national and international debt situation. When countries become excessively leveraged, they frequently turn to slashing imports and boosting exports to generate trade surpluses capable of servicing their debt. Faced with these policies, domestic firms producing for export markets can often no longer import essential inputs. When a debtor country is successful in boosting its exports, domestic firms often encounter a protectionist backlash in foreign countries.

Multinational business strategists can contribute to the solution of economic trade problems and improve their firms' competitive positions by maintaining and strengthening communication channels with domestic and foreign governments. Strategists are commonly on the front line of trade and financial crises around the world, so they often have direct knowledge of the gravity and interrelated nature of particular problems. Strategists should relay this knowledge and experience to political leaders. A steady stream of counsel and advice from international business strategists to policymakers and lawmakers is needed.

Strategists in *multinational corporations* need an understanding of foreign governments' industrial policies. Industrial policies differ from country to country as governments take different actions to develop their own economies. For example, cooperation between business and government in Japan is so good that some experts doubt whether a clear distinction exists there between government and business; some even use the term *Japan, Inc.* when referring to the Japanese government and particularly the Ministry for International Trade and Industry (MITI).

Multinational corporations face unique and diverse risks such as expropriation of assets, currency losses through exchange rate fluctuations, unfavorable foreign court interpretations of contracts and agreements, social/political disturbances, import/export restrictions, tariffs, and trade barriers. Strategists in MNCs are often confronted with the need to be globally competitive and nationally responsive at the same time. With the rise in world commerce, government and regulatory bodies are more closely monitoring foreign business practices. The United States Foreign Corrupt Practices Act, for example, defines *corrupt practices* in many areas of business. A sensitive issue is that some MNCs sometimes violate legal and ethical standards of the home country, but not of the host country.

Before entering international markets, firms should scan relevant journals and patent reports, seek the advice of academic and research organizations, participate in international trade fairs, form partnerships, and conduct extensive research to broaden their contacts and diminish the risk of doing business in new markets. Firms can also reduce the risks of doing business internationally by obtaining insurance from the United States government's Overseas Private Investment Corporation (OPIC).

GLOBALIZATION   Globalization is a process of worldwide integration of strategy formulation, implementation, and evaluation activities. Strategic decisions are made based on their impact upon global profitability of the firm, rather than on just domestic or other individual country considerations. A global strategy seeks to meet the needs of customers worldwide with the highest value at the lowest cost. This may mean locating production in countries with the lowest labor costs or abundant natural resources, locating research and complex engineering where skilled scientists and engineers can be found, and locating marketing activities close to the markets to be served. A global strategy includes designing, producing, and marketing products with global needs in mind, instead of considering individual countries alone. A global strategy integrates actions against competitors into a worldwide plan.

Globalization of industries is occurring for many reasons, including a worldwide trend toward similar consumption patterns, the emergence of global buyers and sellers, and instant transmission of money and information across continents. The European Economic Community (EEC), religions, the Olympics, the World Bank, world trade centers, the Red Cross, environmental conferences, telecommunications, and economic summits all contribute to global interdependencies and the emerging global marketplace.

David Shanks, manager of the Strategic Management Unit of Arthur D. Little, suggests that three major factors are driving many domestic firms into international operations: (1) the maturing economies of industrialized nations, (2) the emergence of new geographic markets and business arenas, and (3) the globalization of financial systems.[6] The typical evolution of a domestic firm into a multinational corporation (MNC) is illustrated in Figure 10–2.

It is clear that different industries become global for different reasons. Convergence of income levels and standardization is what made designer clothing a universal product. The need to amortize massive R&D investments over many markets is a major reason why the aircraft manufacturing industry became global. Monitoring globalization in one's in-

FIGURE 10–2
The Typical Evolution of an MNC

| *Begin Export Operations* | *Conduct Licensing Activities* | *Add Foreign Sales Representatives* | *Build Foreign Manufacturing Facilities* | *Establish a Foreign Division of the Firm* | *Establish Several Foreign Business Units* | *An MNC* |

Source: Adapted from C. A. Bartlett, "How Multinational Organizations Evolve." *Journal of Business Strategy* (Summer 1982): 20–32. Also, D. Shanks, "Strategic Planning for Global Competeition," *Journal of Business Strategy* (Winter 1985): 83.

dustry is an important strategic-management activity. Knowing how to use that information for one's competitive advantage is even more important. For example, firms may look around the world for the best technology and select one that has the most promise for the largest number of markets. When firms design a product, they design it to be marketable in as many countries as possible. When firms manufacture a product, they select the lowest cost source, which may be Japan for semiconductors, Sri Lanka for textiles, Malaysia for simple electronics, and Europe for precision machinery. MNCs design manufacturing systems to accommodate world markets. One of the riskiest strategies for a domestic firm is to remain solely a domestic firm in an industry that is rapidly becoming global.

MEXICO

On December 22, 1994, the Mexican government decided to allow the peso to float in foreign exchange markets, introducing considerable uncertainty into any economic or trade forecast for Mexico. With insufficient capital inflows to finance a current account deficit equivalent to nearly 8 percent of GDP, the Mexican government had little choice but to let the peso devalue in the face of rapidly diminishing foreign reserves. By mid-March, the peso had fallen by roughly half and had not yet stabilized.[7]

On March 9, 1995, Mexico announced its revised economic program to restore business and consumer confidence and stabilize the economy. Major elements of the package are reductions in government spending, tax and price increases, and strict control of credit. The new plan reinforces actions announced on January 3, 1995, which also included accelerated privatization and liberalization of key industries. Moreover, the United States has organized a $50 billion economic stabilization package aimed at restoring confidence and containing the crisis. Participating alongside the United States are the IMF, the central banks of major industrialized nations (via the Bank of International Settlements), the Bank of Canada, and a group of Latin American countries.

The current difficulties follow a year of major developments in Mexico (see Figure 10–3). The Mexican government continued to open the Mexican market to foreign competition following the implementation of the North American Free Trade Agreement (NAFTA) on January 1, 1994. Inflation dropped to about 7 percent in 1994, down from a peak of more than 150 percent in 1987. The inauguration of a new president, Ernesto Zedillo, after elections that were widely viewed as fair, signaled a continuation of economic and political reform. At the same time, however, an unresolved peasant uprising in Chiapas, two political assassinations, and a series of high-profile kidnappings contributed to investor wariness in 1994.

The immediate impact of its economic plan was to cut the current account deficit to $2 billion in 1995 from $28 billion in 1994. However, real GDP declined 2 percent and inflation rose 49 percent.

FIGURE 10–3
Mexico

Population 1995	**92.2 Million**
Gross Domestic Product 1995	**$269 Billion**
Labor Force 1995	**33 Million**
Goods Trade with U.S. 1995	**$107.1 Billion**

Longer-term prospects for the Mexican economy will be heavily influenced by the success of this program. After an adjustment period, however, most analysts expect the Mexican economy's underlying strengths—a balanced budget, a low predevaluation inflation base, a modernizing economy that is no longer insulated from foreign competition, and an improved investment environment—will facilitate a resumption of growth that would allow rising per capita income (see Figure 10–4).

TRADE TRENDS   Mexico is among the fastest-growing export markets for the United States. In 1985, Mexico became the third-largest market for total U.S. exports, after Canada and Japan. In 1992, Mexico surpassed Japan as the second-largest export market for U.S. manufactured goods. Mexico now accounts for nearly $1 out of every $11 of total U.S. exports.

Bilateral trade flows were a record $107 billion in 1995. Bilateral trade in (1994) the first year of NAFTA was quite balanced, with the United States registering a small surplus of $1.3 billion, virtually unchanged from 1993. Notable, however, was the sharp increase in trade opportunities, as both export and import growth exceeded 20 percent. One-fifth of the total trade that occurs between the United States and Mexico was created in 1994 (see Table 10–4).

Since NAFTA's implementation at the beginning of 1994, half of all U.S. exports to Mexico have been eligible for zero Mexican tariffs. These include some of the most competitive U.S. products—computers, aerospace equipment, telecommunications equipment, electronic equipment, and medical devices. The trade figures are replete with examples of U.S. products—automobiles, semiconductors, machine tools, even apples—that realized export increases of between 100 and 10,000 percent when Mexican barriers were sharply reduced or eliminated. U.S. companies also benefited directly from NAFTA's phaseout of Mexican Auto Decree under NAFTA helped to triple U.S. exports of passenger cars and contributed to a shift

FIGURE 10–4
Mexico's Real GDP
Growth, 1987–1995

Source: Banco de Mexico.

TABLE 10–4
Snapshot: Mexico

ITEM	PERCENT CHANGE (ANNUAL RATE)			
	1987–1992	1993	1994	1995
Gross Domestic Product	3.1	0.4	3.5	−2.0
Consumer Prices	35.8	9.9	7.1	49.0

ITEM	1987	1992	1993	1994	1995
Unemployment Rate (Percent)	3.9	2.8	3.4	3.7	18.5
Exports ($ Billion)	20.5	46.2	51.9	60.8	75.0
To United States	20.2	35.2	39.9	49.5	45.4
Imports ($ Billion)	13.3	62.1	65.4	79.3	69.6
From United States	14.6	40.6	41.6	50.8	61.7
Exchange Rate (Mex$ per US$)	1.4	3.1	3.1	3.3	7.7

toward higher-valued units. In October 1994, for the first time in 50 years, Mexico approved the establishment of wholly owned U.S. financial affiliates, including those of such major U.S. banks as Chemical Bank, Bank of America, Chase Manhattan, and NationsBank.

Despite the recent financial crisis, opportunities for U.S. sales exist in many sectors, and are particularly strong in infrastructure development, where the government will invest $20 billion to $35 billion between 1994 and 2000. Consequently, companies supplying infrastructure-related goods and services have good prospects in port privatization, highway construction, railroad services, and water projects.

NAFTA will continue to provide U.S. companies with several advantages in the Mexican market post-devaluation. Access to government procurement, strong intellectual property protection, and the ability to provide services will allow U.S. firms to compete more effectively. Preferential duty treatment of U.S.-origin goods under NAFTA gives them an edge over products from European or Japanese firms, which are often the principal competitors.

TRADE CLIMATE   Mexico joined the GATT in 1986, setting the stage for further trade liberalization. In late 1987, the government went beyond its GATT commitments by unilaterally lowering its maximum tariff rate to 20 percent ad valorem and reduced or eliminated many nontariff barriers (such as import licenses and quotas). NAFTA expands this trade liberalization and gradually dismantles most of the remaining barriers to the movement of goods, services, and capital among Mexico, the United States, and Canada.

NAFTA was a critical factor in Mexico's outward-looking response to its financial problems. In sharp contrast to previous devaluations in which Mexico dramatically raised tariffs and imposed across-the-board import licensing requirements, on January 1, 1995— with the peso crisis in full swing—Mexico quietly implemented the second round of scheduled NAFTA tariff cuts. Later, as the extent of the economic impact of the devaluation on its domestic economy became clearer, Mexico announced that it would raise duties up to 35 percent on selected products and utilize the market protections provided in the Multifiber Agreement. Significantly, Mexico is taking these actions in a manner consistent not only with its WTO obligations, but also with the obligations of NAFTA and similar free trade agreements with other Latin American partners. Thus, U.S. and Canadian companies trading goods produced in North America will continue to enjoy favored access to the Mexican market and certainty as to the rules of the game.

Equally significant, the Mexican crisis has underscored the imperatives of economic reform that led to NAFTA in the first place. In a move to significantly reduce its current account deficit, Mexico plans to accelerate its privitization efforts in the areas of banks, petrochemicals, ports, railroads, and satellite communications. Not only are these the building blocks for a strong commercial infrastructure for the future, but they will also provide immediate export and investment opportunities for U.S. firms (see Figure 10–5).

FIGURE 10–5
U.S. Trade with Mexico, 1987–1994

Source: Department of Commerce.

NATURAL ENVIRONMENT

An Environmental Scoreboard

In July of each year, *Fortune* magazine publishes an Environmental Scoreboard, which lists the ten most improved U.S. companies in reducing hazardous waste and chemicals. The Scoreboard also reveals the ten least improved companies. The most recent rankings of companies are given below.

Source: Adapted from Fay Richards, "Who Scores Best on the Environment?" *Fortune* (July 26, 1993): 114–122.

MOST IMPROVED FIRMS	LEAST IMPROVED FIRMS
AT&T	Ciba-Geigy
Apple Computer	Hewlett-Packard
Church & Dwight	Johnson & Johnson
Clorox	S. C. Johnson & Son
Digital Equipment	Minnesota Mining & Mfg. (3M)
Dow Chemical	Nalco Chemical
H. B. Fuller	Polaroid
IBM	Shell Oil
Herman Miller	Sun Company
Xerox	Union Camp

The United States and Mexico share a 2,000-mile-long border that today is bristling with business in response to passage of the North American Free Trade Agreement (NAFTA). Mexico has 91.2 million people hungry for U.S. products and willing to work hard for low wages. More than 80 percent of Mexico's population is under age 40 and only 3 percent of all Mexicans have a college degree.

The big winners of NAFTA are firms manufacturing high-tech products such as autos, computers, and telecommunications equipment. American banks, brokerage houses, and other financial service firms also benefit as barriers to their entry into the Mexican market are loosened. Apparel manufacturers, shoe companies, and other low-tech industries, however, are hurt by increased competition from cheaper Mexican products. U.S. citrus and vegetable farmers also fear increased competition from Mexico. The agreement brings Mexico into the free trade zone between the United States and Canada. It removes tariffs and other barriers to the movement of goods, services, and investment among the three nations over 15 years. The first day the agreement went into effect, tariffs ended on about half of the more than 9,000 products covered. Tariffs on another 15 percent of the goods will end in five years, and the rest of the products will be duty-free at the end of 15 years. Free trade zones benefit consumers by lowering prices. Manufacturers and workers benefit from expanded markets for their products.

A NEW PRESIDENT   Holding a Ph.D. From Yale, Ernesto Zedillo was inaugurated as President of Mexico in December 1994, succeeding the popular Carlos Salinas, who had a Ph.D. from Harvard. President Zedillo is faced with a country tormented by violence, assasination, class and drug operations. Nearly 80 percent of Mexico's wealth rests with 30 families. About 20 percent of the population lives on roughly a dollar income per day. About 60 percent of Mexican workers take home less than $140 per month. Minimum wage is still 80 cents per hour. Unemployment rates are higher than ever and interest rates hover around 35 percent. Banks are reluctant to make loans because consumer and business delinquency rates are higher than ever.

Since Zedillo's inauguration, corruption in Mexico has worsened as the ruling Institutional Revolutionary Party (PRI) opposes privatization of industries, rigs elections, buys politicians, owns law enforcement officers, hires gangs of murderers, and supports drug traffickers. The PRI has ruled Mexico in this manner since 1924. Shipments of illegal drugs to the United States via Mexico has climbed every year and now exceeds $120 billion per year. This level is more than twice the value of Mexico's legal exports. Over 20 percent of the Mexican population in rural areas is actually employed by drug traffickers, who have built schools and hospitals for their workers and invested in local banks. The U.S. Drug Enforcement Administration estimates that 75 percent of all drugs entering the United States from South America now come through Mexico, up from 25 percent in the 1980s.

President Zedillo, a member of the conservative middle-class National Action Party (PAN), is dedicated to fighting the drug trade, privatizing industry, reducing corruption, promoting democracy, and improving the natural environment. Zedillo is good for Mexico and offers hope, but PAN and PRI are at a crossroads. The Mexican populace and the outside world favor the reforms of PAN, but the drug cartel-backed PRI has private bands of gunmen to intimidate and eliminate rivals. Corruption in Mexico has worsened such that Zedillo may not be able to reverse its stronghold. Pornography, prostitution, pollution, drug addiction, and drug trafficking severely harm both business and society. Mexico in 1995 was much less attractive for business investment than in 1994, and the jury is still out regarding the prospects for 1996 to 1998.

MEXICAN CULTURE   Mexico always has been and still is an authoritarian society in terms of schools, churches, businesses, and families. Employers seek workers who are agreeable, respectful, and obedient, rather than innovative, creative, and independent. Mexican workers tend to be activity-oriented rather than problem solvers. When visitors walk into a Mexican business, they are impressed by the cordial friendly atmosphere. This is almost always true because Mexicans desire harmony rather than conflict; desire for harmony is an overriding social fabric in worker-manager relations. There is a much lower tolerance for adversarial relations or friction at work in Mexico as compared to the United States.

Mexican employers are paternalistic, providing workers with more than a paycheck, but in return, they expect allegience. In addition to pay, weekly food baskets, free meals, free bus service, and free day care are often a part of compensation. Ideal working conditions for a Mexican worker is the family model, with everyone working together, doing their share, according to their designated roles. Mexican workers do not expect or desire a work environment where self-expression and initiative are encouraged. Whereas U.S. business embodies individualism, achievement, competition, curiosity, pragmatism, informality, spontaneity, and doing more than expected on the job, Mexican businesses stress collectivism, continuity, cooperation, belongingness, formality, and doing exactly what you're told.

In Mexico, business associates only rarely entertain at their home, a place reserved exclusively for close friends and family. Business meetings and entertaining is nearly always done at a restaurant. Preserving one's honor, saving face, and looking important is also exceptionally important in Mexico. This is why Mexicans do not accept criticism and change easily; many find it humiliating to acknowledge having made a mistake. Meetings among employees and managers in businesses located in Mexico are a forum for giving orders and directions rather than for discussing problems or participating in decision making. Mexican workers desire to be closely supervised, cared for, and corrected in a civil manner. Opinions expressed by employees are often regarded as back talk in Mexico. Mexican supervisors are viewed as weak if they explain the rationale for their orders to workers.

Mexicans do not feel compelled to follow rules that are not accompanied by a particular person in authority they know well or work for. Thus, signs to wear ear plugs or safety glasses, or attendance or seniority policies, and even one way street signs are often ignored. Whereas Americans follow the rules, Mexicans often do not follow rules.

Life is slower in Mexico than in the United States. People do not wear watches. The first priority is often assigned to the last request, rather than the first. Telephone systems break down. Banks may suddenly not have pesos. Phone repair can take months. Electricity for an entire plant or town can be down for hours or even days. Business and government offices open and close at different hours. Buses and taxis may be hours off schedule. Meeting times for appointments are not rigid. Tardiness is common everywhere. Doing business effectively in Mexico requires knowledge of the Mexican way of life, its culture, beliefs, and customs.

Mexican minimum wage is 80 cents per hour or $100 monthly. Easier access to Mexico's abundant, low-cost, high-quality labor has spurred U.S. firms to locate manufacturing facilities in Mexico. Jerry Perlman, president and chairman of Zenith Electronics Corporation, says, "If we didn't have support operations in Mexico, our annual operating costs would be $350 million to $400 million higher, and we'd be out of business." Despite low wages in Mexico, Mexicans are acquiring a global reputation for quality workmanship, as evidenced by Ford Motor Company's $1 billion Hermosillo plant, which recently tied the Daimler-Benz plant in Germany for the auto industry's first-place award for lowest production defects.

NEW BUSINESS OPPORTUNITIES   Mexico's a good place for business for many reasons, including the fact that Mexicans are a hard-working people; 12-hour workdays are common. Also, the corporate income tax rate in Mexico is 35 percent, there are no taxes on dividends, local governments do not tax corporate income, there are no constraints on dividend and capital repatriation, and franchisers are allowed unlimited repatriation of royalties. Also, the fisheries, petrochemicals, and trucking industries have been deregulated, and more than 100 state businesses from airlines to petrochemicals have been privatized. By law, Mexican children must attend school for 10 years, and 88 percent of the citizenry is literate.

U.S. electronics and garment companies have established maquiladoras—assembly plants on the U.S.–Mexico border. AT&T, for example, recently moved its cordless-phone repair operation to Mexico from Singapore. Du Pont Company and SCI Systems also are expanding their facilities in Guadalajara. Wal-Mart is opening five warehouse clubs, called Club Aurrera, in a joint venture with Cifra, Mexico's largest retailer. Sears, Roebuck is spending $150 million to open new stores in Mexico. Southwestern Bell Corporation of St. Louis recently acquired Telefonos de Mexico, the state phone monopoly, and PepsiCo acquired Gamesa, the huge snack food firm. Unilever Group acquired part of Conasupo, the Mexican commodities company. Nissan plans a $1 billion expansion of its assembly plant in Aguascalientes. Compaq Computer, Lotus Development Corporation, and Microsoft opened large subsidiaries in Mexico City recently.

RUSSIA

Since the breakup of the Soviet Union in 1991, Russia and the 11 other *newly independent states (NIS)* have made uneven progress toward economic reform, free markets, and openness to foreign investment and trade. Each of the countries is pursuing a political and economic reform agenda, although the pace of implementation varies significantly. The majority of these economies are now experiencing declining output, rising unemployment, difficult inflationary battles, and rapidly decaying infrastructures.[8]

Russia has been one of the most successful of the NIS in pursuing economic reforms. By tightening monetary policy, Russia has been able to reduce inflation from about 20 percent monthly in 1993 to just under 8 percent in May 1995. It also has made remarkable progress in privatizing its public sector. An estimated 80 percent of the Russian workforce is now employed in the private sector, and nearly 70 percent of industrial firms have sold some shares to the public. As of early 1995, privatization is being expanded to include particularly attractive investment targets, such as Aeroflot, the United Utility of Russia (national electric utility), and GAzprom (gas production). This process is expected to continue over the next two years.

Despite these reforms, Russia's GDP declined 15 percent in 1994. However, these official data significantly undercount the services sector, where many Russians hold second jobs. Real disposable income grew in 1993–1994 by 12 percent, and some companies producing consumer goods are experiencing growing sales.

Russia's economic reforms will likely have some positive results in 1995. The government's goal is to bring inflation down to 1 percent to 2 percent monthly by the end of 1995, but this target may be difficult to achieve. Inflation was 18 percent in January 1995 and 12 percent in February. The Russian budget deficit is expected to continue to be high—up to 10 percent of the GDP. Russia's goal is to halve this during the next two years. The decline in output is likely to slow, while real disposable income will continue to rise. The future of the ruble will remain largely dependent on domestic inflation; in the near term, the ruble's stability will depend on the central bank's willingness to support it.

TRADE CLIMATE AND TRENDS

In 1995, Russia had a trade surplus of $12.6 billion; exports totalled almost $46 billion. Also in 1995, the United States had a bilateral goods trade deficit with Russia of $1.2 billion. Russia is one of the 10 fastest-growing world markets for U.S. manufactured goods. Many of the largest U.S. manufactured exports will continue to be infrastructure-related, including equipment in the engineering, automatic data processing, and telecommunications sectors. The largest single export to Russia in 1994 was aircraft and related equipment, however. Russia accounts for roughly 60 percent of GDP of the former Soviet Union, but nearly 80 percent of all NIS trade with the United States. Ukrain and Kazakhstan are the next most prominent markets for U.S. exports. Total U.S. exports to Russia have been increasing steadily, and were $2.8 billion in 1995.

The major barriers to increased U.S. exports to Russia are a substantial value-added tax, high import duties, and onerous Russian excise levies. In addition, the government has imposed strict quality and safety standards on the majority of goods entering Russia. However, Russian standards authorities have permitted only a tightly circumscribed number of groups to perform this testing in the United States. The customs clearance process at Russian borders points is frequently cumbersome and unpredictable. Local transportation problems also complicate the process of getting goods to the Russian market.

The 10 best prospects for U.S. exports to Russia during 1995 are telecommunications equipment, computers and computer peripherals, pollution control equipment, oil and gas field machinery, construction equipment, medical equipment, electric power systems equipment, automotive parts and services, building products, and food processing and packaging equipment. The increasing ability of local organizations to pay for substantive improvements in Russia's deteriorated infrastructure also will stimulate imports of more U.S. products.

In terms of population, Russia is larger than all the other NIS combined and is the fifth-largest country in the world. Russia has more oil reserves than Saudi Arabia, as well as vast quantities of timber and gold and first-rate scientists. Russia spans 11 time zones. Donald Kendall, former CEO of PepsiCo, says the Soviet disintegration "means chaos in the short term but immense business opportunities in the long term. If U.S. companies wait until all the problems are solved, somebody else will get the business."

RUSSIA: AN ENTREPRENEUR'S PARADISE

Many American entrepreneurs have gotten ideas for launching businesses in Russia by living in Russia and seeing for themselves how bad the services are. Stories abound about such woes as sheets coming

FIGURE 10–6
Russia

Population 1995	148.3 Million
Gross Domestic Product 1994	$721.2 Billion
Labor Force 1995	72 Million
Goods Trade with U.S. 1995	$6.86 Billion

back from the laundry with holes in them, shirts coming back from the dry cleaners missing buttons, scratchy copies of movie videos and the widespread rudeness of shop employees. Even searching for a good meal is difficult. Lisa Dobbs, a trained French chef and wife of a foreign correspondent turned good food into a money-making enterprise. She called a Western news organization and offered to cook lunch and dinner every day for its Moscow employees. It accepted. Soon she formed Moscow Catering Co./ Kalitnikovski Produkti. Today, the catering firm has 18 employees and is swamped with orders. It recently began selling prepared food.

American entrepreneurs in Russia face numerous roadblocks. Just registering one's company with the Russian government can take six months. Most renovated commercial real estate in Moscow is to expensive for small firms, forcing them to settle in dingy, overcrowded office buildings.

But the opportunities for foreign entrepreneurs in Russia are huge. After-tax profits can be repatriated without restriction. Many entrepreneurs initially in business to meet the needs of foreigners are finding that demand from Russians drives growth.

Today, entrepreneurs in Russia are offering everything from catering services to video rentals to fitness centers. "There's a lot of money to be made," says Michael L. Oster, managing director of Oster & Co., a Moscow real estate and development firm. "Basically, there's still a need for just about everything." The potential for political unrest in Russia is troubling to business men and women in that country, but the opportunities for entrepreneurs are limitless.

MONEY AND POLITICS   Russia now recognizes individual rights, including equality, privacy, freedom of speech, conscience, and religion, and free choice of work. However, these newly won freedoms have contributed to skyrocketing prices and consumer discontent. A major problem facing Russia is economic disarray. The ruble is grossly overvalued at the official exchange rate of $1.79, but the black market rate is three cents. Companies doing business with Russian firms must hedge against the drop of the ruble's dollar value. Many companies will not do business with the former Soviets until the ruble is converted to a gold standard like all major currencies of the world, because the two-tier exchange rate is unwieldy.

CORRUPTION   In 1993 and 1994, Russia privatized nearly 100,000 businesses that employed 70 percent of the nation's workforce. *Privatizing* simply meant giving the firm to its workers. Being untrained and unorganized, these workers most often in turn gave the firm to the top director(s). These top directors today have largely become rich barons, while 90 percent of Russian employees live below the poverty level. "Imagine if Lee Iacocca had thought about nothing all day but how to steal from Chrysler," says Mikhail Harshan. "This is the situation in 99 percent of Russian businesses." Many Russians eat cabbage, bread, and potatoes at nearly every meal; most live in crowded apartments sharing bedrooms and bathrooms with other families.

The climate for business in Russia worsened in 1995 due to further director stealing, the war in Chechnya, continued devaluation of the ruble, high unemployment, high inflation, skyrocketing taxes, and increased crime. Analysts fear the 1996–1998 era will be even worse. It is almost impossible today to run a business in Russia legally. Racketeering, money laundering, and financial scams were perfectly legal until July 1995, when the Russian Duma passed a measure to restrict organized criminal activity. President Boris Yeltsin's greatest failure is the state's forced criminalization of the economy. Organized crime is gaining a stranglehold on the Russian economy; the July 1995 law may be too little too late. More than 500 businessmen were murdered in 1994 alone. More than 40,000 Russian enterprises are connected in some way to organized criminals. Ten of Russia's 25 largest banks are operated by organized criminals. There are daily reports of business disputes being settled fatally. More than 1,000 taxi drivers recently organized themselves in Vnukovo to discuss how to avoid paying protection money to organized crime bosses.

Even President Yeltsin's executive branch of the government is now described as crooked, unpredictable, and capricious in dealing with businesses. But Yeltsin's capitalism and free economy is now so firmly entrenched in Russia that there is little fear of a return to communism.

The risk of business investments in Russia decreases from south to north and west to east. Thus, investments in Siberia and along the Pacific coast are more stable and much less corrupt than those near Moscow or the Russian areas bordering Europe. Because the ruble is virtually of no value in Russia, companies need to pay their workers with something besides money, such as apartments, health care, and medical and food products. Bartering is an excellent way to motivate Russian workers.

THE RUSSIAN CULTURE In America, unsuccessful business entrepreneurs are viewed negatively as failures, whereas successful small business owners enjoy high esteem and respect. In Russia, however, there is substantial social pressure against becoming a successful entrepreneur. Being a winner in Russia makes you the object of envy and resentment, a member of the elite rather than the masses. Personal ambition and success are often met with vindictiveness and derision. Initiative is met with indifference at best and punishment at worst. In the face of public ridicule and organized crime however, thousands of Russians, particularly young persons, are opening all kinds of businesses. Public scorn and their own guilt from violating the values they were raised with does not deter many. Because Russian society scorns success, publicizing achievements, material possessions, awards, or privileges earned by Russian workers is not an effective motivation tool for those workers.

The Russian people are best known for their drive, boundless energy, tenacity, hard work, and perseverance in spite of immense obstacles. This is as true today as ever. The notion that the average Russian is stupid or lazy is nonsense; Russians on average are more educated than their American counterparts and bounce back more readily from failure.

In the United States, business ethics and personal ethics are essentially the same. In the United States, deception is deception, and a lie is a lie, whether in business or personal affairs. However, in Russia business and personal ethics are separate. To deceive someone, bribe someone, or lie to someone to promote a business transaction is ethical in Russia, but to deceive a friend or trusted colleague is unethical. There are countless examples of foreign firms being cheated by Russian business partners. The implication of this fact for American businesses is that they should forge strong personal relationships with their Russian business partners whenever possible, to spend time with them eating, relaxing, and exercising. In the absence of a personal relationship, be exceptionally cautious with agreements, partnerships, payments, and granting credit.

The Russian people have great faith, confidence, and respect for American products and services. Russians generally have low self-confidence. American ideas, technology, and production practices are viewed by Russians as a panacea that can save them from a gloomy existence. For example, their squeaky telephone system and lack of fax machines make them feel deprived. This mind-set presents great opportunity in Russia for American products of all kinds.

Russia has historically been an autocratic state. This cultural factor is evident in business; Russian managers generally exercise power without ever being challenged by subordinates. Delegation of authority and responsibility is difficult and often nonexistent in Russian businesses. The American participative management style is not well received in Russia.

JOINT VENTURES A joint venture strategy offers an excellent way to enter the Russian market. Joint ventures create a mechanism to generate hard currency, which is important due to problems valuing the ruble. Russia's joint venture law has been revised to allow foreigners to own up to 99 percent of the venture and to allow a foreigner to serve as chief executive officer.

The list of U.S. companies that have active joint ventures with Russia include Archer-Daniels-Midland, Chevron, Combustion Engineering, Dresser Industries, Hewlett-Packard, Honeywell, Johnson & Johnson, MCI, Marriott, McDonald's, Ogilvy & Mather, Radisson, RJR/Nabisco, and Young & Rubicam. In the aerospace industry, Russian firms are cooperating with Germany's Messerschmitt Company; in computers, with IBM; in manufacturing, with Combustion Engineering, Honeywell, and Siemens; in nuclear power, with Asea, Brown Boveri, and Siemens; and in telecommunications, with Nokia. PepsiCo Inc. recently formed a joint venture with Moscow Metropolitan to sell PepsiCo food products in Moscow's subway stations.

Most analysts believe Russia will become a market that many U.S. firms will want to enter in the 1990s. Those firms that start mastering the complexities early and keep informed about the latest developments may likely gain the biggest rewards. Thousands of businesses in Russia have been given financial independence and broad management autonomy. Poor telecommunications equipment, however, often isolates foreign managers in Russia from the parent company. Russia's telephone system is comparable to the U.S. phone system of the 1930s.

GUIDELINES FOR STRATEGIC VENTURES   The following guidelines are appropriate when considering a strategic venture into Russia. First, avoid regions with ethnic conflicts and violence. Also, make sure the potential partner has a proper charter that has been amended to permit joint venture participation. Be aware that businesspeople in these lands have little knowledge of marketing, contract law, and corporate law, fax machines, voice mail, and other business practices that Westerners take for granted.

Business contracts with Russian firms should address natural environment issues because Westerners often get the blame for air and water pollution problems and habitat destruction. Work out a clear means of converting rubles to dollars before entering a proposed joint venture, because neither Russian banks nor authorities can be counted on to facilitate foreign firms' getting dollar profits out of a business. Recognize that chronic shortages of raw materials hamper business in Russia, so make sure an adequate supply of competitively priced, good-quality raw materials is reliably available. Finally, make sure the business contract limits the circumstances in which expropriation would be legal. Specify a lump sum in dollars if expropriation should occur unexpectedly, and obtain expropriation insurance before signing the agreement.

A number of organizations in Russia assist foreign companies interested in initiating, continuing, or expanding business operations there. Some of these organizations are Amtorg, the Consultation Center of the Chamber of Commerce and Industry, Inpred, Interfact, and the U.S. Commercial Office (USCO). Inpred, for example, is a consulting firm in Russia that helps Western managers operate within regulations. Inpred also helps foreign firms locate partners in the republics and develop contracts, and contacts officials to set up meetings between Commonwealth and foreign businesspersons. USCO annually sponsors about 25 trade fairs and exhibitions that introduce foreign companies and individuals to the new Commonwealth markets, customers, buyers, and sellers.

CHINA

The Chinese economy continues to score impressive gains. GDP increased 11 percent in 1994 and about 10 percent in 1995, continuing the surge in investment-led growth that began in 1992 (see Figures 10–7 and 10–8 and Table 10–6). Investment in fixed assets, which makes up almost 40 percent of GDP, grew 22 percent in 1993, but public enterprises absorbed 70 percent of total investment. Industrial output jumped 21 percent in 1993 and 18

	PERCENT CHANGE (ANNUAL RATE)			
ITEM	1987–1992	1993	1994	1995
Gross Domestic Product	8.1	13.8	11.0	10.0
Consumer Prices	9.1	13.0	20.0	21.3

ITEM	1987	1992	1993	1994	1995
Unemployment Rate (Percent)	2.0	2.3	2.6	3.0	3.2
Exports ($Billion)	39.4	84.9	91.8	121.0	148.8
To United States	6.3	25.7	31.5	38.8	45.5
Imports ($ Billion)	43.2	80.6	103.9	115.7	136.5
From United States	3.5	7.4	8.8	9.3	11.7
Exchange Rate (Yen per US$)	3.72	5.52	5.76	8.63	8.33

TABLE 10–5
Snapshot: China

FIGURE 10–7
China

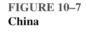
Population 1996 — 1.22 Billion

Gross Domestic Product 1995 — $817 Billion

Labor Force 1995 — 700 Million

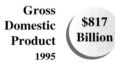
Goods Trade with U.S. 1995 — $57.2 Billion

percent in 1994, due in large part to collectives and firms that are at least partially foreign owned. Inflation, a major problem, was an estimated 21.3 percent in 1995.[9]

The government's key macroeconomic objectives continue to be the maintenance of high growth to generate new jobs and help spread the benefits of economic reform and to control inflation. China's economic program is guided by a November 1993 decision that established a broad framework for the transition to a socialist market economy, including ambitious plans for fiscal, financial, and enterprise reforms to be implemented by the end of the decade. The unification of China's foreign exchange rates has gone relatively smoothly, with the yuan appreciating slightly against the U.S. dollar since January 1994, following a large devaluation. Tax reform has resulted in a simplified code and a smaller gap between rates for state-owned and other enterprises. However, the new structure of tax-sharing between central and provincial governments, a significant improvement over the previous system, has yet to increase (in real terms) the central government's share of GDP, a key objective of China's leaders.

A series of important economic laws have been proposed, some of which apply to commercial and central banking, foreign trade, and securities. Some of these reforms are being introduced because of China's determination to join the WTO; discussions related to its application continued in 1995.

A major question is whether the government will continue its economic liberalization program as the era of Deng Xiaoping draws to a close. Rapid economic expansion has brought mixed blessings and is not without controversy. One immediate concern is to cool an overheating economy without precipitating a drastic slowdown in growth. Longer-term difficulties associated with China's rapid growth include increasing disparities in income, greater regional autonomy, a burgeoning population of migrant laborers, and shortages of key commodities and services.

FIGURE 10–8
China's Real GDP Growth, 1987–1995

Source: International Monetary Fund.

FIGURE 10–9
U.S. Trade with China,
1987–94

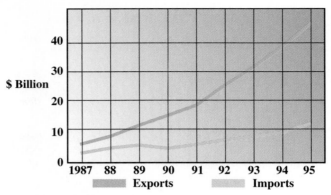

Source: Department of Commerce.

TRADE TRENDS   China's trade moved back into surplus in 1994, with exports growing by 32 percent and imports gaining just over 11 percent. The $12 billion merchandise trade deficit recorded in 1993 became a $12.3 billion surplus in 1995. This turnaround was in part due to the unification and devaluation of China's currency at the beginning of 1994 but also the result of a slowdown in China' economic growth last year. However, China could quickly return to a trade deficit in future years as developmental needs outstrip local production in key areas. Manufactured products led export growth and primary products led import growth.

Foreign invested enterprises and developed coastal areas continued to outpace the rest of the economy in growth of trade. Japan remained China's top trade partner and source of imports, according to Chinese statistics. Filtering out the effect of entrepot trade through Hong Kong, however, the United States moved closer to the top of the list for overall trade and into the top slot as a destination for China's exports.

Imports from the United States grew at nearly triple the overall import growth rate and faster than any partner except South Korea. Nonetheless, in 1994 the United States remained China's fourth-largest source of imports after Japan, the European Union and Taiwan. China's fastest-growing major imports from the United States included cotton, fats and oils, manmade staple fibers, fertilizer, aircraft, wood pulp, and leather.

The United States had a trade deficit of $29.5 billion with China in 1994 and $33.8 billion in 1995. This deficit has increased steadily since 1987—U.S. imports have grown 30 percent a year and U.S. exports 15 percent. The United States has an important stake in the outcome of any government measures to control the economy, because China has become an increasingly important market for U.S. goods and services (see Figure 10–9).

TRADE CLIMATE   China maintains an intricate system of import controls to implement its industrial and trade policies. Many products are subject to quotas, import licensing requirements, or other restrictions. Laws and regulations that affect trade often go unpublished. Some exports to China are hampered by product standards and testing requirements that are more demanding than the ones applied to domestic goods. Other trade-related problems include indirect export subsidies, import substitution measures, and limits on the geographic and business scope of U.S. financial and other services firms. In addition, senior government officials intervene in market activities to preserve social stability or to protect key state companies. However, some liberalization has resulted from negotiations between the United States and China and Beijing's keen interest in fuller integration into the international trading system.

Chinese authorities have announced that state enterprise reform will be the centerpiece of their reform efforts in 1995. If implemented, further market liberalization should occur, and some unprofitable state enterprises may be forced into bankruptcy. A proposed

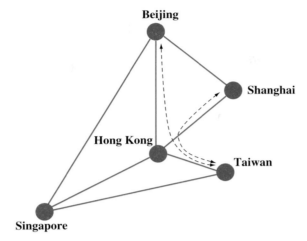

FIGURE 10–10

social insurance system that has received extensive attention could buffer the impact of re-structuring the state sector.

China is the world's fastest growing economy; some analysts predict that in 20 years China will be the world's largest economy. China's 1993–1994 Gross National Product grew at 13 percent; 1994 foreign trade was up 22 percent. Despite its problems and risks, more and more U.S. firms are doing business in China. Holiday Inn has a 448-room hotel in Lhasa, Tibet. Boeing is selling 14 percent of its production to Chinese airlines. Ford and Chrysler are making money manufacturing automobiles or component parts. Playboy Enterprises operates nearly 200 sportswear boutiques in Chinese stores. Nike, Compaq Computer, Hughes, General Electric, and Weyerhaeuser are making money in their opera-tions in China. These firms are successfully operating in a culture of bribery, nepotism, and open disregard for rule of the law. A senior U.S. official says "We're very anxious to have a good relationship with China, but that can't mean we subordinate our interests every time they conflict with Chinese interests."

THE HONG KONG ANNEXATION   On July 1, 1997, Great Britain is scheduled to give control of Hong Kong back to China, based on the *joint declaration* signed in 1983 be-tween the countries. In the document, China pledged to operate Hong Kong for at least 50 years as a separate democratic state with freedom of religion, press, speech, and a fair legal system. However, it is now clear that communist China is not going to fulfill this promise. Revolt, corruption, fear, disorder, emigration, and revolution are accompanying the upcom-ing annexation. As indicated in the map in Figure 10–10, China views Hong Kong as the cen-terpiece of its efforts to expand influence and control throughout Southeast Asia.

The riskiness of doing business in Hong Kong and China is increasing daily. Like the United States during its Civil War, Hong Kong is torn with wrenching human dramas in which friends and family are deeply split over the best means for survival—to cave in to Beijing or fight for continued freedom. There is growing fear among Hong Kong residents that China will turn on, imprison, torture, or even kill persons who are considered to have conspired with the British. The June 1989 Tiananmen Square mass killing of pro-democracy supporters in Beijing is fresh in the minds of many Chinese. The demise of Hong Kong as a global business center is forcing international companies to rethink the way they operate there and in China.

U.S. companies alone have 178 regional headquarters in Hong Kong and $10.5 billion in direct investment. With its 6 million people, magnificent harbor, financial wealth, 500 banks from 43 countries, the world's eighth-largest stock market, and minimum taxation, Hong Kong has served for decades as the gateway to fast-growing South China. However,

Hong Kong today is rapidly becoming just another China city governed by corruption, oppression, favoritism, and political connections. Troops from Beijing are aligning themselves with gangs in Hong Kong. Government officials in Hong Kong are being murdered, bought, exiled, or intimidated, and replaced by Beijing communists. Hong Kong's 52 newspapers are being pressured into strict self-censorship. Beijing may even replace Hong Kong's independent currency pegged to the U.S. dollar with Chinese renminbi.

RISKS IN DOING BUSINESS   Poor infrastructure, disregard for the natural environment, absence of a legal system, rampant corruption, and lack of freedom of press, speech, and religion are part of the risks inherent in doing business in China. Severe human rights violations compound problems. The Chinese have no respect for intangible assets such as patents, copyrights, brands, and logos. Counterfeiting, fraud, and pirating of products such as pop music, software, movies, books, and technology thus is rampant in China. Legal contracts have little meaning in China. McDonald's, for instance, was recently evicted from its site in Beijing after operating its largest store in the world for only two of the twenty years in its lease agreement. DuPont's herbicide Londax, which kills weeds in rice fields, was recently pirated and manufactured extensively in China. Scores of U.S. firms such as DuPont and banks that have lost millions of dollars have begged Beijing to stop such illegal business actions, but to no avail. You can walk into any store in Beijing and buy a pirated copy of Microsoft's Windows 95 software.

Although U.S. corporations pour more than $2 billion annually in new investment into China, there is a growing realization that this investment is at grave risk. William Wendler says, "There are no generally accepted accounting principles in China, nothing that you can understand and trust, nothing that ensures that a Chinese set of books will look anything like a U.S. set of books." James Broering of Arthur Anderson says, "We have to be in China, but we also have to figure that we can lose everything, that we may have to walk away from every investment we make." There is no sign in China that the communist form of government will ever lose its stronghold on society.

More than 50 percent of China's state businesses are insolvent and are not paying their bills. Foreign firms must look carefully at their Chinese partners because many are bankrupt and corrupt. Technological research is almost nonexistent in China. Ninety percent of people in China live below the poverty level; 10 percent are very rich. Unemployment and inflation are soaring.

Newt Gingrich and other congressional leaders back the Democratic Progressive Party (DPP) in Taiwan, which has been calling for independence from China. Some analysts say China would declare war on Taiwan if this were to happen. Beijing regards Taiwan as a Chinese province; this point is very sensitive. When the United States normalized relations with Vietnam in July 1995, China protested. The United States has prohibited China's entry to the World Trade Organization because of its human rights violations and expansionist aspirations. China is intimidating Japan, Indonesia, Malaysia, Korea, Vietnam, and especially Taiwan. Driven by a vision of itself as the leader of Asia, China may be preparing for annexation of Taiwan to follow several years after annexation of Hong Kong. Doomsayers predict that this would lead to a world war.

The minimum wage in China is 12 cents per hour, but many firms pay even less. Chinese workers usually have no health care and no compensation for injury. Few factories have fire extinguishers. Eighty four women were recently killed in a fire in the Zhili Handicraft Factory in Shenzhen. Hundreds of other workers were killed in the trampling panic that occurred because all windows had been barred to prevent stealing. Bribes are often paid to officials to avoid fines and shutdowns. Labor unions are illegal and nonexistent in China. Child labor is commonplace, as are political and religious oppression and imprisonment. Levi Strauss recently pulled all its business operations out of China in protest to its human rights violations.

The Japanese economy is in the fourth year of its most serious slowdown since the early 1970s (see Table 10–6). No GDP growth was recorded in 1993, and only 1.2 was recorded in 1995. The immediate cause of the slump was the collapse of Japan's bubble economy beginning in 1989, during which equity values plunged, followed a year later by careening land prices. The effects are still being felt: Industries have been left with huge amounts of excess capacity, and business investment, having fallen for the past three years, increase somewhat in 1995.[10]

The decline in asset values left Japanese banks with substantial nonperforming loans and precarious balance sheets. As a result, bank lending has been weak despite low interest rates. Residential housing construction has benefited from low interest rates and falling land prices, but constraints on government-supported housing finance may temper this growth. Commercial construction has declined throughout the downturn, although public construction projects initiated as part of four government stimulus packages have compensated somewhat.

Private consumption has given a boost to slowly rising economic activity. Income tax rebates and low inflation have helped bolster consumer expenditures. Business's policy of keeping layoffs to a minimum during economic slowdowns has also helped consumption levels remain steady.

Japan's labor markets are very weak. At 3.3 percent, unemployment is high by Japanese standards. During 1994, total employment fell below year-earlier levels for the first time in 16 years. Recruitment of new college graduates is depressed, and many firms have so much redundant employment that no hiring will occur until at least 1997 (see Figure 10–11).

The trade sector has also been a drag on the economy, as import volumes have outpaced exports. Because of the appreciation of the yen, however, Japan's current account surplus in dollar terms continued to increase during 1993. It peaked in 1993 and fell in 1994 and 1995 (see Figure 10–12).

GDP is expected to increase nearly 2 percent in 1995. The recovery will be led by strong growth in private consumption, although about 40 percent of higher personal income will likely be saved. For the remainder of this decade, Japan's growth is expected to be well below the levels recorded during the past 20 years, when GDP increased more than 4 percent

FIGURE 10–11
Japan

Population 1995	125 Million
Gross Domestic Product 1995	$1.6 Trillion
Employment 1994	65.9 Million
Goods Trade with U.S. 1995	$200 Billion

TABLE 10–6
Snapshot: Japan

| | PERCENT CHANGE (ANNUAL RATE) | | | |
ITEM	1987–1992	1993	1994	1995
Gross Domestic Product	4.2	−0.2	0.9	1.2
Consumer Prices	2.2	1.3	0.7[a]	0.3

ITEM	1987	1992	1993	1994	1995
Unemployment Rate (Percent)	2.8	2.2	2.5	2.9	3.3
Exports ($ Billion)	224.6	330.8	351.3	395.6[b]	418.9
To United States	84.6	97.4	107.2	117.6	125.8
Imports ($ Billion)	128.2	198.5	209.8	274.7	307.2
From United States	28.2	47.8	47.9	62.7	74.2
Exchange Rate (Yen per US$)	144.6	126.8	111.1	102.2[a]	96.3

[a]Estimate.
[b]January–September annual rate.

FIGURE 10–12
**Japan's Real GDP
Growth, 1987–1995**

•Department of Commerce estimate
Source: Economic Planning Agency.

FIGURE 10–13
**U.S. Trade with Japan,
1987–1994**

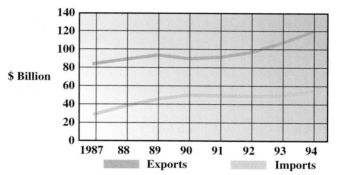

Source: Department of Commerce.

annually. Low rates of labor force growth, excess capacity in manufacturing, and economic restructuring (away from manufacturing and into services and communications) will tend to keep average growth below 3 percent per year during 1995–2000.

The economy could fall short of even these low growth rates if government budget deficits continue to mount and the yen appreciates further. A weaker yen is predicted in the next two years, but continuing trade surpluses could drive it even higher. This would destroy business confidence, undermine export competitiveness, and stall investment spending. (None of these forecasts takes into account the effect of the Kobe earthquake of January 1995.)

TRADE TRENDS   In 1995, Japan was the world's third-largest merchandise exporter and importer (behind the United States and Germany). Machinery and equipment make up about 75 percent of Japan's exports. In 1993, Japan's merchandise trade surplus totalled $141.5 billion, a record for the third consecutive year. However, the volume of Japanese imports increased more than 4 percent in 1993, while export volume shrank 2 percent. The sharp appreciation of the yen with respect to the dollar and price changes in imports and exports tend to conceal these shifts. In 1994, the trade surplus reached nearly $147 billion, but then fell in 1995 to $112 billion.

The United States is by far Japan's single largest trading partner (see Figure 10–13). In 1994, the United States had a 23 percent share of Japan's import market, and 30 percent of Japanese exports went to the United States. Japan has been the second-largest market for U.S. products for many years. In 1993, the U.S.-Japan trade deficit widened to $59.4 billion—more than half of the total U.S. merchandise trade deficit. In 1994 the bilateral deficit was $54.9 billion but in 1995 it was down to $51.6 billion. Between 1987 and 1993, U.S. exports to Japan expanded more than twice as fast (9 percent annually) as Japanese exports to the United States. A relatively smaller share of U.S. exports to Japan are manufactured goods (67 percent in 1995). By comparison, about 84 percent of U.S. exports to the rest of the world are manufactures. In addition, a relatively large share of U.S. exports to Japan consist of intracompany shipments from Japanese subsidiaries in the United States to their parent firms in Japan.

As a group, Southeast Asian countries and the NIEs are now a more important export market for Japan than the United States is. In recent years, Japan's trade surplus with Southeast Asia has grown very rapidly, exceeding its surplus with the United States in 1993. To offset the impact of the high yen, Japan's industries have been shifting the labor-intensive and assembly components of their manufacturing operations to Southeast Asia in the last several years. Most of this investment initially went to Thailand and Malaysia; more recently China and Hong Kong have become the preferred sites. As a result, there has been a surge of reverse imports from these countries to Japan.

TRADE CLIMATE   Japan's large trade surpluses with the United States and other industrial nations have resulted in almost continuous trade friction between Japan and these countries over the last two decades. Consequently, the primary goal of U.S. trade policy with Japan has been to open the Japanese market to imports and foreign investment. Informal obstacles have largely prevented manufactured goods, especially high-technology products, from entering Japan's markets. These barriers include administrative guidance; opaque customs procedures, testing standards, and certification requirements; restrictive public procurement and industrial promotion policies; intellectual property regulations; and impenetrable local distribution channels.

Some deregulation has opened Japan's markets in recent years, but its trade structure remains substantially different from that of any other industrial country. Japanese exports are mainly manufactured goods, and its imports are raw materials, food, and industrial components. Most of Japan's imported goods come from its foreign subsidiaries. Deregulation and other market-opening measures that have resulted from U.S. policy initiatives may lead to some change to this trade pattern during the remainder of this century.

Although no larger in size than California, Japan supports a population five times that of California's. Japan is changing rapidly. Masakagu Yamazaki uses the term *flexible individualism* to summarize the changes occurring in Japanese society and business. Workaholic attitudes in Japan are being replaced by greater emphasis on leisure activities and consumption of leisure products and services. Rising incomes, an aging population, and more women in the workforce are increasing the demand for services in all sectors of the Japanese economy. Japanese people save much more of their income than Americans, averaging 17 percent versus 4 percent, but prices in Japan are among the highest in the world. An apple costs $2 and dinner for four can cost $600.

A comparison of educational levels of Japanese and American young people appears in Table 10–7. Teachers in Japan enjoy much more respect, status, job security, and higher pay than their counterparts in America. Japanese teachers visit their students' homes, are available after school to assist students, and supervise learning on vacation days. Education is compulsory for children ages 6 to 15 in Japan, and 95 percent of 5-year-olds and 70 percent of 4-year-olds go to kindergarten. The school year is 240 days, and many children spend Sunday and holidays being tutored or studying. Some of the forces behind the educational system in Japan are relative homogeneity in the population, an occupational system in which selection and promotion are based on educational credentials, a relatively equal distribution of educational opportunities across the population, steep competition for entry into prestigious universities, and devotion of families to enhancing the life chances of children. Many analysts contend that as we approach the year 2000 and beyond, countries around the world will be as competitive as their underlying education system. U.S. firms

TABLE 10–7
The Educational Levels
of Young Japanese and
Young Americans
Compared

	AMERICANS	JAPANESE
Literacy Rate	80.0%	99.0%
High School Completion Rate	72.2%	90.0%
Length of School Year	180 days	240 days
High School Seniors Spending Less Than Five Hours Per Week on Homework	76.0%	35.0%
Financing of Education:		
National	6.2%	47.3%
State	49.0%	28.1%
Local	44.8%	24.6%
Teacher Salaries	Determined locally	By national law, teachers are paid 10% more than the top civil servant.

Sources: U.S. Department of Education and Japanese Ministry of Education.

could be at a disadvantage compared to Japanese firms if this holds true, because the analysts are primarily referring to secondary education, literacy rates, and average education level of the populace.

More and more Japanese women are pursuing careers outside the home, a practice that was taboo until the mid-1980s. However, women still hold only 1 percent of managerial positions in Japan despite their comprising 40 percent of Japan's workforce. The 1986 Japanese law banning sex discrimination at work established no penalties for violations. Most Japanese men and women still believe that when a woman marries, taking care of her husband and children should be her priority. The Japanese government is encouraging companies to promote more women into managerial positions, but the managerial job in Japan typically requires late hours, afterwork drinking sessions with colleagues, and a pledge of allegiance to the company until retirement. Many Japanese women do not cherish that lifestyle, so women on the career track in Japan still remain an oddity.

Research and development has become a basic mission of the Japanese government and nearly all Japanese firms. It is a mission of the whole country. Japan plans to develop a futuristic space shuttle, a colony of space platforms, and an orbiting factory for manufacturing Made-in-Space products. Aerospace companies in the United States and worldwide consider the Japanese market to be a great opportunity and are developing strategies to capitalize on Japan's commitment to commercialize space.

Some U.S. companies have done especially well in Japanese markets, including Coke, Nestlé, Schick, Wella, Vicks, Scott, Del Monte, Kraft, Campbell, Unilever, Twinings, Kellogg, Borden, Ragu, Oscar Mayer, and Hershey. These are all household names in Japan. Schick razor blades have 70 percent of the safety-blade market there, McDonald's has 30 percent of the fast-food hamburger market, Coca-Cola has 50 percent of the market for carbonated soft drinks, Pampers has 22 percent of the disposable-diaper market, and Kodak has 15 percent of the amateur color film market. IBM has 40 percent of the market for computers, and Caterpillar has 43 percent of the market for bulldozers.

JAPANESE MANAGEMENT STYLE   The Japanese place great importance upon group loyalty and consensus, a concept called *Wa*. Nearly all corporate activities in Japan encourage Wa among managers and employees. Wa requires that all members of a group agree and cooperate; this results in constant discussion and compromise. Japanese managers evaluate the potential attractiveness of alternative business decisions in terms of the long-term effect on the group's Wa. This is why silence, used for pondering alternatives, can be a plus in a formal Japanese meeting. Discussions potentially disruptive to Wa are generally conducted in very informal settings, such as at a bar, so as to minimize harm to the group's Wa. Entertaining is an important business activity in Japan because it strengthens Wa. Formal meetings are often conducted in informal settings. When confronted with disturbing questions or opinions, Japanese managers tend to remain silent, whereas Americans tend to respond directly, defending themselves through explanation and argument.

Most Japanese managers are reserved, quiet, distant, introspective, and others-oriented, whereas most U.S. managers are talkative, insensitive, impulsive, direct, and individual-oriented. Americans often perceive Japanese managers as wasting time and carrying on pointless conversations, whereas U.S. managers often use blunt criticism, ask prying questions, and make quick decisions. These kinds of cultural differences have disrupted many potentially productive Japanese-American business endeavors. Viewing the Japanese communication style as a prototype for all Asian and Oriental cultures is a related stereotype that must be avoided.

Americans have more freedom to control their own fate than do the Japanese. Life is much different in the United States than in Japan; the United States offers more upward mobility to its people. This is a great strength of the United States. Fallows explains:

America is not like Japan and can never be. America's strength is the opposite: It opens its doors and brings the world's disorder in. It tolerates social change that would tear most other societies apart. This openness encourages Americans to adapt as individuals rather than as a group. Americans go west to California to get a new start; they move east to Manhattan to try to make the big time; they move to Vermont or to a farm to get close to the soil. They break away from their parents' religions or values or class; they rediscover their ethnicity. They go to night school; they change their names.[11]

GLOBAL EXPANSION Japan is shifting from a strategy of exports to direct investment in the United States and Europe. Japan surpassed the United Kingdom in 1992 as the largest direct investor in the United States. The number of Americans working for Japanese subsidiaries in the United States doubled from 1989 to 1995, to 400,000. The 10 largest Japanese employers in the United States in rank order are Matsushita Electric, Sony, Toyota, Honda, Hitachi, Toshiba, Nissan, NEC, Mitsubishi, and Fujitsu. However, over 50 percent of Japanese companies operating in the United States today face worker lawsuits on race, color, religion, age, sex, and equal employment.

In Europe, Toyota completed its first auto plant in 1992, a $1.2 billion facility in Britain. Fujitsu is also building a $690 million manufacturing plant to produce computer chips in northeast England. The Japanese are expected to continue investing heavily in Great Britain because the British welcome the Japanese, while other European countries are divided in their attitudes toward Japan. More than 40 percent of all Japanese investment in Western Europe is in Britain. The Confederation of British Industry predicts that by the year 2000, an astonishing 16 percent of British factory workers will have Japanese bosses.

There are only three major industries—pharmaceuticals, chemicals, and telecommunications equipment—in which European companies are more competitive than Japanese companies. Five of the top 10 construction firms in the world are Japanese: Shimizu, Kajima, Jaisei, Takenaka, and Ohbayashi. Until European countries develop a more unified approach towards Japanese investment, England could be "exporting" Japanese products to the Continent in great quantities.

During the 1990–1994 era, Japan's direct investment strategy focused largely on the United States and Europe. However, during the 1995–1998 era, Japan's focus shifted to Asia for several reasons: First, Japan wants to capitalize on Asian countries' growing markets and rapidly developing economies. Japan wants to lessen their dependence on the United States. Finally, Japan wants to be in a position to determine their own destiny in light of China's explosive growth and expansionist policies.

Asians now buy more Japanese exports than the United States, and Japanese firms are plowing these profits back into Asia. Shintaro Ishihara says, "Japan is a nation of Asian people with Asian blood. It seems natural that we recognize that we exist first for Asia." Japan's emphasis on new trade, investment, financial, and technological moves are in Asia.

To support their country's re-Asianization policy, the Japanese people are putting greater emphasis on learning the languages, foods, and cultural habits of their Asian neighbors from Manchuria to Indonesia. Japanese firms are building plants, forming alliances, and making business friends extensively in Korea, Vietnam, Thailand, Indonesia, Malaysia, Philippines, India, Taiwan, and China. Already the world's largest aid donor, Japan has targeted Asian countries as their primary recipient in order to bolster their Asian influence. Indonesia is Japan's largest aid recipient, followed by China, the Philippines, India, and Thailand. There is a growing acceptance of Japanese culture throughout Asia. Projections are for Japan's U.S. investment to declines to just over $30 billion.

FINANCIAL SERVICES   Japan is determined to obtain world leadership and dominance in financial services. The Tokyo Stock Exchange has replaced the New York Stock Exchange as the world's largest, with a market capitalization of over $3 trillion; this is more volume than that of all the exchanges in Europe combined. The Osaka Exchange has surpassed London's as the world's third-largest. The world's largest life insurance company, Nippon Life, the world's largest transportation company, NYK, and the world's largest tourism firm, Japan Travel Bureau, are all Japanese. There are only a few areas of financial services where U.S. and European financial institutions still hold a firm lead over their Japanese counterparts. These areas include trust banking, portfolio management, venture capital, mergers and acquisitions, swap arrangements, and engineering complex financial packages. American and European firms must capitalize on these strengths and begin to offer these services worldwide to compete effectively with Japanese financial institutions. The worst enemy of Western financial instititutions is complacency.

LIFETIME EMPLOYMENT   The principle of lifetime employment is as strong as ever in Japan, despite Westerners' view that this policy will wilt under global competition. Japanese law makes it illegal to fire employees, so firms cannot cut labor costs when demand falls. But this single disadvantage of a lifetime employment policy is counterbalanced by numerous advantages. For example, Japanese workers even view productivity-enhancing technologies and automation as positive because there is no downside risk of them losing their job. With the lifetime employment policy, Japanese firms undertake expensive training programs without fear that any workers will take their skills to rival firms. U.S. firms are only one-seventh as likely as Japanese firms to offer new employees formal training.

Another benefit of the lifetime employment is the long-term accountability built into system; this enhances managerial decision making. Labor unions in Japan work for the business; a strike may last at most an hour. CEOs in Japan are salaried employees compensated at levels of 10 times that of lower-level managers; this compares to U.S. CEOs being paid on average 100 times the salary of lower-level managers. Stock options for CEOs are prohibited in Japan. Japanese workers are paid and promoted according to seniority rather than competence. This system promotes teamwork and eliminates a possible source of friction and jealousy among workers. Because older workers and managers are not going to be leapfrogged in promotion, they mentor and help younger, inexperienced workers and managers much more readily than in the United States. Workers in Japanese firms function as part of a clearly identified team, and assignments are given to the team rather than to individuals. Offenders of team norms risk being ostracized by the group. Lifetime employment in Japan has a bright and stable future. It is a policy that U.S. firms should consider implementing.

THE EUROPEAN UNION

The economies of the *European Union (EU)* grew 2.5 percent in 1995, a notable improvement on 1993's contraction of 0.3 percent (see Table 10–8). Unemployment, which reached 11 percent in the spring of 1994, has begun to decline slowly, although further increases are possible. The EU's economic recovery is good news for the United States. Western Europe, which accounts for 40 percent of all production of goods and services outside the United States, is the largest overseas market for U.S. companies. The EU's per-capita income of $17,000 (about 71 percent of the U.S. figure) is evidence of a rich and broad market for U.S. products.[12]

Europe is undergoing rapid economic and political change. A major development for U.S. commercial interests is the EU membership of Austria, Finland, and Sweden in 1995. Their economies add $380 billion, or 5 percent of GDP, to the EU. Their 20 million consumers result in a 15-member EU with a total GDP of more than $7 trillion and a population of 370 million. This enlargement will create new trade and investment opportunities, but will also lead to increased competition for U.S. firms. Some customs duties in the Nordic countries will rise as they align their tariff schedules with those of the other EU members.

The EU's GDP is projected to grow about 3 percent in 1996, its best economic performance in many years. Rising exports in the major countries, improved business attitudes, and higher consumer demand will fuel this economic recovery (see Figure 10–14). Structural problems remain entrenched, however. Excessive labor costs, economic rigidities that stall the growth of smaller companies and service enterprises, and costly social programs will tend to restrain growth below the EU's long-term potential and keep unemployment high. European governments recognize the necessity of overcoming these basic problems to increase growth and jobs.

FIGURE 10–14
The European Union

Population 1995: 148.3 Million

Gross Domestic Product 1994: $721.2 Billion

Labor Force 1995: 72 Million

Goods Trade with U.S. 1995: $6.86 Billion

TRADE CLIMATE AND TRENDS   The EU is the largest trading area in the world (see Figure 10–15). In 1993, EU exports totalled $1.3 trillion, about the same as its imports. As the United States' second-largest export market, it absorbed $123.8 billion worth of U.S. products in 1995. It is the fastest-growing market for U.S. high-tech exports, the predominant destination for U.S. direct investment, and the largest source of foreign direct investment in the United States. It also ranks as the largest overseas market for 25 U.S. states, including California (see Figure 10–16).

TABLE 10–8
Snapshot: European Union

ITEM	PERCENT CHANGE (ANNUAL RATE)			
	1987–1992	1993	1994	1995
Gross Domestic Product	3.0	−0.3	1.6	2.5
Consumer Prices	4.8	3.3	3.0	2.9

ITEM	1987	1992	1993	1994	1995
Unemployment Rate (Percent)	10.5	9.6	10.6	11.0	–
Exports ($ Billion)	957	1,475	1,300	NA	–
To United States	81.3	94.0	97.9	110.9	129.8
Imports ($ Billion)	957	1,567	1,295	NA	–
From United States	60.6	103.0	97.0	102.8	123.8
Exchange Rate (ECU per US$)	.87	.77	.85	.84*	–

NA Not available. *Estimate.

FIGURE 10–15
**The European Union's
Real GDP Growth,
1987–1995**

•Department of Commerce estimate
Source: Statistical Office of the European Communities.

FIGURE 10–16
**U.S. Trade with the
European Union,
1987–94**

Source: Department of Commerce.

The faltering European economy led to a 6-percent drop in U.S. exports to the EU in 1993; the U.S. bilateral trade balance went from a $9 billion surplus in 1992 to a $1 billion deficit. The U.S. trade deficit with the EU continued to grow in 1994, reaching $8.1 billion, as a 6-percent increase in U.S. exports to the EU was overtaken by a 13-percent rise in EU exports to the United States. The European Union accounted for only 20 percent of U.S. exports in 1994, compared with 25 percent in 1990. However, European economic growth and rise in U.S. exports shrank the U.S. trade deficit with the EU in 1995 to $6 billion. Over the long term, U.S. trade with Western Europe is expected to be roughly in balance, as it has been in the past, with surpluses in some years offsetting deficits in others.

The leading U.S. exports to the EU in 1994 were aircraft ($9 billion); data processing and office equipment ($7 billion); engines and motors ($4.2 billion); measuring, checking, and analyzing equipment ($3.1 billion); and thermonic and cathode valves ($4.1 billion). The most promising U.S. export sectors include telecommunications equipment, computer peripherals and software, electronic components, pollution control equipment, medical equipment and supplies, and aircraft. The continuing trends toward privatization, deregulation, and market decentralization in the EU make prospects for these products bright for the foreseeable future.

Europe's overall importance for U.S. companies and the U.S. economy is much greater than these trade statistics indicate. Most international business takes the form of investment in foreign affiliates that produce abroad, rather than the shipment of U.S.–produced goods to target export markets. (Sales of U.S. companies through overseas affiliates reached $1.9 trillion in 1993; total U.S. merchandise exports that year, valued at $465 billion, were one-quarter that amount.) In 1993, U.S. affiliate sales in Europe exceeded $860 billion. These sales account for more than half of total U.S. affiliate sales worldwide and are four times as large as U.S. affiliate sales in Canada or Asia, and 11 times as large as U.S. affiliate sales in Japan.

U.S. companies' overseas affiliates are major importers of U.S. products. In 1993, sales by U.S. parent companies to their European affiliates made up 38 percent of U.S. exports to Europe and generated a $20 billion trade surplus for the United States. At the same time, U.S. affiliates in Europe contributed $30 billion to the overall U.S. trade surplus in services (dividends, fees, royalties, and other earnings), yielding a total U.S. surplus in affiliate trade of $50 billion in 1993.

Europe is one of the most open markets for U.S. companies, which are in a position to benefit from an integrated and borderless EU. In order to capitalize fully, however, they must be allowed to participate in the coming wave of privatizations. In addition, U.S. exports are threatened by new product standards and rules on testing and certification, growing incompatibility in business regulations, and remaining barriers in such areas as telecommunications, heavy electrical equipment, and audiovisual services. Eliminating these obstacles is a primary trade objective of the U.S. government. U.S. companies also stand to benefit from increased marketing efforts in the EU, particularly in Germany and Italy. In 1995, U.S. firms had a 13.2-percent share of UK imports, but only 6.5 percent in the rest of the EU. Each percentage point rise in the U.S. share of the EU market signifies a $13 billion increase in the value of U.S. exports.

Since World War II, Western European countries have comprised distinct national markets where governments protected their own businesses and imposed stiff tariffs on outside firms. Jealousy, regulation, diverse economic conditions, and tensions among nations have characterized Europe for years. Viewed as separate entities, European countries have not represented a sufficiently large customer base to warrant many international companies establishing business operations in Europe. Consequently, Europe has been economically stagnant since World War II, especially compared with the United States and the Far East. For several years during the 1980s, the combined results of the largest 100 companies in Europe, excluding the oil companies, showed a profit level of 0 percent. Unemployment in Europe still remains high and companies generally are not competitive in world markets.

There are also still wide differences in product tastes across European countries. For example, the French want top-loading washing machines, whereas the British want front-loading washers. The Portuguese eat only 10 kg of beef per capita each year, whereas the French eat 33 kg. Germans eat 9.5 kg of poultry each year, whereas the Spanish eat 22 kg. Electrical outlets in Britain are also different from those in Holland.

With the exception of a few industries such as chemicals, most sectors of the European economy are marked by chronic overcapacity and high fixed costs, such as steel, detergents, pharmaceuticals, transportation, and banking. There is no reason why Europe's $2 billion turbine-generator business should support 10 producers. Similar overcapactiy problems plague other industries, such as locomotive manufacturing. European companies are moving quickly, however, to correct the overcapacity problems, and survivors will likely emerge as strong competitors in world markets. Differences among European countries are narrowing due to a massive increase in the flow of people and information across national borders, and European companies are moving rapidly to develop and market products that will be well received all over Europe. The Europlug, for example, has recently been developed and marketed in Europe as the electrical plug that "will work everywhere."

UNIFICATION   Unification of Western Europe was perhaps the single most important world event affecting business strategies since the formation of OPEC in the early 1970s. Fifteen countries speaking with one voice is more attractive to multinational corporations than 15 countries speaking with 15 voices. A proliferation of cross-border mergers, acquisitions, and alliances in Europe is creating a new generation of European firms large enough to take on U.S. and Japanese companies. In some industries, such as packaging and electric generating equipment, European firms have already replaced American firms as world leaders.

Unification of Western Europe has reduced or eliminated trade barriers between European countries; people, goods, services, and capital now flow freely across national boundaries. European banks can operate in different countries without prohibitive barriers. Trucks pass freely between national borders, instead of having to wait for hours at places such as the Mount Blanc tunnel between France and Italy, where custom agents used to check documents and cargo. The Eurotunnel under the English Channel is spurring business between England and the European mainland. The estimated annual savings to European companies from the unification is $75 to $90 billion.

Unification also brought common licensing of food and beverage products in Europe, common radio and television signals, common health and safety standards, elimination of duplication in distribution systems, and standardization of product lines. It has also prompted increased competitor analysis and alliances, decentralization of businesses, new marketing efforts, new strategies, more emphasis on service, improved telecommunications and information flow, and increased momentum for a single monetary system evolving in Europe.

Perhaps the most far-reaching feature of European unification is the planned establishment of a single financial market. Much stronger competitors in Europe have emerged from unification, and consumers throughout Europe are benefiting from lower prices and better choices. However, European companies still pay the world's highest wages and generally have trouble offering goods at globally competitive prices. The social welfare system in Europe is especially costly to firms. Most European workers and managers enjoy lifetime employment guarantees. There is a fear throughout Europe that rising unemployment, already at 10.5 percent, may bring back overregulation and protectionism, which would hurt firms' efforts to become more globally competitive.

European industries expected to represent the greatest threat to U.S. firms in the near future are publishing, communications equipment, pharmaceutical, and civilian-aerospace. Representing a lesser but still significant threat to U.S. firms will be European banks and producers of food, beverages, computers, electronics, and autos. U.S. industries that appear for the moment to be least affected by European unification are retailing, trucking, airlines, and insurance.

MERGERS AND ACQUISITIONS   Because Brussels is the headquarters of the European Economic Community (EEC), significant business and economic activity has shifted there from other national capitals in Europe. A wave of mergers and acquisitions is sweeping Europe as companies try to consolidate strength in core markets. For example, Banco de Bilbao and Banco Vizcaya, Spain's third- and sixth-largest banks, recently combined to form the only Spanish bank to rank among the top 30 in Europe. Consolidations in the paper industry have resulted in strong competitors such as Stora Kopparbergs Bergslags and Svanska Cellusosa in Sweden and Finnpap and Kymmene in Finland. Nestlé in Switzerland has acquired a number of other food companies in both Europe and the United States. Two large accounting firms in England, Coopers & Lybrand and Deloitte Haskins & Sells, recently merged, creating the largest accounting firm in Europe. Eurocom S.A., France's largest advertising agency, merged with Roux, Seguela, Cayzac & Goudard, creating by far the largest ad agency in Europe.

Some examples of European firms that have acquired U.S. firms are Pechiney of France, which acquired Triangle Industries; Grand Metropolitan of Britain, which acquired Pillsbury, Burger King, and Green Giant; Hoechst of Germany, which acquired Celanese; and Nestlé of Switzerland, which acquired Carnation.

Japanese firms are also making large acquisitions in Western Europe. For example, Fujitsu acquired Britain's last true computer maker, ICL. Mitsubishi Electric has a stated goal to increase its investment in Europe by as much as 30 percent a year. Olivetti in Italy depends on Canon and Sanyo for office equipment, and Fiat depends on Hitachi for construction gear. Nissan, Toyota, and Honda are all building manufacturing plants in Britain and expect to raise overall Japanese market share of automobiles in Britain from 12 percent to 17 percent by 1998.

After Great Britain, the European country receiving the next most extensive Japanese investment is Germany; Germany already imports 40 percent of all Japanese exports to Europe. Dusseldorf, Germany, has Europe's largest number of Japanese residents—over 7,000. Mitsubishi Electric and Toshiba are leading an array of Japanese firms planning investment of over $400 million annually in the Dusseldorf region alone.

GUIDELINES FOR SUCCESS AS A GLOBAL COMPETITOR

As indicated in the Information Technology Perspective, a guideline for success as a global competitor is to make full use of STAT-USA on the World Wide Web at

http://www.stat-usa.gov/ingsample.html

Updated monthly, this is the U.S. government's premier Internet publisher of business information.

Robert Allio offers seven guidelines for winning global battles for customer loyalty and market share:

1. Get to new global markets first. Trying to gain market share from well-entrenched competitors is exceptionally difficult.
2. Counterattack at home. Parent firms often finance expansion into host countries with profits generated at home. Competitor cash flow can be reduced by attacking them at home. A recent example is the 3M attack on Japanese markets for audiotape and videotape.
3. Invest in new technology. Successful firms in the 1990s are going to utilize the most efficient technology.
4. Consider alternative sourcing. Locate manufacturing facilities in low labor cost areas of the world. A recent example of this is Dominion Textile of Canada's building a denim manufacturing facility in Tunisia.
5. Install the right managerial system. Ensure that managers in foreign markets understand the nuances of culture and language in host countries.
6. Take early losses if necessary. Sacrifice short-term profits for long-term rewards. A recent example is Japanese firms' taking losses for seven years in order to capture the European motorcycle market.
7. Join forces with competitors. Collaborate with competitors who have expertise in other parts of the value chain. Recent examples are Chrysler's deal with Mitsubishi and AT&T's linkup with Olivetti.[13]

Jeremy Main says there is no universal formula for going global, but any company serious about joining the race should do most or all of the following:

1. Make yourself at home in all three of the world's most important markets—North America, Europe, and Asia.
2. Develop new products for the whole world.
3. Replace profit centers based on countries or regions with ones based on product lines.

INFORMATION TECHNOLOGY

STAT-USA/Internet

THE ONE-STOP INTERNET SOURCE FOR BUSINESS AND ECONOMIC DATA

The Information Revolution has arrived in full force. The Internet, a worldwide network of interconnected computers, has emerged to become a significant factor in business and personal communications. Every day, thousands of people are joining the "on-line" world to take advantage of the many benefits that the Internet has to offer, such as quick and easy transfer of messages, the ability to search vast libraries of information, and the ability to download files to your own computer for personal use.

STAT-USA, a recipient of the 1994 Government Computer News Award for Excellence in the Application of Information Technology, is leading the way in becoming the U.S. Government's premier Internet publisher of business, trade and economic information. If your business depends on up-to-date economic news and market intelligence . . . if you track the exchange rate for the Mexican peso . . . if you need Gross Domestic Product data, or . . . if you are looking to break into new markets . . .

then you can't afford to miss STAT-USA/Internet.

STAT-USA publishes the best business and economic information that the Federal Government has to offer. Gone are the days of calling from agency to agency to find the report that you need. STAT-USA gathers the most crucial, timely business and economic information from over 50 Federal Agencies and distributes from a central source: true low-cost, "one-stop" shopping, saving you countless hours in research time.

STAT-USA/Internet brings over 300,000 reports and statistical series (the equivalent of 7 sets of encyclopedias) right to your desktop. Those interested in exporting or international trade issues will appreciate STAT-USA's extensive collection of trade reports, which includes:

- Market Research Reports cabled back each day from U.S. embassies and consulates
- Overseas contacts from the Commercial Service International Contacts database (formerly called the Foreign Traders Index)

- Domestic contacts from the Export Yellow Pages
- Merchandise Trade Statistics from the Census Bureau
- Trade Leads

Our collection of domestic economic and business information includes:

- National Income and Product Accounts (including GDP)
- Composite Index of Leading Indicators
- Regional Economic Data including personal income, wages, and employment for states and local areas
- Housing and Population Statistics
- The Economic Report of the President
- The Budget of the U.S. Federal Government

If you are familiar with the other products that STAT-USA provides, you will appreciate the STAT-USA/Internet provides the following and more:

- From the National Trade Data Bank on CD-ROM:
  - All textual data from the CD-ROM's including Market Research Reports, the

4. "Glocalize," as the Japanese call it: Make global decisions on strategic questions about products, capital, and research, but let local units decide tactical questions about packaging, marketing, and advertising.

5. Overcome parochial attitudes, such as the not-invented-here syndrome. Train people to think internationally, send them off on frequent trips, and give them the latest communications technology, such as teleconferencing.

6. Open the senior ranks to foreign employees.

7. Do whatever seems best wherever it seems best, even if people at home lose jobs or responsibilities.

8. In markets that you cannot penetrate on your own, find allies.[14]

David Garfield, president of Ingersoll-Rand Company, offers three strategy suggestions to make domestic firms more competitive internationally:

1. The best defense is a good offense. Companies need to fight tooth and claw for exports and battle foreign competition on foreign ground wherever possible. This is preferable to competing intensely in domestic markets.

2. Investments that will improve competitive advantage should receive priority attention. Domestic firms should strive to reduce labor costs, lower overhead, compress production cycles, and improve the quality of products and services.

3. Domestic industries and firms need to help one another. They should give preference to American suppliers and distributors; they should encourage one another to take action to improve competitiveness in technology, quality, service, and cost.[15]

Commercial Service International Contacts, the Export Yellow Pages, etc.

- The U.S. merchandise and export trade by 10-digit Harmonized System number and country
- From the Economic Bulletin Board dial-in service:
  - The top 25 most popular files from the EBB
  - The Trade Opportunity Program (TOP) leads from U.S. commercial attaches overseas in a full-text searchable form
  - The Commerce Business Daily leads in full-text searchable form
  - The Defense Logistics Agency leads in full-text searchable form
- From the Bureau of Economic Analysis:
  - All major releases

You don't have to be a "techy" to enjoy quick and easy access to STAT-USA/Internet's extensive databases. Searching is made easy with Inquery, an award winning natural-language search and retrieval software that makes locating files as easy as "find me all reports about automobiles in Japan" or "I need total exports of household appliances, especially toasters."

We encourage you to take our service for a free test drive. All you need is a computer with a graphically-based World Wide Web browser (such as the Mosaic or Netscape browser) that supports forms. Connect to http://www.stat_usa.gov, select one of the databases (such as the National Trade Data Bank), select the "Test drive" option, and then enter a sample query, such as "where can I sell metal cutting machinery" Inquery will search through a broad array of STAT-USA/Internet sample documents, and quickly return an accurate, ranked listing of files most relevant to your question. It doesn't get much easier than that.

Full access to STAT-USA/Internet is available to users for a flat rate per year. There are three types of accounts offered:

- Single user: This account allows a specified single user full access to our Web site.
- U.S. educational or U.S. governmental site license: Provides full access to all users within a given e-mail domain.
- Concurrent users: This account allows users to share a userid and password among multiple users provided that you guarantee that you will never have more

than the specified number of users on our site at the same time. For example, a group of five people might want to share one simultaneous user license.

For site and concurrent user licenses, each site has to designate a single contact person at that site. All assistance for users at the site has to be requested through that contact person. The contact person's name and e-mail address have to be provided on the application form itself.

If you need additional information about STAT-USA/Internet, or if you would like to place an order, please call the STAT-USA Helpline at (202) 482-1986, Monday through Friday from 8:30 AM–5:30 PM Eastern Time. Or reach us through e-mail at: stat-usa@doc.gov.

NOTE: All amounts due are in U.S. currency. We cannot accept electronic funds transfer requests.

NOTE: All payments must be received in advance of shipment.

CONCLUSION

Success in business more and more depends upon offering products and services that are competitive on a world basis, not just on a local basis. If the price and quality of a firm's products and services are not competitive with those available elsewhere in the world, the firm may soon face extinction. Global markets have become a reality in all but the most remote areas of the world. Certainly throughout the United States, even in small towns, firms feel the pressure of world competitors. Nearly half of all the automobiles sold in the United States, for example, are made in Japan and Germany.

Culture, industrial policies, joint venturing, and exporting are important in the strategic-management process of international firms. As world economies and consumption patterns become increasingly similar and interrelated, political and economic changes represent major opportunities for, and threats to, U.S. firms. To be successful in the 1990s, businesses must offer products and services that exhibit a price/quality relationship competitive with similar products and services available worldwide.

TAKE IT TO THE NET We invite you to visit the DAVID page on the Prentice Hall Web site at:
http://www.prenhall.com/davidsm
for this chapter's World Wide Web exercises.

KEY TERMS AND CONCEPTS

European Economic Community	(p. 305)	Industrial Policies	(p. 308)	Newly Independent States (NIS)	(p. 316)
European Union (EU)	(p. 331)	Inhwa	(p. 305)	Parent Company	(p. 302)
Guanxi	(p. 305)	Joint Declaration	(p. 323)	Wa	(p. 305)
Host Country	(p. 302)	Multinational Corporation (MNCs)	(p. 302)		

ISSUES FOR REVIEW AND DISCUSSION

1. Compare and contrast American culture with other cultures worldwide. How do differences in culture affect strategic management?

2. Explain why consumption patterns are becoming more and more similar worldwide. What are the strategic implications of this trend?

3. What are the advantages and disadvantages of beginning export operations in a foreign country?

4. Why do you believe the airline industry is only slowly becoming global?

5. What recommendations do you have for firms wanting to do business with Russia?

6. What strategies are most commonly being pursued by Japanese firms? Why?

7. How does unification of western Europe affect the strategies of U.S. firms?

8. What guidelines for success as a global competitor do you believe are most important?

9. Select one of the readings at the end of this chapter and prepare a three-minute report to the class on this topic.

10. Do you believe Guanxi, Inhwa, or Wa would help facilitate strategic management in an organization? Why?

11. Compare and contrast the trade climate in Mexico, China, Japan, Russia, and the European Union.

12. Compare and contrast the political climate in Mexico, China, Japan, Russia, and the European Union.

13. Compare and contrast the culture in Mexico, China, Japan, Russia, and the European Union.

NOTES

1. Gephardt, Richard A. "U.S.–Japanese Trade Relations," *Vital Speeches of the Day* Vol. LV, no. 15 (May 15, 1989).

2. Jon Alston, "Wa, Guanxi, and Inhwa: Managerial Principles in Japan, China and Korea," *Business Horizons* 32, no. 2 (March–April 1989): 26.

3. Rose Knotts, "Cross-Cultural Management: Transformations and Adaptations," *Business Horizons* (January–February 1989): 29–33.

4. Vern Terpstra and David Kenneth, *The Cultural Environment of International Business* (Cincinnati: South-Western Publishing Company, 1985). Also, see: Rose Knotts, "Cross-Cultural Management: Transformations and Adaptations," *Business Horizons* 32, no. 1 (January–February 1989): 31.

5. Ellen Fingerhut and Daryl Hatano, "Principles of Strategic Planning Applied to International Corporations," *Managerial Planning* 31, no. 5 (September–October 1983): 4–14. Also, Narendra Sethi,

"Strategic Planning Systems for Multinational Companies," *Long Range Planning* 15, no. 3 (June 1982): 80–9.

6. David Shanks, "Strategic Planning for Global Competition," *Journal of Business Strategy* 5, no. 3 (Winter 1985): 80.

7. The first three pages of information about Mexico were written by Reginald Biddle at the Office of NAFTA at the U.S. Department of Commerce.

8. The first two pages of information about Russia were written by Trevor Gunn at the U.S. Department of Commerce.

9. The first three pages of information about China were written by Scott Goddin at the U.S. Department of Commerce.

10. The first four pages of information about Japan were written by Edward Leslie at the U.S. Department of Commerce.

11. Stratford Sherman, "How to Beat the Japanese," *Fortune* (April 10, 1989): 145.

12. The first three pages of information about the European Union were written by Lori Cooper at the U.S. Department of Commerce.

13. Robert Allio, "Formulating Global Strategy," *Planning Review* 17, no. 2 (March–April 1989): 27.

14. Jeremy Main, "How to Go Global—And Why," *Fortune* (August 28, 1989): 76.

15. David Garfield, "The International Challenge to U.S. Business," *Journal of Business Strategy* 5, no. 4 (Spring 1985): 28, 29.

CURRENT READINGS

Banks, Philip and Ganesh Natarajan. "India: The New Asian Tiger?" *Business Horizons* 38, no. 3 (May–June 1995): 47–50.

Bouteiller, Eric. "The Emergence of Greater China as an Economic Force." *Long Range Planning* 28, no. 1 (February 1995): 54–60.

Brown, P. R., V. E. Soybel, and C. P. Stickney. "Comparing U.S. and Japanese Corporate-Level Operating Performance Using Financial Statement Data." *Strategic Management Journal* 15, no. 1 (January 1994): 75–89.

Chilton, Kenneth. "How American Manufacturers Are Facing the Global Marketplace." *Business Horizons* 38, no. 4 (July–August 1995): 10–19.

Coplin, William D. "Turning Points in China Over the Next Five Years." *Planning Review* 23 (January–February 1995): 37.

Donaldson, Thomas and Thomas W. Dunfee. "Toward a Unified Conception of Business Ethics: Integrative Social Contracts Theory." *Academy of Management Review* 19, no. 2 (April 1994): 252–284.

Dyer, Jeffrey H. and William G. Ouchi. "Japanese-style Partnerships: Giving Companies a Competitive Edge." *Sloan Management Review* 35, no. 1 (Fall 1993): 51–64.

Fahy, John and Fuyuki Taguchi. "Reassessing the Japanese Distribution System." *Sloan Management Review* 36, no. 2 (Winter 1995): 49–61.

Fram, Eugene H. and Riad Ajami. "Globalization of Markets and Shopping Stress: Cross-Country Comparisons." *Business Horizons* 37, no. 1 (January–February 1994): 17–23.

Hagedoorn, J. "A Note on International Market Leaders and Networks of Strategic Technology Partnering." *Strategic Management Journal* 16, no. 3 (March 1995): 241–253.

Helper, Susan R. and Mari Sako. "Supplier Relations in Japan and the United States: Are They Converging?" *Sloan Management Review* 36, no. 3 (Spring 1995): 77–84

Hitt, Michael A., Beverly B. Tyler, Camilla Hardee, and Daewoo Park. "Understanding Strategic Intent in the Global Marketplace." *Academy of Management Executive IX,* no. 2 (May 1995): 12–19.

Holland, Christopher P., Geoff Lockett, Jean-Michel Richard, and Ian Blackman. "The Evolution of a Global Cash Management System." *Sloan Management Review* 36, no. 1 (Fall 1994): 37–48.

Holt, David H., David A. Ralston, and Robert H. Terpstra. "Constraints on Capitalism in Russia: The Managerial Psyche, Social Infrastructure, and Ideology." *California Management Review* 36, no. 3 (Spring 1994): 124–141.

Hordes, Mark W., J. Anthony Clancy, and Julie Braddaley. "A Primer for Global Start-ups." *Academy of Management Executive IX*, no. 2 (May 1995): 7–11.

Hu, Yao-Su. "The International Transferability of the Firm's Advantages." *California Management Review* 37, no. 4 (Summer 1995): 73–88.

Johnston, Stewart. "Managerial Dominance of Japan's Major Corporations." *Journal of Management* 21, no. 2 (Summer 1995): 191–210.

Karlöf, Bengt. "Strategies for the Emerging European Market." *Long Range Planning* 27, no. 2 (April 1994): 36–44.

Kvint, Vladimir. "Don't Give Up on Russia." World View. *Harvard Business Review* (March–April 1994): 62–75.

Lasserre, Philippe. "Corporate Strategies for the Asia Pacific Region." *Long Range Planning* 28, no. 1 (February 1995):13–30.

Lasserre, Philippe and Jocelyn Probert. "Competing on the Pacific Rim: High Risks and High Returns." *Long Range Planning* 27, no. 2 (April 1994): 12–35.

Li, J. "Foreign Entry and Survival: Effects of Strategic Choices on Performance in International Markets." *Strategic Management Journal* 16, no. 5 (June 1995): 333–352.

Lieblich, Julia. "The Russian Investment Dilemma." Perspectives. *Harvard Business Review* (May–June 1994): 35–45.

Lowry, James R. "A Partnering Approach to Mass Merchandising in Russia." *Business Horizons* 38, no. 4 (July–August 1995): 28–31.

Luo, Yadong and Min Chen. "A Financial Primer for Inventors in China." *Business Horizons* 38, no. 4 (July–August 1995): 32.

Lussier, Robert N., Robert W. Baeder, and Joel Corman. " Measuring Global Practices: Global Strategic Planning Through Company Situational Analysis." *Business Horizons* 37, no. 5 (September–October 1994): 56–64.

Luthans, Fred, Richard R. Patrick, and Brett C. Luthans. "Doing Business in Central and Eastern Europe: Political, Economic, and Cultural Diversity." *Business Horizons* 38, no. 5 (September–October 1995): 9–16.

Malnight, T. W. "Globalization of an Ethnocentric Firm: An Evolutionary Perspective." *Strategic Management Journal* 16, no. 2 (February 1995): 143–160.

Maruca, Regina Fazio. "The Right Way To Go Global: An Interview With Whirlpool CEO David Whitwam." *Harvard Business Review* (March–April 1994): 134–149.

Mathe, Hervé and Cynthia Perras. "Successful Global Strategies for Service Companies." *Long Range Planning* 27 (February 1994): 30–49.

Palich, Leslie E., Peter W. Hom, and Rodger W. Griffeth. "Managing in the International Context: Testing Cultural Generality of Sources of Commitment to Multinational Enterprises." *Journal of Management* 21, no. 4 (Winter 1995): 671–690.

Randall, Doug and Piero Telesio. "China: Five Scenarios for Managing Risks." *Planning Review* 23, no. 1 (January–February 1995): 30–36.

Raudabaugh, Joseph L. "Asian Investment: Lessons from the Japanese Experience." Communiqué from Japan. *Planning Review* 23, no. 1 (January–February 1995): 38.

Redding, Gordon. "Overseas Chinese Networks: Understanding the Enigma." *Long Range Planning* 28, no. 1 (February 1995): 61–69.

Roth, K. and D. A. Ricks. "Goal Configuration in a Global Industry Context." *Strategic Management Journal* 15, no. 2 (February 1994): 103–120.

Sarathy, Ravi. "Global Strategy in Service Industries." *Long Range Planning* 27, no. 6 (December 1994): 115–124.

Shama, Avraham. "Entry Strategies of U.S. Firms to the Newly Independent States, Baltic States, and Eastern European Countries." *California Management Review* 37, no. 3 (Spring 1995): 90–109.

Shane, S. "The Effect of National Culture on the Choice Between Licensing and Direct Foreign Investment." *Strategic Management Journal* 15, no. 8 (October 1994): 627–642.

Simpson, Dan. "Planning in a Global Business." Chief Planning Officer Dialogue. *Planning Review* 23, no. 2 (March–April 1995): 25–27.

Tan, Kong-Yam and Chow-Hou Wee. "A Scenario for East Asia: Recent Trends and Future Challenges." *Long Range Planning* 28, no. 1 (February 1995): 41–53.

Turcq, Dominique. "The Global Impact of Non-Japan Asia." *Long Range Planning* 28, no. 1 (February 1995): 31–40.

Yan, Amin and Barbara Gray. "Bargaining Power, Management Control, and Performance in United States—China Joint Ventures: A Comparative Case Study." *Academy of Management Journal* 37, no. 6 (December 1994): 1478–1517.

Yan, Rick. "To Reach China's Consumers, Adapt to Guo Qing." World View. *Harvard Business Review* (September–October 1994): 66–75.

Yip, G. S. "Exploiting Globalization Potential: U.S. and Japanese Strategies." *Strategic Management Journal* 15, no. 8 (October 1994): 579–602.

EXPERIENTIAL EXERCISES

DETERMINING THE COMPETITIVE ENVIRONMENT FOR HERSHEY'S PRODUCTS IN OTHER COUNTRIES

PURPOSE

Organizations are exploring potential markets in other countries more and more. The purpose of this exercise is to assess the relative attractiveness of various foreign countries for distributing and possibly manufacturing Hershey products.

INSTRUCTIONS

Step 1 Select a European, Asian, African, South American, or Central American country of your choice.

Step 2 Go to your college library. Research your chosen country to identify social, cultural, demographic, geographic, political, legal, governmental, economic, technological, and competitive forces or trends that affect the candy and pasta market there. Decide whether you would recommend Hershey begin or increase export operations or manufacturing operations in that country.

Step 3 Prepare a three-page typed report to Hershey's president of international operations, William F. Christ. Give the results of your research and your specific recommendations.

DETERMINING MY UNIVERSITY'S RECRUITING EFFORTS IN FOREIGN COUNTRIES

PURPOSE

A competitive climate is emerging among colleges and universities around the world. Colleges and universities in Europe and Japan are increasingly recruiting American students to offset declining enrollments. Foreign students already comprise more than one-third of the student body at many American universities. The purpose of this exercise is to identify particular colleges and universities in foreign countries that represent a competitive threat to American institutions of higher learning.

INSTRUCTIONS

Step 1 Select a foreign country. Conduct research to determine the number and nature of colleges and universities in that country. What are the major institutions in that country? What programs are those institutions recognized for offering? What percentage of undergraduate and graduate students attending those institutions are American? Do those institutions actively recruit American students?

Step 2 Prepare a report for the president or chancellor of your college or university that summarizes your research findings.

Experiential Exercise 10C

LESSONS IN DOING BUSINESS GLOBALLY

PURPOSE

The purpose of this exercise is to discover some important lessons learned by local businesses who do business internationally.

INSTRUCTIONS

Contact several local business leaders by phone. Find at least three firms that engage in international or export operations. Ask the businessperson to give you several important lessons his or her firm has learned in doing business globally. Record the lessons on paper and report your findings to the class.

COMPANY INDEX